D1003114

DOPE, INC.
The Book That Drove
Henry Kissinger Crazy

DOPE, INC.
The Book That Drove Henry Kissinger Crazy

by the Editors of
Executive Intelligence Review

Executive Intelligence Review
Washington, D.C.
1992

Cover design: Alan Yue

ISBN: 0-943253-02-2
Copyright © 1992 by Executive Intelligence Review

Library of Congress Catalogue number: 91-78004

Printed in the U.S.A.
For information contact the publisher
Executive Intelligence Review
P.O. Box 17390
Washington, D.C. 20041-0390

Contents

Acknowledgments   viii

Preface: Yuri Andropov Put the Soviet KGB Into the
   Narcoterrorism Business   xi
   by Lyndon H. LaRouche, Jr.

Introduction: The Drug Trade Today   1
1. The Book That Drove Henry Kissinger Crazy   3
2. Dope, Inc. Is Doubling Every Five Years   28
3. Marijuana Is Now the Nation's Major Crop   45

Part I: Our Enemies Proved Us Right   59
1. Why This Book Has Become Famous   61
2. The Dope, Inc. Command Structure   90

Part II: Britain's First Opium War   111
To Sap the Vitality of a Nation   113
1. The East India Company's War Against China   116
2. Britain's 'Noble Experiment'   133
Notes   141

Part III: How the Drug Empire Works   145
The Basis of This Investigation   147
1. Banking and the World's Biggest Business   151
2. How To Hide $200 Billion   166
3. From Opium to Dirty Money   181

4. How the Drug Trade Is Financed   185
5. Britain's Dirty Gold and Diamond Operations   192
6. Hong Kong: The Capital of Heroin Financing   204
7. The Beijing Connection   215
8. How the Royal Institute of International Affairs Runs
   Drugs and Dirty Money   235
9. Canada: North America's Hong Kong   250
10. The Families Behind the Drug Empire   262
Notes   275

Part IV: Moscow Moves In   289
1. Islamic Fundamentalism and the Golden Crescent   291

**Part V: Narcotráfico, SA: The IMF Recolonizes
   Ibero-America   303**
Introduction—Dope and Debt   305
1. The Trilateral Connection   312
2. Jamaica: The IMF Creates the Perfect Free Enterprise
   Economy   317
3. Colombia: Can Dope, Inc. Buy a Country?   324
4. The Cash Connection   331
5. How the *Fondi* Control Ibero-America's Dope Traffic   338
6. The Cisneros Family: The Bronfmans of Venezuela   344
7. Vesco and Castro   359

Part VI: The Nazi-Communist Mafia   365
1. Who Runs the Nazi International Today?   367
2. Stipam: The Real Bulgarian Connection   377
3. The Narco-Terrorists   392
4. Sendero Luminoso: Indigenous Murderers   396
5. The True Horror Story of the Gnostics   403
Notes   409

Part VII: Organized Crime   413
Intro—The Criminal International   415
1. The Bronfman Gang   423
2. The Kennedys: Organized Crime in the Government   441

3. Britain's International Assassination Bureau:
   Permindex   452
4. Permindex Unveiled: Resorts International-Intertel   492
5. Max Fisher: Distributor and Retailer   502
6. The Jacobs Family's Emprise: Sports and Crime   515
Notes   525

Part VIII: Origins of the Counterculture   533
1. The Aquarian Conspiracy   535
Notes   554

Part IX: The Dope Lobby   557
1. Drug Pushers in Government   559
Notes   569

Appendices   571
Appendix A: A Proposed Multi-National Strategic Operation
   Against the Drug Traffic for the Western Hemisphere by
   Lyndon H. LaRouche, Jr.   573
Appendix B: The FBI: An American Okhrana   583
Appendix C: The Anti-Defamation League: Dope, Inc.'s
   Public Relations Firm   603
Appendix D: The Drug Runners in Beijing   652

Index   669

Figures and Tables accompanying the Introduction follow page 44.

Acknowledgments

Special thanks are due to the following individuals:

Jeffrey Steinberg, *EIR Counterintelligence Editor*
Linda de Hoyos
Robyn Quijano
Marcia Merry
Dennis Small
Paul Goldstein
Michael Minnicino
Gretchen Small
John Hoefle
Kathy Wolfe
Scott Thompson
Joseph Brewda
Roger Moore
Michele Steinberg
Karen Steinherz
Carlos Wesley

Dedication

We dedicate this book to our friend Rodrigo Lara Bonilla, Colombian Justice Minister and selfless soldier in the war against drugs, murdered at the hands of the Colombian drug mafia on April 30, 1984, on orders of the board of directors of Dope, Inc.

After August 1983, when he became justice minister, Lara began to gather the moral reserves of his nation to unleash an offensive against the narcotics trade and against the "citizens above suspicion," the merchants of death who buy political power with their "respectable" fortunes.

Rodrigo Lara Bonilla dared to say "Enough!" In an environment in which the drug czars were able to buy people and political posts at their whim, in which former Presidents and Nobel prize winners sang the praises of narco-dollars and drug legalization, Lara Bonilla promised: "I will not cease my battle against drugs. . . . there are risks that one must take in life. . . ."

Since Lara Bonilla's tragic death, unfortunately, the drug mafia has launched, and virtually won, a war for political power inside of Colombia. Countless thousands of Colombian citizens have been killed and wounded in shoot-outs, bombings, and other terrorist actions by the drug gangsters, calculated to bring the civil authority to its knees. Dozens more leading officials have been murdered by the drug mafia, including former attorney general Carlos Mauro Hoyos and 11 justices of the nation's supreme court, who met their deaths during the M-19 guerrillas' 1985 storming of Colombia's justice ministry. Perhaps the most courageous was 1989 presidential candidate Luis Carlos Galán, who had dedicated himself to winning a war against the drug-pushers, before his assassination on the campaign trail.

Did Rodrigo Lara Bonilla die in vain? Will the thousands of deaths of Colombia's anti-drug fighters prove to be in vain? The answer to that question will be determined in large part by whether you, the reader, and millions of other Americans, join with us in crushing the leaders of Dope, Inc.—the "citizens above suspicion."

Preface: Yuri Andropov Put the Soviet KGB Into the Narco-Terrorism Business

The international drug-traffic enters the history books with the rise of the Sufi mystics, Syrian Hashishins (the "Assassins") of Shaykh al-Jabal, in the time of the Assassins' Templar allies. It was spread throughout the Asian littoral by Arab slave-traders. It was taken over from the slave-traders, by the Venetian slave-traders of the Levant Company. When the Levant-Company moved into England and the Netherlands, the Levant Company assumed the new name of the "East India Company" of England and the Netherlands. Adam Smith's employers, of the British East India Company, established world-monopoly in the opium-traffic during the eighteenth century, and Britain ran the international drug-traffic, until Yuri Andropov's Soviet KGB entered the traffic, and launched present-day international narco-terrorism against the West during the 1967–1969 interval.

What are, today, the leading financial families of New England and New York, bridge the transition from British to Soviet control of the international drug-traffic. The Perkins Syndicate of Salem, Massachusetts, were the American drug-trafficking partners of the British East India Company during the late eighteenth and the nineteenth centuries: establishing the drug-traffickers' fortunes which are the foundation of the wealth of the so-called "Eastern Liberal Establishment," the New York Council on Foreign Relations, of today. Not accidentally, these same families of Britain and the United States, typified by McGeorge Bundy's circles, are the leading accomplices of the Soviet dictatorship, both in their connections to the drug-money-laundering banking institutions, and in demanding that the United States appease Soviet strategic demands, today. It is no accident, therefore, that David Rockefeller, the founder of the pro-Soviet Trilateral Commission, entered into a partnership with the late, drug-trafficking Meyer Lansky, to turn the Mary Carter Paint Company, into the mob-linked Resorts International and Intertel. In both Britain and the United States, the "families" which built up their fortunes in the proceeds from the nineteenth-century opium traffic, are at the center of an organization known to insiders as the "Trust," the main channel of present-day Soviet KGB policy-shaping influence into policy-making circles of Western Europe and the Americas. It is no accident, that Boston-based U.S. Attorney William Weld, of the White Weld interests, interceded to cover up the money-laundering organization created under present White House Chief of Staff Donald T. Regan, among Merrill Lynch, Crédit Suisse, and White Weld, prior to Regan's becoming U.S. Treasury Secretary. It is no accident that Donald Regan has become a leading ally of Secretary of State George Shultz, and of Shultz's Bohemian Grove crony, Henry Kissinger, in supporting operations strategically decisive for Moscow, and contrary to the most vital strategic interests of the United States.

The first edition of *Dope, Inc.* pulled together four of the major features of the international drug-traffic: 1) the creation of the modern international drug-traffic, by the British government; 2) the evidence collected by the former U.S. Federal Bureau of Narcotics and Central Intelligence Agency on the international drug-traffic; 3) the role of the special operation, code-named "MK-Ultra," in unleashing a massive drug market inside the United States; and 4) the crucial role of British Commonwealth-based, "off-shore" financial institutions, such as the HongShang Bank, in laundering what was, during 1978, a $200-billions annual revenue from the drug-traffic.

This new edition brings the picture up to date, emphasizing

the dominant role of the Soviet KGB in taking over the traffic from the British, and in securing a dominant role in the international drug-trafficking and narco-terrorist operations of the late 1970s and 1980s.

Americans, and others, are increasingly fearful of international terrorism. Few, unfortunately, understand that terrorism is so tightly integrated with the international drug-traffic that the two can not be separated from one another. If we destroy the narcotics traffic, terrorism's essential logistical base is destroyed. However, destroying the crops and shooting down the planes carrying the drugs is not enough. Unless the hundreds of billions of dollars of the drug-traffickers are confiscated, and the guilty bankers and financial brokers are sent to prison, the United States and Western Europe are helpless against terrorism. As long as such creators of the money-laundering system as Donald T. Regan are allowed to exert influence over the policies of our own and allied governments, there is no serious "War On Drugs," nor is there any serious action against international terrorism.

The following pages give you the facts.

Lyndon H. LaRouche, Jr.
Leesburg, Virginia
April 10, 1986

Introduction
The Drug Trade Today

The Book That Drove Henry Kissinger Crazy

Thirteen years ago, the first edition of *Dope, Inc.* was released. Commissioned by anti-drug American statesman Lyndon H. LaRouche, Jr., it was the first book to reveal that the illegal drug cartel was becoming the world's biggest business; to name the causes of the war "Dope, Inc." has waged against every nation in the world; and to reveal the names of the "untouchable" figures who protect it, including the European monarchs, whom our Hollywood media have sold to the public as veritable deities. The book, which has since come out in several foreign-language versions and a second edition, remains unique.

Its effectiveness is attested to above all by the fact that the kingpins of the U.S. branch of the drug cartel—led by Henry A. Kissinger and the Anti-Defamation League of B'nai B'rith—launched a years-long effort to silence the authors, starting with LaRouche, who was railroaded to federal prison in late

1988 on trumped-up "conspiracy" charges, and is now fighting in the courts to overturn that travesty of justice.

Lyndon LaRouche was jailed within days of George Bush's inauguration as President in January 1989, and Bush has kept him there, for reasons that include a fear by Bush and his backers of the information contained in this book.

Former Secretary of State Henry A. Kissinger ran the risk of federal criminal prosecution as the result of his persistent interference into the conduct of the U.S. Department of Justice, the FBI, and the White House to stoke up the government campaign to silence LaRouche.

The dope lobby's hysteria over LaRouche's campaign to put them out of business was not restricted to the United States. In Venezuela, the Spanish-language edition, *Narcotráfico, SA,* has been banned since 1985 because the local Kissinger- and Rockefeller-linked bankers are terrified that a few bland references in the second edition to the bad company they keep might lead to the exposure of much bigger crimes. Recently, some of Dope, Inc.'s Venezuela operators have been publicly linked to two major terrorist bombings (one in Washington, D.C.) and at least one cocaine bust in Miami. As a result, scores of parliamentarians throughout Ibero-America have publicly demanded the lifting of the ban on this book.

It was in 1977 that Lyndon LaRouche realized Americans must be mobilized against the illegal-drug plague being spread by the Jimmy Carter administration. The campaign drew together a broad coalition of concerned citizens in the United States and abroad. By spring 1978, the coalition's intelligence on the higher-ups behind the narcotics cartel had grown to the point, that LaRouche commissioned a U.S. Labor Party investigative team to draft a comprehensive profile of the international dope trade. LaRouche warned that, unless the United States fought the undeclared war which Dope, Inc. was waging on it, the nation would be destroyed within a generation. There could be no "national security" without a commitment to destroy Dope, Inc., he argued.

Instead, three successive U.S. administrations have made their peace with the dope cartel, and as a result, America is swimming in addictive drugs and the U.S. economy is drowning in narco-dollars.

The Carter-Mondale administration (1977–81) openly embraced the dope lobby agenda of drug legalization. White House drug adviser Dr. Peter Bourne not only pushed "decriminalization" of marijuana, but he claimed, as late as 1978, that cocaine was not a narcotic. Vice President Walter Mondale owed much of his political career to the Minnesota organized crime cronies of Meyer Lansky.

The U.S. Labor Party, an electoral arm during the 1970s of LaRouche's political movement, published the first edition of *Dope, Inc.* and led a nationwide campaign to defeat the Carter White House-backed effort to legalize marijuana on a state-by-state basis. Out of that campaign emerged the National Anti-Drug Coalition, which helped shape the political climate leading to the defeat of the Carter-Mondale team in the 1980 U.S. elections. In 1980, LaRouche challenged Carter for the Democratic Party's presidential nomination, and began building the anti-drug, American System wing of the Democratic Party.

Both President Ronald Reagan and Vice President George Bush, reflecting that popular rejection of the soft-on-drugs policies of their predecessors, mouthed anti-drug slogans. But as their lips were flapping about "war on drugs" and the threat of "narcoterrorism," behind the scenes, White House and CIA officials like National Security Council staffer Oliver North were peddling drugs to covertly finance their favorite secret missions.

Attack the Money-Laundering Capability

And nobody in the White House or the Congress dared to take up the most essential message of *Dope, Inc.*: Shut down the drug money-laundering by the major Anglo-American banks, and the dope cartel would choke to death on its own profits!

When George Bush succeeded Ronald Reagan in the presidency, things got even worse than they were under Jimmy Carter. Not only did Bush keep the dope cartel's most feared enemy, Lyndon LaRouche, in prison, but, as two new chapters in this third edition will detail, Dope, Inc. is doubling every five years and marijuana has replaced food as America's number-one cash crop. George Bush talks about shutting down the dope trade, and then secretly turns over the government of Colombia to the cocaine cartel and joins the narcoterrorist regime of Syria's Hafez al-Assad in an obscene embrace.

In the first edition of *Dope, Inc.*, Lyndon LaRouche also warned that the International Monetary Fund and World Bank were committed to imposing narco-economies on many nations of the developing sector as part of a conscious policy of genocide on a scale worse than Adolf Hitler. LaRouche identified the IMF-World Bank as synonymous with Dope, Inc. These words have been borne out with a vengeance.

The ADL and Kissinger React

Even before the first copies of the first edition of *Dope, Inc.: Britain's Opium War Against the United States,* rolled off the press in December 1978, leaders of the narcotics enterprise were busy trying to stop LaRouche. Beginning in summer 1978, the Anti-Defamation League (ADL), known to well-informed people as the "American Dope Lobby," launched a multi-million dollar campaign to label LaRouche and his political associates as "anti-Semites" for daring to expose the involvement of gangsters like Meyer Lansky and Zionist lobby leaders like Edgar Bronfman and Max Fisher in the dope business. The fact that LaRouche also identified the powerful British Crown bankers as partners in the dope trade along with the Jewish crime syndicate, marked him as one of the most dangerous men alive in the eyes of Dope, Inc.

The ADL's "anti-Semitic" smear against LaRouche was pure Big Lie terrorism in the tradition of Nazi propagandist Joseph Goebbels. Everyone who bothered to look into the matter knew

that LaRouche's political career had been built around his dis-
coveries in physical economy, and that by 1978 he had written
hundreds of articles and several books exposing the fascist economic austerity policies behind the Nazi holocaust which killed
millions of Jews and other victims. The ADL's bizarre slanders
prompted *EIR*'s investigators to scrutinize the history of the
supposed "Jewish civil rights" organization.

The probe turned up a 70-year legacy of intimate ADL ties
with Jewish gangsters, from Meyer Lansky and his "Our
Crowd" sponsor Arnold Rothstein, to more contemporary Dope,
Inc. figures such as Max Fisher, Edgar Bronfman, Edmond
Safra, Meshulam Riklis, and the ADL's own national chairman,
Kenneth Bialkin, the lawyer for the Medellín Cartel's "American connection," Robert Vesco. We also discovered that much
of the ADL's financial backing comes from leading families of
the Anglo-American establishment, whose fortunes trace back
to the British banks and trading companies that ran the opium
clipper ships in and out of China in the last century.

Given the ADL's organized crime pedigree, it was also no
surprise that one of the earliest and nastiest of the ADL-com-
missioned slanders against LaRouche was published in *High
Times* magazine, the unofficial house-organ of the dope lobby.
That article, by Chip Berlet, was run under the headline: "War
on Drugs: The Strange Story of Lyndon LaRouche: Sinister
Mastermind of the National Anti-Drug Coalition—They Want
To Take Your Drugs Away!"

To this day, the ADL holds the key to the corruption of the
American political and judicial system, a corruption that was
bought and paid for by the proceeds of the international dope
trade. Lyndon LaRouche was railroaded to prison on a train
built by drug money and stoked by government officials and
private agencies on the pad of Dope, Inc.

By the summer of 1982, the ADL was joined in its "Get
LaRouche" efforts by Henry A. Kissinger, former secretary of
state and recipient of the ADL's Man of the Year award. Kissinger launched a vendetta to get the federal government to
shut down the LaRouche movement.

The case of LaRouche associate Lewis du Pont Smith illustrates the desperation of the efforts by Kissinger and the Get LaRouche Task Force to stop the LaRouche movement's organizing of a national war on drugs. An heir to the du Pont family industrial fortune, Smith contributed $212,000 to the LaRouche movement in 1985, the bulk of it for the publication of the second edition of this book. Within months, Smith's parents—advised by none other than Kissinger—had secured a judgment in the Chester County, Pennsylvania Court of Common Pleas, depriving their son of control of his inheritance, and suspending his basic human rights—such as the right to sign contracts and be married—on the grounds that Smith was "mentally incompetent." Smith's is the first case in American history in which an individual has been declared incompetent by the courts on the basis of political affiliation.

Kissinger: A British Agent of Influence

Although Kissinger has been historically a close ally of the most rabid factions inside Israel and within the Zionist establishment in the United States, his primary allegiance throughout his political career has been to the British Crown and its intelligence and financial tentacles.

On May 10, 1982, addressing a celebration at the Royal Institute for International Affairs at Chatham House in London, Kissinger boasted that throughout his career in the Nixon and Ford administrations, he had always been closer to the British Foreign Office than to his American colleagues, and had taken all his major policy leads from London. Kissinger set up the international "consulting firm" Kissinger Associates, in partnership with Britain's Peter Lord Carrington, shortly after he delivered that Chatham House lecture.

Chatham House is a successor to the old British East India Company, and serves as the think-tank and foreign intelligence arm of the British Crown. The roots of Chatham House are to be found in Britain's nineteenth-century Opium War policy.

Kissinger is no stranger to the world of international dope-trafficking. The 1978 edition of *Dope, Inc.* told how Kissinger played a pivotal role in covering up the involvement of the People's Republic of China in the Southeast Asia Golden Triangle heroin trade in the early 1970s when he was shuttling between Washington and Beijing playing the "China card." Tens of thousands of American GIs who became addicted to drugs in Southeast Asia during the Vietnam War should hold Kissinger at least partially responsible for their habits. Later, during the 1980s, through Kissinger Associates, Henry became a business partner of some of the same Chinese opium lords he protected from American drug enforcement for over a decade.

Kissinger was furious that LaRouche and his associates widely circulated the official text of his Chatham House speech to document that Kissinger was a loyal asset of the British Crown. He went head-to-head with LaRouche over Reagan administration policy. By 1982, a major battle had broken out within the administration over the emerging Ibero-American debt crisis, a crisis of which LaRouche had been warning senior White House officials for months. A confrontation evolved between LaRouche and Kissinger over whether Washington would negotiate an equitable solution to the debt crisis, on a government-to-government basis, or back International Monetary Fund policies aimed at further looting our hemispheric neighbors.

A paper trail of personal letters from Kissinger to then-FBI Director William Webster during the summer and autumn of 1982 documents Kissinger's role.

'Get LaRouche' Task Force Formed

On August 19, 1982, Henry Kissinger wrote the now-infamous "Dear Bill" letter to Webster, demanding action against the LaRouche movement: "Because these people have been getting increasingly obnoxious, I have taken the liberty of asking my lawyer, Bill Rogers, to get in touch with you and ask your advice, especially with respect to security. It was good seeing you at the Grove [Bohemian Grove, where male invitees dress up as women and romp in the woods—ed.] . . . warm regards."

Kissinger's own efforts, aided by the ADL's so-called Civil Rights Division, were augmented in January 1983 by a Kissinger-solicited intervention on the part of several members of President Ronald Reagan's Foreign Intelligence Advisory Board, led by Edward Bennett Williams, David Abshire, and Leo Cherne. The PFIAB members demanded that the FBI launch an international investigation of Lyndon LaRouche, in effect claiming that LaRouche's exposé of Kissinger's record of selling out the United States to British, Soviet, and Dope, Inc. interests was somehow "subversive."

Government documents catalogue the role of Kissinger's PFIAB cronies. A memorandum from Webster to his chief deputy, Oliver Revell, dated January 12, 1983, stated in part:

"At the PFIAB meeting today, [name redacted] raised the subject of the activities of the U.S. Labor Party and Lyndon LaRouche. He noted that he and a number of other Americans in public life had been the subject of repeated harassment by LaRouche and wondered whether the FBI had a basis for investigating these activities *under the guidelines or otherwise*. A number of members present, including Edward Bennett Williams, raised the question of the sources for these U.S. Labor Party activities. In view of the large amounts obviously being expended worldwide, the question was raised whether the U.S. Labor Party might be funded by hostile intelligence agencies" (emphasis added).

The PFIAB inquiry led in early 1983 to the opening of a formal FBI investigation into Lyndon LaRouche and his associates. That inquiry provided the legal cover for an all-out offensive to drive LaRouche and his associates out of business and into prison. The "guidelines" under which the unconstitutional "Get LaRouche" campaign was conducted, were contained in a little-known White House document, Executive Order 12333, signed by President Reagan in December 1981. EO 12333 gave the FBI and U.S. intelligence agencies a broad mandate to spy on and conduct covert actions against American citizens deemed to be opponents of the incumbent administration. EO

12333 also allowed these agencies to use private citizens as their agents in carrying out these operations. At this point, the ADL became an integral component of the government's "Get LaRouche" task force.

The ADL and Kissinger found their most willing collaborators inside the Reagan-Bush administration among the spooks and White House staffers involved in the illegal, secret Iran-Contra program. Once again, the pawprints of Dope, Inc. were everywhere.

LaRouche Objects to Contra Policy

In the first years of the Reagan administration, LaRouche had collaborated with several senior administration officials in the development of the Strategic Defense Initiative and other national security policies. During the 1982–83 period, LaRouche and his colleagues had been quietly approached and asked to also cooperate with the administration's effort to support the Contra guerrillas fighting to overthrow the Sandinista regime in Nicaragua. LaRouche warned the Reagan administration that the Contras were a wholly owned asset of international gun- and drug-trafficking organizations and that the entire anti-Sandinista program—and the Reagan administration's widely publicized anti-drug efforts along with it—were doomed to disaster if the administration went ahead with its Contra support program. As an alternative plan of action, LaRouche proposed that the administration focus its Central American efforts on an all-out war on drugs which would, among other things, expose Soviet, Cuban, and Sandinista involvement in the dope trade.

By this time, with pressure from Wall Street and the Zionist Lobby, Henry Kissinger had been named to head up the Reagan administration's Blue Ribbon Commission on Central American Policy. A one-time paid employee of the ADL, Carl Gershman, had been named as the chief of the administration's National Endowment for Democracy (NED), a covert operations funding agency housed in the State Department's U.S. Information Agency. The NED was at the center of the secret support for the Contras.

For Kissinger and the ADL-led NED, dealing with cocaine traffickers was no problem. But LaRouche's public exposé of leading drug traffickers on the government payroll was a problem.

A May 1986 memo from White House Iran-Contra operator Gen. Richard Secord to National Security Council staffer Oliver North confirms that the Contra support apparatus—what Sen. David Boren (D-Okla.) labeled the "secret, parallel government"—was gathering "information against LaRouche."

By the spring of 1986, following dramatic electoral victories in the statewide Illinois Democratic Party primary by two LaRouche-backed candidates for lieutenant governor and secretary of state, the "Get LaRouche" forces inside the government had built up momentum, especially inside the deeply corrupted Department of Justice and the FBI.

Two of the most zealous of the Justice Department "Get LaRouche" activists were William Weld and Arnold Burns. Weld was the U.S. attorney in Boston who led the federal government's pioneering strike force against LaRouche. He became head of the Department of Justice Criminal Division in September 1986, the number-two position at the DoJ. Now Governor of Massachusetts, Weld is the scion of a prominent blueblood family that made its fortune in the China opium trade.

Arnold Burns, the deputy attorney general, was a director of the ADL's Sterling National Bank, an outfit founded by mob cronies of Meyer Lansky and implicated in hot-money dealings in the United States, Italy, and Israel. Burns himself was nearly indicted in a money-laundering scheme run by Israel's secret service, the Mossad. It would later emerge that Burns's partners in that scheme were part of the Jonathan Jay Pollard Israeli-Soviet espionage ring.

In October 1986, an army of over 400 federal and state police, accompanied by helicopters, fixed-wing planes, and an armored personnel carrier, conducted a raid against the offices of several LaRouche-associated publications in Leesburg, Virginia. This was the largest domestic paramilitary action by the federal government since the urban and student riots of the late 1960s and early 1970s. The purpose was simply to execute two search warrants and make four arrests of people who had no criminal records!

Over the next several years, LaRouche and dozens of associates were arrested and put on trial. A prosecution of LaRouche and a dozen co-defendants in a Boston federal court ended in a mistrial on May 4, 1988. The Boston jury had heard 92 days of testimony from government witnesses. The defense never got to present its case. However, the jurors, according to press accounts, were so angry at the government's behavior that when they polled themselves after they had been dismissed by the judge, they voted LaRouche and the others "not guilty" on all 125 counts. One juror told the *Boston Herald* on May 5, 1988 that he and his colleagues were convinced the government had committed crimes against LaRouche. LaRouche told the press that he had been defrauded of a verdict of "innocent."

Six months later, the Justice Department re-indicted LaRouche in an Alexandria, Virginia federal district court on nearly identical charges. The judge and the jury were rigged. The jury foreman, a Department of Agriculture official named Buster Horton, had been a member of a secret government task force that also included Oliver North. The judge, Albert V. Bryan, Jr. had been a business partner of the CIA's biggest secret arms dealer, Sam Cummings. In that federal trial and at subsequent state trials in Virginia, leading officials of the ADL operated as de facto members of the government's prosecution team. In one telling incident, the ADL was caught attempting to bribe a Commonwealth of Virginia trial judge with a promise of a state Supreme Court post in return for throwing the book at the LaRouche defendants.

On January 27, 1989, just days after George Bush was inaugurated as President, LaRouche was deprived of bail pending appeal and thrown in federal prison, along with six colleagues. LaRouche was sentenced to 15 years in prison—a life sentence for a man already in his mid-60s. Bush added his imprimatur to the jailing by refusing to release thousands of pages of exculpatory evidence under the control of the White House. Of all his political adversaries and critics, Lyndon LaRouche was the one man whom George Bush desperately wanted out of the way.

But the jailing of LaRouche and some of his closest colleagues was not enough to satisfy the Dope, Inc. crowd. Two LaRouche-linked publications, *New Solidarity,* a twice-weekly newspaper with over 100,000 subscribers, and *Fusion,* a science magazine with over 114,000 subscribers, were seized by the government on April 21, 1987, and shut down in an action that federal courts after the fact declared to have been illegal. Federal Bankruptcy Court Judge Martin V.B. Bostetter wrote in his Oct. 25, 1989 decision, which was upheld on appeal, that the government action had been in "bad faith" and that the government had committed a "constructive fraud upon the court."

Drug Pushers Can't Be Patriots

When Lyndon LaRouche first warned senior Reagan administration officials about the drug cartel links of the Nicaraguan Contras, it was not yet publicly known that the U.S. government was selling dope to American children to fund the secret Contra war in Nicaragua (even at the same time that some well-meaning government officials thought they were genuinely fighting drugs). Within days of the Leesburg raid, the first details of the Iran-Contra scandal surfaced following the crash of an American supply plane over Nicaraguan territory and the arrest of Eugene Hasenfus, a member of the crew. In the months following the Hasenfus capture, more and more pieces of the secret government corruption came out.

The case of Lt. Col. Oliver North is one good example of this corruption, especially because so much media attention has been directed toward building up the image of the Marine-turned-White House superspy as a model of American patriotism.

Evidence made public during the congressional Iran-Contra hearings, through federal and state court cases and international criminal prosecutions, reveals that Oliver North was in the middle of a major international arms-for-drugs trafficking operation which was run out of his National Security Council office at the Old Executive Office Building next door to the White House.

Colonel North was the day-to-day operations officer for the Contra resupply program. But it was Vice President George Bush, the former CIA director, who was formally in charge of the entire Reagan administration Central America covert operations program. Under National Security Decision Directive 3, signed by Ronald Reagan in May 1982, Bush was placed in charge of two little-known White House secret committees: the Special Situation Group (SSG) and the Crisis Pre-Planning Group (CPPG). Oliver North was the secretary of the CPPG, and it was in this capacity that he ran the Central America spook show—under George Bush.

North's personal notebooks, which catalogued most of his meetings, telephone calls, and personal observations during his White House days, betray the fact that he was well aware that the Contras were being heavily financed by Miami-based cocaine traffickers. For example, a March 26, 1985 handwritten entry in North's notebook read: "Rafael Quintero—Secord's Agent should be on shore when arrivals occur—as liaison w/ APLICANO . . . Quintero . . ." Several days later, on April 3, a sequel note read: "0600—RAFAEL QUINTERO—(captured)—known narcotics trafficker—Enrique Camarena . . ."

Camarena was a Drug Enforcement Administration (DEA) agent in Guadalajara, Mexico who was kidnapped and tortured to death in February 1985. In 1990, Juan Ramón Matta Ballesteros, a Honduran national who helped set up Colombian cocaine routes through Mexico, was convicted along with several other men in federal court in Los Angeles of conspiracy to kidnap and murder Camarena. At the time of the Camarena affair, Matta Ballesteros was the owner of a Honduran charter airline, SETCO Air, which was paid over a half-million dollars by the U.S. State Department to airlift "humanitarian aid" to the Contras in a program run by Oliver North from the White House. Other funds, drawn directly from secret North-Secord bank accounts in Switzerland, were also funneled into SETCO Air.

Worse, according to a report published in the *Washington Post* on July 5, 1990, a ranch near Veracruz, Mexico owned by Rafael Caro Quintero, the mastermind of the Camarena torture-murder and the head of the Mexican drug mafia, was used by the CIA to train Central American guerrillas as yet another feature of the North-White House effort. According to DEA informant Laurence Victor Harrison, the CIA used Mexico's Federal Security Directorate (DFS) "as a cover in the event any questions were raised as to who was running the training operation. Representatives of the DFS, which was the front for the training camp, were in fact acting in consort with major drug overlords to ensure a flow of narcotics through Mexico into the United States."

Another North notebook entry on August 9, 1985 removes any shadow of a doubt that Oliver North was fully aware of the Contra-cocaine connection: "Honduran DC–6 which is being used for runs out of New Orleans is probably being used for drug runs into U.S." The Honduran plane referenced by North was owned by Matta Ballesteros.

North and company were aware of the cocaine connection even earlier, according to other government records. On September 26, 1984, the Miami Police Department provided FBI Special Agent George Kiszynski with an investigative report identifying a network of Miami cocaine traffickers which was pouring money into the Contras' coffers. Within days of the report being turned over to Kiszynski, according to congressional testimony, it had been passed on to Oliver Revell, a key player in the "Get LaRouche" effort and North's FBI liaison for the White House Central America program.

That Miami Police Department document stated in unambiguous terms: "Frank Castro is a close associate of an individual by the name of Francisco Chanes. . . . Chanes is a narcotics trafficker. . . . Chanes was giving financial support to anti-Castro groups and the Nicaraguan Contra guerrillas; the monies comes from narcotic transactions. . . . Frank Castro contacted Mr. Coutin to give the Legion Cubana financial support to fight the Nicaraguan Sandinista Marxist government . . . the financial support was from drug monies."

White House Ties to Terrorists

North's collusion with dope peddlers was not limited to Central America. In the spring of 1986, according to the congressional Iran-Contra investigation, North, then-National Security Adviser Robert McFarlane, and other administration officials opened a so-called "second channel" to secretly negotiate the arms-for-hostages swap with the Lebanese-based terrorists holding American hostages. That second channel was a Syrian national named Mansur Al-Kassar. A well-known international heroin, hashish, and cocaine smuggler, Al-Kassar was also implicated in a string of terrorist attacks and kidnappings in the Middle East, including the infamous *Achille Lauro* cruise ship hijacking, in which an American citizen, Leon Klinghoffer, was killed. Al-Kassar provided arms to the Palestine Liberation Front, the group responsible for the *Achille Lauro* attack, and for years ran a mercenary kidnapping ring inside Lebanon with Abul Abbas, head of the PLF. Al-Kassar also sold Soviet-made weapons to the Black September group of Abu Nidal and to the Syrian-sponsored Popular Front for the Liberation of Palestine-General Command of Ahmed Jibril.

Al-Kassar was a black market partner of Syria's Vice President Rifaat al-Assad, the brother of President Hafez al-Assad. In 1986, Spanish authorities obtained photographs of Al-Kassar and Rifaat al-Assad meeting in the city of Marbella with Medellín Cartel boss Pablo Escobar Gaviria. The purpose of the meeting was to establish expanded cocaine-trafficking operations in continental Europe. Al-Kassar, throughout this period, was identified in CIA files as an agent of the Soviet KGB who had been a leading smuggler of Soviet bloc arms into the West.

None of this dissuaded North and company from bringing Al-Kassar into the White House "Enterprise." He never succeeded in winning the freedom of any of the hostages, but he did become one of the suppliers of Soviet bloc weapons to the Contras. In 1986, one transaction alone netted Al-Kassar $1.5 million in payments from the North-Secord Lake Resources Swiss bank accounts.

In return for these favors, Al-Kassar's drug-running and terrorist activities were protected by the National Security Council. This protection continued long after the Iran-Contra scandal had blown up in the faces of North, Secord, CIA director William Casey, et al. And, according to one report, Al-Kassar's cozy ties to the White House may have led to the deaths of 270 people.

On December 21, 1988, just weeks before George Bush's inauguration as President, a bomb exploded aboard Pan American World Airways Flight 103 above Lockerbie, Scotland. Some 259 passengers and crew aboard the plane, and 11 people on the ground, were killed.

It is still not known exactly how the bomb was placed on board the airplane. The full story may never come out. Attorneys and investigators for the airline, as well as U.S. Rep. James Traficant (D-Ohio), have suggested that Mansur Al-Kassar may have been involved. Allegedly, heroin smugglers in his employ at Frankfurt International Airport in Germany placed the bomb on board Flight 103, and Al-Kassar's men were protected by CIA personnel in Frankfurt as part of the hostage release deal and other features of the new "Syrian-American rapprochement."

According to syndicated columnist Jack Anderson, in April 1989, President Bush conferred with British Prime Minister Margaret Thatcher, and the two ordered British and American intelligence to cover up Al-Kassar's alleged involvement in the Lockerbie bombing. Whether Anderson's charges are true or not, the truth about the Lockerbie massacre has been completely covered up, as has the role of Syria in the flourishing multi-billion dollar Middle East heroin and hashish trade.

One reason for the cover-up is that the use of Middle Eastern dope-smuggling networks was as pervasive a feature of the Reagan-Bush era Iran-Contra misdeeds as was the hiring of Colombian cocaine cartel pilots and money launderers to supply the Contras. In fact, the Colombian and Middle Eastern dope connections have one recurring common denominator: a very prominent Israeli component.

During the very month—April 1989—that President Bush and Prime Minister Thatcher were allegedly ordering a cover-up of the Pan Am 103 bombing, a DEA and U.S. Customs Service report was covered in the media alleging that New York's Republic National Bank was serving as a money-laundering facility for Middle East and Ibero-American narcotics-trafficking organizations. Republic National Bank is owned by Edmond Safra, a prominent Jewish banker of Lebanese descent whose worldwide banking operations extend from Aleppo, Syria, to Rio de Janiero, Brazil, to midtown Manhattan.

According to a 13-page memo written by DEA agents in Berne, Switzerland and dated January 3, 1989, Safra and Republic National Bank were implicated in a Swiss-centered drug money-laundering network run out of the Zurich-based Shakarchi Trading Co. U.S. investigators linked Shakarchi to a heroin-smuggling ring that enjoyed the cooperation of the Bulgarian secret police and the state-owned export-import agency, Globus (formerly called Kintex). An earlier DEA report had implicated Kintex's director in the attempted assassination of Pope John Paul II by Mehmet Ali Agca in May 1981. Kintex was identified as the hub of the "Bulgarian connection" international drug-smuggling network. We provide an inside look at this Soviet-Bulgarian dope ring in a chapter that follows. For now, it is sufficient to note the following:

According to the January 1989 DEA memo, "The Shakarchi Trading Company of Zurich, Switzerland, operates as a currency exchange company and is utilized by some of the world's largest drug-trafficking organizations to launder the proceeds of their drug-trafficking activities. . . . Shakarchi Trading Company maintains accounts at the Republic National Bank of New York, a bank which has surfaced in several previous money-laundering investigations. . . . While he was alive, Mahmoud Shakarchi maintained a close relationship with Edmond Safra and the banking institutions in which Safra had an interest, including Republic National Bank. Since the death of Mahmoud Shakarchi, Mohammed Shakarchi, doing business as Shakar-

chi Trading Company, has maintained close ties with the Republic National Bank."

Drug Money Funding ADL

DEA and U.S. Customs investigators tracing the flow of heroin revenues from Lebanon through Turkey and Bulgaria on to
the Shakarchi firm in Zurich found that millions of dollars
made their way into Account No. 606347712 at the main New
York City branch of Republic National Bank. Meanwhile, DEA
agents in Colombia and on the U.S. West Coast busted up the
largest Medellín Cartel cocaine money-laundering scheme ever
unearthed as part of the DEA's Operation Polar Cap. Known as
"La Mina" (The Mine), the money-laundering circuit involved a
string of banks in Colombia and Uruguay and a Los Angeles
jewelry wholesale company called Ropex. Millions of dollars in
Ropex deposits were traced by the Polar Cap team to Account
No. 606347712 at Republic National Bank—the same Shakarchi Trading Co. account!

Not surprisingly, in 1989, as the Shakarchi-Safra story was
grabbing headlines in Europe and the United States, banker
Safra was donating a reported $1 million to his favorite char-
ity—the Anti-Defamation League!

Banker Safra's ties to the Dope, Inc. money-laundering go
back to at least the mid-1970s when Republic National Bank
shepherded Argentine wheeler-dealer David Graiver into the
inner sanctums of Wall Street. Graiver bought up American
Bank and Trust in 1975, and, in less than a year, looted the New
York bank of an estimated $40 million. Graiver conveniently
"died" in a plane crash in Mexico just as bank regulators discovered that American Bank and Trust's cupboard was bare during
an audit of the bank. There was such skepticism over Graiver's
disappearance that, for years, New York State prosecutors continued to list Graiver as a defendant in the bank fraud case.

Of course, Graiver was simply a front man for a Swiss-based
Mossad money-laundering network known as the Centrade

Group, one of whose leading figures, Tibor Rosenbaum, is profiled at length in this book. The point is that for the past 20
years, a large and growing component of Dope, Inc. has been
the combined machinery of gangster Meyer Lansky and the
Israeli Mossad.

If there were any doubt about the pivotal role played by shady
elements within the Israeli intelligence services, in partnership
with British and American counterparts, in the world dope-for-
guns bazaar, it was shattered in a hail of bullets in a desolate
corner of Colombia on December 15, 1989.

On that date, Colombian Army units invaded the compound
of Medellín Cartel capo José Gonzalo Rodríguez Gacha near
the town of Pacho. In a separate shootout at Gacha's bunker
hideout, Rodríguez Gacha and several of his bodyguards were
killed. On January 24 and 28, in followup raids on two other
ranches owned by Rodríguez Gacha, the Army seized large
stockpiles of weapons—the majority of which were made in
Israel. The Galil rifle used to assassinate Colombian presidential candidate Luis Carlos Galán in August 1989 was part of
the shipment.

The discovery of the Israeli weapons caches prompted the
Colombian government to make a formal inquiry to Tel Aviv:
To whom had those particular weapons been sold? The answer
came back from the Israeli Defense Ministry: The guns had
been sold to the government of the tiny Caribbean island nation
of Antigua, in a deal brokered by an Israeli national named
Maurice Sarfati. According to the original Israeli version, Sarfati, a resident of Antigua, had supposedly brokered the deal
for the Antiguan "national security adviser"—a nonexistent
post.

Many months and cover stories later, at least a semblance of
the truth came out. Israeli intelligence—through a string of
front companies—had been providing weapons and terrorist
training to the Medellín Cartel's assassination squads in collaboration with British mercenaries. And the entire program had
been run by senior officials at the Reagan-Bush White House
and administered by the CIA and Project Democracy.

In fact, the funds to purchase the weapons found at Rodríguez

Gacha's farm had been provided by the U.S. State Department through a program personally run by Assistant Secretary of State Elliott Abrams, who pleaded guilty on October 7 to Iran-Contra crimes. The weapons were ostensibly bought to arm a fictitious "Panamanian government in exile" nominally headed by former Panamanian President Eric Delvalle.

That program, which was part of the Reagan-Bush anti-Noriega effort, also involved high-powered Republican Party operators, including John Zagame and Richard Bond. Zagame, a former aide to Sen. Alfonse D'Amato (R-N.Y.) , set up a consulting firm and hired himself out as an adviser to the Delvalle group to the tune of $15,000 per month. The funds came from the same accounts that bought the Israeli Uzis, Galils and other weapons discovered at the Rodríguez Gacha ranches. Zagame, the last time we looked, was running a public relations firm called PanAmerican, which had only one major client: Ollie North.

At the same time that Zagame was hired on to the anti-Noriega program, the same funds were also going to another "consulting" firm, Bond Donatelli, which shared offices with Zagame in Alexandria, Virginia. Richard Bond was Vice President Bush's deputy chief of staff and a former deputy chairman of the Republican National Committee. He was asked in 1991 to become RNC chairman by George Bush, but turned down the offer. Frank Donatelli was at one point political director of the Reagan White House.

Among the casualties racked up to the marriage of the cocaine cartel to the CIA-Israeli intelligence were thousands of innocent Colombian nationals who were victims of cartel gunmen and bombers. During one particular bloody week in June 1990, according to Colombian government reports, over 640 people died violent deaths, the vast majority at the hands of the cartel. In one November 1989 airline bombing that has been linked to Israeli-trained cartel terrorists, 117 people perished. As we already reported, one of the guns provided by the Israeli arms merchants was used in August 1989 to assassinate Colombia's frontrunning presidential candidate, Luis Carlos Galán. Had he survived the armed assault against him at a campaign rally, Galán would have surely been elected President of Colombia, and he was committed to an anti-drug policy dramatically in contrast to the total capitulation that has occurred as the result of his murder.

The trainer of Rodríguez Gacha's killer squads was a reserve Israeli Army colonel named Yair Klein. His company, Spearhead, Ltd. (Hod Hahanit in Hebrew), set up shop in Colombia sometime in the late 1980s. Besides the Israelis, in a parallel operation, a group of British mercenaries also engaged in training the cartel hit squads, and even participated in paramilitary operations inside Colombia. Among the British soldiers of fortune were David Tomkins and Peter MacAleese, a veteran of the Rhodesian Army. Most of the British mercenaries were former Special Air Services (SAS) officers.

The involvement of British intelligence in the CIA-Mossad Colombia deal was further confirmed when Louis Blom-Cooper and Geoffrey Robertson, both officials of Amnesty International, which is funded by British intelligence, were deployed to cover up the official U.S., British and Israeli government sponsorship of the Klein operation and to pin the blame solely on officials of the tiny island of Antigua, a British Crown Colony.

Shortly after the Medellín Cartel assassins school got going, Klein was brought into a sensitive covert action program being run by the Reagan-Bush administration: the plot to overthrow Panama's Gen. Manuel Antonio Noriega. In 1988, Klein was brought to Miami for a series of secret meetings with Col. Eduardo Herrera, the former Panamanian ambassador to Israel. Herrera got the boot from the Tel Aviv assignment after General Noriega discovered that he was working with both the Mossad and the CIA. Colonel Herrera was then relocated to the United States by Elliott Abrams and was put formally on the CIA's payroll. Colonel Klein was assigned to work with Herrera on a plan to create a Panamanian "Contra" force that would be sponsored by the United States to oust the Panamanian general, who had become a thorn in the side of George Bush.

On behalf of this secret project, Klein visited Antigua in early
1989 to solicit permission from the local authorities to establish
a "VIP security guard" training academy. Sarfati, a longstanding Mossad operator who had purchased a melon farm in Antigua with U.S. government funds arranged through Bruce Rappaport, a Swiss-Israeli Iran-Contra figure who was a golfing
partner of the late William Casey, set up the local contacts.

According to Col. Clyde Walker, at the time the chief of
Antigua's tiny national defense force, after he had met with
Colonel Klein and Sarfati in January 1989, he made formal
inquiries with CIA officials in charge of the eastern Caribbean.
In a sworn affidavit, Walker stated, "I prepared an intelligence
report on Colonel Klein and all the other names in the [Spear-
head] pamphlets . . . and I gave the report to United States CIA
agent Robert Hogan in his hotel room at St. James Club and I
requested of him some investigation into Spearhead, Ltd. and
the colonel and his trainers. I also discussed Spearhead, Ltd.
and Colonel Klein with chief of the CIA Eastern Caribbean Mr.
George Kenning, Barbados Embassy, in my office, and also in
the VIP Lounge at Grantley-Adams Airport." Some months
later, says Walker in his affidavit, CIA Chief of Eastern Caribbean George Kenning "told me Spearhead, Ltd. appears to be
all right."

In spite of that CIA green light, the powers that be on Antigua
decided in March 1989 not to approve Klein's request for the
training school.

At that moment, a shipload of Israeli arms were steaming
across the Atlantic on board the Danish-flagged ship *Else TH*.
On April 24, 1989, the arms were transferred at the Antigua
port onto a Panamanian-registered ship, *Sea Point*, and shut-
tled off to Rodríguez Gacha in Colombia.

The money to purchase the 1989 weapons shipment had come
from a State Department-administered account under the control of Assistant Secretary for Inter-American Affairs Elliott
Abrams. The escrow deposit to ensure that the hundreds of
guns left Israel on time had come through the Miami branch of
the Israeli Bank Hapoalim.

Dope, Inc. Installs Governments

If there were any doubt that the arming of the Medellín Cartel hit squads was part and parcel of the same program that included the December 20, 1989 U.S. invasion of Panama and overthrow of General Noriega, consider the following:

After the smoke cleared in Panama—thousands of dead bodies and billions of dollars in bombed-out property later—the Bush administration succeeded in installing into the presidency a local Panamanian lawyer, Guillermo "Porky" Endara. A review of court records shows that President Endara and several of his law partners were the owners of record of the ship *Sea Point* in April 1989 when the ship had delivered the Israeli weapons to Rodríguez Gacha! They still owned the ship in late 1989 when it was stopped off the coast of Mexico and busted for carrying a massive shipment of cocaine. For good measure, over half of the crew members busted by the Mexican authorities were also on board when the gun delivery was made to the Medellín Cartel. Back on dry land in Panama City, Endara was the co-owner, along with Rodríguez Gacha, of the drug money-laundering Banco Interoceánico.

When the lid blew on the Mossad-Medellín connection in early 1990, the Israeli government scrambled to deny that Klein was on "official business" when he trained and armed the narcoterrorists. Unfortunately for this story's credibility, Klein had been not only linked to Sarfati in his Caribbean adventures but, back in Miami, Klein's Spearhead, Ltd. had been managed by two rather important Israeli operatives, Gen. Pinchas Sachar and Pesach Ben-Or. Both men were officially designated representatives of the Israeli government's Israeli Military Industry, and it was Sachar's account at the Bank Hapoalim that had received the funds from Elliott Abrams to purchase the guns routed to Colombia.

Pesach Ben-Or had been installed back during the Carter administration as the Mossad's principal arms merchant in Guatemala City, a hub of later Contra supply action. According to eyewitness accounts, Carter's National Security Adviser

Zbigniew Brzezinski quietly informed the Guatemalan junta in 1978— after Carter shut down all American military aid to the country over alleged human rights violations—that Ben-Or would fill all their arms and military training requirements with the secret blessing of Washington. Ben-Or did just that— at a 600% markup. A decade later, Ben-Or was still wheeling and dealing with Guatemala—out of offices he shared in Miami with General Sachar and Colonel Klein.

Why A Third Edition

Since the second edition of *Dope, Inc.* was published by *Executive Intelligence Review* magazine in 1986, the international narcotics cartel has steadily gained ground, especially inside the United States. On top of that, the nation's fiercest anti-drug fighter, Lyndon LaRouche, was railroaded into jail and the American people let it happen. That was a moral failing.

But more to the point, the editors of *EIR* have decided that the eve of the 1992 presidential elections is an appropriate moment to issue a third edition of *Dope, Inc.* Current events give us a unique historical chance to defeat the drug cartel, a chance we cannot afford to ignore.

The fraud of the Reagan-Bush "economic recovery" is being exposed all over the world—especially inside the United States, where Dope, Inc.'s control over some of the most powerful financial institutions has brought the United States into a second Great Depression. These bankrupt institutions are now ripe to be replaced by new structures, free of Dope, Inc.'s corruption.

In addition, the peaceful revolutions in eastern Europe and the former Soviet Union demonstrate that it is no longer automatically the case that "citizens above suspicion" are free to operate above the law. The images of Ceausescu in Romania or Honecker in the former East Germany being executed or charged with treason offer a clear warning to those still clinging to power that their time in the sun is coming to an end.

In 1985, powerful families were able to suppress *Dope, Inc.;* the Cisneros clan of Venezuela ordered the banning of the Spanish language edition of this book in Venezuela. Today, however, dozens of parliamentarians from Venezuela, Peru, the Dominican Republic and other Latin American nations are demanding publicly that the ban be lifted. Longstanding associates of the Cisneros Group and of President Carlos Andrés Pérez are being accused in congressional hearings of terrorism, dope-trafficking and black market arms-dealing. These developments have turned Venezuelan politics upside-down.

The cracking of Dope, Inc.'s power evidenced by these developments abroad can happen in the United States as well.

This book is your ammunition to fight, and win, a war against Dope, Inc.

* * *

In this third edition, we have retained almost all of the chapters published in the 1985 Spanish language and 1986 English language second editions. Some of this material dates back to the historic first edition of *Dope, Inc.*, subtitled *Britain's Opium War Against the United States,* which sold out almost immediately in 50,000 copies when it was published in 1978. In details, therefore, parts of this text contain inaccuracies, especially in the sections discussing the the size of the drug trade globally and in major producing and consuming areas. Nevertheless, the methodology of our original work—which indentified the institutions and individuals who run Dope, Inc. by tracing the flow of narcotics profits through the international banking system—stands as validated today. And it is as true today as it was when this volume was first released thirteen years ago, that a competent war on drugs must begin with a war against the banking institutions and bankers who "launder" Dope Inc.'s ill-gotten gains.

To this third edition, we have added, along with this new introduction, a chapter detailing the phenomenal growth rates of Dope, Inc., which is now doubling in size every five years, and a chapter documenting the emergence of marijuana as America's number one cash crop. Finally, we have updated Appendix C, on the Anti-Defamation League of B'nai B'rith, and added a new appendix on the role of the People's Republic of China in global drug-trafficking.

2
Dope, Inc. Is Doubling Every Five Years

In February 1991, the Bush White House issued its third annual National Drug Control Strategy report. The document was a compendium of doctored statistics and unwarranted conclusions. At the press conference at which the report was issued, President Bush, flanked by Attorney General Richard Thornburgh and newly appointed drug czar Bob Martinez, declared that the United States had scored a near-total victory in the War on Drugs.

It was one of the most shameless cases of government fraud ever recorded. Even on its face, the report admitted that there were no statistics available on the total volume of illegal drugs circulating on the streets of the United States or the amount of marijuana domestically produced and distributed. The President's claim that hospital emergency room drug overdose admissions were way down was a classic bit of doublespeak. The statistics were down because emergency rooms, hard hit by budget cuts, had simply stopped compiling the data and reporting it to the Drug Abuse Warning Network (DAWN), the federal office responsible for compiling these statistics.

The Bush-Thornburgh-Martinez press conference was in every respect a piece of pure hypocrisy. Martinez was the former Governor of Florida, the favored point of entry of cocaine into the United States for the smugglers of Colombia's Medellín Cartel. Attorney General Thornburgh was at that very moment embroiled in a major scandal involving widespread cocaine use by several of his most longstanding and trusted aides. Henry Barr, the attorney general's liaison to all federal prosecutors handling major narcotics prosecutions, would soon be indicted and convicted for cocaine use and perjury. Richard Guida, who had served as Thornburgh's aide while the attorney general was Governor of Pennsylvania, was indicted on cocaine-trafficking charges by the same federal grand jury that indicted Barr. Guida pleaded guilty to avoid a 100-count trafficking indictment. Witnesses in Pennsylvania named the attorney general's own son as a principal player in the "yuppie" cocaine ring operating in and around the Pennsylvania State House.

Two months after this sorry performance, the Drug Enforcement Administration issued a limited-circulation report which was barred from release to the general public. The report warned that the United States was being flooded with cheap, high-grade heroin from the Golden Triangle region of Southeast Asia. Yet even this report, mindful of State Department and White House "China card" policy, vastly underplayed the role of the Communist regime in Beijing in that Golden Triangle heroin bonanza.

The Bush administration could hardly explain away its Big Lie about drug war "victory" by claiming that adequate documentation could not be obtained. Just three months before the National Drug Control Strategy was released to the public, *Executive Intelligence Review* magazine published a detailed analysis of the drug epidemic. *EIR*'s conclusion: Dope, Inc. is doubling every five years!

The detailed findings were shocking.

Contrary to the self-serving propaganda issued by the Bush administration, consumption of mind-destroying drugs such as marijuana and cocaine is *not* declining in the United States; it is *not* contained; its rate of growth is *not even leveling off*. It is skyrocketing. There are currently about 70 million Americans who have consumed drugs—nearly one-third of the total population.

Moreover, the single, integrated, multinational cartel which runs this trade, and which is properly referred to as "Dope, Inc.," is now engaged in a vast expansion of its markets in Europe and Japan, which, if not checked, will do to their youth, their cities, and their economies what has already been done to ours in America.

In the second edition of this book, back in 1986, *EIR* researchers concluded that the U.S. drug trade grossed a minimum of $250 billion per year, and that if non-U.S. drug-trafficking and other aspects of the "black economy" (such as the illegal weapons and gold trade) were taken into account, the total figure would be in the range of $500 billion per year.

It can now be demonstrated that those figures were, if anything, *too low*. In 1986, world drug trafficking alone was close to $400 billion. By 1989, the last year for which figures are available, that total had leapt to $558 billion. This is much larger than the annual world consumption of oil. It is more than 50% larger than the Gross National Product of Brazil, the largest nation of Ibero-America, and the eighth-largest economy in the capitalist world. It is about half the GNP of Germany, the most powerful economy of Western Europe (*Figure 1*).

These are conservative calculations, based mainly on official production statistics of the Drug Enforcement Administration (DEA), adjusted to assume that 10% of the quantity produced is lost through seizures and spoilage. If we were to also consider other areas of the so-called "black economy"—illegal weapons, gold, and other transactions related to the drug trade—it is likely that the total would be closer to $1 trillion for 1989.

All of it is a cancer; it is a sickness which is destroying

the productive economies of both the advanced and developing sectors of the world.

The drug trade has been growing exponentially over the past 10–15 years. *Table 1,* based on production estimates, shows that Dope, Inc.'s annual revenues from street sales of drugs rose from $175 billion back in 1977, to about $400 billion in 1987, to $558 billion in 1989. It has been growing by an average of about 18% per year over the last few years—more rapidly than any productive economy on the face of the Earth. *At this rate, Dope, Inc.'s size doubles every five years!*

Its main components are cocaine (where Ibero-America is the sole producer worldwide), marijuana and hashish (where Ibero-America and the United States are the biggest producers), opium and heroin (where the largest amounts by far are grown in Southeast and Southwest Asia), and other synthetic chemical drugs such as amphetamines, LSD, and so on. We will look at each of these components in more detail shortly, but for now, notice that Ibero-America currently produces about 55% of the world total value of drugs—up from a 43% share 12 years ago.

This does not mean that Ibero-American nations receive this drug money. Quite the contrary: The large international banks that finance the drug trade get it and launder it, using it to prop up their bankrupt international financial system. *Figure 2* shows that, over the past 12 years, the total cumulative revenue that the banks have received from just the Ibero-American portion of the drug trade, is almost $2 trillion. This dwarfs even the gigantic Ibero-American foreign debt of $430 billion.

In the face of this, the so-called "War on Drugs" of the Bush administration is a cruel joke. Its official purpose is, at best, to reduce the drug trade by 50% over a 10-year period. In practice, this means Washington is picking and choosing which drug mafias will survive and flourish, and which will be driven out of business—all the while confessing that the best solution of all would be to legalize the entire trade. Throughout, the financial controllers of Dope, Inc. are protected from all prosecution.

A very different type of war on drugs is required.

Cocaine: Growth Industry

Where are the world's illegal drugs produced and processed? What are the distribution routes? Let's begin with the case of cocaine.

As we mentioned before, cocaine is the one drug that is produced almost 100% in Ibero-America, as we see in *Figure 3*. The coca leaves are grown here, and the processing laboratories which produce the basic paste of cocaine, and then the refined cocaine, are located here.

In 1989 the continent as a whole produced 703 tons of cocaine hydrochloride, measured in terms of maximum potential cocaine production if all known coca leaf harvested were refined into cocaine. (This is the standard international unit for measuring cocaine.) As the map shows, by 1989 Peru had assumed the lion's share of coca production (373 tons), followed by Bolivia and Colombia. However, the bulk of refining of coca paste or base into pure cocaine occurs in Colombia, followed secondarily by Bolivia and Peru, which refine only a small portion of their coca base. Therefore, the figures should not be misunderstood to imply a lesser role for Colombia in the cocaine trade: They simply indicate that its local production of coca leaves is less than that of Peru and Bolivia.

A critical input to the transformation of coca leaves into cocaine, are certain chemicals, such as ether and acetone. Although these are legal chemicals that have valid industrial uses, they are obtained illegally by the drug runners in large quantities, principally from the United States, Western Europe, and also Brazil.

Figure 4 shows the shocking growth of the volume of cocaine production in Ibero-America. It increased almost sixfold in the decade from 1977 to 1987 (from 90 tons to 513 tons), and grew another 37% since then, to its 1989 total of 703 tons. The estimated amount for 1990 is a staggering 876 tons. These increases are due both to increased hectares under cultivation, and to improved productivity on those already in use.

We see in *Figure 5* what this translates into in terms of

average annual growth rates. In the five-year period of 1982–87, cocaine output grew by an average of 15% per year. In 1988 and 1989, that increased to 16% and 18% respectively; and for 1990, everything indicates that cocaine production will leap by another 25%.

These are hardly the signs of a victorious war on drugs.

Historically, the vast majority of Ibero-American cocaine has been shipped to the United States from laboratories in Colombia and the trinational triangle in the jungle area where Peru, Brazil, and Colombia meet. Up until a few years ago, the principal route was to the Miami area, by both air and sea. But increased surveillance and interdiction along this route have forced the mafia to develop a second major route through Central America and Mexico, before entering the western United States.

Cocaine for the European market is shipped directly from Colombia, as well as through Brazil and Argentina. Brazil is reportedly becoming an important refining center as well, producing 144 tons of cocaine last year, according to one report. Spain is the principal port of entry and logistical staging area for coke bound for all of Europe, for the obvious reason of the historically strong commercial, linguistic, and also mafia links between Spain and Ibero-America.

Anti-drug investigators report that Nigeria has recently become an important new transshipment point in the European route.

What does the future hold for the coke trade?

Take a look at *Figure 6,* which shows how the U.S. coke market was created. You can see that the average retail price of a ton of cocaine was $640 million in 1977, and dropped dramatically to $182 million in 1987, a decade later. In other words, the 1977 price was more than three times greater than the 1987 price.

As a result of this *deliberate marketing decision* by Dope, Inc., the amount of coke sold to American kids increased by almost six times in the same period! This price slashing is the typical way in which any cartel creates and seizes a market. So, coke went from being a high-priced drug for the upper middle class in 1977, to being a cheap dose of death, especially in the form of crack, for a mass market of millions of working-class and poor youth in the 1980s. Of course, Dope, Inc.'s total revenue from coke also rose substantially in the process.

But the picture gets worse. As the American market begins to reach "saturation" levels, as an entire generation is destroyed by this epidemic, Dope, Inc. is turning its attention to what it hopes are the markets of the future: Europe and Japan.

Figure 7 shows the cocaine price and quantity trends for Europe over the last five years: a precise replica of the tragedy that has swept the United States.

In 1987, the retail price of cocaine in Europe was $510 million per ton, about what it was in the United States in 1979–80. In the last two years, the European price has plummeted to $262 million per ton, half of what it was in 1987. What took a decade to achieve in the United States is being executed in Europe by the drug mafia in one-third that time.

The consequences are identical. European consumption of cocaine is skyrocketing, as can be seen in the graph.

If one compares *Figure 6* and *Figure 7,* the similarity of the process is striking—only it is happening far more quickly in Europe.

Figure 8 compares the rate of price decline, and the rate of quantity increase, in the United States and Europe over the indicated years.

It should be noted that, when we refer to Europe, until 1989 we are referring to Western Europe. But now, with the peaceful revolutions that have swept Eastern Europe, and especially with the unification of Germany, there is a new situation. Just as this new Europe is humanity's greatest hope in terms of the potential for economic development, so too is it viewed by Dope, Inc. as a potential new and larger market for drugs. And the traditional European mafias are on board for this project.

Japan is also a prime target of the drug mafia, although so far the drug runners have been unable to cut a deal with that country's traditional organized crime apparatus.

Marijuana and Hashish

The picture is no better when we turn to marijuana. As *Figure 9* shows, Ibero-America is not the only producer—but it is the largest one. Mexico and Colombia are the biggest producers, but Jamaica is also significant, and Brazil has reportedly begun to grow a large, but unspecified, amount. The Mexican figures we employed for this study are particularly high, reflecting both the findings of a U.S. congressional committee, and a new U.S. government methodology for calculating production based on satellite detection of growing areas.

The lion's share of Ibero-America's marijuana production is exported to the United States, but a rapidly growing percentage of the U.S. market is now being supplied by marijuana grown right at home. In fact, DEA sources indicate that U.S. production of marijuana has tripled from 5,000 to 15,000 tons in the last three years.

Southeast Asia is the third important producing region for marijuana, but it is much smaller in size and seems to supply the Asian market principally.

The total world production of marijuana has been growing by about 13% per year between 1987 and 1989.

The relative shares of world marijuana production can be seen in *Figure 10*, for 1987, 1988, and 1989. Particularly noticeable is the growth of the U.S. share, to the point where it is now more than 25% of the total.

The reader should also note the areas of the world where hashish is produced—a derivative of the same cannabis plant which produces marijuana. The majority of hashish production occurs in Afghanistan, Pakistan, and Lebanon (in particular, in the Syrian-controlled Bekaa Valley).

Also note the major distribution routes for marijuana and hashish. Because marijuana is bulkier than cocaine and has a lower dollar value per ton, most producing areas supply nearby consumers. Thus, most Ibero-American production is shipped to the United States, with only a small share going to Europe.

Europe's hashish is supplied by Middle Eastern and Southwest Asian producers, such as Afghanistan, Pakistan, and Lebanon, using Turkey and Communist Bulgaria as major transshipment points.

Southeast Asian marijuana is mainly consumed in that area itself.

Opium and Heroin

Opium is a drug which either can be consumed directly, by smoking it, or can be refined into heroin, which is usually injected into the veins of the addict. The vast majority of world opium is grown in two areas of Asia: the first spanning southwest China, Afghanistan, Pakistan, and Iran (and Lebanon), and the second from China to the Southeast Asian nations of Burma, Thailand, and Laos—the infamous "Golden Triangle" (*Figure 11*). Although DEA statistics show Burma as producing the lion's share here, the fact is that much of this is grown in Communist China, or in areas of Burma and Laos under Communist Chinese control.

The other significant world producer of heroin is Mexico, with Guatemala just beginning to take up an important role.

We can see in *Table 2* that the amount of opium grown in Mexico in 1989 (85 tons) is only a small fraction of the total world output of nearly 5,000 tons. The largest amount (over 3,000 tons, or 60% of the total) comes from the nation listed as "Burma"—i.e., from China. But the Mexican production is actually of greater significance than the tonnage seems to indicate, because 100% of it is converted into heroin, and thus its street sales value was a whopping $18.7 billion in 1989.

Best estimates are that only about 10% of Asian opium is converted into heroin for export to the West, and the remaining 90% is consumed in the area, both in the form of opium and as low-grade "brown" heroin, whose retail prices are only a fraction of Western heroin. Thus, in 1989 Mexico accounted for 17% of the total world value of opium and heroin production,

Southwest Asia was 32%, and Southeast Asia was about 51%. If heroin alone is considered, some sources report that as much as three-quarters of all the high-quality heroin consumed in the West comes from areas controlled by the Communist Chinese, a fact deliberately covered up by the U.S. government since the early 1970s, when Henry Kissinger insisted on that cover-up as part of his famous "secret diplomacy" deals with that country.

The other shocking fact that can be seen in this chart is the gigantic jump in opium production from 1988 to 1989, mainly as a result of a bumper crop in "Burma." It is also noteworthy that Mexico's production of opium rose from 55 to 85 tons that year—a more than 50% increase in one year.

Although most bulk opium is consumed in the general area in which it is produced, refined heroin is exactly the opposite, since it has an extremely high unit price and is more easily shipped. Thus, the United States gets some of its heroin from Mexico and Guatemala, but most is Asian or Mideast heroin shipped to both the western and eastern coasts of the United States.

The route of Southeast Asian, or Golden Triangle, heroin is particularly interesting. The British Crown Colony of Hong Kong is the major entrepôt, and it reaches there both by over-land routes through Communist China, and also via Thailand and Malaysia—a perfect symbiosis between the Communist Chinese and their Western oligarchic counterparts!

As with hashish, Southwest Asian heroin is shipped to Europe and the U.S. via Iran, Turkey, and Bulgaria.

Consumption

There are almost no reliable statistics on either the number of drug users around the world, or the quantity they consume. At best, the evidence is fragmentary.

U.S. government agencies have attempted to present some semblance of consumption statistics through a system known as DAWN (Drug Abuse Warning Network), which makes use of *reported* cases of hospitalization due to different kinds of drug abuse. But this approach is notoriously inaccurate since 1) it deals only with consumption levels requiring hospitalization, and 2) it depends on cases being reported. Informed DEA sources have confided to *EIR* that the latest DAWN statistics are particularly unreliable: The drop in the figures reflects, more than anything, the decline in DAWN's *budget,* and therefore, of its ability to detect even a fraction of the consumption. The same methodological errors and outright biases plague the recent, much ballyhooed consumption surveys, which purportedly show a drop-off in U.S. consumption of certain drugs.

The United States unquestionably has the single largest addict population, with somewhere in the range of 70 million Americans having used drugs at some point in their lives. Many, if not most of these, are now addicts.

Europe is another very large market for all types of drugs, with an unknown number of consumers.

Ibero-America used to be relatively free of widespread drug use, and many politicians and others convinced themselves that their countries could keep on producing drugs, without worrying much about the consumption problem. Not any more. Over the last five years, the period of the sharpest austerity measures imposed by the International Monetary Fund, drug consumption has skyrocketed all across Ibero-America—by and large, consumption of the same drugs that are grown in each area. Thus, Brazil reports a serious jump in domestic marijuana production—and consumption. Peruvian sources say that there is now widespread use of basic paste of cocaine, soaked into cigarettes. "Bazuko," another form semi-refined cocaine, is endemic in Colombia. And so forth and so on.

Perhaps less known are the shocking figures for Asia. U.S. government publications admit that there are 5 million opium addicts in India, 2 million heroin addicts in Iran and 1.2 million in Pakistan, and 1 million opium users in Egypt. No figures are available for China, but researchers believe that opium and heroin use is extremely widespread, perhaps reaching into the tens of millions.

Jail the Drug Bankers

The international drug trade today has amassed such power, wealth, and military might that it almost constitutes a government unto itself, stronger and better supplied than the legitimate governments of many nations. Yet with all its power, the single most effective weapon in the dope trade's arsenal is the Big Lie that it is too big and powerful to stop. But it can be defeated. An all-out military war on drugs must be declared. The means and methods of war must be applied in every sense. Traffickers, and especially drug bankers, must be treated as are traitors in time of war. Consumers and advocates of the legalization of drugs are guilty of giving aid and comfort to the enemy in time of war, and must be prosecuted for such crimes.

Dope, Inc.'s vulnerable flank is the international network of banks and other financial institutions that "launder" the cartel's $558 billion per year in gross revenue. This is the most serious logistical problem faced by the drug trade, where it is most vulnerable. Action by governments against the drug bankers could rapidly shut down Dope, Inc.

Take it from the beginning. A dealer sells cocaine on the streets of the United States for cash, some $100 per gram. He then pays off his supplier, who may supply a network as large as a hundred or more dealers. This supplier may accumulate tens or hundreds of thousands of dollars per week, most of it in $20, $50, and $100 bills. But he can't just go to a bank and deposit it. Under U.S. law, banks must report all cash deposits of $10,000 or more.

Traffickers have turned to high cash-turnover businesses—such as hotels, casinos, restaurants, and sports events—to launder their money. Since banks don't have to report deposits made by these businesses, drug profits are simply mixed in with legal cash flows.

Cash is also frequently shipped out of the United States. Often planes which fly cocaine into the U.S., fly back loaded with $20, $50, and $100 bills. The bills can then either be deposited directly in offshore banking centers—where no questions are asked—or in remote bank branches in the drug-producing countries. These funds are then wire-transferred out to the offshore banks, into secret accounts where there is no government supervision.

Only a tiny portion (at most 10%) of the drug revenues ever stay in the producer countries—and virtually none of that benefits those nations' productive economies. It is simply a lie to say that the drug trade is a "bonanza" for Ibero-America.

Although no precise figures are available, a leading anti-drug prosecutor in Switzerland, Paolo Bernasconi, told Italy's *La Stampa* newspaper in January 1990 that the leading money-laundering centers include the United States (Miami and Wall Street), Canada, Great Britain, and, of course, Switzerland.

Today many Ibero-American governments, including Venezuela and Mexico, are rushing to change their banking laws so that they can capture some of these "hot money" flows. They foolishly view this as a way to help pay their foreign debt, and solve their financial crises.

The world financial system is now as addicted to drug monies as a junkie is to heroin. Without the regular flow of those monies, the system would collapse.

As the London *Economist* wrote proudly in June 1989: "It is obvious . . . that drug dealers use banks. . . . The business . . . has become part of the financial system. . . . If you had morals or ethics in this business, you would not be in it."

U.S. finances are so dominated by money-laundering that Treasury officials cannot locate 80% of all the dollar bills printed by the U.S. Treasury. Cocaine plays such a predominant role in the U.S. financial system that a significant majority of all $20 bills show physical traces of cocaine dust on them!

Yet no government has ever touched the *system* which allowed this to occur. At best, a few accounts here and there have been seized. To this day, money-laundering is not even a criminal offense in 8 out of the 15 industrialized nations. In the United States, the center of the problem, government action is a joke: No top management has *ever* been charged or prosecuted for criminal money-laundering activity.

The banks didn't just take advantage of the drug trade profits; they have *promoted* their "right" to make use of them. As one banker stated in an off-the-record discussion in London in 1986: Dope "is the biggest source of new financial business in the world today. . . . I know banks which will literally kill to secure a chunk of this action."

The banker worked for one of Wall Street's biggest investment houses, Merrill Lynch. The chief executive officer of Merrill Lynch for 12 years was Donald Regan, who served as treasury secretary and chief of staff of the White House for seven years of the Reagan presidency.

The bankers have also sponsored the campaign to legalize drugs. "Cocaine is indeed clearly the most profitable article of trade in the world," the *Economist* wrote in August 1989. "Vast untaxed profits amass in the conspirators' hands." The time has come to legalize the dope trade, the magazine argued.

Instead of prosecuting drug bankers, this crowd has prosecuted anyone who has acted against the drug trade, such as Lyndon LaRouche, the American economist who commissioned the book *Dope, Inc.*, which first exposed how the bankers set up the dope trade.

In 1986, in Panama, Gen. Manuel Noriega closed down First Interamericas Bank after it was proven that the bank was owned by the Cali Cartel. In December 1989, U.S. occupation forces invaded Panama on the pretext of the lie that Noriega himself was a drug runner—and proceeded to place four members of the board of that same First Interamericas Bank in power—as President, attorney general, president of the Supreme Court, and minister of Treasury. The result: Drug running in Panama has *grown* since Noriega's ouster.

The Bush administration's misnamed "War on Drugs" is a major part of the problem, not the solution. Besides turning a blind eye to the laundering of billions in drug profits, Bush's official strategy is to reduce drugs by 50% over the next decade. In practice, this has meant working with one group of drug runners to control or eliminate another.

Specifically, a working alliance has been created between the U.S. government and the Cali Cartel, against the Medellín Cartel of Pablo Escobar and José Gonzalo Rodríguez Gacha. The result has been, as now admitted in such organs of the liberal Establishment such as the *Washington Post,* that the Cali Cartel has become dominant among the different Colombian groups . . . all with behind-the-scenes American approval. Small surprise, when one learns that one of the official Washington lobbyists of the Cali Cartel is Michael Abbell, a 17-year employee of the U.S. Justice Department who became one of its highest officials as director of the department's Office of International Affairs. Abbell was quoted in the *Washington Post* 1990 saying of the Cali Cartel: "The people in Cali have been adamantly opposed to any violence. . . . My impression is you can work with these people."

The drug runners also know where to turn for influence in Washington. The Colombian lawyer Joaquín Vallejo Arbeláez, who has publicly represented the Medellín Cartel "Extraditables" on numerous occasions, told the press that the cocaine cartel was hiring lobbyists in Washington. "Even Kissinger's name was thought of. They knew what Kissinger costs. However, they said they were ready to take on those costs for the purpose of convincing the American government of the appropriateness" of making a deal.

But Washington's role is worse still. The Bush administration is actively promoting the destruction of one of the only Ibero-American institutions capable of stopping Dope, Inc.: the military. Bush has forced on the nations of Ibero-America paramilitary operations by U.S. troops which violate their sovereignty and help dismantle the legitimate militaries of these countries—all using the hypocritical excuse of "fighting drugs." The invasion of Panama was the classic case of such an operation, which constituted a dangerous precedent for the entire Hemisphere.

The scope of such U.S. military actions, both current and planned, can be seen in *Figure 12*.

To actually destroy Dope, Inc. and eliminate the drug problem, it is not a matter of arguing whether consumption or production must be stopped first. The enemy must be hit simultaneously on all fronts—above all on the financial front. The money-laundering aspect must be attacked with special vigor, since this is Dope, Inc.'s jugular—and in war, one must always go for the enemy's jugular.

To do all of this, alliances are needed between those governments, in both consuming and producing nations, who are willing to carry out this war, but with full respect for national sovereignty. Each government shall be responsible for prosecution of this war within its own territory.

The specific measures to be taken can be summarized in the following six points:

1) *Stop drug-money laundering*

■ banking transparency
■ seize the drug traffickers' assets
■ jail the drug bankers

2) *Stop drug production*

■ satellite detection of all production and processing sites
■ air and land military assault on crops and laboratories
■ bomb all clandestine air fields
■ seize all illegal shipments of chemicals used for processing drugs

3) *Stop drug distribution*

■ AWACS and other radar technology detection of shipments
■ X-ray and nuclear magnetic resonance technologies to "search" all shipments

4) *Stop drug consumption*

■ stop the legalization campaign
■ severe jail terms for all traffickers and dealers

5) *Stop pornography and Satanism*

■ make them illegal, and jail all violators
■ promote classical culture among the youth

6) *Develop the Third World*

■ Great projects of infrastructural, industrial, and agricultural development
■ Full productive employment
■ High-technology crop substitution

This study first appeared in Executive Intelligence Review magazine, Volume 17, Number 43, November 9, 1990.

Figures for Chapter 2

TABLE 1
Retail value of world drug trade grew exponentially from 1977-89
(billions $)

	1977	1982	1987	1988	1989
Cocaine					
Total	52	83	99	106	113
Ibero-America	52	83	99	106	113
Marijuana and hashish					
Total	40	60	156	254	273
Ibero-American marijuana	19	15	114	185	178
U.S. marijuana	—	—	30	53	76
Southeast Asian marijuana	—	—	4	6	7
Hashish	—	—	8	10	12
Opium					
Total	50	60	83	89	100
Ibero-America	4	3	11	11	17
Southeast Asia	—	—	38	44	51
Southwest Asia	—	—	34	34	32
Others, total	33	47	65	68	72
World total	175	250	403	517	558
Total from Ibero-America	75	101	224	302	308
Ibero-America as percent of world	43%	40%	56%	58%	55%

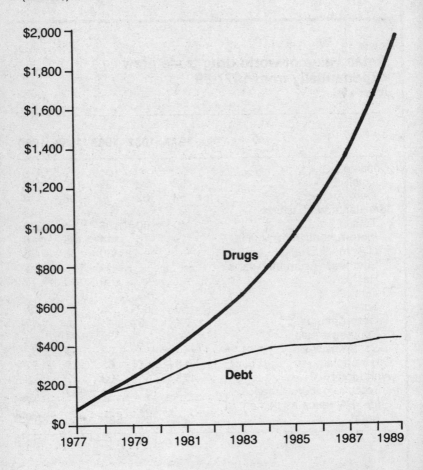

FIGURE 2

Cumulative value of Ibero-America's drug trade is nearing $2 trillion mark

(billions $)

Drugs

Debt

FIGURE 3
Cocaine production sites and distribution routes

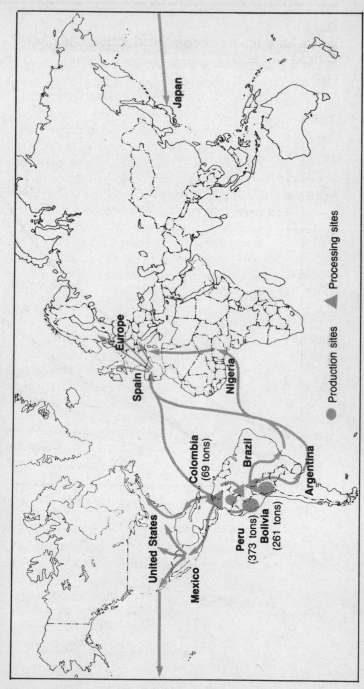

Japan

Europe

Spain

Nigeria

Colombia
(69 tons)

Brazil

Argentina

United States

Mexico

Peru
(373 tons)

Bolivia
(261 tons)

● Production sites

▲ Processing sites

FIGURE 4

Ibero-America's cocaine production has risen sixfold since 1977

(tons)

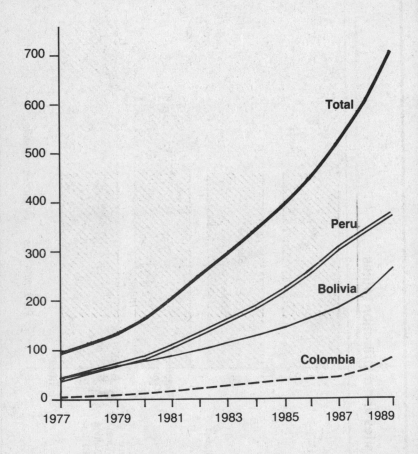

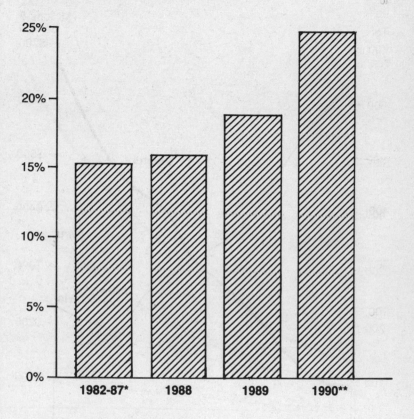

FIGURE 5

Ibero-American cocaine production is growing faster than ever

(annual rate of growth)

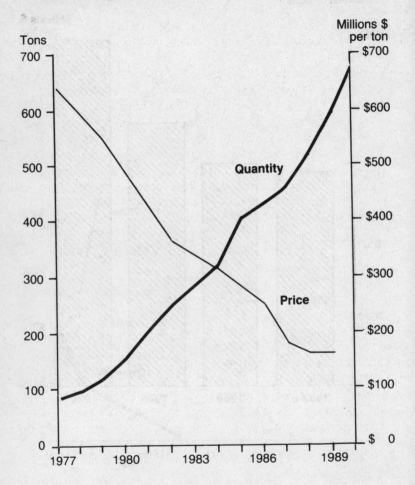

FIGURE 6
Deliberate cuts in U.S. cocaine prices have created a huge market

Tons

Millions $ per ton

Quantity

Price

1977   1980   1983   1986   1989

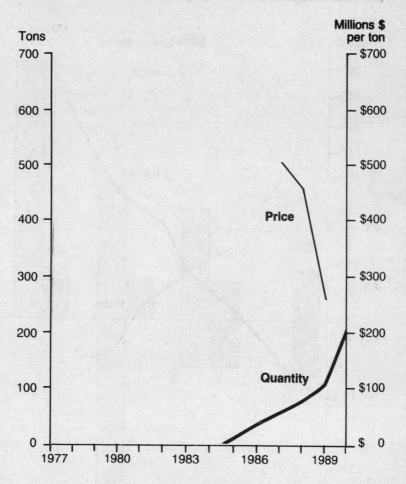

FIGURE 7
Price and quantity of cocaine exported to Europe follows U.S. pattern

Tons

Millions $
per ton

700 — — $700

600 — — $600

500 — — $500

Price

400 — — $400

300 — — $300

200 — — $200

Quantity

100 — — $100

0 — $ 0

1977   1980   1983   1986   1989

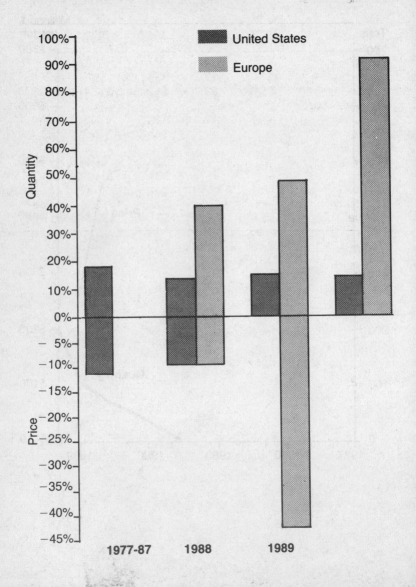

FIGURE 8
Rates of change in price and quantity of cocaine show Europe is targeted

United States
Europe

100%
90%
80%
70%
60%
50%
40%
30%
20%
10%
0%
− 5%
−10%
−15%
−20%
−25%
−30%
−35%
−40%
−45%

Quantity

Price

1977-87   1988   1989

TABLE 2

China produces most of the world's opium and heroin

(tons and billions $)

	1977	1982	1987	1988	1989
Mexico					
Quantity	31	17	55	55	85
Value	$5.0	$3.7	$12.1	$12.1	$18.7
Southeast Asia					
Quantity	—	—	1,575	1,833	3,593
Value	—	—	$41.6	$48.6	$56.7
Southwest Asia					
Quantity	—	—	1,420	1,450	1,310
Value	—	—	$37.6	$38.4	$34.7
Total					
Quantity	—	—	3,050	3,338	4,988
Value	$55.6	$66.7	$91.3	$99.1	$110.1

FIGURE 9
Marijuana and hashish production and distribution routes

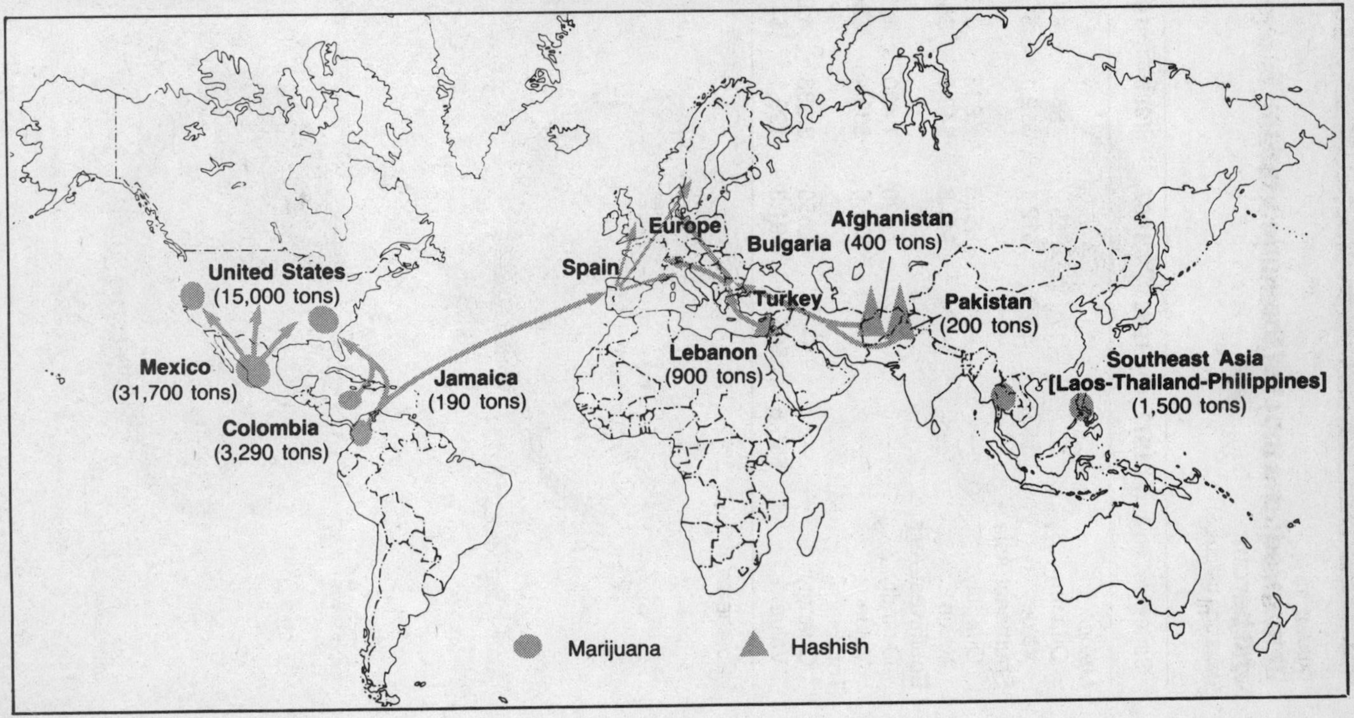

Southeast Asia
[Laos-Thailand-Philippines]
(1,500 tons)

Pakistan
(200 tons)

Afghanistan
(400 tons)

Bulgaria

Turkey

Europe

Lebanon
(900 tons)

Spain

Jamaica
(190 tons)

United States
(15,000 tons)

Colombia
(3,290 tons)

Mexico
(31,700 tons)

● Marijuana

▲ Hashish

FIGURE 10
U.S. share of world marijuana production is over 25%
(percent of total)

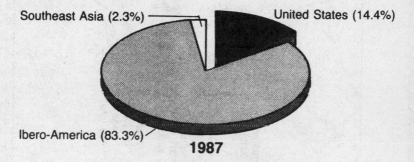

Southeast Asia (2.3%)

United States (14.4%)

Ibero-America (83.3%)

1987

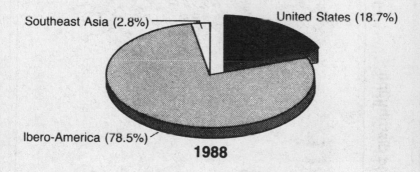

Southeast Asia (2.8%)

United States (18.7%)

Ibero-America (78.5%)

1988

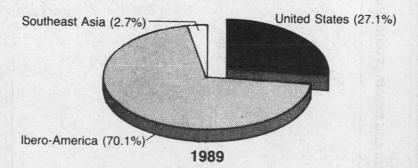

Southeast Asia (2.7%)

United States (27.1%)

Ibero-America (70.1%)

1989

FIGURE 11
Opium and heroin production and distribution

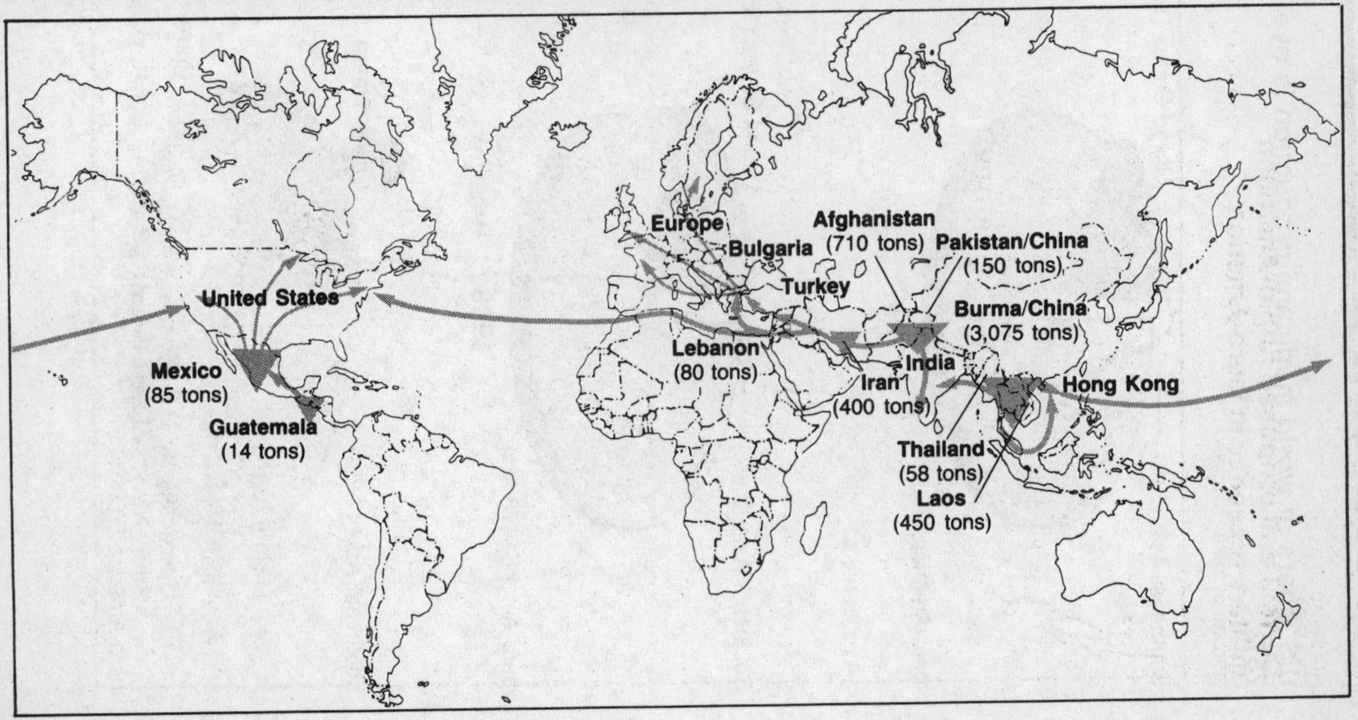

Europe
Bulgaria
Turkey
Afghanistan
Pakistan/China
(150 tons)
(710 tons)
Burma/China
(3,075 tons)
Iran
India
(400 tons)
Lebanon
(80 tons)
Hong Kong
Thailand
(58 tons)
Laos
(450 tons)

United States
Mexico
(85 tons)
Guatemala
(14 tons)

FIGURE 12
Current and proposed Anglo-American military presence in Ibero-America

Legend:

- ● Military Bases
- ▲ Illegal kidnapings
- □ Operations by U.S. Special Forces, Army, Navy, or Coast Guard
- □ Current
- ▨ Proposed

Figures for Chapter 3

FIGURE 1
Value of 1987 U.S. marijuana harvest exceeds all agricultural commodities but one
(millions $)

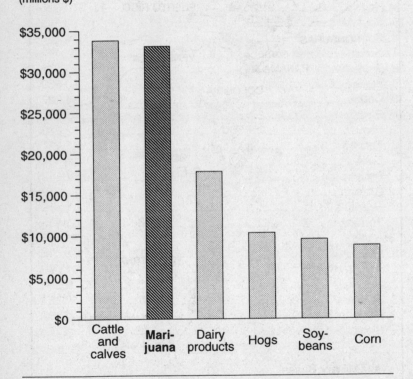

Source: USDA; NORML; *EIR* estimates

TABLE 1
Receipts from marketing of top 25 crop/livestock commodities
(millions of $)

Crop/livestock commodity	Receipts
1. Cattle and calves	$33,829
2. Marijuana	$33,095
3. Dairy products	$17,829
4. Hogs	$10,326
5. Soybeans	$9,565
6. Corn	$8,807
7. Greenhouse and nursery	$6,402
8. Broilers	$6,176
9. Wheat	$4,869
10. Cotton	$4,027
11. Eggs	$3,177
12. Hay	$2,233
13. Tobacco	$1,827
14. Turkeys	$1,701
15. Potatoes	$1,588
16. Grapes	$1,355
17. Oranges	$1,300
18. Tomatoes	$1,283
19. Apples	$1,091
20. Peanuts	$1,016
21. Sorghum grain	$1,009
22. Sugar beets	$942
23. Lettuce	$857
24. Barley	$782
25. Cane for sugar	$778

Source: USDA

FIGURE 2

Ten states produce 42% of U.S. marijuana output
(billions $)

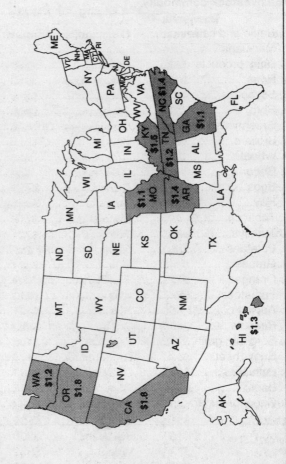

Source: NORML; *EIR* estimates

TABLE 2
State-by-state comparison of marijuana harvest vs. leading agricultural commodity
(millions of $)

State	Marijuana harvest	Leading commodity Commodity	Leading commodity Amount	Marijuana as % of commodity
Alabama	$880	Eggs	$156	564.1%
Alaska	$190	Greenhouse	$13	1,461.5%
Arizona	$640	Cotton	$339	188.8%
Arkansas	$1,375	Soybeans	$369	372.6%
California	$1,750	Greenhouse	$1,464	119.5%
Colorado	$560	Wheat	$221	253.4%
Connecticut	$230	Greenhouse	$95	242.1%
Delaware	NA	Greenhouse	$30	NA
Florida	$825	Greenhouse	$933	88.4%
Georgia	$1,125	Peanuts	$454	247.8%
Hawaii	$1,325	Cane/sugar	$218	607.8%
Idaho	$755	Potatoes	$321	235.2%
Illinois	$485	Corn	$1,858	26.1%
Indiana	$370	Corn	$884	41.9%
Iowa	$475	Soybeans	$1,689	28.1%
Kansas	$845	Wheat	$810	104.3%
Kentucky	$1,550	Tobacco	$441	351.5%
Louisiana	$690	Cotton	$282	244.7%
Maine	$225	Potatoes	$108	208.3%
Maryland	$235	Greenhouse	$176	133.5%
Massachusetts	$375	Greenhouse	$122	307.4%
Michigan	$780	Corn	$196	398.0%
Minnesota	$430	Soybeans	$769	55.9%
Mississippi	$810	Cotton	$532	152.3%
Missouri	$1,100	Soybeans	$808	136.1%
Montana	$790	Wheat	$332	238.0%
Nebraska	$330	Corn	$1,003	32.9%
Nevada	NA	Hay	$46	NA
New Hampshire	$245	Greenhouse	$15	1,633.3%
New Jersey	$195	Greenhouse	$192	101.6%
New Mexico	$565	Hay	$69	818.8%

State	Marijuana harvest	Leading commodity		Marijuana as % of commodity
		Commodity	Amount	
New York	$600	Greenhouse	$208	288.5%
North Carolina	$1,400	Tobacco	$730	191.8%
North Dakota	NA	Wheat	$701	NA
Ohio	$540	Soybeans	$741	72.9%
Oklahoma	$975	Wheat	$290	336.2%
Oregon	$1,825	Greenhouse	$210	869.0%
Pennsylvania	$475	Greenhouse	$298	159.4%
Rhode Island	NA	Greenhouse	$38	NA
South Carolina	$790	Tobacco	$149	530.2%
South Dakota	NA	Wheat	$238	NA
Tennessee	$1,225	Cotton	$178	688.2%
Texas	$835	Cotton	$980	85.2%
Utah	$330	Hay	$45	733.3%
Vermont	$370	Hay	$9	4,111.1%
Virginia	$825	Tobacco	$114	723.7%
Washington	$1,200	Apples	$462	259.7%
West Virginia	$740	Apples	$22	3,363.6%
Wisconsin	$385	Corn	$229	168.1%
Wyoming	$250	Sugar beets	$37	675.7%
U.S. total	**$33,095**		**$20,624**	**160.5%**

Source: USDA; NORML; *EIR* estimates

States in which marijuana production is over 100% of crop/livestock output

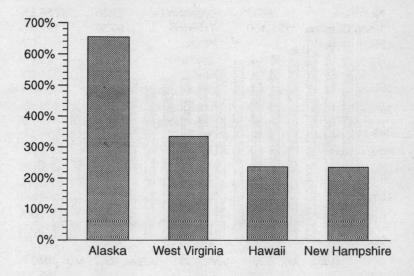

States in which marijuana production is 50-90% of crop/livestock output

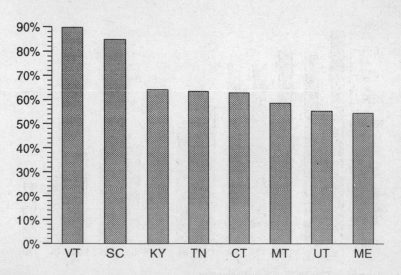

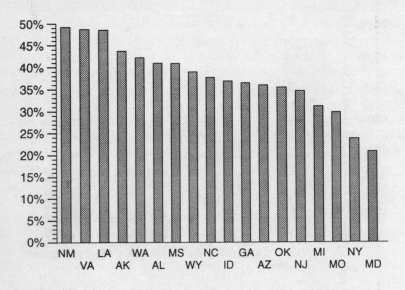

FIGURE 3c
States in which marijuana production is 20-49% of crop/livestock output

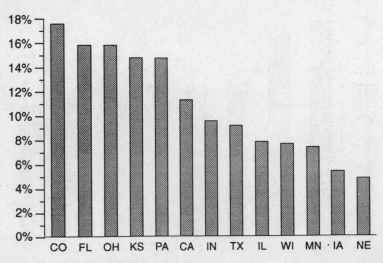

FIGURE 3d
States in which marijuana production is 4-18% of crop/livestock output

Source: USDA; NORML; *EIR* estimates

FIGURE 4

In 37 states marijuana outranks the leading crop in harvest value

(status as of 1987)

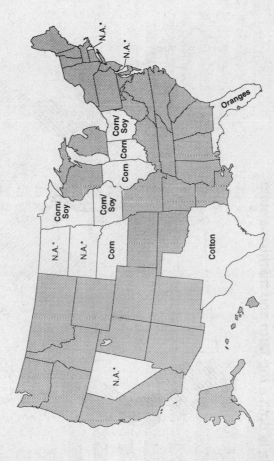

* N.A. = data not available

Source: USDA; NORML; *EIR* estimates

FIGURE 5

Only California is both a top farm and marijuana state

(status as of 1987)

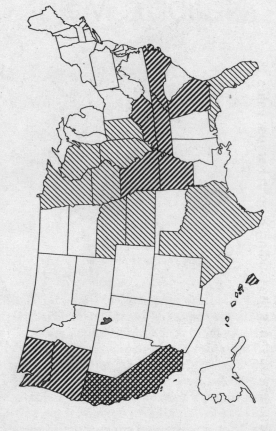

10 top farm states, producing 52% of all U.S. farm/ranch marketings

10 top pot states, producing 42% of U.S. marijuana

Source: USDA; NORML; *E/R* estimates

3

Marijuana Is Now the Nation's Major Crop

In 1988, a Montana farm couple, Dick and Judith Kurth of Fort Benton, were convicted and jailed for switching from cattle to marijuana as their cash crop. *People* magazine, the TV networks, and all major media publicized the incident, in part to promote the view that decent farmers everywhere were turning to pot growing, and were wrongly punished. In 1985, the Kurths were in debt for $1.2 million to Norwest Bank, and the bank cut off their credit. Unable to operate their once-prosperous cattle ranch, they investigated growing marijuana in makeshift hothouses in their farm buildings, in a desperate bid to save their farm.

Over the 1980s, marijuana cultivation in the United States became gigantic, and it continues to soar. For example, in 1987, the total gross value of the crop was an estimated $43.7 billion. Two years later, in 1989, that had risen to $50.1 billion. In part, this reflects the rising street price, particularly as eradication raids periodically kill off significant amounts of cultivation in certain regions. But over three-fourths of the dollar increase is due to increased *physical production* of marijuana. Clearly, the trend is toward increased domestic cultivation of the drug, even as Mexico and other points also continue to increase their production. In terms of percentage of annual estimated world output, the U.S. share of marijuana production in 1989 constituted about 27% of the world total.

America's drug problem is no longer just a *consumption* problem—importing marijuana, cocaine, and heroin from "over there." We now have a major domestic drug *production* catastrophe on our hands as well.

We use 1987 data in our calculations, because, for purposes of assembling a consistent and complete data base for both agriculture and estimated marijuana values, that was the best recent year. The agricultural statistics used in this chapter come from the U.S. Department of Agriculture's Economic Research Service, "State Financial Summary, 1987."

The state-by-state marijuana production statistics come from a June 17, 1988 press release issued by the National Organization for the Reform of Marijuana Laws (NORML), and have been cross-checked in aggregate terms against official U.S. government statistics published by the National Narcotics Intelligence Consumers Committee (NNICC—an interdepartmental committee which includes DEA, CIA, FBI, State Department, and other federal agencies), data provided by U.S. congressional committees, and international statistics provided by various producer nations.

The NORML statistics are substantially higher (3–4 times) than those provided by most U.S. government agencies (NNICC in particular). Both NNICC and NORML start from the official Drug Enforcement Administration figures for tons of marijuana eradicated. NNICC then estimates total crop size based on their assumptions regarding what percentage of the total crop they believe to have been eradicated. Thus, in 1987, they assumed that the DEA eradicated almost two-thirds of all marijuana production; in 1989, they more modestly claimed only one-half was eradicated. NORML's estimate—based on state-by-state budget analyses, *in situ* reports, etc.—is that, from the mid- to late 1980s, only 16% of the crop was eradicated, and they derive their global estimates from this.

So, who is right?

The NNICC notoriously underestimates most drug production statistics, for a combination of political and methodological reasons. Take the case of coca production in Peru. In 1988, *EIR* used official Peruvian statistics to estimate that total 1987 coca production in that country was about 300 tons (maximum hydrochloride of cocaine capacity)—50% higher than the NNICC's estimate for that year. But the 1989 NNICC annual report subsequently revised their own earlier estimates upward, making their 1989 figures consistent with *EIR*'s—and de facto admitting that *EIR* was right all along.

NNICC figures for Mexican marijuana production are also revealing. Their 1989 report states them as follows:

1987 =   4,200 tons
1988 =   4,710 tons
1989 = 42,283 tons

The gigantic, order-of-magnitude jump for 1989, the NNICC admits, is *not* due to that much new production, but to the fact that their earlier numbers were much too low. Or, as they put it: "This increase is the result of improved estimation methodologies and a review of cultivation areas that had not been included in previous years."

In 1986, the House Select Committee on Narcotics Abuse and Control published figures on U.S. marijuana imports (30,000 tons) which were two to three times the standard NNICC figures. These congressional figures are far closer to NORML's estimates than those of the NNICC.

So it is safe to assume that the NNICC is substantially understating U.S. pot production. But are NORML's numbers any more accurate?

It is *EIR*'s view, after careful examination of the data, that, even though NORML has "an ax to grind" (they wish to impress upon the public the size of U.S. pot production, in order to promote its legalization), their global statistics more closely reflect reality than do any other published data series. (We cannot at this time vouch for their state-by-state breakdown.)

To further verify at least the order-of-magnitude accuracy of NORML's figures, *EIR* independently estimated non-U.S. marijuana production in the Western Hemisphere at approximately $115 billion in 1987[2]. If NORML's data are accurate, then U.S. pot production of $33 billion that year would constitute about 22% of the value of the total output from the Western Hemisphere. The vast majority (80–90%) of this hemispheric marijuana is consumed in the United States, so that the proportions that apply to hemispheric production pretty much hold for the proportions of U.S. consumption coming from different hemispheric suppliers. That is, it is safe to assume, based on the above statistics, that the United States itself produces about 22% of the marijuana consumed in this country.

Compare this with the DEA's own estimates on U.S. consumption. They report that about 25% of the pot consumed in the United States is produced domestically. This is in the same ball park as the percentage which results from employing NORML's numbers in combination with *EIR*'s calculations—in fact, it is surprisingly close, given the obvious difficulty of accurately calculating the size and value of what is still an illegal crop.

The patterns have, if anything, worsened over the intervening years, as pot production has kept growing by around 20% per year. Meantime, levels of farm output of food and fiber are depressed, relative to need and potential productivity. In fact, 1987 marked the first year in recent history that, for a month or two, the United States was a net food importer.

Figure 1 shows that the 1987 marijuana harvest ($33,095 million) was almost equivalent to the receipts from the largest agriculture commodity (cattle and calves) that year ($33,829 million), and it was larger than *every other* agricultural commodity, and larger than several major grain crops combined. The relative values are shown for a breakdown of five of the top farm commodities in the bar diagram, and another 20 commodities are shown for comparison in *Table 1*.

What is outstanding is that by 1987, the harvest value of marijuana exceeded that of soybeans and corn combined ($18,372 million)—the two crops in which the United States leads in world production. Even adding in the value of wheat ($4,869 million) and hay ($2,233 million), the $25,474 million total does not begin to rival marijuana.

You would be wrong to expect to see "waving fields of hemp" in Iowa, however. The pattern in these figures does *not* reflect some imputed "natural shift of preference" among farmers away from producing food, into producing dope. The U.S. marijuana harvest reflects a series of deliberate policy decisions by a network of influentials in the mega-banks, the Justice Department, U.S. Department of Agriculture, the International Monetary Fund (IMF) and related agencies, to create the conditions where dope-growing in the United States is encouraged.

Over the 1970s and 1980s, the banks jacked up international interest rates into the stratosphere, and then forced Third World nations to adopt austerity policies. This predictably destroyed the productive sectors of their economies, at which point the bankers told them that they should produce any crop—including drugs, wherever it was lucrative—for the purpose of generating cash to repay their debts to the banks.

The spectacular growth of marijuana cultivation in the United States in the 1980s is a result of the same policies. The same usurious interest rates that destroyed the Third World have also made it nearly impossible for agriculture to survive in the United States. Bankruptcies in the farm sector have skyrocketed, and farmers are being told to grow pot, or lose their farms.

So long as the Bush administration promotes liberal free market economic policies at home and abroad, the drug trade will flourish—at home and abroad—and Washington's so-called War on Drugs will remain a cruel joke.

The example of the conviction of the Montana farmers is a case in point. It is on public record that Dick and Judith Kurth were advised by their local Norwest Bank officer Floyd De-Rusha, that they would have a chance to prevent bankruptcy if they produced marijuana. Once the farmers, very experienced in agronomy, did produce successive years of marijuana crops, they paid off their debts, with money to spare.

According to press accounts, DeRusha was just "joking" when, in 1985, he replied to the Kurths' anguished plea for help to continue ranching, "Well, other than growing marijuana, I don't know what you can do. Why don't you try that?" Norwest Bank President Frank Shaw denies that this was an okay to grow dope, but the bank gladly accepted the Kurths' money to pay off their loan, even though any bank official would have to wonder where the money was coming from, since the Kurths had been insolvent. Dick Kurth further testified that he informed Norwest how he was making his money, and that bank officials even helped him make big cash deposits in such a way as to evade federal rules to detect suspicious sums of cash. According to the bank's behavior, money is money.

Nationally, this "one step removed" policy has prevailed among banks and other agencies connected with taking in or laundering dope money. The big banks caught violating federal reporting laws, and taking in large amounts of cash—such as the Bank of Boston and SeaFirst in Seattle—were given only slap-on-the-wrist fines. No follow-up of the drug money networks was done by the Justice Department. In the marijuana-producing areas, likewise, there are large unaccounted for cash flows, and yet there have been conspicuously few regional raids, indictments, and convictions.

What is one to conclude from the size of the domestic pot economy? Marijuana advocates such as the National Organization for the Reform of Marijuana Laws (NORML) conclude that marijuana output is so big and lucrative that it reflects public support, including that of farmers, and therefore must be legalized. Many of the major media also promote this view. But closer inspection of the patterns of cultivation do not indicate widespread public support or farmer involvement.

In the report that follows, we present a systematic computer-assisted study of the scope and geography of marijuana-growing in the United States. The study shows that there are demarcated areas of cultivation, which any concerted eradication program could obliterate—if the political will to do so actually existed.

The two zones accounting for 42% of U.S. marijuana output (1987) are concentrated in the Pacific states (California, Oregon, Washington, and Hawaii), and in the secluded, poverty-stricken counties of the Ozarks and Appalachians, in a five-state region in the eastern central United States (Arkansas, Missouri, Tennessee, northern Georgia, Kentucky, and also adjacent southwestern Virginia) (*Figure 2*). The other 58% of the pot production is spread around the nation, but in only the most secluded areas.

The figures show that there were not wholesale switchovers to marijuana by traditional farmers in the big farm states. Instead, the marijuana cultivation has been taken up in remote areas impoverished by the shutdown of local coal mines and other industries and by the fall in farm commodity prices. Added to that is the counterculture's "Mother Earth"-type farmer, based especially on the West Coast, but located around the country, as a product of the "New Age."

If, over the 1980s there had been genuine economic growth, instead of "Reaganomics" followed by Bush's equally disastrous free market liberalism, then the U.S. farm sector would be booming, and marijuana would not have become the new crop of "alternative agriculture."

Where Marijuana Is the Top Cash Crop

The 1980s saw a deadly boom in the production of marijuana in the United States. Estimates for the 45 states where statistics are available, show that marijuana is now cultivated in significant amounts everywhere.

The four bar diagrams (*Figure 3*) show the scope of the problem. They rank the 45 states in terms of the harvest value of marijuana as a percent of the total value of all other crop and livestock output of that state.

Figure 3a shows that marijuana is 655% of all other farm

output combined in Alaska, 335% in West Virginia, 237% in Hawaii, and 236% in New Hampshire. *Figure 3b* ranks 10 states where marijuana is 50–99% of farm harvest value, from Oregon and Massachusetts (90% or over), down to 55% in the case of Maine. *Figure 3c* shows 18 states where marijuana ranks from 49% down to 20%. And finally, 13 states where marijuana harvest value is below 20% of other farm output, are ranked in *Figure 3d*.

Table 2 is a master table, listing all states in alphabetical order, and giving the dollar value of marijuana output, the value and name of the leading farm commodity of that state, and the size of the marijuana crop, expressed as a percentage of the leading legal farm commodity. For example, in Vermont, the value of marijuana harvested ($370 million) is 118% of the value of the state's leading commodity—dairy products ($314 million).

Figure 6) gives another comparative view of the spread of marijuana cultivation, by showing that in 37 states, the harvest value of marijuana cultivated exceeds that of the top crop (i.e., excluding non-crop agricultural commodities, such as livestock and dairy) grown in that state.

But this map also indicates an important counter-pattern. In the Midwest corn belt, the marijuana does not outrank the value of the corn and soybean harvests. And it does not outrank cotton in Texas or citrus in Florida—at least not yet.

A deeper look at the state data shows clearly that the top farm states are not the top pot-producing states—neither in percentage nor in absolute terms. The one exception to this is California, which is special in many respects. That state has the largest population in the nation, and an economy larger than that of many nations. It has a rich, varied agriculture, with secluded and favorable growth locations for marijuana. It also has Hollywood and a history of the pro-drug counterculture, and cases of experimentation with hallucinogenic drugs provided clandestinely to masses of people.

The map in *Figure 4* shows the 37 states in which marijuana is now the leading cash crop. The map in *Figure 5* shows the locations of the top 10 farm states in the country, and the top

10 marijuana states. Only California ranks in both. The top 10 farm states account for 52% of the total crop and livestock commodity marketings in 1987. The top 10 marijuana-producing states account for 42% of the harvest value of all marijuana produced in the United States in 1987.

It is clear that the two centers of marijuana production are 1) the Pacific states: Hawaii, California, Oregon, and Washington, and 2) the eastern central states of Arkansas, Missouri, Tennessee, Kentucky, Georgia, and North Carolina. The adjacent counties of southwestern Virginia, and other remote parts of adjoining states, such as West Virginia, could also be included.

The Pacific states were famous in the mid-1980s for what was called the "Emerald Triangle," in Northern California. However, in the past three years, networks of dope dealers have vastly expanded the number of growing areas with high-quality seeds, specialized growing equipment, and other inputs throughout the larger region. Hawaii's climate can sustain three crops a year. Places in Southern California and Arizona have developed underground greenhouses, with grow lights and hydroponics.

The Eastern states marijuana cultivation is spread throughout the remote areas of the Ozarks and Appalachians. Both the farm crisis of the 1980s, and the layoffs in the coal fields, have left thousands with no livelihoods and no hope. In this poverty belt, both local residents and the carpetbagger pothead entrepreneurs have moved to create "marijuana zones." In the atmosphere of economic downturn, there are plenty of state troopers, sheriffs, and deputies, in addition to crooked judges, who are not prepared to root out the dope networks. They are frequently the local "Yo Boys" who get a kick out of packing a gun, having some cash, and looking the other way. The law enforcement officer or citizen who does try to take action in this environment, is targeted for harassment or even death.

Extensive acreage in the national park lands is planted to marijuana, both because of the remoteness of the land, and because the grower calculates thus to avoid personal property seizure in case he is caught. The 661,000-acre Daniel Boone National Forest in Kentucky has had large patches of mari-

juana sown in secluded hollows, behind corn fields, and inside
rows of corn. In Hawaii, on the Big Island, marijuana growers
take advantage of vast tracts of the undeveloped land.

Even the pattern of occasional drug busts provides enough
public information to show the social and geographic characteristics of the marijuana cultivation:

Clay County, Kentucky: As many as 40% of the county's
24,100 citizens grew marijuana as of 1989, according to local
authorities. The county has suffered 25% unemployment, compared with an official rate of 6% nationally; half the population
is living on Social Security, disability, or unemployment payments; there is a 50% dropout rate from high school, compared
with 25% nationally.

This area is a former coal-producing region where the mines
shut down. As of a year ago, Clay County was the largest
producer of marijuana in Kentucky, which in turn is the third-
largest producing state in the nation.

Southwestern Virginia: The same sitation prevails in this 15-
county region, where coal mining is dying out, and there is
nothing else growing in this mountainous area. Last summer,
one raid destroyed 10,753 plants there, with a value roughly
estimated to be $10.7 million.

Two new patterns are apparent in the Pacific states:

Hawaii: For the last decade, this state has been the first or
second largest marijuana producer in the nation. Marijuana
plots as large as a quarter of an acre came to dot the state
forests. Some growers hid their crops amid sugar cane fields.
When a six-month eradication effort called Operation Wipeout
was conducted last year, it was estimated that 800,000 plants
were destroyed. This represents about 80% of the estimated
outdoor plants, and shows the extent of the dope operations,
which press reports of the raid estimated to be $8 billion.

California: Some dope growers from California's Emerald
Triangle have moved south to avoid harassment from law authorities. They have invested in high-tech underground pot
production. The Drug Enforcement Administration captured
130 indoor farms in 1989, and over 260 in 1990. The most
advanced setups are designed to produce four crops a year. One

"farm" raided last fall in the desert near Lancaster cost about $1 million to build, and had the potential to grow 8,500 plants four times a year, for an annual profit of $75 million.

Both the raids and the statistics show that the average farmer is *not* viewing marijuana as an alternative, despite the encouragement that the Reagan-Bush economic "recovery" provides. The map in *Figure 5* shows that the grain belt states are *not* part of the pattern of the 37 other states where the harvest value of marijuana exceeds the value of the state's top crop (excluding dairy or livestock). The corn belt states produce relatively little marijuana—if hundreds of millions of dollars per year can be considered "little." They only look good in comparison to the West Coast and Appalachian "marijuana belt." Typically, various plots of wild types of marijuana are cultivated in the grain belt, and few high-tech greenhouses are used.

In none of the top 10 U.S. farm states does the value of marijuana outrank that of the top farm commodity, as *Table 2* shows. However, in California and Florida, marijuana harvest value exceeds the value of the greenhouse and nursery output— the second-ranking commodity in each state.

The harvest value of marijuana exceeds that of the third-ranking commodity in four states: California (cattle), Texas (wheat), Kansas (grain sorghum) and Florida (tomatoes).

Desperate Farmers Switch to Pot

Last December, the *Chicago Tribune* syndicated an article titled, "Hemp touted as cash crop with side effect of legalized marijuana." It sang the praises of marijuana for making paper, medicine, and other uses, saying that farmers could make huge profits from growing hemp, according to the Illinois Marijuana Initiative (IMI). "This is definitely a cash crop. It could mean billions of dollars for U.S. farmers. . . . It's already the nation's leading illegal cash crop," said the IMI's Mike Rosing.

Such arguments are aimed, not at farmers, but at softening

up the non-farm population for more dope and degradation. No traditional, independent family farmer, in his or her "right mind," is so befuddled that he thinks it is wise to base national farm policy, and individual decisions about what to grow, on dope.

However, U.S. farm policy over the past 25 years has been a disaster. And millions of Americans—farmers included—have been "out of their minds" to have tolerated it. If it continues, they will soon have no choice but to grow pot—or starve.

Over the 1980s decade of the "Reagan-Bush recovery," crisis hit the U.S. farm belt. An estimated 400,000 farmers were bankrupted or forced to quit by selling out or abandoning their operations.

Under orders from the food cartels, whose executives direct the programs of the U.S. Department of Agriculture (USDA), the U.S. government followed a radical free market policy, in the 1985 five-year farm bill and in the General Agreement on Tariffs and Trade (GATT) negotiations. A government study predicts that if the U.S. GATT proposal were to go through (or a domestic farm law equivalent), 500,000 farmers more would be wiped out by 1992.

The mass impoverishment of American family farmers over the 1980s was accomplished by a combination of high interest rates, removal of financing sources, devaluation of farm assets, plus high costs for inputs, and low prices for outputs. This is in exact parallel to the impoverishment of Third World nations.

In 1981, U.S. agriculture had a total assets value of $1 trillion, which dropped to $760 billion by 1990—a 24% plunge. Over this decade, lending agencies devalued the collateral backing farmers' loans, and demanded more collateral and higher interest rates on debt. After Paul Volcker became head of the Federal Reserve in 1979, his high interest rate policy caused some farm lending to exceed a 20% interest rate.

For awhile, in the early 1980s, farmers scrambled to hock everything they owned, and went deeper into debt. Applications soared to the Farmers Home Administration (FmHA), the farmers' lender of last resort.

By the mid-1980s, total agriculture debt reached over $215

billion, held by three major lending groups: the FmHA, the commercial banks, and the Production Credit Association (PCA), a private entity with limited government backing. Then the axe fell. The Reagan-Bush administration ordered creditors to "tighten up" on loans. By 1990, total national agriculture debt was brought down to less than $190 billion, by a process of shutting down hundreds of thousands of farmers, and squeezing others to the bone. The USDA dumped thousands of their FmHA farm borrowers through forced bankruptcy. Hundreds of small, local farm banks went under.

This situation prevails today. Farm communities have become ghost towns. And with the low prices for farm commodities, farmers are still unable to service debt and capitalize their operations.

The prices of all farm commodities in the United States, just as internationally, are artificially depressed by the food cartel companies—Cargill, ADM/Toepfer, Louis Dreyfus, Continental, Bunge, André/Garnac, and a few others—whose policy is to liquidate the independent family farm. Most farm prices are less than half of parity (a fair price covering cost of production, and a return on investment sufficient to guarantee the capitalization necessary for continued food production). The USDA issued a report in 1987 saying that parity is an outmoded concept.

The crisis is exemplified by the current situation of wheat, the staff of life. *Figure 6* shows that wheat prices have plunged over the last eight months. The average price today is $2.38 a bushel, lower than it has been in 20 years, and *half* the minimum cost of production.

Contrary to any propaganda you may hear, this does not represent a glut of wheat on the market, nor any suppression of prices according to some mythical law of supply and demand. Instead, it represents systematic underpayment of farmers by the cartel grain-brokering companies that monopolize the world grain trade and domestic distribution. It has been the policy of London and Washington, D.C. to condone this underpayment of farmers for their food output, in the name of "free market" competition.

Wheat is, in reality, *scarce* relative to need. On a world basis, less grain of all types was harvested from 1987 to 1989, than was consumed. While over 2 billion tons of grains of all types were needed for consumption, only 1.6–1.75 billion tons were produced. Of this, wheat output leveled off at about 420 million tons. For the minimum for decent diets, over 3 billion tons would be required for direct consumption as cereals, and indirect consumption through livestock products.

Grain reserve stocks of all types were drawn down from 1986 to the present. Therefore, the first decent harvest year during that period, 1990, does not make up for this drawdown, nor for the fact that millions have been deprived of adequate nutrition. Over the 1980s, food output per capita declined in Ibero-America. Food output per capita in Africa has declined so drastically over the past 20 years that starvation is occurring on the scale of genocide.

The graph shows that the "stocks-to-use ratio" for wheat is low. This illustrates that prices to the farm should be much higher.

With minor changes, the wheat and grain picture holds true for other dietary staples—oils, sugars, meat, milk, fruits, and vegetables. Prices have fallen to the farmers while shortages are forcing millions to go hungry.

In this depressed environment, the "marijuana industry" has taken hold.

PART I
Our Enemies Proved Us Right

1
Why This Book Has Become Famous

When the first edition of *Dope, Inc.* made its appearance in December 1978, it sent shock waves through the international capitals of organized crime—from London to Moscow, from Geneva to Boston and Lower Manhattan, from Tel Aviv to Milan, Sofia, and Montreal. More than seven years later, the multinational narcotics cartel is still desperately scrambling to cover up the truth our book exposed. But fortunately, while several government agencies were confirming the reality of our charges for themselves, the enemy's furious response to the 100,000-copy circulation of the first edition of *Dope, Inc.*, produced much new evidence, implicating a broader net of powerful international figures.

In the spring of 1978, Lyndon LaRouche had commissioned the original investigation which led to publication of *Dope, Inc.*, on the basis of his conviction that unless the U.S. government and the American people moved quickly to crush the international drug mafia, the United States would, within a generation, cease to exist as a nation, and, with its collapse, Western civilization would fall into a new dark age.

The book was conceived as a military intelligence report, a first step toward launching a full-scale war on drugs, employing all of the military, technological, and moral resources which the Allied nations employed in World War II to defeat Nazism. That is still our aim. By the mid-1980s, although the Reagan administration had adopted the phrase "war on drugs" as a slogan, the most energetic battles in the war LaRouche had proposed were being fought in Ibero-America, by such nations as President Alan García's Peru and President Belisario Betancur's Colombia—with scant aid from the U.S.A. On March 9, 1985, LaRouche presented to a Mexico City conference a battle plan for a hemispheric war on drugs that would bring the U.S. armed forces into the fight. The LaRouche plan is published as Appendix A in this book. On March 3, 1986, the President's Commission on Organized Crime recommended to Ronald Reagan: "The Joint Chiefs should be instructed by the highest levels of government . . . that hostile or destructive action from within or without—overt or covert—shall include the . . . invasion of this country by drug smugglers." This conclusion is bitterly opposed by the FBI and the corruption-riddled U.S. Justice Department presided over by Attorney General Edwin Meese, and the go-ahead for the U.S. military's participation in the war on drugs has not been given.

The battle terrain of the drug wars has shifted significantly in the intervening years since the first publication of *Dope, Inc.*

In 1978, the Carter administration was championing the decriminalization and legalization of marijuana and cocaine. "Recreational" drug abuse was being touted as a "victimless crime." Today, with every population group victimized by the dope trade—congressmen, junior high school students, industrial workers, housewives, professional athletes, Wall Street businessmen—such claims of "victimless crime" ring increasingly hollow.

When *Dope, Inc.* was first published, the Latin American

"cocaine bonanza" that would open a new, ugly chapter in the annals of organized crime, and boost the annual revenues of Dope, Inc. toward the half-trillion-dollar level, was still a year or two in the future. Indeed, in 1978, Carlos Lehder Rivas, the kingpin of today's Colombian narcoterrorist rebellion and an avowed collaborator of the murderous M–19 terrorist army, was just getting out of jail in Miami on car theft and marijuana charges, and was only first establishing contact with Dope, Inc. financier Robert Vesco.

The concept of narcoterrorism—first elaborated in the first edition of *Dope, Inc.*—was scoffed at in intelligence and law enforcement circles, where images of Sicilian mafia "moustache Petes" and leftist Robin Hoods still blocked officials from discerning a single worldwide underground economy servicing the illegal arms and drug trade. Revelations growing out of the attempted assassination of Pope John Paul II in May 1981 began to open the eyes of a few, particularly with respect to the active role of the Soviet KGB.

With the Soviet invasion of Afghanistan in 1979, the international heroin trade, centered in the Golden Triangle of Southeast Asia where it had operated so successfully during the Vietnam War, began to diversify and expand rapidly in Soviet-occupied Afghanistan and neighboring Pakistan. The coming to power of "Islamic fundamentalism" in Ayatollah Khomeini's Iran, under the auspices of Soviet specialist G. A. Aliyev, together with Soviet-British fostering of separatist insurgencies such as the Sikh "Khalistan," turned southwest Asia into a "Golden Crescent" for Dope, Inc. rivalling the Far East.

In this new edition of *Dope, Inc.*, we have taken account of the changed landscape, by adding new sections on the dope cartel's command structure, the drug traffic in Ibero-America and Southwest Asia, and the major role of the worldwide Soviet Empire.

In one respect, however, the story of *Dope, Inc.* is the same today as it was seven years ago—the unparalleled corruption of so many of the world's "respectable" financial institutions. Since its original publication, this, the central charge leveled in *Dope, Inc.*, has been massively re-documented by official sources—and by the drug bankers of Dope, Inc. themselves, whose uncontrolled and savage attacks on us have demonstrated repeatedly that they regard our efforts as the most serious threat to their continued existence.

'Apocalyptic Vision' or Everyday Reality?

The idea that some of the world's leading private financial institutions were deeply implicated in the witting laundering of hundreds of billions of dollars a year in illegal dope money was seen as the single most shocking fact brought to light with the first release of *Dope, Inc.* We demonstrated that dope was the largest commodity in international trade, with the exception of petroleum, and that the annual revenues of the narcotics traffic exceeded the national product of most of the world's nations, and the revenues of the largest multinational companies.

The American weekly magazine *Saturday Review* described our view as "a truly apocalyptic vision." The intervening years and their unbroken string of revelations have shown that the apocalypse is here. After the November 1984 publication of the report on money laundering of the President's Commission on Organized Crime, the March 1983 report of the Permanent Investigations Subcommittee of the U.S. Senate, and countless congressional hearings on the subject of banks and money-laundering, the core contents of *Dope, Inc.*'s first edition have been restated by official sources.

Among the earliest confirmation for *Dope, Inc.*'s charges came from New York State's banking superintendent: On the basis of evidence presented by its authors, this regulatory body refused to permit the Hongkong and Shanghai Banking Corporation to purchase control of New York's Marine Midland Bank in 1979, delaying what was, until then, the largest foreign takeover plan in American banking history.

The superintendent, Muriel Siebert, demanded detailed accounting of the HongShang's hidden profits, silent subsidiaries, and other paraphernalia of money laundering, and refused its application when the Hong Kong institution predictably refused. HongShang was compelled to employ a subterfuge—ultimately sanctioned by Paul Volcker's Federal Reserve Board—in order to consummate the takeover: it arranged for Marine Midland Bank, one of America's largest, to change its status from a state-chartered to a nationally chartered bank, in order to circumvent the regulatory powers of New York State. The Federal Reserve threw out the rule books and accepted the takeover of Marine Midland in early 1980, preferring to ignore the law and the banking regulator of America's financial center, New York State, rather than jeopardize the plans of Dope, Inc.

In 1978, we asked, "How is it possible that $200 billion and up in dirty money, crisscrossing international borders, can remain outside the control of the law? Again, only one possible answer can be admitted: a huge chunk of international banking and related financial operations have been created solely to manage dirty money. More than that, this chunk of international banking enjoys the sovereign protection of more than a few governments."

Half a decade ago, the charge seemed adventurous to many. Measure it against the conclusions of the study entitled, "Crime and Secrecy: The Use of Offshore Banks and Companies," issued by the Permanent Investigations Subcommittee of the U.S. Senate in March 1983 after two years of investigations. The investigators estimated the illegal economy of the United States at up to 10% of reported Gross National Product, or over $300 billion. The study reported that London is the leading center worldwide for the concealment of funds, a charge first made in *Dope, Inc.;* that two-fifths of all foreign banking activities conducted out of Switzerland are performed with other offshore centers, Switzerland being the center for the practice of "layering" secret financial accounts so that beneficial ownership is impossible to determine.

We had subtitled the 1978 work, "Britain's Opium War Against the United States." The Senate investigators went to London to ask for British cooperation in dismantling criminal activities in the offshore centers, and complained that British officials rejected the proposal out of hand, asserting for the record that organized crime was an internal American problem and no concern of London's. The British told the Senate investigators:

> As London sees it, the crime problem for the most part rests with the U.S., for whether it is drug money or other fraud it derives primarily from U.S. sources, i.e., criminal transactions in the U.S., and is processed offshore on behalf of American citizens and companies. It is argued by London that control efforts will incur only costs but no benefits. Given these conditions, whatever the U.S. policy, it behooves the U.K. not to involve itself collaboratively.

The SPIS study summarizes the charges of American prosecutors against Swiss, British, and Canadian banks during the preceding several years, with multiple mention of the three big Swiss banks, Britain's largest commercial bank, Barclays, Canada's Bank of Nova Scotia, as well as offshore divisions of American banks. Referring to the Bank of Nova Scotia, nestled into the coziest reaches of the British establishment, the SPIS report complains, "For example, in the Caribbean, one major Canadian international bank has a consistent reputation for encouraging dirty money. ... Senior bank officials describe instances where headquarters banks have removed competent offshore managers for their failures ... to optimize profits through corrupt relationships."

Not merely in the specifics, but in the scope of its conclusions, the Senate report corroborated the most controversial judgments we offered in 1978. We had argued that a large part of the world banking structure had come to exist in order to handle dirty offshore-money flows. The SPIS report concluded that illegal financial operations are now so closely meshed with the offshore banking system in general that the movement of illegal funds may constitute a threat to the security of the world banking system as a whole. Citing the case of the 1982 bankruptcy of Banco Ambrosiano, Roberto Calvi's ill-fated vehicle for dirty political and financial operations, SPIS wrote:

In 1982, Banco Ambrosiano of Milan, Italy, collapsed, crippled by a $1.4 billion exposure in loans to several mysterious Panamanian "shell" companies. . . . The Euromarket is a critically important . . . feature of international commerce. But in the haven countries where money is laundered, it is unregulated. Thus, the same conditions which facilitate international commerce also create criminal opportunites. The criminal use of offshore facilities poses a problem to the stability of entire national banking systems. The fragile condition of the world's banking system today is a result in part of questionable loans, poor controls and the country risk occurring when so many nations cannot pay the interest or principal on their debt. It is not inconceivable that it could be a criminally derived loss, not the failure of repayment of a loan from a sovereign nation, which could be the backbreaking straw to the banking system.

As we will report below, the Senate committee's specific concern in the case of Calvi's Banco Ambrosiano was not merely conjectural. When the financing of the American banking system derives from international flight capital, it is no exaggeration to state that the vagaries of the financial underworld may determine the fate of the entire world banking system.

By October 1984, the role of some of Boston and New York's most prestigious commercial banks and investment houses in washing drug money had become such a public scandal that the Reagan administration drafted model legislation allowing for criminal prosecution of bank corporate executives. And the President's Commission on Organized Crime, a blue ribbon panel established by Ronald Reagan by Executive Order 12435 on July 23, 1983, devoted the entirety of its first published report to "The Cash Connection: Organized Crime, Financial Institutions, and Money Laundering." Among the big league financial houses cited in the commission's report for washing hot money were Chemical Bank, Merrill Lynch, Chase Manhattan Bank, and Deak-Perrera.

When the President's Commission on Organized Crime released its report, the bag of tricks of the narcotics traffic was put on display, at least the best known of them: the use of casinos to launder drug money, the corruption and virtual take-over of banks, the participation of such august firms as E.F. Hutton (which sent security guards to the Waldorf-Astoria Hotel to help a Colombian client bring suitcases full of cash to its offices, and then tipped off its client when informed that he was under investigation as a money-launderer for Colombian cocaine-traffickers).

This corroboration of our original conclusions would be a greater consolation were it not for the continued, massive expansion of narcotics traffic and dirty-money networks. With the consumption of $75 billion per year of cocaine in the United States alone, and the rapid growth of heroin addiction in Western Europe, our original estimate of $100 billion per annum in narcotics sales in the United States and $200 billion worldwide is dwarfed by the present reality. Narcotics traffic grosses a minimum of $200 billion per year in the United States and $500 billion worldwide, and the associated illegal traffic in arms, contraband, and so forth has grown in proportion.

For the first time, the nations of Ibero-America are fighting openly, in their national parliaments and their international gatherings, for their sovereignty, against the professed allies of the narcotics mafias, who dare to openly challenge the power of duly-constituted legal governments. In Colombia, where former president Alfonso López Michelsen has bragged of meeting with the narcotics mafia and advised the government to accept their terms, the narcoterrorist M–19 has carried out an armed attack on the Justice Ministry, taking hostage and then murdering 11 Supreme Court justices. In Peru, President Alan García has conducted an all-out war on the drug traffickers, but the terrorist guerrillas of Sendero Luminoso have repeatedly crippled the electrical power supplies of major cities, and murdered officials and burned homes in countryside. The Andean Pact countries have been plunged into the same type of inconclusive warfare which has plagued Southeast Asia—the opium region called the "Golden Triangle"—since the middle 1960s, where well-armed and well-organized military bands have exerted control over the territory where the poppy is planted.

Despite President Reagan's promise of a war on drugs, despite the heroic efforts of the Italian police against the Sicilian mafia, despite the destruction of the Calvi gang in Italian freemasonry, despite the mopping-up of money-laundering operations of Florida banks—despite all of this, the international network we called Dope, Incorporated has not merely flourished; it has risen to commanding heights in the world economy. The International Monetary Fund shamelessly does its bidding among the debtor nations of the developing sector.

In June 1983, the International Monetary Fund made its first published comment on the subject, in an appendix buried in its World Economic Outlook report. In its bland, malevolent way, the IMF noted that about $200 billion per year was disappearing from the accounts of national governments who report their balance-of-payments data to the international financial organization. This is referred to in the arcane interchanges of governmental accounts as the "statistical discrepancy in the global current account payments balance." It represents the difference between all countries' surpluses and deficits once they are totaled up. In theory, one country's deficit must be another country's surplus. By 1982, however, the total excess of deficits over surpluses had risen to $89 billion. If all the discrepancies between countries' payments and receipts on current account were totaled up individually, rather than aggregated on a global basis, the total for 1982 would be in the range of $200 billion—representing almost one-fifth of world trade. In other words, the net deficit reported by all countries is $89 billion; the funds not accounted for by all countries is almost $200 billion. Since 1973, the IMF added, the total volume of such discrepancies has accumulated to the fantastic sum of $800 billion.

This is no surprise to the Ibero-American nations hit by waves of flight capital during 1982 and 1983. What the gross numbers state is that the movements of international capital are out of the hands of governments entirely; governments can no longer even identify $200 billion per year in capital flows, much less attempt to influence them!

The IMF report leaves little to the imagination: The origin

of the "statistical discrepancy" is international flight capital and related illegal money flows. The 1983 document states:

> The principal factor accounting for the growth of the world payments asymmetry on current account has been the fairly rapid increase in the negative balance on invisibles. After being approximately balanced in 1973, estimated payments and receipts for services and private transfers have diverged progressively more widely in subsequent years, and the excess of recorded payments over receipts in these accounts reached some $800 billion in 1982.

The IMF reports directly that the "invisibles" which account for the "statistical discrepancy," i.e. "shipment," "reinvested earnings," and "other earned income," boil down to flight capital:

"The most readily identifiable part of this large excess of debits over credits is that rooted in the services provided by fleets flying so-called flags of convenience. The payments for services of these fleets are, for the most part, duly recorded in the balance of payments statistics of the countries using such services. The corresponding credits, on the other hand, are typically not entered in any country's balance of payments," that is, they enter the banking system illegally.

The IMF, the supposed lawgiver of international finance, explains that international finance is now lawless.

The implications of these admissions are breathtaking. After ruining the economies and undermining the political stability of most of Ibero-America, as well as Nigeria, the Philippines, and numerous other nations of the developing sector, the International Monetary Fund admits that the provocation for its actions—the mass exit of capital and associated burgeoning of foreign debt of the victim countries—is out of the victim countries' control. Indeed, according to the IMF, it is out of the control of any national government.

Dope, Inc. Answers the Charges

Long before the law enforcement and intelligence services of the Western nations responded to the challenge posed by the publication of *Dope, Inc.*, the dope cartel itself issued its response. Lyndon LaRouche and his closest associates became the immediate targets of a brutal campaign of libels, attempted murders, kidnappings, and, eventually, an attack by elements of the U.S. Department of Justice, the federal courts, and the Federal Bureau of Investigation, who were themselves under the thumb of the international dope mafia.

Dope, Inc.'s first response came in the form of simultaneous published attacks penned by the Anti-Defamation League of B'nai B'rith and the British import Heritage Foundation, the latter a nominally "conservative" lobbying group that is in fact pushing the British East India Company policies of the opium trade apologist Adam Smith.

While the original edition of *Dope, Inc.* had exposed ADL patrons Edgar Bronfman and Max Fisher among the leading American and Canadian "citizens above suspicion" with deep ties to the international drug trade, it was only as the result of the ADL libel campaign that the full extent of the ADL's role as a public relations front for the dope interests came to the surface.

Current ADL National Chairman Kenneth Bialkin, of the New York law firm of Willkie, Farr & Gallagher, according to U.S. federal court proceedings in the Southern District of New York, was the gray eminence behind dope trafficker Robert Vesco's bilking of Investors Overseas Service (IOS) out of hundreds of millions of dollars, money Vesco then used to build his Caribbean dirty money empire. The Havana-headquartered Vesco, the heir apparent to the U.S. syndicate's original "financial wizard," Meyer Lansky, has most recently fulfilled Lansky's own dream of turning Castro's Cuba into the capital of a hemispheric guns-for-dope and dirty money conglomerate. And, in the course of so doing, ADL Chairman Bialkin's most notorious client became an honorary commissar in Yuri Andropov's army of KGB narco-pushers.

A former ADL chairman, Sterling National Bank President Theodore Silbert, was sued by the Italian government in New York district court in 1983, for alleged criminal conspiracy with mafia financier Michele Sindona. The Italian government's legal brief charges that Silbert knowingly assisted Sindona's looting of the Banca Privata and other companies Sindona controlled, prior to their bankruptcy. Sterling National Bank, which allegedly laundered Sindona's looted funds, manages the ADL's investment and checking accounts.

In February 1985, when *Dope, Inc.* was published in Spanish as *Narcotráfico, SA,* and distributed in countries all over Latin America, the Rockefellers' closest financial allies in Venezuela, the Cisneros family, indulged themselves in a remarkable public tantrum. Pulling wires, the Cisneros clan deployed agents of the Venezuelan political police, the DISIP, to carry out a 2 a.m. raid on *EIR*'s offices in Caracas, arrest its correspondents in their homes, subject them to more than 48 hours of illegal jailing, interrogation, threats, and physical abuse, and finally, expel them from the country. Their offense was simply their employment by *EIR*, the authors of *Narcotráfico, SA*. The Cisneros family, an agent of the DISIP announced to *EIR*, "will not permit one single copy of the book to circulate." Shortly thereafter, thanks to a compliant judge, *Narcotráfico, SA* became the first book since the end of the military dictatorship in 1958 to be banned in Venezuela.

You can read what we had to say about the Cisneros family, word for word, later in this book—including the family connection to Castro's Cuba that so embarrassed the Cisneroses.

In August 1985, another Rockefeller ally, the former prime minister of Peru, Manuel Ulloa, brought a slander suit against the Peruvian Anti-Drug Coalition and its head, Luis Vásquez Medina, for repeating the charges against Ulloa made in *Narcotráfico, SA*. With the García government investigating the financial and political interests in the past government which had protected the dope trade, Ulloa hoped to silence his accusers, who had charged his policies had paved the way for the takeover of the Peruvian economy by Dope, Inc. But on October

17, 1985 the court rejected Ulloa's suit, and absolved the ADC and Vásquez of all charges.

On March 22, 1986 a three-judge panel of Peru's Superior Court unanimously upheld the lower-court ruling. The court ruled that the Anti-Drug Coalition's publications, including *Narcotráfico, SA*, were "in the spirit of criticism of the economic policy which the plaintiff executed, . . . which is described as 'superliberal' . . . [and] whose policy permitted the proliferation not only of the drug trade, but also of bingo, finance companies, and real estate which are interconnected and which make up the 'illicit economies.' "

Dope Lobbyists Invade the Halls of Justice

On October 22, 1984, the Boston offices of U.S. Attorney William Weld opened a bogus criminal investigation into the presidential campaign committee of independent Democratic presidential candidate Lyndon LaRouche, on the excuse of several purported cases of credit card irregularities at the campaign's local Boston office.

The Boston "probe" provided the pretext ten days later for First Fidelity Bank of Newark, New Jersey to seize $200,000 on deposit in two LaRouche campaign accounts, thereby blocking a nationwide prime time TV broadcast scheduled for election eve. First Fidelity was the leading institution responsible for bringing Dope, Inc. into Atlantic City under the cover of legalized casino gambling. First Fidelity chairman Robert Ferguson financed the first boardwalk casino construction through an $11 million loan to Resorts International, a notorious front for the old Meyer Lansky syndicate. Ferguson's Newark attorney, Albert Besser, had been the attorney for Robert Vesco in the same series of IOS cases that featured the ADL's Kenneth Bialkin as a virtual unindicted co-conspirator.

Nearly 18 months, and hundreds of thousands of dollars in taxpayers' money later, Weld's "Get LaRouche" witchhunt con-

tinues on an expanded scale. The goal? To bankrupt and set up
for potential assassination America's leading drug fighter—
before the 1986 midterm congressional elections place
LaRouche, already a declared and registered candidate for the
1988 Democratic Party presidential nomination, in the political
limelight with access to nationwide television advertising.
LaRouche's sixteen half-hour nationwide prime time TV broad-
casts during the 1984 presidential race prompted Dope, Inc. to
loudly declare, "Never again." By the time the reader finishes
this book, the reasons for the syndicate's declaration of war will
be very clear.

The designation of William Weld as the grand inquisitor was
a "family decision" by the Dope, Inc. elite that has ruled New
England since the clipper ship days of the opium and slave
trade and the traitorous Hartford Convention. Weld's grandfather was the founder of the Lower Manhattan and old Boston
investment house of White, Weld and Company. His father,
David Weld, was the firm's chief executive officer during a long
period in which the company was intermarried with the elite
of the Swiss money-laundering institutions, Crédit Suisse.

Under its chairman Donald Regan, Wall Street giant Merrill
Lynch bought White, Weld in 1978, leaving the White, Weld
partners who stayed with Merrill to take over the bigger firm;
Merrill's chief administrative officer and next-in-line to the
chairmanship is now the former White, Weld legal counsel
Stephen Hammerman. But Crédit Suisse, which had bought a
controlling 31% share in White Weld from David Weld and his
partners, took full control of White, Weld's Geneva and London
operations. These operations had provided an estimated two-
thirds of White Weld's revenues. Crédit Suisse then turned
around and bought 38% of the old Rockefeller-Mellon investment bank, First Boston Corporation, bringing White, Weld's
foreign operations under a new umbrella, First Boston-Crédit
Suisse.

The same old White, Weld network now dominates the $150
billion per year "Eurobond" market, the biggest haven for dirty
money in the world, and now the most important source of
funds for U.S. corporations. Crédit Suisse-First Boston is the

dominant market maker for "Eurobonds," a form of anonymous international security favored by criminals everywhere. Swiss banker Robert Genillard, the man who set up David Weld's old link to Crédit Suisse in the late 1960s, is still chairman of the old White, Weld bank in Geneva, now renamed Clariden Bank under 100% Crédit Suisse ownership. Genillard is still a friend and business associate of former White, Weld partner George S. Moore, one of the group that sold White, Weld to Don Regan; Moore is the official advisor to the tainted Cisneros interests of Venezuela.

In fact, on February 7, 1985, Crédit Suisse was caught red-handed in a multi-billion dollar money-laundering scheme directed out of the staid offices of the First National Bank of Boston, the flagship institution of the Boston Brahmins' Bank of Boston Corporation. Fortunately for the dope bankers, the case was handled by William Weld, who collapsed 1,163 separate documented cases of criminal felony, involving $1,218,682,281 in hot money, laundered in and out of nine foreign banks, into a one-count indictment—for which Bank of Boston was fined a slap-on-the-wrist $500,000 in a plea bargain! The penalty imposed on the bank amounted to an absurd 1/20 of 1% of the amount of money laundered in just these documented cases. Bank of Boston chairman and chief executive officer William Brown was forced to admit in testimony before a congressional committee early in 1985 that the bank made enormous profits from the laundering of the dirty money—even after the fine was paid.

The whitewashing of the Bank of Boston was accompanied by no action whatsoever against the nine foreign correspondent banks, led by Weld's own Crédit Suisse Bank of Zurich, and including Swiss Bank Corp. of Basel, Union Bank of Switzerland in Zurich, Barclays Bank International of New York, Bank of Boston S.A. of Luxembourg, Bank Leu of Zurich, Die Freie Osterreichische of Vienna, Canadian Imperial Bank of Commerce of Ottawa, and Standard Chartered Bank Ltd. of New York. Meanwhile, a flood of other cases opened up revealing the deeper role of the Bank of Boston in the international narcoterrorist conspiracy.

On February 28, 1985, just weeks after the Bank of Boston case had been swept under the rug by U.S. Attorney Weld, the Venezuelan daily newspaper *El Mundo* published an investigative report by journalist José Cupertino Flores revealing that between October 1983 and February 1984, more than $12 billion in capital had gone from Caracas, Valencia, Barquisimeto and San Cristóbal, Venezuela—all favorite money-laundering holes for Latin America's cocaine and marijuana traffickers—into the coffers of the Bank of Boston. Flores suggested that a study of the "passenger lists of flights between New York and Miami and the Boston airport would find famous names and surnames," although "others come by private jets. . . . After last year's intervention into Continental Illinois, the funds of innumerable personalities of our country were transferred with speed to the vaults of the Bostonian institution."

On February 20, 1985, the Irish High Court in Dublin announced it had seized $1.64 million in cash that belonged to a secret Irish Republican Army fund laundered through Swiss banks, into London, on to the Bank of Boston, before arriving at the secret IRA account at the Bank of Ireland. The laundered money, according to Irish Justice Minister Michael Noonan, represented the revenues of kidnappings, death threat extortions, and robberies.

An earlier investigation by the Senate Permanent Investigations Subcommittee had uncovered another illegal money funnel passing from the Banco Nacional de Panamá through the Federal Reserve Bank of Boston into the Bank of Boston International division during 1982–83. Once again, the hot cash wound up in numbered bank accounts at the Zurich offices of the Weld family-linked Crédit Suisse. According to the already-cited report of the President's Commission on Organized Crime, "the cash flow from Panama to the United States is the most significant recorded flow of currency that is likely to be drug money."

If the issue of computer- and electronic mail-generated cash flows between the elite of the offshore international financial community was too pristine a business to warrant the attention of U.S. Attorney Weld, the Boston federal prosecutor had little excuse for blocking the probe into the Bank of Boston's ties to the organized crime Angiulo family, an investigation that Weld apparently had jurisdiction over from no later than 1983. Using an exemption loophole in the federal codes demanding that banks report all cash transactions of $10,000 or more, officials of the Bank of Boston passed tens of millions of dollars in and out of Angiulo family front accounts, taking in cardboard cartons and shopping bags full of ten, twenty, and fifty dollar bills, and issuing cashier's checks. Officials of the U.S. Treasury Department, including the recently departed Assistant Secretary of the Treasury for Enforcement, John Walker, have stated in public forums their belief that the cash laundered by the Bank of Boston, on behalf of the Angiulo family and other shady clients, was dope money.

Testifying before the House subcommittee on financial institutions on March 5, 1985, Walker stated, "There's every indication that the $600 million of small bills that the bank took in was the laundering of drug money. Why else would the money be $20 bills?"

In an earlier public statement, carried by the *Boston Globe* on February 8, 1985, Walker had declared, "The patterns that we saw, which were small bills coming back from Switzerland and large bills going out to Switzerland, are consistent with money laundering going on. There was definitely money laundering in the air."

So confident were the executives of the Bank of Boston in Weld's loyalty to the Dope, Inc. cause that, after the initial flurry of congressional and Treasury Department activity against the bank's laundering adventures, bank officials "discovered" another $73 million in illegally washed funds. The bank executives apologized for the "honest" mistake and Weld took no prosecutorial action.

If there was any doubt that Weld was acting as a defender and advocate of the interests of the Bank of Boston and the Dope, Inc. Brahmins, the U.S. Attorney, who took the federal post only after he was defeated in a statewide election for Commonwealth of Massachusetts Attorney General, received campaign contributions from at least two current officials of the

Bank of Boston, honorary director William C. Mercer and Peter M. Whitman—in addition to Canada's Dope, Inc. magnate Edgar Bronfman.

U.S. Attorney Weld's complicity in whitewashing the role of the big Boston banks—including banks associated with his own family business affairs—in the laundering of billions in dope revenues is perhaps only surpassed by the criminal zeal with which he has targeted the enemies of Dope, Inc. for frameup prosecutions.

In addition to the already cited case of Lyndon LaRouche, Weld conducted a brutal five-year-long assault against the Democratic Party political organization of Boston Mayor Kevin White, a campaign that prompted White to retire from the city post when his term expired in 1981, rather than run for a fifth term in a climate defined by Weld's inquisition. Thomas Anzalone, White's leading fundraiser and campaign coordinator, was indicted by Weld's office and convicted before Federal District Court Judge A. David Mazzone, the same judge handling the LaRouche assault. The Weld-Mazzone team committed such a battery of acts treading on criminality that a three-judge panel in the First District Court of Appeals, on July 1, 1985, threw the Anzalone conviction out, characterizing Weld's methods as bordering on the Soviet legal principle of "guilt by analogy." The appellate decision concluded, "We cannot engage in unprincipled interpretation of the law unless we foment lawlessness instead of compliance."

Even as the "Get White" operation was unfolding, the *National Law Journal* published an article on June 13, 1983 describing the Weld action as a "textbook example of a prosecutor misusing his powers to bully witnesses and manipulate the political process." Weld was cited for using improper pressure tactics, unfounded allegations, leaks to the press, and harassment of witnesses, including late-night sweeps by dozens of subpoena-serving FBI agents. These are the identical methods being repeated in the LaRouche case today.

Yet, in early April 1986, according to press reports citing Attorney General Edwin Meese, Weld was about to be promoted to Washington—to head the U.S. Justice Department's Criminal Division!

The role in all this of White House chief of staff Don Regan, the former Merrill Lynch chairman, certainly merits further investigation. According to evidence supplied in the October 1984 report by the President's Commission on Organized Crime, titled "The Cash Connection: Organized Crime, Financial Institutions and Money Laundering," business procedures at Don Regan's Merrill Lynch have been anything but conservative. The report states:

> In 1980 . . . couriers were observed transferring enormous amounts of cash through investment houses and banks in New York City to Italy and Switzerland. Tens of millions of dollars in heroin sales in this country were transferred overseas in this fashion. . . .
>
> One of the couriers for this laundering operation was Franco Della Torre, a Swiss resident. In March 1982, Della Torre deposited slightly more than $1 million in $5, $10, and $20 bills in the "Traex" account at the Manhattan office of the brokerage firm Merrill Lynch Pierce Fenner & Smith. Thereafter, Della Torre made four additional cash deposits totalling $3.9 million in the "Traex" account. . . .

Merrill Lynch even helped make security arrangements, according to the President's Commission report: "In making large cash deposits at Merrill Lynch, Della Torre's practice was to request that security personnel accompany him from his hotel to Merrill Lynch offices. After several such deposits . . . arrangements were made to escort the money from Della Torre's hotel directly to Bankers Trust, where Merrill Lynch maintained accounts."

According to federal indictments of Della Torre and others in this heroin ring, Merrill Lynch moved the funds directly to Switzerland, where one of the major depositories was—Crédit Suisse.

Some direct evidence of Don Regan's attitude toward narcot-

ics trafficking surfaced in March 1984, when he was questioned
by Congress on why, as Treasury Secretary, he had dismantled
an air interdiction anti-drug program, while shifting $18 mil-
lion in funds for the program to an administrative fund, to
remodel his office.

Marvin Warner Buys a U.S. Attorney

On April 15, 1985, nearly six months into the Weld witchhunt
against LaRouche, an associate of the three-time presidential
candidate wrote to Attorney General Edwin Meese III demanding an official Justice Department probe into Weld's conflict of interest in the coverup of the Bank of Boston's multi-
billion dollar money-laundering schemes. Shortly after the Department of Justice's Office of Public Responsibility opened a
brief probe into the Weld-Crédit Suisse conflict of interest, a
parallel federal grand jury was suddenly opened into the
LaRouche campaign in Cincinnati, Ohio, a city where the campaign did not even maintain an office.

What common thread bound the Boston and Cincinnati juris-
dictions? Whereas U.S. Attorney Weld hob-nobbed with the
elite of the dope bankers in the wood-paneled supper clubs of
Harvard Square, the U.S. Attorney's office in Cincinnati was
virtually a private fiefdom of Marvin Warner, Jimmy Carter's
U.S. ambassador to Switzerland. Warner's dirty-fisted dealings
with some of Latin America's biggest cocaine smugglers
grabbed coast-to-coast headlines between 1980 and the spring
of 1985, when Warner's Ohio banking empire went belly up,
triggering a near-collapse of the entire U.S. savings and loan
sector.

What the Weld-Warner combination proved, above all else,
was the existence of a powerful dope mafia underground pulling
the strings from within the U.S. Department of Justice. When
push comes to shove, Dope, Inc. occupies the Attorney General's
chair.

At the time that the Cincinnati office of the U.S. Attorney

obligingly opened a second grand jury against Lyndon LaRouche, the U.S. Attorney was Christopher Barnes, who, at 32 years old, was perhaps the youngest federal prosecutor in the United States. Barnes's father, Earl Barnes, the former chairman of the Ohio Republican Party, handpicked his son for the job—in large measure to protect his financial "godfather" Marvin Warner from federal prosecution for a string of money-fleecing operations generally linked to the Ibero-American drug trade.

According to testimony delivered before an Ohio state legislative committee probing Warner's role in the collapse of his Home State Savings Bank, Earl Barnes was the recipient of a $1 million unsecured loan from Warner, a loan he had never paid a penny on.

While Warner's "contributions" to GOP kingmaker Barnes, and his equally generous treatment of the Democratic Party state machine of Governor Richard Celeste (Warner is widely credited with the multi-million dollar vote fraud operation that stole the Ohio electoral college for Jimmy Carter in 1976) ensured that both the Democratic and GOP-appointed U.S. Attorneys would look the other way when Warner dipped his hands into the Ohio taxpayers' pockets, on December 13, 1985, a special state grand jury sitting in Hamilton County, Ohio handed down a 50-count indictment of Warner for willful misapplication of funds, theft of securities, and theft by deception. That indictment was put together without a stitch of cooperation from the U.S. Attorney's office, from the Department of Justice in Washington, or from the FBI.

If the Feds had not covered up for Warner, one of the most protected and hermetically sealed drug-money-laundering operations ever put together in the United States might have been crushed.

It is no coincidence that the Warner money-laundering apparatus can be traced directly back to the Boston Brahmins and White, Weld.

In 1976, a White, Weld securities whiz kid, Allen Nowick, went to Fort Lauderdale, Fla. to help set up ESM Government Securities. The three "out-front" partners of Nowick in ESM were Ronnie R. Ewton, Robert Seneca, and George Mead. In much the same way that White, Weld took control of the vastly larger Merrill Lynch and First Boston Eurobond laundering apparatus, it was White, Weld special operative Nowick who transformed the ESM-Marvin Warner group into a vast hot-money-washing complex over the period from 1976–81, through a string of buyouts and hostile takeovers of banks and other lending institutions stretching from Florida to New Jersey to Ohio.

The merry-go-round got started in 1977, when Warner's Home State Savings Bank, a Cincinnati-based S&L, loaned $17 million to Ewton and Seneca, permitting them to take over the Great American Bank group of Florida. Warner's son-in-law, Steven Arky, a Florida attorney, had put Warner together with Ewton, a close associate of Arky from the National Guard. Warner ignored the fact that Ewton had already been under investigation by the SEC for ESM's unlicensed securities trading.

Warner's cavalier attitude toward his intimate dealings with suspected criminal Ewton was born of two factors. First, by 1978, Warner's Home State already had one federal fraud conviction under its own belt—for issuing phony commercial standby loan commitments (at a lucrative commission) to 47 contractors and developers in 11 states. $800,000 in paybacks, and a paltry $11,000 in fines were ordered. No bank officials were indicted by name. A spinoff personal tax fraud probe into Warner by the IRS was short circuited by a September 1980 plea bargain arranged by Warner's attorney, Edward Bennett Williams, a prominent Democratic Party fixer, and Justice Department officials John Keeny, head of Carter's Criminal Division, and James Cissell, U.S. Attorney for the Southern District of Ohio.

Second, Warner was richly rewarded for his role in stealing the 1976 presidential elections for Jimmy Carter. In early 1977, he was named U.S. ambassador to Switzerland, a position that never got in the way of Warner's continuing money-laundering activities. It was not merely that Warner enjoyed the political protection and diplomatic immunity of the Carter administration. Warner proved to be a centerpiece of the Florida dirty money machine implicated in the Billygate affair and the drug empire of fugitive Dope, Inc. financier Robert Vesco.

In 1978, Warner bought back Great American Bank Corp. from Ewton and merged it with ComBank, another Florida banking group he had previously purchased in partnership with Hugh Culverhouse, Sr. In the meantime, Warner issued standing orders to all of his bank officers to conduct their government securities purchases exclusively through ESM. Subsequent investigations by federal and state regulators in the wake of ESM's March 4, 1985, $300 million collapse, revealed that Warner and Arky were the exclusive holders of personal investment accounts with ESM. In effect, ESM was Warner's private little *fondo*.

A review of newspaper accounts and federal court records suggests that Warner used the facilities of his burgeoning empire of Florida banks to draw in the revenues of Ibero-American drug traffickers and wash the funds through ESM and other conduits en route to numbered accounts in Switzerland, Panama, and other offshore havens.

In addition to his own position as ambassador to Switzerland (and lover of Jimmy Carter's personal White House secretary, Susan Clough), Warner enjoyed the protection of the Florida state comptroller, Gerald E. Lewis—his second cousin—and his lifetime friend and business partner, Hugh Culverhouse Sr., whose son, Hugh Jr., up through 1982 directed the division of the U.S. Attorney's office in Florida responsible for prosecuting money-laundering cases.

It was precisely this combination of "guardian angels" who closed ranks to protect Warner when agents of the IRS, DEA, and U.S. Customs Service moved in on the Great American Bank of Dade County on February 27, 1981 as part of Operation Greenback, an early Reagan administration effort to crack down on some of the most egregious instances of drug money-laundering by U.S. banks. In fact, Florida Comptroller Lewis, whom federal officials described as notoriously soft on drug-money-launderers, complained bitterly that the DEA had not informed him in advance of the pending raid.

On December 10, 1982, a federal grand jury in Miami indicted
the Great American Bank and three middle level employees—
Vice President Lionel Paytuvi, head teller Carlos Nunez, and
teller Elaine Kemp—on charges that during the 14-month period leading up to the February 1981 raid, over $94 million had
been illegally laundered through the bank on behalf of three
Latin American drug-trafficking organizations.

By far the most notorious of the three drug rings was that
of Isaac Kattan-Kasin, a Syrian Jew from the smugglers'
enclave of Aleppo, who, after spending the early 1960s living
in New Jersey as an employee of Robert Vesco, became a
Colombian citizen and ran the largest Latin American cocaine
smuggling organization of the 1970s. Kattan laundered an
estimated $350 million a year into southern Florida, according
to Operation Greenback veterans. Those funds were then
transferred to numbered accounts at the Swiss Bank Corp.
in Zurich, the Banco de Ibero-America in Panama and Banco
Internacional, Banco del Crédito and the Bank of Tokyo, all
in Lima, Peru.

Although Warner screamed he was only a victim, and managed to sidestep indictment in the Kattan affair, Operation
Greenback officials said privately they were convinced that
Warner was a mastermind of the laundering scheme. In fact,
according to one federal law enforcement source, within days
of the arrest of Kattan, Hugh Culverhouse Jr., fresh out of
the Miami U.S. Attorney's office, paid a personal visit to the
Department of Justice headquarters, lobbying for the International Affairs Section to unfreeze the funds in eight Swiss bank
accounts maintained by Kattan.

Once the smoke cleared on the Great American Bank scandal,
Warner quietly sold his majority holdings in the bank to Barnett Banks of Florida—at a handsome 325% profit.

Simultaneous to the Great American Bank bust, another one
of Warner's flagship institutions, ComBank, surfaced in the
middle of yet another DEA investigation, codenamed Operation
Groper. On April 13, 1982, a Winter Park, Florida businessman,
Robert Govern, and 12 others were indicted for smuggling more
than four million pounds of marijuana from Colombia into the

United States between 1975–81. Govern laundered the drug proceeds through ComBank into a string of sham corporations in the Grand Caymans and Netherlands Antilles.

According to an investigative report published in the *Cleveland Plain Dealer* on June 18, 1985, one of Warner's prize investors was the Venezuelan Cisneros group that is the subject of another chapter. Suffice it to say here that a Cisneros family retainer, Vincente Pérez Sandoval, was a client of Steven Arky who tried unsuccessfully to take over Freedom Savings and Loan Association of Tampa shortly after Warner, a shareholder in the bank, maneuvered the S&L into buying ComBank at a price estimated to be more than double the book value of the banking group.

Another Florida bank, Metropolitan Bank of Tampa, came under intensive federal investigation on suspicion of laundering drug revenues from the World Finance Corp., a Meyer Lansky-Robert Vesco linked Coral Gables firm also tied to the Cisneros interests in Venezuela through Arky client Pérez Sandoval. Then Warner stepped in through Great American Bank to buy up the Tampa bank. Prior to this "friendly" takeover, overseen by Florida State Comptroller Gerald Lewis, Warner's cousin, Metropolitan had been owned by Edward J. DeBartolo, a Youngstown, Ohio multi-millionaire whose name has often been linked to organized crime.

In fact, Warner's association with the very same Ohio-centered criminal circles provoked speculation that the title transfer was a cosmetic change, aimed at clearing the books on Metropolitan's unexplained "loss" of $51 million, drawn from a discount window at the Federal Reserve.

In June of 1985, a Hamilton County judge approved an almost identical "lateral" takeover of Warner's own Home State Savings by Hunter Savings Association, a Cincinnati S&L owned by Carl Lindner. A subsidiary of Lindner's American Financial Corp., Hunter is one of 40 corporations—including the notorious United Brands and Penn Central Railroad—under the control of a holding company board that lists Warner's ComBank partner Hugh Culverhouse, Sr. as one of only three directors drawn from outside Lindner's immediate family.

The taxpayers of Ohio paid for the Hunter takeover of Home State—through a grant of $100 million from the state of Ohio.

This chain of events began on March 4, 1985, when the SEC obtained a federal court order to close down ESM, on the grounds that the Fort Lauderdale hot money laundromat was $300 million short of its current obligations. Within 48 hours, panicked depositors began a three-day run on Home State, which had $570 million admittedly tied up in ESM. By the time Home State Chairman David J. Schiebel announced on March 8 that the Cincinnati thrift was closing its doors, $154 million had been withdrawn.

In early April, a New Jersey government securities firm, Bevill, Bresler, and Schulman folded up in a repeat of the ESM blowout. An even bigger run on the banks seemed possible. Two of the firm's former brokers, Ronnie Ewton and George Mead, had left the firm in 1975 to link up with White, Weld's Nowick in founding ESM. In return, ESM later deployed one of their chief brokers, Andrew Ledbetter, into Bevill, Bresler, and Schulman.

The First Fidelity Case

On November 1, 1984, immediately after U.S. Attorney William Weld announced his investigation of the LaRouche campaign on NBC television, Boston-based FBI special agent Richard Egan contacted the First Fidelity Bank of Newark, New Jersey, then holding deposits for two LaRouche campaign committees. Within hours of the call, First Fidelity had illegally seized $200,000 from the two accounts, thus blocking a scheduled LaRouche election eve half-hour nationwide broadcast on CBS-TV.

At the time of the theft, LaRouche campaign spokesmen charged that top officials of First Fidelity, including bank Chairman Robert Ferguson, were implicated in an organized crime network involving the old Meyer Lansky syndicate and corrupt leading officials of the Democratic Party. The spokesmen documented that the bank's organized crime ties revolved around the Lansky mob's invasion of Atlantic City through the legalization of casino gambling, a project in which bank head Ferguson had played a pivotal role. That Ferguson and First Fidelity shared a lawyer with dope financier Robert Vesco merely added to an already rich mosaic of evidence. The LaRouche campaign committees sued the bank for their money, and the bank countersued for libel.

Fifteen months and thousands of pages of court papers, depositions, affidavits, and motions after the bank's ripoff of LaRouche campaign contributors, the *Wall Street Journal* published a pair of front-page stories putting First Fidelity in the middle of loan-sharking, bigtime dope-trafficking, a rash of gangland beatings, at least two murders, shakedowns of legitimate—and not-so-legitimate—businesses. First Fidelity bankers had systematically passed $22 million in cash into the mob, and managed, so far, to walk away from the scene scot free.

The January 14 and 15, 1986 *Wall Street Journal* pieces by reporter Jonathan Kwitny exposed First Fidelity's relationship with Richard Mamarella, a professional con man who apparently was picked up by the Gambino organized crime family and assigned to manage a New Jersey loan-sharking and drug-financing operations that made use of the Atlantic City casinos—and the accommodating facilities of a south Jersey branch of First Fidelity. Between early 1982 and September 1983, when he was found guilty of fraud and extortion and sentenced to seven years in federal prison, Mamarella received a total of $22 million in loans from First Fidelity Bank of South Jersey. A total of 139 such loans, all personally approved by the president of the south Jersey branch, John Petrycki, were issued to Mamarella on collateral consisting of non-existent insurance policies, all fraudulently written by shell insurance companies owned by Mamarella himself, on behalf of non-existent corporate clients.

According to court documents and Mamarella's own testimony in a summer 1985 trial of two of his "business associates," the bulk of the $22 million passed into the hands of organized crime to finance loansharking operations from Atlantic City to

Chinatown, and to purchase Golden Triangle heroin from mafia refineries in Palermo, Florence, and Milan on behalf of the south Jersey "Pizza Connection."

Was First Fidelity the victim or the perpetrator of the $22 million crime spree? According to *Wall Street Journal* reporter Kwitny, throughout the duration of the theft and fraud, Mamarella's principal front company, IFA Inc., was legally represented by Nathaniel Yohalem of the prominent Newark, New Jersey firm of Greenbaum, Greenbaum, Rowe & Smith—a firm that had represented First Fidelity Bancorp. for the past 20 years. It was Yohalem who submitted the original letters to First Fidelity assuring the bank that Mamarella and IFA were worthy of millions of dollars in credits—no questions asked.

The Mamarella fraud and organized crime ties came out publicly, following his April 29, 1983 Chinatown arrest on extortion charges. Mamarella and four associates were grabbed by the FBI while in the process of beating up a recalcitrant borrower who had fallen behind on his payments to Chinatown dope financier and loan shark Louis Chung. First Fidelity responded to the "news" that it had handed $22 million to a mafia hoodlum—by hiring Mamarella and his mob "toughs" to get the money back! At a time when Mamarella was under federal indictment for extortion, he and his gang were put on the payroll as "consultants" to aid in the collection of an estimated $14.5 million in outstanding loans from the bank to Mamarella.

The "special arrangement" with Mamarella was sanctioned by no less an official of the bank than First Fidelity's chairman Robert Ferguson, according to the July 19, 1983 issue of *American Banker*.

In a statement issued to the shareholders of the bank, Ferguson stated:

In February of 1982, one of our banks began purchasing a third party paper from a corporation licensed by the Department of Banking of the State of New Jersey, engaged in the business of insurance premium financing. . . . In early June of this year [over a month after Mamarella's extortion arrest in Chinatown—ed.], we began to question and investigate

the authenticity of that paper. . . . At the present time, outstanding obligations total approximately $15.5 million. . . .
We are continuing to receive payments and, in the opinion of
our counsel, unpaid balances, if any, after comprehensive
collection efforts, will be covered by our blanket and fidelity
bonds.

And what were those "comprehensive collection efforts" referred to by Ferguson?

According to Kwitny and other sources, from the very outset
of the scam, Mamarella regularly reached out to his mob sponsor Joseph Paterno, a New Jersey syndicate captain who had
fled to Fort Lauderdale, Florida to avoid state court subpoena,
and to other criminal elements, to help with "collections" on
funds lent by First Fidelity.

For Mario Stacchini, a New Jersey restaurateur, and Anthony Turano, a New York shoe manufacturer who used his
business as a distribution point for Sicilian-refined heroin,
these "comprehensive efforts" cost them their lives. Both Stacchini and Turano were forced by Mamarella's mob higher-ups
to take out personal life insurance policies as "collateral" on
their First Fidelity loans, once they had fallen behind on their
payments.

Anthony Turano was arrested by U.S. Drug Enforcement
Administration agents in late 1982 in New York City, as he
was about to take possession of 15 kilos of Golden Triangle
heroin, purchased with $290,000 provided by Mamarella.
Clearly Turano was in no position to keep up his payments.
However, when his bullet-riddled body was found wrapped in
a deserted lot in Queens, New York, the mob, Mamarella, and
First Fidelity all collected on his $1 million life insurance
policy.

Such are the characteristic methods of Dope, Inc. In our next
chapter, we travel up the ladder from casino bankers and mafia
hoodlums to the top command of Dope, Inc., where the moral
atmosphere is somewhat worse.

2
The Dope, Inc. Command Structure

The international drug traffic works like a single multinational firm, not unlike the Swiss-based pharmaceuticals cartels—controlling production, supply, distribution, stockpiling, and financing through a single, integrated management. Its objective, at least at the highest level of its command structure, is not profit. What we call Dope, Incorporated constitutes a strategic capability in the service of a deal between the Western European financial oligarchy and the masters of the new Russian Empire known as the U.S.S.R. The deal is the same one concluded between Bertrand Russell and representatives of the Soviet Union through the so-called back-channel discussions initiated through the Pugwash Conferences of the late 1950s, among other locations. The world shall be redivided, according to this deal, which the late Soviet President Yuri Andropov characterized as a "New Yalta" in early 1983: The Western European nations shall become a satrapy of the Soviet Empire, and the United States shall be reduced to 25% of its former post-World War II influence, and relegated to the Western Hemisphere, the brutal debt-collector for Anglo-American and Swiss banking interests which hold Ibero-America's debt.

Through global control of the means of exchanging dirty money for clean money, through control over the supply of narcotics, through a dominant position in the international markets for precious metals and gemstones, and, above all, through its ability to bring a multi-hundred billion dollar annual cash flow to bear upon the corruption of the legal organs of sovereign national states, Dope, Inc. exercises a unique sort of political control. What American intelligence in the 1920s called the "Nazi-Communist synarchist international," works alongside the Italian, Jewish, Chinese and other branches of organized crime in the United States, the criminal wing of Italian masonry, the narcoterrorists of Ibero-America, the Sikh separatists of Southwest Asia, and separatist movements throughout Europe and the developing sector.

Beyond the specifics of this or that business deal or political arrangement, is a shared world outlook of a sort that has been around since at least the days of the Chaldean-Babylonian empire. It is an *oligarchical* outlook that views man as essentially a "talking beast," a creature of appetites to be governed through the manipulation of a priesthood whose business it is to apply pleasure and pain to achieve desired results. Narcotics have always played a central role for oligarchs.

It is therefore hardly surprising that the same oligarchy that controls the filthiest elements of the financial underworld today, dominates, and bends to the same purposes, the leading institutions of international finance: the International Monetary Fund and the Basel-based Bank for International Settlements. The same international political figures who, conceding world supremacy to the oligarchs of the new Soviet Empire, advance the policies of "New Yalta"—policies of depopulation, destruction of national sovereignty, debt collection, decoupling of the Western alliance—are enmeshed, in their private business affairs, with the dirtiest elements of the financial underworld. Henry Kissinger, together with his international political directorate known as Kissinger Associates, is the individual who stands at the intersection point of every one of these networks: the back-channel with the Soviet Union, the drug and terror networks from Italy to Ibero-America, and the highest levels of finance—including his directorship in American Express, the entity into which has merged a major portion of Dope, Inc.'s command structure.

This command structure contains the following main groups:

■ The British combination that controls offshore banking and precious metals trading, i.e., the Hongkong and Shanghai Bank, the Oppenheimer gold interests, top British financial institutions such as Eagle Star Insurance and Barclay's Bank, and their Canadian cousins such as Bank of Montreal and Bank of Nova Scotia;

■ The major Swiss banks;

■ The continuity of Venetian-Genoese financial manipulations in the personage of the late Roberto Calvi of Banco Ambrosiano, and the shadowy Edmund Safra of American Express;

■ The combined offspring of the Swiss bankers and the old European *fondi,* the international grain cartel of Cargill, Continental (Fribourg family), Bunge, and Louis Dreyfus;

■ The Boston Brahmin families and the big American financial institutions associated with Henry Kissinger, including Citibank, Chase Manhattan Bank, and American Express.

This monster has devoured North American finance. The United States is now financially dependent upon capital inflows exceeding $120 billion per year (as of the third quarter of 1984). It is also a matter of the International Monetary Fund's official admission that the major source of such capital flows is the so-called "flight capital," i.e., funds moved across borders despite tax or foreign-exchange laws of national governments.

The London Network

In the following chapters taken from the 1978 edition, we identify a tightly closed financial network whose origins lie in the Dutch and British East India Companies and the modern origins of the narcotics traffic in the British Opium Wars of the 1840s. The paradigm for this network is the London Committee, or British-based directors, of the Hongkong and Shanghai Bank, the central bank for Dope, Incorporated. It ties in directly and immediately to the five big London clearing banks, the five London "gold pool" dealers, and the big Canadian international banks.

This network, we demonstrated, provides the offshore banking, precious metals, and related capabilities to cause several hundred billion dollars per year to disappear from the streets of New York, Amsterdam, Frankfurt, and Hong Kong, and reappear as apparently legitimate assets wherever convenient. We showed further that Anglo-Chinese collaboration in the Asian opiates traffic was a matter of official policy on the part of the People's Republic of China, and "business arrangements" of the British elite dating back to the first corruption of the Imperial Chinese bureaucracy by the British East India Company.

As noted, the core of this evidence has been confirmed multiply by the official U.S. reports cited above, among others. Six years of additional research by the hundreds of researchers and correspondents of the *Executive Intelligence Review* has reconstructed the three-dimensional character of Dope, Inc., whose most obvious, outward facade is British. Its other dimensions, equally integrated into the single world command structure, are Swiss-centered continental European, and Soviet.

The Hongkong and Shanghai Bank, as reported, now controls the twelfth-largest American bank, and its close collaborators among the British clearing banks have moved massively into American banking, through the Midland Bank takeover of Crocker National Bank in California, the Rothschild takeover of California's BanCal-TriState, and similar expansion into the American market.

The Oppenheimer mining group, heirs to the empire of Cecil Rhodes, is the dominant force—in collaboration with Hong-Shang and its Mideast subsidiaries—in the illegal traffic in gold and diamonds through which so much dirty money is turned into untraceable, portable assets. Through its diamond monopoly, De Beers, its mining corporations, Anglo-American Mining and Consolidated Gold Fields of South Africa, through its commodity trading organization, Phibro, the Oppenheimer group has expanded its tentacles across the world and, most of all, in the United States.

Eagle Star Insurance, the mediating link between the British oligarchy and the Canadian banks, has extended its branches to the continental insurance companies, and sunk deep roots into the United States at the same time. In the chapters taken from the 1978 edition, the reader will find that Eagle Star controls the family trusts of those barely rehabilitated Prohibition-era mobsters, the Bronfman family. The Bronfmans, in turn, control a variety of lower species of criminal life in Canada and the United States. The Canadian real estate firms which operate under the umbrella of Eagle Star control have come to dominate the major urban real estate markets in the United States, from New York to Texas.

But even more important is the role that Eagle Star assumed as of November 1983, when it became the principal overt link between the British high command of the narcotics traffic, and the Swiss-German financial interests centered around the great South German family fortunes. Allianz Versicherung of Munich, continental Europe's largest insurance company, bought 30% of Eagle Star in a well-publicized takeover battle whose sound and fury disguised the underlying cooperation and identity of interests between the British and German sides. Close financial relationships had existed for some time between the HongShang in the Far East and the nastier elements of German finance.

Allianz represents a coalition of the oldest and nastiest German family *fondi,* or trust funds, including those of the old Bavarian Wittelsbach dynasty, and the most evil family in German-speaking Europe, Thurn und Taxis. It is the Thurn und Taxis family and their in-laws, the defunct Portuguese royal family of Braganza, who created and funded the terrorist organization Tradition, Family, and Property, implicated in plans to assassinate Pope John Paul II. TFP's Venezuelan chapter was banned by the Venezuelan government.

The old United Fruit Company, renamed United Brands in the 1960s, has been the center of American organized crime since the turn of this century, we showed in 1978, through a merger between the Sicilian mafia of New Orleans and the shipping interests of the Boston Brahmins; since the beginning of the Ibero-American narcotics traffic, United Fruit's banana boats coming into Baltimore harbor have been the freest vehicle for the physical passage of contraband into the United States. In its successive corporate reorganizations, United Brands has since wound up in the hands of Cincinnati, Ohio insurance financier Carl Lindner, the principal business partner through the last three decades of Michigan organized crime heir Max Fisher. And through an entanglement of financial interests that might have been invented by a gaudy but unimaginative mystery novelist, the fate of United Brands has been intertwined with that of American Express, the world's most efficient silent money-mover, and the prince of Levantine money-laundering, Syrian-Swiss financier Edmund Safra. American Express, the monster that devoured half the old great houses of Wall Street, ties together the United Brands crime and smuggling capability, the financial networks who created and funded the Argentine Monteneros and other terrorist organizations, as well as the Swiss-based interests who have acted, for a generation, as the private couriers of the Soviet Union in the international gold markets.

But more ominous than the spectacular rise of the tainted financial institutions of the West is the role of the Soviet Union, the subject of a chapter newly written for this edition. There was a pattern to the failure of narcotics-related financial enterprises during the years 1973–1975, when the great shakeout occurred. At the same time that Watergate disposed of Richard Nixon's administration, and the American intelligence services were abandoned to the claws of the U.S. Senate's Church Committee, a grand reorganization came about in the affairs of the financial underworld.

The rotund Bernie Cornfeld was unceremoniously expelled from the money-laundering organization par excellence of the 1960s, Investors Overseas Services, with the connivance of Baron Edmond de Rothschild and the Swiss authorities, to be replaced by Rothschild "discovery" Robert Vesco. Fugitive from justice Vesco is now the guest of Fidel Castro's Cuba, vigorously and personally defended by Castro, and documented to be a key ally of Cuban efforts to milk the narcotics traffic as a slush-fund for dirty political operations in the Caribbean, as we show in a later chapter.

Romanian banker Tibor Rosenbaum, reportedly a senior official of the Israeli Mossad and a principal crony of former Israeli Finance Minister Pinhas Sapir, died in disgrace after the failure of his Swiss-based BCI. His role in the Israeli covert weapons traffic fell to such men as Ariel Sharon and his unpleasant runabout, Meshulam Riklis of Rapid-American Corporation. It is not merely that Riklis and his company have been a top-priority target of U.S. Customs narcotics investigators since the mid-1970s; his patron in Israeli politics, the bloodthirsty Ariel Sharon, belongs to an evil faction which believes that Israel, in order to maintain itself, must cut a deal with the Soviet Union to betray the United States.

Michele Sindona's fall in 1974 was no loss to humanity. But the man who stepped into his role as the Vatican's private banker was the doubly unfortunate Roberto Calvi of Banco Ambrosiano, and his allies in Italian Masonry, Licio Gelli and Umberto Ortolani. We will document in later chapters that Gelli, the ex-fascist enforcer, was the Italian leg of the now-infamous "Bulgarian connection," the heroin-for-armaments network uncovered by Italian police in 1982, and the source of the protection for the would-be assassin of Pope John Paul II.

The great shakeout of the mid-1970s was the point at which the Soviet Union muscled its way into a critical partnership position in the underground of world finance. Through the expansion of its own imperial banking apparatus, through the emplacement of organized crime elements under Soviet influence, and, most of all, through deals with such Western interests as the Oppenheimer group, the Soviet Union took over dirty-money networks. It did this in the service of its global strategic aim: the imposition of Soviet hegemony over the Eurasian landmass, and the relegation of the United States to a hemispheric power presiding over the social collapse of the entire Ibero-American world.

How Dope, Inc. Bought Up American Finance

Parallel to the shakeout of the financial underworld during the mid-1970s was a much more publicized shakeout—the weeding out of the big Wall Street brokerage firms, a process which has continued through to the present. It is no less relevant to the transformation of the world financial system into the instrument of the allied European and Soviet oligarchy. It is no longer possible to tell how much American equity is, in fact, American; it can only be stated as a matter of public record that investment banking in the United States is now almost wholly controlled by the ancient European *fondi*, that is, family trust funds whose pedigree goes back to the financing of the Crusades by Genoa and Venice.

From 1971 to 1981, in the decade after then-Treasury Undersecretary Paul Volcker removed its gold backing, the U.S. dollar fell to a mere 60% of its pre-devaluation level, while the combined effects of inflation and lower stock prices devalued American equity to about 30% of its 1971 level in terms of gold. From the standpoint of the old oligarchical *fondi*, secured through gold, American equity could be had for a fifth of its pre-1971 price during the late 1970s. This is the period of the grand reflow of capital to the United States, measured by the International Monetary Fund as the "statistical discrepancy in the world current account balance."

A similar collapse of the dollar and equity values occurred during the years 1929–1933. With stock prices at a fraction of their previous values, and the economy in ruins, President

Franklin Roosevelt was persuaded by the American friends of John Maynard Keynes to force a devaluation of the dollar in 1932, giving the old *fondi*—particularly the fortunes of the Franco-Swiss-Italian "gold bloc"—the chance to buy into American equity at distress prices comparable to those available during the late 1970s.

Among modern financial institutions, the Assicurazioni Generali of Venice, the heir to the old Venetian fortunes, provides the most clues to the operations of the *fondi*. The "Generali," as an insurance organization, is a clearing house for the operations of numerous *fondi*, each one represented by its frontman, one of the principal European investment banks. Its board of directors consists of the principal banking fortunes of Western Europe, each of whom is to be found in the succeeding chapters drawn from the 1978 edition of *Dope, Inc*. These directors included:

■ Baron August Von Finck, reputedly the richest man in Germany until his recent death (with the possible exception of Johannes von Thurn und Taxis), owner of the Merck und Finck investment bank. However large Finck's personal fortune might be, the bank's importance is a function of the *fondo* of the old Bavarian royal family of Wittelsbach.

■ Elie de Rothschild, of the French Rothschild family;

■ Baron Pierre Lambert, the Belgian cousin of the Rothschild family and proprietor of the Banque Bruxelles-Lambert (and a force on Wall Street through Drexel Burnham Lambert);

■ Jocelyn Hambro of Hambro's Bank, which owned a quarter of Michele Sindona's Banca Privata when it went under in 1974;

■ Pierpaolo Luzzatto Fequiz, of the ancient Venetian Luzzatto family, whom we shall encounter later in this chapter in the company of the notorious Banco Ambrosiano;

■ Franco Orsini Bonacossi of the ancient Orsini family, whose origin includes members of the ancient Roman senate.

Europe's two most powerful investment banks, Lazard Frères (of the thousand-year-old David-Weill family) and the Banque Paribas (founded by Venetian Jews based in the Ottoman Empire trade) are the largest stockholders in the Assicurazioni through a variety of shells. The sister Venetian insurance company of the "Generali," the Riunione Adriatica di Sicurtà, includes among its directors members of the Giustiniani family of Genoa and Venice, descendants of the vile Roman Emperor Justinian; the Doria family, the chief Genoese financiers of the Spanish Hapsburgs; as well as the current Duke of Alba, descendant of the brutal Spanish marcher-lord whom the Genoese bankers sent to the Netherlands four centuries ago to crush their independence.

Assicurazioni Generali and the Bank for International Settlements of Basel (the "central bank for central banks"), are the world's only financial institutions to keep their books in the old pre-war Swiss gold franc, the "hard currency" which the *fondi* employed to buy American equities at a dime on the dollar during the first fumbling years of the Roosevelt administration.

They waited long to avenge themselves against the upstart United States. Their chance came with the break of the dollar from its gold backing in 1971.

Given the collapse of Wall Street stock prices during the long agony of the dollar between the 1967 collapse of the pound sterling and the aftermath of the 1971 debacle, it is not surprising that every major brokerage firm ran into trouble no later than the mid-1970s. Lehman Brothers, once the most powerful firm on the Street, was the first to raise the white flag. It secured, through offices of George Ball, a 7% investment from Banca de la Svizzera Italiana, a Swiss bank which functioned as a virtual Swiss subsidiary of the Banca Commerciale d'Italia—the bank at whose headquarters the infamous Propaganda–2 lodge of Italian freemasonry had been founded years earlier.

The Banca de la Svizzera Italiana (BSI), based in Lugano, Switzerland, specialized in covert movement of Italian flight capital into the United States.

One by one, the other major Wall Street houses fell under the control of the old European *fondi*. The dominant mergers and acquisitions operation on Wall Street, Lazard Frères, had never been an American house in any event; it was always dominated by the French-Jewish David-Weill family, and only managed for the interim by its then chairman, André Meyer, when no suitable family member was available.

Drexel Burnham Lambert, the sixth-largest house, sold out its entire capital to the Lambert family of Brussels, the Belgian cousins of the Rothschild family.

A.G. Becker, an old-line Chicago brokerage firm, merged into a *ménage-à-trois* with S.G. Warburg, the supposedly independent branch of the Warburg banking family, and the ancient French-Ottoman Empire firm, the Banque de Paris et des Pays-Bas (Paribas), to create Warburg-Becker-Paribas (subsequently merged into Merrill Lynch during 1984).

With virtually no exceptions, Wall Street's major houses sold out to the *fondi*. Finally, in 1981, Wall Street's most powerful investment bank (with the possible exception of Henry Kissinger's employer Goldman Sachs), Salomon Brothers, merged with Phibro, the trading arm of the Oppenheimer interests. As we shall see below, the absorption of Salomon Brothers, investment bankers to New York's Citibank, had the most devastating implications of all.

In a July 1981 study, *Executive Intelligence Review* applied the results of an ingenious measure of foreign investment designed by the Securities Industry Association to available data for foreign control of U.S. equities. The Securities Industry Association showed the absurdity of Treasury data: Under the law, brokerage houses must report the nationality of securities transactions of foreign origin. The results of this survey proved enlightening; the Treasury data showed that foreign investors turned over their stock portfolios several times as fast as American investors. This was unlikely, the association argued; it was more likely that the Treasury had badly misestimated the total of foreign investment. If foreign investors behaved the same way as American investors, then the total foreign equity investment in U.S. stocks as of 1980 was $225 billion, three times the $75 billion figure estimated by the Treasury! That rough figure represents 20% of the value of all U.S. stocks. However, 20% of the total appeared to represent a much greater concentration of effective control.

We know that the European *fondi* and their investment banking frontmen launder funds from deficit countries, and turn these into anonymous investments in surplus countries, creating the supposed "statistical discrepancy." Once the nature of the swindle is known, the discrepancy disappears. Armed with a rough and ready estimate of the extent of Dope, Inc. infiltration of the American financial system and control over American corporate equity, we may complete the sordid tale of the dope traffickers' intimate relations with the most prestigious American financial institutions.

Hong Kong, Oppenheimer and Banco Ambrosiano: Flight Capital is King

Salomon Brothers was the last of the big Wall Street firms, and most important, to go, merging in 1981 with the trading arm of the Oppenheimer empire, Phibro. In the process, the Oppenheimers acquired effective policy control of the largest American commercial bank, Citibank. A month after the Phibro-Salomon merger, Costanzo's deputy George Vojta quietly left for Phibro, to cement a transatlantic relationship between the biggest American bank and the biggest Anglo-South African raw materials empire. Harry Oppenheimer had stated earlier that year, "We mean to expand into North America," and proceeded to create a $3 billion vehicle with which to do so: the Bermuda-based investment firm Minorco, which Oppenheimer created the same year. Both Citibank Chairman Walter Wriston and Citibank's chief lawyer, Shearman and Sterling managing partner Robert Clare, joined the board of Minorco. A year earlier, Oppenheimer had taken control of 28% of the only South African gold firm to rival his Anglo-American, Consolidated Gold Fields of South Africa, the country's second-largest gold producer. With 28% control also of Engelhard Minerals, the largest American precious metals refiner and the parent organization of Phibro, Oppenheimer came to dominate world precious metals and related markets in a way that Anglo-American's nineteenth-century founder, Cecil Rhodes, could only have dreamed of.

Even more obscure than the ultra-secret operations of Phibro is Anglo-American's role in the Caribbean offshore market, the main dumping ground for international flight capital in transit to a more permanent home. About $100 billion in banking assets in the Bahamas alone, as well as substantial operations in the British Virgin Islands, Netherlands Antilles, Cayman Islands, and other Caribbean banking centers, move the money that disappears from the world's balance sheet in the form of the $200 billion "statistical discrepancy" described earlier. Chief investment banker to the region is the International Trust Corporation, or Itco, created by Anglo-American in consortium with Barclays Bank of the U.K., the Royal Bank of Canada, and N.M. Rothschild of London—whom we will meet again and again in the pages that follow. Itco creates banks, investment companies, commodities firms, tax shelters, trust funds, and insurance and reinsurance outlets throughout the Caribbean, smoothing contacts with local bank regulators and back-stopping the legal position of the offshore market operators with which it deals. Itco is, in effect, the offshore-banking sister subsidiary of Phibro.

Citibank, Oppenheimer's direct partner in the Caribbean funny-money business and indirect partner in the Phibro-Salomon combination, was not new to the flight capital game. In the early 1960s, Robert Meyjes of First National City Bank suggested to Chairman Walter Wriston that the bank establish a division for "private international banking" to conduit funds from wealthy individuals abroad into U.S. investment markets. Wriston backed the plan.

When the new division for international private banking opened, it had a staff of six, and managed $250 million. Twelve years later, the "private banking" division of the renamed Citibank was responsible for a $12.5 billion investment pool, and contributed 10% of the bank's annual profits.

The individual who had first proposed the new department was a Dutchman named Robert Christopher Portomas Meyjes.

In a 10-year period, Meyjes rotated 600 bank trainees through his division. Today, his protégés manage the private banking divisions of most of the big American banks from Boston to San Francisco. Meyjes is now based at Citibank's Paris office.

The former bank trainees to whom Meyjes played Fagin during the 1960s maintain an active "old boys'" network, according to participants. Many have gone into business for themselves, handling private investments for clients referred to them by associates at the big commercial banks. Each "private international banker" keeps a black book of former colleagues who now operate on their own as "investment advisers." When a client abroad requests services that are too sensitive for the bank to handle—e.g., the creation of dummy subsidiaries or the chartering of non-existent aircraft—the banker will refer the client to one of the "advisers." The adviser will accomplish the required skulduggery, and the funds extracted by the client from his business or investment portfolio in his home country are then invested through the "private banking division" of the commercial bank which made the referral.

David Rockefeller's Chase Manhattan Bank did not take long to imitate Citibank's imaginative program for obtaining new deposits. In 1966, a memo circulated in Chase's international division arguing explicitly that the bank should seek illicit international funds as new sources of deposits. In Chase's international department, this became referred to as "looking for mafia money." Chase found that this was more easily proposed than accomplished. It had made the Asian market a priority, but found that Hong Kong, the central, Asian offshore market, was too closed a club to afford easy access to an American bank. Until Chase brought the billionaire shipowner Y.K. Pao onto its own board of directors, establishing a link to the Hongkong and Shanghai Bank (where Y.K. Pao is vice chairman), Chase could not begin its subsequent expansion into the Hong Kong market.

Bank of America, looking westward from its headquarters in San Francisco, also made Hong Kong its top priority. Rudolph Peterson, its former international chief, once told a reporter, "The Hongkong and Shanghai Bank is the dominant institution there, but we found a way to work with them so that they wouldn't see us as a threat."

When the now-infamous Banco Ambrosiano went down in the financial scandal of the 1980s, the chairmen of the major American commercial banks could not have been more embarrassed were they forced to tell their wives that they had contracted a social disease. Ambrosiano was a financial brothel; by itself it is of no interest past the police blotter, were it not for the fact that its ownership and clientele included the financial elite of Europe and the United States. Not merely the major Italian banks, including the Banca Commerciale Italiana and its Swiss offshoot Banca della Svizzera Italiana, but Bank of America and Chase Manhattan Bank were up to their ears in the scandal.

The most prominent financier of the Italian Socialist Party and the treasurer of the Propaganda–2 lodge of Italian freemasonry, Calvi built the $6 billion Banco Ambrosiano into the core of a $20 billion international empire of merged and associate companies. But Ambrosiano itself fit tightly into a larger series of Chinese boxes, a publicity-shy but powerful international syndicate called "Inter-Alpha," i.e., "among the first." Inter-Alpha was founded as the bridge between the Levantine money-wash of Roberto Calvi and the Far Eastern operations of the Hong Kong dope financiers: its British members are the Royal Bank of Scotland and its English counterpart, the Williams and Glyns clearing bank. At the time of the Ambrosiano bankruptcy in 1982, the Royal Bank of Scotland was negotiating for a merger with none other than the Hongkong and Shanghai Bank.

Remarkable are the intimate ties between Calvi and the major American banks. The Inter-Alpha group capitalized a small securities firm in New York under the name "Ultrafin," leaving the management to Roberto Calvi and his close friend, the late Club of Rome founder Aurelio Peccei, the former chief of Fiat's Argentina operations. At Peccei's suggestion, Calvi brought in the chief economist of David Rockefeller's Trilateral Commission, Professor Richard Gardner, to act as intelligence chief for Inter-Alpha in New York. Gardner became a board member of Ultrafin in New York with this special assignment.

Richard Gardner, personally close to Chase Manhattan chief Rockefeller, drafted all the major financial documents of the Trilateral Commission, including the 1976 plan to replace national governments' control of economic policy with a truly global central bank. His wife, Daniele Luzzatto, is the daughter of Bruno Luzzatto, the aristocratic Venetian who controlled the Paris office of the Marshall Plan after World War II.

Bank of America, meanwhile, together with the Banca Nazionale della Agricoltura, the Banca d'America e d'Italia had capitalized a joint venture with Banco Ambrosiano, the $3 billion assets Interbanca Spa.

Almost to the end, Bank of America defended its connection to Calvi. As reported in *EIR* July 7, 1981, the chief of the San Francisco bank's international department, Rudolph Peterson, said, "Banco Ambrosiano is a fine upstanding bank of good reputation." Peterson, whose close ties to Italy earned him the country's Grand Order of Merit, added, "I'm sure this scandal concerning them will wash away. Even when there is chaos all around them, the bankers and especially the central bankers know how to get through. The banks and central bank will continue with their direction, while they pull through and the scandal washes away."

Kissinger and the New Directorate of Dope, Inc.

The Bank of America's Peterson was wrong. Calvi ended up hanging underneath Blackfriars Bridge in London, and Dope Inc. was reorganized again—this time from the top.

These capabilities, as we reported them six years ago, were impressive in their day. But they are no longer needed. The grand redeployment of the oligarchical *fondi* onshore to the United States made them superfluous.

When Henry Kissinger was elected to the board of directors of American Express in March 1984, a circle was completed which had begun with the wave of foreign takeovers of American securities houses during the 1960s and 1970s. George Ball's old firm, Lehman Brothers, had long since been absorbed by its great rival among the old-line German-Jewish Wall Street houses, Kuhn Loeb, to form Lehman Brothers-Kuhn Loeb. Shearson Hayden Stone, the second retail broker after Merrill Lynch, had repeated Merrill Lynch's march into investment banking by absorbing the third of the old-line German-Jewish firms, Loeb Rhoades. Now American Express, in turn, swallowed up Shearson-Loeb Rhoades and Lehman-Kuhn Loeb, bringing under a single umbrella a large part of what we identified in 1978 as the supposedly respectable interests behind organized crime and the drug traffic. The American Express board member and chief attorney responsible for handling the serious of mergers is Kenneth Bialkin, the current chairman of the Anti-Defamation League of B'nai B'rith; his predecessor, Theodore Silbert of the Recanati family's Sterling National Bank, currently faces a civil suit initiated by the Italian government, charging that Silbert helped Michele Sindona to launder money for the bankrupt Banca Privata.

Shearson Lehman American Express, as the ultimate Wall Street merger calls itself, is the phoenix which has arisen from the ashes of the offshore money markets. The new entity is effectively controlled, in turn, by two of the world's shadiest financiers, Edmund Safra and Carl Lindner, each of whom owns about 4% of the stock. Lindner, as noted earlier, owns the old United Fruit dope-pushing apparatus. Safra's case is more interesting.

Safra's controlling share of American Express derives from the January 1983 merger of his Trade Development Bank of Geneva with American Express International Bank where Safra briefly served as chairman. Amex took control of the Swiss institution and its global network, in return for 4% of its outstanding shares. Safra is the reported frontman for the Syrian-

Jewish banking families who served the Venetian-Genoese *fondi* from Aleppo through the long history of Levantine finance.

Safra's Republic National Bank of New York, in the person of its chairman, Theodore Kheel, made the introductions that permitted shady Argentine banker David Graiver to buy up the American Bank and Trust. Graiver subsequently looted $45 million from the American Bank and Trust, in cooperation with John Samuels, a New York frontman for Safra's original backers, the Recanati family of Israel Discount Bank. The Argentine swindler subsequently disappeared after his plane crashed over Mexico. Graiver had been the principal financier for the Argentine terrorist organization, the Monteneros, and functioned as the Argentine connection for the old Tibor Rosenbaum-Meyer Lansky money wash, before his short-lived fling in New York.

These are current employers of Henry Kissinger, who also serves as vice chairman of the International Advisory Board of Chase Manhattan Bank (he was chairman until David Rockefeller retired from the bank and moved to its International Advisory Board); adviser to Goldman Sachs; and a consultant to dozens of leading corporations and financial institutions through Kissinger Associates.

The members of Kissinger Associates represent a de facto board of directors for the entity we call Dope, Incorporated. Just as Kissinger is represented on the board of American Express, it is represented on Kissinger's, in the person of Mario d'Urso. D'Urso came to Shearson Lehman American Express through the old Kuhn Loeb firm, whose international department he directed before it merged into Lehman. He is also the New York chief for the Jefferson Insurance Company, the joint arm of the Venetian insurance giants Assicurazioni Generali and Riunione Adriatica di Sicurtà; as we saw earlier, these are the central clearing-houses for the ancient Venetian *fondi*. The New York chairman of Jefferson Insurance is an old State Department crony of Kissinger, Nathaniel Samuels, also of the old Kuhn Loeb firm; Nathaniel Samuels is also the New York chairman of the Banque Louis-Dreyfus Holding Company in the United

States and director of the Banque Louis-Dreyfus of Paris. This bank owns the grain company of the same name, one of the grain-cartel firms which hook into the Venetian insurance companies. Another board member of Jefferson Insurance for many years was the former British Intelligence station chief in New York City, financier Arthur Ross, an intimate of Lazard Frères' late Chairman André Meyer.

Britain's Lord Carrington, the cofounder of Kissinger Associates until his move to NATO headquarters in Brussels, is a former director of both Hambro's Bank (one of the constituent *fondi* of the Assicurazioni Generali) at the time that Hambro's bought 25% of Michele Sindona's Banca Privata, and also former director of Barclays Bank, the principal financier and partner in Caribbean skulduggery of the Oppenheimer interests.

Lord Carrington was replaced on the Kissinger Associates board in mid-1984 by the chairman of the London merchant bank S.G. Warburg, Lord Eric Roll of Ipsden. Lord Roll had just completed a reorganization of London Warburg interests under the umbrella of the Warburg holding company Mercury Securities.

The Oppenheimer family's London vehicle (which we shall encounter later when we examine the offshore finances of the Soviet Union), Charter Consolidated, meanwhile bought a 9% stake in the new Warburg consortium. Warburg has a mutual ownership with the Paris Banque de Paris et des Pays-Bas, the major stockholder of the Assicurazioni Generali of Venice.

In Asia, Kissinger Associates is represented by Sir Y.K. Kan of Hong Kong, who represents the four overseas Chinese families which control the Hong Kong-based Bank of East Asia.

The staff of Kissinger Associates is headed by Lawrence Eagleburger, the former highest-ranking member of U.S. foreign service, and a Kissinger protégé since the Nixon days. In a 1984 series on Jamaica's marijuana economy, the *New York Times* ridiculed Eagleburger's claims that, in supporting the Edward Seaga regime in Jamaica, he had no idea that Seaga had intentionally made marijuana the country's principal cash crop. Seaga had announced his intention to the *Washington Post* and on the U.S. network television program "Face the Nation."

The intertwining of interests represented in Kissinger Associates is not new. On the contrary, these are representatives of the ancient *fondi* who have collaborated for centuries. What is new and ominous is that the men who perform the dirty work of the *fondi* have moved out of shadows of Caribbean offshore banking and Hong Kong smuggling, and into the board rooms of the most powerful American financial institutions, and close to the councils of the United States government itself. It is even more ominous that the major conduit for the political influence of the Soviet Empire in American politics has now become the point of interchange of the constituent parts of Dope, Inc., doubly so in the context of the Soviet move into the financial underworld which we shall document in a later chapter.

As the International Monetary Fund attempts to destroy, one by one, the friends of the United States in the developing world, creating the conditions in which Soviet influence may extend itself to nations inherently hostile to Soviet designs, so the dope-peddling policies of the IMF finance the Soviet Empire's covert operations. The monster we identified in 1978 has moulted, shedding such skin as the Banco Ambrosiano and Investors Overseas Services, only to multiply in extent and influence. Six years ago, the narcotics traffic menaced all future generations of youth. Now it is the center of the gravest threat to Western civilization since the fourteenth century. Slowly, belatedly, the governments of the West have acknowledged the extent of the problem, and, in their lumbering fashion, accepted parts of the analysis we offered six years ago. But effective, ruthless, action has yet to be taken, against the citizens and institutions who have brought the dregs of the financial underworld to the apex of power in political life.

PART II
Britain's First Opium War

Introduction

To Sap the Vitality of a Nation

This is the setting for what follows below: narcotics are pouring in from abroad through a well-organized, efficient group of smugglers. One-fifth of the population abuses drugs, an epidemic surpassing any known since the Great Plagues. Not only the poor, but the wealthy and the children of the wealthy have succumbed. Within the nation, organized crime displays its drug profits without shame, ruling local governments, and threatening the integrity even of national government. None of their opponents is safe from assassins, not even the chief of state. Law enforcement is in shambles. The moral fiber of the nation has deteriorated past the danger point.

And one of the leading dope-traffickers writes to his superiors abroad, that as along as drug use continues to dominate the country, "there is not the least reason to fear that she will become a military power of any importance, as the habit saps the energies and vitality of the nation."[1]

The familiar description is not of America in 1986, but China in 1838, on the eve of the First Opium War, when Great Britain landed troops to compel China to ingest the poison distributed by British merchants.

During the last century, British finance protected by British guns controlled the world narcotics traffic. The names of the families and institutions are known to the history student: Matheson, Keswick, Swire, Dent, Baring, and Rothschild; Jardine Matheson, the Hongkong and Shanghai Bank, the Chartered Bank, the Peninsular and Orient Steam Navigation Company. Britain's array of intelligence fronts ran a worldwide assassination bureau, operating through occult secret societies: the Order of St. John of Jerusalem, its Zionist branch centered in the Jerusalem Foundation, Mazzini's Mafia, the Triads, or Societies of Heaven in China.

Paging back over the records of the narcotics traffic and its wake of corruption and murder, the most uncanny feature of the opium-based Pax Britannica is how shamelessly, how publicly the dope-runners operated. Opium trading, for the British, was not a sordid backstreet business, but an honored instrument of state policy, the mainstay of the Exchequer, the subject of encomia from Britain's leading apostles of free trade—Adam Smith, David Ricardo, Thomas Malthus, James Mill, and John Stuart Mill. The poisoning of China, and, later, the post-Civil War United States, did not lead to prison but to peerages. Great sectors of the Far East became devoted to the growing of the opium poppy, to the exclusion of food crops, to the extent that scores of millions of people depended utterly on the growing, distribution, and consumption of drugs.

The Keswicks, Dents, Swires, and Barings *still* control the world flow of opiates from their stronghold in the British Crown Colony of Hong Kong. Jardine Matheson, the Hongkong and Shanghai Banking Corporation, and the Peninsular and Orient Steam Navigation Company *still* control the channels of production and distribution of the drugs from the Far East, through the British Dominion of Canada, into the United States. By an uninterrupted chain of succession, the descendants of the Triads, the Mafia, and the *Hofjuden* of the British Chamber of Jewish Deputies *still* promote drug traffic, dirty money transfers, political corruption, and an assassination bureau that has claimed the life of an American President. Of course, the drug revenues of this machine are no longer tallied in the published accounts of the British Exchequer. But the leading installations of the drug traffic are no more hidden than they were a hundred years ago. From the Crown Colony of Hong Kong, the Hong-Shang bank does what the Keswicks set it up to do: provide centralized rediscounting facilities for the financing of the drug trade. The surnames of senior management are still the same.

Even today, the grand old names of Prohibition liquor and dope-running rouse the deep awareness of Americans: Bronfman, Kennedy, Lansky. Arc the denizens of the India opium trade, of the Prohibition mob, imprisoned in the history books and behind the movie screen? Not infrequently, the observer feels a momentary lapse in time, and sees not a history book, but the morning newspaper, not the late-night movie, but the evening television newscast.

The story we have to tell happened twice. It first happened to China, and now it is happening to the United States. Emphasizing that neither the names nor the hangouts of the criminals have changed, we begin by telling how it happened the first time.

The East India Company's War Against China

In 1715, the British East India Company opened up its first Far East office in the Chinese port city of Canton and began trading in opium. Between that time and the First Opium War against China in 1840, Great Britain did not take over the dope trade. The dope trade took over Britain. The vehicle was the 1783 near coup d'état by Lord Shelburne (the British prime minister who concluded peace negotiations with the American colonies after Yorktown), which brought to power in London the financial and political faction that had conducted the Asian opium trade.

Shelburne's ruling combination centered on the East India Company, a group of Scottish merchants, and an alliance on the continent with the chivalric order of the Knights of St. John of Jerusalem and the Society of Jesus. Unable to rule in his own name—he was known as the "Jesuit of Berkeley Square"—

Shelburne wielded the power that kept William Pitt the Younger in the prime ministership for twenty years.

The East India Company had begun its business in dope in 1715, but they were not the first. Since the original Jesuit mission had established itself in Beijing in 1601, the Society of Jesus had held the key to the Far East trade—including the dope trade. The first report of large-scale cultivation of opium came from India, then under the Mogul empire at the end of the sixteenth century, when the Jesuits—following the trail of the first Portuguese traders—had achieved positions of unquestioned authority in the Mogul court.

With the Jesuits as their contact point between the Manchu rulers of China and the Mogul empire, the Portuguese and later the Dutch took over the centuries-old dope-trading routes paved by Arab and Indian traders, including opium trade between Canton, and Portuguese-controlled Macao. The Dutch later negotiated an opium monopoly for the entire northern part of the Indian subcontinent that included Bengal, Bihar, Orissa, and Benares. The Dutch traders were permitted to force-draft Indian peasants to produce opium in exchange for taxes paid to the Mogul court. By 1659, the opium trade had become second only to the trade in spices, for which opium was a medium of exchange. By 1750, the Dutch were shipping more than 100 tons of opium a year to Indonesia.

Opium has always been an extraordinarily lucrative commodity, but the Dutch did not fail to notice its side benefits. According to one historian, the Dutch found "opium a useful means for breaking the moral resistance of Indonesians who opposed the introduction of their semi-servile but increasingly profitable plantation system. They deliberately spread the drug habits from the ports, where Arab traders used opium, to the countryside."[1]

The East India Company remained on the sidelines of this trade until the 1757 military victories that made Bengal a crown colony. But the beneficiary of the new move into the opium trade was not Britain, nor even the company itself. The company had paid the costs of the 1757 military expeditions, but saw none of the profit, as the lucre from the opium trade went to line the pockets of the company's officials in India. Repeatedly, the East India Company had to apply for a parliamentary bailout, until Shelburne moved in, reorganized the company, and made it the central instrument of loot for the maintenance of the British Empire.

Shelburne took two bankrupt entities, the East India Company and the British Empire, and combined them to make a going concern. By the end of the Revolutionary War with the American colonies, Britain's national debt had swollen to the then-stupendous figure of £240 million. Like today's underdeveloped countries, Britain's yearly debt service consumed more than half of all government tax revenues. More serious, through the League of Armed Neutrality, the European alliance that had formed against Britain during the war, England had lost to France most of the European market in staple items such as linens, textiles, and ironware.

To alleviate the crisis, Shelburne proposed a two-pronged strategy: expand the opium traffic and subvert the United States—both under the banner of free trade. The first achieved crowning success with the Chinese Opium War; the second not until the twentieth century.

First, Shelburne struck an alliance with the East India Company faction around Laurence Sullivan, whose son had subcontracted for the private opium monopoly in Bengal, and Francis Baring, the Anglo-Dutch banker prominent in the Atlantic trade. With the money from the opium trade and the monarchy's patronage machine, Shelburne bought the Parliament in 1783 lock, stock, and barrel, and consolidated a financial power that far outweighed the landed families of the 1688 Glorious Revolution that had so bungled British policy toward the American colonies.

Shelburne's chief propagandist was Adam Smith, the paid official of the East India Company, whose 1776 tome *The Wealth of Nations* set forth British policy to maintain the American colonies as backward raw materials producers and the mandate to expand the opium trade. Smith blasted the East India Company's practice of "ordering a peasant to plough up a rich field of poppies and sow it with rice or some other grain," in order to maintain high opium prices in the existing restricted markets. Opium was to be transformed from the source of fortunes for a few East India Company officials into the lifeblood of the Empire. Wrote Smith in *The Wealth of Nations:*

> The servants of the company have upon several occasions attempted to establish in their own favour the monopoly of some of the most important branches, not only of the foreign, but of the inland trade of the country. . . . In the course of a century or two, the policy of the English company would in this manner have probably proved as destructive as that of the Dutch. . . . Nothing, however, can be more directly contrary to the real interest of those companies considered as the sovereigns of the countries which they have conquered. . . . It is in [the sovereign's] interest, therefore, to increase as much as possible that annual produce. But if this is the interest of every sovereign, it is peculiarly so of one whose revenue, like that of the sovereign of Bengal, arises chiefly from a land rent. That rent must necessarily be in proportion to the quantity and value of the produce, and both one and the other must depend upon the extent of the market.[2]

The "produce" was opium.

In 1787, British Secretary of State Dundas had proposed that Britain storm China for the creation of the opium market. The East India Company meanwhile established a set of cutouts, or intermediaries, to conduct the exports of opium from India to China on the Company's covert behalf. Among the first of these was Jardine Matheson, which maintains an active hand in Far East heroin-trafficking to this day.[3]

Under the direct sponsorship now of the Crown, Jardine Matheson and others fostered an epidemic of opium-trafficking into China. By the year 1830, the number of chests of opium brought into China increased fourfold, to 18,956 chests. In 1836, the figure exceeded 30,000 chests. In financial terms, trade figures made available by both the British and Chinese governments showed that between 1829 and 1840, a total of 7 million silver dollars entered China, while 56 million silver dollars were sucked out by the soaring rise in opium trade.[4] In fact, by 1830, opium was the largest commodity in world trade.[5]

'The Chinese Have Fallen Into the Snare'

In 1840, the Chinese Emperor, confronted with a drug addiction crisis that was destroying the Mandarin class and the nation, tried to restrict the British trading companies. Britain's answer was war.

The year before, the Emperor had appointed Lin Tse-hsu commissioner of Canton to lead a war against opium. Lin launched a serious crackdown against the Triad gangs, who were sponsored by the British trading companies to smuggle the drugs out of the "Factory" area into the pores of the communities. The Triad Society, also known as the "Society of Heaven and Earth," was a century-old feudalist religious cult that had been suppressed by the Manchu Dynasty for its often violent opposition to the government's reform programs. The Triad group in Canton had been profiled and cultivated by Jesuit and Church of England missionaries and recruited into the East India Company's opium trade by the early nineteenth century.[6]

When Lin moved to arrest one of the British nationals employed through the opium merchant houses, Crown Commissioner Capt. Charles Elliot intervened to protect the drug smuggler with Her Majesty's fleet. And when Lin responded by laying siege to the factory warehouses holding the tea shipments about to sail for Britain until the merchants turned over their opium stockpiles, Elliot assured the British drug-pushers that the Crown would take full responsibility for covering their losses.

The British Crown had its *casus belli*. Matheson of the opium house Jardine Matheson joyously wrote his partner Jardine—then in London conferring with Prime Minister Palmerston—on how to pursue the pending war with China:

The Chinese have fallen into the snare of rendering themselves directly liable to the Crown. To a close observer, it would seem as if the whole of Elliot's career was expressly designed to lead on the Chinese to commit themselves, and produce a collision.

Matheson concluded the correspondence: "I suppose war with China will be the next step."[7]

Indeed, on October 12, 1839, Palmerston sent a secret dispatch to Elliot in Canton informing him that an expeditionary force proceeding from India could be expected to reach Canton by March 1840. In a followup secret dispatch dated November 23, Palmerston provided detailed instructions on how Elliot was to proceed with negotiations with the Chinese—once they had been defeated by the British fleet.

Palmerston's second dispatch was, in fact, modeled on a memorandum authored by Jardine dated October 26, 1839, in which the opium pusher demanded: (1) full legalization of opium trade into China; (2) compensation for the opium stockpiles confiscated by Lin to the tune of £2 million; and (3) territorial sovereignty for the British Crown over several designated offshore islands. In a simultaneous memorandum to the prime minister, Jardine placed J&M's entire opium fleet at the disposal of the Crown to pursue war against China.[8]

The Chinese forces, decimated by ten years of rampant opium addiction within the Imperial Army, proved no match for the British.

The British fleet arrived in force and laid siege in June of 1840. While it encountered difficulties in Canton, its threat to the northern cities, particularly Nanking, forced the Emperor to terms. Painfully aware that any prolonged conflict would merely strengthen Britain's bargaining position, he petitioned for a treaty ending the war.

When Elliot forwarded to Palmerston in 1841 a draft Treaty of Chuenpi, the prime minister rejected it out of hand, replying, "After all, our naval power is so strong that we can tell the Emperor what *we* mean to hold, rather than what *he* should say he would cede." Palmerston ordered Elliot to demand "admission of opium into China as an article of lawful commerce," increased indemnity payment, and British access to several additional Chinese ports.[9]

The Treaty of Nanking, signed in 1842, brought the British Crown an incredible sum of $21 million in silver—as well as extraterritorial control over the "free port" of Hong Kong—to this day the capital of Britain's global drug-running.

The First Opium War defined the proliferation of and profiteering from mind-destroying drugs as a cornerstone of British imperial policy. Doubters need only consider this policy statement issued by Lord Palmerston in a January 1841 communiqué to Lord Auckland, then governor general of India:

> The rivalship of European manufactures is fast excluding our productions from the markets of Europe, and we must unremittingly endeavor to find in other parts of the world new vents for our industry [opium]. . . . If we succeed in our China expedition, Abyssinia, Arabia, the countries of the Indus and the new markets of China will at no distant period give us a most important extension to the range of our foreign commerce. . . .[10]

It is appropriate to conclude this summary profile of Britain's First Opium War by quoting from the fifteenth edition of the *Encyclopaedia Britannica,* published in 1977. This brief biographical sketch of Lin Tse-hsu—the leader of the Chinese Emperor's fight to defeat British drugging of the Chinese— makes clear to the intelligent reader that British policy to this day has not changed one degree:

> He [Lin] did not comprehend the significance of the British demands for free trade and international equality, which were based on their concept of a commercial empire. This concept was a radical challenge to the Chinese world order, which knew only an empire and subject peoples. . . . In a famous letter to Queen Victoria, written when he arrived in Canton, Lin asked if she would allow the importation of such a poisonous substance into her own country, and requested her to forbid her subjects to bring it into his. Lin relied on

aggressive moral tone; meanwhile proceeding relentlessly against British merchants, in a manner that could only insult their government.

Britain's Opium Diplomacy

Not a dozen years would pass from the signing of the Treaty of Nanking before the British Crown would precipiate its Second Opium War against China, with similar disastrous consequences for the Chinese and with similar monumental profits for London's drug-pushers. Out of the Second Opium War (1858–1860), the British merchant banks and trading companies established the Hongkong and Shanghai Corporation, which to this day serves as the central clearinghouse for all Far Eastern financial transactions relating to the black market in opium and its heroin derivative.

Furthermore, with the joint British-French siege of Beijing during October 1860, the British completed the process of opening up all of China. Lord Palmerston, the High Priest of the Scottish Rites of Freemasonry, had returned to the prime ministership in June 1859 to launch the second war and fulfill the "open China" policy he had outlined twenty years earlier.

Like the 1840 invasion of Canton, the Second Opium War was an act of British imperial aggression—launched on the basis of the first flimsy pretext that occurred. Just prior to his ordering of a northern campaign against Beijing (which permitted the British to maintain uninterrupted opium-trafficking even while a state of war was under way), Lord Palmerston wrote to his close collaborator Foreign Secretary Lord John Russell (grandfather and guardian of the evil Lord Bertrand Russell). "We must in some way or other make the Chinese repent of the outrage," wrote Palmerston, referring to the defeat suffered by a joint British-French expeditionary force at Taku Forts in June 1859. The expeditionary fleet, acting on orders to seize the forts, had run aground in the mud-bogged harbor, and several hundred sailors attempting to wade to shore through the mud had been either killed or captured. "We might send a military-naval force to attack and occupy Beijing," Palmerston continued. Following Palmerston's lead, *The Times* of London let loose a bloodcurdling propaganda campaign:

> England, with France, or England without France if necessary . . . shall teach a lesson to these perfidious hordes that the name of Europe will hereafter be a passport of fear, if it cannot be of love throughout their land.[11]

In October 1860 the British-French expeditionary force laid siege to Beijing. The city fell within a day with almost no resistance. Despite French protests, British commander Lord Elgin ordered the temples and other sacred shrines in the city sacked and burned to the ground—as a show of Britain's contempt for the Chinese.

Within four years of the signing of the Treaty of Tientsin (October 25, 1860), Britain was in control of seven-eighths of the vastly expanded trade into China. This trade amounted to over £20 million in 1864 alone. Over the next twenty years, the total opium export from India—the overwhelming majority of which was still funneled into China—skyrocketed from 58,681 chests in 1860 to 105,508 chests in 1880.[12]

With its war against China, Britain established its method of control over the international opium trade:

1. Sponsorship of mass-scale opium addiction of targeted colonial and neocolonial populations as the way "to sap the vitality of the nation";

2. Willingness of Her Majesty's government to deploy Britain's national military forces to protect the opium trade; and

3. Use of the gigantic profits reaped from the trade to fund allied terrorist and organized criminal infrastructure within the targeted nation to carry out the trade and to act as a fifth column of British interests.

Beachhead in the United States

Plantation cotton, of the Southern states of the United States, was not merely a facet of the same trading operation that produced the dope trade; for all purposes, it was the dope trade.

Opium was the final stage in the demand cycle for British-financed and slave-produced cotton. British firms brought cotton to Liverpool. From there, it was spun and worked up in cloth in the mills in the north of England, employing unskilled child and female labor at extremely low wages. The finished cotton goods were then exported to India, in a process that destroyed the existing cloth industry, causing widespread privation. India paid for its imported cloth (and railway cars to carry the cloth, and other British goods) with the proceeds of Bengali opium exports to China.

Without the "final demand" of Chinese opium sales, the entire world structure of British trade would have collapsed.

It is around the slave production and transport of cotton that Britain gathered allies in the United States into the orbit of the East India Company's opium trade cycle. The southern cotton and slave trade were run to a significant degree by the same Scottish-based families that also ran the opium trade in the Orient. The Sutherland family, which was one of the largest cotton and opium traders in the South, was first cousin to the Matheson family of Jardine Matheson. The Barings, who founded the Peninsular and Orient Steam Navigation Company that carried the dope, had been the largest investors in U.S. clipper shipping from the time of the American Revolution. The Rothschild family, as well as their later "Our Crowd" New York banking cousins, the Lehmans of Lehman Brothers, all made their initial entry into the United States through the pre-Civil War cotton and slave trade.

In the North, John Jacob Astor became the first "American" to make his fortune in Chinese opium sales. "We see that quicksilver and lead from Gibraltar and opium from Smyrna, as well as some iron and steel from the North of Europe, began in 1816 to take a conspicuous place in the list of Astor's imports into China," reported one of Astor's biographers. "Since according to Dr. Kenneth Latourette, quicksilver and opium did not become regular articles of import into China by Americans until 1816, Astor must have been one of the pioneers in their introduction."[13]

Astor poured his opium profits into Manhattan real estate— an arrangement between the two fields of enterprise that still remains intact.

Participation in the China opium trade, a de facto monopoly of the East India Company at the time Astor took part in the traffic, was a privilege extended only to Americans the East India Company thought deserving. Other American firms active in the Canton trade did not touch opium. Possibly, Astor's trading privileges were a British pecuniary reward for services as a British intelligence operative in the United States. Astor provided funds for the escape of his attorney Aaron Burr after Burr murdered Alexander Hamilton: At the time, Burr was a British intelligence agent. Burr's controller and the man to whom he fled after the murder of Hamilton, was East India Company employee Jeremy Bentham.[14]

Apart from the Astor group in New York City, the East India Company developed similar networks in Philadelphia and Boston, among other American cities. The leading British merchant bank, Baring Brothers, acquired a group of business partners (and brothers-in-law) in Quaker Philadelphia. The family the Barings married into was William Bingham's, reportedly the richest in the United States at the turn of the nineteenth century. One historian describes how closely the Bingham group aped the British oligarchy:

Bingham was a most enthusiastic admirer of the British financial system which he desired to see copied in America. . . . Immense wealth enabled the Binghams to import fashions, and copy the Duke of Manchester's residence in Philadelphia . . . they gave the first masquerade ball in the city, encouraging what soon became a mania among the American rich—a passion for dressing up as aristocrats.

The Binghams finally achieved their ambitions by uniting two daughters to foreign aristocrats: one to Count de Tilly, and the other to a member of the London banking house of the Barings, who later became Lord Ashburton.[15]

Another Philadelphia family that united itself with Baring Brothers was that of millionaire Stephen Girard,[16] whose interests survived under the family name, in Philadelphia's multi-billion dollar Girard Bank and Trust.

Several of the old "Boston Brahmin" families, however, made it into the mainstream of the nineteenth-century opium traffic, alongside the well-remembered British names of Jardine, Matheson, Sassoon, Japhet, and Dent. The Perkins and Forbes families achieved notoriety in the traffic after the East India Company's monopoly expired in 1832, and after the Astors had ceased to be an important factor. William Hathaway Forbes became so prominent an associate of the British trading companies that he joined the board of directors of the Hongkong and Shanghai Bank in 1866, two years after its founding.

Hathaway, Perkins, and Forbes operated through a joint outlet, Russell and Company, formed around the Perkins family shipping empire, a "business reaching from Rio to Canton." The fortunes of these families, as with the Philadelphia group, began with the slave trade—handed to them when the British dropped it as unprofitable in 1833. The China clippers of Russell and Company made not only Perkins's fortune, but most of the city of Boston's. A biographer reports, "By merging and creating Russell and Company, he was responsible to a large degree in the establishing of all of Boston's merchant families—Cabots, Lodges, Forbes, Cunninghams, Appletons, Bacons, Russells, Coolidges, Parkmans, Shaws, Codmans, Boylstons and Runnewells."[17]

Baring Brothers, the premier merchant bank of the opium traffic from 1783 to the present day, also maintained close contact with the Boston families. John Murray Forbes (1813–1898) was U.S. agent for Barings, a post occupied earlier by Philadelphia's Stephen Girard: He was the father of the first American on the HongShang board.

The group's leading banker became, at the close of the nineteenth century, the House of Morgan—which also took its cut in the Eastern opium traffic. Thomas Nelson Perkins, a descendant of the opium-and-slaves shipping magnate who founded Russell and Company, became the Morgan Bank's chief Boston agent, through Perkins's First National Bank of Boston. Morgan and Perkins, among other things, provided the major endowments for Harvard University.[18] Morgan's Far Eastern operations were the officially conducted British opium traffic. Exemplary is the case of Morgan partner Willard Straight, who spent the years 1901–12 in China as assistant to the notorious Sir Robert Hart, chief of the Imperial Chinese Customs Service, and hence the leading British official in charge of conducting opium traffic. Afterwards he became head of Morgan Bank's Far Eastern operations.[19]

Morgan's case deserves special scrutiny from American police and regulatory agencies, for the intimate associations of Morgan Guaranty Trust with the identified leadership of the British dope banks (see Part III, Section 8). Jardine Matheson's current chairman David Newbigging, the most powerful man today in Hong Kong, is a member of Morgan's international advisory board. The chairman of Morgan et Cie., the bank's international division, sits on the Council of the Royal Institute of International Affairs. The chairman of Morgan Grenfell, in which Morgan Guaranty Trust has a 40% stake, Lord Catto of Cairncatto, sits on the "London Committee" of the Hongkong and Shanghai Bank.

But perhaps the most devastating example of continuity among the corrupted American families involves the descendants of old John Jacob Astor. American citizen Waldorf Astor, his direct descendant, was chairman of the Council of the Royal Institute of International Affairs during World War II, while Harvard-trained American citizens of its branch, the Institute for Pacific Relations, smoothed the transition to People's Republic of China opium production.

The Chinese Entry

The first shipments of opium into the United States for consumption were not brought in Astor's clipper ships, but via the "coolie trade," referred to by its British Hong Kong and Shanghai sponsors as the "pig trade."

Even before the Civil War, the same British trading companies behind the slave trade into the South were running a fantastic market in Chinese indentured servants into the West Coast. In 1846 alone, 117,000 coolies were brought into the country, feeding an opium trade estimated at nearly 230,000 pounds of gum opium and over 53,000 pounds of prepared (smoking) opium.[20] Although Lincoln outlawed the coolie trade in 1862, the black marketeering in Chinese (the term "Shanghaied" referred to the merchant company kidnapping—through the Triad Society—of impoverished and often opium-addicted Chinese) continued at an escalating rate through to the end of the century. Often these Chinese "indentureds" would put their entire earnings toward bringing their families over to the United States. This traffic in Chinese immigrants represented one of the earliest channels of opium into the country, and laid the foundations for the later drug trade out of the Chinatowns developed in San Francisco, Vancouver, and other West Coast cities during this period. The amount of opium coming into the United States during the last quarter of the nineteenth century is measured by the fact that in 1875, official government statistics estimated that 120,000 Americans—over and above the Chinese immigrant population—were addicted to opium![21]

Adding to the opium addiction, British pharmaceutical houses had begun commercial production of morphine in the years leading up to the Civil War and made large quantities available to both armies. The British firms misrepresented the morphine as a "nonaddictive" painkiller and even had the audacity to push it as a cure for opium addiction.

Protecting the Opium Market

In 1911, an international conference on the narcotics problem was held at The Hague. The conference participants agreed to regulate the narcotics trade, with the goal in mind of eventual total suppression. The conference was a major step forward; in the early days of the dope trade, neither opium nor morphine were considered illegal drugs, and heroin would not be outlawed as a prescription drug until 1924. But this conference and subsequent efforts to stem the opium plague ran up against Britain's open diplomatic posture on behalf of its unrestricted profiteering from a commodity known to destroy its consumers.

The success of the Hague Convention, as it was called, depended on strict enforcement of the earlier Anglo-Chinese agreement of 1905. Under that agreement, the Chinese were to reduce domestic opium production, while the British were to reduce their exports to China from British India correspondingly.

The Chinese, who had subscribed enthusiastically to both the 1905 and 1911 protocols, soon discovered that the British were completely evading both by sending their opium to their extraterritorial bases, Hong Kong and Shanghai. Opium dens in the Shanghai International Settlement jumped from 87 licensed dens in 1911 at the time of the Hague Convention to 663 dens in 1914![22] In addition to the trafficking internal to Shanghai, the Triads and related British-sponsored organized crime networks within China redoubled smuggling operations—conveniently based out of the warehouses of Shanghai.

In yet another act of contempt for the Hague Convention, Britain issued a large new loan to Persia in 1911. The collateral on that loan was Persia's opium revenues.[23]

Even with the post-Versailles creation of the League of Nations, Britain flaunted its drug-trafficking before the world. During this period, His Majesty's opium trade was so widely known that even the Anglophile U.S. newsweekly *The Nation* ran a series of documentary reports highly critical of the British role.[24]

At the Fifth Session of the League of Nations Opium Committee, one delegate demanded that the British government account for the fact that there were vast discrepancies between the official figures on opium shipments into Japan released by the Japanese and British governments. The British claimed only negligible shipments, all earmarked for medical use, during the period from 1916 to 1920; while the Japanese figures showed a thriving British traffic. When confronted with this discrepancy as prima facie evidence of British black market smuggling of opium into Japan, the British delegate argued that such black marketeering merely proved the case for creating a government-owned opium monopoly.

As late as 1927, official British statistics showed that *government opium revenues*—excluding the far more expansive black market figures—accounted for significant percentages of total revenue in all of the major Far East Crown colonies.[25]

British North Borneo	23%
Federated Malay States	14%
Sarawak	28%
Straits Settlements	37%
Confederated Malay	28%

In India as well, official Crown policy centered on protection for the opium market. According to one recently published account, when Gandhi began agitating against opium in 1921,

> his followers were arrested on charges of "undermining the revenue." So little concerned were the British about the views of the League of Nations that after a commission under Lord Inchcape had investigated India's finances in 1923, its report, while recognizing that it might be necessary to reduce opium production again if prices fell, went on to warn against diminishing the cultivated area, because of the need to safeguard "this most important source of revenue. . . ."
>
> While the British government was professing to be taking measures to reduce consumption of opium and hemp drugs, its agents in India were in fact busy pushing sales in order to increase the colony's revenues.[26]

Lord Inchcape—who chaired the India Commission which endorsed continued opium production in British India—was a direct descendant of the Lord Inchcape who during the previous century had founded Peninsular and Orient Steam Navigational Company and subsequently helped establish HongShang

as the clearinghouse bank for opium trade. Through to the
present, a Lord Inchcape sits on the boards of P&O and the
HongShang.

In 1923, the British-run opium black market was perceived
as such a serious international problem that Congressman Stephen Porter, chairman of the U.S. House of Representatives
Foreign Affairs Committee, introduced and passed a bill
through Congress calling for country-by-country production
and import quotas to be set on opium that would reduce consumption to approximately 10% of then-current levels. The
10% figure represented generally accepted levels of necessary
medical consumption.

Porter's proposal was brought before the League of Nations
Opium Committee—where it was publicly fought by the British
representative. The British delegate drafted an amendment to
Porter's plan, which called for increased quotas to account for
"legitimate opium consumption" beyond the medical usage.
This referred to the huge addicted population in British colonies
and spheres of influence (predominantly in Asia) where no regulations restricted opium use. The enraged U.S. and Chinese
delegations led a walkout of the plenipotentiary session; the
British rubberstamped the creation of a Central Narcotics
Board designated with authority to gather information and
nothing more; and the journalists stationed in Geneva hence-
forth referred to what remained of the committee as the "Smugglers Reunion."[27]

Nothing had been accomplished; the U.S. and Chinese governments were powerless in face of the fact that the deal between organized crime in the United States and the operatives
of Hongkong and Shanghai Bank for a dope pipeline into the
East Coast of the United States had already been set.

2

Britain's 'Noble Experiment'

In the years 1919 and 1920, two events of critical strategic importance for Britain's opium war against the United States occurred.

First, the Royal Institute of International Affairs was founded.

The purpose of this institution had been set forth over forty years before in the last will and testament of empire-builder Cecil Rhodes. Rhodes had called for the formation of a "secret society" that would oversee the reestablishment of a British empire that would incorporate most of the developing world and recapture the United States. Toward this objective, Rhodes's circle, including Rudyard Kipling, Lord Milner, and a group of Oxford College graduates known as "Milner's Kindergarten," constituted the Roundtable at the turn of the twentieth century. In 1919, the same grouping founded the Royal Institute

of International Affairs as the central planning and recruitment agency for Britain's "one-world empire."

The second event occurred on January 6 of the next year.
Britain declared its opium war against the United States.
Americans knew it as Prohibition.

Prohibition brought the narcotics traffic, the narcotics traffickers, and large-scale organized crime into the United States.
Illegal alcohol and illegal narcotics made up two different product lines of the same multinational firm. The British "Company" networks, through their distilleries in Scotland and Canada, and the British, from their opium refineries in Shanghai
and Hong Kong, were the suppliers. The British, through their
banks in Canada and the Caribbean, were the financiers.
Through their political conduits in the United States, the British created the set of political conditions under which the
United States might finally be won back.

Two tracks led to the drug epidemic in the United States, one
in the Far East, and the other in the United States and Canada.
Against the outcry of the League of Nations and nearly the
entire civilized world, the British stubbornly fought to maintain
opium production in the Far East, expanding the illegal supply
of heroin, just as the drug went out of legal circulation in
America in 1924. In North America, Canada—which had had
its own period of Prohibition—went "wet" one month before the
United States went dry.

In interviews with the authors, Drug Enforcement Administration officials have emphasized the similarity of the alcohol
and narcotics modus operandi. When the agents of Arnold
Rothstein and Meyer Lansky made their first trips to the Far
East in the 1920s, they purchased heroin from the British with
full legality. What the American gangsters did with the drug
was their own business; the British opium merchants were
merely engaging in "free enterprise." When Britain's leading
distilling companies sold bulk quantities of liquor to Arnold
Rothstein and Joseph Kennedy—for delivery either to the Bahamas or to the three-mile territorial limit of the United States
coastal waters—they had no responsibility for what happened
to the liquor once it reached American shores. (The identical

explanation was offered by an official of the British Bank of the Middle East, which now services the Far East drug traffic through a smugglers' market in gold bullion in Dubai, on the Persian Gulf. "We only sell the gold, old boy," the banker said. "What those fellows do with it once they get it is up to them.")

Which of the American syndicates obtained this month's franchise for drug or liquor distribution was immaterial to the British traffickers. The greater the extent of intergang bloodshed, the less obvious their role would be. In fact, the British distillers could provoke such events at will by withholding needed inventory of bootleg alcohol.

The "Noble Experiment" was aimed at degrading the American people through popular "violation of the law" and association with the crime syndicate controlled by the Our Crowd banks of Wall Street. New York's Our Crowd is an extension of the London Rothschild banking network and British Secret Intelligence into the United States. For example, Sir William Wiseman was the official head of British Secret Intelligence in the United States throughout the World War I period. He became a senior partner in the investment house of Kuhn Loeb immediately on demobilization. Wiseman was a personal protégé of Canadian Roundtable founder Lord Beaverbrook and one of the most prominent public figures in the Zionist movement.[1]

With this lower Manhattan-Canada centered grouping acting as the political control, the Prohibition project was launched during the early 1910s under the shadow of the United States' entry into World War I.

It is a fraud of the highest order that Prohibition represented only a mass social protest against the "evils" of alcohol. The Women's Christian Temperance Union (WCTU) and its Anti-Saloon League offshoots enjoyed the financial backing of the Astors, the Vanderbilts, the Warburgs, and the Rockefellers.[2] Then as now, the funding conduits were principally the tax-exempt foundations—especially the Russell Sage Foundation and the Rockefeller Foundation. John D. Rockefeller I was hoodwinked by Lord Beaverbrook colleague and former Canadian Prime Minister Mackenzie King into not only bankrolling the

WCTU, but providing it with the services of the foundation's entire staff of private investigators.[3]

One strand of the Temperance Movement was run by Jane Addams, who studied the Fabian Society's London settlement house Toynbee Hall experiment, and came to the United States to launch a parallel project which later produced the University of Chicago.[4]

These three British-spawned cults agitated nationally for Prohibition. While the WCTU and Anti-Saloon League staged well-publicized raids against saloons, the more sophisticated Fabian settlement house social workers of Jane Addams used the unique conjuncture of the recently passed Seventeenth Amendment certifying women's voting rights in national elections and the concentration of much of the adult male population on the war effort to vote up the Eighteenth Amendment making Prohibition the law of the land. The amendment was fully ratified by 1917; however, the Volstead Act that defined the federal enforcement procedures was not scheduled for implementation until January 6, 1920.

In Canada, a brief Prohibition period (1915–1919) was enacted by order of His Majesty's Privy Council principally to create the financial reserves and bootlegging circuit for the U.S. Prohibition. In this period, Canada's Bronfman family established the local mob contacts in the United States and consolidated contractual agreements with the Royal Liquor Commission in London.

In New York, primarily out of Brooklyn, teams of field agents of the Russell Sage Foundation conducted a reorganization and recruitment drive among local hoodlum networks—already loosely organized through Tammany Hall's New York City Democratic Party machine. "Legitimate" business fronts were established, replacing neighborhood nickel-and-dime loan-sharking operations, and specially selected individuals—largely drawn from the Mazzini "Mafia" transplanted to the United States during the late 1800s Italian migrations—were sent out of Brooklyn into such major Midwest cities as Chicago, Detroit, and St. Louis in the twelve months leading up to the

Volstead enforcement. One such Brooklyn recruit was Al Capone.

The British oligarchy did much more than supply the gutter elements of the crime syndicates with their stock in trade. To a surprising extent, the Anglophile portion of America's upper crust joined the fun. The case of Joseph Kennedy, who owed his British contracts for liquor wholesaling to the Duke of Devonshire, and later married his daughter into the family, is notorious. In some respects more revealing is the strange case of Robert Maynard Hutchins, the president of the University of Chicago from 1929 to 1950. Hutchins had American citizenship, but was so close to the British aristocracy that he became a Knight Commander of Her Majesty's Venerable Order of St. John of Jerusalem, swearing an oath of chivalric fealty to the head of the order, the British monarch.

Under the guise of "social studies research," several well-known University of Chicago postgraduate students received their apprenticeships in the service of the Capone gang.

In 1930, University of Chicago graduate student Saul Alinsky, the godfather of the "New Left," entered the Capone mob in Chicago. Alinsky for several years was the accountant for the gang—at the height of the Prohibition profiteering.[5] Alinsky went on to be one of the most important British Fabian-modeled social engineers in the United States for the next thirty years, specializing in the creation of dionysian cults among the nation's youth and ghetto victims.

Alinsky, in fact, used the organizational model of the Capone mob to build up a criminal youth gang infrastructure in Chicago during the early 1960s that assumed street-level control over drug-trafficking and related criminal operations run thirty years earlier through the Capone gang. When the Our Crowd sponsors of Capone's initial deployment to Chicago determined at the close of Prohibition that a more "civilized" cutout was desired, Alinsky was the channel for bringing Frank Nitti into the mob.

As late as the 1960s, retired University of Chicago President Hutchins himself was under investigation for his involvement with drug-trafficking and other black market enterprises. Through the late 1960s his Center for the Study of Democratic Institutions was financed principally through Bernie Cornfeld's Investments Overseas Service (IOS)—an international pyramid swindle and drug money-laundering enterprise. Furthermore, Hutchins was simultaneously the president of a little-known Nevada foundation called the Albert Parvin Foundation, which several congressional committees investigating organized crime cited as a front for Las Vegas gambling receipts.[6]

Mounting the Drug Invasion

The United States' fourteen-year experiment in Prohibition accomplished precisely what its British framers had intended. Ralph Salerno, an internationally recognized authority and historian on organized crime, a law enforcement consultant and former member of the New York City Police Department's intelligence division, succinctly summarized the effect of Britain's Prohibition gameplan in his book, *The Crime Confederation:*

The most crucial event in the history of the confederation "organized crime" was a legal assist called Prohibition. . . . Prohibition helped foster organized crime in several ways. It was the first source of real big money. Until that time, prostitution, gambling, extortion and other activities had not generated much capital even on their largest scale. But illegal liquor was a multibillion dollar industry. It furnished the money that the organization later used to expand into other illegal activities and to penetrate legitimate business. Prohibition also opened the way to corruption of politicians and policemen on a large scale. It began the syndicate connection with politics and it demoralized some law enforcement groups to the point where they have never really recovered. . . .

The manufacture and distribution of illegal liquor here

and the importation of foreign-made liquor gave the men who were organizing crime experience in the administration and control of multi-billion dollar world businesses with thousands of employees and long payrolls. Men who had never before managed anything bigger than a family farm or a local gang got on-the-job training that turned them into leaders developing executive qualities.

Mass evasion of the Volstead Act also put the average citizen in touch with criminals, resulting in tolerance and eventually even romantic approval of them. It permanently undermined respect for the law and for the people enforcing it. Ever since Prohibition the man in the street has accepted the idea that cops can be bought.[7]

The combined revenues of the illicit whiskey and drug trade during Prohibition had constituted a multibillion dollar black market booty. While families like the Kennedys and Bronfmans "made out like bandits" in the early 1930s transition to "legitimate" liquor trade, the overall financial structure for maintaining an organized crime infrastructure demanded diversification into other areas of black market activity only marginally developed previously. The market for illicit drugs in the United States—though significantly expanded as the result of the Prohibition experience—was not to become the foundation of multibillion dollar traffic for several decades.

In the interim, the Our Crowd-British crime syndicate turned to casino gambling and associated enterprises as the immediate area for expansion. The Lansky syndicate took the opportunity of Nevada's 1933 passage of specific regulations legalizing casino operations to turn that no-man's-land into a desert resort to house all the West Coast criminal operations that had previously been run on pleasure boats twelve miles off the coast of Hollywood. Lansky also moved into the Caribbean, preparing the way for the British offshore complex of unregulated banking.

Through the investment of the phenomenal profits derived from Prohibition into gambling casinos, professional sports stadiums, and racetracks, organized crime established the support

structure during the 1930s and 1940s for the drug-trafficking
that would begin in the mid-1950s—once a cultural climate had
been created that was conducive to fostering drug addiction.

Nixon's War on Drugs

It is not widely known that President Nixon was a casualty
in the war against Britain's drug invasion of the United States.
Had Nixon not taken up the most basic interests of the nation
in launching a wholesale effort to shut down the drug-trafficking—from the top down—it is likely that he would not have
been unceremoniously forced out of office by Henry Kissinger,
Edward Kennedy, and their British masters. Documents are
available in the public domain from the Drug Enforcement
Administration and other executive agencies showing that Nixon's "War on Drugs" was directed *at the top*—at the banking
institutions, the transportation grids, and only then at the distribution channels delivering the volumes of drugs onto the
streets of the country.

At the same time that Nixon generically understood the top-
down nature of the problem, he and his assistants scarcely
understood that by going after the drug infrastructure they
were taking on the British oligarchy and the entire underpin-
nings of the Eurodollar market, the Soviet KGB, recently reorganized under Yuri Andropov, and the People's Republic of
China. Had Nixon understood the drug problem as a London-
Moscow-Beijing problem, he would have perhaps been better
prepared to deal with the "inside-outside" attack against his
presidency.

Tracing that connection is the first step in fighting against
Britain's Opium War against the United States, and that is our
next task.

Notes: Part II

Introduction: To Sap the Vitality of a Nation
1. As quoted in Jack Beeching, *The Chinese Opium Wars* (New York: Harvest Books, 1975), p. 258.

1: The East India Company's War Against China
1. Philip Woodruff, *The Men Who Ruled India* (London: J. Cape, 1953).
2. Adam Smith, *Wealth of Nations, Representative Selections* (New York: Bobbs-Merrill, 1961).
3. Beeching, *Chinese Opium Wars.*
4. Ibid, p. 43.
5. Ibid.
6. In addition to the Chinese Hong Kong merchants who collaborated with the British opium houses and the run-of-the-mill pirates and river rats that the British recruited into their service as the "eyes and ears" in Canton and the interior, the Hakkas, a people living in the southern province of Kwangsi who were under the strong influence of the Heaven and Earth Society (Triads) were particularly important to the British operations. The Triads, who were devoted to the days of the Ming Dynasty—and who were very similar to the Freemason organizations in Europe and North America—wanted to overthrow the Manchu Dynasty. The Hakkas were used by both the British and their Triad allies as a grassroots bludgeon against the Emperor. The key figure in the joint Anglo-Triad venture was a religious fanatic named Hung Hsui-Ch'uan.

Hung, having suffered public "loss of face" on four occasions—he failed the examinations that would allow him to join the Mandarin class and become a governmental official—suffered a nervous collapse. He was in a trance for forty days in which he was supposedly born again and then, using a translation of the King James Bible, he created a new religion based on the notion of "The Chosen People." The Hakkas were to be the Chosen People, and the Triad identification of the

Manchus as the enemy was fully incorporated into Hung's quasi-Protestant religion.

Hung served as the "prophet," and a Hakkas Triad member, Yang Hsin-Ch'ing, served as the recruiter and military commander of the movement. Yang was in the employ of the British as an opium runner on the Pearl River.

In 1851, Hung and Yang launched a full-scale assault against the Manchu Dynasty—called the Taiping Revolt, or "The Triad War"—which drained China's treasury, shook the government, and demoralized China's pathetic army. The Taiping-Triad forces also played a significant role in the 1911 overthrow of the Manchu Dynasty that led to the Republic of China under its president Dr. Sun Yat-sen (also a member of the "Hung Society"), although the organization was outlawed as treasonous and terrorist in 1890.

7. Beeching, *Chinese Opium Wars,* p. 80.

8. Ibid., p. 98.

9. Ibid., p. 127.

10. Ibid., p. 95.

11. Ibid., p. 272.

12. Ibid., p. 264.

13. Kenneth Wiggins Porter, *John Jacob Astor, Business Man* (New York: Russell and Russell, 1966).

14. Ibid., p. 604.

15. Miriam Beard, *History of Business, Vol. II* (Ann Arbor, Mich.: University of Michigan Press, 1963), p. 162 *ff.;* see also Joseph Wechsberg, *The Merchant Bankers* (Boston: Little, Brown and Company, 1966), 104 *ff.*

16. Wechsberg, *Merchant Bankers,* p. 123.

17. Brett Howard, *Boston: A Social History* (New York: Hawthorn Books, 1976).

18. Ibid.

19. Brian Ingles, *The Forbidden Game: A Social History of Drugs* (New York: Charles Scribner, 1975), chapter 11.

20. Beeching, *Chinese Opium Wars,* p. 178.

21. Ibid.

22. Ingles, *Forbidden Game,* chapter 11.

23. Ibid.

24. Ibid.

25. Ibid.

26. Ibid.

27. Ibid.

2: Britain's Noble Experiment

1. *Who's Who in America* and *Who's Who in World Jewry*.

2. John Kobler, *Ardent Spirits* (New York: G.P. Putnam's Sons, 1973).

3. Ibid.

4. Jeffrey Steinberg, "Robert Hutchins: Creator of an American Oligarchy," *The Campaigner* (May–June 1978) 10:73–77.

5. Saul Alinsky, *Reveille for Radicals* (New York: Random House, 1969).

6. Hank Messick, *Lansky* (New York: Berkley Medallion Books, 1971), p. 172.

7. Ralph Salerno and John S. Tompkins, *The Crime Confederation* (New York: Doubleday and Company, 1969), pp. 275, 278–279.

PART III

How the Drug Empire Works

Introduction
The Basis of This Investigation

In the following pages we will take the reader from the opium-growing mountains of the Far East's Golden Triangle, to the offices of opium wholesalers in the expatriate Chinese districts of Bangkok, Rangoon, and Singapore; we will take him through the bonded warehouses, shipping lines, and air freight companies of old-line British trading companies that control the Chinese expatriate wholesalers; we will lead him through the maze of financial channels that fund the Far East's opium trade, to the august portals of the Hongkong and Shanghai Banking Corporation and other top British banks that control the financing top down; we will take him across the Pacific to the ports of entry for heroin into the United States, to the skyscraper offices of the Canadian banks and corporations that finance, ship, and protect the heroin en route to the United States; and, finally, we will guide the reader through the pedigrees of the Canada-based financiers, to their contact-points in the world of organized crime and heroin distribution. When this is done, we will have reconstructed a major portion of the annual report of Dope, Inc.

At the conclusion, the reader will know and understand more about the personnel and operations of illegal drugs—the world's second-biggest business—than the law enforcement authorities of the United States and other countries knew until recently. In the files of these agencies, in the minds of solitary investigators, and, to a surprising extent, in the public record itself, the pieces of the puzzle have existed for years. Fitting them together into a single picture is the task of this investigation. But the puzzle is not a jigsaw game, in which the picture is assembled by fitting the pieces together side by side. As a first approximation, it would be better for the reader to imagine a set of clear plastic overlays, each of which contains part of the picture; laid one on top of the other, they complete the puzzle.

The different overlays of this puzzle are these:

1. The detailed record assembled by American and other investigators of the mechanics of the opium trade from the Golden Triangle down to opium's ports of departure to the rest of the world;

2. Pinpointed identification of opium wholesalers, largely in the Chinese expatriate community, including the names of leading bankers;

3. A comprehensive profile of British finance in the Far East, revolving around the Hong Kong financial center and its leading bank, the Hongkong and Shanghai, including the web of British ties to the Chinese expatriate banking community throughout the area;

4. An exhaustive grid of the British control over means of laundering dirty money in the hundreds of billions of dollars, including "offshore" banking, gold, and diamonds;

5. A grid of the huge quantity of public record material showing the integration of British Far East and dirty money financial operations worldwide with the top level of British foreign

policy-making, centered in the Royal Institute of International Affairs;

6. The similar public record of evidence of strategic agreement between Great Britain and the People's Republic of China, going back to negotiations between British opium-runners and Mao Zedong, under the auspices of the Royal Institute of International Affairs;

7. Twenty years of official documentation—from American, Japanese, Taiwanese, and European sources—that the People's Republic of China grows and exports opium not only to earn foreign exchange, but to fund secret intelligence operations;

8. A comprehensive grid of the intimate links between all these elements—British old-line opium-runners, British dirty-money operations, Chinese expatriate overseas operations, British-Chinese policy agreement—with the "Canadian" connection to American organized crime;

9. The international web of the British-centered "Zionist lobby," and its special function in gold and diamond-related dirty money operations, laundering of dirty money, financing of international terrorism, and financial control of the Canada-U.S. drug channels.

The resulting picture is comprehensive: The entire mass of detailed, documented evidence fits together into a single picture, stretching from the present day back through the British origins of the opium trade in the time of Adam Smith.

The Hongkong and Shanghai Bank and related companies finance the opium trade. In this, they are acting as designated agents of the British monarchy through such agencies as the Royal Institute of International Affairs. Not only do they control the expatriate Chinese legmen of the opium trade, but they do so as part of an agreement negotiated between Mao Zedong and the Royal Institute of International Affairs, by the Hongkong and Shanghai's leading representatives!

The gold and diamonds side of the dirty money-laundering operations, under the immediate control of Britain's faction of Zionists, is part of the same machine. Through the highest circles of British policy, all the important branches of the drug machine—the Chinese connection, the old-line British opium traders, the dirty "offshore" banking sector, and the Anglo-Zionist *Hofjuden*—run Canada from the top.

From there the trail leads directly into the American crime syndicate, through the Bronfman family.

The world's illegal drug traffic is not only the world's biggest swindle and subversive agency: It is controlled by a group of evil men whose names and organizational affiliations are printed below, and who retain longstanding intimate ties of ownership, family, and political collaboration. We know their names and addresses, and how to mop them up.

1

Banking and the World's Biggest Business

Assembled as one picture, the hard evidence available from the Drug Enforcement Administration and other law enforcement agencies leaves only one possible conclusion: The drug "industry" is run as a single integrated world operation, from the opium poppy to the nickel bag of heroin sold on an American inner-city street corner. The price of opium in the Golden Triangle has remained essentially stable at approximately $40 per kilo since the late 1960s, indicating the central control of this basic commodity. Not only is the illegal drug traffic under the control of a single world network, but opiates traffic in particular is without doubt the best-controlled production and distribution system of any commodity in international trade, illegal or legal. De Beers' Central Selling Organization's 85% control of world diamond wholesaling—an example not irrelevant to the drug trade—pales by comparison to the orderly marketing arrangements for heroin demonstrated by the hardest figures available.

Investigators are daunted by the fact that the solution to the problem is so obvious. Imagine Edgar Allan Poe's fictional purloined letter, photographically enlarged to 8 by 20 feet, and used as wallpaper; then, imagine the French police attempting to find it with magnifying glasses.

When we speak of the drug-related illegal economy—for drugs are the pivot on which most other illegal activity turns—we are talking of a $500 billion per year business. That is net, not gross, annual sales of drugs, plus related illicit payments.

How can such activity avoid sticking out wildly, especially in areas of concentration such as the Far East? Because the British monarchy organized most of the Far East to conform to the drug traffic! How can $500 billion in illegal payments get through the international banking system past the eyes of law enforcement authorities? The answer is: the British "offshore" banking system. This and related precious metals and gems trade were designed around illegal money in the first place!

Mere consideration of the obvious—or what will quickly become obvious when the evidence of the public record is assembled below—gives the financial specialist the equivalent of an inner-ear disorder. The financial world, remember, is one in which the stock market will do flips over a measly few hundred million dollars' difference in the weekly reported figures for the U.S. money supply. Although most of the necessary evidence has long been available, both investigators and the public prefer to see world drug traffic and related illegal activity as a montage of movie villains: Far Eastern warlords, freelance smugglers, jowly gangsters, and corrupt politicians. Such individuals figure into the world drug traffic, but as the arms and legs headed by British and allied monarchies.

The most striking single fact for this conclusion is that the price series for heroin at the retail level in major American cities shows virtually total uniformity.

Law enforcement records show that, within the acceptable

range of 3 to 6% purity at the street level, the price of heroin has been constant between widely disparate distribution points during the past ten years. Arrests of local distribution chains, internecine warfare among drug traffickers, interdiction of smuggling routes, the nearly total elimination of the Turkish opium supply after 1972, the scouring of Asian and European transit points, and local changes in political and growing conditions in the Golden Triangle growing area, all have failed to have any effect on the single world heroin price![1]

Where Does It Go?

Closely related to the striking uniformity of inner-city heroin prices at the retail level in the United States is the gigantic discrepancy between known levels of opium production for illegal purposes and its consumption by the world's addict population. Fairly reliable statistical data are available for both. Within great margins of fluctuation depending on weather, enforcement, and other conditions, available supply exceeds demand by roughly a factor of ten. The same ratio holds true for the cocaine bonanza of the post-1975 period.

Approximately 740 tons annually are produced and transported out of the world's largest opium-growing area, the Golden Triangle.[2] Seven hundred tons of raw opium, in the form of balls of opium gum, are the equivalent of about seventy tons of refined heroin. In practice less than half this amount is refined into heroin; the remainder is sold in the form of either opium or morphine base, largely for smoking purposes, and largely to an addict population in the Orient itself. However, by all estimates of the American addict population, approximately three tons per year of refined heroin arc more than sufficient to meet annual consumption "requirements." About that much again is required to maintain all other heroin addicts in the non-Communist advanced sector.

DEA and other official sources affirm the cited production figures through direct monitoring of opium shipments and other sophisticated intelligence methods. Consumption and sales are obviously limited by the possible size and financial resources of the addict population in the advanced sector. To use a rough example: If the full 30,000 kilograms of annual Golden Triangle heroin production obtained the full street price for heroin, the total retail value would be about $150 billion. But most estimates of annual illegal purchases of retail heroin are under $15 billion. In short, most of it is never sold, because production capacity is enormous relative to the market's absorption capacity.

What happens to the rest of the heroin? Only a small portion of the total comes into the hands of law enforcement agencies, whose capture of a few pounds of heroin is a matter for celebration. We still must account for tens of tons. The law enforcement records indicate that the drug is warehoused in huge stockpiles against contingencies and to prevent oversupply on the market. For example, during the height of the crackdown on Southeast Asian heroin traffic in 1972, a single refinery captured by Thai police had on hand a stockpile of 3,000 kilograms, roughly one-tenth of Southeast Asian production. At the time, twenty-one refineries were known to be operational in the area.[3]

The Market Analysis

The law enforcement record shows that Dope, Inc. does its best to avoid mishaps through careful research—done on the streets of American cities—which is transmitted back to the poppy fields. Poppy growers in the Burmese or the Chinese Yunnan Province mountains and foothills do not plant what they feel like, but what they are told to plant. This facet of the production cycle is well known to law enforcement investigators. If for some reason the market research is off, chaos will ensue, as it did in 1972, when the Golden Triangle yielded a bumper harvest, after wholesalers told poppy-growing peasants to increase their acreage by 50 to 100%. The wholesalers counted on the continuing exponential expansion of heroin consumption among American soldiers in Vietnam. Nixon pulled the rug out from under them by pulling the troops out, leaving the world heroin market in an unprecedented state of oversupply.

Reckless price-cutting and competition for sales outlets in this case might have provoked serious consequences for Dope, Inc. were it not for "government regulatory intervention." The Thai government stepped in and sold twenty-two tons of opium to the United States. The opium was burned in a public ceremony attended by giggling Thai officials, thus restoring "equilibrium" to the market. (In any case, the Thais were only repeating the action of the imperial Chinese in 1839, who purchased and burned more than 3,000 tons of opium to the great relief of oversupplied British traders, who sent special fleets to India to bring additional opium back to get the imperial government's attractive price.)

Once world illegal opiates traffic comes under scrutiny as an integrated, centralized "monopoly," the discrepancy between the huge oversupply and relatively restricted demand presents no further difficulties. We are looking at an "industry" based on the same principles as the world diamond cartel controlled by De Beers, or the so-called club among leading pharmaceuticals manufacturers. Diamond production capacity is so large relative to the absorption capacity of the world market that De Beers' Central Selling Organization, running 85% of world diamond wholesale trade, limits availability in order to obtain essentially the price it wants. Pharmaceuticals are, ironically, an even better example. Since the knowledge to manufacture more of the commonly used prescription drugs is widespread among the pharmaceuticals companies, and since the costs of production are insignificant compared to the retail prices of most drugs, elaborate legal arrangements are necessary to prevent a price collapse. Notoriously, the profits of the pharmaceuticals industry owe not to chemists but to patent lawyers.

How Big an Industry?

Heroin trade is the ideal commodity cartel; its price is more reliably controlled than that of crude oil, and its world volume of sales, is substantially higher than that of most of the commodities the United Nations Conference on Trade and Development is presently considering for cartelization.

In the United States alone, the illicit drug trade, not counting laboratory drugs such as hallucinogens, is at least $233 billion.

According to the House Select Committee on Narcotics Abuse and Control, the following amounts of illicit drugs will enter the United States during 1986:

Heroin	12 tons
Cocaine	150 tons
Marijuana	30,000 tons

Virtually no heroin or cocaine are produced in the United States, but a substantial amount of marijuana is. A conservative estimate is that domestic production would increase the House Committee's estimate by one-third, giving a total of 40,000 tons.

The street value of these drugs, using standard estimates for street value, can be calculated as follows:

DRUG	VOLUME	STREET PRICE	TOTAL VALUE
Pot	40,000 tons	$100/oz.	$128 billion
Heroin	12 tons	$5 million/ kilogram*	60 billion
Cocaine	150 tons	$240/gram**	45 billion
Subtotal			$233 billion
PCP	n.a.		n.a.
"Uppers"	n.a.		n.a.
"Downers"	n.a.		n.a.
Hallucinogens	n.a.		n.a.

*diluted to street-level purity of 4 percent
**Diluted to street-level purity of 20 percent.

Heroin, marijuana and cocaine account for *potential* sales of $233 billion. No accurate data are available for other drugs, which may be produced cheaply in domestic laboratories, or siphoned from the stream of otherwise-available prescription drugs. A rough estimate of the street value of all available narcotics is $300 billion. Assuming that what accountants call "inventory shrinkage" reduces total sales by a considerable margin, we can estimate that total narcotics sales in the United States are somewhere between $200 and $250 billion.

Add to this figure the drug trade internationally, and also include means of barter for drugs—gold, diamonds, armaments, and so forth—and the $500 billion estimate appears conservative. The $500 billion international narcotics trade today is second only to the world oil trade. Total world trade volume is $1.7 trillion. (*See* Dope, Inc. Doubling Every Five Years, p. 28 for updated statistics on the world drug trade.)

Where Does the Money Go?

The question that emerges now is: "How is it possible that $500 billion and up in dirty money, crisscrossing international borders, can remain outside the control of the law?" Again, only one possible answer can be admitted: A huge chunk of international banking and related financial operations has been created solely to manage dirty money.

These conclusions are obvious. If the entire resources of the largest private bank in the world, at $120 billion, had no other use but the financing of illegal world drug traffic and related illegal activity, those resources would be grossly insufficient.

In the following sections of this report, the British banking operations that control illegal drug and related trade are documented in detail. Below, we will demonstrate through several chains of evidence that this is the only possible banking network that could handle the requisite volume of illegal traffic. The British oligarchy's banking operations—including the Boston-New York "Tory" banking establishment of the United States—have the following qualifications:

1. They have run the drug trade for a century and a half.
2. They dominate those banking centers closed off to law enforcement agencies.
3. Almost all such "offshore," unregulated banking centers are under the direct political control of the British monarchy and their allies.
4. They dominate all banking at the heart of the narcotics traffic; the Hongkong and Shanghai Bank, created in 1864 to finance the drug trade, is exemplary.
5. They control world trade in gold and diamonds, a necessary aspect of "hard commodity" exchange for drugs.
6. They subsume—as documented below—the full array of connections to organized crime, the prodrug legislative lobby in the United States, and all other required elements of distribution, protection, and legal support.

The Offshore Cover-up

Financial specialists, who have lived too long with the smell of the West Indies backwaters to mind it any longer, will choke on the above assertion. The general reader, by contrast, only needs to know a few facts in order to realize that something is wrong. All the offshore international banking operations—including the clean side—are such a speculative whirlpool, that virtually the entire deposit base changes hands every week. Hundreds of billions of dollars in the offshore centers, and further hundreds of billions elsewhere, circle the world through teletyped bank transfers.

No banking reserves are kept on any of this, as insurance against sudden withdrawals; in the United States, by contrast, commercial banks must hold 15% of their checking account balances and 4% of their savings balances on reserve. The offshore banks just assume that if they are short of cash, they can borrow what they need on the enormous "interbank" market. This mind-boggling financial procedure involves banks lending funds to each other in order to obtain fractional advantages in interest rates. Perhaps 40% of the total market is interbank money. Deposit maturities are so short, and money transfers are so rapid, that $50 billion changes hands every business day through the New York banks' Clearinghouse system alone. In the foreign currency markets, $150 billion per day changes hands.

The offshore banking markets are precisely what the name implies: either Britain's old island colonies refurbished for international banking, or inland feudal relics like Andorra and Liechtenstein. Federal bank regulators will only stare at their shoes when asked what goes on in such locations.

In the Cayman Islands, one of the largest offshore centers, the only government is the official "Tax Haven Commission." Law enforcement officers have absolutely no way of getting hold of bank records in such places. Repeatedly, they have identified the offshore centers as the place to look for dirty money. They have not been able to investigate, because almost all the centers are under British political protection.

American banks do a land office business in the offshore centers, precisely because no reserves are needed, and every dollar of deposits can be lent out for interest.

Even clean banking operations have moved offshore because present federal banking regulations virtually force them to do so. The big movement offshore began under the Kennedy administration, when anglophile Treasury officials C. Douglas Dillon and Robert V. Roosa railroaded legislation through Congress that taxed loans made to foreigners by U.S. banks. The tax did not apply to loans made offshore; and that is where the bankers went. By the time the Dillon-Roosa legislation was lifted in 1974, the banks were "hooked" through the difference in reserve requirements. In a 1978 interview in *Euromoney* magazine, Citibank's chairman Walter Wriston denounced the Dillon-Roosa taxes as a "pure gift to London."[4]

According to the estimates of the Bank for International Settlements, the total assets of the so-called Group of Ten offshore banking centers, the unregulated islands and enclaves

where "bank inspector" is a dirty word, amounted to close to
$300 billion, as of 1984. The figures break down as follows:

Deposits of Group of Ten Banks in Offshore Centers
(in millions)

Andorra	$ 3
Liechtenstein	466
Bahamas	87,639
Barbados	723
Bermuda	2,970
Caymans	62,368
Hong Kong	41,068
Panama	25,609
Singapore	10,000
Lebanon	1,426
Liberia	6,584
Vanuatu	103
West Indies UK	4,725
Total	$283,789,349

Source: Bank for International Settlements

The above figures do not show the actual size of the offshore
banking centers, because they include only the assets of
branches domiciled in the largest ten industrial countries. They
do not include such entities as the three large banks in Thailand's capital, Bangkok, which figure prominently in financing
Golden Triangle opium production. Nor do they include thousands of smaller, offshore finance companies based only in the
offshore centers themselves. Expatriate Chinese banks in the
Far East, which have long been known to be a key point of
contact with illegal drugs and other contraband traffic in the
Far East, also do not show up on these tables; there is no
available data on these institutions at all. Furthermore, the
above table does include a great deal of legitimate banking
business which American and other industrial country banks
bring to the offshore market for tax and other reasons. However,
the round figure of nearly $300 billion is a useful starting point.

Another set of figures is provided in the Bank of England's quarterly report, although it contains the same unwanted additions and deletions; it shows the large volume of interchange between London, which in major respects functions as the world's biggest offshore center, with the previously mentioned outposts for illegal money. Unfortunately, the available figures mix in both British banks' dealings and those of American and other banks that have offices in London.

More important than these numbers—which give a meager understanding of the volume of business in the offshore centers—is the political control of the unregulated banking centers. With very few exceptions, offshore banking as a whole is under the thumb of the British oligarchy.

The British preeminence makes the world picture of offshore banking and dirty money more comprehensible. If the world offshore banking sector appears to run as a single operation under British monarchy control, that is because the same group of people who run it, also run the opium traffic, whose proceeds this banking sector was created to handle.

London and Switzerland are not normally considered offshore banking centers, although in practice both centers function that way. Although Switzerland has signed a treaty with the United States permitting law enforcement officers to investigate and seize funds relating to illegal narcotics traffic, Swiss banks are notorious depots for dirty money. However, the Swiss side of the operation, typified by Lombard Odier and Edmond de Rothschild's Banque Privée in Geneva and the Baseler Handelsbank, is more specialized. Its most important activity is conduiting funds for international terrorism. European authorities, for example, traced the funding of the 1978 Aldo Moro assassination through Swiss channels back to Israel.

London is the largest center for Eurodollar banking under the encouragement of the Bank of England, which permits the foreign branches of U.S. and other banks to hold external accounts in London without reserve requirements, and with minimal inspection. As of 1978, international banks had $90 billion in assets in London. The Bank of England can do as much or as little as it wants in the way of regulation, under British law.

For self-evident reasons, even the best-protected institutions of the British oligarchy prefer to launder their dirty money through the Caribbean, Hong Kong, and similar branch operations, rather than in London itself.

Because the British suppliers of narcotics have ironclad control over offshore bank operations, American organized crime marketers of those narcotics have had a field day in the Cayman Islands and the Bahamas. American drug enforcement authorities know that most of the dirty money arising from the U.S. drug trade and related illegal activities ends up in the Bahamas. There has been, unfortunately, little public heat against the British officials who control the operations.

This level of control reaches the flagrant. For example, the chief of all banking regulation and licensing in the Cayman Islands, a close third behind Hong Kong and Macao in the big league of dirty money, is one Mr. Benbow. Mr. Benbow is a retired official of Britain's National Westminster Bank, which shares two directors, J.A.F. Binny and R.J. Dent, with the Hongkong and Shanghai Bank. Benbow got his present job at the recommendation of the British-influenced International Monetary Fund, according to a source at the Fund's Exchange and Stabilization division. Direct British "hands-on" management of the Caribbean offshore operation dates back to the 1940s, when E.D. Sassoon, Ltd. of Hong Kong—which had made its fortune from the opium trade over the preceding century— picked up, moved, and became E.D. Sassoon, Ltd. of the Bahamas.

Virtually the only one of the offshore centers not under *official* British control is Panama; not coincidentally, Panama is the only offshore center where American banks strongly outnumber British banks. That is not to say that Panama is clean; on the contrary, funds derived from the Colombian trade in marijuana and cocaine are laundered through Panama, including through the three large Colombian banks resident there. However, American banks have a measure of maneuvering room that they do not have in the Cayman Islands or the Bahamas, under the snooping eyes of the British authorities.

West German banking sources believe that the British banks behind Dope, Inc. want to move in on Panama and close the gap. The West German sources identify a special feature of the drug-ridden Hongkong and Shanghai Bank's takeover of a controlling share in New York's $20 billion Marine Midland Bank: Marine Midland is the transactions agent for the central bank of Panama. All of the national accounts clear through Marine Midland. The Hongkong and Shanghai can thus exercise a decisive margin of control over the Panama offshore market, and bring British control over the offshore centers full circle.

Longstanding ties between Marine Midland and Panama were reflected in the fact that a former board member of Marine Midland Bank, Coudert Brothers lawyer Sol Linowitz, negotiated the Carter administration's 1978 treaty concerning the Panama Canal.

Far East Chokepoint

The next sections will concentrate on the Far East offshore banking connection to the drug traffic as a model for the world operation. It is the Far East that acts as a chokepoint for dirty money, in such volume that it dwarfs legitimate economic activity in the region and in the British Crown Colony of Hong Kong in particular.

London has seduced and jostled American banking operations into the Caribbean to such an extent that there is a vast amount of legitimate money mixed in with the proceeds of the drug traffic, and many who made their original fortunes in drugs have now turned exclusively to legitimate businesses. However, Hong Kong was set up by the British, literally from bare rock, as a center for the drug trade, and remains to this day purely British, and purely a center for the drug trade.

The Laundering Cycle

The Drug Enforcement Administration and other law enforcement organizations know how the cycle of dirty money in the United States works. The $200 billion retail proceeds of the total drug traffic in the United States are partly recycled into the drug operation in the United States itself, with large "offtake" by each level of the crime machine. The net profits, in cash, are laundered through hotels, restaurants, gambling casinos, and sports events—the "corporate profile" of the Max Jacobs family and other field officers of the drug machine.

After the cash is laundered through these nominally legitimate channels, it is transferred to offshore banking operations or their equivalent. Then, according to DEA officials, the funds take several trips around the world over the telex machines of offshore banks, passing through at least a half-dozen, and usually more, different bank accounts and corporate fronts, from the Caymans to Liechtenstein, from Liechtenstein to the Bahamas, from the Bahamas to a "nonresident corporation" in Canada, from Canada to Panama, and so forth.

At various points in the process, the funds will purchase diamonds, gold, paintings, or similar portable valuables. At a further point, the valuables will be translated back into cash, eliminating even the trace of a bank transfer. For this reason, the use of undercover agents, in place even at fairly high levels in known branches of narcotics-trafficking, has a poor record of detecting either the source or ultimate destination of narcotics-related funds.

Once laundered, the proceeds of the drug traffic and related illegal activities divide into three channels. First, between 10 and 20% of the total is recycled back to the opium wholesalers in the Far East and the marijuana and cocaine wholesalers in the Caribbean and Latin America, constituting the net profits of the wholesale drug trade. A second part is invested in expansion of offshore operations, particularly gambling casinos, resorts, and other profitable operations that are also useful for further laundering of dirty money. The remainder is reinvested in the United States in "legitimate" racing, gambling, hotels, restaurants, and other business appropriate for cash-laundering and expansion of the domestic drug traffic.

As noted, Hong Kong and related Far East operations are the chokepoint in the entire traffic. We will focus on the Far East, the point of origin of world heroin traffic, and work backwards through the maze of Dope, Inc. fronts and subsidiaries, to arrive at the British-controlled syndicates in the United States.

2

How to Hide $200 Billion

In 1975, New York City police arrested the managers of a small branch of Chemical Bank in the borough of the Bronx, who had been accepting the cash flow of the Paul Lucas heroin mob. Lucas was a small-time operator who drew limited supplies from returning Vietnam veterans, retailing a few million dollars a year in heavily cut heroin and laundering the dirty money through the corrupted branch. When police moved in, they found the bank's entire vault piled ceiling to floor with small bills. The branch was at the limit of its physical capability to handle additional cash.

What makes these facts so extraordinary is that the $3 million a year passing through that single branch, clogging its vaults, represented barely one-fifth of 1% of New York City's annual drug money flow of $15 billion. (The figure is an estimate of New York Drug Enforcement Administration officials as of

1977. It has skyrocketed in recent years.) If all the dope traffic
in the city went through similar channels, 500 bank branches
would be required to handle the volume of cash!

Again, during 1980, Treasury investigators announced a
"crackdown" on a group of small Miami banks, which, they
said, accepted a large volume of funds over the counter from
narcotics traffickers. Eighteen banks were named in hearings
before the Senate Banking Committee on June 6, 1980, where
Treasury officials bragged of the success of their enforcement
operations. But the banks involved had allegedly accepted sums
in the magnitude of $1 to $2 million each. Compared to the size
of Florida's dope traffic, estimated by the Senate Permanent
Investigations Subcommittee to exceed $13 billion, the scale of
operations the Treasury says it uncovered is extremely modest.
Again, if we assume that this is the dope trade's modus operandi, we are forced to imagine that thousands of banks are
involved in this traffic.

Prior to the Senate hearings, the national press was filled
with stories about drug money laundering in Florida, citing
Treasury sources. These articles spoke of teenagers in jeans
and T-shirts walking calmly into banks with suitcases full of
cash for deposit, and even phoning in advance, at the bank's
request, to be sure that sufficient tellers were on hand to count
it all.

Lurid as this information is, on closer inspection it fails to
tell us very much about the way $200 billion could be hidden
from the eyes of the tax and drug enforcement authorities. On
the contrary, if it were all so simple, the dope trade would stand
out like a sore thumb. Under federal legislation, every bank
must file a report with the Internal Revenue Service on every
cash deposit in excess of $10,000. Even if the dope traders
funneled smaller amounts than $10,000 into their accounts, the
sudden buildup of cash in a bank account would immediately
arouse the suspicion of bank officials, according to investigator
Robert Potter, the IRS assistant director for criminal investigation.

Large commercial banks with computerized internal operations employ supersophisticated methods to monitor what hap-

pens to their internal cash flow, mainly to prevent embezzlement. Any unusual cash transfer out of the bank, and especially cash transfers out of the country, would be picked up and audited by the banks' computers, which are programmed to pick up any unusual disturbances in the banks' normal pattern of operation. Using an advanced mathematical technique called "spectrum analysis," these programs are highly effective against embezzlers—unless the embezzlers are equipped with their own computer programs to fool the banks' computers, and so forth.

In the good old days of the dope trade, the Meyer Lansky syndicate operation was able to transfer huge amounts of cash by suitcase on airplanes to safe offshore banking havens. There was a group of corrupt entities, including Bernie Cornfeld's Investors Overseas Services and Tibor Rosenbaum's Banque du Crédit International in Geneva, which handled mammoth amounts of dirty money. We will meet these gentlemen in later chapters. However, it is fair to point out that we know about them in such great detail because they were closed down in 1974 and audited after-the-fact with a fine-toothed comb. Rosenbaum is reportedly in a jail in Tel Aviv; Cornfeld, after a short spell in a Swiss prison, is in retirement in Los Angeles; and his successor at IOS, Robert Vesco, has been a fugitive from justice in the Bahamas, Costa Rica, and most recently, in Cuba. Yet the dope trade continues.

Airline hijackings, ironically, wrecked Dope, Inc.'s primary means of laundering its money. Close inspection of all baggage makes it impossible to transfer physical cash abroad in sufficient amounts to make a dent in the $200–500 billion the dope traffic must hide.

Superficially, the maze of checkpoints and controls arrayed against mere tax evaders, let alone narcotics traffickers, appears insurmountable. Yet these controls have a flaw. They are designed to spot the *abnormal*, the unusual funds transfer, the big cash deposit, the suitcase full of small bills. If the reader is beginning to suspect that thousands of bankers and IRS officials are all in on the game, we emphasize that no such thing is, or could possibly be the case. Dope, Inc. is a tightly run little network. What makes it effective is that there is nothing "abnormal" about it; it is built into the business structure of the United States and a number of other countries.

The mystery may seem even more impenetrable, but we are actually at the starting point of its solution. Let us view this part of the narcotics cycle from the top: Retail dope dealers take well over $200 billion a year off American streets and school corridors. Most of this money, though not all, flows in one way or another back to wholesale traffickers who need to "launder" it. They start with close to $200 billion in cash, and end up with bank accounts in the British-protected offshore banking havens in the Caribbean or Asia.

Here is what one senior Drug Enforcement Administration officer had to say about the laundering process, in an interview with the authors:

Q: How much in dope revenues comes out of New York City each year?
A: $10, 12, 15 billion, perhaps. That's $1 billion in heroin and who knows how much of everything else.
Q: How can that much money be hidden from public view or the Internal Revenue Service?
A: Most of it is washed [turned into legitimate bank accounts] in Miami.
Q: How does it get down there—in cardboard cartons?
A: What cartons? It gets sent down there through normal bank transfers.
Q: How does it get into New York City in the first place?
A: Through legitimate businesses—that's the best cover possible.
Q: Wasn't the biggest money-washing operation ever busted in New York, the case where the Lucas mob in the Bronx was using a branch of the Chemical Bank to launder $5 and $10 bills right off the street? They had to launder an entire vault filled up with dope money.
A: That's right.
Q: But the total capacity of that operation, which used an

entire branch of a commercial bank, was no more than $3 or
$4 million a year.

A: That's my recollection.

Q: In other words, it only handles less than half of 1% of all
dope revenues going through New York?

A: That appears to be correct.

Q: So what kind of legitimate businesses are we talking
about?

A: Very big legitimate businesses. That's all I can say about
it.

This is a good start. Who has the cash flow to siphon in small
bills off the street in large volume, camouflaged in an even
larger volume of cash? Gambling casinos, sports stadium concessions, department stores, and so forth. Later, we will trace
the history of Resorts International, America's biggest gambling operation, into the command structure of Dope, Inc. When
casinos go to the bank at the end of the day, they deposit cash
in the form of several giant canvas bags, wheeled in on what
looks like an immense clothes rack. An extra million or two a
day starts to add up to big money. But it is not merely gambling
casinos, which are under fairly intense scrutiny, but a host of
other "legitimate" fronts. We will meet shopping-mall czar Max
Fisher, the stadium concessionaire Jacobs brothers, and other
operators later in this volume.

Even if a large "legit" business manages to get its illegal
money into a bank account, it runs into the maze of controls
described earlier. How does it evade it?

"The thing every company is most afraid of is that it will—
inadvertently—become a host for some sort of criminal operation," a senior official of one of New York's largest financial
houses told the authors. "But it can be very hard to track down,
what with the pressure to keep down the cost of operations. You
just can't check into every transaction."

What sort of financial business is typically used to handle
large amounts of illicit money without detection? the question
came back.

"There are certain sorts of accounts," the executive said,

"which are virtually foolproof means of moving illicit funds. The most reliable is the type of account maintained by someone dealing in the financial market, buying and selling large amounts of securities every day. You will be cashing in stocks, bonds, or commodities futures, and using the proceeds to buy new securities, almost every minute. Tens of millions could go through the account every day, even if the balance at the end of the day is only a few thousand dollars. No one would notice an extra few million dollars passing through."

How can banks stop this? he was asked.

"You can't do much after you let them open an account," the financier concluded.

Someone in the bank must be witting, usually the corporate banking officer who clears the business relationship in the first place. The rest of bank management may know nothing about it. One well-placed employee of Dope, Inc. in a high position may be enough.

The Strange Case of Midwest Air

In following the trail of physical narcotics shipments into the United States, the investigator almost stumbles upon the secrets of Dope, Inc.'s money laundering.

There was a small "air taxi" and charter cargo airline company based in Elyria, Ohio, outside of Cleveland, called Midwest Air Charter, Inc. Twenty percent of Midwest Air was owned by Airborne Freight out of Seattle. Airborne is controlled by the New York investment bank Allen and Co.

According to the *New York Times,* Allen was Meyer Lansky's investment banker. Charles Allen's number-two man, Allen and Co. President F. William Harder, sat on Airborne Freight's board. Detroit's Max Fisher, Allen's closest business associate, also controlled a major block of shares in Airborne.

Two things are of special interest about Airborne Freight.

First, according to Midwestern law enforcement officials, it handled a large volume of dope coming in from the Far East, and used Midwest Air Charter for its distribution throughout the United States.

Second, its story takes us into the executive suite of New York's Chase Manhattan Bank, and into the Federal Reserve System itself.

Airborne's widespread Pacific network made it almost inspection-proof, according to U.S. Customs officials. Containerized shipments brought in through Seattle, Airborne's headquarters, were not closely inspected by airport customs, who do not have a tenth of the manpower required for this sort of work. The containers were taken directly off Airborne's planes, loaded onto trucks, and broken down well out of the way.

Alternately, drug shipments may be brought into the United States from Canada's northwest province, crossing the border into Alaska, and then shipped—free of customs—to the port of Seattle. A subsidiary of the Hongkong and Shanghai Bank, Canadian Pacific Transport, moves this freight across remote Alaskan border points, according to law enforcement sources.

But Airborne's subsidiary, Midwest Air, is even more interesting. Its biggest client was the Federal Reserve System. The line's average flight was, by its own estimate, 40% Federal Reserve business.

The Fed ships huge numbers of canceled checks every day between the twelve regional Federal Reserve banks, in the process of collecting payments between different localities. Large commercial banks employ fleets of private planes to handle their own collections, and the Federal Reserve provides a service either for smaller banks, or for low-priority collections of the larger banks. The bags of checks were shipped by Midwest Air, under a contract that began in 1973.

Midwest's service had not been good. According to Cleveland Federal Reserve Bank officer Norman Hagen, who managed part of the Fed's clearing system, "When Midwest Air bid for renewal in July 1978, they underbid incredibly, by almost $2 million. Of course they got the new contract. But since then, their service to the Fed System has collapsed. They just stopped shipping our checks, which would pile up at airports. They seemed more interested in shipping the growing freight contracts of their other customer, Airborne Freight. They claimed to be shipping at least 40% Fed cargo, 60% Airborne cargo on the average flight. I don't believe it. I think Airborne, which would like to own Midwest 100%, is dumping their cargo instead on our flights."

Hagen continued, "By early 1979 this lag in service was causing a major problem with the 'float,' that is, the balance of unsettled checks outstanding in the Fed system. All Midwest Air has to do is delay shipments by four or five hours a day and at one point some $14 billion in unsettled checks a day, was ballooning up in the money supply. Midwest then insisted we had to pay them more money—of course they had only submitted the original low bid because Airborne is subsidizing their flights—so they could buy more planes. But the problem is still there."

Midwest's service to the Federal Reserve became so bad that it threw the accounting of money supply off-kilter, and occasioned an investigation by a displeased House Banking Committee panel. No one showed the company the door, however, and the firm continued to carry the Fed's canceled checks.

Midwest Air Charter did not make money from the Fed's business, nor did it have much interest in fulfilling its obligations. But it had a major advantage in maintaining the contract. The Fed's priority cargo was never inspected by law enforcement officers, nor delayed by airport officers. It is immune to any normal checkpoints. If Midwest planes were also transporting narcotics, that was an extremely useful feature of the business.

It makes sense that Max Fisher and Charles Allen would run outfits like Airborne Freight and Midwest Air. It does not make sense that the Federal Reserve would tolerate shoddy service—or does it? Upon examination, Midwest turned out to have some powerful friends in the banking sector.

"We set up Midwest Air," retired Cleveland National City Bank Senior Vice President Fred Hogg has bragged. "Joseph Garrigy, the founder and now president of Midwest, came to me in the early sixties with no money, no customers, and one plane. I gave him National City's business of moving our checks around the state, and I called up every other Cleveland bank and got their business. Then I introduced him to the Fed."

Hogg introduced Garrigy to his friend Clifford G. Miller, then senior vice president at the Cleveland Federal Reserve. By 1967, Miller, whose number-two man in charge of Cleveland Fed transportation happened to be Hogg's son-in-law Norman Hagen, had gotten Midwest the contract to carry all checks and other "time-sensitive" financial documents for the entire Cleveland Fed district.

By late 1972, Hogg and Miller arranged with Harry Schultze, senior vice president at the Chicago Fed, to set up a unified national Interdistrict Transport System (ITS) headquartered in Chicago to transport all "time-sensitives." They advised Schultze to give Midwest the national contract.

"They submitted the lowest bid by far," said Schultze, and besides, "they were given clearance from the national headquarters of the Air Force Military Airlift Command. We didn't bother to check them out any further."

It is likely that the clearance was arranged through the National Bank of Cleveland's board member Claude Maclary Blair, who was a major general in the elite Air Force Intelligence Signal Corps. Also on the board of Midwest Air's sponsor, the Cleveland National City Bank, was Carl S. Ablon. Ablon is chairman of New York's Ogden Corporation, which in turn, was Charles Allen and Co.'s privately financed metals firm, whose directors include not only Allen himself but also Airborne's F. William Harder.

Also on the bank's board was James C. Donnell II, chairman of the Marathon Oil Co., of which Max Fisher was a founder and part owner.

What, precisely, do these high-ranking gentlemen know about Airborne Freight's illegal operations? Their business relationship with Max Fisher and the Allen brothers started with Midwest Air, and went all the way up to the National City Bank's board of directors. Either they were stupid, or criminal.

The Banking Nest

One character on the Airborne Freight board of directors is of even greater interest than the company's friends at National City Bank of Cleveland: one James H. Carey, then an executive vice president of the Chase Manhattan Bank in New York City. Carey was the top man in the corporate banking department who determines which companies may open accounts with the Chase Manhattan Bank. He had another distinction: Carey was a Knight of St. John of Jerusalem, the ultra-elite British chivalric order over which Queen Elizabeth presides. He was the only Chase Manhattan officer to hold that title.

Our investigators began to dig into Carey's history. During the early 1960s, he was a faceless junior executive in Chase's loan department. Then, in 1969, Carey left the bank to join the local branch of Hambro's, the leading British merchant bank. He quickly became the chief executive officer at First Empire Bank, a joint venture between Hambro's and R.H. Macy's in Buffalo, New York. First Empire boasted two directors from Macy's Department Stores. It also did the banking for Emprise, the Jacobs brothers' shady firm, and for most of the Buffalo dry-goods trade.

Chase Manhattan rarely promotes officers who leave the bank in mid-career and then return. Carey was the one exception among Chase's executive vice presidents, the rest of whom are bank career men. His connections were unusual. "We knew him through family connections up at Brown University," said British banker Richard Hambro, who now runs the family's American operations. "Then we sent him back into Chase. With his Brown University background and family, he was just the sort of person to impress [Chase Manhattan Chairman] Rockefeller and [Chase President Willard C.] Butcher." Among his colleagues, Carey was known as a corporate glad-hander without special banking talent.

But his sponsors at Hambro's were among the best-connected of Britain's elite: Richard Hambro's uncle, the late Sir Charles Hambro, was chief of Britain's Special Operations Executive during World War II, the superior of Sir William "Intrepid" Stephenson. That they brought their American protégé James Carey into the Order of St. John of Jerusalem is an indication that Carey performed more than off-hand services for his British friends to merit the highest symbolic honor that the British royal house can confer on an American.

What the Airborne Freight story thus led to was a tight little circle of anglophile bankers, sometimes in top management but often in the key secondary positions. The allegations made concerning Airborne's role in distributing narcotics are of less fundamental interest than the insight it provides us into how types such as Max Fisher and Charles Allen can establish relationships with major banking institutions, such as National City Bank of Cleveland and Chase Manhattan. The same set of characters keeps bumping into each other.

For example: Allen and Co. financed the first real estate purchases in the Bahamas to build Meyer Lansky's Hogg Island casino, which, with a deft change of hats, became Resorts International's Paradise Island Casino. Resorts created a new security firm, Intertel, to ensure things ran on track. Somehow the vice chairman of Macy's and a senior officer of Prudential Life Insurance ended up sitting on Intertel's board of directors. Prudential owned 15% of Hambro's, Macy's business partner in the career of James Carey.

Macy's is a strange company, for that matter. "Strictly speaking," said one of their managers, "Macy's is not a retail store. They don't make their money by selling goods. They use retail sales as an excuse to make short-term loans, overnight or one week loans, or to play the money markets. A lot of these short-term loans finance the pornography business in New York."

Macy's owned its own bank—the R.H. Macy bank—to manage all of its money-market operations. Hypothetically speaking, Macy's is the ideal entity through which to conduct really gigantic dirty-money transfers. At the retail end, its stores take in gigantic amounts of cash, enough to mask a very substantial flow of funds through illegal sources. At the high-finance end, Macy's does enough high-turnover securities business to pass billions of dollars per day through its innumerable bank accounts.

How Computers Can Lie

When we enter the brave new world of electronic funds transfer,[1] through which scores of billions of dollars change hands every day by the switching of computer-generated signals, the possibilities for dirty-money laundering are even greater. According to Robert Morris, a computer scientist at American Telephone and Telegraph's Bell Laboratories, here is how it works:

Any illegal owner of funds wants to put them into a bank account in order, for example, to transfer them abroad. He establishes a dummy corporation and gets an account at the bank. But if he builds up a big account through cash deposits, the bank will normally tell the Internal Revenue Service that the company has had an unusual flowthrough of funds.

Then how are the illegal funds transferred? If the dope trafficker has a collaborator inside the bank who works in the computer money transfer divisions and knows the bank's system for data coding, it is easy.

The dope trafficker writes a $10,000 transfer from his account at, say, Chase Manhattan to his account in an IRS-proof offshore banking center, perhaps at the Standard Chartered Bank branch in the Cayman Islands. His confederate at the computer adds one more message unit, transferring another $1 million, to the regular string of message units going from Chase Manhattan to the Standard Chartered Bank in the Bahamas. Simultaneously, the dope trader deposits $1 million of "laundered" illegal money in his "legitimate" account at Chase; $1 million came in, and $1 million—plus the $10,000 decoy transfer—go out. The bank's computers pick up no unusual movement of funds, particularly if the account is one where large sums of money come in and are withdrawn every day.

In 1979, a computer programmer at Security Pacific Bank in Seattle was arrested by the Federal Bureau of Investigation for doing exactly this. He simply had the bank's computer credit his account in Zurich, Switzerland with a nonexistent $11 million. The problem was that he did not leave the country fast enough, and was found out when the Swiss bank tried to collect the $11 million from the Security Pacific head office. The system is a tricky one for embezzlers, who wish to "create" money transfers out of thin air. But it is almost fail-safe for hiding large amounts of money. Once transferred, the illegal money disappears into the offshore banking havens, where no IRS men go.

Let us summarize the requirements for laundering $200 billion in dirty money:

1. The dope traffickers must have control of major legitimate business with cash turnover in the tens of billions per day, overall.

2. The dope traffickers must have a sophisticated money-market operation that trades a much greater volume of securities than the cash to be laundered.

3. The traffickers must have well-placed contacts inside the commercial banks themselves, international banking contacts, Cayman Islands accounts, and so forth.

From the Field to the Bank

When we read in the newspapers of a Treasury crackdown against a small group of Florida bankers who allegedly "wash" a few million in dope money, we should consider both what this tells us, and what it does not tell us.

Who, for example, are the teenagers who hand satchels of small bills over to bank clerks? For the most part they are the sewer rats of the dope trade, the smugglers who bring the physical goods in. They are highly paid, are highly expendable, and often greedy enough to be incautious. They do not have the infrastructure to launder their payments quietly through the channels described. Of the $13 billion Florida dope trade—if the 1980 Senate Committee's figure is accurate for that year—probably less than $300 million, or 30% of the wholesale cut, accrued to the smugglers themselves. From what the Treasury has alleged, somewhat less than this has been deposited by traffickers in the eighteen banks cited before the June 6, 1980 panel.

The smugglers are paid off by the growers in Latin America, in the case of the Florida-based marijuana and cocaine traffic. These are almost entirely old landed families, who also grow sugar, which needs the same terrain as marijuana, and coffee, whose growing conditions are identical to those of coca. These are major powers in nations like Colombia or Bolivia or Peru. The old landed oligarchy has direct channels into the New York, London, and Caribbean banking markets, and accounts on the world's major commodities exchanges.

Take the example of the Italian firm of Mocca Coffee, controlled by one of Italy's oldest oligarchical families, that of Count Barnabo. Count Barnabo came to international attention when Italian authorities arrested him in 1979 for helping to arrange the escape from a Costa Rican jail of two right-wing Italian terrorists, Fredda and Ventura. Those two had fled Italy after planting a bomb in a public piazza that had killed dozens of bystanders.

Mocca Coffee dealt with the landed oligarchy in Central and South America. It also used its large shipments of coffee into the United States to transport a fair volume of cocaine, according to commodity market sources. Mocca was paid for the drugs in New York, in cash. The cash never left the United States.

Mocca went to a British national who controls the coffee market division of one of New York's larger commodities trading houses. It paid cash for a futures contract betting both for *and* against the same month's, or adjacent month's, contract on coffee futures. The British national who made the order wrote two tickets, one of which would go up in value, the other of which would go down, as the market fluctuated. When Mocca wanted to collect, the corrupt commodity trader tore up the

losing ticket. The loss was met with Mocca's original cash deposit—and commodity brokers did not have to report cash, unlike commercial banks. The record of the transaction, however,
disappeared from Mocca's account at the brokerage house.
Mocca cashed in the winning ticket, and walked away with
what appeared to be legitimate commodity market earnings.
Not exactly simple, but highly effective.

The actual dope growers use a myriad of means to launder
their funds. It is an entirely different world than that of the
penny-ante smuggler with a few hundred thousand dollars
burning a hole in his pocket. Back during Prohibition, old Sam
Bronfman had the same problem with the petty racketeers who
drove the trucks across the border. They were greedy, and too
numerous. Meyer Lansky's Murder, Inc. provided the essential
service of weeding their ranks. It appears that today the same
service is performed for the dope traffic by the United States
Treasury.

While the Treasury has been poking around at small Florida
banks, several of the names encountered most often in this book
moved into Florida beginning in 1978, Standard Chartered,
Bank Leumi, and Bank Hapoalim, among others. According to
the Florida State Banking Commission in a June 1980 interview, "No one is even looking at the international banks." Why
should they? Standard Chartered Bank is not so stupid as to
accept suitcases full of cash over the counter. They are simply
following their clientele, including some large Latin American
cocaine planters, into the Miami area, banking their funds, and
helping them to invest in real estate or diamonds.

3

From Opium to Dirty Money

The starting point for the drug cash flow is the cash size of the opium and heroin traffic in the Far East, before the drugs obtain the stupendous price markups available in Western markets. The price pyramid, as the editors found it in 1978, was the following:

1. Raw opium, the gum of syrup extracted from opium poppies, is produced in the Golden Triangle, the conjunction of the southern border of the People's Republic of China (Yunnan Province) and the northern borders of Thailand, Burma, and Laos. The mountainous terrain, largely above 4,000 feet in elevation, provides ideal growing conditions. Mountain peoples, rather than ethnic Chinese (including those in Yunnan Province), grow the opium and collect the gum. The merchant pur-

chasing the gum pays roughly $100 a pound, at collection points such as Lashio or Mae Sai in Burma.

2. By the time the merchant, typically a Yunnanese, has brought the gum by mule train to the triborder area, for example, to Tachilek or Chiengmai in Thailand, the price has doubled, to $200 a pound.[1] At this point, the opium is either refined into heroin at refineries located in the triborder area itself, or earmarked for the large Far Eastern market for smoking-opium and related derivatives.

Existing data permit the estimate that a division of an average 700-ton crop into 300 tons for heroin refining and 400 tons for opium shipment for Far Eastern smoking purposes is usual.[2]

The $200 pound price at the triborder area is the price paid to the local agent by a wholesaler based either in Bangkok, Rangoon, or Hong Kong. Any distinction among these cities is meaningless. The business structure of the area is under the control of two principal groups that straddle the Far East. The first is the old British banks and trading companies, including the HongShang, Jardine Matheson, Charterhouse Japhet, Swire's, and the Peninsular and Orient Lines. The second, their satellites, are the overseas Chinese networks, under the joint control of London and Beijing.

The wholesale value of the 700 tons of annual opium produced in the Golden Triangle, prepaid in the triborder area, is roughly $280 million. But this wholesale figure is only a small portion of the cash flow of the Far East drug traffic. The next wholesaler, the Bangkok merchant who buys from the first wholesaler, pays about $1 billion for the equivalent of 700 tons of opium in the form of either raw opium or refined heroin. This is roughly four times what the opium was worth at the first wholesale round. The majority of production is retailed locally at large markups (although the markups are much smaller than in the case of heroin retailed in Western countries).

While no hard estimates are possible, the cash flow in the Far East related to this first phase of opium production alone was not less than $1 billion in 1978. That by itself is 15% of the 1978 assets of foreign banks in Hong Kong, or 10% of estimated bank assets of foreign banks in Singapore, or precisely Thailand's 1977 balance of trade deficit!

Measured against the size of economic activity in the region, there is no possible way to chalk these numbers up in the "Errors and Omissions" column. The cash must go through nominally legitimate channels, in such volume that the nominally legitimate channels—like the HongShang—cannot possibly be unwitting as to the origin.

Even these numbers do not sufficiently reflect the scale of the cash flow derived from crude opium sales alone. It must be added that most of this cash flow is seasonal; nearly all wholesaling must be completed during the two months following the March poppy harvest. Correspondingly, the visible flow of drug-related funds is several times as large during those two months.

4. Finally, the 1978 wholesale and local retail cash figures presented above exclude what is possibly the largest component of Far Eastern narcotics money: the reflow of funds back to the Far East from sales made in the West. The narcotics wholesaler in Bangkok or Rangoon or Hong Kong with direct contacts with the growers and control of refineries has paid about $2,000 a pound for the refined heroin. Between him and the street corner, the same pound of heroin will undergo three markups of 1,000%. Its ultimate retail value (for pure heroin) will be close to $5,000,000 per kilogram, according to official DEA figures, or *$2.27 million a pound,* with a total of $25 billion for Western sales.

What portion of this markup, and in what quantity, accrues to the Far East wholesaler? There is no possible way to estimate this. According to the record of arrests of heroin smuggling, a substantial portion of such smuggling is conducted directly through expatriate Chinese channels, like the Hong Kong to Vancouver route,[3] and the notorious activities of the Hong Kong Seamen's Union. However, it is this markup that pays the wholesaler's out of pocket costs, including the original purchase from the highlands merchant, the refining, the huge quantity (perhaps 300 tons annually) of acetic anhydride used in heroin

refining, security, bribes, transportation, warehousing, and so
forth.

If the annual profit of the Golden Triangle operators is in the
range of $5 billion—or a mere one-fifth of the annual retail
sales of heroin in the West—then the total cash flow in the Far
East related to drugs is not $1 billion, but $6 billion. The actual
reflow is probably several times that sum. Some of the $5 billion
may be banked elsewhere than in the Far East. The comparisons to the size of the region's economic activity become all the
more grotesque: Thailand's 1976 total exports were only $2
billion. Even the $6 billion figure does not include the huge Far
Eastern market for opium and heroin consumption. Added in,
the retail volume brings the total close to $10 billion—twice
Hong Kong's money supply in 1978.

There is another way to arrive at the same $10 billion figure:
The *official* estimate for bribes paid annually to Hong Kong
police during the period of 1978 is an astonishing $1 billion,
more than the annual police budget. From a hard business
standpoint, that $1 billion in payoffs is a major part of the
overhead cost of both wholesale and retail drug operations in
Hong Kong, the area's drug capital. Since the known profit
margin in the drug trade is 500 to 1,000%, it is fair to state that
the $1 billion bribe figure is no more than 10% of the local drug
revenues. If $1 billion is 10% of the total, the total is $10 billion.

4
How the Drug Trade
Is Financed

The chain of financial control of world opium traffic begins in Hong Kong, with billions of dollars in Hong Kong dollar loans to expatriate Chinese operators in the drug-growing regions.

Hong Kong also provides essential logistical support, including:

1. Smuggler-sized gold bars, obtainable through Hongkong and Shanghai Bank subsidiaries;
2. Diamonds, available through Hong Kong's Anglo-Israeli controlled diamond monopoly; and
3. Warehousing facilities, dominated by a subsidiary of the Hongkong and Shanghai Bank.

The HongShang

The Hongkong and Shanghai Bank is the semi-official central bank for the Crown Colony, regulating general market conditions, holding excess deposits of the myriad smaller banks, providing rediscount facilities, and so forth. The Hongkong and Shanghai Bank is also the financial hydra unifying the production, transportation, and distribution of Asia's opium.

Not only does it dominate financial activity in Hong Kong, with 50% of total banking business on the island, but "bank and government often work closely together," the London *Financial Times* commented.[1] The colonial government in Hong Kong makes virtually no statistics on banking activity available. Commenting on the $8.3 billion figure for the Group of Ten bank operations in Hong Kong at that time, the *Financial Times* noted that "the official figures are also just the tip of an almost certainly greater volume of business, which is conducted by international banks with finance company subsidiaries in Hong Kong, or organized from Hong Kong but routed through entirely offshore accounts in such places as Vila [New Hebrides]."[2] To be precise, there were 213 deposit-taking finance companies in the colony, as well as 34 local banks and 104 bank representative offices. Over these squatted the HongShang, and it performs the same function today.

The Chinese Middleman

The essence of the bank's drug control is its intimate relationship to scores of expatriate Chinese banking families scattered throughout the Far East. The British and Dutch connection to these families dates back to the first East India Company penetration of the region. The central banking role of the Hong-Shang expresses an agreement that grew out of a century of official opium trade and continues through to the present.

First, consider the financial and logistical requirements of the trade. Planning for the March opium harvest begins in September. The Bangkok or Hong Kong drug wholesaler must estimate the size of his market during the next summer, and after the market research is completed, inform his agents in the triborder area. (That market research must come from the United States and other retailers.) They, in turn, will communicate to the Yunnanese and other merchants who operate in the poppy-growing highlands to the north what the market will bear for the next harvest. The merchants then inform the Meo peasants what acreage they may plant.

At this point, the wholesaler must consider the following. First, the physical means of payment must be obtained, including American or Soviet armaments, gold in appropriate small-bar or jewelry form, or whatever, and this to the tune of $140 million worth. Golden Triangle peasants cannot use American dollars. Thousands of mules and muleteers must be made ready for the treks into the highlands. Bribes must be paid, routes monitored, border conditions observed, smuggling routes mapped, contacts opened in the West, and other loose ends secured. The required seed money is in the range of the wholesaler's $2,000 a pound price for refined heroin.[3]

What portion of the investment is made through "internal resources" of the drug wholesalers, and what portion borrowed, is a matter of guesswork. It is known that a very large amount is borrowed seasonally to finance drug wholesaling, largely from expatriate Ch'ao Chou Chinese banking networks. Since the Ch'ao Chou category includes Thailand's most prestigious bankers, very considerable financial resources are at the traffic's disposal. It is a matter of a 200% annual rate of interest—agreed and no questions asked.

Known "angels" of the narcotics trade have included Chen Pi Chen, a.k.a. Chin Sophonpanich, chairman of the board of the Bangkok Bank; and Udhane Tejapaibul, former chairman of the board of the Bangkok Metropolitan Bank. Udhane, whose bank handles most of Thailand's chemical imports, developed the Golden Triangle's major source of acetic anhydride, the chemical required to refine opium into heroin, through a Hong Kong subsidiary of the Bangkok Metropolitan Bank. It is well known in Bangkok that Udhane also ran the city's opium dens, before they were shut down.

Such scandalous relationships are not much of a surprise in the region. At the time of the 1973 Thai coup, the premier's son and chief of the narcotics bureau, Narong Kittikachorn, was found to be a prominent investor in drug-wholesaling, part of an operation which also involved American figures to cash in on the Vietnam War.

The annual credit line that must be extended to drug wholesalers, assuming the figures presented above and that they finance half their operations through credit, probably comes to about $150 million. Through pure chance, that was the average annual growth of the Bangkok Bank's "Loans and Advances" over the decade 1968 to 1978.

Wherever the Ch'ao Chou expatriate banking community has surfaced in leading positions of influence, Beijing, British, and opium trade connections are evident. In 1958, the Thai authorities issued a fraud warrant against Bangkok Bank's Sophonpanich. He fled to Hong Kong and remained there until 1965, after which he returned. According to area sources, Sophonpanich still maintains close contact with the Beijing regime.

As one among several Bangkok financiers who finance the drug wholesalers in the volume of $100 to $200 million per year, Sophonpanich's contacts include several names that have frequently appeared on the "Opium Watch List" of American law enforcement agencies: Ying Tsu-li, General Lo, and the brothers Hutien-Hsiang and Hutien-Fa, leading refiners of heroin in the triborder area.

In addition, area sources report that Sophonpanich has direct links to the so-called Triads, the expatriate Chinese secret societies that do most of the legwork in the opium traffic.

Yet, Sophonpanich is actually nothing more than a subcontractor of the Hongkong and Shanghai Bank.

The HongShang-Chinese Deal

Bangkok Bank illustrates the way the chain of financing leads back to the HongShang. In 1978 its volume was $5 billion, much larger than the savings capacity of the area could justify. Banking sources reported that most of its credit-generating capacity came from rediscounting of the trade paper of the Singapore and Hong Kong financial markets, and mostly with the HongShang itself. The HongShang controls 50% of Hong Kong deposits and acts as the ultimate rediscount agency for the entire colony and much of the rest of Southeast Asia. Most of the Bangkok Bank's lending volume was subcontracted business, controlled by the HongShang. This relationship became somewhat attenuated after 1978 when the Bangkok Bank became a full-fledged commercial bank.

The British-Chinese expatriate link goes back as long as the British have been in the Far East. The British organized the systematic colonization of tens of thousands of Chinese expatriates throughout the area, and started them out in the lower levels of the business otherwise conducted by the East India companies and their successors.[4]

Even where Britain displaced early overseas Chinese financial interests from positions they had enjoyed in the precolonial period, they left them in local control or in a junior status in such areas as opium trading, and often virtually restricted them to those areas. As W.J. Cator notes in his book *The Economic Position of the Chinese in the Netherlands Indies*[5] and Purcell notes in *The Chinese in Malaya*,[6] Chinese monopolies of local opium and alcohol distribution continued in many Southeast Asian colonies, under the aegis of the colonial authorities, into the first decades of the twentieth century.

Colonial powers divested Chinese merchants of control of many trading monopolies granted by the precolonial local authorities, but left them in control of gambling and local drug and alcohol distribution because Chinese secret societies were uniquely equipped to handle them. The secret societies, representing branches of societies operating in southern China, theoretically pursued the aim of their founding—the overthrow of the Manchu Ch'ing Dynasty in Beijing. But as time wore on and the regimes remained in power, the societies abroad became less interested in the politics of their homeland and more in the instruments of overseas economic interests. As anthropologist William Skinner notes in his book *Chinese Society in Thailand, An Analytical History,*[7] the immigrant societies were usually headed by influential monopoly owners—opium traders, keepers of gambling and prostitution houses—who used the societies to further the interests of their monopolies.

In other economic sectors besides opium, it is common knowledge that overseas Chinese business interests were often employed as compradors, middlemen in the service of colonial banking and trading operations, indispensable due to their knowledge of the local market and their language abilities. The close economic relationships that certain sections of the Chinese business community enjoy with particular British banking interests date from that experience. At every point in the postwar political history of the region, the Chinese expatriate financiers have acted as consistent allies of the British and the Dutch. According to standard estimates, Chinese expatriate financiers currently control 60 to 80% of the economies of Indonesia, Thailand, and Malaysia.

What the size of Chinese expatriate dependency on the Hong Kong market is can only be guessed. However, the existing financial data show that the Hong Kong financial market is enormously oriented to foreign lending, in roughly the same proportion as the American banking system. One-third of all Hong Kong dollar-denominated loans—excluding the so-called Asiadollar market—are to foreign borrowers. Foreign lending stood at HK $18.47 billion in March 1978, against HK $39 billion in local loans.

Since the borrowers' market for Hong Kong, rather than American, dollars is limited to the areas of the Far East still under British financial sway, the HK $18.47 billion figure of overseas loans reflects the immense financial dependency of Burma, Thailand, and Malaysia on Hong Kong. The business is largely conducted through Chinese expatriate family ties.

In fact, most of Hong Kong's 250 locally registered finance companies are owned by Chinese expatriates.

The scale of expatriate Chinese operations, centered in Hong Kong and dependent on the Hongkong and Shanghai Bank, is gigantic. In 1978, the overseas Chinese community controlled 42% of the foreign trade of the Southeast Asian countries, compared to 32% of Western business, 18% of non-Chinese local firms, and only 8% of state-controlled trading companies. As of the most recent figures available, Chinese expatriate investments in the area totaled only slightly less than combined American, Western European, and Japanese investments (although recent Japanese expansion in the area may have shifted the proportion somewhat).

The activities of the corrupted section of the expatriate Chinese community in Southeast Asia have provoked a long series of clashes with national authorities—who have not generally been successful in limiting illegal traffic. The one exception is the British possession of Hong Kong, the center of illegal operations in the area, where the smugglers are members of Hong Kong's high society, as in the case of Macao gambling overlord Stanley Ho, who made his career smuggling strategic materials from Hong Kong to China via Macao during the Korean War.

5

Britain's Dirty Gold and Diamond Operations

One feature of the financing chain of the Far Eastern drug traffic—the Asian gold market—is a tipoff of the British (and especially Hongkong and Shanghai Bank) control over the entire process. It might seem strange to the general reader, but the gold connection was one of a handful of critical clues that led investigators up the chain of evidence that will eventually put the management of the HongShang and a few other long-established institutions behind bars.

Vast quantities of gold are absorbed into the Asian drug trade—an inestimable percentage of the 400 to 600 tons of the metal that pass through the Orient in a year, mainly through Hong Kong, and mainly through subsidiaries of the Hong-Shang. The trade could not run without it and other precious, portable, untraceable substances—like diamonds.

First of all, peasants of the Golden Triangle poppy fields do not appreciate secret accounts in the Bahamas. Furthermore, since the end of the Vietnam War, and the end of the widespread traffic in contraband and American arms and American dollars, the U.S. dollar in the form of acceptable currency is no longer an acceptable medium of exchange. They must be paid in food— which they do not produce themselves—goods, and gold or the equivalent.

Second, and more important, gold cannot be traced, although any bank transfer ultimately can. One bar of gold looks like any other; changing a bank balance into gold or diamonds, and then changing it back into a bank balance, is like crossing a river to avoid bloodhounds.

Gold is so important to the entire business that the metal's price is pegged to the price of raw opium in the Golden Triangle highlands. The dollar's fall in terms of the gold price from $35 an ounce before 1971 to about $225 in 1978 and $350 in January 1986 has also dramatically escalated opium wholesale prices. The escalation of the gold price over the past years has been so steady that all the numbers regarding the size of the opium trade would tend to be *underestimates*. One indication of the closeness of the gold-opium relationship is the well-known story that the CIA fieldmen in northern Laos carried both gold and opium, to use as means of payment to the local Meo population in case of need.

How Illegal Gold Travels

The American public will be shocked at how openly the Hong-kong and Shanghai Bank uses its monopoly in the Far Eastern gold trade to feed smuggling operations. Prior to the official opening of the Hong Kong gold market in 1974, HongShang openly financed the gold markets of Macao, the flagrantly crime-ridden island that plays "offshore" to Hong Kong's own "offshore" operations. Today the Hong Kong market is run top-down by Sharps Pixley Ward, a 51%-owned subsidiary of the HongShang. The Hong Kong market's current daily trading volume is in the hundreds of millions of dollars, on a par with London and Zurich.

Apart from Hong Kong, the other route for smuggled gold to the Far East is through the Persian Gulf sheikhdom of Dubai. The dominant commercial and gold market force in Dubai is the British Bank of the Middle East, a 100% subsidiary of the Hongkong and Shanghai Bank.

A 1972 description from one of Britain's best-known experts, Timothy Green of Consolidated Gold Fields, Ltd., is instructive on how the illegal flow of gold travels:

"It may indeed sound romantic, but it is a fact that both in 1970 and 1971 at least 500 tons of gold—that is to say half of all South Africa's production, or 40% of total gold production in the noncommunist world—passed through unofficial channels on the way to its ultimate destination."[1]

"Unofficial" channels, as the author proceeds to make clear, mean *illegal channels*. Most of the world's existing gold is held by central banks; prior to 1971, gold was the basis of central bank reserves. Gold dealings among banks, industrial users such as jewelers, and so forth, are also counted as "official" channels.

Despite this, judging from the activity of the Hong Kong market, the proportion of gold running into illegal channels has, if anything, increased, and the drug-related proportion of the illegal gold increased with it.

Green continues:

These unofficial channels usually start in gold markets such as Beirut [since defunct], Dubai, Vientiane, Hong Kong, and Singapore which I am discussing today. Their chief role— their raison d'être—is as distribution centers for the smuggling; they are entrepôts convenient to nations, which for a variety of reasons, forbid the official import of gold for commercial or hoarding uses. . . .

Dubai has become the largest gold market in the world, except for London and Zurich—no mean achievement for a sheikhdom with a population of around 60,000. Both in 1970 and 1971 Dubai had well over 200 tons of gold—indeed in

1970 the equivalent of a quarter of all South African production found its way along this golden pipeline to India and
Pakistan [and further East. Since the beginning of official
gold sales by the Indian government in 1977, and the reopening of the Hong Kong gold market, Dubai's importance
has attenuated somewhat]. . . .

By contrast to Dubai, a gold market that developed very
quickly to meet a special short-term need was Vientiane in
Laos. The market there grew with the escalation of the war
with Vietnam. And it grew because it was the nearest and
cheapest source of gold. . . . This gold which was bought as a
hedge against the constant devaluations of the Vietnamese
currency and to hide the vast black market profits made from
pilfered American arms and equipment, was paid for almost
entirely in cash. [Throughout the 1960s and 1970s, pilfered
American arms and equipment formed a major part of the
barter goods exchanged for opium in the Golden Triangle
highlands.]

Vientiane's short success made some impact on the oldest
gold market in the Far East—Hong Kong, or more correctly
Hong Kong-Macao, for the two are held together as it were by
a golden chain. Hong Kong, as a British Crown Colony, forbids
the private holding of gold bullion; only commercial gold of less
than 945 purity may be traded. To get around this regulation,
gold bullion has for more than twenty-five years made a curious sideways shuffle from Hong Kong to Macao and back again.
The gold bullion—in 995 good delivery bars—that comes into
Hong Kong by air from Europe and Australia . . . is transferred
in Macao, where it is melted down into Chinese 1.5 and 10 tael
bars. It then returns, stealthily, to Hong Kong. This traffic has
been presided over for many years by the Wong Hong Hon
Company which negotiated a series of two-year contracts with
the Portuguese authorities in Macao for exclusive rights for
the gold traffic. *The traffic was financed by the Hongkong and
Shanghai Bank.* [emphasis added]

That is, in the testimony of Britain's leading gold expert, the
HongShang financed illegal gold trade in Hong Kong itself,

prior to the reopening of the Hong Kong gold market, after which the HongShang subsidiary Sharps Pixley Ward took over the legal trade.

An Underestimation

Digging into the back archives, it is clear that Consolidated Gold Fields' 40% figure for smuggled gold in 1972 represents, if anything, a *moderation* of past trends. Earlier figures are much higher. For example, British author Paul Ferris in *The City*[2] claimed that in 1951 only 17% of all world gold production went through official channels; Ferris's report was based on interviews with the London gold pool. "What happens to the gold when it disappears into the economic undergrowth of the East is of no concern to the London bullion dealers," Ferris claimed, but as we will demonstrate, the London bullion dealers know precisely what happens to the gold in the Far East. The London bullion market is merely a subsidiary of Dope, Inc.

In the July 22, 1952 issue of *The Reporter,* an article under the byline of H.R. Reinhart, then the Far East correspondent of the *Neue Zürcher Zeitung,* estimated Asian gold smuggling at $150 million in that year. At today's gold prices, the figure would be over $1 billion for the same quantity of gold. The account bears impressive credentials, since first, *The Reporter* editor at the time was Harlan Cleveland, now a senior official of the Hubert Humphrey Institute after a stint at the top oligarchical think tank, the Aspen Institute; and second, the *Neue Zürcher Zeitung,* Switzerland's top daily paper, is linked through European aristocratic ties directly to the British monarchy.[3]

Reinhart identified a "Golden Loop, the circuitous path that leads from North Africa to the coast of Red China and back again as far west as India." The center of gold smuggling was the Portuguese-controlled island of Macao, where gold smuggling is legal, and "anyone who dares call a smuggler a smuggler can be sued for libel." Then the gold is smuggled into Hong Kong, and thence to the rest of Asia.

A mere 3% of the smuggled gold is seized by Hong Kong authorities, Reinhart noted, even though customs officials receive a 20% commission on all seizures; presumably, bribes to customs officials are more substantial.

Standard Western and Soviet sources estimate the smugglers' commission at 30 to 50% in such transactions. Soviet economist M.A. Andreyev reported: "According to a Chinese businessman in Singapore, smuggling yields a profit of up to 100% on invested capital, which is several times higher than the profit received in the basic branches of the island's economy. In Hong Kong the commission paid to smugglers amounts to from 30 to 50%." The point is that the gold trade itself would not be profitable, *unless it were only a bridge transaction in a much more profitable operation*—for example, narcotics traffic! That is the case.

But as Reinhart reported, "British justice, as dispensed by the magistrates' court in Hong Kong, extends even the benefit of the doubt to a suspected smuggler caught with the goods." That should not be a surprise at this point; as noted before, it was a matter of public record for a quarter-century that Britain's Hongkong and Shanghai Bank itself financed the gold smuggling!

One further crucial point—whose full importance will only emerge in the following sections—is that the People's Republic of China has been in on the illegal gold market since the 1949 Maoist takeover.

Gold flown into Macao, as noted above, was (before Hong Kong opened up its gold markets in 1974) resmelted into bars of less than 95% purity, whose trading the Hong Kong authorities hypocritically endorsed. The resmelting, Reinhart reported, was the business of the Kan Kuam Tsing Company in Macao. "On the Hong Kong exchange," the Swiss journalist added, "the buyer is not unlikely from the People's Republic of China." Since the P.R.C. buyer wants metal of monetary-reserve purity, above 95%, he takes the gold *back* to the Kan Kuam Tsing Company, and reconverts the gold back to a higher purity level.

Reinhart identified the firm Pao San and Co. as a regular vehicle for Beijing gold purchases during the early 1950s.[4]

According to Reinhart, the PRC entered the Hong Kong gold
market in 1950. The July 1978 announcement that thirteen
Communist-owned banks in Hong Kong would be permitted to
trade directly in the Hong Kong gold market thus only extends
an agreement that has been in force since the founding of the
People's Republic of China.

One Big Gold Pool

Apart from a relatively insignificant flow of gold into Hong
Kong from mines in Australia and the Philippines—insignificant compared to the 300 tons of gold traded in Hong Kong
during 1977 and the 600 tons traded during 1978—Hong Kong
depends entirely on the London gold pool for its supplies.

The London gold pool is the same operation as the Hongkong
and Shanghai Bank, controlled by the same London families
whose drug-running activities go back 150 years.[5]

There are two major South African gold producers, Anglo-
American and Consolidated Gold Fields (whose gold specialist
was quoted above); there is one major South African diamond
producer De Beers, largely owned by Anglo-American; and five
major London gold pool firms, who meet every day in the trading
room of N.M. Rothschild at New Court, St. Swithin Street,
London, to set the world gold "fixing." Examining these firms
individually, we discover such a manifold of connections that it
is meaningless to speak of the London and Hong Kong gold
markets as anything but branch offices of the same operation.

Hongkong and Shanghai's own gold-trading outlet is Sharps
Pixley Ward, of which the bank owns 51%. One of the five
London gold pool firms, Sharps Pixley, owns the remaining
49%. But Sharps Pixley itself is a fully owned subsidiary of
the London merchant bank Kleinwort Benson, whose deputy
chairman is Sir Mark Turner, the chairman of Rio Tinto Zinc.

Kleinwort Benson's George Young was the number-two man of British intelligence throughout the 1960s.

Rio Tinto Zinc itself was founded a century ago with the opium-trading profits of Jardine Matheson by a member of the Matheson family; the Mathesons are still large shareholders in the HongShang. The Matheson family's heirs, the Keswick family, still have their traditional seat on the HongShang board. Sir Mark Turner spent World War II at Britain's Ministry of Economic Warfare, which also employed Sir John Henry Keswick, and another HongShang board member, John Kidston Swire.

Hong Kong's second largest bank, the Standard and Chartered Bank, owns a majority share of another member of the London gold pool, Mocatta Metals. Standard and Chartered's predecessor, the Standard Bank, was founded a century ago by the British "race imperialist" Cecil Rhodes. Standard and Chartered is not only a close collaborator of the HongShang in such matters as the transfer of Red Chinese opium money, but heavily interlocked since the days of the official British opium trade.

One of Standard and Chartered's directors is the current Lord Inchcape, of Inchcape and Co. and the Peninsular and Orient Navigation Company, the latter dominating ocean freight in the Far East. Both companies are heavily represented on the HongShang's board of directors. Inchcape's father wrote the notorious 1923 Inchcape Report recommending continued British sponsorship of the opium traffic—despite the outrage of the rest of the League of Nations—in order to "protect the revenues" of then-British colonies in the Far East.

This example also indicates why the London gold pool's dirty money operations are a worldwide, not merely a Far Eastern, problem. Mocatta Metals, a subsidiary of Standard and Chartered's Mocatta and Goldsmid, operates one of New York's biggest dirty money-laundering operations.

Mocatta Metals' current chairman, Dr. Henry Jarecki, has been under investigation for years for illegal activities, although no indictment has yet been handed down. According to European intelligence sources, Jarecki's dirty money operation helps fund the activities of the Mossad, Israel's foreign secret intelligence service, in one of its key operating locations, New York City.

Jarecki is no small fry: He is a frequent gold columnist for British financial publications such as *Euromoney,* and rated a lengthy profile in the September 1978 issue of *Fortune* magazine. Nonetheless, he is eminently suited for the role of bagman for Israeli intelligence. In addition to law enforcement source reports of a shady personal past, including an involvement with drugs, according to published sources, approximately half of Jarecki's present staff of twenty-eight gold traders started out in the same Harvard Psychology Department that featured LSD-pushers Dr. Timothy Leary and "Baba Ram Dass," Richard Alpert, in the early 1960s.[6]

Midland Bank stands behind both Standard and Chartered and Mocatta and Goldsmid, with a 20% ownership of Standard and Chartered. It also wholly owns another London gold pool bank, Samuel Montagu. Sir Mark Turner is a director of both Midland Bank and Samuel Montagu. The Montagu family is heavily intermarried with the Rothschilds, Montefiores, and Samuels. One of the family's protégés is HongShang board member Philip de Zulueta.

N.M. Rothschild and Sons, which opened up operations in Hong Kong in 1975 to take advantage of the newly liberalized gold trading laws, and Johnson Matthey, the remaining members of the London gold pool, are also interlocked several times over with both the HongShang and the major South African gold producers, Consolidated Gold Fields and Anglo-American, who control between them 90% of South Africa's gold output.

The Diamond Black Market

Second in importance in the money-laundering process is the world diamonds market, whose single presiding manager is Sir Harry Oppenheimer of the De Beers Corporation. Oppenheimer is also the chairman of the larger South African gold producer,

Anglo-American. The Anglo-American and De Beers complex runs the Hong Kong side of the money-laundering diamonds operation on two levels—wholesale and retail. De Beers runs 85% of the wholesale diamonds market; through his intimate Israeli connections, Oppenheimer also runs the Hong Kong diamond market.

There are two points of special relevance for diamonds to the international heroin traffic. The first is that, in value relative to size and weight, diamonds are the closest approximation to heroin as a store of value for furtive use. Second, the De Beers-controlled international diamond cartel operates according to a pyramidal structure identical to that of the world heroin trade.

The use of expatriate ethnic networks for the dirtier side of the operations is also homologous, except that in the case of diamonds, largely Jewish networks take the place of Ch'ao Chou Chinese networks. Not coincidentally, there is almost as little publicly available information on international diamonds trade as on the heroin traffic.

South Africa's largest producer, De Beers, was the 1888 creation of Cecil Rhodes; in 1929, the company underwent reorganization by Sir Ernest Oppenheimer, of the Anglo-American family. De Beers controls the Central Selling Organization (CSO), which handles 85% of international diamond trade.

At ten "sights" each year, 300 clients purchase stones from the CSO. The list of these select clients is secret. After their purchase by the secret list of clients, the diamonds are sent to cutting centers for further preparation. The two dominant cutting centers are Antwerp and Ashqelon, in Israel. Antwerp's diamond-cutting and related trade is financed by the Banque Bruxelles-Lambert, controlled by the Lambert family, the Belgian cousins of the Rothschilds. Israel's (and also New York's) diamond business is financed by Bank Leumi.[7] In this context, it is also interesting to note that according to several informed sources, the Belgian banks have become prominent in Far East financing.

Within the individual centers, dealers trade among themselves on such exchanges as the New York Diamond Dealers

Club, the Ramat Gan in Tel Aviv, and the Antwerp Diamond
Bourse. No written records are kept of any transactions on these
exchanges; the agreements are sealed with a handshake. No
aspects of this trade are available for scrutiny by law enforcement agencies, even under American law, before the diamonds
reach the jewelry store level.

As *EIR* investigators discovered in 1978, Hong Kong's own
substantial wholesale diamond market was the virtual monopoly of the Union Bank of Israel; this bank was wholly owned by
Israel's largest finance house, Bank Leumi. Bank Leumi, in
turn, was under the control of Barclays Bank, on whose board
sat Harry Oppenheimer and the Oppenheimer family itself.
Bank Leumi's own chairman was Ernst Israel Japhet, of the
Charterhouse Japhet family whose fortune derived from the
official British opium trade during the nineteenth century!

Ten times a year, representatives from the Ramat Gan, Tel
Aviv's diamond exchange, go with Union Bank financing to the
De Beers Central Selling Organization "sights" in London, and
purchase one-third of the world diamond output.

Like the Beijing-British controlled Ch'ao Chou networks in
the Far East, Britain's Anglo-Zionist financiers are a cult unto
themselves, with their own family networks, rituals, and language. New York's diamond market consists, at the lower levels, mainly of members of the Hasidic sects resident in the
area. This exotic feature of the diamond traffic received public
notoriety after several unexplained thefts and murders occurred in the diamond trade during 1977.

Here again, the various firms involved are so closely intermarried, interlocked, and interowned with the major dirty
money banks, that the working of the dirty money apparatus
is totally integrated.

A case in point is Canada, the dumping ground for all aspects
of Dope, Inc. that feed into the United States. The Bank of Nova
Scotia, for example, was both the major gold dealer (and banker
for the second largest gold dealer, Noranda Mines), and the
major dirty money operator in the Caribbean.

The Bank of Nova Scotia has been notorious for bribing its
way into new branch offices in the Caribbean, violating local

currency laws, running flight capital against currency restrictions, "investing" in local businesses known to be intelligence fronts, and so forth. Nova Scotia's branch network in the Caribbean is the largest of any bank in the world, save Barclays, which has a similar pedigree. Gold is a useful medium for the special case of the Caribbean, where official restrictions make some bank transfers difficult. Conveniently, Nova Scotia leads the Toronto gold market.

The other leading gold market operator in Toronto at the time of the *EIR* investigation was Noranda Mines; its vice president, E. Kendall Cork, was a member of the board of directors of the Bank of Nova Scotia.

6

Hong Kong: The Capital of Heroin Financing

On August 27, 1985, Crocker National Bank of San Francisco was slapped by the U.S. Treasury Department with a fine of $2.25 million, the largest fine ever imposed on a bank by the federal government. The crime: Crocker had failed to report cash transactions totaling nearly $4 billion over a period of four years, in violation of the Bank Secrecy Act of 1980, which requires that a report be filed for all currency transactions over $10,000. Between 1980 and October 1984, Crocker failed to report 7,877 separate transactions, totalling $3.98 billion, about $3.88 billion of which involved shipment of U.S. currency from overseas banks. Crocker's general counsel Harold P. Reichwald explained the violations as an "honest mistake."

But Treasury officials thought otherwise. In fact, they believed that Crocker's transactions were linked to the heroin trade in Hong Kong. Out of the 7,877 transactions not reported, those totaling $3.43 billion, all involved six Hong Kong banks. These banks shipped large amounts of cash in small denominations to Crocker's central cash vault in San Francisco. These transactions "appeared to be evidence of large-scale money-laundering by international heroin traffickers," Treasury officials said. As the Treasury's Art Siddon put it, "Hong Kong is a major banking center and is also known as a major center of drug money. We're assuming that some of that money is laundered drug money."

The Hongkong and Shanghai Banking Corporation was one of the banks that sent the small-denominated cash deposits to Crocker. Indeed, the HongShang is the parent company of Crocker Bank. Since May, Crocker has been a wholly owned subsidiary of the London-based Midland Bank, which previously owned 57% of Hongshang. In his press conference announcing the fine, John M. Walker, Jr., assistant treasury secretary for enforcement and operations, noted that large volumes of Southeast Asian heroin that come into the United States are "financed out of Hong Kong."

In testimony before the House Select Committee on Narcotics Abuse and Control in 1984, Assistant Secretary of State Dominick Di Carlo pointed to Hong Kong as "the major financial center for Southeast Asia's drug-trafficking. Hong Kong-based trafficking organizations operate throughout the world. . . . Large numbers of heroin-trafficking ventures throughout the world are financed and controlled from Hong Kong. There is evidence that Hong Kong-based groups are involved in directing the smuggling of heroin into Europe and North America."

Hong Kong, and its premier bank, the Hongkong and Shanghai Banking Corporation, sit on top of the Golden Triangle drug production and trafficking. In 1979 and 1980, the trade suffered a drought, losing its share in the U.S. heroin market. In 1981 the rebound began—10% in 1981, 14% in 1982, and 19% in 1983. In 1983, heroin from Southeast Asia accounted for 41% of the heroin encountered in the Western United States.

Not so oddly, increases in U.S. currency repatriated from Hong Kong to the United States from 1982 to the first half of 1984, paralleled the consistent rise in Southeast Asian heroin marketed in the United States from 1981 to 1983, according to an investigation conducted by the President's Commission on Organized Crime released in October 1984. According to the report, "One U.S. financial institution in Hong Kong handled approximately $700 million in U.S. currency in 1982, more than $1 billion in 1983, and more than $600 million in the first half of 1984. While half this currency is shipped to the United States, the balance, all in $100 bills, is shipped to other countries, principally Switzerland," where the banks are about as secretive as those in Hong Kong. "Approximately 65% of the currency repatriated to this country is in $100 bills," the report noted. "The remainder is in smaller-denomination bills"—like those Crocker had taken in—"a telltale sign of drug-trafficking and money-laundering."

"This high volume of smaller denomination bills exceeds the total volume of all currency transactions with any European country," including West Germany and France, the report notes, looking askance at the proffered explanations for the repatriatiother than dope money. Evidently Crocker is not the only American bank involved in this business!

The British Crown Colony of Hong Kong, with the British Hongkong and Shanghai Banking Corporation at the top, is considered the number-one money-laundering center for the heroin trade. This was true when this book was first issued in 1978 and it is true today. Here is what we said about this extraordinary place in 1978:

Illegal drugs are the biggest business in the Far East—and close to being the biggest business in the world—but in Hong Kong, drugs do not merely dominate the economy: They *are* the economy. A look at the British Colony of Hong Kong gives us a picture in microcosm of the drugs and dirty money economy worldwide.

First, start with the fact that Hong Kong is the most drug-ridden place in the world, per capita. Official British police estimates have it that 10% of Hong Kong's population or 500,000 people, are hardcore addicts. Unofficial estimates run this figure up to 50%. A safe, conservative estimate is 20% or 1 million people—more than New York City's addicts. Assuming the daily cost of a serious opium or morphine habit in Hong Kong to run to about $10 U.S., the annual cash flow of retail drug sales at HongShang's back porch runs to about $3.7 billion.

As the region's central bank, the Hongkong and Shanghai Bank provides banknotes to its clients, among other services. Any reasonable estimate of Hong Kong's dirty money operations including the retail drug trade, as well as the notorious bribes to police officers, international drug-wholesaling based on the island, illegal gambling, and other forms of illicit transactions, must yield a shockingly large number. With a drugged-up population of that size, the life of Hong Kong's population must be organized around illegal activity.

Shifting focus to New York City for a moment indicates the magnitude of the world's drug-centered illegal economy. Most estimates put the city's addict population at 500,000 (and another 250,000 nationally). Assuming a $50 per day habit is average—which the federal estimates apparently do—this addict population must obtain $9 billion a year out of New York City's faltering economy to meet its needs.

Where does it get $9 billion? Not substantially through well-paying jobs. With rare exceptions that is physically impossible. Not from muggings; however bad matters seem, neither 500,000 muggings, nor a combination of muggings and burglaries, take place daily in New York City. Even prostitution could contribute only a small portion of the $9 billion annual habit of New York City's addicts.

Where does the money come from? From organized crime activity: the numbers racket, bookmaking, protection rackets, auto theft, stolen auto parts distribution, prostitution, pornography, arson-for-hire, and similar occupations. Drug addiction could not possibly exist without organized crime to provide the means of financing addiction. Law enforcement authorities estimate that 80% of all crime in New York City is drug-related.

The National Educational Television's 1978 series on the narcotics trade demonstrated irremonstrable nerve by repeatedly citing the view of the (well-paid) Royal Police of Hong Kong that the narcotics traffic will always exist as long as there is a market. The market for the worst form of human misery not only *is* the most centrally organized of any market in the world, but could not possibly exist in any other way. If the demand provokes the supply, one might ask, why do narcotics wholesalers produce roughly ten times what addicts can consume annually?

Hong Kong is the capital of the world's illegal drug economy. This explains some of its most notable characteristics: the biggest illegal market in dirty money, drugs, and gold; the world's biggest liquidity ratio; and the world's biggest bribe rate.

The annual exports of the Colony this year (1978) will be no more than $8 billion; as we have seen, it will take in more than $10 billion in drug and drug-related financial activity.

Apart from retailing and wholesaling of drugs, huge sectors of the island's economy are indirectly dependent on the drug traffic. Exemplary is the booming gold market, whose turnover doubled from 305 tons in 1976 to 600 tons (worth $43.6 billion) in 1977. Some several hundreds of millions of dollars of gold go directly to the Golden Triangle; hundreds of millions more absorb and hide the profits of drug traffickers across the Far East.

Highest Liquidity Ratio

Hong Kong's drug traffic and the regionwide illegal dealings surrounding it undoubtedly account for the Colony's chronic excess of liquidity (see *International Currency Review,* vol. 10, no. 4, for a descriptive analysis). Year-to-year growth in money supply as of April 1978 was 25%; however, some of that is attributable to inflows of foreign currency related to the opening of an offshore Hong Kong bond market. Over the past fifteen years, the huge volume of external lending tended to suppress the otherwise huge money supply needed to finance several billions of illegal activity on an island whose reported money supply is now about $4.5 billion. According to an article in the London *Financial Times,* July 4, 1977, offshore business booked through Hong Kong was formerly so large that the liquidity ratio of the banks (taking into account both cash and redis-counted offshore bills of exchange) stood at an extraordinary 50%. Most of the local money supply was in the form of cash.

In effect, the cash-based local drug traffic in Hong Kong created a reserve base for offshore lending to finance the drug traffic in the rest of Asia! Since 1975, however, the development of the offshore bond market and the influx of foreign capital has led to the reduction of the liquidity ratio to a still extraordinary 43%.

Understandably, even *public* business practice in Hong Kong is politically corrupt. The HongShang's entirely open role in gold smuggling between Hong Kong and Macao was noted above. The *Financial Times* article reported a scandal of that year in which Wheelock Marden, a trading company listed on the Hong Kong Stock Exchange, provoked an investigation by the Securities Commission, after a "modestly optimistic state-ment" was followed by "revelation of huge profits drop, dividend cut, write-offs and liquidity problems."

The *Financial Times* wrote, "Insider trading is rampant. . . . These flurries may be attributable to leaks by clerks, secretaries and translators, rather than to insider trading at the top. But who can blame these lesser lights when Mr. John Marden is still chairman of Wheelock Marden, still sits on the board of the Hongkong and Shanghai Bank, is still a pillar of 'respectable' colonial society?"

Biggest Bribe Rate

Law enforcement sources report that the "lesser lights" are generally taken care of through the world's most efficient brib-ery system. At least $1 billion is passed out to Hong Kong's officialdom.

According to a report in the same London *Financial Times* article cited above:

Perhaps a billion dollars a year flow into the syndicates, admits Mr. Jack Cater, Hong Kong's head of the Independent Commission Against Corruption (ICAC), started in February. The sum gives one clue to the size of the problem the ICAC has to tackle. Another, Mr. Cater points out, is the extent of official and in particular police corruption in the Colony. With membership varying from 10 to 300, there are at least 28 identifiable public sector syndicates, and 25 of them are in the Royal Hong Kong Police Force. . . .

The ICAC has considered about 9,500 reports on corruption, about 85% of them involving Her Majesty's service. Reports of police crime (4,000) have regularly accounted for more than half the reports of government crime. . . . Mr. Cater has failed to bring back the many wealthy and mostly Chinese noncommissioned police officers who left Hong Kong before the ICAC cast its net.

The largest concentration of the last-mentioned is in Vancouver, British Columbia, where they are still active in the narcotics traffic, according to law enforcement specialists.

The $1 billion figure cited can be counted as overhead on the narcotics and related drug traffic in the area. Earlier, the local Hong Kong and related drug traffic was estimated at about $4 billion, and the area's drug-wholesaling business at $3 million and more. Assuming that bribes of police and other officials—what most of the $1 billion cited represents—amount to no more than 10 to 15% of the volume of drug traffic, retail and wholesale combined, then the estimates for the size of the drug traffic already made are unquestionably on the low side. The $1 billion in Hong Kong corruption annually estimated by the authorities, indicates drug traffic in and through Hong Kong of close to $10 billion. That figure, of course, does not include bribes to customs officials at Bangkok, Rangoon, Singapore, and elsewhere, let alone bribes to Thai and Burmese army officials.

To the extent that limited efforts at giving the appearance of honesty have come to pass in Hong Kong, both the police and the Chinese expatriate community have risen in revolt against them. In 1977 police rioted uncontrollably against so-called anti-corruption efforts. The July 4, 1977 *Financial Times* account noted that the crusade "enraged Chinese business in particular. . . . In a rare display, the Chinese Manufacturers Association [pro-Beijing] and the Kowloon Chamber of Commerce held a mass rally to protest against 'interference in Chinese ancient customs.' "

Such ancient customs indicate the nature of Hong Kong and its bank. According to custom, no bribes are solicited, none offered. Instead, couriers make their rounds through the Royal Hong Kong Police and other official buildings early each Monday morning, leaving an envelope containing between one and five hundred-dollar bills in the top drawer of every desk. Any policeman who refuses to take his envelope will probably be dead within forty-eight hours, according to law enforcement officials.

1986: Hong Kong and Free Trade

Is it any wonder that Hong Kong, the fully deregulated heroin financial capital of the world, the crowning achievement of the East India Company, is the model for the "free trade" ideologues that infest Washington? Take the testimony of one such ideologue—Milton Friedman, who declared in his 1980 book, *Free to Choose:*

In today's world big government seems pervasive. We may well ask whether there exist any contemporaneous examples of societies that rely primarily on voluntary exchange through the market to organize their economic activity and in which government is limited. . . . Perhaps the best example is Hong Kong—a speck of land next to mainland China containing less than 400 square miles with a population of roughly 4.5 million people. Hong Kong has no tariffs or other restraints on international trade. . . . It has no government direction of economic activity, no minimum wage law, no fixing of prices. . . . It is somewhat ironic that Hong Kong, a Crown Colony of Great Britain, should be the modern exemplar of free markets and limited government.

Friedman is not unaware, of course, that the main prop on the Hong Kong economy, is the drug trade. However, that does not bother Friedman, any more than it bothered the Crocker National Bank that the $3.48 billion in small denomination bills they were taking in had been made off the destruction of a generation of American youth. True to his values, Friedman advocates the legalization of marijuana and heroin. In an interview on the Phil Donahue show April 16, 1980, Friedman enunciated his libertarian brand of immorality. Arguing first that suicide is a basic human right, Friedman then continued:

Even if on ethical principles, you believe it is right to prevent somebody else from smoking marijuana, as a matter of expediency, it's a terrible mistake. . . . I mean, it's a terrible mistake for society to render heroin illegal, because that increases the harm which heroin does. Why do we have so much crime in the inner cities and in the cities? Over 50% of it is attributed to crime for the sake of acquiring money to buy heroin.

Friedman's advocacy of the dope trade stems not only from his personal credentials as a public relations officer for Dope, Inc. Dope right now, it can be shown, is the only thing keeping the U.S. economy afloat—after the collapse the productive economy has suffered from Friedman's free trade theories! As of 1986, the volume of global foreign exchange trading stands at $150 billion per day! However, in all such speculation, there are (by definition) as many losers as winners; everyone can't make a living out of a floating crap game. What has held the Eurodollar market together is Friedman's brand of free trade—that is, the underground economy. This includes the $500 billion a year in global narcotics traffic; the $100 billion a year in illegal arms-trafficking; and several hundred additional billions in flight capital, tax evasion, and other sorts of "free trade."

Skeptics are referred to the U.S. balance of payments tables. During the first half of 1985, according to official government numbers, almost half of America's $120 billion a year balance-of-payments deficit was financed by parties unknown, who took precautions to ensure their investments in the United States were hidden. Analysts at the Federal Reserve Board, the Commerce Department, and the International Monetary Fund believe that the biggest source of revenues from the parties unknown is narcotics traffic, and that the second biggest is flight capital from developing countries.

That is, in hard numbers: The United States was importing $124 billion per year more than it was exporting, as of the first half of 1985. Of that, $50 billion in financing of the trade deficit is reported in the official data, as "net errors and omissions." In other words, the U.S.A. could not account for $50 billion a year in money coming into the United States, enabling the country to pay its trade deficit.

That is not the end of it. American companies, and various U.S. government agencies, are borrowing at a $35 billion annual rate from the offshore entity known as the "Eurobond market," founded in the first place to enable parties unknown to buy income-yielding securities without being traced. This market used to be a relatively small, dirty corner of the world financial market; it is now "closely lagging" behind the U.S. government debt market, the largest market for securities in the world, according to Crédit Suisse-First Boston, the London firm which dominates the market.

Fifty billion dollars a year of "errors and omissions," plus $35 billion a year of "Eurobonds,"adds up to $85 billion, or more than two-thirds of the United States' annual external financing requirement, from sources the U.S. government cannot identify.

The U.S. economy and banking system are therefore being propped up by the international dope trade, which at the same time acts as a cancer on the productive economy. It is not, as Milton Friedman argues the case, that toleration of the dope trade is a natural philosophical outgrowth of commitment to free trade. The converse is the case. From the East India Company's Adam Smith down to his progeny Milton Friedman and former Treasury Secretary Donald Regan, the idea of fully deregulated economies—which the free trade paradise of Hong Kong represents—is a practical necessity for the international narcotics trade. After all, in Hong Kong, Crocker National Bank never would have been caught.

7

The Beijing Connection

Some of them [U.S. troops in Vietnam] are trying opium. And we are helping them. . . . Do you remember when the West imposed opium on us? They fought us with opium. And we are going to fight them with their own weapons. . . . The effect this demoralization is going to have on the United States will be far greater than anyone realizes.

Chinese Prime Minister Zhou Enlai, in conversation with Egyptian President Nasser, June 1965[1]

The Hong Kong-British-China connection that controls the Far East drug trade is personified in the figure of Sir Y.K. Pao, the British knight who sits on the board of the Hongkong and Shanghai Bank as well as the board of Chase Manhattan, runs the world's largest merchant fleet, his Worldwide Shipping Group, and has equal access to the Queen of England and China's most powerful leaders. He was made a knight of the British Empire in 1979 for "breathtaking ascent to the pinnacle of world trade" and was the first overseas Chinese to be officially received in Beijing, in 1980.

In 1982, the events surrounding the visit to China of British Prime Minister Margaret Thatcher give a flavor of the tight relationship that exists between the British and the Chinese businessmen of Hong Kong and the mainland. As Reuters reported it on September 25, 1982, in a story datelined Shanghai:

> British Prime Minister Margaret Thatcher named a ship for a Hong Kong millionaire in a Chinese shipyard today and described it as a symbol of the close relationship between China, Britain, and Hong Kong. Mrs. Thatcher earlier flew to Shanghai from Beijing where she had talks with Chinese leaders on the future of Hong Kong. . . . In a joint statement after her final discussion with elder statesman Deng Xiaoping, the two sides agreed to open negotiations through diplomatic channels on the question. Britain and China had the common aim of maintaining the prosperity and stability of Hong Kong, the statement said. On arrival in Shanghai, China's biggest city, Mrs. Thatcher had lunch with Sir Y.K. Pao, head of Hong Kong's Worldwide Shipping. She then went to the Jiangnan shipyard and performed the naming ceremony for his 27,000-ton freighter, *World Goodwill*. She told Shanghai's Mayor Wang Daohan: "The ship is the symbol of the close relationship between China, Britain, and Hong Kong."

It is through this triad, that the People's Republic of China reaps its share of the profit in the international drug trade, in keeping with the strategy of Zhou Enlai, whose protégés are in power in Beijing today. Only since Henry Kissinger's 1972 trip to China has the Chinese role in the world opium trade been out of the headlines. The American, European, and Japanese authorities had long insisted that Beijing was a major primary producer and exporter of opium and its derivatives, and the British, under extreme pressure from abroad, had to assent.

The highlights of the public record to this effect follow below in this section. However, even the most compelling documentation of Beijing's role in opium production misses the point.

Red China's revenues from opium exports, as we will demonstrate, are a mere $800 million annually.[2] Beijing makes its real profits in the wholesaling, retailing, and financing of the opium traffic, mainly through Hong Kong, where the big money is made. The People's Republic of China has taken active part in the gold-smuggling side of drug-financing in the Orient since 1950.

But since the late 1950s, Beijing has deliberately integrated its external financial affairs with the top British drug-running firms in Hong Kong and Macao, and the overseas Chinese drug wholesaling and dirty money networks throughout the Orient. Y.K. Pao, member of a banking family who fled Shanghai in 1949, is at the pinnacle of the relationship that exists between the overseas Chinese and the government on the mainland, a relationship which China's Open Door policy of the Deng era has made all the easier.

Beijing's financial dependence on Hong Kong is a matter of public record. On October 2, 1978, Chase Manhattan's newsletter *East-West Markets* estimated that the financial flow into mainland China in 1978 (excluding exports) through Hong Kong would total $2.5 billion, up from $1.3 billion in 1977. This $2.5 billion includes income on Beijing's foreign investments in Hong Kong and other Southeast Asian centers, plus remittances back to relatives on the mainland from Chinese expatriates. This flow into China has not decreased, but increased, as the "Open Door Policy" of Chinese leader Deng Xiaoping has been extremely successful in attracting overseas Chinese money into the mainland.

Apart from the purely financial offtake, most of Red China's exports pass through Hong Kong. In 1976, Beijing earned $2.4 billion in exports through the British Colony, or sufficient to cover 40% of the PRC's total import requirements for that year. Beijing does all its banking through Hong Kong, largely through the Hongkong and Shanghai Bank, and secondarily through the Standard and Chartered Bank.

The astonishing $2.5 billion financial reflow back to Communist China represents the fruits of Beijing's twenty-year program of moving into the higher echelons of the drug traffic, by agreement with the British. Combining American and Soviet sources, we will demonstrate that this estimation of foreign drug revenues through Hong Kong is a good approximation of Beijing's income from drug wholesaling, retailing, and financing, as well as gambling, real estate, and other shady joint ventures with British and expatriate Chinese finance, closely related to the drug trade.

Even the $2.5 billion figure does not include the $800 million that Beijing earns as a primary opium producer. To estimate Beijing's gross revenues from the drug traffic, an additional sum of several hundred millions of dollars must be added: the overhead cost of maintaining one of the largest and best-financed intelligence and sabotage operations in the world, the Chinese Communist Intelligence Service (CCIS).

Old Ties Grown Stronger

Beijing's current policy represents a direct line of continuity between the current regime and Britain's nineteenth-century corrupt collaborators in China. Correspondingly, the fortunes of the Beijing Communists are linked to the opium trade and the British oligarchy. They have staked China's economy—its capacity to import urgently needed foreign goods—on the opium trade.

Among the first major foreign credit arrangements the Beijing government has accepted was a $200 million deposit in the summer of 1978 in the Bank of China by a consortium of banks led by Standard and Chartered. Then, in October 1978, the venerable opium traders Jardine Matheson concluded a $300 million agreement with Chinese Communist firms in Hong Kong to develop a real estate complex adjoining a branch station of Hong Kong's new mass transit system. Apparently, the joint investment came as part of a package deal including the largest-ever export package to China, also announced at the beginning of October by Jardine Matheson, which handled the negotiations on behalf of a consortium of British firms. The $300 million real estate development in Hong Kong's New Territories includes an 80% stake on the part of two PRC-owned firms in Hong Kong, the Sun Company and the Kui Kwing Company; a 15% stake from the Hong Kong Land Company, Ltd., headed by Jardine Matheson's ex-Chairman H.N.L. Keswick; and a 5% share from Jardine Matheson itself.[3]

The PRC's roughly $3 billion in foreign exchange reserves are banked through HongShang, Standard and Chartered Bank, and other British banks through Hong Kong. In 1978 Beijing began large purchases of gold through the Hong Kong gold market, according to the London *Economist*'s *Financial Report*.[4]

The *International Currency Review* reported in September 1978: "China's increasingly open economic policies are likely to have a further impact on other Hong Kong balance-of-payments items . . . the Bank of China's announcement in early July that the 13 Communist-owned banks in Hong Kong would be able to purchase bullion, debentures and possibly equities, should generate further hard currency revenue for Hong Kong's financial community—and will also probably encourage a great deal of additional business. . . . The Chinese Government's initiative in this connection represents one of several financial liberalizing measures recently implemented by Beijing. In June, for example, the Bank of China and the Vanying Bank issued guarantees for a real estate project in Tsuen Warn, located in the New Territories."[5]

London's current view of Hong Kong's relationship to the mainland is rosy. "By its acceptance of the status quo, China shows that it is happy to keep the Hong Kong show on the road," wrote the London *Financial Times*. "The existence of the communist banks [in Hong Kong] is an indication of the continuing commitment, as the establishment of a machinery manufacturing plant on Tsing Yi island, one purpose of which is to modify mainland machinery which fails to meet the requirements of potential buyers in the region.

"This sort of commitment is understood by even the most nervous businessmen and helps remove the cloud of uncertainty which would otherwise start to gather. . . . It may be the final irony of the Hong Kong paradox that to ensure Hong Kong's well-being, Beijing will have to increase its own investment and participation in the colony."[6]

The same *Financial Times* report then specified what it meant by increased Beijing participation in the colony, citing the exemplary case of a leading Hong Kong and Macao entrepreneur, Mr. Stanley Ho:

> It is a widely accepted allegation that Mr. Ho and his partner, Mr. Henry Fok, started their fortunes at the time of the Korean War running strategic materials into China. Certainly, both men became prominent during that era of smuggling. Indeed, Mr. Ho seems to have weathered the 1967 riots [following the Cultural Revolution] without taking sides, and he even managed to bolster his friendship with Beijing authorities. The relationship, and Mr. Ho's wealth, can be traced to the award of China's sand monopoly in Hong Kong to his partnership with Mr. Fok. Later, in 1962, Mr. Ho was awarded the 25-year gambling franchise in Macao, where he had worked during World War II for a Japanese company. It is fair to say that the gambling franchise was a present from Beijing.

The *Financial Times* could have cited other cases, like the Shaw brothers (anglicized Chinese name), Hong Kong's premier producers of Kung Fu films for distribution throughout the world. Apart from their chain of theaters in Chinese communities across the world, the Shaw brothers control most of Hong Kong's prostitution.[7]

Beijing-owned businessmen and British bankers rub shoulders in the Hong Kong Jockey Club and other havens of Hong Kong's elite. In any corner of the world but Hong Kong, Beijing's relationship to the British elite would be a source of international outrage.

Beijing controls the Chinese General Chamber of Commerce

in the colony, the same organization that produced riots in 1977 to protest the Independent Commission Against Corruption's "interference in the ancient Chinese practice" of bribing police officers. Its chairman, Dr. Wang Kwan-cheng, is a frequent visitor to the mainland, and has been identified in intelligence reports as a Chinese political intelligence operative. Wang's position has been described as "the most prestigious in the colony, along with the British Governor-General." Among other things, Wang is among the wealthiest men in Hong Kong, with interests in the retail trade, restaurants, real estate, and transportation. According to his entry in *Who's Who in Hong Kong*, Wang is "chairman of the Board of Directors of Magna Development Company, Chinese Arts and Crafts (Hong Kong)," and a member of the Hong Kong Jockey Club.

The vice chairman of the Chinese Chamber of Commerce is C.H. Kao, who, like Macao gambling czar Stanley Ho, amassed great wealth by running strategic materials into China during the Korean War. Other known Beijing agents include Ho Yin, chairman of the Macao Chamber of Commerce, and Macao's representative to PRC's People's Congress, the organization that centralizes the political activities of Chinese expatriates through Beijing. Another is K.C. Jay (or Choi), formerly with the Bank of China in Beijing, and currently a resident financial intelligence operative and currency specialist for the Bank of China in Hong Kong.

As Richard Deacon, the British author of *The Chinese Secret Service,* puts it:

What is abundantly clear is that Beijing has a great reservoir of strength and talent among its supporters in Hong Kong. Its Secret Service activities there are low-key, as in many other centers, and have avoided clashes with the authorities. Indeed, the only espionage scandals to break in the Colony for several years past are attributable to other powers altogether, some of them at least manufactured by the Chinese to embarrass another nation. Perhaps the subtlest of these was when in 1973 a Chinese Intelligence agent tipped off the British about two K.G.B. agents, who had been taught

Chinese at the University of Vladivostok, arriving in Hong Kong. In their possession were found documents containing valuable information about the Soviet espionage network in the Far East.

And as Deacon remarks, "There may be even some unofficial contacts on an intelligence level between the British and Chinese Secret Services. . . .[8]

Deacon also reports that when China's narcotics smuggling operations were at their height, they were controlled by the Central External Liaison Department and the Ministry of Investigation. According to Deacon, the major secret agents were employed through the pro-Beijing Hong Kong Seamen's Union. The union was responsible for bringing in a large shipment of heroin discovered by the New York police in January 1973. "The International United Front operations, controlled by the CELD, included drug-pushing with the aim of creating disruption and demoralization in carefully selected target areas indicated by the CELD."

Deacon adds: "From Italian sources, diplomatic and otherwise, comes confirmation that the heroin traffic between Hong Kong and Europe is master-minded by Chinese secret agents. It is even suspected that there may have been undercover deals between the Chinese and the Mafia for distribution of the stuff."

Deacon identifies Keng Biao as the chief of the cited Central External Liaison Department. Whether Keng, in fact, coordinates Chinese drug-pushing cannot be independently corroborated at this time. Since the 1974 publication of Deacon's account, however, Keng was elevated to the Politburo, China's highest political body, in August 1977. In August 1978, he toured some of the prime marijuana-growing regions of the Caribbean, including Jamaica. Keng also made a stop at the island of Malta, the old base of the drug-pushing Maltese order, for unexplained reasons, on his return home.

The renowned Mr. Stanley Ho, mentioned above, who as controller of Macao gambling is the proprietor of what law enforcement agencies consider the world's dirtiest financial operation, is a bona fide member of Hong Kong's social elite.

Macao's relationship to Beijing became a public scandal in 1974, when the revolutionary Portuguese government offered to cede the colony to the PRC. The Beijing government refused, because Macao is much more useful to Beijing as a source of illicit foreign exchange earnings through opium and other forms of smuggling than as a people's commune.[9]

Only in rare instances have the links between the Hong Kong opium firms, British intelligence, and the Chinese Communist Intelligence Service come to public light. Where they have, the results put the best pulp thrillers to shame. One illustration is the story of the luckless Rennie family, Scots traders who sold their operation to Jardine Matheson in 1975. The Rennies are old Africa and Asia hands both in merchant ventures and the British colonial service, with major operations in South Africa, through Rennies Consolidated Holdings, Ltd.[10]

A relative, Sir John Rennie, resigned as head of Britain's foreign secret intelligence organization D16. Normally the identity of the chief of D16—"M" in the James Bond movies—is one of Britain's best-guarded secrets. But Rennie's identity came to light after his son, Charles Tatham Ogilvy Rennie, was arrested for heroin-trafficking in London on January 15, 1973. Official British press censorship, the infamous "D-notices" sent to newspaper editors, delayed press coverage of the blue-blooded drug bust until February 7, 1973, when London's *Evening Standard* reported that "the previously unnamed son of the head of D16, who is facing drug charges in London, is Charles Tatham Ogilvy Rennie."

Significantly, on the same day, West Germany's *Stern* magazine blew Sir John Rennie's cover—in a dispatch from Hong Kong, the base of the Rennie family's business partners, Jardine Matheson. *Stern* magazine's information could have come either from Rennie family channels through Jardine Matheson or through the Chinese Secret Service, or both. According to a Chinese Communist intelligence source cited by a British author,

In the case of Sir John Rennie I believe the Chinese were so cautious that they refused to accept their own suspicion [that

Rennie was head of D16] for a long time. Confirmation finally came when Sir John's son was arrested. They did not have far to look as his son's wife used Gerrard Street—almost a 100% Chinese quarter of London—as a rendezvous for obtaining Chinese heroin.

The British author, Richard Deacon, commented, "I suspect that some of the leakages to the press of this information came from the Chinese, who have a very high regard for the British Secret Service."

Of course, nothing is proven; British author Deacon guards his version of this story with an elaborate description of the Chinese Communist Intelligence Service's purported method of discovering the chiefs of British intelligence branches through a careful reading of *Who's Who*. Nonetheless, we have the fact that the head of D16 was a member of a family with intimate business ties to the core of the Hong Kong drug traffic; that his son dealt in narcotics through Beijing intelligence agents in London; and that the ultimate public announcement of his son's arrest came via Hong Kong sources, either British or Chinese.

On September 2, 1978, the London *Economist* reported,

One after another, top South African businessmen have been falling foul of the country's strict foreign exchange laws. This week's man in the spotlight was Mr. Charles Fiddian Green, chief executive of the country's leading transport conglomerate, Rennies. ... He was convicted of currency offenses on August 29 and fined Rand 10,000.

Last week Mr. Gordon Rennie [Sir John's relative and Rennies Consolidated chairman] cut his throat and wrists after police came to talk to him. He went to hospital and was charged with currency offenses. Four other Rennies executives have been questioned by police; another has already been charged with currency smuggling; and two, including Mr. Laurence Parry, have been sacked after apparently leaving the country.[11]

Also significant is the implication of Laurence Parry in the recent Rennies scandal; Parry was chief of Rennies Holiday Inn franchise in Swaziland and Lesotho, where rich South Africans spend weekends gambling and watching fleshy floorshows that are prohibited in puritan South Africa. Rennies, a 53% owned subsidiary of Jardine Matheson since 1975, has an almost classical dirty money profile, apart from its casino gambling and fleshpot operations. Rennies' subsidiary in the security field, Fidelity Guards, is South Africa's leader in armored car services and payroll preparations, and has its own computer facilities—tailor-made for the currency smuggling operations of which Rennies has been accused. In addition Rennies owns its own air and cargo shipping facilities, making it the leading transport group in South Africa.[12]

At the time of Rennies' merger with Jardine Matheson, South Africa's magazine *Management* wrote, "For both, it's a getting together of like people, like lifestyles, and remarkably similar management philosophies. Good solid Scots tradition abounds in both groups." Apart from its affinity to the leading Hong Kong dynasty, Rennies is part of the South African mining establishment. Two of its board members, the arrested Charles Fiddian Green and Fred G. Wolmarans, were previously senior officials of Consolidated Gold Fields of South Africa. Consolidated Gold, as quoted extensively above, wrote the book on currency smuggling—literally.

Beijing's Opium Weapon

Gold trading, banking, property, gambling—and roughly half of Beijing's foreign trade. That is the bottom line of the Beijing investment in Hong Kong. Since the early 1950s, it was the official view of American law enforcement agencies that Hong Kong was the main outlet for heroin grown in Red China. In 1961, just before the Kennedy administration kicked him out, U.S. Narcotics Bureau Chief Harry Anslinger stated, *"One primary outlet for the Red Chinese traffic has been Hong Kong."*[13]

The police blotter's record of Red Chinese opium traffic through Hong Kong is comprehensive. Even the British and Hong Kong police have been forced, on occasion, to admit this is the case. Scotland Yard attributed a large quantity of heroin seized in a 1969 bust in London's West End to Chinese shipments through Hong Kong. On October 15, 1970, the chief of Hong Kong's notoriously corrupt narcotics bureau, Shih Tiehpi, told a press conference that his force had confiscated 10,500 pounds of raw opium, 320 pounds of heroin, and 250 pounds of morphine, all of Red Chinese origin, during 1969. The quantities just cited compare dramatically with the largest-ever U.S. bust of heroin—the so-called French Connection bust involved a mere 100 kilograms.[14]

Without knowing the quality of the heroin seized, or the veracity of Mr. Shih Tieh-pi, comparisons are difficult. But if the 320 pounds of heroin seized so close to the original source were fairly pure, which is likely, and the rule of thumb applies that roughly one-tenth of illegal narcotics shipped are seized by police—then 3,200 pounds of heroin passed through Hong Kong in 1969. That is roughly what American narcotics addicts consumed in 1969.

Beijing's connection is not a matter of convenience, but the expression of a quarter-century-long policy agreement between the Beijing government and the highest levels of the British oligarchy. The best-known source for the unexpurgated views of China's elite is former *Al Ahram* Editor Mohammed Heikal. Heikal reported the following 1965 conversation between Nasser and visiting Chinese Prime Minister Zhou Enlai:

One of the most remarkable statements Chou En-lai made on that evening [June 23, 1965] during our discussion of the demoralization of American soldiers was that: "Some of them are trying opium and we are helping them. We are planting the best kinds of poppies especially for the American soldiers in Vietnam." Nasser appeared to be somewhat disturbed, but Chou continued: "We want them to maintain a large army in Vietnam that will serve us as a hostage, and we wish to demoralize the troops. The effect of this demoralization on the United States will be much greater than anyone can imagine." Nasser thought that Chou might be exaggerating somewhat, but Chou's concept was clear. He left no doubt that this was his course of action.[15]

For whatever reason, American intelligence ignored field reports throughout the 1960s that indicated a gigantic step-up ofjing's narcotics-trafficking. One of the most extraordinary of the stories that got lost in the intelligence bureaucracy involved an airfield in northern Laos, seventy-five miles south of the Chinese border, built by PRC troops during the summer of 1964. According to American intelligence sources, the airfield appeared in Phong Sally province, between Luang Prabang, Thailand's religious capital, and the border of Red China's Yunnan province. Meo guerrillas operating in the area under American direction discovered the Chinese building the airstrip far into Laotian territory, and reported back in June 1964.

However, the intelligence chain-of-command showed little interest in those reports. An enterprising mercenary pilot flying a T-28 aircraft obtained clear-as-daylight reconnaissance photographs of the airfield, including shots of Chinese soldiers pushing wheelbarrows. The photographs were duly sent through channels, where they disappeared. American officers, however, believed that the airstrip was intended to link up with an asphalt highway the Chinese had been building from Yunnan province into northern Laos for some time. Initially, thinking among American intelligence officers centered on the possibility that the airstrip had been intended as a forward fighter base for Beijing involvement in the Indochinese conflict. Only later, when no Chinese fighters appeared did the truth emerge: The Chinese road and connected airstrip were built to ship opium out of Yunnan province.

Today, Chinese control of the Golden Triangle opium production is limited. In Burma, the White Flag (Chinese-controlled) Burmese Communist Party now controls most if not all of the Kokang opium-growing district. Khun Sa, a.k.a. Chiang Chi Fu, controls the Shan States United Army located near Lashio. Although Khun Sa is now known to have received weapons

from the Soviets, likely via Indochina, the actual business man-
agement of this notorious outfit is in the hands of the She Pa
Lang (a.k.a. Sao Fa Lan), whose Chinese name is Chang Chu-
Chun.

From Hong Kong

Until the "China card" strategic policy found favor in Wash-
ington under Kissinger, the official American view, among others, was that the Chinese Communists grew and exported large
quantities of opium. Harry Anslinger, the first chief of the U.S.
Federal Bureau of Narcotics, said in 1961: "Heroin made in
Chinese factories out of poppies grown in China is smuggled
into Hong Kong and onto freighters and planes to Malaysia,
Macao, the Philippines, the Hawaiian Islands, the United
States, or, going the other direction, India, Egypt, Africa, and
Europe. A prime 'target area' in the United States was California. The Los Angeles area alone probably received 40% of the
smuggled contraband from China's heroin and morphine
plants. The syndicate crowd does not object to dealing with the
Reds as long as the profits are big in terms of dollars."[16]

U.S. investigators have succeeded only in putting heat on the
Hong Kong authorities, provoking token busts of local drug
operations. The last major scandal raked up by American authorities—immediately before the "opening to Beijing"
slammed the lid on further action—came in 1973, when U.S.
Congressman Lester Wolff visited Hong Kong on behalf of the
House Select Committee on Narcotics Abuse. Citing the Nixon
administration's effective crackdown on Turkish heroin entering the U.S. East Coast through the so-called French Connection in Marseilles, Wolff charged, "All the narcotics entering
the United States must be coming from somewhere else, the
center of which is Hong Kong."[17]

Why has no action been taken against Hong Kong, when the
evidence is so well known? There are two reasons. First, no
American law enforcement or intelligence agency has ever had

operational access to Hong Kong. Hong Kong, as British territory, was strictly off limits to American investigators. To our direct knowledge, American intelligence never tries to circumvent this feature of the "special relationship" between Britain and the United States.

The more important reason is that, to a great extent, the actual refining of heroin—which moved lock, stock and barrel to Hong Kong from Shanghai after the Communist takeover in 1949—is no longer done in Hong Kong. Rather, Hong Kong's importance is overwhelmingly in the sphere of dirty money operations, and secondarily in transshipment of heroin. The great shift of the production-refining cycle from the Shanghai to Hong Kong route to the Golden Triangle (including substantial portions of China's Yunnan province) occurred in the context of the Vietnam War. Vietnam provided a gigantic captive market with easy access from the Burmese-Thai-Laotian growing areas, some of which had alrown substantial quantities of opium during the British colonial period.

The Ch'ao Chou Connection

The key to the Far Eastern drug traffic—the link that ties the entire operational picture together—is the Chinese expatriate connection. Law enforcement investigators have known for years what the Ch'ao Chou Chinese networks were up to, but the law enforcement agencies never followed through the maze of financial connections: To do so would have violated standing American intelligence agreements with British intelligence.

As the *DEA Quarterly* of winter 1984 described the dirty money operations in Hong Kong: "Responsible for moving most heroin money in Southeast Asia, it operates through gold shops, trading companies, and money changers, many of which are operated in various countries by members of the same Chinese family. Recordkeeping susceptible to standard audit rarely exists in this underground banking system, and coded messages, 'chits,' and simple telephone calls are used to transfer money

from one country to another. Nonetheless, the system has the
ability to transfer funds from one country to another in a matter
of hours, provide complete anonymity and total security for the
customer, convert gold or other items into currency, and convert
one currency into that of the customer's choice."

Crucial clues to the inner operation of drug traffic—the joint
operations of the Chinese Communist Intelligence Service
(CCIS), British intelligence, and Chinese and British finance—
have been gathering dust in police files for years. One such clue
is the arrest of a Chinese Communist Party official in Djakarta,
the Indonesian capital, in 1972. The Indonesian authorities
arrested a Ch'ao Chou Chinese, complete with Chinese Communist Party card and other documentary evidence, in possession
of 30 kilograms of heroin—worth between $60 million and $150
million in terms of American street value, depending on the
quality. The investigation, employing the combined efforts of
Indonesian and American drug enforcement officials, showed
that the purpose of the heroin imports was the financing of the
Indonesian Communist Party (PKI) through the creation of a
drug ring in Djakarta.[18]

A handful of similar incidents are on record. At the same
time, American police busted a Filipino diplomat carrying
seven pounds of pure Number Four white heroin in his country's
diplomatic pouch. He had been followed from the Philippines
to a New York City hotel room. His contact man, arrested with
him, was a Ch'ao Chou Chinese.[19]

A November 1978 interview with a Malaysian intelligence
source is worth printing in full here for the insight it gives into
this particular type of operation:

Source: It is definitely a fact that China distributes narcotics
to its fraternal communist parties in Southeast Asia as a
means of raising funds for their activities. The most recent
case is that of North Korea. Their diplomats have been kicked
out of several European countries for smuggling and distributing heroin. Opium is not grown in North Korea. It is obviously given to them by the Chinese. In Singapore, Communist
agents were reported selling narcotics to American students

at the American school for lunch money. Imagine, they were giving fixes out for 20 or 30 cents—just to get the kids hooked for their return to the U.S.

Question: Can you substantiate that?

Source: It's on the Singapore official record. There is more information at the local Kiwanis Club. They keep a file on narcotics. Also there was a DEA report written on how the PRC distributes narcotics through local party functionaries in the region. The report was never released, but photostats exist.

Question: There is a lot of accumulated evidence that the Hongkong and Shanghai Bank is at the center of the entire Far Eastern narcotics trade.

Source: HongShang is the largest bank in the region and particularly in Singapore. China's biggest agent is Pang Hock-lim. He is instrumental in trafficking Chinese opium into India, Thailand, Singapore, and Malaysia.

Question: Has he been arrested?

Source: Sure. He's been arrested plenty of times, but every time a fix is made and he is released.

Question: Who makes the fix?

Source: He's directly linked with the Hongkong and Shanghai Bank. That's a fact.

The North Koreans mentioned in this account might just as well have gotten the heroin from the Soviets as the Chinese. Soviet drug-related operations in Asia, have taken off especially with the increased Soviet presence in Southeast Asia. According to law enforcement sources in the region, the Soviets are fully backing a state policy on the part of Laos to grow opium for foreign exchange purposes.

The Chinese expatriate population's close ties to the Beijing regime are well documented. According to a British author writing in 1965, two-thirds of the Chinese expatriates in Southeast Asia supported the Beijing regime, and only one-third Taiwan.[20]

American authors like A. Doak Barnett have drawn the same conclusion.[21] These impressive figures are the result of assiduous cultivation of such ties on the part of the Beijing government.

Beijing's insistence on the continuity of ties between the 12 million Chinese residing abroad and the Great Han motherland achieved notoriety through such incidents as the recent border disputes with Vietnam. The system of remittances from Chinese residents abroad to families on the mainland, and the more recent system of joint investments between the Beijing regime and Chinese expatriates, are not only a major source of foreign exchange for China; they are the financial infrastructure of Chinese Secret Intelligence. The network of financial ties between Beijing and the expatriates overlaps the networks that control the wholesale drug trade in the Golden Triangle.

Forging the Hong Kong-Beijing Link

Until the Sino-Soviet split period, the ties that bound the expatriate Chinese to the mainland were the strongest of all: family. This link was expressed in the large-scale transmission of remittances back to families on the mainland. According to the limited available data, the largest volume of such remittances, for which special remittance transfer agencies had been created, was to the small city of Swatow on the northern Chinese coast; Swatow is the home city of the Ch'ao Chou Chinese. The Ch'ao Chou, seafaring and commercial people with a special dialect, evidently maintained the closest family links with the mainland. That is the background to the wholesale recruitment of expatriate Ch'ao Chou Chinese into Chinese secret intelligence during the postwar period.[22]

In the late 1950s, the volume of reported remittances dropped off sharply. Instead of paying remittances directly to relatives, expatriate Chinese invested heavily in both mainland China and in foreign joint ventures with the Beijing government. The flow of remittances was *capitalized* in joint ventures with Beijing, and relatives back home received dividends from these investments.

The point of decline of remittances coincides with Beijing's orientation to joint investments with expatriate Chinese. That policy goes back to 1951, when the South China Enterprise Company, the forerunner of the present Overseas Chinese Investment Corporation, sold 100,000 shares to Chinese businessmen in Hong Kong and Macao. However, until 1957, the attractions for such investors were limited; overseas Chinese investment could only find opportunities in agriculture, the least profitable sector of the economy.

But in 1957 new regulations came into effect that guaranteed a 12% dividend investment, against a normal 8% dividend in ordinary mixed companies. The Beijing government also made provision for repatriation of part of the profits to the overseas Chinese investor.

By the mid-1950s, this capital was concentrated in the Overseas Chinese Industrial Construction Company and related companies, which merged into the Overseas Chinese Investment Corporation (OCIC) in 1955, with initial capitalization of $50 million. The board of directors of the OCIC included leading Chinese businessmen resident in Southeast Asia. By 1966, there were 140 businesses under the OCIC aegis operating in China.

By the mid-1960s, however, the policy of using the hard currency of expatriate Chinese to invest in China gave way to a much more efficient form of raising vitally needed foreign exchange. Beijing took a stake in the expatriate Chinese community's expanding operations in drug-pushing and dirty money operations, centering on the boomtown in Hong Kong.

In 1980, for example, Y.K. Pao traveled to Beijing, where he held five days of talks which resulted in the groundbreaking joint venture, International Shipping and Investment Co. The venture was believed to be the first time Beijing had put its money directly into a project outside of its borders. Chairman: Y.K. Pao. But even more interestingly, the idea had been born out of a discussion held between Pao and then Chinese Premier Hua Guofeng. The venue: a private dinner at 10 Downing Street with British Prime Minister Margaret Thatcher.

Or, take the case of China Everbright Holdings Ltd., whose

chairman is Wang Guangying, the premier "red capitalist" of Hong Kong. The brother-in-law of the late Liu Shaoqi, China's head of state in the 1960s and one of the early "capitalist roaders," Wang was dispatched with a sack of capital to Hong Kong to show that thirty years of communism had not blunted Chinese business expertise. Wang has since made millions in primarily real estate deals in the city, and joint ventures with overseas Chinese.

Everbright's success however is not all based on entrepreneurship. A client of Kissinger Associates, on whose board sat Lord Peter Carrington until he took over the post of NATO secretary general, Everbright receives top-rate advice and connections through personal association with Kissinger. Among Kissinger's other clients are some of the top names in Dope, Inc., including American Express, Chase Manhattan, and Britain's Midland Bank, the overseer for the Hongkong and Shanghai Banking Corporation. "Why do companies go to Kissinger Associates instead of an investment bank," asked a December 2, 1985, article in *Business Week*. "Because they know you keep your mouth shut," the article quotes Kissinger's reply. "Each contract his firm signs with a corporate client contains a clause pledging mutual confidentiality. Neither party is supposed even to acknowledge it has any ties to the other."

8

How the Royal Institute of International Affairs Runs Drugs and Dirty Money

Now we will take the reader up through the chain of command of the world drug and dirty money business, to the top level of political control: to Chatham House, St. James Square, London, the headquarters of the Royal Institute of International Affairs. We have inspected the books of Dope, Inc., met the operating personnel, visited its subsidiaries in Hong Kong, Bangkok, and Beijing, as well as its farms and factories in the Golden Triangle, on the common border of Burma, Laos, Thailand, and the People's Republic of China. The Far East drug traffic emerges as a single business operation, a British-Chinese joint venture, in which Britain is the senior partner.[1]

It is obvious, by now, that an operation of this scope could not exist without the political approval of the British government, nor without the gigantic supporting facilities of the world's offshore credit markets, the world's gold and diamonds trade, and "hands-on" management of the retail distribution, or organized crime aspects of the operation.

The Hongkong and Shanghai Bank is not an independent malefactor, but a special operation of the British oligarchy's top banks, specializing in the Far Eastern drug traffic. The Hongkong and Shanghai Bank's governing body, the London Committee, is the British oligarchy's delegated group assigned to the Far East drug traffic.

More specifically, it is an economic warfare operation. Two of its directors, J.H. Keswick, of the family that founded Jardine Matheson in 1828 to trade opium, and J.K. Swire, of the Swire family of hereditary opium traders, were senior officials in Britain's Ministry of Economic Warfare during World War II. Another senior official of that ministry is Sir Mark Turner, the chairman of Rio Tinto Zinc, the HongShang's partner in numerous fields, including gold. Turner is now a key figure in the Royal Institute of International Affairs, founded by Lord Alfred Milner, an earlier chairman of Rio Tinto Zinc.

The Royal Institute of International Affairs (RIIA) and its leading personnel control not only the Far Eastern drug traffic but every important dirty money operation on the surface of the globe.

The next section will further document the British monarchy's control of the Canadian banks and corporations, the same installations responsible for channeling drugs into and illegal funds out of the United States. It demonstrates that the direct agency of control over Canada's huge financial warfare apparatus is the Canadian Institute of International Affairs (CIIA), a mock-up creation of Britain's Royal Institute. Included in the Canadian operation are the Bank of Nova Scotia's domination of Canada's gold market, Canadian banks' huge role in Caribbean Silver Triangle dirty-money operations, and—most important—the direct links between the hard-core Far East drug wholesalers, and the Canadian institutions that have participated in the wholesale drug traffic on the North American continent since the closing days of Prohibition. Through the Canadian outpost of the British monarchy, the drug traders close the circle between the Keswick family of Hong Kong, the founders of Jardine Matheson in 1828, and the Bronfman family, the immediate sponsors of so-called organized crime in the United States.

From their base in the dirty money traffic, the institutions assembled in force on the leading committees of the Royal Institute dominate:

1. All of Britain's leading commercial banks;
2. Both big British oil companies, British Petroleum and Royal Dutch Shell;
3. All the leading British merchant banks;
4. The world's gold and diamonds trade;
5. Every leading old-line opium trading firm, including the Peninsular and Orient Company, Jardine Matheson, John Swire and Sons, and Charterhouse Japhet.

Goal: Rebuild the Empire

We are going to examine the content of the Royal Institute of International Affairs' subversive activities, following through the careers of some of its leading operatives—including Sir John Henry Keswick, member of the family that controls the Hongkong and Shanghai Bank, and from the old Jardine Matheson opium trading firm; and the current chairman of the Council of the RIIA, Lord Humphrey Trevelyan, member of the board of directors of HongShang's gold-smuggling subsidiary, the British Bank of the Middle East. These are the men who created the Beijing Connection in its modern form.

According to the charter of the RIIA published in 1920, the Royal Institute of International Affairs is "an unofficial and nonpolitical body," whose object is "to advance the sciences of international politics, economics, and jurisprudence," to "provide and maintain a means of information upon international questions," and "to promote the study and investigation of such questions." Few times in the history of the written word have so many lies appeared in so few lines.

However, a concise summary of the RIIA's purposes appears in its de facto founding document, Cecil Rhodes's 1877 bequest. Rhodes, who founded both the gold and diamond mining empire that still dominates world markets under the aegis of Anglo-American and De Beers, and also founded the dope-trading Standard Bank (the African partner of the Asian-based Chartered Bank, since merged), is the starting point for the present form of the disease. Rhodes left his wealth to the Rhodes Trust, administered by Lord Milner. Milner's collection of Oxford trainees, called the "Milner Kindergarten," made up most of the 1916 Lloyd George government, and formed the RIIA at a meeting in Versailles on May 30, 1919.

Rhodes's 1877 will was:

> To establish a trust, to and for the establishment and promotion and development of a secret society, the true aim and object whereof shall be the extension of British rule throughout the world, the perfecting of a system of emigration from the United Kingdom and the colonization by British subjects of all islands wherein the means of livelihood are attainable by energy, labor, and enterprise, and especially the occupation by British settlers of the entire continent of Africa, the Holy Land, the valley of the Euphrates, the islands of Cyprus and Candia, the whole of South America, the islands of the Pacific not heretofore possessed by Great Britain, the whole of the Malay Archipelago, the seaboard of China and Japan, the ultimate recovery of the United States of America as an integral part of the British Empire, the consolidation of the whole Empire, the inauguration of a system of colonial representation in the Imperial Parliament which may tend to weld together the disjointed members of the Empire, and finally, the foundation of so great a power as to hereafter render wars impossible and promote the best interests of humanity.[2]

The secret society concept was passed on by Milner, Rhodes's successor as high commissioner in South Africa, through Milner's trainees Lionel Curtis (of the Roundtable group), and Lord Robert Cecil—whose family dates back to the Genoa-Amsterdam coup against Elizabethan humanism in 1601. Curtis and Cecil both participated in the May 1919 meeting at Versailles that founded the RIIA.

The Royal Institute of International Affairs is the secret society.

1949: The British-Beijing Deal

Let us backtrack, for a moment, to the point of origin of the London-Beijing joint drug-running venture in the Far East, the wartime deal between the RIIA and Zhou Enlai. Detailed records of the relevant years have recently been made available. In August 1978, the U.S. State Department released 1,300 pages of documents to the public dealing with American diplomacy in China at the time of the Maoist takeover.[3] From the British side, the RIIA in 1977 released its own records of its wartime and postwar operations group in the region, the Far East Committee—the real British Foreign Office.

Both sets of documents yield the same interpretation: the creation of the People's Republic of China included an alliance between the British dope-runners and the Chinese dope-runners. This was negotiated from the British side by Sir John Henry Keswick and from the Chinese side by Chou En-lai. The Chinese team also prominently included top figures in the opium trade, such as the Bank of China's Chi Ch'ao-ting, Shanghai Commercial Bank's K.P. Chen (who also headed the Chinese wing of the Institute for Pacific Relations), and elements of the so-called Green Gangs. The Green Gangs, which could be called the Chinese mafia, ran the opium trade not only in the Far East but through the far-flung Chinese expatriate community.

Mao Zedong, in fact, owed a lot to his links with the opium trade, and one of the principal links between him and the opium runners involves one of the puzzles of his rise to power within the Chinese Communist Party. The usual coterie of China "hands" such as J.K. Fairbanks, Edgar Snow, and Anna Louise

Strong, were either ignorant of, or deliberately ignored the critical links between Mao and the two military leaders who were critical to his accession to the CCP leadership. These two military leaders were Chu Teh and Ho Long, who led the only cohesive military forces within the Communist movement of the latter half of the 1920s. These two, and their soldiers, were members of the Ko Lao Hui, the "Elder Brothers Society," a secret society that had been in existence since the 17th century. As an indication of how little the U.S. government is aware of these matters, the Foreign Broadcasting Information Service, published by the State Department, mistranslated the term repeatedly during its coverage of the trial of the "Gang of Four," referring to this well-known secret society as the "Old Tie Veterans Association." It is through such societies, which were essentially mafias, with links to the CCP, that the People's Republic carried on the drug trade.

From both the British and the Chinese side, the alliance was explicitly against the United States. The Chinese knew it, and said so, the British knew it, and said so, and American diplomats cabled home that the United States had been shafted.[4]

When the top representatives of Britain's RIIA began soundings in the Chinese Communist stronghold of Yenan and at Zhou Enlai's Chungking legation during the World War II period, they had reasons dating back a century to expect results.

But the credit for the re-creation of the alliance between Britain and the modern equivalent of the Triad gangs must go to Sir John Henry Keswick, the Royal Institute's man-on-the-spot at the British Embassy in Chungking during World War II. It is known that Keswick was in regular contact with Chou En-lai in his capacity as a prominent businessman and through his attachment to the British embassy in Chungking. Chou was in Chungking from 1937 through the 1940s.[5]

Keswick, of the hereditary drug-trading family that founded and still controls Jardine Matheson, also represented the Royal Institute and its subbranch, the Institute for Pacific Relations, to the United States.[6] Sir John Henry was Britain's number-one man for China policy, chairman of Britain's China Association, vice president of the Sino-British Trade Council, and a member of the Great Britain-China Committee. (His predecessor at the China Association from 1951 to 1955 was John Kidston Swire, of that opium-trading family, who still sits on the HongShang's London Committee.)

Two pieces of eyewitness testimony from Mao Zedong's wartime hideout in China's northern Yenan province bear comparison. The first is the report by Peter Vladimirov, who was the Soviet liaison to Mao's headquarters in Yenan from 1941 to 1945. According to the Soviet-published *Vladimirov Diaries,* the Chinese Communist Party operating in Yenan grew opium for profit, not only for medicinal uses. Opium had been a major cash crop for Yenan before Mao's arrival; Vladimirov claimed that Mao continued the practice. The Soviet representative also suspected the Chinese chairman's close contact with American visitors connected to the Institute for Pacific Relations.[7]

A second account appeared in the January 1978 issue of *International Affairs,* the Royal Institute's journal:

> Victor Farmer, who was a director of Imperial Chemical Industries (China) and who in 1944 had recently returned from a visit to the Far East [stated]: "I have met some [Chinese] Communists and their ideas are very open-minded. If you could get rid of this ultra-nationalist clique in the saddle at present in Chungking, and many Government officials are extremely broad-minded, I think that the way would be open for a compromise with the Communists; and an effective compromise."

The view Farmer expressed on behalf of the Royal Institute's Far Eastern Committee had already surfaced in the United States through the Committee's American branch, the Institute for Pacific Relations (IPR), the organization that produced the pro-Maoist group in the State Department centered around John S. Service and John Carter Vincent. Although the IPR included American citizens and was funded through the Rockefeller and Carnegie Foundations, it functioned as a branch of the RIIA and British policy-making. Now called the Asian Research Institute, the IPR's two most prominent general secretaries, Edward Carter and William Holland, had extensive British pedigrees. Carter, whose reign as IPR chief lasted until 1946, was a leader of the international Young Men's Christian Association, while his successor Holland was a citizen of New Zealand until 1943 and a member of London's Royal Institute.

The dead giveaway on the IPR's British character is the organization's move to Canada subsequent to the 1950 McCarran Committee investigation, which mistook pro-British treason for pro-Communist treason. With hearty British cheers, the disgraced Institute for Pacific Relations moved to Canada.

Britain's support for the IPR was further expressed by the chairman of the RIIA's Far Eastern Group, Sir Andrew McFadyean (who in 1947 became the chairman of S.G. Warburg, the merchant bank). In a 1952 letter McFadyean wrote: "The fact that I have criticized certain activities and certain officers of the IPR entitles me to say with greater emphasis, firstly that it would have been a useless body if it had not represented a wide variety of political views, and secondly that throughout my acquaintance with the Institute, its governing body, while respecting the rights of free expression, has never encouraged or countenanced subversive views."[8]

Once in Canada, the IPR came under the official sponsorship of the Canadian Institute of International Affairs, the local RIIA subsidiary, and its chairman—now "honorary Chairman for Life"—Walter Lockhart Gordon. During the last thirty years, Gordon has been the most consistent North American apologist for Maoist China. Gordon currently has direct personal ties to Canada's "old China hands," including Dr. Paul Lin, Chester Ronning, and James Endicott. All three served as advisers to Chinese Premier Chou En-lai; Paul Lin's official duties as an aide to Chou terminated only in 1965. Lin, in turn, is a power in the expatriate Chinese community in Vancouver, British Columbia, one of the most important transshipment points for opium entering the United States.

The ties run back the other way across the Pacific as well. Gordon sponsored the initial founding of the Chinese People's Institute of Foreign Affairs in China, an official Red Chinese organization that currently maintains links with the Canadian

Institute of International Affairs. Gordon also arranged funding for the Norman Bethune School at York University in Toronto, Canada, the most overtly pro-Maoist institution on the North American continent. That is the pedigree of the British-created, British-defended, and still British-run Institute for Pacific Relations.[9]

Squeeze Play

According to the RIIA's official account cited above, the RIIA-IPR's function at the close of World War II was to propose the John Service-John Keswick policy of fostering Maoism as the "alternative" to Britain's shrill insistence on her colonial rights in the area. Prime Minister Winston Churchill still balked at the self-determination provisions of the Atlantic Charter, namely that Britain give up its Southeast Asian colonies. Feeling against the British ran so high in the United States, the *International Affairs* study points out, that Henry Luce's *Life* magazine urged the British people "to stop fighting for the British Empire and fight for victory . . . if you cling to the Empire at the expense of a United Nations victory, you will lose the war because you will lose us." A poll taken in 1942 revealed that 56% of Americans questioned agreed that the British could rightly be described as "oppressors . . . because of the unfair advantage . . . they have taken of their colonial possessions."

The RIIA and the IPR's "alternative" posture was a retreat under fire from an imperial position in the Far East to an alliance with the Great Han chauvinists of the Communist Party of China. Any suggestion that an actual policy difference intervened between the "hidebound reactionary" Winston Churchill and the openly pro-Maoist Victor Farmer of the RIIA's Far Eastern Group is made silly by the role of Jardine Matheson's John Henry Keswick.

Keswick was a prominent figure in the Shanghai International Settlements, of which his brother, Sir William Johnston

Keswick, was chairman throughout the 1930s and until 1949. Britain had owned a chunk of the city of Shanghai by the treaty that ended the Second Opium War. The status of the Shanghai International Settlement was one of the major policy conflicts between Roosevelt and Churchill, since it represented a foreign colonial intrusion in an allied nation. Britain's concern for Shanghai may also have been motivated by the fact that it was the world's center for refining opium into heroin. Keswick and the refineries both picked up and moved to Hong Kong in 1949.

In January 1945, pro-Maoist Victor Farmer and John Henry Keswick (with Andrew McFadyean) together led Britain's delegation to the Institute for Pacific Relations's most important conference at Hot Springs, West Virginia. Ten British officials went along in tow with the RIIA officials. The British delegation presented a softer front to the Americans than the Churchill government was then willing to officially concede. RIIA documents show that the queer combination of Chinese Communist Party apologist Victor Farmer and old-line opium trader John Keswick did the trick of mollifying the Americans.

"The general atmosphere here [at Hot Springs] is very much better than [at the last Institute for Pacific Relations conference at] Mont Tremblant. . . . There is much less disposition to twist British tails just for the fun of seeing how the animal reacts," McFadyean wrote back to the Royal Institute in relief.[10] American delegates included Treasury official Harry Dexter White, responsible for selling to the United States John Maynard Keynes's British blueprint for the International Monetary Fund.

Not until Mao's army marched into Shanghai in 1949 did the Americans realize what they were in for. The new mayor of Shanghai, Chen Yi, summoned John Keswick for secret talks, the State Department documents reveal, virtually as soon as the mayor arrived in the city. After a lengthy round of discussion, Keswick departed and called on the American consul-general. The stunned diplomat later telexed back to Washington that Keswick "made a statement that he did not expect Americans to fare well under the Communist regime, but did not indicate whether this opinion was formed as a result of the conversation with the mayor." Keswick was either threatening the United States or relaying what the Chinese had told him, the consul-general wrote. "He would hardly have invented this as a bluff to frighten away American competitors," the American concluded optimistically.[11]

How ingenuous that evaluation was became clear within days. Behind the backs of the Americans, the British negotiated a deal to keep Hong Kong under London's control, and opened up confidential lines of communication between the mainland and Hong Kong. In wires to Washington, American diplomats accused the British of tearing up the standing Anglo-American agreement that all decisions respecting the Communist government would be made in close consultations. "The Communists are obviously trying to play off the British against us and seem to have succeeded somewhat," one American official wrote.[12]

The British added insult to injury by maintaining an official pro-Maoist propaganda campaign, which began far before the Communists took over. British officials gave awards to leading members of the CCP, even while maintaining "official" diplomatic relations with Chiang Kai-shek, and gave lavish public receptions for dissident elements of the Kuomintang, such as the widow of Sun Yat-sen, the Chinese nationalist leader who died in 1925. (Sun's wife is currently an official of the Beijing government.)

Shortly before the Communist takeover, one journalist wrote: "The British have a reputation for very smart diplomacy in Asia. Part of this comes from their ability to spot key groups and get on the right side of them. It is generally believed by observers that the British now figure the intellectual left wing to be one of the groups that will gain rather than lose strength in the political changes of the next few years, and are preparing for this eventuality."[13]

American intelligence dispatches from 1947 reprinted in the State Department release read: "It is significant to note that shortly after the Communist takeover of the key city of Shanghai, the Maoists halted all anti-British propaganda."[14]

Creation of the Hong Kong Drug Nexus

Under the public cover of Anglo-Chinese mutual seduction, and before the horrified eyes of American observers, the British and Maoists created the financial infrastructure of what would later underwrite the Far East narcotics traffic. Keswick's opening of channels between Beijing and Hong Kong permitted a division of the Shanghai banking families between mainland China and Hong Kong; this 1947 division founded the expatriate Chinese connection between Beijing and London. (Apparently, other expatriate networks, like the Thai bankers who date back to the 1930s, were consolidated in the same fashion, although the same degree of documentation from the period is not yet available.)

The Senate investigation of the Institute for Pacific Relations revealed indirectly the role of the Royal Institute of International Affairs in the creation of the drug-financing networks. The McCarran Committee made public some of the correspondence of IPR General Secretary William Holland. Holland, before his ascendance as IPR chief in 1946, took over the China stations of the U.S. Office of War Information, an organization closely tied to the wartime predecessor of the Central Intelligence Agency, the Office of Strategic Services. Holland was in frequent touch with the head of the Royal Institute in London, which as noted above, had created Holland's IPR in the first place.

In one of the letters available from the 1950–1951 McCarran proceedings, Holland informed the Royal Institute that a top Chinese Communist banking official "may turn out to be one of the best friends we have."[15] The official in question, Chi Ch'ao-ting, was a top officer in the Nationalist Bank of China, until the Maoist victory. At that moment, he shifted allegiance to the Maoist Bank of China. Moreover, Chi's defection was preceded by that of a whole faction within the Nationalist Bank, which chose to "make a deal" with the Communists rather than flee to Taiwan. This faction, according to the 1949 State Department papers, made arrangements to communicate with Chinese IPR leader and Shanghai banker K.P. Chen, who had left Shanghai for Hong Kong, even after the Communist takeover.[16]

Chi's defection to Mao's Bank of China began an illustrious career, during which he rose to a high position in the bank and participated in international conferences for the PRC as well. As noted, the Bank of China's financial connections to the West are through Hong Kong; its reserves were and still are held with the Hongkong and Shanghai Bank and the Standard and Chartered Bank, its remittances payments conducted through the same banks, and so forth. Chi's move—under the approving eyes of Holland—only typified what went on in the Shanghai banking community at large. In the same dispatch to the RIIA cited above, Holland reported on his contacts with leading Shanghai bankers, citing the case of Chinese Shanghai Commercial Bank chief K.P. Chen. Chen fled to Hong Kong shortly before the Communists took over, Holland reported, adding, "Impossible as it now seems, I have an idea Chen will later go to Shanghai."[17]

One of Holland's close associates during the period was the Canadian representative in Chungking, Chester Ronning—still prominent in the Canadian connection to the London-Beijing drug apparatus. Utterly enamored of the Maoists, Ronning met almost weekly with Chou En-lai's chief deputy, Wang Ping-nan, during his 1945–1947 tour of duty.[18]

Ronning's relationship with Wang Ping-nan has a special importance, which we will indicate momentarily. Ronning went on to act as midwife in the Institute for Pacific Relations's 1950 rebirth in Canada after the scandal.

At the outset of the Korean War, the public amity between Great Britain and China was reduced—for purposes of public consumption. However, the leading individuals who created the Beijing Connection continued to hold all the important strings, and maintained the full continuity of the narcotics traffic. Despite the public hostilities, Beijing operated freely on Hong Kong's illicit gold exchanges, and present-day luminaries like Stanley Ho made their fortunes smuggling strategic goods into China from Hong Kong.

The Emergence of the 'China Card'

In 1951, Lord Humphrey Trevelyan took his post as British ambassador to China, the same man who today sits on the board of the British Bank of the Middle East. Public contacts between Lord Trevelyan and the Beijing regime were necessarily low-key, by the dictates of what even the British and Chinese consider public decency. To cover their tracks, the British claim that Trevelyan did not meet Premier Chou En-lai during the first two years of his stay in Beijing, although they do admit that Trevelyan's fellow diplomat John Henry Keswick had had regular access to Chou during the early 1940s in Chungking.

However, Trevelyan's stay in Beijing was not without great importance. Trevelyan set up the beginnings of the so-called American opening to China, laying the basis for the "China card." His partner in this maneuver was Chester Ronning's old Maoist contact, Wang Ping-nan. By this time, Chou En-lai's old deputy of the Chungking days was Beijing's ambassador to Poland. Trevelyan set up the first American diplomatic contacts with the People's Republic of China, through China's embassy in Poland, during the mid-1950s. America's contact man with the Beijing government was Ambassador Wang Ping-nan.

Trevelyan's further career is remarkable. After a brief stay in West Germany, he went on to become Britain's ambassador to Egypt during the Suez Crisis—the British-French-Israeli invasion of Egypt that wrecked President Eisenhower's world development plan, the Atoms for Peace program. After a tour at the British Foreign Office, he was Britain's ambassador to the Soviet Union from 1962 to 1965, during the Cuban missile crisis. Currently, he sits on the board of directors of British Petroleum, along with John Keswick's brother Sir William Johnston Keswick, and various other members of the boards of the HongShang and the RIIA council.

Lord Trevelyan completed the circle by taking the chairmanship of the Council of the Royal Institute, while keeping an active hand in the opium business, through the British Bank of the Middle East.

Direct experience in the drug trade is apparently a standard qualification for chairmen of the Council of the RIIA. When Trevelyan, Keswick, Holland, and Ronning were young men setting up the Beijing Connection during World War II, the chairman of the RIIA Council was Waldorf Astor. Astor's great-grandfather, John Jacob Astor, was a British agent-of-influence in the first years of the American republic; according to his biographer, J.J. Astor was the first American to get in on the drug trade alongside the British East India Company, starting in 1816.

9

Canada: North America's Hong Kong

Much of the heroin entering North America comes through Canada. This is the estimate of authoritative law enforcement sources.

Virtually everything the reader now knows about the British Crown Colony of Hong Kong applies to the British Dominion north of the American border. The idea that Canada is a nation—in the sense that Americans understand the term—is the product of low-grade, if persistent, public relations efforts. Politically and financially, Canada is run straight from the top by the British monarchy, starting with the Governor-General whom the Queen appoints, the Privy Council, and including the core group of Knights of St. John of Jerusalem who control the bulk of Canadian business.

Canada's role in the drug flow to the United States is not much different from its role during Prohibition. Canada transships much of the heroin entering the American market, because it was created and maintained as a British Dominion on the northern flank of the United States to carry out precisely such operations.

Despite the British monarchy's iron grip over the highest levels of Canadian public life, there are a few individuals well placed in Canada, including in its law enforcement services, who look to America rather than Britain as a model for Canada's future. At great risk to themselves, they have fought a long rearguard action against criminal activities that enjoy near-official sanction. The American public has heard little of their efforts because of Canada's Official Secrets Act, modeled on Great Britain's own 1911 Official Secrets Act. That legislation prevents any publication or public discussion of what the government—that is, the British-appointed Governor-General—chooses to regard as a state secret. Given Canada's makeup, most drug-running, dirty money-laundering, and organized crime activity, including political terrorism, fall into that category. Anyone who writes about this in Canada will go to jail immediately and could, under the law, be executed. But without the help of Canadian citizens with access to official sources, willing to take the risk, this report could not have been written.

Three Crucial Cases

Before examining the structure of Canada's drug and dirty money operations, a few leading examples will suffice to indicate the nature of the problem. One is the personage of Walter Lockhart Gordon, honorary chairman for life of the Canadian Institute of International Affairs (CIIA), the Canadian offshoot of the British Royal Institute of International Affairs. The CIIA receives most of its funding directly from the office of the Governor-General. Every Canadian secretary of state for external affairs since the CIIA's founding has been a CIIA member. The CIIA is also the official sponsor of the Institute for Pacific Relations, the nexus of Britain's Beijing Connection, after pub-

lic scandal forced the Institute for Pacific Relations to leave the
United States after 1947.

1. Walter Lockhart Gordon

Walter Lockhart Gordon's fingerprints show up throughout
this section. Apart from his lifetime post at the top of the CIIA,
he is a past chairman of the Privy Council, the Governor-General's
select operations group for running Canadian politics
(1967–68); he was finance minister from 1963 to 1965; and a
director of some of the dirtiest corporate operations in Canada.

His father founded Clarkson and Gordon, the accounting firm
that audited three of the five Canadian chartered banks: Bank
of Nova Scotia, Toronto Dominion Bank, and Canadian Imperial
Bank. Steven Clarkson of Clarkson and Gordon has been
a leading member of the Canadian Institute of International
Affairs, as well as a leading sponsor of the Institute for Pacific
Relations. Through a network of accountants dispersed through
these banks, Clarkson and Gordon functioned as a command
center for the most extensive dirty money-landering operation
in the world, stretching from the heroin-receiving points in the
Pacific Northwest, to the branch operations of the Canadian
banks in the Caribbean Silver Triangle.

Gordon, as we shall detail below, was also Canada's chief
contact-man for the Beijing Connection.

2. The Eagle Star Insurance Company

A second example is the group of British "spooks" who run the
Eagle Star Insurance Company. Eagle Star is one of Britain's
largest financial corporations, and a joint operation between
Britain's top financial firms, including Barclays Bank, Lloyds,
Hill Samuel, and N.M. Rothschild and Sons.

Eagle Star runs the Bronfman family operation from the top,
through its control of English Properties, and English Properties'
control of the "Bronfman" Trizec Corporations.

The Bronfmans are what is known in intelligence jargon as
"cutouts," or controlled front-men. What is significant here is
Eagle Star's special qualifications for controlling the Bronfman
family's corporate group, which, in turn, has been the seat of

Canada's rum and dope-running, dirty money, and terrorist operations since Prohibition.

Eagle Star's management is British intelligence, by an arrangement that traces back to World War II.

Two Eagle Star directors, Sir Kenneth Strong and Sir Kenneth Keith, were number-one and number-two men, respectively, in British intelligence immediately after World War II—when the Bronfman family created its "legitimate" front Trizec with Eagle Star funding.[1] Both men have kept up their close ties to Britain's foreign intelligence service, MI6.

In a pattern that has already become familiar, Sir Kenneth Keith moved between the secret world of British intelligence and the opium politics of the Far East. Keith was also a leading member of the Canadian Institute of International Affairs. Among other leading corporate positions, including a directorship at Canada's Bank of Nova Scotia, he was the chairman of the Hill Samuel group of companies, one of the leading British merchant banks, and an incarnation of the old Samuel banking family's interests.

Sitting with Sir Kenneth Keith on the board of directors of Hill Samuel was the Hongkong and Shanghai Bank's Sir Philip de Zulueta, member of the HongShang's controlling London Committee. Zulueta was private parliamentary secretary to a string of British Conservative prime ministers while Sir Kenneth Strong was completing his career at British intelligence.

Eagle Star is a sterling example of Canada's role in drugs because it contains every element of the drug machine: the Bronfman family, which has spokes tying into the dirty money and terrorist apparat; the top levels of British intelligence; and the core of the opium trade, the HongShang itself.

3. The Hudson's Bay Company

The Hudson's Bay Company is the appropriate starting point for a look inside the operations of Canada's drug machine. During Prohibition, it was the partner of the Bronfmans' Seagram's in the "Pure Drug Company," the main source of bootleg liquor during Canada's dry period.

The Hudson's Bay is also a front for the grand old families

of the opium trade, the Inchcape and Keswick families, the proprietors, respectively, of the Peninsular and Orient Navigation Company, the world's largest shipping fleets, and Jardine Matheson, Hong Kong's dominant trading company. The second Earl of Inchcape, whose son still runs the P and O lines, wrote the notorious 1923 Inchcape report advocating the continuation of opium production in the Far East to maintain British revenues. The number-two man today at the P and O, vice chairman of the board Eric Drake, sits on the board of Hudson's Bay.

Jardine Matheson's Sir William Johnston Keswick—the chairman of the Shanghai Municipal Settlements during the 1930's peak of Shanghai heroin traffic—was a director of the Hudson's Bay Company.

William Johnston Keswick and Sir Eric Drake also sat together on the board of British Petroleum, next to Lord Humphrey Trevelyan, the chairman of the council of the Royal Institute of International Affairs and Britain's chargé d'affaires in Beijing during the critical years 1951 to 1953.

Drake was also a director of the top British merchant bank Kleinwort Benson. Kleinwort Benson's wholly owned subsidiary Sharps Pixley Ward jointly runs the Hong Kong gold market with the Hongkong and Shanghai Bank, a crucial support operation for the Far East drug traffic. Drake's fellow director, the deputy chairman of Kleinwort Benson, was Sir Mark Turner of Rio Tinto Zinc. Rio Tinto Zinc, in turn, was founded by Matheson family money in the 1840s, and the Mathesons ran Rio Tinto Zinc until the turn of the century. To complete the circle, William Johnston Keswick sits on the board of Jardine Matheson, along with several directors of Sir Eric Drake's P and O Navigation Company.

In short the Hudson's Bay Company, the most "Canadian" of companies, has been run from the top by a combination of Far Eastern old-line drug traffickers and their closest London contacts.

The Hong Kong opium connection goes even further. Sir William Keswick's son, Henry Neville Lindley Keswick, a board member of the Hongkong and Shanghai Bank, is also a director of Macmillan Bloedel, one of Canada's biggest pulp and paper operations, closely tied to the Macmillan publishing interests. The Macmillans took off as a Canadian family when Harold Macmillan—British Prime Minister at the time of the Kennedy administration—married the daughter of Canada's Governor-General, the Queen's personal representative. The Governor-General in question was the ninth Duke of Devonshire, Victor C.W. Cavendish, who held office from 1916 to 1920 at the outset of Prohibition; his son-in-law Harold Macmillan became his chief assistant in Canada in 1919, the same year that Arnold Rothstein set up the big liquor delivery contacts in England. The Governor-General's son William helped Joe Kennedy make contacts among big English distilleries. The Macmillan interests started with Prohibition. Today, through their association with William Johnston Keswick—who personally ran the Shanghai heroin traffic during the 1930s—they take a place in Dope, Inc.

Canadian Pacific, Ltd., the biggest company in Canada, holds a controlling interest in Macmillan Bloedel.

Dope Goes In; Dirty Money Goes Out

According to high-level Canadian intelligence sources, large quantities of heroin that reach North America are flown in through Canadian Pacific Air. There is no "smoking gun" evidence to substantiate this, but a November 1978 trial in Vancouver revealed evidence that Canadian Pacific was involved in the smuggling of twenty-two pounds of cocaine from Hong Kong.

The drugs come in through Canadian Pacific and then are conduited to points south of the border. Heavily interlocked with the Western Canada connection is the Bronfman group, whose corporate center is Seagram's, and whose financial center is the Trizec group. Since Prohibition, Seagram's has handled the flow of smuggling into the United States.

Both Seagram's (and its old Prohibition rum-running partner, Hudson's Bay) are interlocked through a maze of contacts
with all five of the big Canadian chartered banks: the Bank
of Montreal, the Royal Bank of Canada, the Bank of Nova
Scotia, the Toronto Dominion Bank, and the Canadian Imperial Bank of Commerce. Thus, the dirty money gleaned from
the drug trade is conduited through these banks to points
further south: The banks' offshore centers in the Caribbean,
and from there the money makes its whirlpool round of
worldwide laundering.

Canada's Big Five dominate all Canadian banking as
fiercely as the British Big Four—Barclays, National Westminster, Lloyds, and Midlands—do in Britain. Unlike the United
States, which has a relatively broadly spread base of regional
banking, Canadian and British banking is run from the top
by the institutions named. The Canadian institutions are
barely distinguishable in their current practice from the
British buccaneers who plied the Caribbean during the seventeenth century. Along with the British banks, which have
numerous joint ventures with the Canadians—for example,
the Royal Bank operates in the Bahamas under the "RoyWest"
cover in a joint venture with National Westminster—they
are the core of the dirty money operations offshore of the
United States.

In 1978, the Royal Bank of Canada had twenty-one affiliates
in offshore banking and subsidiaries—more than any other
bank in the world save Barclays Bank. Its "RoyWest" connection to the National Westminster Bank tied it closely to the
Hongkong and Shanghai Bank itself; HongShang had two mutual directors with National Westminster, J.A.F. Binny and
R.D. Dent. Dent is the descendant of the old-line British opium-
trading family that founded Lancelot Dent about the same time
that Jardine Matheson appeared.

Among other links, the Royal Bank of Canada is tied to the
Bronfmans through Neil Phillips—son of Lazarus Phillips, the
Bronfman family's lawyer and most trusted aide from Prohibi-
tion until the 1950s.

Canada's Silver Triangle

Royal Bank has the dirtiest reputation of any bank in the Caribbean. According to authoritative diplomatic sources, the Royal Bank of Canada directly ordered the Guyanese government to plant marijuana in order to raise foreign exchange income. In 1976, when Guyana went flat broke and applied to the International Monetary Fund for emergency assistance, Royal Bank of Canada officials met with senior members of the Guyana government. The Royal Bank insisted that Guyana transform its economy into a "cash crop" producer before it, or any other major bank, would issue loans. The Guyanese were desperate and did what they were told. Northwest Guyana, in consequence, became a major producer of marijuana for the North American market.

Second in the Caribbean offshore centers to the Royal Bank is the Bank of Nova Scotia. A top Bronfman aide and figure in Canadian Zionist organizations, R.D. Wolfe, sat both on the board of Seagram's and the Bank of Nova Scotia. Scotiabank has thirteen branches in offshore centers, as well as innumerable joint ventures and similar fronts.

Banking and diplomatic sources agree that the Bank of Nova Scotia has been the number-one handler of flight capital out of Caribbean countries, especially troubled countries such as Jamaica. Apart from funds fleeing difficult political situations, much, if not most, of all illegal money transfers out of the Caribbean. In the late 1970s, a large portion of Jamaican illegal funds was conduited through a Jamaican national employed in a senior position at the big New York brokerage house Drexel Burnham Lambert.[2]

Scotiabank's Jamaican trade is a particularly filthy business, since it involves shifting funds earned in Jamaica by local criminals into safe havens. The cash side of the Jamaican operations, according to law enforcement sources, is done more with arms than drugs. Planes fly into Jamaica with loads of small arms, and take loads of marijuana out. The retail side in Jamaica is arms-selling. The ultimate cash proceeds of the selling chain are then laundered through Scotiabank.

The Bank of Nova Scotia's role in Canadian gold markets, is through its own trading operations and its interlock with the chairman of the second largest Canadian gold trader, Noranda Mines. According to informed New York gold market sources, a substantial proportion of Nova Scotia's flight capital operations are accomplished through illegal purchases of gold by Jamaican and other nationals. The same sources add that Dr. Henry Jarecki's Mocatta Metals in New York has a substantial share of Caribbean dirty money traffic.

The Canada-Beijing Connection

The starting point of any examination of Canadian drug traffic is Walter Lockhart Gordon's close relationship to Canadian Pacific. Gordon was Canada's grand old man, honorary chairman of the Canadian Institute of International Affairs for life, top leader of the ruling Liberal Party, finance minister after 1963, and chief foreign policy-maker in Canada for the past thirty years. He is also on the board of directors of the Canadian Corporate Management Corporation, a holding company interlocked with the Hudson's Bay Company.

Authoritative Canadian intelligence sources further identified Gordon as the controller of Canada's three leading China specialists, Paul Lin, James Endicott, and Chester Ronning. The association went back in the cases of Endicott and Ronning to the end of World War II, when the two returned from close collaboration with Chou En-lai, to become the core of the transplanted Institute for Pacific Relations in Canada.

Based in Montreal, Paul Lin was the go-between for Walter Gordon and the Vancouver, British Columbia, drug wholesaling and transshipment operations. Lin's most important contact was the former president of drug-shipping Canadian Pacific, John C. Gilmer, a Knight of St. John of Jerusalem. Paul Lin was the attorney for Canadian Pacific.

In addition, there were two open representatives of the People's Republic of China in Vancouver, B.C., the Chinese Commercial Corporation and the Chinese Cultural Center. The latter received funding from another Knight of St. John, John Robert Nicholson, a close associate of Gilmer.

All these men have been working together since the Institute for Pacific Relations served as the Royal Institute of International Affairs' bridgehead into the United States, and Chester Ronning was meeting weekly with Wang Ping-nan and occasionally with Chou En-lai in Chungking.

Endicott, now an old man, created the leading North American center of explicit Maoism, the Norman Bethune Institute at York University. Walter Gordon was the university's chancellor for many years. Gordon personally arranged the funding of the Bethune Institute, named after a Canadian doctor who served in Mao's armies.

Gordon's accounting firm, Clarkson and Gordon, tried to keep its nose clean of overt involvement in the drug trade. But one of its escapades caused a public scandal in Canada some years ago. Clarkson and Gordon put together the funding for Rochdale College in Toronto, an experimental university that quickly became the most drug-ridden college campus in Canada. By the early 1970s Rochdale College had become not only a main center of illegal drug consumption, but also the retail distribution point for marijuana and hallucinogens throughout most of Eastern Canada. When the story inevitably became headline material in the early 1970s, Canadian police were compelled to shut it down, as a matter of public decency. Clarkson and Gordon, who had created Rochdale College, sadly took the drug-ridden remnant back, acting as its receiver and liquidator.

Who Rules Canada

But the company to which Gordon was closest is Canadian Pacific, which controlled most of the dominion's air, sea, and land transportation. It is interlocked three ways with Seagram's, Ltd., the core of the Bronfman group. No fewer than fourteen of Canadian Pacific's directors sat on the boards of the five major chartered banks.

Most important, Canadian Pacific featured no fewer than four members of the Most Venerable Order of the Knights of St. John of Jerusalem on its board. They included the aforementioned J.C. Gilmer of Vancouver; W.E. McLaughlin, the chairman of the board of the Royal Bank of Canada; and J.P.W. Ostiguy.

Only one other corporation in the world, Barclays Bank, contains more members of the British monarchy's most elite order among its directors. That fact alone establishes Canadian Pacific's vassalhood before the feudal rights of the British monarchy. In terms of Canada's real chain of command, it is an honor for Charles R. Bronfman to sit on Canadian Pacific's board.

The concentration of Knights of Malta on the council of the Canadian Pacific Company also clears up—from a professional intelligence standpoint—why that company has special access to the Far Eastern narcotics traffic. The chairman of the board of the Hongkong and Shanghai Bank from 1962 to 1970 was Sir Michael Turner. When the current chairman, M.G. Sandberg, replaced Turner in 1970, he remained on the London Committee of the HongShang (as well as on the board of directors of National Westminster Bank, with two of his fellow HongShang directors). Sandberg was created Commander of St. John, a high-ranking position in the elite order, in 1960. He is still the chairman of the Council of St. John—the organization of the Knights—in Hong Kong. The company most under the direction of the Knights of Malta in Canada deals directly with the chief of their order in Hong Kong.

At the other end of the Canadian drug cycle, each of the five Canadian dirty money banks had in 1978 at least one Knight of Malta on its board. The Canadian Imperial Bank and the Bank of Nova Scotia were directed by three Knights of Malta each.

The Canadian Institute of International Affairs—which has picked every Canadian foreign minister of this century—is not a Canadian institution, but the local branch of the British monarchy's most elite chivalric order. Canada's former Governor-General and chairman of the CIIA, Roland Michener, was also a Knight of St. John. A board member of the Italian branch of the Order of St. John, the Order of St. Lazarus, was a member of the CIIA's board, Henry R. Jackman. J.J. Jodrey, another board member, was also a Knight of St. John.

The Order of St. John respects the same chain of command as Canada's Governor-General and Privy Council: the Queen of England, who is the titular head of the Order, and the Queen's cousin, the Duke of Gloucester, who is Grand Prior of the Order. These men control the finances and logistics of Canada's economy. Through a series of "cutouts," like the Bronfman family, they also control much of the drug-running, the organized crime, and the political terrorism directed against the United States.

10

The Families Behind the Drug Empire

Why, if so much detailed evidence on the world narcotics traffic exists in the public record or in the files of law enforcement agencies, has this picture remained hidden for so long? One answer is that the HongShang and other top traffickers who mingle freely in the business world were designed specifically to hide the drug trade behind a facade of legitimate finance. The more important answer lies deeper.

The answer takes the reader behind the oh-so-respectable corporate boardrooms and precious metal exchanges, to the international oligarchy—in particular, the British elite. What we now present is the real *family* operation responsible for the financing and directing of the opium trade, including every crucial juncture in the development of Dope, Inc.: from the expansion of opium production in India, through the Opium

Wars against China, up through the Opium War against the United States.

Popular accounts of organized crime families, give the reader a starting point whence to look at Great Britain's oligarchy, but the British dynasty is far more sinister.

The Family Religion

The sinister element that sets the British oligarchy apart from the popular image of the mafia family is its unshakable belief that it alone is fit to rule the world—the view reflected in Cecil Rhodes's 1877 Testament. Their religion is not the Anglican Christianity they publicly profess, but a hodgepodge of paganism, including satanic cults such as Theosophy and Rosicrucianism. The central, syncretic ideology of the oligarchy's inner cult life is the revived Egyptian drug cult, the myth of Isis and Osiris, the same anti-Christian cult that ran the Roman Empire. And like the ancient Isis-worshipping Egyptian dynasties, the British ruling family networks have maintained power for centuries by keeping the secrets of their intrigues *within the family*.

The Cult of Isis, dredged up in modern format, was the official ideology of leading British politicians, financiers, and literary figures during the previous century. The Isis cult also formed the core of Lord Palmerston's Scottish Rite of Freemasonry. Its great public exponent was the colonial secretary during the Second Opium War, Edward Bulwer-Lytton, the author of *The Last Days of Pompeii*, which first popularized the Isis cult, and the mentor of Cecil Rhodes's whole generation of British imperialists.[1]

The Royal Institute of International Affairs was the "secret society" called for in Rhodes's will and is the body that provides the command structure for the drug trade. But the Royal Institute itself was founded by an even more secret group: the "Circle of Initiates . . . devoted to the extension of the British Empire,"

in the description of one of its historians.[2] The Circle of Initiates
included Lord Milner; Cecil Rhodes, the founder of Britain's
African mining empire; future prime minister Arthur Balfour;
Albert Grey; and Lord Rothschild.

All these men celebrated forms of the Isis cult. Their
worldview was largely designed by Bulwer-Lytton and his protégé John Ruskin. Britain's high priest of Isis, Bulwer-Lytton,
was also the British government's chief drug-runner.

The words of American Founding Father Thomas Paine to
characterize British King George III, against whom America
fought the Revolutionary War, thus are highly appropriate: "I
rejected the hardened, sullen-tempered *Pharaoh of England*
forever . . . and disdain the wretch."[3]

The Beginning: The Knights of St. John of Jerusalem

The elite of the elite in Britain's secret dynastic life is Her
Majesty's Most Venerable Order of St. John of Jerusalem—the
"Christians who are not really Christians."[4] We have already
highlighted the Knights' prominence in the centers of the world
drug traffic: from the Hongkong and Shanghai Bank to the
Canadian Pacific in Vancouver to Barclays Bank in London.
Although Queen Victoria reconstituted the Most Venerable
Order in the 1880s as the Protestant British branch of the
Knights of Malta, our tale properly begins much earlier with
the original order of the Knights of St. John, founded in Jerusalem in 1070. The Order of St. John inherited what British
authors smirkingly call "the wisdom of the East" from the
Coptic, Gnostic, and Manichean networks of the Eastern Mediterranean. The Order of St. John thus maintained direct continuity with the ancient Cult of Isis.

However distant from the familiarity of the American reader,
the area we have entered must be viewed the way the families
themselves see it. The brooding evil of Walter Scott or Robert

Louis Stevenson romances, or their cheap Gothic novel imitations, gives the reader a basis for insight into the inner history of the families, and the need to begin with cobwebbed history in order to get to the bottom of Dope, Inc.

To begin at the beginning: In the fourteenth century, the Order of St. John's emergence in England was part of a project to annihilate its humanist opposition, the Knights Templar. Total warfare had broken out on the continent. The oligarchs in France and Italy, Philip the Fair and Pope Clement V, slaughtered hundreds of Templars, and burned the Templars' courageous Grand Master, Jacques de Molay, at the stake in 1314.

A renegade group of Templars under the command of an adventurous thug, King Robert Bruce, grabbed Scotland—Europe's least civilized outpost—as an "offshore" stronghold, as a form of insurance against their uncertain fortunes on the European continent. King Robert Bruce is the spiritual founder of the Scottish Rite of Freemasonry.

> After the death of Jacques de Molay, some Scottish Templars . . . at the instigation of Robert Bruce ranged themselves under the banners of a New Order [The Royal Order of Scotland] instituted by this prince. . . . *It is there that we must seek the origin of the Scottish masonry.*[5]

This statement by a leading historian of the Masonic movement is the standard interpretation of the origin of the Scottish Rite.

The Family's Opium Wars

There is in fact a direct lineage from King Robert Bruce to the British officials who ran the first opium wars against China. James Bruce, the eighth Earl of Elgin—after supervising the Caribbean slave trade as Jamaican Governor-General from 1842 to 1846—was appointed ambassador and minister plenipotentiary to China from 1857 to 1861—the period covering the

Second Opium War against China. His brother Frederick Bruce had been colonial secretary at Hong Kong during the mopping-up operations following the First Opium War and returned to China in 1857 to assist his brother in delivering the British government's ultimatum to the Chinese emperor.[6]

The British *Dictionary of National Biography* summarizes the Chinese career of the elder Bruce succinctly:

> In 1857 Elgin was sent as envoy to China. On reaching Singapore he was met by letters from Lord Canning informing him of the Indian mutiny, and urging him to send troops to Calcutta from the force which was to accompany him to China. With this requisition he at once complied, sending in fact the whole of the force, but he proceeded himself to Hong Kong in the expectation that troops would speedily follow. . . .
>
> He repaired to Calcutta. . . . Later in the year he returned to China, fresh troops having been sent out [to replace those which had been directed to India]. . . . Canton was speedily taken and some months later a treaty was made at Tientsin, providing, among other matters, for the appointment of a British minister, for additional facilities for British trade [opium] . . . and for a war indemnity.

Elgin returned to England in 1859.

> In the following year he was again sent to China, the Emperor having failed to ratify the treaty of Tientsin and having committed other unfriendly acts. . . . The military opposition [to Elgin's mass addiction policy] was not effective, but the Chinese resorted to treachery. [Chinese forces killed some British troops enforcing opium distribution.] In retribution for his treacherous acts, the summer palace, the favorite residence of the Emperor at Beijing, was destroyed. A few days later the treaty of Tientsin was formally ratified.[7]

The account concludes that Elgin's "letters show he was a man of warm affections, eminently domestic, with very decided convictions on religion. . . ."

Who was running England at the time? The Prime Minister was the same Lord Palmerston who turned the Scottish Rite into Britain's leading cash-producing export product. The foreign secretary was Lord John Russell, son of the sixth Duke of Bedford, and grandfather of Britain's most dangerous twentieth-century intelligence operative—Bertrand Russell.

Palmerston and Russell were relatives of the Bruce brothers, the Elgin peerage, by marriage into the direct line of Order of St. John control over England. The branch that encompasses Britain's two leading cabinet ministers during the Second Opium War is the Villiers line. The line began with George Villiers, who assisted Robert Cecil and Edward Bruce in seizing the English throne for another descendant of Robert Bruce— James I of Scotland—in 1603.[8]

Lord Russell's daughter, Victoria, married into the Villiers family. Russell's grandson, Bertrand, among his other covert operations, maintained liaison with Chou En-lai throughout the postwar period on behalf of British intelligence.[9]

Even more significant is the third member of the London team during the Opium Wars—Colonial Secretary Edward Bulwer-Lytton, a relation by marriage of the Duke of Wellington. His son married Edith Villiers, of the same branch of the leading Order of St. John dynasty.

The Imperial Cultists and Opium

Bulwer-Lytton is best known to Americans through his 1838 novel, *The Last Days of Pompeii*, but he is also both the spiritual father of the Cecil Rhodes-Lord Milner secret societies and of Nazi fascism. Bulwer-Lytton led the English Rosicrucians, a branch of the Scottish Rite Masons headed by Prime Minister Palmerston.

Unlike the comparatively closed-mouth members of the British elite around him, Bulwer-Lytton was an outspoken exponent of the Isis cult, which formed the subject of his famous novel. His popularized Isis myth was the inspiration for an entire array of warped imitations.

Included among these was Helena Blavatsky's book, *Isis Unveiled,* and her Theosophist cult. Theosophy was the Satanic bible of the mystic secret societies, including Germany's "Thule" group, which produced most of Hitler's SS.[10]

Another Bulwer-Lytton protégé was satanist Aleister Crowley, of the "Thule" group's equivalent in England, the "Isis-Urania Hermetic Order of the Golden Dawn." Both of these groups traced their lineage back to Palmerston's Scottish Rite Masons through Bulwer-Lytton.[11]

Aleister Crowley was the tutor of Aldous Huxley, the prophet of mind control, who later introduced the LSD cult into the United States during the 1950s.[12]

Britain's imperial link to Nazi fascism is even more direct in the case of Bulwer-Lytton's other published work. His novel *Rienzi,* about the Knights of St. John, provided the text of Richard Wagner's first opera. His 1871 novel, *Vril: The Power of the Coming Race,* contained virtually everything that Houston Stewart Chamberlain later had to say on racial theory; Professor Karl Haushofer, who ghost-wrote most of *Mein Kampf* in Hitler's prison cell fifty years later, named his first secret organization the "Vril Society."[13] Bulwer-Lytton's Nazi German and British secret societies met officially for the last time when Nazi minister Rudolf Hess attempted to make contact in 1941 by flying to Britain.

Bulwer-Lytton directly influenced John Ruskin at Oxford University and established the lineage that leads—through such names as Milner and Rhodes—to the present-day Royal Institute of International Affairs. Ruskin's students included Milner, Rhodes, Albert Grey, and the future director of research for the RIIA, Arnold Toynbee.

Ruskin's inaugural speech at Oxford in 1870, inspired by Bulwer-Lytton, left such an impression on Cecil Rhodes that he carried a handwritten version of it with him until he died.

The speech—which set the tone for Rhodes's 1877 will—stated in part:

> There is a destiny now possible to us—the highest ever set before a nation, to be accepted or refused. We are still undegenerate in race; a race mingled of the best northern blood. . . . We are rich in an inheritance of honour, which it should be our daily thirst to increase with splendid avarice. . . . [England] must found colonies as fast and as far as she is able . . . seizing every piece of fruitful ground she can set her foot on, and teaching these her colonists that their . . . first aim is to advance the power of England by land and sea. . . .[14]

Bulwer-Lytton's son Edward Lytton was Viceroy and Governor-General in India from 1876 to 1880. Two aspects of the younger Lytton's rule in India are important to this report. First, Lytton supervised the single greatest expansion period in the history of opium production in British India.[15] Palmerston had set forth this task as a means of compensating for Britain's industrial decline relative to the United States.

Second, Edward Lytton's rule in India provided a home for the most important of the crackpot cultists inspired by his father. Lytton himself was the closest friend of Rudyard Kipling's parents, members of the circle around A.P. Sinnett's Allahabad journal *The Pioneer*.[16] The elder Bulwer-Lytton's follower, Madame Blavatsky of the Theosophy cult, appeared in India in 1879, and recruited A.P. Sinnett to her belief-structure.[17] Both Kipling and Blavatsky employed the swastika as their personal mystic symbol. From Kipling, Blavatsky, Haushofer, and others, the swastika found its way into the German cults that formed the core of later Nazism.

Kipling's last major official post was under press czar Lord Beaverbrook at the wartime Propaganda Ministry; working side-by-side with him was a relative of the Lyttons' by marriage, Sir Charles Hambro. Hambro went on to run Britain's dirty operations during World War II as chief of the Special Operations Executive from 1942 onward. Kipling also served as a trustee of the Rhodes Trust from 1917 until 1925.

Kipling's cousin, Stanley Baldwin, was Prime Minister from 1923 to 1929 and from 1935 to 1937; during his second tenure, the Baldwin government groomed Hitler as a "marcher lord" against the Soviet Union, setting the stage for Munich in 1938.[18]

Another well-known British literary figure, also with a mystical bent, deserves mention in this context: Alfred, Lord Tennyson. Tennyson married the niece of the eighth Lord of Elgin (James Bruce), and remained a close personal friend of the commander-in-chief of the Second Opium War. Tennyson was a founding member of the Metaphysical Society, with Bulwer-Lytton's protégé John Ruskin, Lord John Russell's uncle Lord Arthur Russell, future prime minister Arthur Balfour, and Thomas Huxley.[19] In 1880, the Metaphysical Society was reorganized, and became the Aristotelian Society. Lord John Russell's grandson Bertrand Russell became the Aristotelian Society's president: One of his successors was Sir Karl Popper.

Tennyson's unambiguous endorsement of opium abuse was expressed in his well-known poem, "The Lotus Eaters":

Let us swear an oath, and keep it with an equal mind.
In the hollow Lotus-land to live and lie reclined,
On the hills like Gods together, careless of Mankind.[20]

Today's Opium Dynasty

The closing days of the Baldwin government and the opening days of World War II are an appropriate place to pick up the contemporary trail of the leading opium families—the Inchcapes and Keswicks. In 1939 the creation of Britain's Ministry of Economic Warfare offered a meeting place for the old families: Sir John Henry Keswick, later the architect of the Beijing Connection; Sir Mark Turner, the current chairman of the old Matheson-Keswick firm Rio Tinto Zinc; Gerald Hyde Villiers, a leading scion of the evil old family; and John Kidston Swire, of the old Swire dope-trading family.

Starting from the Matheson family's role in the First Opium War and tracing through to the World War II period and up to the present, the fortunes of the Matheson and Keswick line of the dynasty run the entire gamut of political developments surrounding the drug trade.

The Rio Tinto Zinc Company was founded in 1873 by James Sutherland Matheson's nephew Hugh Matheson—taking the lineage of that firm all the way back to the days of George III and the American Revolution through then-Prime Minister Spencer Perceval. The younger Matheson founded the firm with his uncle's opium profits and help from the Schroeder banking family—who in 1931 funded Bulwer-Lytton's ideological spawn, Adolf Hitler. The Lyttons and Mathesons are relatives by marriage, through the Villiers family and the Sutherland family.

Hugh Matheson's successor at Rio Tino Zinc in 1898 was J.J. Keswick, a partner in the opium-running Jardine Matheson firm, and a relative of the Mathesons by marriage through the Fraser family.

Apart from their leading role in Jardine Matheson, J.J. Keswick's family had a leading role in the British governance of the official opium trade. His cousin, William P. Keswick, was British consul-general in Hong Kong during the same years that Edward Lytton, Governor-General in India, was expanding opium output according to the Palmerston program.

William P. Keswick's son Henry Keswick, a past chairman of the Hongkong and Shanghai Bank at the height of its dope-trading glory, had three sons: David, John H., and William J. David Keswick, who is still among the largest shareholders and a partner of the London merchant bank Samuel Montagu. Sitting with him on the board of Samuel Montagu is Rio Tinto Zinc's Sir Mark Turner. Turner, as noted, also worked with brother Sir John Henry Keswick in the Ministry of Economic Warfare. Later, John Henry went on to the British embassy in Chungking, picking up the opium trail where World War II had cut it off.

The third brother, Sir William Johnston Keswick, is a prominent figure in Dope, Inc.'s Canadian connection. Keswick ruled the Shanghai Municipal Settlements at the height of Shanghai's heroin traffic, and set up the first big heroin connection, via intermediary Jacob "Yasha" Katzenberg.

The family history of the Keswicks intersects the story of the Russells, Villiers, and Bruces through their most senior political operatives, notably Lord Milner. Milner, Cecil Rhodes's protégé, bridged the gap between the establishment of the Rhodes Trust and the creation of the Royal Institute of International Affairs in 1920. Milner became a director of Rio Tinto Zinc in 1921 and served as chairman from 1922 until his death in 1925.

During World War I Milner worked closely with wartime British Commissioner in St. Petersburg, Frederick Lindley, and William Boyce Thompson in setting forth a geopolitical policy most advantageous to Britain's free hand in drug-running.[21]

Frederick Lindley was the grandfather of Henry Neville Lindley Keswick, who currently occupies the traditional family seats at the head of Jardine Matheson's directors and on the board of the Hongkong and Shanghai Bank.

The third member of the Milner team, William Boyce Thompson, was the head of the Red Cross delegation in Russia; the Red Cross is, officially, the "charitable" side of the Order of St. John of Jerusalem.[22] After the war, Thompson, with funding from the Morgan bank, established the Anglo-American mining firm in South Africa—which now controls 60% of world gold output outside the Soviet Union, and, through its controlling interest in De Beers, virtually all the diamond output. That is the origin of London's control over the precious metals and gems channels for laundering dirty money.

To tie these strands back into the main line of the narcotics traffic: Milner's hand-picked successor at Rio Tinto Zinc, whose original mines were in Spain, was Sir Auckland Geddes. Geddes, who ruled until 1952, was a sponsor of Francisco Franco's fascist coup in Spain.[23] His nephew, Ford Irvine Geddes, was a director and then chairman from 1971 to 1972 of the Inchcape family's huge shipping complex, the P and O Navigation Company, which has shipped more opium than any other entity in the world.

One of P and O's officers, deputy chairman Sir Eric Drake, is a close associate of Sir William Johnston Keswick, also of the old Rio Tinto Zinc family. Drake and W.J. Keswick jointly control Canada's Hudson's Bay Company, which established the rum-running routes from Canada into the United States during Prohibition, together with the Bronfmans.

The old Inchcape family, whose current scion, the third Earl of Inchcape, still is chairman of the P and O Lines, is closely related to the Matheson family of Jardine Matheson. The founder of Jardine Matheson, James Sutherland Matheson, was the son of Katherine Mackay and Donald Matheson; Mackay is the family name of the Earls of Inchcape. The third Earl, J.W. Mackay, is the son of the second Earl of Inchcape who authored the 1923 Inchcape Report, insisting that the opium trade must be maintained to "protect the revenues" of the British Empire—despite the outcry of the League of Nations.

Through the current Lord Inchcape, the old opium dynasty married into the highest level of British banking. The afore-mentioned J.W. Mackay of the P and O Lines married Aline Pease: His brother-in-law, Richard T. Pease, has been the vice chairman of Barclays Bank since 1970. Barclays Bank, as noted, is the controlling institution for the entire array of Israeli financial operations, through its control over the current Japhet family bank—Charterhouse Japhet. The current senior Japhet family member, Ernst Israel Japhet, is now the chairman of Israel's biggest commercial bank, Bank Leumi. Barclays Bank controls outright Israel's second largest commercial bank, the Israel Discount Bank.

Taken together, the Inchcapes, Keswicks, Peases, and related families' control over London's banking establishment becomes a swirl of intermarriages, to the point that the top London banks and the scions of the drug trade appear as a single family entity, rather than competing or even parallel institutions. For example, the current deputy chairman of Inchcape and Co.—the family holding company that owns majority stock in the P and O Lines—is Sir Hugh Mackay-Tallack. Mackay-Tallack is also the deputy chairman of the Standard and Chartered Bank, the second-largest bank in the Far East after the HongShang. The third Lord Inchcape himself, J.W. Mackay, is also a director of Standard and Chartered, along with cousin Sir Hugh.

The Pease branch of the Family is further closely related to:

■ The Schroeder Bank, whose chairman, the tenth Earl of Airlie, is the brother-in-law of A.D.F. Lloyd, of the bank that bears his name.

■ Kuhn Loeb, whose leading partner was Otto Kahn; his granddaughter is the wife of the tenth Earl of Airlie, the chairman of Schroeder Bank.

■ The family of Winston Churchill, whose mother-in-law was an Airlie;

■ The Lazard group, related to the Churchills by marriage; Lazard controls the London *Financial Times,* the *Economist,* Penguin books, as well as one of Britain's top merchant banks. It should be remembered that the Lytton family and the Keswick family are related to each other, via marriage through the Fraser family, whose current leading member is deputy chairman of Lazard.

Notes: Part III

1: Banking and the World's Biggest Business

1. Based on interviews with Drug Enforcement Administration sources. The typical deviation from the price trend resulted from the importation of several kilograms of high-grade number-four (85 to 95%) heroin from Vietnam by individual returning soldiers, who would attempt to start their own distribution chain. Such incidents stood out because the novice distributor tended to dilute the heroin too little—often distributing heroin at 30% purity and above, rather than 5% purity, the normal dilution. The freelance pusher would therefore occasion an extraordinarily large number of drug overdoses, enabling the authorities to spot him quickly.

2. The 740 ton figure comes from the U.S. Drug Enforcement Administration. Approximately this figure is also used by the most widely circulated sources on the subject.

3. *The New York Times,* January 20, 1971, p.1.

4. *Euromoney* (London), April 1978.

2: How to Hide $200 Billion

1. Electronic funds transfer refers to the introduction of computerized interbank transfers, thus far within the New York Clearinghouse system of the twelve largest New York City banks. The Clearinghouse International Payments System (CHIPS), run through a large Burroughs computer at the New York Clearinghouse office in lower Manhattan, is seeking, through the Federal Reserve, to extend itself to the entire national banking system, in association with unregulated "free banking zones."

3: From Opium to Dirty Money

1. Calculated on the basis of price markups as reported by law enforcement sources in interviews with the authors.

2. The estimate was derived from the following calculations: At the 1971–1972 peak of heroin production in the Golden Triangle, much of which was intended for American soldiers in Vietnam, twenty-one refineries were in operation; since then the number has declined.

Assuming that ten are still in operation, and that the annual output of each is equivalent to the 3,000 kilograms of heroin seized in one major bust on record, then they produce roughly 30,000 kilograms a year of heroin, derived from about 300 tons of raw opium.

3. Richard Deacon, *The Chinese Secret Service* (New York: Ballantine Books, 1976), p. 447.

4: How the Drug Trade Is Financed

1. London *Financial Times,* April 24, 1978.

2. Ibid.

3. A close examination of the price markup structure of the Golden Triangle's primary wholesalers demonstrates that the increased prices at various stages merely account for substantial additional expenses, including the livelihoods of an inestimable number of Thai and Burmese policemen and customs officials. The real profitability—the enormous profits associated with the traffic—depends on the process of cutting the pure heroin into "decks" of street quality for sale in the West. The profits of the Hong Kong syndicates who wholesale heroin are not accrued through the difference between primary and secondary wholesale prices, but as a percentage of the profits obtained through distribution of the drugs in the West. In other words, the Hong Kong networks are directly represented in the Western "organized crime" segment of Dope, Inc. and take their cut in the form of a reflow of the retailing profits. Scattered bits of evidence—the most prominent of which is the activities of the expatriate Chinese community in Vancouver—indicate that this is, in fact, how these syndicates operate.

4. Certain aspects of the expatriate Chinese activity antedate the British. The predominance of Chinese compradors in the region, however, dates to the turn of this century. The Soviets also play a role in the expatriate Chinese community.

5. W.J. Cator, *The Economic Position of the Chinese in the Netherlands Indies,* pp. 97–98.

6. Victor Purcell, *The Chinese in Malaya,* p. 189.

7. William Skinner, *Chinese Society in Thailand, An Analytical History,* p. 140.

5: Britain's Dirty Gold and Diamond Operation

1. Timothy Green, "Other World Markets," speech at the Gold Conference of the London *Financial Times* and *Investors Chronicle,* the London Hilton, October 24, 1972.

2. Paul Ferris, *The City* (London, 1951).

3. H.R. Reinhart, *The Reporter,* July 22, 1952.

4. Ibid.

5. The information below is from 1978, and although some of the names may have been changed, the picture of financial incest that emerges is as true now as it was then.

6. This information is a by-product of an *Executive Intelligence Review* investigation of the operations of the Israeli intelligence agency Mossad, for which Jarecki appears to be a "bagman." The details were cross-checked with law enforcement officials.

7. According to interview with leading diamond traders in New York.

7: Beijing Connection

The current "standard reference work" of the Far East traffic is *The Politics of Heroin in Southeast Asia,* by Alfred W. McCoy, with Cathleen B. Read and Leonard P. Adams II (New York: Harper and Row, 1972). In dismissing the claims of former Bureau of Narcotics and Dangerous Drugs chief Harry Anslinger, McCoy quotes an unnamed BNDD agent who dismisses Anslinger's accusations against Beijing, saying that the People's Republic of China has no role whatsoever in the opium trade, and that Anslinger's accusations are substantiated by nothing more than Taiwanese propaganda. McCoy cites no other evidence, and merely brushes the issue aside.

In fact, McCoy and his co-authors went so far out on a limb that even sympathetic experts were forced to correct them. In a review published in the *Bulletin of Concerned Asian Scholars* in September 1973, Peter Dale Scott wrote:

"McCoy quotes U.S. narcotics officials today to ridicule the 1950s claims by then-U.S. Narcotics Commissioner Anslinger (and his government) about Communist China's 'twenty-year plan to finance political activities and spread addiction' in the United States. But McCoy subscribes to the equally dubious 'Turkey hypothesis' which replaced Anslinger's in the 1960s; namely, that all of the U.S. plague of heroin produced in the laboratories of Marseilles could be attributed to opium grown in the Middle East. McCoy even claims that

Throughout the 1960s . . . the U.S. Bureau of Narcotics paid almost no attention to Asia, there were few seizures of Asian heroin and little awareness of the colony's growing role in the international traffic. It was not until American GIs serving in Vietnam began using . . . heroin refined in the Golden Triangle region that any attention was focused on the Asian heroin trade. (pp.223–224)

"That is an important claim," reviewer Scott continued, "and it is quite false. In 1960, as he knows, the United States officially listed Hong Kong as the first of the 'principal sources' of the diacetylmorphine (heroin) seized in the United States; and the Federal Bureau of Narcotics showed its concern by opening a branch office in Hong Kong in 1963. Anslinger himself, while transmitting KMT [Kuomintang, or Taiwanese] propaganda about a Red Chinese opium conspiracy, proved himself to be well-informed about the worldwide significance of the Northern Thailand traffic, even to such details as the roles played by a Macao financial syndicate, and a Bangkok official of the Soong Bank of Canton." Peter Dale Scott's references are to Harry J. Anslinger, "The Opium of the People's Government," in *Soviet Total War,* 85th Congress, House Document No. 227, pp. 759–761.

The accuracy or inaccuracy of Harry Anslinger's presentation is not what is in question at the moment. Rather, it is a simple point of fact that McCoy and his co-authors have no facts whatever to indicate that the PRC is *not* involved in the drug traffic; and furthermore, that their treatment of U.S. authorities who presented facts implicating the PRC is wildly inaccurate. As the Scott review demonstrated, that is a matter of the published record.

Experts on the Southeast Asian theater at the time McCoy wrote simply doubt the author's integrity. McCoy had available to him a mass of documentary evidence showing that roughly half of the Golden Triangle growing area lay within the confines of Communist China's Yunnan province. He also had available a substantial portion of corroborating facts contained in this report. McCoy simply chose to ignore this evidence, or, more accurately, to attempt to refute it with unsubstantiated assertions. According to individuals who knew McCoy when he was a regular in the anti-Vietnam War movement, McCoy was in close friendly contact with North Vietnamese legations in Western Europe at the time of writing of *The Politics of Heroin in Southeast Asia,* and intended his efforts to undermine the American war effort. In that context he deliberately excised references to PRC opium-trafficking. Since the PRC and Vietnam have come to blows over the status of the expatriate Chinese comprador community in the latter country, it may be that McCoy's political judgment, rather than Vietnamese views, were faulty on this subject. *McCoy's book cannot be taken seriously as far as the PRC issue is concerned.*

1. Heikal, Mohammed Hassanein, *The Cairo Documents* (Garden City, N.Y.: Doubleday and Company, 1973), pp. 306–307.

2. Figures in this chapter are based on 1978 data.

3. The significance of the investment, which occasioned widespread commentary in the Western press, is not so much the novelty of the joint-venture format, but the surfacing of longstanding business relationships between Jardine's and the PRC.

4. Beijing's influence on the international gold market has been the subject of considerable commentary in the financial press; during 1977, the Bank of China suddenly released about 80 tons of gold onto the international markets, a move which commentators believed depressed the gold price. What commentators were then at a loss to explain is how the PRC, which runs a chronic balance-of-trade deficit, was able to obtain the gold in advance of selling it off. Beijing's role in the gold-related aspects of opium financing provides some explanation.

5. *International Currency Review,* vol. 10, no. 4, p. 146.

6. London *Financial Times,* July 4, 1977, p. 20.

7. Interviews with law enforcement officers. Law enforcement authorities suspect, but have never proven, that the Shaw Brothers' international film distribution network also conduits narcotics.

8. Deacon, *Chinese Secret Service,* pp. 437–438.

9. In 1949, according to recently released American diplomatic cables, the newly formed PRC was happy to permit Britain to retain control over Hong Kong for the same reason.

10. *Management Magazine* (South Africa), December 1975. The Rennie and Matheson families' relations go back much further than the recent merger of business operations. They are intermarried through the Ogilvie family, which is itself intermarried with the current British royal family.

11. The *Economist,* September 2, 1978.

12. The authors benefited from an unpublished letter, "Jardine's Octopus in Southern Africa; Rennie's Consolidated Holdings," by David Cherry of the Africa staff of *Executive Intelligence Review.*

13. Harry J. Anslinger, *The Murderers* (New York: Farrar, Straus, and Cudahy, 1961).

14. "World Drug Traffic and Its Impact on U.S. Security," Hearings before the Subcommittee to Investigate the Administration of the Internal Security Act and Other Internal Security Laws of the Committee on the Judiciary, United States Senate; 92nd Congress, Second Session; Part 3. The International Connection; September 13, 15, 1972, p. 101.

15. Haikal, *Cairo Documents*.

16. Anslinger, *Murderers*.

17. Harold Chang, "U.S. Sanction Threat to HK Over Drugs," *South China Morning Post,* August 18, 1977.

18. Reported in the Indonesian journal *Buana Minggu,* December 12, 1972.

19. Virtually the only published source indicating the Ch'ao Chou operation is John Le Carré's *The Honourable Schoolboy* (New York: Alfred A. Knopf, 1977). Its leading character is Drake Ko, supposedly a Hong Kong kingpin of narcotics traffic with an Order of the British Empire and a brother in the Chinese Politburo. "They'd come up from Swatow, the two of them," a Le Carré character remarks of Ko and his brother. "They were boat people, Chiu Chow." Le Carré's novel, according to highly informed sources, is a straight *roman à clef* from the files of British intelligence; most of the individual characters are scarcely disguised real figures in the Far East drug traffic and mercenary scene. The book's apparent intent, to portray fictionally the replacement of British intelligence-power in the Far East by the CIA, is patent nonsense. The interesting question is how Le Carré became so well informed; his acknowledgements are to British intelligence and police sources.

20. Daniel Insor, *Thailand: A Political, Social, and Economic Analysis,* (London: 1965), p. 135.

21. A. Doak Barnett, *Communist China and Asia,* (New York: 1960), p. 186.

22. Apparently, the relatively small city of Swatow was the center of an extraordinary prerevolution network of mainland financial links with expatriates that was maintained intact after the PRC was established. The remittance agencies, based in Swatow, Amoy, and Canton, had 1,000 branches throughout Southeast Asia as of 1950. After the revolution, the PRC government transformed them into an intelligence operation, employing the agents of the remittance companies abroad for intelligence-gathering pruposes. Once the external financial operations of Beijing's state banks got off the ground, however, the remittance companies were merged into the new apparatus.

8: How the RIIA Runs Drugs and Dirty Money

1. All names of members of the boards mentioned here are from 1978, but the picture of the interlocking directorates still stands. All figures in this chapter are also from 1978.

2. John Flint, *Cecil Rhodes,* (Boston: Little Brown and Co., 1974).

3. U.S. State Department, *Foreign Relations of the United States,* 1949, vol. VII: "The Far East: China."

4. State Department, *Foreign Relations,* pp. 1289–1292.

5. Chou En-lai represented the Chinese Communist Party in its "United Front" in Chungking with the Kuomintang during these years.

6. Christopher Thorne, "Chatham House, Whitehall, and Far Eastern Issues: 1941–45," *International Affairs,* January 1978, p. 20. The authors were compelled to rely on this summary rather than the original documents of the Royal Institute itself. However, the Thorne article is by a member of the RIIA, and published in the RIIA's own journal, and may be considered an authoritative representation of the RIIA's views concerning its own history.

7. Peter Vladimirov, *Vladimirov Diaries,* (New York: Doubleday and Co., 1976).

8. Ibid.

9. The ties of Ronning and Endicott to China go back very far and have served as a crucial contact between British policy and the PRC. Endicott was born of missionary parents in China in 1899, and worked there as a Methodist minister for many years. By the time of the 1927 Shanghai massacre of Communists by the KMT, Endicott admitted in a discussion that he was already working as an adviser to Chiang Kai-shek. In the early 1940s Endicott underwent a "Damascus Road" transformation to Marxism and became a supporter of the CCP. He became close to Chou En-lai during this time. Following his return to Canada, Endicott formed a newsletter which reported on the PRC and was a founding member of the Norman Bethune College at York University, working closely with Chester Ronning.

Ronning, also born in China of missionary parents, was in the Royal Canadian Air Force Intelligence during World War II. With the end of the war, Ronning became a Canadian foreign officer in China, during which time he developed close relations with CCP leaders, especially Chou En-lai, and current PRC Premier Huang Hua. Ronning argued strongly for Western recognition of the PRC after 1949, as did the leaders of the Far East Group of the RIIA, and was recognized as a friend by PRC leaders. Ronning served as translator for Huang Hua, who was the official spokesman for the PRC in the aftermath of the Communist victory. When China began diplomatic openings to the West in the early 1970s, Canada was one of the first countries chosen for normalization. Ronning's friend Huang Hua was the PRC's first ambassador to Canada.

Investigations have shown that both Paul Lin and Endicott maintain extensive ties to Canadian Maoist organizations, and through them, to international terrorist organizations. Ronning is known by professional intelligence officers to play a higher "coordinating" role at the government level of terrorist deployment; Endicott and Lin handled the "field work" with the Maoists. (The information here is derived from team interviews with Endicott himself and associates of Paul Lin.)

10. Thorne,"Chatham House," *International Affairs,* p. 27.

11. State Department, *Foreign Relations,* pp. 1289–1292.

12. Ibid.

13. Christopher Wren,*New York Herald Tribune,* January 16, 1948.

14. State Department, *Foreign Relations,* pp. 1289–1292.

15. U.S. Senate, Committee on the Judiciary, 82nd Congress. First Session, Subcommittee on Internal Security, Hearings on the Institute for Pacific Relations, Part I.

16. State Department, *Foreign Relations,* pp. 331–332.

17. U.S. Senate, Hearings on the Institute for Pacific Relations, Part I.

18. Ibid.

9: Canada: North America's Hong Kong

This chapter is from the 1978 edition of *Dope, Inc.* Most of the source material from this section came from analysis at that time of bank and corporate annual reports and *Who's Who* entries; a simple cross-correlation of such information produced an unbroken trail of dope and dirty money from the Far East, through Canada, into the United States. The business, legal, and accounting relations noted here are all a matter of public record. In addition, the authors interviewed several former and serving Canadian and American law enforcement officers, who have had Walter Lockhart Gordon and his Canadian "China Lobby" under scrutiny for years.

1. An egregious example of British intelligence activity in Canada is the formation of the British Newfoundland Corporation (Brinco) in the early 1950s. This project was planned by Winston Churchill, the Rothschilds, and Newfoundland's Premier Joseph "Joey" Smallwood, a Master Scottish Mason. According to Virginia Cowles's book on the Rothschilds (1973):

In 1951 shortly after Winston Churchill had become Prime Minister for the second time, he received Mr. Smallwood, the Premier of Newfoundland. Smallwood unfolded plans for a vast development scheme in Labrador and Newfoundland. To carry it out British capital was needed on a truly mammoth scale. . . . When the consortium of firms was formed [Churchill] was delighted that N.M. Rothschild & Sons should head it.

Participation in the founding of Brinco included the following leading firms involved in Dope, Inc.: Morgan Grenfell, Kleinwort and Sons, Rio Tinto Zinc, Anglo-American Corp., and Prudential. Cowles adds, "Brinco's terms of reference were breathtaking: the exploratory right to sixty thousand square miles in Newfoundland and Labrador, an area larger than England and Wales. . . ."

In Smallwood's autobiography (New American Library, 1973), he identified himself: "In 1967 [I] enjoyed immensely the distinction of being installed in office [as Master Mason] by the Grand Master Mason [Scottish Constitution] Lord Bruce, who came from Scotland especially for the purpose. So I met the direct descendant of King Robert the Bruce. Proud? Oh, yes."

2. This piece of information was an incidental product of a counter-surveillance operation against a number of individuals associated with the top management of Drexel Burnham Lambert.

10: The Families Behind the Drug Empire
1. The cult of Isis was developed in ancient Egypt no later than the Third Dynasty of the Old Kingdom, approximately 2780 B.C., and represents one of the earliest formal articulations of the entropic and backward ideology of mother-worship. As known to the Priesthood of the Temple of Isis—true believers themselves—the Isis cult formalizes the elements of a capability for social control, exploitation, and destruction of creative free will in subject population. The elements include:

■ Use of various schizophrenia-inducing drugs:
■ Use of repetitive, heteronomic sounds in "music" to supplement the effect of psychotropic drugs, and to create a societal aesthetic that endorses and encourages use of the drugs;
■ Creation of synthetic cults based on the original reactionary Isis myth, but specific to the psychological profile of the population which the priesthood has targeted for subversion;

■ Enforcement of a political-economic model antagonistic to general human progress, and containing targeted populations within noncreative, manual slave-labor projects such as pyramid-building.

This combination of Pharaonic cult capabilities was taken as a model for further refinement in this century by the British Secret Intelligence Service's Tavistock Institute in London—an institution which launched the "counterculture" in the United States and Europe, based on the very drugs, mescaline and hashish, the ancient priesthood had employed.

2. Carroll Quigley, *Tragedy and Hope,* (New York: Macmillan, 1974), p. 131. The "Circle of Initiates" formation was explicitly modeled after the ancient Isis Priesthood.

3. R.S. Clymer, *The Book of Rosicruciae,* (1947), vol. II, p. 106.

4. See Lyndon H. LaRouche, Jr., "Is Jimmy Carter Truly a Christian?" *New Solidarity,* October 13, 1978.

5. Cited in Nesta H. Webster, *Secret Societies and Subversive Movements,* (London: Boswell Printing and Publishing Co., 1924), p. 115.

6. Their father, the seventh Earl of Elgin, was famous for his theft of the "Elgin Marbles" from Greece, smuggling them to the British Museum.

7. *Dictionary of National Biography,* (London: Oxford University Press, 1968), vol. III, p. 104 *ff.*

8. Jean de Villiershad was the Master of the Knights of St. John of Jerusalem from 1285–1293, when the preparations for the slaughter of the Knights Templar were undertaken. Philippe Villiers de l'Isle Adam was the Grand Master of the Knights of St. John in France from 1521–1522, and was the first Grand Master in Malta from 1530–1534. Today, Sir Charles Villiers, who was the managing director of J. Henry Schroder Wagg from 1960–1968, is the chairman of the British Steel Corp. Sir John Michael Villiers, a Knight of St. John, was the Queen's Harbour Master of Malta from 1952–1954, and Lieutenant-Governor of Jersey, an offshore banking center, from 1964–1969.

9. By his own testimony in various writings, Lord Russell was in periodic contact with the Communist Chinese regime and Premier Chou in particular after 1949.

10. For example, Rudolf Hess and Professor General Karl Haushofer, ghost-writer of *Mein Kampf;* Alfred Rosenberg, Nazi minister of foreign services; Max Amann, editor-in-chief of Nazi publications; Hans Frank, Nazi Governor-General of Occupied Poland during World

War II; and several members of the Wittelsbach family (the Bavarian royal family) who sponsored much of Adolf Hitler's career. Hitler himself was an associate of the society, known as a "Visiting Brother."

11. The connection is visible in the 1866 founding of the "Masonic Rosicrucian Society" whose leaders, Mathers, Wescott, and Woodman, also formed the Isis-Urania Temple of the Hermetic Students of the Golden Dawn in 1886. The Golden Dawn group, by 1890, included the mystic poet William Butler Yeats, former secretary of the Theosophist Society. Aleister Crowley was the order's historian during the period of Yeats' association with it.

12. The LSD cult was a creation of the Royal Institute of International Affairs and its psychological warfare arm, the Tavistock Institute.

During the late 1960s—at the height of the "counterculture" and "hippy movement" in the United States—the Director of the RIIA, Andrew Schonfield, was a member of the Tavistock Institute's Governing Council. In 1967, during Schonfield's tenure at RIIA and Tavistock, Tavistock's leading staff psychologist, R.D. Laing, published his book, *The Politics of Experience,* which advocated schizophrenia ("madness is the only sanity") and drug use. Laing writes:

> I want you to taste and smell me, want to be palpable, to get under your skin, to be an itch in your brain and in your guts that you can't scratch out and that you can't allay, that will corrupt and destroy you and drive you mad.

During the 1960s, the Tavistock Institute received large grants from the Ford Foundation, the British Center for Environmental Studies, the British Defense Ministry, Harvard University, and at least £22,797 from the Social Science Research Council, of which Schonfield was chairman at the time.

13. See Robert Cohen and L. Wolfe, "Karl Haushofer's *Mein Kampf,*" *New Solidarity,* August 7, 1978.

14. Cited in John Flint, *Cecil Rhodes,* p. 27.

15. Martin Fido, *Rudyard Kipling* (New York: Viking Press, 1974).

16. Ibid., p. 35.

17. See Harbans Rai Bachchan, *W.B. Yeats and Occultism,* (Delhi: Motilal Banarsidass, 1965).

18. See Lyndon H. LaRouche, Jr., "Hitler: Runaway British Agent," *New Solidarity,* January 10, 1978.

19. Tennyson in 1820 had been a member of the "Cambridge Apostles" which initiated the Metaphysical Society in 1868–69. Other members of the Metaphysical Society included H.Q. Ackland, the Duke of Argyle, Alexander Campbell Fraser, William Gladstone, Shadworth Hodgson, and Walter Bagehot. This group included prominent members of the Society for Psychical Research, *Mind* magazine, and the Fabian Society.

20. Verse 8 of the Choric Song of the poem "The Lotus Eaters."

21. *History of the Times,* vol. IV: 1912–1920 (New York: Macmillan Co., 1952), p. 244. The relevant section reads:

> On Jan. 19, 1917, Milner left London at the head of an Allied mission which, during three weeks in Petrograd, laid down a suitable scheme for keeping the Russian forces supplied with Western munitions. . . . It was widely believed at the time that the February Revolution [installing Kerensky] was hatched at the British embassy.

22. After the destruction of the Knights Templar in the fourteenth century, the Knights of St. John appropriated the Templars' Red Cross symbol into their own iconography.

According to Ferdinand Lundberg, *America's 60 Families* (New York: Vanguard Press, 1937), p. 146 *ff.*

> The Russian mission of the Red Cross was headed by Col. William Boyce Thompson and Col. Raymond Robbins [who] used the Red Cross to forward the war aims of Wall Street in a way unsuspected by the American people. The purely political function of the Red Cross is not generally appreciated even today. . . .
>
> Thompson and Robbins, according to their own statements, functioned in Russia as a political arm of the War Department. Their crowning achievement was the purchase of enough delegates to the All-Russian Democratic Congress [to support Kerensky]. The cost of seducing this congress was $1,000,000.

Winston Churchill's wife, Clementine, a Commander of the Order of St. John, served as the chairman of the Red Cross Aid to Russia Fund from 1939–46. The same uses of the "Red Cross" cover for intelligence operations is implicit in the fact that a direct descendant of King Robert Bruce of Scotland, David Bruce, was the chief representative of the American Red Cross in Britain in 1940, and one year later, in 1941, became head of Office of Strategic Services (OSS) operations in the European Theatre; the same David Bruce, during the Nixon administration years, was selected by Secretary of State Henry Kissinger to be chief of the U.S. Mission to the People's Republic of China from 1973 to 1974, and then became U.S. ambassador to NATO from 1974 to 1976.

23. For example, in his April 1938 Annual Report to the Shareholders of Rio Tinto, chairman Geddes noted that:

Our company has received recently a great deal of attention in the press of many countries. Propagandists possessed of lively imaginations but devoid of respect for accuracy have told the world of our doings. In result a lot of nonsense has been published, evidently designed to suggest that your Board is composed of violent fascists actively participating on the side of General Franco. I read the other day an article in which it was stated as a fact that we had sent in a year 300,000 tons of copper to Germany and 65,000 tons to Italy to pay for supplies from those two countries to General Franco. . . . This is just rubbish. . . . I have seen it stated in the press that we . . . your Board . . . "gave" . . . help to General Franco's cause. It depends on your meaning of the verb "to give."

Significantly, in 1923's Annual Report by then-Chairman Lord Alfred Milner, it was stated, "The constantly increasing burden of taxation, especially in Spain, where the [republican] government is evidently convinced that it can never kill the goose that lays golden eggs. . . ." (See David Avery, *Not On Queen Victoria's Birthday: The Story of the Rio Tinto Mines,* London, 1973, pp. 371 *ff.*)

Auckland Geddes's grandfather had been the Hudson's Bay Company's official agent in Scotland. His second nephew, Anthony, was a member of the Governing Council of the Royal Institute of International Affairs in 1949, alongside Sir Mark Turner, Rio Tinto's current chairman. The same Anthony is a director of the Midlands Bank.

PART IV
Moscow Moves In

Islamic Fundamentalism and the Golden Crescent

In 1979 the Carter administration, in collaboration with British intelligence and with the glowing approval of the Soviet KGB, overthrew the Shah of Iran and installed the Islamic fundamentalist regime of Ayatollah Khomeini in power.

That year, the Carter administration displayed its total paralysis when Islamic terrorists linked to the KGB seized over 50 hostages at the U.S. Embassy in Teheran, and the Soviet Red Army installed a puppet regime in Afghanistan reinforced by the active presence of Soviet military forces.

Much of the Southwest Asian region fell under the bloody hand of Islamic fundamentalism and Soviet occupation. It was promptly labeled the "Arc of Crisis" by President Jimmy Carter's National Security Council chief Zbigniew Brzezinski, who argued insanely that "anti-Marxist" Islamic hordes would eventually overrun the southern frontiers of the Soviet Union and help overthrow the Russian government.

To narcotics and law enforcement officials on both sides of the Atlantic Ocean, the same area—Iran, Afghanistan, and the Northwest Frontier Province (NWFP) of Pakistan—came to be known, with increasing horror, as the Golden Crescent. The Golden Crescent emerged in the months immediately following the Khomeini coup as the fastest-growing opium production, processing, and transshipping zone in the world.

With Soviet occupation and continuous warfare between the Russian Army and Western-backed Afghani rebels, and the 1981 outbreak of a meatgrinder war between Iran and Iraq, the statistics of opium production in the Golden Crescent soared. It is impossible to account for this Dope, Inc. bonanza without the highest-level complicity of the governments of the Golden Crescent region—and the backing of the Russian imperialists in Moscow.

The 1978–79 Golden Crescent harvest yielded more than 1,600 metric tons of opium, or 160 metric tons of pure heroin. In March 1980, in response to the panic created when that harvest was unleashed into the Western European and American marketplaces, the U.S. Drug Enforcement Administration (DEA) wrote a confidential report called "Operation: CERBERUS." The DEA report, leaked to the public, warned that the U.S. was about to be hit with a heroin epidemic surpassing even the crisis of 1969–70, when the U.S. had over 700,000 heroin addicts.

By the time the "Operation: CERBERUS" report hit the streets, local law enforcement authorities had already sounded the alarm bell. Cities like New York were experiencing a shocking increase in heroin overdoses, caused by a flooding of low-cost, high-quality Golden Crescent smack onto the streets.

Even Manhattan District Attorney Robert Morgenthau, reacting to the DEA report, stated publicly that the anticipated heroin epidemic had already arrived, citing statistics that showed that the amount of heroin available in New York was ten times the amount available at the height of the 1970 glut. D.A. Morgenthau, himself allied to the pro-dope legalization

New York Times, went even further by harshly criticizing the Carter administration for its lack of funding for anti-narcotics law enforcement efforts.

Top narcotics officials within the Carter administration dismissed the calls for action, claiming that they were powerless to deal with the Golden Crescent heroin epidemic. Said DEA chief Peter Bensinger in spring 1980: "Candidly, we're not in as strong a position as we'd like to be because of the tremendous instability in the growing regions. We've been cut off from the type of cooperative enforcement efforts we had going."

Bensinger failed to mention that under the Carter administration, the majority of DEA international offices—including offices responsible for the suddenly flourishing Golden Crescent region—had been shut or pared down to meaningless desk posts. Given the Carter administration's avid support for drug legalization, it is not unreasonable to accuse the Carter national security establishment of having given their quiet blessing to the opium bonanza that followed the Khomeini revolution.

The black market routes that flooded the Persian Gulf and Southwest Asia with billions of dollars in sophisticated weaponry, arming Afghani rebels, Sikh separatists, Tamil separatists, and an alphabet soup of insurgency groups backed by the United States, Russia, and the People's Republic of China, became indistinguishable from the drug-smuggling underground in the wake of the U.S.-sponsored Khomeini revolution.

The connection between illegal arms-trafficking and the dramatic jump in opium and other dope production in areas devastated by regional wars, is one of the most fundamental points for the reader to understand about today's Dope, Inc. And nowhere is this case more glaringly shown than in the Golden Crescent region. When it comes to the fabulous war-profiteering from the guns-for-drugs trade, all distinctions between East and West melt.

One example suffices. On June 6, 1985, five Sikhs were arrested in Queens, New York in possession of over $40 million in drugs. The arrests spun out of a June 5 bust by DEA and U.S. Customs agents of Branjandan Singh while he was waiting at Newark International Airport to receive a shipment of "spices" from Bombay, India. Among the "spices" the federal agents found 10,000 pounds of hashish and 22 pounds of heroin.

Just one week earlier, Ludovicus Vastenavondt, third secretary of the Belgian Embassy in New Delhi, was arrested in Queens, New York when he delivered another 22 pounds of pure heroin to U.S. federal agents working undercover. Followup investigations showed that the Belgian's partner in the dope ring was a Bulgarian national. The ring also involved a Montreal, Canada-based Sikh activist, Mehta Singh Gulati, and a Garden City, Long Island Indian national, Rajan Patiwana.

The Belgian daily *Le Soir,* in January 1985, had already exposed the Belgian-Bulgarian-Sikh heroin and hashish ring as working with a Belgian counterfeiter named Antoine Michel. It seems that Michel was smuggling counterfeit U.S. dollars into India to buy heroin, which were then smuggled into the United States and sold for real U.S. currency. That money was earmarked for the purchase of Belgian weapons for the Khalistani separatists inside India.

Surpassing the Triangle

According to a 1984 DEA public report, by 1981 Iran had emerged as the largest opium-producing country in the world, accounting for between 400–600 metric tons of opium per year. In 1981, Afghanistan was already producing 225 metric tons of opium. Within two years, that figure had jumped to between 400–575 metric tons. Between Islamic fundamentalist Iran and Soviet-occupied Afghanistan, well over half of the world's heroin supply was being generated, according to those DEA figures.

And in the Northwest Frontier Province of Pakistan, the Pushtun tribes involved in opium production and laboratory processing are part of the Soviet separatist project of Geidar Aliyev. The Pushtun have been agitating for years for a separate Pushtunistan entity—with full backing from Moscow. When the Pakistani government of Zia ul-Haq attempted in early 1986 to win parliamentary support for a military offensive into the separatist-held opium-producing region, a political brawl broke out that effectively sabotaged the campaign. When Pakistani military units attempted to enter the poppy plantations, the Pushtun separatists put hundreds of children in front of the army trucks, blocking their access.

The Case of Sadegh Tabatabai

On January 8, 1983, Sadegh Tabatabai, the son-in-law of Ayatollah Khomeini and the former Deputy Prime Minister of Iran, was arrested at the Düsseldorf, West Germany airport for possession of 3.3 pounds of raw opium. In the investigation and ultimate cover-up that ensued, Tabatabai emerged as the chief of Khomeini's illegal arms-procurement effort, an effort that showed Tabatabai to have been knee-deep in both Bulgarian and Israeli black market arms- and drug-trafficking.

In the first effort to cover up the Tabatabai heroin connection, the Iranian Foreign Ministry sent a letter to West German officials on January 31, 1983 claiming that Tabatabai's status as a "special trade emissary" constituted diplomatic immunity. Foreign Minister Hans Dietrich Genscher, of the West German Free Democratic Party, immediately intervened on behalf of the Iranian request, providing experts from the foreign ministry to testify in support of Tabatabai's claim of diplomatic status. When a West German court in Düsseldorf ignored Genscher's intervention and found Tabatabai guilty of drug-trafficking on March 9, Genscher again intervened within hours of the conviction by expelling Tabatabai from the Federal Republic—before he could be thrown into jail.

The January 1983 arrest of Tabatabai was not his first acquaintance with West German police authorities, nor was it Foreign Minister Genscher's first intercession on Tabatabai's behalf. Once before, in June 1981, Genscher had prevented

Tabatabai's arrest. In that case, Tabatabai and several accomplices had conspired to violate West German laws against exporting weapons to war zones. Tabatabai was granted diplomatic immunity.

That June 1981 deal had involved a $50 million attempted illegal procurement of 50 American M–48 tanks for Iran. Tabatabai's accomplices in the deal were two Swiss nationals, Walter Gnaedinger and Roland Huber. The company used in the deal was the London-based Botco Ltd. At least part of the payment was deposited in the Düsseldorf Global Bank.

The close brush with prosecution in 1981 did not deter Tabatabai from pursuing his illegal weapons trade. Tabatabai had maintained several international connections for obtaining sophisticated weapons for Iran—and did so even at the time that Khomeini's supporters were holding American personnel hostage.

The major connection for those armaments was Israel. According to the Argentine news magazine *Siete Días,* the Iranian government was able to purchase motors for Skorpion tanks through a French company called Sati, as early as 1980. Through an Israeli embassy official in Paris, spare parts for 250 F–4 Phantom jets were obtained and transported from Tel Aviv to Nimes in southern France, then delivered to Teheran. According to documents shown on West German television during the Tabatabai 1983 trial, the Iranian contact point to Sati was Sadegh Tabatabai.

Siete Días also reported that through a Kent, England gun merchant, Ian Smalley, the Iranians directly approached the Israelis, who agreed to provide military equipment, on condition that shipping be conducted through two Israeli companies: Mivtza B.M., based in Yavne, Israel, and Soltam B.M., which is part of the powerful Koor industrial combine in Israel.

According to the investigation conducted by Italian magistrate Carlo Palermo, one of the largest arms deals for Iran was concluded in August 1982, involving 500 Soviet T–72 tanks, captured by the Israelis from the PLO and Syrian forces in Lebanon. Those tanks were provided to Iran in exchange for cheap Iranian oil, which was conduited to Israel through British Petroleum and Royal Dutch Shell.

To cover this transaction, a Swiss firm, Draycott Trading and Finance Ltd., operating out of Fribourg, Switzerland, was engaged.

The first meeting to map out the deal had occurred in April 1981, when Draycott President Lovatt MacDonald attended a meeting at the Hotel President in Geneva with Sadegh Tabatabai, Hans Albert Kunz, and Stefano Delle Chiaie.

It was this meeting that placed Tabatabai at the center of the illegal arms and drugs running Propaganda–2 (P–2) secret freemasonic lodge headed by Licio Gelli, and the overlapping Bulgarian connection to the Soviet KGB.

Who were the two men joining MacDonald and Tabatabai at the Geneva session?

Hans Albert Kunz was the personal representative of the P–2 associated Italian banker Roberto Calvi, head of the Banco Ambrosiano. According to investigations by magistrate Carlo Palermo, Kunz was the last person to see Calvi alive before his departure for London, where he was found hanged from Blackfriars Bridge.

Stefano Delle Chiaie is one of the leading neo-Nazi terrorists controlled by P–2. In 1969, Delle Chiaie was convicted for the Piazza Fontana Italian terrorist bombing which was part of a P–2 organized attempted coup d'état. Following the 1980 Bologna train station bombing in which over 80 people were killed, Delle Chiaie fled to Bolivia, where he found sanctuary under the cocaine colonels regime. In Bolivia, he operated as part of a cell of neo-Nazi terrorists assigned to the Interior Ministry of Arce Gómez. His immediate superior was Klaus Barbie, the Nazi war criminal extradited to France in February 1983 to stand trial for mass murder in Lyon.

The Tabatabai-Draycott smuggling ring was identified by Italian magistrate Palermo as merely one component of a Bulgarian-centered dope-for-guns empire involving the Milan-headquartered Stipam International Transport, discussed later in this volume.

The Aliyev Project

If Iranian Sadegh Tabatabai was typical of the top government officials responsible for directing the multi-billion arms-for-dope trade fueling the Gulf wars, the key to the cultivation and smuggling of illicit substances in the Golden Crescent was the tribal elements that populate the region.

According to intelligence developed by the DEA in the aftermath of the Golden Cresent heroin flood, smuggling operations among the Crescent countries were conducted by the nomadic Baluchi tribesmen. Opium poppy cultivation itself and the early clandestine opiate refining were being carried out by the Pathan tribesmen of the Northwest Frontier Province of Pakistan, and in western Iran by ethnic Kurds and Azerbaijanis. Smuggling of the opiates between Iran and Turkey was being conducted by the Kurds and Azerbaijanis as well.

Since 1979, farmers in India's Punjab region, under the domination of the Sikh separatists, have taken to growing the illicit crop as well.

In virtually every case of "separatist" groups involved in international narcoterrorist activities, intelligence services have found these groups to be under heavy Soviet influence or direct control. The master of the Soviets' "Islamic Card" and other "separatist" operations from the outset was Geidar Ali-Reza ogly Aliyev, the career KGB officer of Shi'ite Muslim origin, who was promoted in 1982 to be the First Deputy Prime Minister of the Soviet Union and a full member of the Politburo. Prior to his Moscow assignment, Aliyev had operated for 15 years in Soviet Azerbaijan, based in Baku, first as its KGB chief and then as First Secretary of the Communist Party of Azerbaijan. The party's approach, later perfected by Aliyev, was to exploit indigenous belief structures, to tame the ethnic/tribal elements away from disruptive excesses and fashion them into a means for the outward expansion of influence.[1] Azerbaijan supplied organizers and administrators to Soviet Central Asia proper, making Baku a point from which Soviet influence radiated into the Islamic world. The Turkish, Iranian, and Iraqi Communist parties were organized from Baku; the Indian party from Tashkent. The years spent building the Soviet-Islamic infrastructure have paid off in numerous ways, not the least of which were the huge revenues secured through the illict drug trade.

By Soviet admission, Geidar Aliyev had been assigned to develop the Russian "Islamic strategy" almost immediately following Yuri Andropov's arrival at Dzherzhinsky Square as director of the KGB in 1967. This coincided with Andropov's orders to the security chiefs of all of the Warsaw Pact countries to begin actively pushing drug addiction on the Western nations.

This Andropov-ordered project represented the revival of a Soviet strategy toward the Persian Gulf first spelled out at a Bolshevik conference in Baku in 1921, in which the Soviets heralded the "revolutionary peoples of the East" and emphasized that the key to Asia was the encouragement of Islamic fundamentalist and regional separatist movements as battering rams against the incursion of Western industrial and cultural values.

The Golden Crescent

Reports from Pakistan's Northwest Frontier Province and from incursions into Soviet-controlled Afghanistan establish that opium cultivation is under the control of Soviet military forces. There have been many reports of systematic Soviet destruction of villages and crops—except the poppy fields. In its most recent Narcotics Intelligence Estimate (1984), the U.S. National Narcotics Intelligence Consumers Committee reported that its estimates for Golden Crescent production were lower in 1984, "due to the availability of better data on Afghanistan." The drop in production for Afghanistan is due not only to the change in data compilation but also to the fact that drought had hit not only in Afghanistan but in Pakistan as well. Drought has been to date, the only major destructive force affecting the opium harvests in the Golden Crescent and Southeast Asia's Golden Triangle.

There were also unconfirmed reports of "significant cultivation" in Lebanon surfacing at that time. Kurdish and Armenian traffickers reportedly remain active in Syria, directing a string of heroin refineries. They have tended to concentrate in the Aleppo and Latakia areas.

Within Lebanon itself, the Baalbek area is known for cultivation and drug-refining. Clandestine labs are also known to be in Beirut and in Tripoli, Lybia.

The role of Baalbek as the center of hashish and other drug cultivation and processing adds another dimension to the Soviet hand in Dope, Inc. Since the renewed outbreak of the Lebanon civil war in the late 1970s, the Baalbek area has been under the total control of Syrian Intelligence and of the Khomeini-controlled Hezbollah (Party of God) under Fadlallah. Eyewitness accounts by Western journalists confirm that the warehouses holding a large amount of the world's hashish supply are maintained under the watchful eye of Syrian Army guards.

In the early days of the Golden Crescent resurgence, traditional organized crime groups took the lead in refining and trafficking. The revival of the French Connection was attributed to this 1978–79 opium cultivation shift. Police in Europe, particularly France and Italy, found chemists from the days of the French Connection refining Golden Crescent opium in sophisticated labs in Milan and Sicily. Western intelligence sources, corroborated by U.S. narcotics enforcement, also noted the deployment of French and later Italian chemists into the Northwest Frontier Province, a factor that coincided with the emergence of the clandestine laboratories in this area. It was the French Connection-Sicilian Connection that dominated in distribution, having built an organized criminal apparatus in the Western nations. According to DEA International Intelligence digests, the center of the renewed French Connection into the Golden Crescent was located in Sofia, Bulgaria, under the control of the KGB.

The notorious Pizza Connection, which accounted for millions of dollars in high-grade heroin flooding the East Coast markets of the United States through the early 1980s, was just one well-known case in which a Bulgaria-centered operation was caught trafficking in Golden Crescent Iranian, Afghani, and Pakistani opium.

The 1984 Narcotics Intelligence Estimate reported, "There were numerous active heroin laboratories in eastern Afghanistan. Most of their output was exported to or through Pakistan. The laboratories in southwestern Afghanistan may have been the sources of some of the heroin smuggled to Iran. Laboratory activity in Iran was believed to have been concentrated in or near the cities of Tabriz, Teheran, and Zahedan, as well as along the Iran Turkey border."

In addition, the Northwest Frontier Province remains the major regional refining, trafficking, and stockpiling depot for drugs and weapons. According to the Narcotics Intelligence Estimate, "Despite the decrease in the regional opium poppy harvest in 1984, there were no indications that major opium shortages resulted. Stockpiles held in the North-West Frontier Province of Pakistan may have prevented large price increases. Prices for opium at the cultivation level, however, have more than doubled compared with 1983. Whereas in 1983 a farmer received about $30 to $35 per kilogram, in 1984 he was paid at least $70 for the same quantity."

Countries within the Golden Crescent have paid a heavy human toll in terms of domestic addiction. And, despite the Ayatollah's threats and public hangings, the Iranian opium addict population has remained at about one million, and the number of heroin addicts has increased to about 100,000, concentrated predominantly in the urban centers. In Afghanistan there are an estimated 100,000 to 125,000 opium addicts, but heroin smoking is reportedly increasing. Pakistan toward the end of 1984 had an estimated 200,000 to 300,000 heroin addicts, and another 300,000 opium users.

Soviet Russia, in line with its Third Rome quest for a Eurasian empire, has borrowed a leaf from the British Archives and has launched in the Middle East and Southwest Asia what may be known to future generations as the Third Opium War.

PART V

Narcotráfico, SA: The IMF Recolonizes Ibero-America

Introduction:
Dope and Debt

Ibero-America is at war. The casualties are in the millions. Some fall victim to Sendero Luminoso, the narcoterrorist guerrillas in the Altiplano of Peru. Others suffer brain damage from bazuco, the cheap drug of slave populations that kills more surely than the more sophisticated products that make it onto New York City streets.

The victims are the starving children in the northeast of Brazil, in Chiapas, Mexico and in the slums of every capital city in every nation of Ibero-America.

During the last ten years, food production in Ibero-America has collapsed. At the same time, drug mafias have sequestered fertile lands and enslaved campesino populations—to grow coca, amapola (poppies), and marijuana. Bolivia produces 200,000 metric tons of coca per year. That nets $2 billion, far more than its Gross National Product. Virtually all of the 61 metric tons of cocaine consumed in the United States in 1983 came from Ibero-America. Nearly 13,000 metric tons of marijuana were exported to the United States from the countries south of the Rio Grande, which also supplied 33% of the U.S. consumption of heroin.

The suppliers have created internal markets. Drug consumption inside the Ibero-American nations themselves has increased radically over the past six years, and the human wreckage caused by addiction now rivals in size the percentages of addiction in the populations of the "advanced sector" nations. The only difference between the new opium war against Ibero-America, and the old Opium Wars of the nineteenth century, is that some nations are simultaneously sharing the fate of China, the consumer nation, and its opium supplier, India.

The proper name for what is happening in Ibero-America today is "recolonization."

The inheritors of the old British East India Company—the same British monarchy and some of the same banking houses—have launched the new Opium War just as they did the first: to loot nations, destroy them, and exalt the power of the Empire.

Today the International Monetary Fund (IMF) has replaced the British East India Company, and the Soviet Empire—inheriting the designs of the old Russian oligarchy to become the "Third and Final Rome"—has negotiated a partnership in Dope, Inc.

The year 1978 was a watershed for the operation to turn Ibero-America into a vast drug colony. By then, Trilateral Commission President Jimmy Carter had set the terms for the U.S. banking system to emulate the world's biggest dope banks, or be gobbled up by them.

In October 1979, Paul Adolph Volcker, the Carter-appointed Federal Reserve chief and intimate of the Trilateral Commission's David Rockefeller, legalized usury by forcing interest rates up to 20%. Ibero-America and the whole developing sector fell hostage to the dope bankers. As national debt quickly doubled and tripled, the IMF accelerated the process of recolonization.

Nations looking forward to entering the 21st century as developed countries, were forced to cancel their future. The great industrial projects that were the hope of the 1970s—nuclear energy, water management, ports, and other infrastructural projects basic to building healthy economies—were dismantled on orders from the IMF.

The great champions of "free enterprise," the followers of Friedrich von Hayek and Milton Friedman who argue the case for genocide much as Parson Malthus wrote the apologetics for the barbarities carried out by the British East India Company, all lauded the not-so-free dictatorship of the IMF over the entire Southern Hemisphere.

This same "free enterprise" dictator, the IMF, accelerated its campaign to legalize the black market economy, to "free" the narcodollars to infiltrate national banking systems, and to promote cultivation of "cash crops"—cannabis, coca, and poppies.

Destroying Cultural Optimism

The cultural optimism that accompanied the partially successful development of the '70s in Ibero-America was the product of a religious and cultural heritage that reflected a deep-seated belief in progress. The continent's aspirations were profoundly expressed by Pope Paul VI in his 1967 encyclical *Populorum Progressio* when he said, "Development is the new name for peace."

The truth of his words was never more apparent than today, when the lack of development enforced by the current economic collapse has produced a state of undeclared war on the continent.

With the debt crisis of the 1980s, came the hopelessness of mass unemployment, chronic malnutrition, and economic marginalization of ever-larger sections of the Ibero-American population. This imposed a climate of cultural pessimism appropriate for the spread of drug addiction, terrorism, and social chaos.

Although the social scientists and anthropologists call the

current terrorism and demoralization a "sociological phenomenon," it is the direct result of actions by the international oligarchic families, actions that are both premeditated and predictable. Look, for example, at the "1980s Project," a series of policy papers put out by the New York Council on Foreign Relations, in which the CFR proudly declared "controlled disintegration of the world economy is a legitimate objective for the 1980s." To the oligarchs, nations have become expendable.

The looting operations of the 1980s were as devastating as British eighteenth-century colonial methods. Capital flight, engineered collapse in Third World commodity prices, and brutal devaluations forced nation after nation to give up development projects, and submit to recolonization.

While the United States, under the Kissinger influence, has time and again supplied the political muscle behind these policies of Paul Volcker and the IMF, no one has benefited more from them than the Soviet Empire. Moscow, whose declared goal is the crushing of Western civilization, has not only a "business interest" in the drugs-for-arms smuggling in Ibero-America; it is allied with the racist Western oligarchy in its readiness to see the population of the Southern Hemisphere wiped out through wars, pestilence, and famine. The genocide the Soviets are carrying out against the Afghan people and the massive increase in drug production from Afghanistan and the Golden Crescent since 1980, is only a part of the story.

Crimes Against Humanity

Ibero-America took important actions in 1984 and 1985 against Dope, Inc.

The largest drug busts in history were carried out in Ibero-America during those years, ranging from the March 1984 dismantling of Colombia's vast complex of "cocaine cities" buried in the jungles of Caquetá, to the spectacular raids of Mexico's giant marijuana-processing plants in northern Chihuahua in November 1984, and the Operation Condor military sweeps against drug plantations carried out by Peru in August and September of 1985, beginning with a joint attack by Peru and Colombia on the gigantic narco-complex of Callarú.

The initial cocaine busts in Colombia dumped nearly 10 tons of refined cocaine powder in the Yari River, and began to dissolve the dope mafia's ten-year-old stranglehold on Colombia. In Mexico, the military burned hundreds of tons of marijuana, and along with it the seed money that powerful interests were counting on to buy the elections in 1985. The lightning raids on drug plantations initiated by Peru's President García during his first two months in office, alone wiped out some $5.6 billion of the U.S.A.'s yearly cocaine consumption. All in all, drugs that would have brought tens of billions of dollars when sold in the United States, were destroyed.

But it wasn't enough, and Ibero-American nations knew it. They called repeatedly for joint action among nations in the war on drugs:

■ In Quito, Ecuador, Ibero-American presidents from seven leading nations met on August 11, 1984 to call for the creation of a "multinational war against drugs" and to declare drug-trafficking "a crime against humanity with all applicable juridical consequences."

■ The OAS Special Task Force on Narcotics convened on August 20, 1984 to call for an inter-American conference to carry forward the Quito resolutions.

■ During the week of September 24, 1984 the U.N. General Assembly heard Venezuelan President Jaime Lusinchi, Colombian Foreign Minister Augusto Ramírez Ocampo, and other prominent Ibero-Americans demand global attention to the "universal plague" of the drug trade.

On November 6, 1984, justice ministers from throughout Ibero-America met in Bogota to formulate a uniform legal code against drug-trafficking and to establish a continent-wide intelligence exchange to assist in the persecution and capture of drug felons.

Again and again, Ibero-American nations have called on the

United States for assistance—not for handouts, but for a serious, all-out commitment to eradicate the drug plague.

On July 12, 1984, Colombian President Belisario Betancur pointed out that the advanced sector countries

> demand of us colossal efforts, sometimes beyond our human and financial possibilities, and nevertheless, there have been in certain societies that have become natural markets for drugs and which foster their production, no more than secondary police efforts and even an undisguised political reticence toward eradicating the evil.
>
> But even worse: When countries like ours, making enormous sacrifices, turn to where we are supposedly offered collaboration, equipment to reinforce our prosecution of these criminals and so forth, we are given miserable trade conditions and they even try to impose unacceptable financial conditions. . . . In Colombia, despite such obstacles, we will continue the war without truce, not only in defense of our own dignity and our own people, of our youth, but for all of humanity, because we are facing a world threat.

More than a year later, on September 23, 1985, President Alan García of Peru addressed the United Nations General Assembly. García called the drug traffic "an activity that corrupts institutions and degrades man," and pointed out that in recent years in Ibero-America:

> The only raw material which has increased in value has been cocaine. The only successful multinational originated in our countries has been the drug traffic. The most advanced effort of Andean integration has been achieved by drug traffickers.
>
> To what can we ascribe this? According to liberal economics, production is regulated by demand, and in terms of drugs, the main consumer market is that of the United States of America.
>
> For Peru, drug consumption is not a national problem, but I can say that within the first 50 days of my administration, we have dealt the most successful blows against international

vice. Twenty-two airports, three helicopter landing strips, five long-range light aircraft, hundreds of kilograms of drugs, and eight large factories have been discovered and seized— all of which signifies that the consumption of drugs in the U.S.A. will suffer a yearly reduction of approximately 80 tons, valued at $5.6 billion.

We could therefore ask the American administration, if we have done that in 50 days, what is it doing for the human rights of the individuals keeling over in Grand Central Station and so many other places, and when will it legally and in a Christian fashion fight to eradicate consumption?

A liberal economist would recommend that we keep our hands off this risky subject, but we believe that democracy must also have an ethical dimension, in which the state cannot look on indifferently at corruption and vice.

That is why we are taking up the fight against the drug traffic. Because it is a crime against humanity. We are not doing this for the granting of a loan or the aid amounting to a few million dollars which are offered to us, and which in the future we will not accept, because our own conscience is all we need to defend the youth, whether Peruvian, American, or from any other part of the world.

But I say from this rostrum, that another crime against humanity is to increase interest rates, to reduce prices of raw materials, to waste economic resources in technologies of death, while hundreds of millions of human beings are living in misery and are encouraged to violence.

When will the United States and other nations take up the challenge issued by Betancur and García? With every moment of delay, more victims are counted in every country of the Hemisphere.

1
The Trilateral Connection

Chase Manhattan Bank chief David Rockefeller's bid for "mafia money" started in the mid-1960s, at the same time that Citibank cranked up its "international personal banking" group to manage illegal capital movements, and Bank of America bankrolled the Banco Ambrosiano in Italy. But not until David Rockefeller bought himself a U.S. administration in 1976, as the ancient European *fondi* installed themselves in Wall Street, did narcotics traffic start to become serious business for the world's biggest banks. Almost at the moment the Jimmy Carter administration took office, the Ibero-American dope traffic exploded into the big time, producing havoc in the distribution of cash throughout the Federal Reserve System by the end of 1978. After a mere two years of Jimmy Carter's White House, an extra $3.3 billion per year in cold cash was piling up in the Florida offices of the Federal Reserve, the $13 billion dope traffic had become Florida's largest industry, and American narcotics consumption had jumped to $100 billion per year by *EIR*'s estimates, perhaps triple the level of the early 1970s.

The strategic consequences were devastating. While President Carter's brother Billy took bribes from the Libyan government, through the intermediation of Armand Hammer's Charter Oil Company, Fidel Castro found a source of income to finance terrorism throughout Ibero-America, courtesy of the Carter White House.

Nor was the Carter White House content to sit back and let the dope traffickers get to work. Through Dr. Peter Bourne's White House Office of Drug Abuse, the Carter administration allied with the official proponents of "drug decriminalization" at *High Times,* the journal of the U.S. narcotics trade, to propagandize on behalf of the dope industry throughout the Caribbean and the Andean countries. Through G. William Miller's Treasury and Paul Volcker's Federal Reserve, the United States backed the International Monetary Fund's campaign to force Ibero-America to produce dope to pay its debts, and with redoubled energy after the 1979 oil price increase threw Third World debtors into penury.

Volcker had been Rockefeller's vice president for strategic planning at the time the "mafia money" memoranda circulated in 1966, and Chase went begging to the likes of Y.K. Pao and the HongShang Bank for a cut in the Hong Kong dirty money pool. Now the Trilateral Commission, the Rockefeller front organization which had nominated its mascot Jimmy Carter for the presidency, hit Ibero-America from all sides. Chase's international advisory board Chairman Henry Kissinger, also the Trilateral Commission's chairman, set in motion the Caribbean policy which culminated in the 1980 marijuana coup in Jamaica, with the backing of Trilateral Commission member Cyrus Vance's Department of State. Dr. Peter Bourne, before his dismissal for dispensing "recreational drugs" to his staff like candy, teamed up with the likes of Ernesto Samper Pizano in Colombia to push narcotics as a growth industry. David Rockefeller's private network of business associates, like the

Gran Colombiano Group in Bogota, Manuel Ulloa's associates in Peru, and the Organización Diego Cisneros in Caracas, created the channels through which spectacular sums of dirty money could move in and out of different Western Hemisphere capitals, in the name of "free enterprise" and the "open market economy."

Above all, the International Monetary Fund turned the financial screws on the Ibero-American debtors, with special emphasis on Jamaica, Colombia, Bolivia, and Peru—the major suppliers of marijuana and cocaine to the U.S. market.

The International Monetary Fund is the instrument by which the United States was forestalled from pursuing Franklin Roosevelt's desire for global industrial development following the Second World War. Lord Keynes conceived it as an expansion of the Bank for International Settlements, founded in 1931 by the same representatives of the *fondi* whose descendants now sit on the boards of the Assicurazioni Generali and the Riunione Adriatica di Sicurtà. And the Bank for International Settlements was conceived in 1922 in Genoa at the Palazzo San Giorgio, the ancient headquarters of the Doria and Giustinian banking operation, the Cassa San Giorgio. The Genoese and their Venetian partners, militarily insecure in the northern Italy of the late eighteenth century, created modern Switzerland as a bank with an army attached, an arrangement ratified by the evil Russian foreign minister Capo d'Istria, a Venetian nobleman, at the Congress of Vienna. Switzerland remains the *fondi*'s strongbox. There the Bank for International Settlements has been headquartered since its founding in 1930.

The great family *fondi* which stand behind the BIS supervise the traffic in narcotics at the ground level. The instruments of this supervision have been the enormous dirty money network of the *fondi* themselves; the governments of Cuba, Nicaragua, Bulgaria, and the Soviet Union; and Theology of Liberation networks within the Society of Jesus, which have control over sizeable financial assets, especially in Ibero-America.

All of the military, financial and social convulsions which have wracked Ibero-America since Lord Carrington's Malvinas War of 1982 have, as their model, a return to the genocidal conditions of the sixteenth and seventeenth century, and as their objective, a new division of the world. But the division this time will not allocate territory between the empires of Spain and Portugal, but between the Soviet Empire of the East, the would-be inheritor of the entire Eurasian land mass, and the Western oligarchy served by Carrington and his partner Henry Kissinger, free to loot Ibero-America at will. Correspondingly, everything dirty in Ibero-America that belongs to Moscow either directly or by way of Havana has joined the army of irregulars who service the "parallel economy" of the International Monetary Fund.

By 1978, the dope economy was the stated policy of the IMF. John Holdson, a senior official for Latin America in the World Bank's International Trade and Monetary Flows department, told *Executive Intelligence Review,* "I know the coca industry there is highly advantageous to producers. In fact, from their point of view, they simply couldn't find a better product. Its advantages are that no elaborate technology is required, no hybrid seeds, and land and climate are perfect."

A Colombia specialist at the International Monetary Fund put it this way: "From an economic viewpoint, marijuana is just a crop, like any other. It brings in foreign exchange, and provides income for the peasants. Legality is a relative concept. In a few years, marijuana may become legal anyway."

An international banker in New York explained in 1978, "Coffee prices are simply too unstable, always fluctuating on the world market, you know. Drugs, on the other hand, provide a stable source of income at all times. With coffee prices like they are, Colombia will never get its development going, can't make plans, like the oil producers can. I happen to know that the World Bank has been pressuring some Latin American countries to find some way of statistically accounting for their contraband flows."

In an interview with *EIR,* the former foreign minister of Guyana, Frederick Wills, explained, "The countries hope that, by getting the IMF seal of approval, this will open the gates for credit from other countries and private banks. But the IMF seal of approval requires *successful* acceptance of the IMF program.

And since you didn't succeed, the flow of funds from money markets and banks is dried up. This means that, first of all, the government ministers started to think, 'What export drive could we have which could realize a quick cash flow, to stem this balance of payments gap?' There is only one commodity that satisfies that requirement: dope, heroin, marijuana.

"In several countries," Wills continued, "officials from the IMF and the Bretton Woods system would come down and say 'your future lies in agriculture.' But in agriculture you have the following problems: High technology is expensive, that increases your import bill. So you have to use the 'appropriate technology' that you do have to produce those goods which can satisfy your local market and a bit for export. You cannot compete with the great agricultural countries like Argentina, Canada, the United States, and Australia. Therefore, the kind of crop you have to produce for export has to be one in which you have the edge and they don't, and that's dope."

2

Jamaica: The IMF Creates the Perfect Free Enterprise Economy

After four years of International Monetary Fund control, Jamaica's marijuana income is conservatively estimated at $3.5 billion per year, more than the country's Gross National Product in 1980, when the International Monetary Fund put Edward Seaga into office. That sum is just short of the $5 billion "production potential" figure circulated in 1979 by the National Organization for Reform of Marijuana Laws (NORML), White House drug adviser Peter Bourne's roving irregulars in the campaign to create the Caribbean drug economy. Unlike Colombia and Peru where, to different degrees, nationalist forces have offered resistance to bankers' plans to turn them into marijuana and coca plantations, Jamaica is the IMF's unchallenged success story.

Edward Seaga was only a gleam in the Trilateral Commission's eye when Sol Linowitz, Carter's Panama Canal negotiator, chaired a small and unpublicized White House meeting on the Caribbean in 1979. Linowitz, whom we shall encounter later in his capacity as a United Fruit company official and intermediary in HongShang's move into the United States, formed a "Caribbean/Central American Action" group inside the Reagan administration, the kernel of what later became David Rockefeller's much publicized Caribbean Basin Initiative, and Henry Kissinger's National Bipartisan Commission on Central America. As a spinoff of Linowitz's group, David Rockefeller's protégé in Venezuela, Gustavo Cisneros, headed up the Venezuelan/Jamaican Businessmen's Committee to back Seaga in 1981.

Officially, the U.S. State Department's excuse for the campaign to install Seaga was the friendly ties between former Jamaican Prime Minister Michael Manley and Fidel Castro. Former Undersecretary of State Lawrence Eagleburger, now the senior staff member of Kissinger Associates, was asked by the *New York Times* on September 10, 1984, why the State Department had not pressured Seaga to curtail the drug traffic. His reply: "Our emphasis has been: Can Jamaica be made economically viable so that we don't face the Manley kind of problem in the next election? To be honest, I wasn't aware that Jamaica was that large a marijuana producer. To the best of my knowledge, it didn't come up."

Eagleburger can have his choice: He is either criminally incompetent, or he lied outright. Seaga had announced his pro-drug policy to millions of Americans on U.S. national television. On the CBS-TV program "Face the Nation" on November 23, 1980, Seaga stated that marijuana "has almost been the lifeline economically to providing dollars and foreign exchange" to Jamaica. Shortly before, Seaga had told the *Washington Post:*

Regardless of whether we want it or not, the industry as such is here to stay. It is just not possible for it to be wiped out, and if it is here to stay, then we have to make up our mind from that point as to how to best deal with it . . . the question of legalizing it so as to bring the flow of several hundred million dollars in this parallel market through official channels.

It is not merely that the Kissinger group in the State Department and the International Monetary Fund installed Seaga for the explicit purpose of maximizing Jamaica's dope revenues. The result of the Kissinger plan for the Caribbean and the Andean countries has been to hand Fidel Castro a partnership in a drug-smuggling operation estimated by some sources at $20 billion per year, as documented below. In effect, Kissinger, Linowitz, and Rockefeller arranged lavish financing for every terrorist movement in Ibero-America.

Two years after oil prices quadrupled in 1974, Manley's government accepted IMF conditions for a loan, including a 30% devaluation of Jamaica's currency in April 1977. The ensuing chaos in the Jamaican economy gave the drug lobby its chance: A Jamaican parliamentary commission was established to study marijuana decriminalization, and NORML director Keith Stroup met with commission member Percival Broderick to devise a model decriminalization plan. Broderick announced: "We must realize that ganja [marijuana] is a primary export product of Jamaica, with possibly more export potential than bauxite ore." Illegal ganja exports were a mere $50 million that year; they were to double in each of the ensuing years until the $3.5 billion jackpot was registered in 1983.

By March 1978, the IMF had declared Jamaica in violation of its austerity agreements. The country faced a $34 million per month cash shortfall, imports of basic foodstuffs were endangered, and the IMF was demanding an additional 10% devaluation as a condition for even reopening talks. The leading newspaper, the *Daily Gleaner,* wrote on March 21, "The salvation of this country lies in ganja. . . . We should stop producing so much sugar cane and produce more ganja instead. . . . We can make the tourists come for it and bring their dollars. . . . You would just pass loads of tourists all over the island puffing the thing and because they feel good, they just smile with you, spending money. . . ."

This was precisely what the International Monetary Fund

had in mind, the London *Observer* wrote a few months later. "In the complicated and topsy-turvy world of international finance," said the British newspaper—owned by Kissinger associate Robert O. Anderson—"the International Monetary Fund is now effectively helping those who want to legalize pot." In May 1978, Kingston accepted a 50% devaluation, in a program which officially proposed to reduce households' consumption by 10% in the ensuing year.

The entire basis of the economy shifted to pot. The London *Economist* reported June 21, 1984, "Ganja is grown mostly by small farmers, who do not want to be paid in American dollars, so the traffickers sell their dollars to industrialists in exchange for local currency . . . and then pay the farmers in Jamaican dollars." Canada's Bank of Nova Scotia, later cited by the President's Commission on Organized Crime as a major dirty money conduit, handled the transfer of cash from marijuana sales, and Mocatta Metals in New York City provided precious metals for cash-laundering purposes.

Prime Minister Manley was still wavering on the bankers' major demand, a crash program for marijuana production. He told *High Times* in 1980, "The question of marijuana exposes me to extreme temptation. As you know, Jamaica has a balance of payments crisis, and we have never been able to get marijuana sales to pass through our central bank."

Edward Seaga, his successor in 1981, created a base for himself among small farmers dependent on ganja income and the local branch of the British financial oligarchy. As a businessman, Seaga owned a record company promoting "reggae" music, the cult sound of the ganja-smoking Rastafarians; as a politician in the Kingston slums and minister of culture and welfare in the early 1960s, Seaga had promoted the Rastas as the syncrescence of Jamaican culture. Now Prime Minister, he arrived in the United States as the Great White Hope of the Trilateral Commission, the man who would usher in the era of free enterprise in the Caribbean. To the U.S. press and on television, Seaga extolled the virtues of the ganja "lifeline" of dope dollars.

To the extent that Kissinger has infiltrated the Reagan administration, through the State Department and other channels, the continued "success" of the Jamaica experiment has made a mockery of the President's promise of a war on drugs. The Report of Kissinger's National Bipartisan Commission on Central America, released January 21, 1984, is an undisguised formula for gunboat diplomacy on behalf of Dope, Inc. The report starts with a warning to the Central American governments:

> For the most part, U.S. policy toward Central America during the early part of this century focused primarily on promoting the stability and solvency of local governments so as to keep other nations out. This was reflected in Theodore Roosevelt's corollary to the Monroe Doctrine, which held that the U.S. should take action to prevent situations from arising that might lead to interventions by extra-hemispheric powers.

Specifically, Roosevelt used the U.S. Marines as a collection agency for debts owed to European financial agencies, so they would not be put to the trouble of sending in their own forces. Today, according to the Kissinger report, U.S. muscle will enforce the Hong Kong model upon the Caribbean. The economy of the region is to be "restructured" to fit the model of dirty money laundromats like "Hong Kong, Singapore, and others." Private sector "initiative" must replace government "as the engine of growth." United Brands—whose ships carried a substantial portion of the cocaine reaching the U.S.A. during the 1970s, according to U.S. law enforcement sources—is cited as a "model employer and model citizen." The Jamaican model can be enforced through a "multinational body including eminent Central Americans," which "can most effectively—and least offensively—assess progress, evaluate program objectives, and measure external resource needs. In addition, the multilateral body should exercise some degree of control over development funds to give its assessments added weight, even though donors would retain a veto."

Peru, another early victim of the IMF, meanwhile lost 70% of its national economy to the so-called underground since accepting IMF conditionalities in 1976. General Francisco Mo-

rales Bermúdez, whose coup against President Velasco began
Peru's descent into the financial underworld, complied with
IMF demands in 1979 to open up Peru's interior to "foreign
investment," as a means of attracting capital to the bankrupt
country; the result was that the international narcotics traffic
gained access to huge tracts of land for coca leaf production.
Peru's Gross National Product is only $20 billion; $6 billion of
narcotics revenues (a tiny fraction of what Peruvian cocaine
sells for abroad) make narcotics the dominant industry in the
national economy.

By 1980, the major international dope banks had moved into
Peru's capital. With the help of former Prime Minister Manuel
Ulloa, former Oppenheimer representative Alvaro Meneses,
chief of the government-owned Banco de la Nación in the late
1970s, opened the way for the Banco Ambrosiano to move into
Lima. Its branch was intended to serve as the central narcotics
bank of the Andean region, with the official participation of
central banks from drug-producing countries.

Manuel Ulloa, twice Prime Minister and finance minister
and a long-standing associate of the Rockefeller empire in Ibero-
America, played a critical role in creating the conditions under
which Peru's narcoeconomy has flourished. He was largely responsible for imposing IMF conditionalities on Peru; he is a
vocal advocate of Mont Pelerin-style "free enterprise"; and he
has even gone on record suggesting that the legalization of
the cocaine trade might be advantageous. In a December 1983
interview with the Lima magazine *Debate 24,* Ulloa said:

> Since the era of Unanue, developing the medical and health
> potentials of this unique plant [coca] has been proposed, sug-
> gesting since that time the possibility of its substitution for,
> or at least having a similar importance, as a drink, to that of
> tea or coffee. . . .

Ulloa continued:

> The economic implications are both varied and significant. It
> begins with the livelihood of the peasants and ends, albeit

indirectly, reflected in our balance of payments. Its importance could reach figures equivalent to a minimum of three or even 5% of the Gross National Product. . . .

Undoubtedly this perspective would open unsuspected horizons and would allow for the channeling of a major portion of illegal coca production towards a legal market.

3

Colombia: Can Dope, Inc. Buy a Country?

In Colombia, the dope traffickers have openly proposed a takeover of the country's finances. In July of 1984, the top honchos of the Colombian mob floated an offer "too good to refuse"—they proposed repatriating $3 billion in narcodollars in return for full amnesty and acceptance into the good graces of the Colombian political and business community. What they were not counting on, however, was President Belisario Betancur, whose administration beginning in 1982 took up the challenge of reversing eight years of capitulation to and/or open collaboration with the drug mob.

Of course, the dope trade would not have made such an outrageous offer without the backing of the international banking community. What makes this backing all the more outrageous is that it is entirely public and open. On November 3, 1983, the Swiss bankers' newspaper *Neue Zürcher Zeitung* responded to

Colombian President Betancur's aggressive war on drugs—in which Justice Minister Lara Bonilla was to fall victim to an assassin's bullets a few months later—with the following outrageous encomium:

Colombian products are of limited interest for the industrial countries. 1983 is expected to result in an all-time low for exports. Comparing its export earnings to its approximately $9.6 It billion foreign debt, the stretched currency situation, and the low level of reserves at the central bank are already reflected in the exchange rate on the parallel [black] market. In the past decade, Colombia could depend annually upon $2 to $3 billion, which, following uncontrolled exports [i.e., the drug traffic] were available to the country. Were the moralizing campaign of the government to reduce this source of funds, Colombia would find itself no longer in a position to earn the foreign exchange necessary for its economy.

Betancur's predecessor and chief antagonist is Alfonso López Michelsen. As President of Colombia from 1974 to 1978, López virtually organized the expanding narcotics traffic from the top. His most outrageous action was to direct his finance minister, Rodrigo Botero Montoya, to create a *Ventanilla Siniestra,* a black market window at the central bank, enabling the dope traders to bring dollars into the above-ground economy with no questions asked. Belisario Betancur shut it the week he took office.

López's cousin, Jaime Michelsen Uribe, head of the country's largest financial conglomerate, the Grupo Grancolombiano, which he created through a 1972 merger, rapidly rose to become Colombia's top mobster. The assets of the Grupo swelled through the laundered inflows of the blossoming narcotics trade, tripling in the first six months of 1976 alone—as drug sales took off, and dirty money flows into Florida went through the ceiling.

Despite significant funding from such known, convicted dope traffickers as Carlos Lehder—whom we will meet later as Robert Vesco and Fidel Castro's business partner—López's 1982 attempt at a political comeback failed. Newly elected President Betancur promptly revived investigations of stock fraud and other financial chicanery of the Grupo Grancolombiano which previous administrations had dropped. In a dramatic personal confrontation with Michelsen on December 31, 1983, Betancur confronted the former President's cousin with the evidence against him and demanded his resignation from the director-ship of the Banco de Colombia, flagship of the Grupo Grancolom-biano. Michelsen promptly fled the country with his family and closest associates. Within a week, 11 officers of the Banco de Colombia were in jail.

The most sensational revelation of all, however, came in the July 29, 1984 edition of the Bogota daily *El Tiempo,* from the lips of former President López Michelsen himself. The interview with López revealed that on the weekend of May 6, just one week after narcotics traffickers had assassinated Colombia's courageous Justice Minister Lara Bonilla, López had arrived in Panama to meet secretly with the men who had ordered Lara's death. Present were such czars of Colombia's drug under-world as Pablo Escobar and Jorge Ochoa. López and the mafia chiefs discussed what terms they could credibly offer to buy the country out from under the control of President Betancur, who had vowed in a graveside eulogy to his slain justice minister to continue Lara Bonilla's war on drugs. A second follow-up meeting was arranged in Panama for later that month between Colombian Attorney General Carlos Jiménez Gómez and the dope mob. Jiménez Gómez later admitted that he had acted on his own authority in meeting with the country's most wanted fugitives.

When the mafia offer was made public, President Betancur responded that "the government has been explicit that under no circumstances would there ever be dialogue concerning the situations that are clearly defined by law. As a consequence, there have not been, nor are there, nor will there be negotia-tions, nor any form of understanding between the government and the authors of the proposal."

Then, on July 29, López Michelsen emerged in public to defend the dope traffickers, in the pages of *El Tiempo*. López Michelsen stated:

> It's true, the interview took place only a few days after Dr. Lara Bonilla's murder. And that's why people of ill will ask, while Rodrigo Lara's corpse is still so fresh, how could I talk to people who could be his murderers? Obviously they sought me out because they were tangled up in that situation. They were afraid of being accused. . . .
>
> They began by asserting that the organization they represented was equally important and of the same size as the National Coffee Growers Federation. They said that they represented some one hundred persons who were the leadership of the cocaine organization, an organization which they said had taken 10 years to form and which worked in coordination with people from Brazil, Bolivia, Peru, Ecuador, and with accomplices in the United States. . . . Some of them asserted that one of the people they represented had a $90 million profit during the last quarter.

López concluded by urging the government to accept the mafia offer:

> If these gentlemen want to surrender their laboratories, landing strips, and plantations and sell their planes, then I think the road to reducing the narcotics traffic is probably easier through some form of arrangement than by the more difficult path to reach the same goal.

Just how brazen the López Michelsen crowd got can be seen in the notorious 1983 case of Félix Salcedo and Jairo Slebi, two Colombian congressmen from López's wing of the Liberal Party who were caught trafficking coke in neighboring Venezuela. According to press accounts and police blotters at the time, the two congressmen were arrested with two kilograms of cocaine in a Caracas shopping center. They were striking a deal with a well-connected Venezuelan national named Alberto Abello, who was also arrested by the police.

Abello told the police a completely unbelievable story:

I was having breakfast in the hotel Caracas Hilton with the citizen Félix Salcedo, where we were discussing business, in dollars and bolívares. At one point in the conversation, he asked me to lend him my briefcase in which he supposedly put a quantity of dollars, which we were to change into bolívares in the course of the day. . . . And while they were taking care of some business I went to meet with the person who would give me the bolívares, adjacent to the Hotel Tamanaco. That other person asked me to go with him to the Unicentro El Marqués, and when we reached the soda fountain there the police arrived and seized the cocaine, which belonged to the citizen Félix Salcedo.

Asked how long he had known the drug-trafficking congressmen, Abello answered shamelessly, "About twenty years."

Abello was the private secretary of a well-known senator from Venezuela's Copei party, Valmore Acevedo, and was supposedly a special envoy of the finance minister and the secretary of the President, Gonzalo García Bustillos.

Within 72 hours after his arrest, a new judge was appointed to the case—according to some reports, through the intervention of García Bustillos. This judge ordered Abello released, and investigation of the two Colombian congressmen was abandoned.

If You Can't Buy It, Burn It

On November 6, 1985 some 40 commandos from the M–19 terrorist army invaded Colombia's Justice Ministry in Bogota, heavily armed. The M–19 are international narcoterrorists, public collaborators of Colombian cocaine king Carlos Lehder. They are in the habit of carrying out murderous military actions against those who have sought to attack the drug trade, like President Betancur. For example in March 1984, the M–19 "occupied" the provincial capital of Florencia in retaliation for a large government raid on cocaine factories in Caquetá province. M–19 equipment and literature has been captured in similar raids in Peru.

When the M–19 invaded the Justice Ministry in Bogota, they seized hundreds of hostages, including most of the country's Supreme Court judges. They demanded that President Betancur go to the Justice Ministry to be tried by a "people's court." Betancur refused to bargain with the terrorists. So the M–19 turned downtown Bogota into a war zone, conducting a 28-hour gun battle with Colombian troops in which nearly 100 people died. Most of the judges who were being held hostage were executed by the terrorists, and 80% of the ministry was destroyed.

President Betancur reported on national television that the international narcotics mafia was behind the attack. Justice Minister Enrique Parejo González told the international press the same thing—three times in three days. The drug mafia, Parejo reported, had threatened six weeks before to assassinate the Supreme Court judges and their families—unless they reversed their earlier decisions upholding an extradition treaty between the United States and Colombia, under which many drug runners had been sent to the United States. Upon entering the building, the narcoterrorists moved at once to seize the four judges who had taken the lead in upholding the extradition rulings. The M–19 commandos destroyed the records of the extradition suits, and demanded the repeal of the extradition treaty, in a "press release" issued after the gun battle. But the M–19 admitted only to being "friends" of the drug traffickers.

The liberal news media in the United States—led by the *New York Times* and the *Washington Post,* who have persistently editorialized on behalf of drug decriminalization—reported the event as if the M–19 were a band of erring teenagers guilty of a wild party, and the Colombian government a tyrannical parent. "Many Colombians were stunned by President Belisario Betancur's rejection of repeated offers to negotiate with the re-

bels," the *New York Times* fumed November 10. An interview
with Justice Minister Parejo on the same day, contained the
phrase "The *New York Times* insists, why didn't the President
get on the phone?" to open negotiations with the terrorists by
speaking to their hostages. At another point, when Parejo spoke
of the burning of the files as among the drug traffickers' objectives, the *Times* reporter called Parejo a liar: "The *New York
Times* correspondent is aware that that affirmation you are
making lacks reality. . . ." Eventually a reporter sneered, "The
government says that the assault was undertaken to defend
Colombian institutions and democracy. Is allowing the death
of more than 50 innocent people democracy?"

At that point, Justice Minister Parejo had had enough.
"Please let us not so distort the facts, let us not distort the
truth," he replied. "If someone breaks into your home to rob
and kill you, and a neighbor, attempting to defend you, should
cause the death of some relative of yours, but in good faith, with
the intent of defending your life, are you going to forget the
criminals who entered to kill you, and lay the blame solely on
those who sought to defend you and came to protect you? By
God, let us not distort the truth. . . . Let it not be thought that
the criminal assault here was by the government, that it was
the government that seized the Justice Ministry, that it was
the government which went in there shooting, that it was the
government which murdered the judges of the court. . . . What
should worry you is that a band of criminals went in there to
murder. That's what you should keep in mind."

Undaunted, the next day the *New York Times* commented,
"Many Colombian political analysts and foreign diplomats said
they were skeptical of the minister's theories partly because
there were numerous copies of the destroyed records."

4

The Cash Connection

In a November 1984 report entitled, "The Cash Connection: Organized Crime, Financial Institutions, and Money Laundering," the U.S. President's Commission on Organized Crime sought to quantify the financial implications of the U.S. narcotics traffic as follows:

Some $5 to $15 billion of the $50 to $75 billion in illegal drug money earned in the United States probably moves into international financial channels each year:

More than two-thirds of the $5 to $15 billion of the $50 to $75 billion is moved on behalf of foreign traffickers bringing drugs to the United States, as well as Colombians and Mexicans involved in distributing cocaine and heroin in the United States. The remainder comes from funds earned by U.S. drug dealers and distributors.

More than two-thirds of the $5-$15 billion probably passes
through Colombia, or the offshore banking centers of the
Caribbean Basin, mainly Panama, the Bahamas, and the
Cayman Islands.

Since 1980, the government has been tracking information
which points to Panama as a banking center for the cocaine
trade, and Hong Kong as a banking center for the heroin
trade. While the international list of offshore havens is
lengthy, Panama and Hong Kong deserve special attention
because, in addition to being banking centers for the narcotics
trade, they are also notorious transshipment and meeting
points for the traffickers. In addition, they well illustrate the
international aspects of the money-laundering problem.

The U.S. government estimates are misleadingly small, as we
shall indicate in a moment, but the identification of Hong Kong
and Panama was on the mark. About this, the Commission's
report has the following to say:

In 1982, the Department of the Treasury examined Federal
Reserve receipts from the Banco Nacional de Panama, the
Panamanian state bank, in an effort to quantify the amount
of cocaine money accumulated in Panama. The examination
revealed that the amount of U.S. dollars that the Federal
Reserve receives from Banco Nacional de Panama had increased substantially in recent years. This fact indicates that
the amount of cash received by the Banco Nacional de Panama from other banks or individuals in Panama also increased. Banco Nacional de Panama acts much like the Federal Reserve in that it is a clearinghouse for cash. It receives
and disburses U.S. dollars to various banks in Panama, just
as the Federal Reserve receives and disburses dollars to U.S.
banks. The Department's review of Federal Reserve receipts
from Panama shows a more than fourfold increase in the
reported cash flow from 1980 to 1983.

The 1984 analysis by Federal law enforcement agencies
and the intelligence community . . . concludes that the cash

flow from Panama to the United States is the most significant recorded flow of currency that is likely to be drug money.

In comparison, some Treasury analysts have estimated that more than $2.2 billion in unreported cash was transported to Panama from 1980 to 1983. While this money is moved to Panama through a wide variety of methods, pilots often simply fly the unreported cash out of the United States in private aircraft.

Recall, before we proceed to consider the implications of these numbers, the 1978 report of Frankfurt banking sources regarding the intent of the Hongkong and Shanghai Bank takeover of Marine Midland: that HongShang was after Marine Midland's specific function as the clearing agent for the central bank of Panama. To the extent that American banks, as reported elsewhere in this volume, have sought out dirty money flows as a principal source of deposits, the Hong Kong bank showed remarkable prescience in its choice of Marine Midland. Panama's offshore banking apparatus was, of course, set up by Nicolás Ardito Barletta, former World Bank director and the President of Panama until he resigned in September 1985.

The data made available from the Treasury and Federal Reserve, fragmentary and outdated as they are, indicate that annual receipts for Ibero-American narcotics sold in the United States are in the range of $100 to $150 billion per year—twice the estimate quoted above. The flaw in the U.S. government's reasoning lies in the unfounded assumption of all Treasury calculations (which other agencies accept as the government's authoritative word on the subject) that the objective of dope traffickers is to accumulate a big pile of dollar bills in their mattress. In fact, cash circulating among the drug traffickers represents merely the transactions balances (checking accounts) of the narcotics traffickers. Just as a $10,000 average balance in the account of a retail merchant will reflect an annual turnover of many times that amount, as the checking balance is drawn upon and replenished, a given volume of cash employed by a narcotics gang will reflect a larger turnover.

This is evident from a study performed by the Federal Reserve

System on net cash payout from its branch offices during the
period 1970–1978. The study shows an exceptional excess issue
of $9.2 billion in $100 bills by the New York Federal Reserve
Bank over this period, and admits this is related to the "underground economy." Compare this to the official data on narcotics
traffic, issued by the National Narcotics Intelligence Consumers Committee in 1978, the source also for the President's Commission estimates cited earlier:

Sold in U.S. (Highest Estimate)

Drug	Highest Estimate: Cash Sales
Mexican Heroin	$3.66 billion
Cocaine	$16.25 billion
Marijuana	
Mexican	$4.18 billion
Colombian	$16.88 billion
Jamaican	$0.86 billion
TOTAL	**$40.98 billion**

This 1978 estimate is roughly half of our 1978 figure, based on
congressional investigations (which put the volume of Florida
traffic, overwhelmingly from Ibero-America, at $13 billion
alone), as well as interviews with police and U.S. intelligence
officials. Cocaine and marijuana, in our estimate, brought $80
billion on the street in the United States.

The street sales, of course, represent a huge multiple of the
original wholesale price. In the case of heroin, the markup is
close to 500 times. To be extremely conservative, let us estimate
25 times for cocaine, and 10 times for marijuana. The government numbers cited above imply a wholesale turnover of merely
$650 million for cocaine, and $2.2 billion for marijuana. Against
this we have an estimated $9.2 billion of additional hundred-
dollar bills in circulation, which volume must turn over several
times a year, in the manner of a transactions balance. For
example, the total $3.3 billion of excess cash reported in Florida
during 1978 reportedly reflects a $13 billion narcotics traffic in
that state, which is to say that the cash used by the traffickers
turns over four times per year (i.e., that a $3.3 billion transac-

tion balance can handle four times that amount of gross annual sales). On this basis, we should say that the $9.2 billion of extra hundred-dollar bills in circulation should be able to handle almost $40 billion in wholesale transactions.

Conservatively, we may estimate that the current volume of narcotics sales' in the United States deriving from Ibero-America is in the range of $150 billion per annum, including close to $100 billion of cocaine. Perhaps another $50 billion is sold in Europe and other parts of the industrial world. Perhaps a tenth of that income is repatriatable to Ibero-America (should they so choose) by the *fondi;* that is roughly equivalent to the combined annual debt service of Mexico, Colombia, and Venezuela. (*See* Dope Inc. Is Doubling Every Five Years, p. 28 for an updated estimation of the size of the drug trade.)

If this seems exaggerated, consider the following: On November 9, 1984, some 1,000 Mexican troops, 30 helicopter gunships, 6 planes, and 60 land vehicles descended upon a stretch of 100,000 hectares in the northern states of Chihuahua and Sonora. The soldiers destroyed 10,000 tons of marijuana, with an estimated street value of $10 billion; this represented the equivalent of two marijuana "joints" for every inhabitant of the Earth. Fourteen thousand Mexican peasants were employed in growing the drug; their employers had the logistical capability to move about 20 tons per day. That is one raid, on one day.

If the volume of cash involved seems unmanageable, consider the following report drawn from the President's Commission study cited earlier:

> Over a four-year period ending in November 1982, Eduardo Orozco and a number of associates deposited approximately $151 million in cash in eighteen bank and currency exchange accounts, and transferred it to accounts elsewhere in the United States, Panama, the Bahamas and the Cayman Islands. While much of the money came from Colombian cocaine dealers, Orozco's laundering customers also included Sicilian heroin traffickers of La Cosa Nostra. . . .
>
> Orozco used several methods to conceal the source and amounts of currency in his operation:

- Small-denomination bills were converted into larger-denomination bills;
- Amounts just under $10,000 were deposited, many times using couriers, to avoid the filing of CTR's [cash reports to IRS].
- Shell corporate entities were set up, and deposits into these accounts were made through inter-corporate transfers, adding another level of insulation.
- False "bills of lading" were used to substantiate the deposit and transfer of funds among export-import companies.
- More than two-thirds of the money moved by Orozco—approximately $97 million—went through his accounts with Deak-Perrera, a currency exchange based in New York City. [Deak was forced into bankruptcy by this exposé—ed.]
- Four of the New York banks used by Orozco [were] Chase Manhattan Bank, Marine Midland Bank [owned by Hong-Shang], Irving Trust, and Crédit Suisse. . . . In interviews with knowledgeable bank officials, the Commission found that with the exception of Marine Midland Bank, none of the banks took active steps to notify law enforcement officials about Orozco's suspicious transactions.
- Orozco opened an account for the Calypso Travel Agency at Chase Manhattan Bank, with a $60,000 cash deposit. . . .
- Crédit Suisse allowed an Orozco nominee, Alvarez Segura, to make a cash deposit of $57,795, which was followed the next day by a cash deposit of $249,000. . . .
- Marine Midland Bank's branch in Jamaica, Queens accepted a cash deposit of $830,000, which Orozco's couriers had brought into the bank in a bag. . . . The next day, Orozco's attorney again asked the bank to accept a $1 million cash deposit. The branch manager was then instructed by his superiors to close the account. In spite of a request from the FBI that Marine Midland keep the account open and accept the deposits from Orozco's attorney, the account was closed.

Orozco's tale is of special interest for another reason: the convicted dope money launderer was the benefactor and first employer of Alberto Duque, the Wunderkind of Colombian banking, whose father was the treasurer of López Michelsen's unsuccessful 1982 presidential campaign.

On May 19, 1982, Duque, the leading financier of the Colombian community in Miami and majority owner of the City National Bank, filed for personal and corporate bankruptcy. His little corporate empire, which included such firms as General Coffee, Allsun Juices, Corporate Jets, Domino Investments Ltd., as well as City National, was being sued by 20 banks for an aggregate sum of $135 million. It came out in the course of these suits that Duque had falsified collateral in the form of false bills of lading for coffee shipments from Colombia.

The method of fraud is not surprising; as noted above, it was a specialty of the man who trained Duque, Eduardo Orozco. Duque had arrived in the U.S. ten years earlier with a bankroll and letters of introduction from his father, a friend of Orozco. Orozco took him in at the Wall Street offices of Colombian Coffee, the firm Orozco used to launder dope money, and within six months made young Alberto vice president of the firm, starting him on his road to the big time.

5

How the Fondi Control Ibero-America's Dope Traffic

We will take the reader "From heaven, through the earth, to hell," as the poet said, beginning with the Olympian families of the ancient European *fondi,* proceeding downwards to such parvenu as the Cisneros family of Venezuela, and the expendable thugs who accept cardboard boxes full of cash at banks in Florida. The latter have received considerable attention from American law enforcement agencies; their masters have not. We will demonstrate how the surrogates of the Soviet Union in Ibero-America are integrated into the narcotics traffic at every level, from the Venetian insurance companies we introduced earlier on, down to the security services of the Cuban state.

Since the 1858 Sepoy Rebellion gave a bad name to Britain's East India Company, the Company's sponsors have prefered to spin off the dirtier side of its operations into separable entities which may be disowned when necessary. For Asia, the new incarnation of "John Company" became the Hongkong and Shanghai Bank, still the central bank for the world opium traffic. For Ibero-America, it became the New Orleans and Boston-based United Fruit Company. United Fruit, later United Brands, was believed by American intelligence officials to be the principal mechanism through which cocaine was transported into the United States during the 1970s.

The sometimes bewildering change of faces at United Fruit—from the old, odd alliance of New Orleans gangsters and Boston Brahmins described in the historical section of this book, to the Max Fisher-Carl Lindner combination now at the helm—does not really disguise a long-term continuity of operations.

It represents a bridge between apparently respectable finance and a ground-level ability to conduct coups d'état, arrange political assassinations, farm and market large quantities of narcotics, and launder the resulting cash flow back into the apparently respectable channels of banking. The corporate form of United Fruit as such is a "black box" through which the complex requirements of this activity may be brought together.

This corporate umbrella shelters virtually every corporate miscreant who has made headlines in the last ten years. Reliance Corporation's Saul Steinberg, the business parter of London's Jacob de Rothschild, is 40% owned by Lindner. Meshulam Riklis's Rapid-American Corporation, number one on the watch-list of the U.S. Customs Service for dope-smuggling across the U.S.-Canadian border, and heir to the old Louie Rosenfeld bootlegging empire, is 40% owned by Lindner. Corporate asset-stripper Victor Posner, reputedly an investment partner of organized crime's late "financial wizard," Meyer Lansky, is 10% Lindner-owned. Gulf and Western, the conglomerate of Charles Bludhorn, the man who arranged Michele Sindona's takeover of the Franklin National Bank, is 8% owned by Lindner. And so the list goes on.

Lindner took over United Brands in February 1975, when its chairman Eli Black walked out of his 44th-floor office window in New York City for unexplained reasons. Within two months, Detroit "ex-"mobster Max Fisher was the new acting chairman of the company; Lindner, Fisher and their immediate associates had garnered 48% of the UB stock. Fisher's appointment was sponsored by two men: Sol Linowitz and Donald R. Gant, a Goldman Sachs partner and Henry Kissinger associate. Linowitz, who later became the Carter administration's special envoy for Panama Canal treaty negotiations, as well as the principal promoter of the dope economy in the Caribbean, was a director as well of Marine Midland Bank, instrumental in promoting Marine Midland's merger with the HongShang.

It is hard to further blacken United Brands' reputation in Ibero-America. Its role in the 1954 Castillo Armas coup in Guatemala, where United Brands financed an expeditionary force to overthrow the Arbenz government when it tried to expropriate United Fruit Company lands, is well documented. What is less well known is United Brands' role in sponsoring the Cuban-allied insurrectionary movements in Central America, including the present government of Nicaragua. Their partner in this venture? Theology of Liberation networks within the Society of Jesus.

During the 1960s and 1970s, the Jesuits' principal training center for Central America was the Inter-American Center of the Institute for Human Relations at Loyola University of New Orleans. The Inter-American Center seeded "liberation theologists" into the guerrilla movements of the area; the Vatican belatedly cracked down on this scandal during 1984.

According to Fr. Janer, S.J., the assistant director of the Institute, United Brands was the principal source of student referrals to the Institute, which brought bright young individuals from El Salvador, Nicaragua, Guatemala, and other countries to New Orleans for training. At the Institute, the inmates were subjected to propaganda lectures, "sensitivity training," and other forms of activity which suggest intensive psychological manipulation. Then they were sent home to lead insurrections. "I would not be surprised if some of them are fighting in there right now," Fr. Janer said in a discussion published by *Executive Intelligence Review* on December 8, 1981.

United Fruit Co.'s funding and ground-level collaboration with the Jesuits' New Orleans institute is not the first instance of support for supposed "leftists." It funded Socialist International member José Figueres's 1947 putsch in Costa Rica, through the mediation of Ernando Castro Cervantes, a Costa Rican businessman. Figueres did the company two important favors during his second term. First, he arranged government purchases of United Fruit Company lands at both his and the company's profits, reportedly making his son-in-law, Danilo Jiménez Nevia, a substantial stockholder in the company. Secondly, he granted asylum to Robert Vesco, now Fidel Castro's drug-runner in chief, then on the lam after the collapse of Investors Overseas Services. Vesco put substantial funds into Figueres' ranch, "La Lucha." Figueres, at the same time, permitted the opening of a large, well-staffed Soviet embassy in San José.

These Theo-Lib Jesuits do not work for free. Their overall Jesuit financial presence in Ibero-America is massive: Their holdings of land and other assets there have been variously estimated at upwards of $50 billion. All Jesuit financial functions in Ibero-America are conducted through the Banque Sudameris in Paris, or to give its full name, the Banque Française et Italienne pour l'Amerique du Sud. Paribas—the extension of the old Ottoman grain-trading de Comondo family—owns a 12% share. The Assicurazioni Generali di Trieste owns a somewhat smaller share; this is a redundant link in any event, since Paribas is the largest shareholder in the Generali. The other main Italian share is held by the Banca Commerciale Italiana, the owner of George Ball's Banca della Svizzera Italiana, which we encountered earlier.

Some continental European banking sources argue, hyperbolically, that Sudameris "owns Argentina," in the same sense that some argue that the Montevideo collaborator of Roberto Calvi and Licio Gelli, Umberto Ortolani, "owns Uruguay." Sudameris maintains 24 branches in Argentina, but its presence elsewhere is enormous.

At the beginning of this account, we reviewed the case of Alvaro Meneses of Phibro and his role in the takeover of the Banco Andino by the dirty Banco Ambrosiano. At the time of Ambrosiano's entrance onto the scene, Banque Sudameris owned a share of the Banco Andino.

The case of the Jesuits' sometime financial adviser, Dr. Franz Pick of New York City, illustrates to what extent such networks within the Jesuits maintain a hands-on relationship to the flow of narcotics money. "I am a friend of the Black Pope," Dr. Pick said of the former Jesuit General Fr. Pedro Arrupe, in a July 21, 1981 discussion with *EIR*. He was introduced to Arrupe by one of the casualties of the Sindona and Ambrosiano scandals, convicted swindler Luigi Menini. Before his jail sentence, Menini was a close associate of Michele Sindona, and enjoyed the protection of the controversial Bishop Paul C. Marcinkus. Menini's most celebrated financial transaction was the sale of the real estate holdings in Immobiliare Roma through the Istituto per le Opere Religiose, the Vatican's bank, to the former Italian royal family, the Savoys. Dr. Pick is a former consultant to the Assicurazioni Generali, the Banque Louis-Dreyfus, and the Banca Commerciale Italiana. In the early 1930s, he was also an adviser and frequent visitor to the infamous Juan March, the dirtiest figure in Spanish finance, and the prototype of the "Shepherd Boy" character in Robert Ludlum's bestseller, *The Matarese Circle*. In this capacity, Pick was a colleague of Col. Louis Mortimer Bloomfield, the protagonist of this volume's chapter concerning the International Assassination Bureau known as Permindex.

Still active as the publisher of *Pick's Currency Yearbook*, the 85-year-old Jesuit adviser describes himself as an expert on the "underground economy."

Pick told *EIR*, "The transfers of sales results of narcotics and other things out of the United States and back into the United States requires a special technique and a special knowledge, and, if possible government connections and customs connections. Of the money supply which exists today, one-third belongs to the underground economy." Pick has such special knowledge; Banca Commerciale Italiana called on him to advise them on the operations of their Bahamas outlet, BCI Overseas Bank. "Half the suitcases on airplanes coming in and out of the Bahamas are filled with cash," he said. Banco Ambrosiano's defunct Bahamas branch was one of the handful of foreign banks with the domestic banking license required to conduct cash transactions in the Bahamas, along with the local branches of Bank of America and Citibank, as reported earlier.

A director of BCI Overseas Bank was Pick's cousin, Felice Pick, the longtime private secretary to former Italian central bank chief Guido Carli; Carli, in turn, spent 20 years on the board of directors of Banque Sudameris.

6

The Cisneros Family: The Bronfmans of Venezuela

Until recently, Venezuela maintained a "privileged" relationship to South America's drug traffic. Largely exempt from producing and processing narcotics until 1983, Venezuela served instead as a transshipment center and "banking house" for the drug trade. It was Venezuelan drug money, for example, which led the way in laundering proceeds into Florida real estate, even before the Colombian mafia got the idea. Laundering from Venezuela into the United States through Florida grew so extensive it became a common joke to say that Florida seceded from the Union—joining Venezuela as a new state. By 1980, public estimates placed Venezuelan real estate assets in Florida at over $1.1 billion. A total of some $5 billion was "washed" through Venezuela in 1983, according to early 1984 public estimates of one Venezuelan police official.

Venezuela's "privileged" relationship is long lost: Processing laboratories, cocaine production, and an estimated half-million addicts (among them, many children of the narcofinanciers), now accompany the banking houses profiting from the trade. But tracking the money-laundering machine and its controllers remains the most efficient tool for identifying Venezuela's dope mafia as a whole.

Cisneros Connection

On July 20, 1984, the Venezuelan magazine *Resumen,* reported on a story alleging that a member of Venezuela's Cisneros family, one of the country's most powerful monied families, was up to his neck in dope money-laundering in Florida. According to the story, taken wholly from left-wing journalist Penny Lernoux's book *In Banks We Trust,* Oswaldo Cisneros Fajardo had been associated with the World Finance Corporation, an international money laundromat. Caught in one scam too many, the WFC eventually collapsed, and its Cuban-American president, Guillermo Hernández Cartaya, landed in jail on lesser charges of income tax evasion. Details of the seamier side of the WFC operation—arms for drugs in the Caribbean, financial capabilities made available to the Castro government in Cuba—were included in the story. Interest was heightened by the fact that a Caracas newspaper, *Diario de Caracas,* had just printed a picture of Venezuela's President Lusinchi reading the Lernoux book with two of his advisers: The caption asserted that the readers were concentrating on the Cisneros links to the drug world.

This provoked as much outrage as if *Newsweek* had accused David Rockefeller of laundering dirty money. The Organización Diego Cisneros, the Cisneros family holding company, published full-page advertisements in the Caracas press denying any connection to World Finance Corporation, Credival, or Mr. Hernández Cartaya. Oswaldo Cisneros, in an interview with *Resumen* magazine telling "his side" of the story, admitted he had hired Hernández Cartaya in 1975 to reorganize the investment company, Inversiones Fénix, later renamed Credi-val, and that the two had jointly incorporated a subsidiary of the WFC in Caracas. But he insisted that that was the last of their business association and that he had no knowledge that Hernández Cartaya was involved in drugs or drug money-laun-dering.

Others defended the good name of Cisneros by attacking the credibility of Lernoux, an easy enough proposition given that her "journalist" career was sponsored by the KGB and British intelligence-linked assets in the United States and Ibero-America. Yet most of the evidence presented by Lernoux on the WFC came from the records of the lengthy investigations into WFC and Hernández Cartaya by numerous U.S. agencies, in-cluding Congress, the Drug Enforcement Administration, Cus-toms, and a federal grand jury.

The true story of the Cisneros family goes far beyond the ugly WFC affair. The mistake is in looking only down from the Cisneros family's position of power, rather than across, and up. What would the reader say if we were to inform him of the existence of a prominent Ibero-American family that:

■ Got its start by being sponsored by one of the leading Dope, Inc. Canadian banks, the Royal Bank of Canada;

■ Has a longstanding association with the Rockefeller family, which has favored it by selling it crumbs of the Rockefeller empire in Ibero-America and by placing family members on the boards of directors of various Rockefeller international hold-ings, and which permitted the consolidation of these ties through marriage into the Rockefeller-linked Phelps family;

■ Has a strong relationship to the Florida banking circles found at the heart of the Carter administration's dope scandal;

■ Was a partner in a Florida finance corporation with docu-mented ties to terrorists and drug runners, and which received millions of dollars from Moscow's Narodny Bank;

■ Has for decades promoted the libertarian economic theories of Friedrich von Hayek's Mont Pelerin Society, which advocates the legalization of the drug trade; and

■ Has joined David Rockefeller's campaigns to promote drug-producing Jamaica as the "model" for the whole Caribbean Basin.

Now the reader is thinking in the right way to be able to understand the real Cisneros story, and the fact that we are dealing with the Venezuelan equivalent of the Bronfmans. And cousin Oswaldo's involvement with the dirty Hernández Cartaya ceases to be a surprise.

Family Empire

The Cisneros family fortune is centralized today in the Organización Diego Cisneros (ODC), a holding company worth an estimated $3 billion. It was described recently by one New York banker close to the group as "a Gulf and Western-type" company uniting some 50 companies producing everything from disco records, sports equipment, computers, and cosmetics to processed foods, and owning real estate, agriculture, communications, and finance. "The Cisneros group, which has always had an international orientation to its investments, went acquisition-crazy in the past two-three years," the banker commented. Informally, he added, it is now estimated to have placed at least $1 billion outside Venezuela.

Like Gulf and Western, which owns Paramount Pictures, the ODC has its "entertainment" company: Venevisión, purchased in 1961 when television was taking off in Venezuela. The Cisneros family has used Venevisión to promote the kind of rock and pornography *Playboy* culture needed to create a "feel-good," hedonistic drug movement in any country. Skyrocketing sales of rock and disco stars recorded by the ODC's recording company, Sonoroven, are one lucrative spinoff of the advertising capabilities Venevisión provides to ODC.

It was the Royal Bank of Canada which gave the pater familias, Diego Cisneros, his start in Caracas after he emigrated from Cuba in 1929. The association with the Canadian dope bank continues to this day; ODC executive vice president (and president of Venevisión) José Rafael Revenga represents Cisneros interests on its board of directors. In 1939, Diego went "independent," and set up the first Pepsi-Cola bottling franchise in Venezuela with his brother, Antonio. Pepsi and Cisneros are synonymous in Venezuela today. Antonio's son, Oswaldo, is the company's current president.

It was Diego Cisneros, however, who built the ODC into a business and financial empire. In Venezuela, the inevitable word-association with the name Cisneros became "Rockefeller." Along with other wealthy families, the Cisneros family took over many of the business operations originally developed by the Rockefellers. These include the local outlets for the Sears Roebuck retail chain; National Cash Register; and Nelson Rockefeller's pet project, Cada Supermarkets. Acquired along the way as ODC "international adviser" was George S. Moore, former president of Citibank and director emeritus of W.R. Grace. Son Gustavo also acquired a wife well-connected to the Rockefeller empire: Patricia Phelps, of the U.S. Eastern Establishment Phelps family.

Diego Cisneros was also proud of his membership in the elite Mont Pelerin Society, the leading international ideologues of "legalizing the illegal economy." Diego Cisneros frequently sponsored visits of Mont Pelerin libertarian propagandists to lecture Venezuelan businessmen, and his lifelong motto, according to son Gustavo's own report, was pure Mont Pelerin ideology: "Give me the right man, and I'll make the deal."

With the father's death in 1980, sons Gustavo and Ricardo Cisneros Rendiles took over the family business, as president and vice president, respectively, of the ODC. Gustavo became heir-apparent of the empire, and has continued the work of his father as a leading promoter of the "free enterprise" model in the Caribbean Basin. When David Rockefeller created the U.S.-Jamaican Businessmen's Committee in 1981 to promote the "Jamaican model" of dope and free enterprise, Gustavo Cisneros announced the founding of a parallel "Venezuelan-Jamaican Businessmen's Association," with himself as co-chairman.

Gustavo's career as an international businessman is rising. He is vice president of the Venezuelan Chapter of the Knights

of the Sovereign Order of Malta. By 1981, he was put on the
International Advisory Board of Chase Manhattan Bank, join-
ing Henry Kissinger and his business associate, Per Gyllen-
hammer of Swedish Volvo, Argentina's "Joe" Martínez de Hoz,
Y.K. Pao of Hong Kong's Worldwide Shipping Corporation, Ian
D. Sinclair, chairman of Canadian Pacific Enterprises, Ltd.,
the chairman of Royal Dutch Petroleum Co. G.A. Wagner—all
headed, of course, by David Rockefeller. In November 1983,
Gustavo was added to the International Advisory Board of Pan
American World Airways, joining United Brands' Sol Linowitz,
Gulf and Western lawyer Cyrus Vance, Notre Dame University
President Theodore Hesburgh, and Hong Kong's Bank of East
Asia head Yet-keung Kan, among others. Now a seat on the
International Advisory Board of Beatrice Foods has been added
to his "credentials."

Cisneros's links to the Vance-Carter nexus are not new. Under the Carter administration, Washington sources report,
then-Secretary of State Vance frequently used Cisneros as his
interlocutor with other political players in the region.

Operations in Florida

From Caracas, Cisneros and Venezuelan banker and longtime ally Pedro Tinoco, Jr. did their part in sponsoring the
Venezuelan money boom in Florida. When Florida Governor
Robert Graham, an avid proponent of the "offshore" scheme for
Florida, came to Caracas in October 1980 to promote increased
Venezuelan investment in Florida, it was Gustavo Cisneros
and Pedro Tinoco, Jr. who threw the big reception for the governor and his Florida promoters. Ties extended, of course, to the
business world as well. Around 1978, the Cisneros bought a
minority share of Florida National Bank of Jacksonville, the
major member of a statewide holding company called Florida
National Banks of Florida. He placed Tinoco, whom we shall
know better in a moment, on the bank's board to represent
Cisneros interests.

Florida National, it turns out, is one of three Florida banks which led the battle to force the deregulation of Florida banking at the end of the 1970s—the legislative changes required to turn Florida into a virtual "offshore" international banking haven for drug money.

Florida National Bank had another interesting feature: It was the principal bank for Charter Oil Co., which had two directors representing it on Florida National's board, Edward Ball and Charter Oil's chairman, Raymond Mason. Charter, which went bankrupt during 1984, became notorious when the news broke that it served as a conduit for Libyan oil sales promoted by President Carter's brother Billy—the scandal that went down in history as "Billygate."

Gustavo Cisneros, however, was not harmed by the scandal. He reportedly sold off his shares in 1981, for a multi-million dollar profit.

WFC and The Cuban Connection

It would seem that Oswaldo Cisneros, Gustavo's cousin, runs a great deal more than the Pepsi-Cola Company in Venezuela. According to a report appearing in the Venezuelan daily *Diario de Caracas* on July 1, 1984, Oswaldo is the point man in a scheme to re-establish commercial and diplomatic relations between Venezuela and Cuba, hoping to legitimize his present middleman role in U.S.-Cuban trade, in violation of the U.S. embargo of Cuba. *Diario de Caracas* claimed that Cisneros visited Cuba in a Pepsi company plane on June 7, 1984, and met personally with Fidel Castro. In an August 12, 1984 interview with *Resumen* magazine, Cisneros did not deny the trip to Cuba, but insisted that it was for family and personal reasons, and that the meeting with Castro occurred by "pure chance" and that only "a series of generalities" were discussed. Oswaldo added that he had several other Pepsi board members who had participated in the Bay of Pigs invasion, and that the whole story was an attempt to discredit his well-cultivated anti-Castro credentials.

But Oswaldo Cisneros has other explanations to make. His wife is Ella Fontanals de Cisneros, a Cuban whose brother, José Fontanals Pérez, currently sits on the Board of Directors of the Banco Nacional de Cuba in Havana, and serves as economic adviser to Fidel Castro. Ella's ties with her brother are not a thing of the past; her husband Oswaldo admitted in his *Resumen* interview that he facilitated at least one quiet visit to Caracas by José Fontanals, to attend the funeral of the Fontanals' mother.

Ella reportedly divides her time between Caracas and New York, and sources close to the U.S. DEA report her to be part of a close social circle in New York which brings together current and former Cuban diplomats and Colombian drug runners, including Jemel Nassel de Lehder, former wife of Colombian mafia kingpin, Carlos Lehder.

How can the anti-Castro Cisneros clan socialize with current Fidelista diplomats, the reader asks? As various U.S. congressional committees have told the World Finance Corporation story, the overlap between anti-Castro and pro-Castro networks in the friendly underworld of drugs is not as "impossible" as Oswaldo Cisneros would have investigators believe.

A Cuban-exile banker named Hernández Cartaya founded WFC in 1971 in Coral Gables, Florida. Hernández Cartaya had some sort of intelligence connection from the beginning; he fought in the Bay of Pigs invasion, was captured, was released, and went to work for the Citizens and Southern Bank of Atlanta until he left to set up his own shop. WFC's lawyer, whose signature appears on WFC's incorporation papers, was a well-connected former OSS operative, Walter Sterling Surrey, who remained with WFC until 1976. Surrey was also the lawyer for Ronald Stark—a terrorist now jailed in Italy for ties to the Red Brigades. Stark, before his activities in Italy within narcoterrorist circles, had been a member of the Brotherhood of Eternal Love, an organization involved in producing a substantial portion of the hallucinogenic drugs peddled in the United States through the 1970s. The Brotherhood was one of the first drug-running and money-laundering channels into the U.S. from the Caribbean and Central America.

From the beginning, according to various accounts, WFC was a money laundromat. By 1977, it owned nine companies plus a bank in Miami, as well as subsidiaries in eight Ibero-American countries. A Panamanian subsidiary, Unibank, controlled outlets in the Netherlands Antilles, Cayman Islands, London, the United Arab Emirates, and Texas. WFC's balance sheet, in the seven years of its existence, was more than $500 million. A bad (and allegedly illegal) investment in the United Arab Emirates brought the group down in 1977, costing investors $55 million. Hernández Cartaya fled the country using a phony Colombian passport. The collapse of the WFC revealed, upon investigation, that a 98%-owned subsidiary, the National Bank of South Florida, was involved in money-laundering, so-called insider loans, and sundry other abuses.

But before any of this happened, the WFC obtained a $2 million loan from the Moscow Narodny Bank in 1975. From the available evidence, Hernández Cartaya had done more than enough to earn it.

WFC's network included the scum of the continent's financial underworld. The Colombian representative of WFC's Panama holding group, Unibank, was Jaime Mosquera, a Colombian banker jailed for fraud in 1982. Mosquera was a contact of Hernández Cartaya since both worked for Citizens and Southern, Mosquera as C&S's representative in Bogota. One of WFC's first actions was to buy a small Colombian bank, Banco del Estado, and install Mosquera as chairman. In 1975, Unibank negotiated for a lead-managing role in a $100 million loan to Colombia's state-owned agricultural institute, Idema, with the inside support of Mosquera's brother Christian, then Colombia's banking commissioner. According to testimony to a U.S. congressional committee investigating the WFC scam, Hernández Cartaya was also acting as a covert representative of the Cuban government, and sought to use the loan as an incentive for the López Michelsen government to cooperate with Cuba on the "northern" drug routes.

Drugs and Terrorism

Unibank in Panama also acted as a conduit for Sandinista arms purchases, before the Cuban-sponsored rebel group ousted Anastasio Somoza in 1978. Unconfirmed reports also have it that Unibank was a mediator for arms-for-drugs exchanges in both Venezuela and Colombia.

Hernández Cartaya was a versatile individual. He was also accused of financing terrorist activities by Orlando Bosch's notorious anti-Castro terrorist group. A WFC official, one Duney Pérez Alamo, was a member of the Bosch group, and an intimate of Gaspar Jiménez, the Bosch operative arrested in Mexico in 1976 when he attempted to kidnap the Cuban consul-general in Mexico City. Mexican government sources quoted by Lernoux claim that the government had evidence that WFC put up $50,000 to break Jiménez out of jail, on condition that Jiménez keep his mouth shut about WFC.

WFC's ties into major narcotics traffickers were extensive.

Drug Enforcement Administration files record that one of Hernández Cartaya's closest associates was a narcotics wholesaler working with the Santos Trafficante mafia group. In any case, a finance company linked to Trafficante, Dominion Mortgage Corporation, listed its offices at the same address as Hernández Cartaya's WFC. The DEA also claimed that a WFC employee named Enrique "Kaki" Argomaniz was a suspected drug and gun runner, and the brother of a known drug wholesaler, Alberto Argomaniz.

Oswaldo Cisneros confirmed to Venezuela's *Resumen* magazine on August 12, 1984, that he had worked with WFC's Hernández Cartaya, but insisted, "I never knew, nor can I affirm that Hernández Cartaya has been tied" to the drug trade. According to his account, Hernández Cartaya and Cisneros did indeed jointly found a subsidiary of WFC in 1975–1976; the relationship lasted a year, after which Hernández Cartaya's relationship with Inversiones Fénix ended, and nothing more allegedly was heard from them.

Cisneros Partner Tinoco

Gustavo Cisneros's partner in a wide range of enterprises is
Pedro Tinoco, Jr., a lawyer and the Venezuelan representative
of the Banque Sudameris, the bank of Jesuit financial interests
and the Venetian insurance companies. Informally, Tinoco is
referred to as "Chase Manhattan's man" in Caracas, as well as
the main contact of the Rothschild family. As chief executive
of Venezuela's Banco Latino, he is a major figure in the informal
"Grupo Occidente," the dominant business power on the Vene-
zuelan-Colombian border, one of the most concentrated sites for
drug cultivation in the world.

Tinoco is described by Caracas bankers as "the smartest
banker in town—young, sharp, and on the move." He may also
be one of the dirtiest. His ties to the Cisneros Rendiles family
are such that they are perceived as one group. In 1981, for
example, Gustavo Cisneros appointed him chairman of the
board of directors of the Cisneros' Cada Supermarket chain.

When Banco Latino decided to build a new Caracas headquarters in 1980, Tinoco borrowed the funds from Banque Sudameris, Banca della Svizzera Italiana, American Express International Banking Corporation, and Araven Finance Ltd. (a joint
partnership of Kuwait International Investment Co., Morgan
Grenfell, Venezuela's Banco Consolidado, and Tinoco's Banco
Latino).

As documented throughout, this is the group which handles
very large amounts of illegal money. The offices of Sudameris,
American Express, and the more venerable Venetian insurance
companies are omnipresent through Ibero-America. They dominate the insurance and re-insurance business and a great deal
besides. Ibero-America lost over $100 billion in "flight capital,"
most of it illegal, during 1981–1983, and continues to lose funds
to the offshore banking system. Phony invoices, phony insurance policies, phony subsidiaries employing phony consultants
and chartering phony ships and planes, turn into offshore bank
accounts, and thence into condominiums in Miami or whatever.
There is a ghost economy whose purpose is to extract funds from
Ibero-America, and it is maintained by billion-dollar companies

like Assicurazioni Generali. As noted, the Cisneros group itself has $1 billion outside Venezuela.

Gustavo Cisneros Rendiles, Oswaldo Cisneros Fajardo, Pedro Tinoco and their friends have one foot planted in this ghost economy. They operate at a level well above that of the country's mere politicians, whom they may grace on occasion with financial backing to obtain a favor here and there. They rub shoulders continuously—perhaps with a slight shudder—with the likes of Hernández Cartaya and World Financial Corporation. As reported earlier, the Hongkong and Shanghai Bank does not keep bags of heroin in its vaults, nor does it habitually lend to the merchants who gather the opium harvest; it provides a central banking function and currency for the hundreds of overseas banks who do. Citibank does not wittingly handle illegal flight capital, directly; its "international personal banking" officers maintain a short list of former colleagues to do this for them, so that Citibank may be the ultimate recipient of these deposits. The HongShang describes this as "free enterprise," and ideologues like the Mont Pelerin Society offer philosophical justifications.

The point is not so much that Oswaldo Cisneros got his hand stuck in the cookie jar, which is amusing enough, but rather, that the Organización Diego Cisneros, the Grupo Latino, and the rest of their ilk collaborate with the bankers of the Jesuit order and the clearinghouses of the ancient European *fondi* to order the affairs of nations and their financial systems, such that an Hernández Cartaya will be available any time they snap their fingers. In the cesspool of the financial underworld, thugs and crooks like Hernández Cartaya vie with each other for the good graces of the Olympians, who pick their servants from among the survivors.

Postscript: The Cisneros Family Responds

On February 4, 1985, little more than a week after publication of this chapter on the Cisneros family in *Narcotráfico, SA,* the Spanish-language edition of this book, four correspondents from *Executive Intelligence Review* were illegally detained by Venezuela's political police, the DISIP. The DISIP agent in charge of this action was one Leovigildo Briceno, a.k.a. "Comisario Amilcar," on a warrant issued by Judge Ana Luisa Gandica. The correspondents were held for three days, and then expelled from the country. DISIP agents raided the Caracas apartment of Mexican citizens Carlos and Lucia Méndez at 2 a.m. on February 4 and at 10 a.m. that same morning raided and emptied out *EIR*'s Caracas bureau offices. The Venezuelan newspaper *El Mundo* reported on February 6, "The four journalists were held incommunicado by the DSIP following a complaint by the Cisneros family." Judge Ana Luisa Gandica had also served as legal counsel to the Cisneros-owned Pepsi-Cola of Venezuela.

In their haste to respond to the wishes of the Cisneros clan, the DISIP agents flagrantly violated international accords regarding the treatment of foreign nationals. The correspondents were stripped and body searched by police. For 36 hours, they were denied their internationally recognized right to contact their embassies. They were subjected to intensive interrogation, always about the book, and especially about the origin and author of the chapter on the Cisneros family, who according to one DISIP agent, would "not permit one single copy of the book to circulate."

Correspondent Carlos Méndez, who was officially registered at the Interior Ministry as a foreign journalist, was physically abused by a DISIP agent. Méndez was presented with what one DISIP agent said was a half-kilo bag of cocaine and told that it had been "found" in his apartment. Agents took several photographs of him holding the bag and threatened that they would publish the pictures in the newspaper *2001* (associated with the Cisneros interests) along with the charge that the publication of *Narcotráfico, SA* was a cover-up for drug-running activities.

Simultaneously, Venevisión and other media outlets controlled by the Cisneros clan erupted in an orgy of vilification and lies about *EIR* and contributing editor Lyndon LaRouche, centered on the theme that *Narcotráfico, SA* was intended to undermine the Venezuelan government by attacking "respect-able" public figures in accordance with the designs of Soviet-Castro expansionism"—a remarkable charge, considering the Cisneros family's personal relationship with Fidel Castro's central banker. (Meanwhile, LaRouche reaffirmed "my support for the good work of the government of Venezuela under President Lusinchi" in fighting drugs.)

According to a report in *Diario de Caracas,* on Feb. 14, ten days after the raid on *EIR*'s Caracas office, U.S. Customs officials seized a Venezuelan Lear jet in Hollywood, Florida, and after a search of the plane, identified as YV–12-CP, uncovered an undisclosed amount of cocaine in a life-preserver float. The owner of the jet was a front company for Pepsi-Cola of Venezuela—and the fleet it belonged to was frequently used by Pepsi President Oswaldo Cisneros!

One month after the raid on *EIR*'s offices, on March 5, 1985, *Narcotráfico, SA* was officially banned throughout Venezuela—the first time a book had been proscribed since the military regime of Pérez Jiménez ended in 1958. The complaint which resulted in the banning of the book was brought by attorney Augusto Matheus Pinto, on behalf of David Rockefeller's friend, Gustavo Cisneros, and José Rafael Revenga, of the Cisneros media outlet, Venevisión. In an argument that turned reality on its head, presiding Judge Alirio Abreu Burelli claimed that the book "could lead to the mistaken belief that drug-trafficking is a possible and highly profitable business, which is run under the cover of legal activities and is carried out with impunity and directed by persons or institutions that society holds to be honorable. So interpreted, the text could constitute a stimulus, a subliminal message"—to the promotion of drug-trafficking!

But this was not the end of the story. In April 1986, the DISIP agent who directed the raid on *EIR*'s offices, Leovigildo Briceno a.k.a. "Comisario Amilcar," was suspended from the police and put under arrest, after he was caught appropriating 15 kilos of cocaine and a fortune in jewels which had been taken into police custody during raids in which he participated. Venezuelan deputy Carlos Tablante accused Amilcar's lawyer, Gabriel Enrique Soto Pacheco, of being a partner of Pablo Escobar, the top Colombian drug-runner wanted for the April 30, 1984 assassination of Colombian Justice Minister Rodrigo Lara Bonilla. The 15 kilos of cocaine, Tablante charged, were to pay Soto his legal fees.

Amilcar worked as a team with Judge Ana Luisa Gandica, the judge from Cisneros Pepsi-Cola who had issued the judicial order against *EIR*. She also ordered the raids of the jewelry stores from which 3 million bolívars worth of jewels were later found missing. (Although Amilcar was charged with the theft, his lawyer claimed Judge Gandica stole the jewels.) In March 1986, it was decreed that Judge Gandica must leave the bench because she had never met the educational requirements to be a judge, but she continued to function as a judge nonetheless. Her brother, Luis Gregorio Gandica, who had served as public attorney in the *EIR* case, was fired in December 1985, for having stolen the files of an investigation in progress.

The banning of *Narcotráfico, SA* has been appealed to the Venezuelan Supreme Court.

7

Vesco and Castro

Among the thugs who did, for a time, obtain the favors of the Olympians was a Colombian named Carlos Enrique Lehder Rivas, now a fugitive from Colombian justice. Lehder funneled substantial amounts of money into the 1982 presidential campaign of former President Alfonso López Michelsen through the good offices of Ernesto Samper Pizano, López Michelsen's 1982 campaign coordinator. In 1978, with financing from Lehder and his fellow drug traffickers, Samper had launched an international campaign for marijuana and cocaine legalization. Jaime Michelsen Uribe's Grancolombiano group and its front organization, the National Association of Financial Institutions, provided Samper with the required vehicle for pressing his case for legalization. The drive kicked off with a March 15, 1979 forum in Bogota entitled, "Marijuana: Myth and Reality," with the participation of *High Times* magazine and its lobby group, the U.S. National Organization for the Reform of Marijuana Laws (NORML), as well as Carter White House drug adviser Lee Dogoloff. *High Times,* in its account of the meeting, quoted Samper threatening that failure to legalize marijuana would lead to a military coup and a police state controlled by the narcotics mafia; that is, by such men as Lehder.

Lehder and Samper found sympathy with White House drug adviser Peter Bourne, later expelled for writing false prescriptions for staff members who wanted to use "recreational drugs." Bourne later turned up as U.S. contact man for the Cuban puppet regime in Grenada, where his father, Geoffrey Bourne, ran an offshore medical college.

Lehder has also worked for the Cubans, through the intermediation of Robert Vesco, whom we met earlier in his capacity as frontman for an attempted Soviet takeover of the "French connection" Intrabank in Lebanon. According to one report, by Ernest Volkman in the April 25, 1984 *Family Weekly,* "Castro and Vesco sit at the center of a huge drug-smuggling operation that is responsible for a significant portion of the illegal narcotics coming into the United States. . . . [A]ccording to admittedly imprecise estimates, believed to be on the conservative side, the operation has generated nearly $20 billion in profits during the past four years alone, and Castro is believed to have made about $50 million thus far on his side of the deal."

Castro, according to the Volkman article, wanted to form a second, ultra-secret Cuban intelligence service apart from the DGI, run by the KGB. Whether this wrinkle of the story is true or not is immaterial. In any case, "the connections with drug-runners provided one source of secret income, and Vesco then proposed another lucrative scheme. Cuba was the target of an American trade embargo, which meant that Castro lacked the kind of high technology he needed for modernization of the Cuban economy, especially the sugar industry, the country's staple. Vesco proposed a plan under which he would arrange to smuggle into Cuba advanced American technology, the kind the Soviets could not provide—in exchange for which Castro would protect the drug-traffickers. As an added bonus, the Cubans would be paid a cut of the cocaine and marijuana traffic moving into the United States."

The most important connection for the Cubans was the same Carlos Lehder who had played the legalization game with Peter Bourne in 1979, the account continues. In 1982, the Cubans hooked up with Lehder. "The Cubans needed Lehder; they were trying to run guns to leftist M–19 guerrillas in the Colombian countryside. Lehder, with his extensive smuggling operation, was perfect for the job, and a deal was struck: Lehder would aid Cuban arms-smuggling into Colombia, while the Cubans would provide protection, anchorages and other help for his drug-smuggling operations into the United States."

Vesco's arrangement with Lehder involved the financial side of the operation. Vesco "set up a series of small banks in the Caribbean, where secrecy laws make it easy to protect the identities of depositors. Working in concert with corrupt lawyers and accountants in the southeastern United States, Vesco then devised a complex scheme to launder all that drug money through a series of bank transactions that converted cash into holdings in offshore corporations, based mostly in the Caribbean."

By 1981, Volkman asserted, Vesco and Lehder "were the most important suppliers of cocaine" to the United States.

Since United Fruit Company ally "Pepe" Figueras gave Vesco asylum in Costa Rica in 1972, the fugitive embezzler has led an unsteady existence; he was expelled from Costa Rica by another government in 1978, and refused re-entry in 1982. According to numerous press accounts, he finally settled in Havana that year; according to the *New York Times* of May 7, 1984, Vesco was spending $50,000 per day in Havana, providing the Cubans with badly needed foreign exchange.

Forbes magazine wrote on September 4, 1984:

Federal authorities are certain that Vesco is the brains behind what appears to be the large-scale, illicit two-way trade between Cuba and the continent of North America. Records from federal narcotics trials in Florida and a "Trading With the Enemy Act" case in Texas seem to back them up. So far, as the coincidences pile up, at least four people with some connection to Vesco are dead.

This is no ordinary gang organization. Vesco's operations are reportedly run with the complete cooperation of Castro and the Cuban Intelligence Service. Vesco helps arrange for shipments of heroin, cocaine and marijuana from South America to Cuba, has it transferred to smaller boats and planes there, and delivered to the U.S. and Canada. The money is laundered through offshore banks, and the Castro government is said to get payments of $500,000 or more per large boatload of drugs. Vesco also helps Castro get American goods, which the U.S. prohibits selling to Cuba. In exchange, the fugitive swindler gets safe harbor in the workers' paradise, living quarters at a yacht club and in a beach house near Havana, and his profit.

On August 4, 1985—after Vesco's presence in Cuba was publicized in *Narcotráfico, SA*—Fidel Castro himself admitted Robert Vesco's residence in Havana, and delivered a passionate defense of the drug baron as a misunderstood man-without-a-country. "Is it just to hunt down a man who no longer has even a place to hide, as if he were a beast?" Castro asked reporters. "Is it just, that the country where people speak so much of human rights, and shelter is given to all drug-traffickers, all thieves, all terrorists, goes after someone said to have evaded paying taxes? I don't know this gentleman, nor do I know what he did. But I know that he was here, that he received medical treatment, and that he can come back again." Castro added that he had told Vesco, "If you want to live here, live here."

Mr. Vesco has come full circle, and so has this narrative, from the "Bulgarian Connection" of the Levant, of Moscow Narodny's Intrabank and Edmund Safra; to the "French connection" of Marseilles; through the Caribbean money-laundromat of Resorts International and Oppenheimer's Anglo-American; to the banking networks shared by Banco Ambrosiano and Soviet intelligence; and finally to Fidel Castro's bright idea that he can make more money trading other things than sugar. Human trash like Vesco, Carlos Lehder, Hernández Cartaya, Eduardo Orozco, Alberto Duque, and Jaime Michelsen Uribe are of no interest in themselves. Their job is to do the dirty work and, ultimately, to get caught. But when we cast a strong light on the human trash, the thin marionette-wires become visible; and when we follow these wires upward, we encounter, again, the board of directors of Dope, Incorporated.

1   A victim of Britain's opium war against the U.S.A.

2   Henry A. Kissinger

3   Ariel Sharon

4   Yuri Andropov

5   Jimmy Carter

6   Dr. Peter Bourne

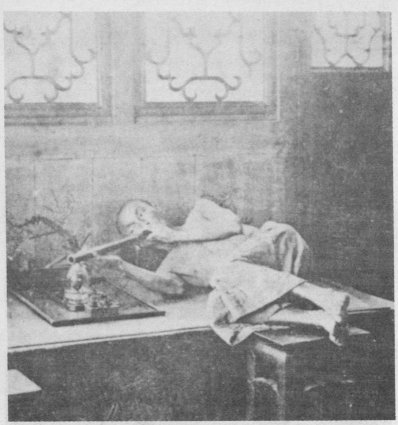

7   A Chinese opium smoker of the 19th century

8   Edgar Bronfman

9   The Seagram's empire was built on smuggling whiskey to the United States during Prohibition.

10   Max Fisher

11 Resorts International and other gambling casinos: ideal instruments for laundering dirty money.

12 Chase Manhattan Bank

13 Hongkong and Shanghai Banking Corporation

14 Michelsen's Grancolombiano financial empire

15 Paul A. Volcker

16 Adam Smith

17 Milton Friedman

18   The Russian Orthodox Church operates in full partnership with the Soviet state bureaucracy."

19   An investiture ceremony of the Knights of Malta in New York City in 1982.

20 Hernando de Soto (center), the Peruvian economist whose promotion of the so-called informal economy justifies the legalization of drugs.

21 The attempt to assassinate Pope John Paul II. Here, a hand holding a pistol, at left in photo, aims from the crowd in St. Peter's Square in Rome on May 13, 1981. AP Wide World Photo

22 Colombian Justice Minister Rodrigo Lara Bonilla, to whom this book is dedicated, before his April 1984 assassination by Dope, Inc.

23 A spectacular drug seizure in the state of Chihuahua in Mexico.

24 Alfonso López Michelsen   25 Jaime Michelsen Uribe

26 Carlos Lehder Rivas   27 Pablo Escobar Gaviria

28   The Hare Krishna cult

29   The Aquarian Conspiracy: the rock group, KISS (Knights in Service of Satan).

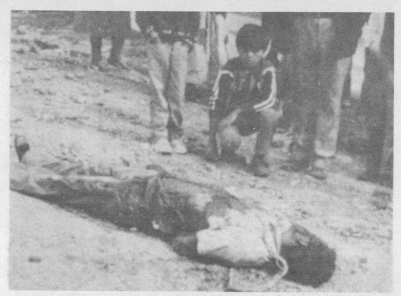

30 One of the many victims of the Nazi-Communist terrorist group in Peru, Sendero Luminoso.

31 Supporters of Sikh terrorism demonstrate outside the White House.

32 Robert Vesco

33 Kenneth Bialkin, Vesco's lawyer

34 Irwin Suall of the ADL

35 William Weld

36 First Fidelity Bank chief Robert Ferguson tried to shut the door on a LaRouche supporter who wanted to know what happened to the $200,000 in campaign funds the bank illegally pocketed.

37 A demonstration against the Bank of Boston.

38–39   Scenes from the founding meeting of Permindex (Permanent Industrial Exhibitions) company in Paris 1958. Documentation shows that Permindex—which was expelled from France for assassination plots against Charles de Gaulle—employed all of the principal players in the assassination of JFK.

PART VI
The Nazi-Communist Mafia

1
Who Runs the Nazi International Today?

Having taken the reader into the board rooms of the international banks and secret societies directing the international dope cartel from both sides of the Iron Curtain, it is now appropriate to descend into the black market gutters through which the poison is passed. Here we will discover the most deeply held secret behind the $500 billion Dope, Inc. empire: International drug-trafficking, arms-smuggling, and terrorism are centralized through the networks that control the Lausanne, Switzerland-based Nazi International.

It should come as no surprise to the reader who has fully grasped the murderous impact of the multi-billion dollar narcotics cartel that the very same oligarchical families, East and West, who sponsored Hitler's rise to power and who were never brought to the dockets at Nuremberg, hatched the postwar

Opium War against the United States to continue the same
genocidal policies by different means.

In the course of unraveling this previously untold story of
how "organized crime" is politically organized, the reader will
discover:

■ Swiss Nazi François Genoud, under the protective umbrella
of Allen Dulles and British Special Operations Executive Sir
William Stephenson, transferred the Hitler and Goebbels trusts
into Swiss banks under a "secret peace" that began two years
before the end of World War II and became the basis for the near
instant revival of the postwar Nazi (Malmoe) International.

■ Genoud's Nazi International—along with the Tashkent Institute of the Soviet Union's KGB Islamic Division and the
British Arab Bureau—sponsored and controls the Islamic fundamentalist apparatus running a major international assassination capability as well as the multi-billion dollar "Golden Crescent" route of heroin and hashish running from West Asia and
the Persian Gulf into Western Europe.

■ The same Nazi-Communist connection runs an international army of smugglers and assassins organized into integrist
and separatist cells banded together under the Endangered
Peoples Society. These integrist cells are today carrying out a
secret war against every sovereign nation in the West, all financed through the revenues of Dope, Inc. In fact, these integrist groups, following on the "Golden Triangle" model, have
become the preferred international smuggling apparatus for all
forms of drugs.

■ This Nazi-Communist connection makes up the heart of the
International Assassination Bureau that we will discover in
detail in a later chapter. Among its victims and near-victims:
President John F. Kennedy, Prime Minister Indira Gandhi,
President Anwar Sadat, President Charles de Gaulle, President
Ronald Reagan, Pope John Paul II.

The key to understanding the pivotal role of the Nazi International today is the concept of "derivative networks." British
Secret Intelligence, the Swiss Dope, Inc. bankers, the Soviet

Union's ruling elite, the "British East India Company" faction within the United States, and even a faction of Israeli intelligence, all have a standing agreement to foster, protect and jointly reap the benefits of the "dirty business" run through the Nazi International. By virtue of this arrangement, none of the controlling partners show their hands directly in some of the most hideous crimes of the postwar period, crimes ordered by the Anglo-Swiss-Soviet "Hobbesian alliance" but carried out—at a respectable distance—by Nazi International-run derivative networks.

From the Archives

For the average reader, and even many intelligence professionals today, the term "Nazi-Communist" seems a strange contradiction. Yet, from the 1920s through to the end of World War II, U.S. military intelligence maintained an ongoing high priority file classification "Synarchist International; Nazi/Communist." A decade before the short-lived public alliance called the Hitler-Stalin Pact, American G–2 documents now publicly available at the National Archives in Washington, D.C. showed that in every far corner of the globe, Anglo-Soviet Comintern agents were in active collaboration with leading figures in the Nazi Party and, later, the Gestapo.

The case of Dr. Herman Erben is exemplary. Born in Austria around the turn of the century, Erben joined the Nazi Party in Austria in 1926 shortly before he moved to the United States. From the United States, he renewed his party status. As a Hitler spy in the U.S.A., Mexico and the Far East, Erben financed his activities by smuggling morphine and other drugs, using his cover as a ship physician to facilitate the trade. By 1930, he was on every Federal Bureau of Narcotics (FBN) watch list in Latin America and the Pacific. Throughout the 1930s, Erben traveled with his lifelong friend, actor Errol Flynn, to Spain, where they served on the republican side in the Spanish Civil War. While Erben's "switching sides" has been passed off by some authors as yet another Nazi spy mission, by no later than the mid-1930s, Erben was working on behalf of both Nazi *and* Soviet interests.

According to U.S. Naval Intelligence reports filed in Mexico City during the period of the Hitler-Stalin Pact (1939–41), Erben was at the center of a Gestapo-Comintern plot to destabilize the southern border states of the U.S. through acts of sabotage and a potential limited military incursion. Forced to flee North America, Erben next surfaced in Shanghai, where he spent the duration of the war working for both the Gestapo and ace Soviet spy Richard Sorge.

Arrested by U.S. Army Counterintelligence in Shanghai at the close of the war, Erben was shipped back to Bremerhaven, West Germany to be put on trial for war crimes. On his arrival, however, he was mysteriously freed and placed on medical assignment in Austria. Circumstantial evidence points to the Allen Dulles grouping in Anglo-American intelligence, who had by 1943 initiated a "separate peace" with a faction of the Nazi apparatus in anticipation of recruiting the Nazis into postwar Anglo-American efforts, including a postwar "universal fascism" project.

In 1950, we find Erben living and working in Iran, probably under the sponsorship of former Nazi economics minister and Dulles crony Hjalmar Schacht. During this period, Erben converted from Judaism (he was born into an Austrian Jewish family that included a cousin who was the first wife of Anglo-Soviet "triple" agent H. Kim Philby) to Islam.

Curiously, during the same period, Erben applied to have his United States citizenship reinstated (it had been pulled by the U.S. attorney general in the early 1930s based on his Nazi espionage activities). The application was rejected—on grounds that Erben was a known Soviet spy!

The closest Erben ever got to the U.S.A. was the Caribbean island of Barbados, where he spent much of the 1970s working for the Bronfman family's Space Research Corporation, a Dope, Inc. front involved in smuggling sophisticated arms into South Africa, Latin America, and the East bloc. Space Research was shut down in the late 1970s as the result of a joint criminal investigation by the U.S. and Canadian governments.

The reader protests: "The case of Dr. Erben is an exception, a fluke. Certainly the Nazi International, if indeed it exists today, cannot be in bed with both Moscow and London."

Be patient, the authors respond. Follow the drug routes from the opium fields of the Islamic fundamentalist havens in Iran, Afghanistan, Pakistan, into the refineries in Turkey. Follow the drug-trafficking routes—unimpeded—through the Iron Curtain into Bulgaria and Yugoslavia before the drugs pass into the West through northern Italy—into Bavaria, Sicily, and Corsica, on to their ultimate destination on the inner city streets of North America. Trace the arms routes over the same path from Western and Eastern Europe into the terrorist havens of the Middle East. Then, trace the trail of the assassin Mehmet Ali Agca—back and forth over the same East-West trail. Illegal drugs, illegal arms, professional killers and terrorists of every political stripe all traversing the same Dope, Inc. underground railroad.

Now, return to the archives. Study the contraband routes as they existed during the Byzantine, Ottoman, and British Empires' undisputed dominions over Asia Minor. The black market trails remain unchanged over centuries.

Finally, ask yourself: Could such a trade flourish today to the point of being the world's biggest business unless powerful interests of both East and West were fully complicit?

The Case of François Genoud

During 1978–79, the authors and researchers of *Dope, Inc.* were the first to expose publicly the intimate interlinks between terrorism and the major drug-running and gun-running networks. With much help from U.S.A. official drug enforcement agencies' files, we tracked the drug-running networks around the world, and traced these historically to the opium-trafficking practices of the British East India Company, into the elaborate offshore financial operations controlling the drug traffic today. Where was the center of this international traffic—exceeding $200 billion a year in the international side of its operations— as distinct from wholesale and retail trafficking within nations such as the United States?

Gradually, the laborious process of triangulation focused our attention in Switzerland and, then, more exactly on the headquarters of the present day Nazi International organization of banker François Genoud, in Lausanne, Switzerland.

Genoud is an authentic hard-core Nazi. He was a prominent Nazi official in Switzerland during Adolf Hitler's rule in Germany and emerged as a kind of general secretary for the reconstituted Nazi (Malmoe) International when that was reassembled as a public association in Rome, Italy at the close of the 1940s. At about the same time, in 1949, Dr. Armin Mohler, formerly a Swiss volunteer in Hitler's Waffen SS, produced his book *The Conservative Revolution in Germany, 1918–1933* as a doctoral dissertation under pro-Nazi Swiss philosopher Dr. Karl Barth.

According to European accounts, François Genoud joined the Swiss Nazi Party, the National Front for Switzerland, at age 21. Financed by the Oltramaire family of the Lombard-Odier Bank of Geneva, the NFS would serve as a channel of contact between Allen Dulles and his "former" Nazi clients.

In 1930, Genoud set up a nightclub in Lausanne called the Oasis, as a front for the German Abwehr. As the result of previous trips to the Middle East, in which he cultivated personal ties to the fanatically pro-Nazi, anti-Semitic Grand Mufti of Jerusalem, Genoud's Oasis became a center for espionage and drug-smuggling into the Middle East.

By 1942, Genoud's Lausanne operations had expanded into the banking world. He facilitated the transfer of millions of marks from German to Swiss banks. These funds would later underwrite the ODESSA organization that smuggled countless top Nazi officials out of Germany into Spain, North Africa, South America, and the Middle East. These networks to this day make up the hard core of the international drug-trafficking organization.

For this banking transfer and safe transit project, a front company, Diethelm Brothers Import-Export, was founded in Lausanne under the personal direction of Hitler's private secretary Martin Bormann. Bormann, while loyally serving Hitler, was almost undoubtedly also a Soviet agent (who pushed as late as 1943 for a revival of the Hitler-Stalin Pact). The importance of this will become apparent as the Genoud file unfolds.

By 1943, Genoud was in regular contact with SS General Karl Wolff and with Berne OSS station chief Allen Dulles. The former attorney for Nazi interests including I.G. Farben and Schroeders Bank, Dulles used Genoud to mediate the postwar safe passage of thousands of top Nazis. Several unconfirmed reports place Genoud in contact with Lyons, France Gestapo chief Klaus Barbie during these wartime "separate peace" negotiations.

After an apparently brief legal detention for his wartime Nazi activities, Genoud revived his Arab world ties in the early 1950s, traveling to Morocco, Egypt, and Algeria with such Nazi notables as General Wolff, Hjalmar Schacht, Dr. Hans Reichenberg, and Otto Skorzeny. It was also during this period that Genoud facilitated the flow of millions of dollars to ex-Nazis in hiding in South America; and launched the first attempt at reviving the Nazi International in the form of the Buenos Aires-based magazine *Der Weg*.

By 1960, Genoud had created a string of "trading companies" and political fronts including Société Interlogin S.A., a Freibourg-based export-import company, and the Lausanne-headquartered International Association of the Friends of the Arab World. The latter was co-founded by a longtime British Intelligence agent with deep ties to the Muslim Brotherhood, Benoist-Mechin. Under the direction of St. John Philby, top British Arabist and father of Kim Philby, Benoist-Mechin had exhaustively profiled the Saud dynasty.

Through this apparatus, Genoud became a primary weapons trafficker to the Polisario (National Union of Popular Forces of

Morocco) and the Algerian FLN. In 1960, using funds still remaining from the Hitler and Goebbels Trusts, and his more recent arms revenues, Genoud set up the Banque Commerciale Arabe in Lausanne. One of BCA's correspondent banks in Lebanon, Intrabank, has been deeply implicated in arms and drug smuggling.

Genoud, in conjunction with Otto Skorzeny, was deeply involved in arms sales to the French Secret Army Organization (OAS) of Jacques Soustelle. At the same time Genoud and Skorzeny were providing arms to Ahmed Ben Bella's FLN. One of Genoud's cutouts in this trade was the Casino de Liban, the Beirut gambling resort owned by Intrabank and notorious as the center of Middle Eastern hashish-trafficking.

Genoud's banking tie to the OAS raises an important question concerning his ties to the French anthropologist and OAS leader Soustelle. According to exhaustive documents in the files of the U.S. Army G–2 and the Office of Naval Intelligence, Soustelle was a leading Comintern agent in Mexico and South America throughout the 1940s, his name appearing on lists of known members of the Soviets' Red Orchestra spy net. Soustelle's name comes up peripherally as well in the 1940 assassination of Leon Trotsky in Mexico City.

In 1941, however, Soustelle, his Comintern mentor Paul Rivet, and Jean de Menil all showed up in prominent positions within de Gaulle's Free French apparatus in Caracas, Rio de Janeiro, Mexico City and Honduras, only to later facilitate the arrival of scores of Nazis and Vichyites into South America at the close of the war. It would be out of this Latin American swamp of ex-Nazis, Vichyites, and Comintern agents that the OAS would recruit and wich would simultaneously make up the backbone of the infamous French Connection heroin ring.

Nazi Genoud and his BCA were in no way lacking in their own direct ties to Soviet intelligence and finance. For its own part, Moscow had not missed any opportunities at war's close to recruit major Nazi assets into Soviet and Eastern European military and intelligence ranks. Whole SS units were integrated intact for a period of time into the East German Army secret police apparatus.

One longtime Genoud collaborator, Lt. General Otto-Ernst Remer, has emerged as a leading neo-Nazi advocate of reunification of Germany under Soviet hegemony. But Genoud's primary known Soviet channel developed through his Arab terrorist ties. Beginning in the early 1970s, Genoud expanded his arms and drug business in the Middle East—in partnership with Intrabank. During this time, in part to cover his arms-trafficking to a string of terrorist and separatist groups, Genoud was brought into the Arab Union of Lawyers. In April 1969, at a Barcelona meeting of the neo-Nazi New European Order, founded by Genoud agent Gaston Guy Amaudruz, the Lausanne banker sponsored a delegation from Al-Fatah and from the Popular Front for the Liberation of Palestine (PFLP). At that meeting, Genoud arranged for the Palestinians to receive training from several ranking ex-Nazis including Karl Van De Put and Johann N. Schuller.

In September 1969, Genoud was brought in as special adviser to the legal team defending three PFLP terrorists who had attacked an Israeli El Al plane in Zurich. The lead attorney defending the terrorists was Jacques Verges, also known as Jacques Mansur.

By no later than 1949 Verges was a Soviet agent. At that time he headed the Paris branch of the Liaison Committee of Anti-Colonialist Students. One year later, Verges was in Prague as a director of the International Student Union. His immediate boss was Alexander Shelepin, later head of the KGB. By 1957, back in Paris, Verges was part of the KGB underground then headed by Egyptian Communist Henri Curiel, cousin of George Blake, soon to defect from British intelligence to the KGB as part of the Kim Philby network. Sponsored first by the Comintern and later by the International Secretariat of the Communist Party of the Soviet Union, Curiel's Solidarity group was the recruitment and logistical base for Soviet terrorist operations throughout Europe, North Africa, the Middle East, and even Latin America. Curiel is credited with recruiting the "Carlos" terrorist network, the Organization of Armed Struggle and Action Directe.

European sources have confirmed that by no later than 1958,

Curiel and Genoud were in active collaboration, in conjunction with Ahmed Ben Bella and the FLN. Recall that during this same period, Genoud was arming the OAS. With the founding of Genoud's Banque Commerciale Arabe, Curiel laundered funds provided through his KGB control into the FLN through Genoud's bank.

Through Curiel, Verges was installed in 1962 as an adviser to the Ben Bella government of Algeria, at which time he converted to Islam and took the name Jacques Mansur. For the next 15 years, Verges floated between Maoist China (Mao sponsored a Verges publication, *Revolucion,* with offices in Beijing, Lausanne, New York and Havana), Pol Pot's Cambodia (Pol Pot and Verges were communist students together at the Sorbonne in the 1940s and retained personal ties afterward), Black September and PFLP training camps in the Middle East, and Paris. In 1977, Verges and Genoud jointly pressured the Israeli government into releasing "Carlos"-linked terrorist Bruno Breguet, a Swiss national jailed for participation in a terrorist attack against an El Al jet. By 1982, Breguet was back in jail in Paris for terrorist actions by the Action Directe group and for possession of sophisticated Czech explosive devices.

Verges also served as the attorney for Nazi Klaus Barbie, who was put on trial in Lyons for war crimes including the 1941 assassination of Jean Moulin, the head of the Gaullist resistance. Verges's introduction to Barbie came from François Genoud on February 6, 1983—just one day after Barbie's extradition to France from Bolivia, where he was an official in the interior ministry and deeply involved in cocaine-trafficking.

Barbie was but one Nazi-turned-narcoterrorist whose postwar career was fathered by Genoud. Genoud's apparatus encompasses scores of currently active terrorists and narcotics traffickers in South America, Europe, and the Middle East. When it comes to the world's biggest business—Dope, Inc.—Red terrorists, Black terrorists, East bloc secret police, and professional mafiosi all swim together.

2

Stipam: The Real Bulgarian Connection

On Tuesday, November 23, 1982, an international law enforcement team under the direction of Italian magistrate Carlo Palermo of Trento carried out a series of arrests of individuals responsible for running the Milan center of "the biggest arms-dealing network in the world." According to Palermo and other Trento magistrates at a press conference the following day, the eight arrests marked the dramatic climax of a three-year investigation during which it was discovered that the Milan-based firm of Stipam International Transports was the channel through which huge quantities of arms were shipped to bands of terrorists and integrists throughout the Middle East. The standard form of "barter" payment for the arms? Hashish, heroin, and other drugs principally produced in the "Golden Crescent" region of Iran, Pakistan, and Afghanistan.

By the time the dust had settled on the Stipam bust, more

had been unearthed than even a multi-billion dollar arms-for-dope ring. At the very heart of the Stipam operation was the arrangement between top government and "family" channels in the East and the West to share in the revenues and political power of Dope, Inc.

As the direct result of the Stipam bust, the Bulgarian Connection to the assassination plot against Pope John Paul II was demonstrated. As a result of the Stipam revelations, the "marriage" between the ruling families of the East—such as Bulgaria's Zhivkov dynasty—and the oligarchical "fondi" of Central Europe and Britain—such as the Braganza clan and the Duke of Kent—was most disgustingly flaunted in the black market bazaars of Varna, Istanbul, Sofia, Palermo, Trieste, and London. Weaving in and out of this mosaic of guns, narcotics and political assassins we find the ever-present shadow of the Nazi-Communist International.

History of the Case

An undated report issued in the fall of 1984 by the chief of the Strategic Intelligence Section of the U.S. Drug Enforcement Administration provides a history of the Stipam International Transports case and the plot to assassinate Pope John Paul II. According to that document, "The Involvement of the People's Republic of Bulgaria in International Narcotics Trafficking," a high-level defector from the Bulgarian State Security Service (KDS), code-named Sverdlev, had told U.S. intelligence of a 1967 meeting in Moscow of the Warsaw Pact Security Service chiefs to develop plans to "exploit and hasten the inherent corruption of Western society." A subsequent meeting of KDS officials in Sofia, Bulgaria established a three-year action plan to implement the "exploitation." According to Sverdlev, a KDS directive was issued in June 1970 assessing the status of the East bloc plan to "destabilize Western society through . . . the narcotics trade."

How would this Moscow-ordered Opium War be carried out?

According to the same DEA document, in 1968, through the Bulgarian government founded KINTEX, the official import-export agency of the communist state:

> KINTEX is structured as an umbrella organization which orchestrates the trafficking of contraband through Bulgaria. KINTEX has been identified as the principal narcotics-and-weapons-shipping agency. Other government agencies have been identified as operating in conjunction with KINTEX primarily as distribution outlets. Each of these agencies reportedly is headed by Bulgarian State Security officials. . . .

Among the "distribution outlets" identified by U.S., Turkish, and Italian authorities were Interkommers, Dap-Ek, and Balkan Tours. Balkan Tours, the official Bulgarian travel bureau, gained instant notoriety on November 25, 1982—just two days after the Stipam raid—when Serge Ivanov Antonov, an official of Bulgarian Airlines posted as the deputy director of the office of Balkan Tours in Rome, was arrested by Italian magistrate Ilario Martella and charged in the conspiracy to assassinate the Pope.

From its inception, KINTEX went about implementing its criminal mandate with a degree of thoroughness and ruthlessness that marks the East bloc secret services. Lists of "sanctioned clients" in the West—arms-smuggling rings, narcotics-trafficking organizations and terrorist cells spanning the neo-Nazi right to the anarchist left—were accumulated and screened. Preferred safe locations—usually nondescript hotels and bars in Sofia—were established as havens for the black market transactions.

Evidence suggests that KINTEX's worldwide dope-for-arms dealings were run top down through a chain of command running back to the Dzherzhinsky Square headquarters of the Soviet KGB in Moscow.

KINTEX reportedly fell under the jurisdiction of the First Directorate of the KDS headed by Colonel General Grigor Shopov. The First Directorate was responsible for all foreign and domestic intelligence operations—including terrorism. A can-

didate member of the Bulgarian Communist Party central committee, Radoslav Todorov, was appointed KINTEX's director
general. According to accounts of a drug smuggler working for
KINTEX, the boss of contraband operations was a high-ranking
KDS officer named Terziev, whose deputy, "Colonel Ivan," was
responsible for all heroin and morphine purchases and sales.

Circumstantial evidence suggests that the shadowy "Colonel
Ivan" may be Ivan Slavkov, the son-in-law of Bulgarian premier
Todor Zhivkov and the widower of Lyudmila Zhivkova, herself
a former member of the Bulgarian Communist Party central
committee and an international cult heroine described by one
observer as a latter-day Madame Blavatsky, the Russian
founder of the occult Golden Dawn movement.

The former director of Bulgarian Television and head of the
Bulgarian National Olympics Committee, Slavkov is widely
identified as the liaison between KINTEX and the drug mafias
of Latin America and the Caribbean. In October 1979, Slavkov
and Lyudmila hosted then-Colombian President Alfonso López
Michelsen, the political "godfather" of the Colombian cocaine
trade, in a state visit to Sofia. KINTEX activities in Colombia
dramatically expanded. Through the Colombian "foot in the
door," Slavkov established "good relations" with governments
in the Caribbean and South America, allowing KINTEX to
become major suppliers of heavy military equipment including
T–54 tanks to Chilean dictator Pinochet and the Sandinista
junta in Nicaragua.

This would be neither the first nor the last time that KINTEX
facilitated massive arms sales to "ideological enemies" of the
Communist state. In 1975, on the eve of the outbreak of civil
war in Lebanon, the Lebanese Communist Party issued a strong
protest to the Bulgarian Communist Party when KINTEX provided tons of heavy weapons to the Lebanese Christian militias,
arms used to kill members of the Communist Party and allied
Palestinian and Shiite Muslim factions. While the DEA report
suggests the KINTEX arms flow to the Falange was cut off
immediately following the protest, as late as 1983 the Bulgarian Litex Bank, the financial arm of KINTEX, still held 40%
ownership of a Beirut bank otherwise owned by the Chamoun

clan of former Lebanese President Camille Chamoun, and known to be a channel for contraband money. It was the Caracas branch of the Chamoun-Litex bank, the Banco Caribe, that financed the 1982 Green Book conference of Libyan dictator Qaddafi in Venezuela. The Chamouns, Pinochet, and Qaddafi— all assets of the Nazi-Communist International—all did their arms-for-dope dealings with KINTEX.

On April 27, 1984, CBS Evening News and Danish television "blew" the Slavkov connection to the KINTEX dope-for-arms bazaar. Slavkov was identified as the mediator between KIN-TEX official Dinef and a Miami, Florida-based West German arms dealer, Peter Mulack, in arms deals to yet another "ideological foe" of Sofia and Moscow, the Republic of South Africa. The transaction exposed by Danish television involved over 100,000 weapons, including rocket launchers, rifles, grenades, and mines, all manufactured in the Soviet Union. In a letter dated April 26, 1979, from Mulack to Dinef, the Miami-based smuggler stated, "I can deliver the required electronic material. However, as the material is under embargo it will take at least three months to deliver. Payment for the consignment may be made in part in heroin or morphine base." The Danish TV broadcast credited Slavkov with the delivery of 6,000 tons of Russian military hardware to South Africa.

Henri Arsan

When Italian authorities raided the offices of Stipam International at Milan's Via Olfredi 2, and arrested the firm's president Henri Arsan, a Syrian national, one of the key "back-channels" between Britain's Dope, Inc. directorate and the KINTEX Bulgarian Connection was blown sky-high.

The Stipam headquarters occupied a good portion of a building owned by the Banco Ambrosiano. Ambrosiano's Branch 18 occupied the ground floor, and the floor below Stipam contained the residence of Roberto Rosone, deputy chairman of the bank until his dismissal several months before the Milan raid and

days after bank president Roberto Calvi was found dead, hanging from Blackfriars Bridge in London.

The Stipam-Ambrosiano connection opened up a Pandora's
Box, leading from the Propaganda–2 secret Freemasonic lodge
founded by Italian ex-Gestapo spy Licio Gelli, back to London,
where the Duke of Kent presided over the Grand Mother Lodge
of Scottish Rite Freemasonry, the same lodge that directed
Britain's Opium War policies for two centuries and that chartered P–2's predecessor lodge, Mazzini's Propaganda–1.

When Judge Palermo's raiding party completed its search of
Via Olfredi 2, they carted off three suitcases filled with documents. The documents consisted mostly of telex transactions
during the 16 years of Stipam's activities, messages sent by
Arsan to and from Milan, New York, Istanbul, Beirut, Damascus and Saigon. Through them, the tight links between Stipam
and Ambrosiano were reportedly reconstructed.

We shall return shortly to the Ambrosiano-Propaganda–2
and London connections of Stipam's Henri Arsan. It is first
necessary to tug further at the Bulgarian string we began unraveling with the 1968 founding of KINTEX.

According to the already cited DEA document, by no later
than 1971, Henri Arsan had been provided with a rent-free
villa in Sofia—courtesy of KINTEX. A known and respected
trafficker in morphine, Arsan had been one of the principal
dope suppliers to the notorious French Connection. By the mid-
1970s, however, the French Connection was no more. Many
of the key players, former Vichyites integrated into François
Genoud's post-war Nazi International through the Union Corse
and the OAS, were either dead or behind bars. Christian David,
for example, the number-two man in the Montevideo-centered
Golden Triangle heroin ring, was in prison in Leavenworth,
Kansas. He had been identified as the organizer of the 1960s
assassination of Moroccan opposition leader Ben Barka, a job
carried out by the Genoud Nazi International.

By 1975, Arsan was in the middle of a regroupment of the
heroin connection in the company of another Milan-based Syrian national, Sallah Aldin Wakkas. Wakkas was the designated

Milan representative of the Turkish mafia, working in league with an old French connection partner of Arsan, syndicate boss Gerlando Alberti.

According to Judge Palermo, the Alberti-Wakkas ring sorted out drugs entering Italy from Turkey, using money that often came from kidnappings and other criminal activities, and depositing funds in accounts in banks in New York, Zurich, Frankfurt and London. Alberti "deposited" the drugs in the Trento-Bolzano-Verona triangle; from there it was shipped to Palermo, Sicily for refinement and transshipment.

Stipam was then in charge of procuring and shipping the weapons requested as payment for the drugs to terrorist groups in Turkey, Lebanon, and elsewhere. Ironically, among the guerrilla movements receiving Stipam's arms deliveries were Afghanistan rebel groups fighting against Soviet troops. According to the DEA, those arms shipments between 1975–82 were made under the protection of Bulgarian State Security. For that service, Stipam deposited tens of millions of dollars in narcotics revenues with KINTEX.

The identification of Stipam and Arsan as the nodal point of this drugs-for-arms traffic was made possible, according to the arresting Italian magistrates, thanks in part to the cooperation of Turkish authorities. The November 23, 1984 Italian arrests were preceded by the arrest in Turkey of the three individuals said to direct the Turkish side of the drug flow. "Not one gram" of heroin left Turkey that was not under the control of this specific mafia, said Judge Palermo at his press conference on November 24. The individuals arrested were Kisakis Mustafa, Hehir Hasan, and Cil Huseyn. This troika had dispatched Sallah Aldin Wakkas to Milan.

The Arsan-Wakkas arms-for-narcotics deals were arranged in a string of second-rate hotels around Milan's central train station and in cafes, bars, and hotels in Sofia, Bulgaria. The Berlin Café, the Japan Hotel, and the Hotel Vitosha were all named by Judge Palermo as safe spots in Sofia. Palermo himself traveled on several occasions to Sofia to personally observe dope-for-arms transactions at the Berlin Café.

Enter Mehmet Ali Agca

Had Judge Palermo been on one of his covert forays to Sofia in the summer of 1980, he might have stumbled upon a neo-Nazi assassin and drug "mule" for the Turkish mafia who discreetly checked into the Hotel Vitosha. The Turk, a member of the right-wing extremist paramilitary group Grey Wolves of Colonel Alparslan Turkes, had escaped in November 1979 from Kartal-Maltepe military prison in Turkey where he had been awaiting execution for the assassination of Abdi Ipekci, editor of the leftist Turkish newspaper *Milliyet*. One day after his escape, arranged by Oral Celik, Grey Wolves hitman Mehmet Ali Agca sent a letter to *Milliyet* threatening that if Pope John Paul II's visit to Istanbul were not called off, "I will definitely kill the Commander-Pope."

As events would later show, Agca's summer 1980 arrival in Sofia signaled the activation of the assassination plot that culminated on May 13, 1981 with Agca's near-fatal shooting of the Pope in St. Peter's Square.

Two things stand out about Agca's meetings at the Hotel Vitosha during the summer of 1980.

First, Agca entered Bulgaria, according to the DEA, on a phony Indian passport in the Sikh name Yoginder Singh. The fact that Agca was traveling as a Sikh raises perplexing questions: Was there also a "Bulgarian Connection" to the more recent brutal assassination of Indian Prime Minister Indira Gandhi by Sikh members of her own security force? Circumstantial evidence points to just such a thread, a thread that leads us back to the Anglo-Soviet Dope, Inc. alliance and to the Nazi International.

According to reports published in the Indian media at the time of the Indian Army's siege of the Golden Temple—the Sikh shrine which had been taken over by fanatical fundamentalist Sikhs—some of the Sikh terrorists were believed to have fled the city of Amritsar aboard Bulgarian Airlines planes. The Punjab region, which the Sikh fanatics seek to turn into a separate, independent, quasi-religious state of "Khalistan," has been a center of opium production in India. That places the

Sikh insurgents in the orbit of the Golden Crescent opium routes known to be part of the Bulgarian Connection.

Even more to the point, Jagjit Singh Chauhan, the head of the Khalistan separatist movement and the self-avowed author of the Gandhi assassination, is a shared "derivative" asset of the Soviet intelligence services, British Secret Intelligence and the Swiss Nazi International. Until late 1968, the year KINTEX was formed, Chauhan was finance minister of the Punjab province. At that time, following a series of pilgrimages to Tashkent in the Soviet Union, the center of the KGB's "Islamic Division," Chauhan resigned his post with the Indian government and began agitating for an independent Khalistan. Since that date, Chauhan, who shifted the center of the Khalistani movement to London, has also become an asset of British subject Richard Hauser.

An Australian by birth, Hauser was recruited to the British Special Operations Executive (SOE) during World War II, serving as part of the SOE team sent into Milan, Italy immediately after the city's liberation by Allied forces. As part of that Milan team, Hauser was in on the ground floor of what later emerged as the P–2 connection into London. Hauser today is an executive of the François Genoud-linked Society for Endangered Peoples, the principal logistics and recruitment support organization for over 200 separatist and integrist movements worldwide. As we shall see, the Endangered Peoples movement constitutes the backbone of the "Golden Crescent" heroin underground.

Is there a "Bulgarian Connection" to the assassination of Mrs. Gandhi that would suggest a link to the Agca attempt on the life of the Pope?

Perhaps.

Jagjit Singh Chauhan's "American Connection" runs through a dubious character named Jon Speller, nominally an asset of U.S. intelligence services. A self-described "Anglophile" and "Russophile," a second-generation product of the Jacob Riis financier circles of lower Manhattan, Speller boasts of extremely close ties into the East bloc, principally through the Russian Orthodox Church's espionage window into the West, the monasteries at Mount Athos. According to eyewitness reports, Speller's Mount Athos channels place him in close association with the Bulgarian Orthodox Church and with the circles that gathered around the late Lyudmila Zhivkova.

According to the DEA, in a late 1982 confession to Italian authorities, Agca stated that in the summer of 1980 he was offered three million German marks by Bekir Celenk to kill the Pope. The assassination weapon was provided by Oral Celik, the Grey Wolves terrorist who arranged Agca's prison break. On November 25, 1982, Italian magistrate Martella indicted both Celenk and Celik for the assassination plot—along with Balkan Tours official Antonov.

According to Turkish government records, Celenk was a "mafia boss" in the Turkish mafia sought by Turkish officials since 1977 for fiscal fraud and illegal flight capital. Celenk owned a fleet of ships—registered in Panama—and a string of hotels believed to be safehouses for the dope-for-arms traffickers.

In March 1981, one of Celenk's top smugglers, Abuzer Ugurlu, turned himself in to Turkish authorities. By his own admission, Ugurlu was an employee of KINTEX functioning as a liaison between the Turkish mafia "heroin connection" and the Milan-based Stipam International and syndicate chieftain Gerlando Alberti. Among Ugurlu's assignments was the delivery of bribes to the former Turkish customs minister in order to secure the deployment of corrupt customs officials to posts along the Bulgarian-Turkish border assuring the safe passage of arms and narcotics. Using loopholes in the TIR European-wide trucking convention, the complicity of customs officials at the Turkey-Bulgaria border assured the contraband safe transit to final destinations in continental Western Europe.

Ugurlu's boss Celenk—Agca's host in Sofia during the summer of 1980—has been singled out by Judge Martella as the direct liaison between Agca and the authors of the papal assassination plot. According to the already cited DEA document, Celenk was reporting directly to a KDS official named Marienov.

The profile of the dope-for-guns mafia—the assassination arm of Dope, Inc.—is not complete until we have directed our attention west to some of the leading partners of the Bulgarian Connection.

For our purposes here, two other events will sufficiently highlight the point.

Oil-for-Guns

One of the most revealing of the dope-for-guns transactions pulled off by Stipam brings us full circle back to the landlords of Henri Arsan at Via Olfredi 2: Banco Ambrosiano and its chairman Roberto Calvi. Until the moment of his Freemasonic ritualistic death at London's Blackfriars Bridge, Calvi had been one of the key financiers of the P–2 Lodge. While the Lodge's membership encompasses some rather complex and contradictory networks, the role of Calvi, Licio Gelli, and a handful of other key players is relatively clear. Italian police files have placed Calvi and Ambrosiano as the funding conduit to a Red Brigades hit team that assassinated a string of top police officials and magistrates in the Milan area when those officials began to turn up evidence linking the P–2 Lodge to the drug trade and to a number of aborted neo-fascist coup plots, including the 1969 Borghese coup attempt and the mid-1970s "Rosa Dei Vente" plot, which also involved a massive outbreak of neo-fascist and anarchist "blind" terrorism known as the "Politics of Tension."

At the time of the U.S. Embassy hostage siege in Teheran, Stipam International facilitated a major arms-for-oil deal between the Israeli government and the Khomeini regime. In exchange for Israeli arms desperately needed by Khomeini to prosecute the war with Iraq, Khomeini provided a flow of Iranian oil to Israel at rock-bottom rates. The oil was delivered to Israel through the full cooperation of British Petroleum and Royal Dutch Shell, in effect the Middle East division of the old British East India Company crowd.

The intermediary for this secret deal among British Petroleum, Royal Dutch Shell, Israel, and Khomeini was Banco Ambrosiano. According to *Middle East* magazine and the Italian daily *La Repubblica,* the specific Ambrosiano "cutout" was a Swiss concern, Dreikot Driving and Financial Company, owned by the Hans brothers and Albert Kunz, Roberto Calvi's Swiss business agent.

But who did Kunz, Calvi, the Hans brothers, British Petroleum, et al. turn to in order to secure the deliveries? According to several European sources, they turned to Stefano Delle Chiaie. The Nazi International's in-house Murder, Inc. executive for Europe and Latin America, Delle Chiaie fled his native Italy in 1969 after being condemned for the Piazza Fontana massacre in Milan that took dozens of lives. That bombing, which was the trigger of the aborted Borghese coup attempt, was carried out by Ordine Nero, the Italian terrorist arm of the revived Nazi (Malmoe) International.

Named as a secret member of the Alpina Lodge of Switzerland, reported to be the controlling "inner elite" behind P–2, Delle Chiaie was at a meeting of the Alpina Lodge somewhere in Uruguay in early 1980 at which he was ordered to carry out a bombing attack against the train station in Bologna. That bombing claimed over 80 lives and over 200 injuries. Swiss publications have named P–2 founder Licio Gelli, Club of Rome founder Aurelio Peccei, and former U.S. Secretary of State Henry Kissinger as leading members of the Alpina Lodge. Gelli was reportedly the person who directed Delle Chiaie to carry out the Bologna attack.

At the time of the 1980 Bologna massacre, Delle Chiaie was based in Bolivia, enjoying the protection and patronage of the cocaine colonels and a crew of ex-Nazis including Klaus Barbie. When the colonels fell in October 1982, Delle Chiaie barely escaped capture and extradition to Italy. His fellow Nazi International fugitives Klaus Barbie and Pier Luigi Pagliai were grabbed by the new Bolivian authorities, backed up by U.S. and Italian anti-drug officials, and extradited to Paris and Rome.

At last report, Delle Chiaie was still in hiding in South America. During 1983 he spent time in Peru training the Sendero Luminoso (Shining Path) Maoist terrorist band and reportedly serving as a bridge between the terrorists and the international dope syndicate. It was Delle Chiaie who was blamed by Italian and Peruvian law enforcement officials as the mastermind of the Sendero Luminoso sabotage and terror campaigns against the capital city of Lima. Delle Chiaie, in keeping with his Sendero cohorts, now proclaims himself to be a devout worshipper of both Adolf Hitler and Mao Zedong.

Tradition, Family and Patricide

On May 13, 1982, one year to the day after Mehmet Ali Agca's attempted assassination of Pope John Paul II in St. Peter's Square, a Spanish priest linked to a fanatical right-wing movement within the Catholic Church attempted to stab the Pope to death as he conducted a Mass over the statue of the Virgin of Fatima in Portugal. Juan Fernández Krohn, a follower of the fundamentalist Archbishop Lefebvre and an agent of the Tradition, Family and Property quasi-terrorist group, had been groomed for nearly a year—as Agca had been—to assassinate the Pontiff on a most symbolic occasion, the celebration of the third vision of Fatima, a vision that proclaims the rechristianization of Russia and the crowning of Moscow as the Third Rome, seat of a world empire. This vision, which to Russian believers signifies Russian world domination, has been dramatically put forward in the Western Church as a portent of the end of the Communist rule in Russia. The fact that in both 1981 and 1982 fanatical assassins tried to murder John Paul II on the same day, may shed some light on the interface between cultist networks of the East and West whom we have seen functioning as the architects of Dope, Inc.

We have traced the trail of assassin Mehmet Ali Agca through the fringes of the Turkish neo-Nazi movement into the service of Bulgarian secret police agents and the heroin syndicate. In the case of Father Krohn, the trail takes us back to familiar territory, the Portuguese royal family Braganza. After training at the Lefebvrist monastery in Regensburg, Ger-

many, Krohn was drawn into the TFP. Traveling throughout
Spain, Portugal and Brazil, Krohn was provided with terrorist
training and weapons and logistics backup through the TFP
group.

The Golden Crescent

In 1978, when the first edition of *Dope, Inc.* was being prepared, Ayatollah Khomeini was still living in exile in Paris.
The Soviet Union had not yet tried to absorb Afghanistan into
its territorial grab-bag. The Indian subcontinent had not yet
been racked with separatist insurgencies. The center of the
world opium production was still the Golden Triangle region of
Southeast Asia.

Within two years, dramatic changes occurred. According to
the best available statistics, as the integrist insurgencies swept
through Western Asia, a new opium production zone encom-
passing the mountainous regions of Khomeini's Iran, Russian-
occupied Afghanistan and an increasingly fragmented Pakistan had taken a huge share of the world market. According to
Drug Enforcement Administration estimates generated by a
special investigative program, Project Cerberus, opium production in the "Golden Crescent" by 1980 had reached a level of
500 tons per year, nearly triple the production of the Southeast
Asian region.

Instead of the old Canadian Pacific and Jardine Matheson
routes out of the Golden Triangle, a new heroin trail was suddenly being cut from Iran-Afghanistan-Pakistan into Turkey,
through the Iron Curtain into Bulgaria, Yugoslavia and back
into Western Europe at the Bolzano-Venice corridor in northern
Italy. And at every step along the way, the "new warlords" of
the Society for Endangered Peoples of Nazi François Genoud
and the Bulgarian connection were running the show on the
ground.

Thus, when Italian authorities stormed into the Verona Red
Brigades safehouse where the terrorists were holding NATO

General James Dozier on January 28, 1982, it was on the basis
of raids of heroin refineries in nearby towns that the location of
the kidnappers was determined. It seems that the Red Brigades
captors were part of the "heroin connection" running a string
of laboratories in the shadow of NATO installations in Italy—
in partnership with the Ordine Nuovo "black international"
terrorists and the mafiosi of the Camorra.

3

The Narco-Terrorists

"Narcoterrorism" dominated the headlines of the Ibero-American press throughout 1984. In Peru, the terrorist Sendero Luminoso, by simultaneously attacking the several electrical generators that supplied electricity to the capital city of Lima, showed that it possessed a capacity far beyond the potential of the indigenous movement it pretends to be. It is not accidental that the area subjected to the most barbarous Sendero massacres also proved to be the largest drug-producing zone in the world. In Colombia, the March 1984 government raid on Tranquilandia, until then the world's largest cocaine refinery ever discovered, triggered the bloody "reprisal" of the M–19 terrorist in Florencia, Caquetá shortly thereafter. On November 15, 1984, federal agents backed by Mexican army troops raided a vast marijuana production and processing center in the northern state of Chihuahua. Later, they burned the marijuana seized, valued at some $10 billion. It was rumored at the time that a large part of the profits from this enormous operation were slated to go to the pro-drug electoral candidates.

The investigator who follows the trail left by Dope, Inc. in its comings and goings in Ibero-America, uncovers the guns-for-drugs traffic essential to the mafia-financed terrorist onslaught against the nations of the region. The trail of the drug trade in Ibero-America necessarily leads to the gigantic arms-smuggling operations of the old Nazi networks shared by their Soviet accomplices.

Where there is drug production, there has to be war. In the drug regions, the mafias can only be safe if they are running the country—as occurred during the rule of the "cocaine colonels" in Bolivia—or if they have provoked a level of guerrilla insurgency or mass violence sufficient to divert any interference with their operations.

This chapter introduces us to a study of the creation and deployment of the so-called "liberation" movements of the drug traffickers, as well as of the growing number of well-financed pseudo-religious sects which create a climate of moral degeneration propitious to the victory of the drug mafias.

A brief look at the career of the Colombian drug czar Carlos Lehder Rivas, will give the reader a clear idea of what was defined as International Synarchism and Nazi-Communism in the introduction of this section.

Carlos Lehder is one of the rich new gangsters who made their fortune in the drug trade. Together with Pablo Escobar Gaviria and the Ochoa and Rodríguez clans, he hired and financed the assassination of Colombian Justice Minister Rodrigo Lara Bonilla. Lehder and his accomplices have also financed housing for the poor, sports stadiums, public and private zoos, and both municipal and national electoral campaigns. Lehder was about to launch his own candidacy for the Colombian Senate when Lara Bonilla was named minister of justice and launched his bold campaign to stop the mafia from taking power in Colombia.

Lehder is not only a part of the Vesco operation, run from Cuba, but from Armenia, his native city, runs his own "National

Latin Civic Movement." His newspaper, Quindío Libre, published a eulogy of Adolf Hitler in June 1983, in the same issue in which he compared his own Latin Movement to the Green Party of West Germany. Lehder considers Hitler one of his heroes.

In an interview with *El Espacio* of Bogota, granted on July 13, 1983, Lehder was asked: "Do you admire Hitler?" to which he responded, "Logically. Adolf was one of the greatest men in our history. A man who has been deformed by the Jews and the imperialists."

In another interview, Lehder plunged even further into anti-semitism and racial fantasies:

Adolf eliminated 21 million Communists and six million allied enemies. He is the greatest warrior that humanity has ever had. What happens is that the Jews tell history the way they want the world to see it, but ask the Germans what really happened. I for example, half of my blood is German and it is as if a Brazilian were asked to speak about Colombia. He couldn't do it. He has to be a Colombian to speak about Colombia. The Jews never should have come to Germany, they should have stayed in their land.

The same Lehder who publicly endorsed the creation of the MAS (Death to Kidnappers) assassination squad, now presents himself as "the true opposition to the obsolete farce of the monarchical oligarchy" and a follower of the Jesuit leftist Camilo Torres, inspirer of the ELN guerrilla movement. "When I was a child, they executed Father Camilo, because he dared to denounce the traitors. His spirit today illuminates the path of the brave popular masses. . . . We are 28,000 brothers, the sole inheritors of the race of Bolívar, of the thousands of Indian races of our land and our destiny."

That declaration could just as well have been made by Abimael Guzmán, one of the founders of the Sendero Luminoso guerrillas of Peru.

Lehder's praise for the environmentalists in the Green Party has the same motivation and origin as the hostility of Sendero

Luminso to progress and Western civilization. With their exhortations to "learn from brother Hitler," Green Party leaders Rainer Langhans and Rudolf Bahro, at the Greens' November 1984 Hamburg conference, expressed the Nazi-Communist ideology in a similar form.

If we research the cultural and intellectual current called "Indigenism"—the racist promotion of a specific "Indian identity" of the blood; the exaltation of black magic, people's medicine and "magical realism"—we will find its priests not in the jungles of Peru, but among the anthropologists of the Sorbonne in Paris. And we will discover the origin of the fascist doctrine of blood and soil shared by the Nazis and the Communist anthropologists of the 1920s, an ideological affinity which preceded the Hitler-Stalin pact.

We will see that there is more than just a marriage of convenience between the old Nazi networks and the Bulgarian-Soviet and Cuban networks which provide the arms and infrastructure to the narcoterrorists.

4

Sendero Luminoso:
Indigenous Murderers

The Peruvian terrorist organization Sendero Luminoso (Shining Path) credits its existence to José Carlos Mariátegui, founder of the Peruvian Communist Party. He was a classic Nazi-Communist ideologue who pushed Sorelian socialism, developed, Mariátegui said, according to "the wishes of Friedrich Nietzsche," the intellectual predecessor of Hitler's fascism. Mariátegui focused on "primitive peoples" and collaborated with some of the leading anthropologists of his time.

Sendero Luminoso identifies itself as a radical Maoist group, following the tenets of Mao Zedong's Cultural Revolution and the Gang of Four. The ideology of Sendero Luminoso is Mother Earth cultism, based on the alleged superiority of the "indigenous" cultures, at one with nature and naturally "communistic." Celebration of the magical death cult of the Wari culture, which preceded the Inca civilization in Peru, is part of the

Sendero Luminoso belief structure. The Wari lunar calendar—and the coca growing season—are used by the terrorist group to plan its guerrilla actions.

While Sendero Luminoso's range of actions has spread rapidly to include most of Peru, its base of operations remains the desolate, geographically isolated and difficult terrain of the Andean highlands in the Department of Ayacucho. The group has demonstrated an ability to move quickly and clandestinely around the rugged country, including the areas known to be under the control of the drug-runners.

Sendero Luminoso has followed a strategy of laying siege to Peru's cities in order to bring about "a collapse of the bourgeois state." Sendero Luminoso terrorists have attempted to cut off the flow of food supplies into the cities, sometimes through razing farms and butchering livestock, attacking electrical power stations and lines, and blowing up bridges. The group has targeted for attack and assassination, local authorities who represent the "bourgeois state": mayors, police, teachers.

Anthropology and the Nazi-Communist Alliance

The Sendero Luminoso terrorists are a far cry from the defenders of the "indigenous" Quechua-speaking Indians of the southern highlands that their international fellow-travellers paint them to be. Their leaders are French-speaking graduates of the Sorbonne University—the same institution that produced the President of butcher Pol Pot's Kampuchea, Khieu Samphan.

Sendero Luminoso was created deliberately, in a decades-long project by anthropologists, sociologists, and erstwhile missionaries. One of these, the proclaimed father of Peruvian "ethnology," theosophist-cultist Luis E. Valcárcel, penned an article in 1960 titled, "Peru, Paradise for the Anthropologist."

EIR founder Lyndon LaRouche outlined the needed approach to investigation of Sendero Luminoso in a February 1984 research memorandum, "The Influence of Gnostic, Sufi, and 'Nativist' Cults in Recruiting and Controlling Terrorist and Separatist Insurgencies." LaRouche wrote:

> To combat the evils deploying terrorism and separatist insurgencies against civilization today, it is indispensable that we understand the enemy and his methods much better. . . . It is necessary to map the networks of anthropologists, sociologists, missionaries, and others who operate such Sufi networks among designated "pre-Columbian" varieties of "blood and soil" cult-stocks in Latin America as a whole, to be able to target counter-operations and appropriate cultural-warfare countermeasures against all of these cult operations, not merely the Sendero Luminoso.

But the power of the Sendero Luminoso does not come only from demented "action anthropologists." They are the intellectual controllers; but the Nazi International's drug-and-weapons trade provides the logistics and protection; the International Monetary Fund and allied financial interests create the conditions of misery and desperation upon which terrorism and separatist insurgencies can thrive; and the Soviet Union encourages the guerrillas in order to hasten the demise of the nation-states of the Western world.

By analyzing the belief-structure of the cults, LaRouche wrote in the cited memorandum, the full extent of this outside sponsorship can be discerned.

> It is necessary to do this to discover where to cut the fabric, with a few well-selected cuts, to cause the larger net to unravel. Once the map is developed, the Nazi-Soviet connection into these "nativist" insurgencies is more precisely defined.

By the 1970s, while the new underground structure of Sendero Luminoso was being constructed, the anthropologists' "new indigenism" moved toward the activist phase of "liberation" struggle. Meeting in Mexico City in 1974, the Société des Americanistes issued the battle cry:

We anthropologists . . . gathered in Mexico City on the occasion of the 41st International Congress of Americanists, consider it an opportune moment to clarify a problem of theoretical definition which implies a political conception for the liberation struggles of the indigenous populations, as part of the liberation projects of the American peoples. At this time, we reassert the necessity for specialists in the social sciences to commit themselves to support, *at a level of efficient practice,* the liberation struggles of the oppressed minorities (emphasis added).

In 1980, the same year that Sendero Luminoso surfaced as a terrorist movement, an umbrella organization for continental "Indian liberation," the Indian Council of South America (CISA), was founded. Representatives from Indian separatist and activist groups from across the continent met to plan a strategy for "taking power."

At the March 1983 Second Conference of the South American Indian Peoples, an organization sponsored by CISA, held outside La Paz, Bolivia, CISA representatives reported the successful completion of initial phases of organization. Expansion operations across the continent, recruitment of youth and training for both urban and rural "liberation" movements were announced as the next phase of "Indian" operations.

The conference consisted of one diatribe after another attacking the idea of the nation-state, lashing out at the "uncontrollable development of destructive and anti-human technology," and glorifying the most brutal aspect of "Indianidad" (Indian-ness)—coca-leaf chewing—as "one of the cultural values most immersed in the Andean ceremonial and ritual world." It was a pure expression of the "Indianidad" ideology espoused by the fanatical Sendero Luminoso gang. The battle cry of the conference: "Let us organize and prepare ourselves physically and ideologically so that when we install our people in power, we totally change the juridical and governmental system: In power, we will change the Western system and thought."

Soviet support for CISA, and the Indian separatist movement throughout Latin America, was restated as policy most recently by Anatolii Shulgovskii, director of the Political and Social Problems Division of the Latin American Institute of the U.S.S.R. Academy of Sciences. In the December 1982 edition of the Institute's magazine, *Latin America,* Shulgovskii wrote that "the characteristic trait of Latin America today is the broad incorporation of the indigenous masses into the liberation movement."

The Narco-Fascist Connection

Investigations by Peruvian police have determined that Italian fascist terrorist Stefano Delle Chiaie, wanted for the 1980 bombing of the Bologna train station which killed more than 80 people, is one of the controllers of Sendero Luminoso, according to an exposé published in the Italian weekly *Panorama.* This highly significant lead conclusively establishes the link between the drug-runners of the Nazi International and Sendero Luminoso.

"According to a report by the Peruvian police," reports *Panorama,* "Delle Chiaie organized one of the most spectacular actions of Sendero Luminoso, the assault against Lima on May 28, 1983. In the northeast of Lima, the government is trying to convince the campesinos to drop drug cultivation, and, through the advice of Delle Chiaie, the narco-traffickers merged their forces with Sendero Luminoso. According to Bolivian police, the latest action of Delle Chiaie was the coup attempt in La Paz, when President Siles [Zuazo] was kidnapped."

Panorama makes reference to the joint U.S.-Peruvian coca eradication program in the Tingo María region northeast of Lima, which was canceled in August following Sendero Luminoso attacks. Tingo María is Sendero Luminoso's second front. The joint program involved eradication of 4,000 acres of coca cultivation and aid to encourage cultivation of alternative crops. Sendero Luminoso mounted a major counterorganizing drive, recruiting an estimated 2,000 people in the valley to support their "right" to grow coca. On July 4, 1983 a large band of guerrillas attacked the American AID compound. Five Americans and several dozen Peruvian workers were withdrawn and the project canceled, because the 224-man police strike-force trained by the United States was unable to provide protection.

Delle Chiaie is a top operative of the Nazi International, who got his start at the University of Rome in the 1960s where he founded a group named the "Nazi-Maoists." He served as "lieutenant" to Nazi Klaus Barbie (the Gestapo "butcher of Lyons," who stood trial in France for his World War II crimes) in running the cocaine trade in Bolivia, where the "cocaine colonels" have seized government power more than once.

Bolivian sources had warned *EIR* in 1983 that the cocaine mafias of the Andean region had set into motion plans to organize a region-wide "Indian rights" movement to facilitate their narco-trafficking operations.

There is no doubt that Sendero Luminoso has worked out a deal with the Peruvian dope-traffickers: logistical support, money, and arms in return for "protection" against government war on drugs operations. Interior Minister Luis Percóvich stated on June 4, 1983 that intelligence agencies possessed positive proof of cooperation between cocaine-traffickers and Sendero Luminoso terrorists, citing as one example Sendero Luminoso's 1983 attack on the Ayacucho jail in which the terrorists took care to release the drug-runners first.

Intelligence experts point to the following patterns of the Sendero Luminoso drug connection.

- Sendero Luminoso's base of operations maps precisely onto the major coca-producing area of Peru, in the south-central highlands around Ayacucho.
- Investigators have been unable to locate any outside supply routes for weapons, funds, and other logistics for the terrorists.
- Sendero Luminoso's ability to deploy up to 2,000 terrorists in all corners of a country in which transportation remains a critical problem, indicates a depth and sophistication in logistical capability which only the narco-traffickers possess, e.g. aircraft.

Peru has been, with Colombia and Bolivia, one of the big three cocaine producers in Latin America. Its net income from cocaine production is estimated at $6 billion annually. With a total GNP of about $20 billion, this makes cocaine the most profitable business in the land.

Sendero Luminoso's area of strongest control, its base of operations, is precisely the prime coca-growing region of Peru: the south-central highland Department of Ayacucho, and the Valle de Alto Huallaga, which cuts through the Departments of Huanuco and San Martín. In fact, the areas of Sendero Luminoso's strength have registered an abrupt increase in production, while other areas have maintained their traditional rates of production. Exemplary is Alto Huallaga, which emerged as a rapidly growing coca producer in the mid-1970s and which, by 1983, was the number-one producing region.

Sendero Luminoso's "liberated zone" in the Andean highlands, the desolate and nearly impassable terrain which separates the urban coastal region from the eastern jungle drug corridor, provides a tight line of defense against law enforcement actions for the drug-runners.

The Sendero Luminoso interface with narco-traffickers probably goes back to the beginnnings of the terrorist cult activities run out of the University of Huamanga. By 1964, the coca plantation of Ayacucho Senator Parodi was reportedly being used as a base for jungle survival training for Huamanga professors and students belonging to the Sendero cult. Shining Path's first bloodletting operation in 1979 was the assassination of the police stationed along Parodi's access road. It is additionally reported that the Guzman group was collecting taxes on the drug trade moving through their zone of control outside Ayacucho in 1971.

5

The True Horror Story of the Gnostics

On July 26, 1984, Patricia Paredes de Londoño, leader of the Colombian National Anti-Drug Coalition, was kidnapped on the streets of Bogota by agents of the drug mafia. Paredes de Londoño disappeared after suffering harassment and intimidation, including death threats, telephone taps, robberies, and druggings, throughout the previous year. The threats and dirty operations were intended to intimidate Maximiliano Londoño, the victim's husband and vice president of the National Anti-Drug Coalition, and Fausto Charris, its president, and were designed to paralyze the investigative, organizational, and cultural activities of the group.

Thanks to an intensive international information campaign, Patricia Paredes de Londoño was released after seven days of captivity, in which she had been drugged and submitted to Patty Hearst-style brainwashing, in conformity with the Gnos-

tic methods of brainwashing detailed in the book of Gnostic
guru Samael Aun Weor, *Keys to Mental Dynamics*.[1]

But long before Paredes de Londoño recovered from her pain-
ful experience and was able to leave the psychiatric ward of the
Departmental Hospital of the University of Valle, the National
Anti-Drug Coalition and *EIR* investigators had been able to
put together a detailed picture of the links between the Gnostics, the Colombian mafia, the Bulgarian connection of narcoterrorism and arms-smuggling, and those "citizens above suspicion," such as former Colombian President Alfonso López Michelsen, who gave legal status to the Universal Christian Gnostic Church of Colombia in 1974—the same year the Colombian
drug bonanza took off.

In carrying out the kidnapping, the godfathers of the Colombian mob exposed the structure behind an international narcoterrorist conspiracy. On the fifth day of Mrs. Londoño's captivity,
EIR had already placed in the hands of influential individuals
around the world a dossier on the connection between the Bul-
garians, Gnostics and López Michelsen.[2]

EIR discovered, in addition, that the dirty Bulgarian operations not only were intended to "destroy the West," but have
the specific purpose of imposing the anti-Christian ideals of the
pagan Gnostic sect, which through the present time is the actual
religion of the state of Bulgaria.[3]

The cultural paradigm known as Gnosticism goes back centuries. It appeared in ancient Rome, reappeared as the ideology
of Adolf Hitler[4] and currently is disseminated around the world
by those international oligarchic circles who seek to replace the
Western Judeo-Christian tradition with the satanic assassin
cults which worship the "Great Mother."

Since the days of Saint Augustine, the oligarchy has drawn
on the Gnostic belief structure, with its deep hostility to the
Western moral values of technological progress and the sacred
worth of the individual, to do battle with the Christian faith,
whose teaching that man can share in the divinity of God by
continuing his creative work is anathema to the oligarchy.

Just as Saint Augustine fought the moral degeneration personified in these irrational sects, so those who would fight the

international drug trade today must recognize in the proliferation of these refurbished sects, the transmission belt of moral corruption so indispensable to the drug culture.

The Universal Christian Gnostic Church

Those who kidnapped, drugged, and tried to brainwash Patricia Paredes de Londoño, are members of the Universal Christian Gnostic Church of Colombia. Arturo Cortés Cadena, who presented himself as the "lawyer" of Patricia Paredes while she was still in captivity, and protected her kidnappers from police intervention, is an active member of the Universal Christian Gnostic Church, according to his own admission.

Cortés Cadena implicated one José Vicente Márquez, bishop of the Gnostic Church, in the Londoño kidnapping, when he stated that Márquez "will get me out of here" in case the police arrested him while Patricia de Londoño was still being held. The infamous Gnostic brainwashing manual, *Keys to Mental Dynamics,* by the master Samael Aun Weor (Víctor Manuel Gómez), which details the step-by-step process for "annihilating the ego," is dedicated among others to José Vicente Márquez.

Márquez was later to become famous as the "cleverest and most influential" partner of Julio Medina Vizcaíno, leader of the Universal Christian Gnostic Church unmasked in the October 9, 1984 edition of the mass circulation Colombian magazine *Cromos,* under the headline "A rapist, forger. . . ."

The trail of the Gnostics led to the doorstep of such personalities as the now-deceased head of the M–19 terrorist movement Jaime Bateman, and the notorious terrorist "La Chiqui," who played a scandalous role during the M–19 occupation of the Dominican Embassy in Bogota. Both were "believers," heavily indoctrinated by the Gnostic Church.

More important than the evidence brought to light by this investigation of key individuals in the narcoterrorist conspiracy is that an awesome weapon of cultural warfare was uncovered. Belief in the essentially bestial nature of man, in astrology and in black magic, the consumption of hallucinogenic drugs and hatred of the creative capacities of man, all define the world of the drug culture shared equally by the victims and raw recruits of the new paganism, as well as by those "respectable" individuals who use the Church as a center of narcoterrorist deployment. Such beliefs have been the secret weapon of the oligarchy for centuries. It is for this reason that we find such strange and repugnant coincidence in the world views of Sendero Luminoso, M–19 terrorist leader Jaime Bateman, drug-trafficker Carlos Lehder, and Adolf Hitler, as well of those anthropologists and bankers who have controlled them.

The Gnostic sect, which claims to have more than 20,000 adherents in Colombia alone, is committed to "world revolution." Through the perverse sexual rites and annihilation of the individual personality, people are brainwashed to accept and participate in the disintegration of their own societies. Preliminary investigation has shown that wherever the Gnostic sect has gained ground, it is there you will also find the principal sites of drug production or trafficking.

Jaime Bateman, the deceased head of the M–19, described the Gnostic support for his gang of terrorists in an interview published on November 28, 1983 by the Peruvian magazine *Caretas:*

> Look, I basically believe in my mother. . . . My mother is Gnostic. My mother was responsible for the organization of Gnosis in Santa Marta, and every Saturday they make a chain to protect us, the organization. . . . The executive committee, or whatever you call them, regularly send us congratulations.

In another interview published after his death, in the book *Listen Brother,* Bateman explained the "idealist" basis for his alliance with the mafia:

> Those who produce coca are not oligarchs; they are the popular sectors. Thus to carry out a repressive action against the trade, these are the sectors directly affected, without ever

enriching themselves. They produce it like any other product, because there is more profit in sowing coca than yuca. . . .

In December of 1984, M–19 leader Iván Marino Ospina repeated the ideas of his dead commander. Endorsing the threat of mafia chieftains like Carlos Lehder to "kill five North Americans for every Colombian extradited," Marino Ospina continued, "The drug trade has acquired special characteristics in my country, because many Colombians live and are benefitted by that activity."

Jaime Michelsen Uribe, founder of the Grancolombiano financial consortium and first cousin of former President Alfonso López Michelsen, couldn't agree more. Of all Colombians, Michelsen Uribe has most benefitted from such activities. Michelsen supported the marijuana legalization campaign of Ernesto Samper Pizano, friend of the Gnostics and director of López Michelsen's 1982 presidential campaign.

Samper admitted having accepted 20 million Colombian pesos for that campaign from Carlos Lehder and his friends, a contribution that, according to the mafia itself, constituted a first down-payment for the legalization of drugs and dirty money. Michelsen Uribe told *El Tiempo* im May 1981 that Samper Pizano's proposals were "eminently respectable . . . perhaps a solution to the problem." The hot money accumulated by the illegal drug trade "has been useful for the country, it has been channeled toward poles of development . . . and has offered solutions to people who would otherwise not find any."[5]

The novelist Gabriel García Márquez, Nobel Prize winner, ideologue of the pessimist movement in Colombia, a Gnostic by belief structure, and intimate of both the M–19 and Fidel Castro, also shares this view. He also campaigned actively for López Michelsen during his 1982 presidential bid.

In an interview in the *Village Voice,* published in August 1984, García Márquez called the drug trade "part of Colombians' self-defense. . . . Some write, some make movies, some are presidents of the republic, but no one lets himself die of hunger. . . . Who knows where our country would be without drugs?

Who knows what levels of common crime we would have if it weren't for the breathing space afforded by the drug trade?"

The International Monetary Fund (IMF) couldn't agree more. The Jamaican model, in which the profits from "ganja" are applied to debt payment, is the IMF's "free enterprise" model for the world.

In 1976, according to well-informed diplomatic sources, the IMF and its affiliate, the Royal Bank of Canada, directly ordered the government of Guyana to sow marijuana in order to earn foreign exchange. Within the year, Guyana had become a marijuana supplier to the United States, and was paying its debts to the IMF. One of the "discrete" conditions that the IMF imposed on Guyana was that the government host the People's Temple of the "Reverend" Jim Jones, the fanatical Gnostic who murdered hundreds of his followers with cyanide. Jones was presented as a friend of the family of President Jimmy Carter.

Milton Friedman, the monetarist economist who designed Chile's current economic model, also agrees. All drugs, says Friedman, including heroin, should be legalized in the name of "free enterprise." The Unification Church of Rev. Sun Myung Moon, a right-wing sect which bases itself on Gnostic beliefs, also favors legalization of heroin.

Where left and right meet, where the Communists and the fanatics of "free enterprise" come together, there we find the trail of narcoterrorism. Just like the National Latin Civic Movement of Carlos Lehder, which calls itself anti-imperialist, non-aligned, a people's leader, indigenist, pro-Green Party, and a fervent admirer of Adolf Hitler, the coherence of all these claims can be found in the doctrines of the Gnostic church.

Notes: Part VI

5: The True Story of the Gnostics

1. The following are extracts from the book *Keys to Mental Dynamics,* a review of brainwashing techniques, written in the third person as dictated by the "Master Samael Aun Weor."

We will give you the key for you to rapidly destroy the ego using the marvelous force of sexual energy. Says Master Samael: "Most Gnostic couples act in the following way: when they are at the moment of their maximum union in the practice of the Great Arcane, the man is annihilating a defect; he is thinking of annihilating the defect of envy (for example). Meanwhile, his wife, his priestess, is working on the defect of rage (for example). . . .

"Positive force works alone, the negative force or negative pole works alone, and the third force also acts independently.

"He who desires final liberation must achieve the destruction of egos or psychic aggregates of past existences, because otherwise he will not have total triumph. . . . On the road to gnosis, man feminizes, he acquires the feminine force; and woman masculinizes. Great men are put before women of strong temperaments, and the man who wants to triumph must subdue his pride. If all men who wish to realize themselves along the road I have shown you subdue the I of their pride and do not rebel against their women, logically they will achieve christifaction. As a man, one has to come to prostration before a woman."

2. On the afternoon of August 21, 1984, the Colombian news media was inundated with the complaints of Alfonso López Michelsen, scarcely a month after he had presented to the population the "amnesty" proposal demanded by the Colombian drug-traffickers. The text of López's protest is as follows:

In Panama, New York, Copenhagen, and presumably all over the world, an Intelligence Executive Review [sic] story is being circulated, according to which I have been in the service of the drug mafia, threatening Your Excellency, and sponsoring the so-called kidnapping of Mrs. Paredes de Londoño, who is supposedly married to the president of the Andean Party and the Anti-Drug Coalition and who has emerged to explain her absence as a dispute with her husband. They add information that, being the cousin of Jaime Michelsen, I sponsored legislation favoring him during my government.

I think that I—as an ex-president of Colombia and friend of your Excellency, whom I informed about every step related to the Panama meeting, and, according to the book by Hernán Echeverría I proceeded rigorously within the law in the Grancolombiano case—have the right for my honor not to be so damaged universally and in newspapers such as *ABC* of Madrid, in the face of the indifference or silence of the agents of the Colombian government, whatever their political affiliation might be.

3. That Gnosticism is flourishing in Bulgaria today is demonstrated by the career of Lyudmila Zhivkova (1942–1981), daughter of Todor Zhivkov, current President of Bulgaria and first secretary of the Bulgarian Communist Party. Zhivkova, member of the Politburo since 1979, presided over a transformation of official cultural policy in the direction of Gnosticism. As director of the government's Committee on Art and Culture in the 1970s, she glorified the pre-Christian death cults of Thrace (where Bulgaria is now), revived Bulgarian herbal folk medicine, built monuments to historical figures from the Gnosticism-shaped Bulgarian Orthodox Church, and preached a classically Gnostic doctrine of "the path to light and truth."

The speech that she gave before a group of children in Sofia is one of the most insane flights into Gnostic rhetoric:

Clad in the fire of the indestructible. . . . May consciousness embrace the infinity of the Cosmos. There will glow the vibration of electrons filling the vast expanse of iridescent spheres with their harmony and rhythm. . . . May the happiness of being eternally new as you create be . . . the most magnificent garment sparkling on you in the vibration of the seven-modal harmony of Eternity!

After her death in 1981, the Lyudmila Zhivkova International Foundation (LZIF) was established to continue her work.

4. Adolf Hitler's Nazi Party is the paramount case in the West of a Gnostic movement come to power. Hitler's world conception was specifically Gnostic. As a child, Hitler attended the Lambach Abbey School in Lambach-am-Tram in upper Austria. Since at least 20 years before Hitler's birth, Lambach had been a center of Gnostic practice. Its abbot, Father Theodore Hagen, was adept in astrology and in the fundamentals of the Gnostic heresy, with particular affinity for thirteenth-century Catharism and Islamic Sufism. This Benedictine monk caused a swastika to be engraved over the entrance to the abbey school.

When Hitler went to the abbey in 1899, there was also a young Cistercian monk, Adolf Joseph Lanz, who was later to lead Hitler through the racialist cult networks of Vienna. In 1900, Lanz threw aside his habit, went to Vienna and founded the Order of the New Temple, inspired by the Knights Templar. In 1905, using the name of Georg Lanz von Liebenfels, he began to publish the racist cult journal *Ostara,* dedicated to propagandizing in favor of the war between the "Sons of Light" and the "Sons of Darkness"; that is, the war between the blond, blue-eyed Aryan and the dark, scheming Jew.

In Munich, Hitler was routed into Gnostic circles revolving around the Thule Society, named after the mythical "Ultima Thule" homeland of the Aryans in the north, and made up of south German, Swiss, and British oligarchs dedicated to creating a mass-based party to indoctrinate defeated Germany with Gnostic ideas. Hitler became its chosen spokesman.

Hitler's mission was to destroy Christianity and Judaism in favor of the ancient pagan religion. When the war was lost, Germany being invaded on every front, catastrophe looming, Hitler's lieutenants clustered around him to know what the Führer would do. Hitler told them that, whatever the outcome of the war, the greater war had been won. One hundred years after his death, he predicted, Christianity would no longer exist as a significant force in the world. That was victory, he said. To destroy Christianity, Hitler reasoned, one must first destroy its "agent," the "bacillus the Jew"; that "nation of priests," as Nietzsche had angrily called them. The Holocaust was planned to do just that.

5. Jaime Michelsen Uribe is currently a fugitive from Colombian justice, and is hiding with his family and closest collaborators in Miami, Florida. Michelsen fled Colombia on New Year's Eve 1984, following a "discussion" with President Betancur in which he was

presented with the evidence of his massive financial frauds. The banker was asked to resign his post as president of the Grancolombiano flagship bank, Banco de Colombia, in order to avoid prosecution. Michelsen instead chose "exile in luxury" in Miami, but runs the risk of being extradited to Colombia to answer for his multi-million dollar crimes.

PART VII
Organized Crime

Introduction
The Criminal International

The powers and aims of Dope, Inc.'s top distributors have always been explicitly political. They invest in spreading the anti-industrial counterculture of drugs, environmental kookery, pornography, gambling, speculation, and all the dolce vita trappings of "leisure society," so beloved of European titled nobility, and increasingly absorbed by ordinary Americans. They invest the revenues of the narcotics trade in destruction of the culture and morality of progress on which the industrial nations' governments rest.

Sodom and Gomorrah backed by international financial power and political dirty tricks; this is, in fact, the only precise definition of organized crime. This is the purpose for which it is "organized." Local family-centered crime rings existed, of course, made shifting, temporary alliances, tried to divide turf within cities, and so on. But there is nothing in this sort of criminal activity which deserves the term "organized." Nor did it consume any measurable fraction of America's national income—not until the British-directed syndication process centered on the Canadian Bronfman family, from the 1920s onward.

The objective and method of that syndication, as we shall see, was the effective seizure of the U.S. government, beginning with its law enforcement and intelligence capabilities.

We will scrape off the coat of whitewash, less than twenty years old, over the Bronfman corporate financial empire. Beneath it we will uncover Dope, Inc. subsidiaries that control the criminal underworld of North America. We will look closely at Meyer Lansky and other "mafia" figures and discover that, like China's Green Gangs, the mob is a secret army, a fifth column controlled by the British oligarchs against the United States.

We will trace the drug money to the gambling casinos and other "legitimate" enterprises that are the syndicate's indispensable store-front cover for the drug trade. From these respectable enterprises we will trace the drug money into the halls of the state assemblies, city councils, congressional offices, and into the pockets of America's contemporary Benedict Arnolds and Aaron Burrs.

We will then take a grand tour through the Anglo-Dutch offshore banking centers, watching money being laundered through Basel, Liechtenstein, Tel Aviv, and the Bahamas; tracing it carefully as it finances international terrorism and a privately owned worldwide assassination bureau.

By the time we finish, the reader will have a view of organized crime that tears to shreds all the fairy tales of the drugstore novels and grade-B Hollywood productions. The much portrayed local "godfather," whose "families" resist the drug trade or oppose the use of political assassinations, is no real part of this syndicate, nor could he ever prevail on its policy. He does not even conceive of its basic objective, the complete legalization of crime internationally by the dissolution of law enforcement and national government.

Similarly, the citizen who thinks of organized crime in terms of the local city's political machine, has been fooled. That political machine has been targeted by a national "war room" with international connections and goals. Some of the local officials are likely to have been entrapped by agents of the national command of organized crime—which now sends still higher-level agents, "above suspicion," to prosecute those officials!

The truly typical alliances we will trace are not those constantly drummed into the citizenry, by media run by Dope, Inc. itself. They are the apparently strange, recurring alliances epitomized by Bernie Cornfeld's funding of Robert Hutchins: the IOS lieutenant of Robert Vesco and the president of the University of Chicago, founder of the Center for the Study of Democratic Institutions; the convicted international swindler and the world-class liberal intellectual. What brings them together? Drug counterculture, and one-world government.

Special Operations Executive

Since the 1920s, British Dope, Inc. gangsters have struck from their Canadian base to seize effective governmental power throughout the islands of the Caribbean, the countries of Central America, and certain watering holes in Mexico. The casino hotels sprang up, the titled nobility took up residence, the banking shells proliferated. As the U.S. media enticed Americans to spend more and more "leisure" money in these offshore principalities of Meyer Lansky's syndicate, Dope, Inc. struck directly at the U.S. post-war economy, and the U.S. government's executive branch.

The turning point in Britain's opium war was the five years following World War II. The key operational capability implanted by Dope, Inc. in the U.S.A. at that turning point was the Special Operations Executive (SOE) of British secret intelligence.

The law enforcement official confronts today two major obstacles in going after the narcotics trade. The first is the extraordinary degree of "inside" protection enjoyed by Dope, Inc. within the national intelligence and security establishment. The history of Col. William Stephenson's SOE is key to this protection.

Col. Sir William "Intrepid" Stephenson, the real deployer of Meyer Lansky's syndicate, and patron of Lucky Luciano's postwar rehabilitation; Col. Louis Mortimer Bloomfield, attorney and controller for the Bronfman liquor and drug fortune; Gen. Julius Klein, sponsor of United Brands Chairman Max Fisher—these commanding cadre of Dope, Inc., all British and Canadian officers, took control of the most sensitive area of U.S. intelligence during and after World War II.

David Sarnoff, whose RCA communications conglomerate formed the core of the National Security Agency (NSA); NSA Counterintelligence chief Walter Sheridan, who later coordinated political protection and intelligence services for the Resorts International-Lansky casino empire; Col. Clay Shaw, NSA officer prosecuted by New Orleans District Attorney Jim Garrison in the JFK assassination;—these were the kind of special operations capabilities the SOE used to pursue its ultimate objective: the complete freedom of operation of Dope, Inc. throughout North America.

Stephenson worked together with the Canadian networks of the celebrated British triple agent Harold "Kim" Philby, who commanded the top level of agent training for OSS and the new Central Intelligence Agency, and then "defected" to the Soviet Union. He is today a KGB general. Stephenson and Philby together used their networks to begin the transformation of American security-intelligence forces into the mess we find them in today.

Beginning with J. Edgar Hoover's all-too-willing FBI, Stephenson's command took over the Justice Department, and elements of the CIA. They made the entire apparatus into a giant sieve, leaking U.S. military intelligence; and they transformed it into a protection agency for gangsters and terrorists, that entraps and prosecutes honest Americans.

We shall look at FBI Division Five, the counterintelligence division of the FBI. This unit was created top-to-bottom by Col. Stephenson, Walter Sheridan, Col. Bloomfield and Gen. Julius Klein, using British methods of "targeting" political enemies,

NSA-RCA communications capabilities, and personnel combined from J. Edgar Hoover's favorites and Eastern European emigré fascists.

Headed personally by Canadian citizen Louis M. Bloomfield, FBI Division Five was the starting core of Stephenson's command.

We shall see the recruitment of Dope, Inc.'s assassination bureau, Permindex, from the "assets" of Division Five combined with the financial holdings of the Bronfmans. We shall learn how Permindex gained the capability, by 1963, to murder an American President, command a coverup, and crush the New Orleans District Attorney who later tried to prosecute that crime.

The Cutouts

The second problem for the law enforcement investigator confronts him because of his habit of working his way up, from the street level to the large-scale suppliers and then toward the real financial and political power of the international narcotics cartel. He confronts what the intelligence trade calls "cutouts"—layers of operatives who are political camouflage for their masters—on a scale that becomes more dense and complex as he goes up. Only District Attorney Garrison, fresh on the trail of a presidential assassination, reached far enough up through the "cutout" layers to hit at the top. His efforts were rewarded by drawing out into public confrontation the layers of direct British intelligence control.

Should the law enforcement official, however—with aid of this report—start at the top, then the picture becomes quite simple.

The British financiers of Dope, Inc. employ three major layers of political camouflage to run the drug trade in North America. The first is a front for Jewish-surnamed criminal elements.

This cutout begins at the top with a cohesive grouping of "Hofjuden" (court Jews) who have served British monarchs and

Venetian doges for generations. These families have a centuries-long unbroken tradition of attaching themselves to the predominant noble houses of Europe; the Venetians and Genoese, the nobility of Amsterdam, and then when the Dutch nobility was merged with the British in the so-called Glorious Revolution of 1688, the Hofjuden centered themselves around the British and have served it to this day.

The Hofjuden have less than nothing to do with the Jewish people, their well-being and aspirations for themselves and their posterity. These families' only relation to the Jews has been to periodically call down persecution upon them, and then to excuse their own role in it by their surnames. One cannot condemn the Jewish people for the centuries of crimes committed by the Hofjuden, whose primary victim has been that people itself.

Among these top families are the Montefiores, servants of the Genoese nobility since thirteenth-century operations in Italy and Spain; the Goldsmids and Mocattas, leading bullion merchants for the British royal family since the seventeenth-century Stuart Restoration; the Oppenheimers, controllers of a large proportion of the diamond and gold mining in South Africa; the Sassoons, the first Hofjuden to settle in India and devote their resources primarily to opium production, now also among the Caribbean jet set; the Canadian de Hirsch family, bankrollers of Jewish emigration from Eastern Europe to Canada; the Rothschilds, with a longstanding special interest in subverting the American republic; and the other "Our Crowd" banking families of Warburg, Schiff, Meyer, Loeb, Schroeder, etc.

Immediately below the Hofjuden elite are the "initiate" families they selected and sponsored to run the criminal underworld and its "legitimate" front organizations in North America. It is these families we put under a microscope in this section. Their open criminal activities are very recently, but with heavy-handed force and blackmail, camouflaged against the police investigator under color of "activities on behalf of Israel," causing the drug fighter who pursues them to be labeled "anti-Semitic."

The second major layer of cutouts, who we shall meet in our report on Permindex, is of an apparently different religious camouflage. These are the emigré nobility and pseudo-nobility of Eastern Europe and the Mediterranean—the Jesuit/Russian Orthodox, or "Solidarist" nobility.

This layer of families, and their empire hangers-on, operate under protective camouflage of "captive nations" anti-Communist crusades, and of reactionary pseudo-churches of an Eastern Orthodox color, particularly in the American Council of Christian Churches.

Nearly all of these families directly collaborated with Central European fascism and manned the dummy governments of Hitler and Mussolini in Eastern Europe and the Balkans. After World War II, they went to work for Soviet or Anglo-American intelligence, sometimes for both. Some of them, like the Sassoons, exemplify the jet set counterculture which is the crown jewel of Dope, Inc.'s drug, pornography, and casino rackets. All of them, from the most chic to the most paranoid clutchers at titles to Eastern European duchies, play an active role today in the drug, political dirty tricks, destabilization, and assassination operations of Dope, Inc.

Typical of these families are the Radziwills, leaders of the Polish Solidarists; the unreconstructed fascist Ferenc Nagy of Permindex; the de Menils, who have involved portions of perhaps unsuspecting Texas fortunes in Permindex through marriage; the di Spadaforas, representatives of the Italian House of Savoy in the Permindex assassination bureau; and of course, the families of minor nobility such as one well-known Brzezinski. The political family of William F. Buckley, Jr. and James Buckley are permanent hangers-on of the Jesuit emigré circles, and promoters of drug decriminalization.

The third and most active "cutout" the investigator of Dope, Inc. confronts is the Socialist International front organizations in North America. These operate under a camouflage of "anti-fascist" coalitions and campaigns targeted against political and law enforcement forces who want to clean drugs and terrorism out of America's cities and restart industrial growth.

Some of the Socialist International organizations, like Social

Democrats U.S.A. and the League for Industrial Democracy, have operated for years under pretended "conservative" cover. They seldom conduct public operations under their own name, in order to penetrate conservative labor and political organizations. But these pseudo-conservative fronts are the funding sources for pro-drug and pro-terrorist organizations: the Institute for Policy Studies, the Communist Workers Party, Yippies, and the rotten American Civil Liberties Union networks epitomized by William Kunstler.

The primary connection point for these "right" and "left" pro-drug front groups of the Socialist International is the organizational dirty-tricks front known as the Anti-Defamation League of B'nai B'rith , a joint creation of Socialist and Stephenson-FBI networks. The ADL is also the "civil liberties" link between the publications of the drug and pornography trade—*Playboy, Hustler, High Times,* etc.—and the pro-drug and pro-terrorist groups which they publicize and fund.

Since the first edition of this volume appeared in 1978, this entire Socialist International drug-pornography lobby has rallied around a curious slogan created for it by the Anti-Defamation League. This is the claim that the national war on drugs to which American citizens are now being roused, represents a "fascist resurgence of the Ku Klux Klan!"

1

The Bronfman Gang

The Bronfman family is best known to Americans through its ownership of Seagrams, the biggest liquor company in North America. The family's holdings stretch from whiskey, banking, mining, to real estate, and—although somewhat less publicized—narcotics. Today they are regarded as respectable and outstanding "philanthropists" whose name is attached to everything important in Canada—and Israel—be it government, business, or cultural affairs.

This was not always the public profile of the Bronfman family. Less than fifty years ago, they were known to be the biggest bootleggers in North America and were referred to by the less prestigious title "the Bronfman gang."

The Bronfmans have always been beholden to the Hofjuden elite. The first member of the family to come to North America was Yechiel Bronfman, a grist mill owner from Bessarabia,

Romania, who later anglicized his name to Ekiel. Yechiel emigrated to Canada in 1889 under the sponsorship of the Moses Montefiore Jewish Colonization Committee.[1]

This enterprise had been initiated at an 1872 meeting between Baron Maurice de Hirsch, Baron Alfred de Rothschild, and other Zionists who established a Jewish Colonization Association to bring selected Russian and Eastern European Jews to agricultural settlements (kibbutzim) in the Canadian provinces of Manitoba and Saskatchewan.[2] The same period marked the transfer of the Warburg, Kuhn, Loeb, and related Our Crowd migration from Germany and Britain into lower Manhattan. In 1912, William Sebag Montefiore arrived in Montreal where he lived until his death in 1950. Lord Harold Sebag Montefiore, current head of the Jerusalem Foundation (the Zionist wing of the Most Venerable Order of St. John of Jerusalem) was sent to Canada for his early education. In the same period, Baron de Hirsch established the de Hirsch Foundation in Canada as the umbrella for all Canadian Jewish "philanthropic" activities, and the Montefiores created a club (named after the family) to service the resident elites. The Rothschilds, too, planted a branch of their family on Canadian soil.

Meanwhile, in Saskatchewan, the Bronfman family found little interest in eking a living out of the plains of midwestern Canada. The family first turned to selling wood, then to horse trading, and then most successfully to the hotel business (and prostitution).[3]

In Yiddish Bronfman means "liquorman," and the hotel business put the Bronfmans in a good position to take advantage of the 1915 advent of Canadian prohibition. Bronfman hotels became "boozeriums." Prohibition—enacted on orders from the Privy Council as the prelude to the 1920s Prohibition in the United States and the birth of organized crime—catapulted the Bronfmans into the multi-millionaire bracket and a status as the untouchable kingpins of crime in North America.

During Canada's four dry years from 1915 to 1919, the Bronfmans established their contacts with U.S. criminal figures for illegally importing liquor into Canada. In 1916, the Bronfmans established their first link with the opium trade proper. Samuel and Abe Bronfman, two of Ekiel's four sons, collaborated with the Hudson's Bay Company—in which the Keswick family of Jardine Matheson had controlling interest—to buy the Canadian Pure Drug Company. In this way the Bronfmans rushed into the loophole in the War Measures Act that permitted the distribution by pharmacists of alcohol for "medicinal" purposes.

When Prohibition in Canada ended in 1919 and Prohibition in the United States began, the Bronfmans simply turned from whiskey importing to whiskey exporting. After it was all over in May 1936, the Bronfmans agreed to pay $1.5 million to settle their account with the U.S. Treasury; the sum amounted to an admission that half the liquor that came into the United States during Prohibition was from the "liquormans."[4]

The "Seagram's Chickencock" the family poured across the border was a mixture of pure alcohol, sulfuric acid, caramel, water, and aged rye whisky. Between 1920 and 1930, 34,000 Americans died from alcohol poisoning.

Their control of the liquor flow during Prohibition U.S.A. gave the Bronfmans life-and-death control over American crime. Refusing to play ball with the Bronfman gang usually spelled death, and independent-minded gang bosses were often known to be executed by their lieutenants on the Bronfmans' behalf. One of the buyers best liked by the gang was New York City beer baron Arthur Flegenheimer, a.k.a. Dutch Schultz, who succeeded in wiping out his competition, including the notorious killer Legs Diamond. Schultz himself was later rubbed out when he took it into his head to murder crusading New York District Attorney Thomas Dewey. (There is some question about what Dewey was crusading for, as we shall see in the story of the Mary Carter Paint Company.)[5]

In the first years of Prohibition, Ekiel Bronfman's four boys ran all bootlegging from the prairie states of Canada to major distribution sites south like Chicago. To secure the shipment lines, Harry set up a dummy firm, Transcanada Transport Company. Transcanada was a protective cover for the Canadian Pacific Railway owned by respectable gentlemen back in London, which ran the whiskey across the border.[6] The Bronfmans also bought up stretches of barren farmland along the border and even built an underground pipeline to pump their "chick-encock" into the United States.

In 1922, Bronfman brother-in-law Paul Matoff was executed gangland-style by the Chicago mob in a dispute over profit-splitting. A scandal ensued, public hearings were convened, and the Bronfman crimes came spilling out into the light of day. The Bronfmans received a mild reprimand from the Canadian government and relocated their operations to Montreal.

The year 1922 also marks the point when the Bronfmans procured their own distillery, hauled, with workmen included, from Kentucky to Montreal.

Since 1920 the Bronfmans had been importing British whis-key from the Distillery Company of London (DCL), which con-trolled more than half the world market in Scotch whiskey. DCL was owned by the higher echelons of the British nobility, including Field Marshal Haig, Lord Dewar, Lord Worlavington, and others. The dispensation of distribution rights was a deci-sion made by His Majesty the King. In 1926, upon the request of Samuel Bronfman, the DCL agreed to go 50–50 in the Bronf-mans' distillery, and the Distillery Corporation Limited was formed as a holding company with Bronfman and Seagram's distilleries. Headquarters were established at the Bronfmans' corporate castle in Montreal, but it was the Distillery Company of London's William Ross who was installed as president with Sam Bronfman as vice president. The British elite had given the green light to the Bronfmans.

Despite the big infusion of capital and the newly gained legitimacy the link-up with DCL afforded them, the smell of Bronfman smuggling and bribery grew too strong. In 1928, the Royal Commission on Customs recommended the immediate prosecution of Harry Bronfman on charges of attempted brib-ery. Shortly thereafter, the Bronfmans created the Atlas Ship-ping Company and moved their smuggling operations to the French islands of St. Pierre and Miquelon, fifteen miles off the Newfoundland coast. With licenses in Bermuda, Saint John, New Brunswick, Belize, and British Honduras, the Atlas Ship-ping Company was one of the first ties nailed down in the dirty money-drug underground railway between Canada and the Caribbean.[7]

A little ditty popular during the time indicates the amusement with which the British viewed the entire operation:

> Four and twenty Yanks
> Feeling very dry,
> Went across the border
> To get a drink of rye.
> When the rye was opened,
> The Yanks began to sing:
> "God bless America,
> But God save the King."

Organized Crime Comes of Age

With Prohibition, crime became a bigtime business. It was no longer based on small-scale prostitution, loan-sharking, or petty protection rackets. Now it was centralized around the marketing of one precious and outlawed commodity whose supply was controlled from London and from the British colony of Canada. Crime was reorganized from top to bottom into an integrated wholesale and retail distribution chain with well-defined marketing districts, quotas, and uniform pricing. Crime became syndicated.

Hundreds of movies spewed out of Hollywood about the "Roaring Twenties" have glamorized the truth: With Prohibition, Britain—through its Bronfman gang cutout—had created a nationally syndicated crime cancer. Within a decade of the Roaring Twenties, the Bronfman syndicate would be peddling heroin, cocaine, and every other available poisonous drug through the same wholesaling, transporting, and retailing system that bootlegged booze.

Bronfman's counterpart in the United States was one Arnold Rothstein. Just as Bronfman made it into the bigtime under the auspices of the Hofjuden elite, so Arnie Rothstein was sponsored by Our Crowd Zionist investment bankers who arrived in New York as the Montefiores were setting up business in Canada. Arnold Rothstein—the godfather of organized crime—was the son of a wealthy Our Crowd dry goods merchant.

At the turn of the century, the Russell Sage Foundation had issued a well-publicized field study of loan-sharking in New York City.[8] The report's wide publicity resulted in the bankrupting, jailing, or takeover of the petty gangsters by Rothstein, who emerged as a powerful Tammany Hall figure with a fabled loan-sharking business estimated at several million dollars.

Regionwide combines were formed up and down the East Coast for smooth distribution. The Reinfeld Syndicate—named after the Newark, New Jersey bootlegger and accused murderer Joseph Reinfeld—functioned as the middleman between the British liquor distilleries and the "rum rows" of Boston and New York. Its controlling shareholders were the four Bronfman brothers, Allan, Sam, Abe, and Harry. The U.S. leg was handled by Reinfeld and Abner "Longie" Zwillman, later the boss of Atlantic City, and Rothstein's gangs in New York.[9]

In 1927, the Big Seven combine consolidated the entire East Coast distribution system. Its organizer was John Torrio—a dapper little gentleman who, without benefit of family, racket, or turf had gained notoriety for eliminating any local crime bosses who stood in the way of national syndication. Torrio was a Bronfman man who had murdered his own uncle to prove it. Brought into Chicago in 1910 by his uncle, racketeer "Big Jim" Colosimo, Torrio sniffed the wind on the eve of Prohibition and demanded that his uncle start making the right contacts to get into the lucrative business of bootlegging. When "Big Jim" refused, Torrio had him murdered and took over the Chicago mob as the distribution point for the Bronfman liquor.[10]

In 1925, Torrio suddenly left Chicago, heading for Havana and then landing in Italy. Returning to the United States in 1927 after he miraculously escaped Mussolini's purges of the Mafia, Torrio came back with one goal: to build a nationally organized crime syndicate.

While the mad killers and punks like Dutch Schultz, Legs

Diamond, and Al Capone made the headlines every day and provided good material for gangster movies, John Torrio quietly continued the work that Arnold Rothstein (assassinated in 1928) had begun, now with the aid of Rothstein's successors Meyer Lansky and Lucky Luciano. Torrio could do what Lansky and the Bronfmans were prohibited from doing for reasons of ethnicity: Discipline the scores of family local crime chieftains and "moustache Petes" into one centralized business that could penetrate every sector of the economy. Known as the "assassin who never carries a gun," Torrio presented himself as the elder statesman of organized crime and commanded respect from the Mafia locals. "Cooperation is good for business" was his slogan.

The Big Seven had been Torrio's first step. The cooperative of East Coast bootleggers controlled from the top down to the local levels all prices, membership, centralized distribution points, corruption, and protection.

By 1928 Torrio was able to call a Cleveland meeting to establish a nationwide crime syndicate.[11] The gathering was unique in that it had succeeded in bringing together into one room all the crime bosses of every major organized city. There were three items on the agenda. First, how to use the huge profits of Prohibition and invest them in legitimate businesses that would permit a steadily increasing take for the syndicate. Second, how to deal with the Italian question. The ritual vendetta murders of the mafioso families were good for the newspapers, said Torrio, but bad for business. Immediately after the meeting the Castellammarese gang wars broke out in New York as the test case for Torrio's syndicate. Under the auspices of Lansky and Torrio, Lucky Luciano succeeded in wiping out all recalcitrant godfathers. During the last night of the war—the infamous "Night of the Sicilian Vespers"—over forty people were gunned down.[12]

With cartelization came the need for more long-lasting regulation—gangland style. In the early 1930s, Murder, Inc. was formed as a regulatory commission of sorts to police any overzealous "free enterprise" advocates who might try to buck the syndicate. A special assassination bureau was set up by Meyer Lansky and Benjamin "Bugs" Siegel. The "Bugs and Meyer

Gang" had been distinguished by the fact that it owed allegiance to no one (except maybe Arnold Rothstein); it had originally been used to protect Bronfman liquor shipments across
the border against "freelance" hijackers.[13]

By 1932, Torrio was strong enough to pull together another
meeting of the syndicate, this time in Atlantic City, where
a National Commission—the board of directors of organized
crime—was officially formed. Aside from the leading Italian
mafiosi who had survived the transition, Meyer Lansky, now
regarded as the financial and enforcement wizard of the syndicate, and Atlantic City's Zwillman were in attendance as honored guests.

For the British, Prohibition was a roaring success. What had
begun as a three-way contract between Britain (the supplier),
Bronfman (the cutout), and Rothstein (the distributor) had become within the space of a decade a nationally organized crime
syndicate, a private, secret army under British banking and
political control.

The Rothstein-Hong Kong Connection

To pick up the story of the modern-day Dope, Inc., let us
return to Cleveland and John Torrio's first 1928 meeting of the
syndicate. The third item on the agenda was what to do after
Prohibition. The commodity, Torrio proposed, that would replace liquor as the black-market, big-profit taker was narcotics.

When Prohibition began in 1920 Arnold Rothstein had personally gone to Great Britain to establish the liquor pipeline
with the British distilleries. At the same time he had dispatched
his underling Jacob "Yasha" Katzenberg to Shanghai to begin
negotiations for a dope pipeline from the Far East into the East
Coast of the United States.[14] (The West Coast had been sewn
up in the 19th century with a pipeline from Shanghai straight
into the Pacific Chinese coolie communities.)

It was projected that the same networks established to bootleg
liquor could just as easily smuggle and retail narcotics. By

1926, U.S. narcotics agent-on-the-scene in the Far East, Ralph Oyler, wrote back to his boss Levi Nutt, chief of the U.S. Narcotics Division, that the opium market had expanded so much that to meet market demand, Britain was "even taking shipments of crude opium from the Near East to add to her gigantic supply of Asian opium." The traditional opium families of Keswick, Sassoon, and Inchcape were preparing for the future.[15]

Let us now stand back and review—in light of this history—the jigsaw puzzle pieces that fall into place with Yasha Katzenberg's trip to Shanghai and the sealing of an opium pact.

First, Arnold Rothstein, Yasha Katzenberg's employer, was a product of the Rothschild dry goods empire that included the Seligman, Wanamaker, and Gimbel families. During Prohibition, according to the Bronfmans' own testimony, Rothstein, Meyer Lansky, and Lucky Luciano were the Bronfmans' main distributors. As Prohibition came to a close, Bronfman associates traveled to Shanghai and Hong Kong to streamline and expand the drug trade into the United States, negotiating with the foremost Chinese drug runners who were not only encouraged but pressured by the British business community to pull together an opium cartel.

The man dictating the opium policy to China in this period was Sir William Johnston Keswick of Jardine Matheson and the Hongkong and Shanghai Bank. From the period of the Shanghai Massacre to 1942 when he was interned by the Japanese, Keswick directed the International Settlements of Shanghai—the period of gross expansion of Shanghai heroin into the United States. The same Sir William Keswick was until very recently the director of the Hudson's Bay Company of Canada, the same company, it will be recalled, that collaborated with Sam and Abe Bronfman in 1916 to found the Pure Drug Company for illegal distribution of whiskey into Canada.

Working for Hudson's Bay along with Keswick is Sir Eric Drake, who not only sits on the board of several Bronfman-run banks and companies, but is also an employee of the Inchcape family and presently the deputy chairman of the Inchcapes' Peninsular and Orient Navigation Company. The current chairman of the board is the son of the Lord Inchcape who in

1923 called for the expansion of "that most valuable source of revenue"—the opium trade.

Sir Eric Drake is also a member of the board of Canadian Pacific, which plays a most vital role in the transshipment of drugs through Canada into the United States, just as it did with alcohol during Prohibition. Along with Lord Trevelyan, who heads up the HongShang's "gold for dope" exchange from his position at the British Bank of the Middle East, and Lord Inchcape, Sir Eric Drake sits on the board of British Petroleum, as does Sir William Johnston Keswick.

Sitting on the board of the Bank of Montreal along with Charles Bronfman and two Seagram's directors are J. Bartlett Morgan, William Arbuckle, and F.S. Burbridge, who in turn sit on the boards of Hudson's Bay, Canadian Pacific, and a host of other banks and corporations in which the drug families of the HongShang nexus play a policy-making role.

We are not charging guilt by association, but rather making note of the fact that the series of legitimate enterprises the Bronfmans moved into toward the close of Prohibition are indistinguishable from and intermeshed with companies controlled by Keswick, Inchcape, and other leading opium traders. During the same period, these gentlemen openly supervised the drug trade into the United States. This association not only continues to this day, but it remains the mainstay of the Bronfman empire.

Going Legit

With the repeal of Prohibition, the Bronfmans, like so many of their partners across the border, "went legit." Organized crime sunk its millions in legitimate businesses that both acted as cover for illegal activities and set up the laundry networks for dirty money. The new phase of respectability signaled that the most successful bigtime whiskey bootleggers were switching to bigtime narcotics.

In the early days, the Bronfmans had to run all the risks of the smuggler's profession. They had to dodge the law, stay one step ahead of the desperados on the other side of the border, and whenever things went wrong, face the humiliation of public exposure and scandal. As a result, the family acquired a considerable reputation.

Looking expectantly toward the fast increase in drug trade in America, the British could not afford to leave their leading cutout in such an exposed and precarious position. Nor could they simply dispose of the Bronfmans after Prohibition. The family had become irreplaceable due to its in-depth control over the syndicate. Yet, the Bronfmans would be a liability if they continued to work as openly with their distributors in narcotics-trafficking as they did running Prohibition.

The problem was resolved by bringing the Bronfmans into the lower rungs of the Hofjuden caste. Almost overnight, the Rothschilds, Montefiores, de Hirsches, et al. took Mr. Sam, the crime czar of North America, and transformed him into a rising star of the Canadian Zionist movement.

■ In 1934, Mr. Sam was given his first respectable post as chairman of the National Jewish People's Relief Committee (Canada).

■ By 1939 he had been appointed head of Baron de Hirsch's Jewish Colonization Association, the same association that had brought Yechiel to Canada.

■ In the same year, the Canadian Pacific Corporation invited Mr. Sam to establish a new refugee organization for Eastern European Jews.

■ Within five years, the prince of crime was transformed by the good grace of His Majesty's oligarchists into a Zionist philanthropist. One post followed after another. He became head of the Canadian Jewish Committee, replacing Lyon Cohen, the son of Lazarus Cohen, the founder of the Jewish Colonization Association and the official agent of the de Hirsch family interest.

After World War II, Mr. Sam established the National Conference of Israeli and Jewish Rehabilitation, using his considerable smuggling skills to run guns to the Haganah.

Similar posts were awarded to the other Bronfmans. Allan
Bronfman was named president of the Zionist Organization of
Canada, a member of the board of trustees of the Federation
of Jewish Philanthropists and of the national council of the
Canadian Jewish Congress. Abe Bronfman was posted to the
Joint Distribution Committee and also to the national council
of the Canadian Jewish Congress.

Finally, in 1969 the Bronfmans were given the highest reward issued by Her Majesty. Sam was made a Knight of Grace
of the Most Venerable Order of St. John of Jerusalem. His
brother Allan and his son Charles were appointed to the highest
rank, Knight of Justice of the order. These appointments are
emphatically not ceremonial, but are only bestowed on those
who have carried out the most dangerous and fruitful missions
for the British Crown.

The Bronfmans' time had truly come. Sam's children were
welcomed into the Hofjuden elite by intermarriage. Minda married Baron Alain de Gunzberg, himself an extension of the
Rothschild family tree. De Gunzberg sits on the board of Seagram's, is managing director of the Banque Louis Dreyfus, and
controls the Seligman-Louis Hirsch investment house that has
close Rothschild ties. Edgar Bronfman's first marriage, to Ann
Loeb, brought him instantly into a command position within
the Wall Street house of Loeb, Rhoades, and Co. While taking
over the Seagram's main branch in New York, Edgar's marriage clinched the tie to Our Crowd that had begun during
Prohibition. His second marriage, to Lady Caroline Townshend,
was unsuccessful. Phyllis Bronfman married Jean Lambert of
the Belgian banking and mining interests.

Yet, despite their mountains of wealth, despite their hard-
won entry into the realms of good breeding, it would be a mistake to think the Bronfmans were a power in their own right.
When it comes to the question of control, they are treated as if
the money were not their own.

Take, for example, the case of Trizec, the holding company

through which the Bronfman brothers ostensibly run their various corporations, including Seagram's. Since it was formed in 1960, the Bronfmans have never held a majority position within Trizec! Trizec is run by Eagle Star Ltd. of London, a holding company whose directors have been described by one author as "the most notable of the British aristocrats."[16] Evelyn de Rothschild, the earls and dukes who control Lloyds of London and other banking and insurance firms, and leading lights of British intelligence such as Sir Kenneth Strong and Sir Kenneth Keith, all converge on the board of Eagle Star. This extraordinary company owns English Property Corp. Ltd.—whose principal individual shareholder, Laurie Marsh, has gained notoriety in Britain as the Prince of Pornography, for his ownership of the majority of pornographic movie theaters, massage parlors, and red light district real estate in London.[17] English Property Corp. Ltd. owns majority holdings in Trizec.

Neither are the brains behind the Bronfman empire situated between the ears of the members of the Bronfman family. The source lies elsewhere—in the family's law firm of Phillips, Bloomfield, Vineberg and Goodman (now called Phillips and Vineberg).

The personage of family arbiter and attorney Lazarus Phillips, in particular, was a constant sore to Mr. Sam. Born into the upper crust of the Zionist elite, Lazarus Phillips succeeded in gaining all the recognition and respect that Mr. Sam could never seem to win. Phillips was a holder of the Order of the British Empire, a senator in the Canadian Parliament, a member of the board of directors of the Royal Bank of Canada, invited into the exclusive Mount Royal Club as a member, and was a powerbroker for the Liberal Party.

But without Phillips, the Bronfman family empire could not survive. It is likely that through him the Bronfmans received the input of cash that allowed them to proceed steadily from bootlegging to a "legitimate" corporate empire. Certainly it was Phillips who unfroze enough funds under export control from the grip of the Bank of Canada to finance Seagram's wartime expansion into the United States. As the final judge in all family matters—legal and otherwise—Phillips has sat on the board of

Seagram's since 1940 and on every other company and philanthropic front nominally run by Mr. Sam. He is still the codirector of Trizec and the other major Bronfman holding company, Edper (named after Edgar and Peter Bronfman). Phillips is also the expert who managed to get the Bronfmans off every legal hook on which they ever got caught.[18]

Phillip F. Vineberg is part of the Vineberg family of Abraham Moses Vineberg, chairman of the Moses Vineberg Investments firm and the De Hirsch Institute. Cochairman of all the Bronfman holding companies, Vineberg runs the Canadian Israeli Bond Drives and the Canadian Council of Christians and Jews. He is also a member of the Hofjuden elite's Montefiore Club.

Major Louis Mortimer Bloomfield, also of the firm Phillips, Vineberg, and Bloomfield is the most colorful of the Bronfman brains behind the scenes, and this may explain why his name was left out of Peter Newman's 1978 book *The Bronfman Dynasty* (rumored to have been commissioned by the Bronfmans themselves). In addition to his position as a Bronfman family lawyer up to the late 1960s, Bloomfield remained a close banking associate until his death in the mid-1980s. The major was involved in a nest of corporations including the Israeli Continental Company. He was chairman of the Canadian Histadrut Campaign, and a president of the Israeli Maritime League. He also held the post of consul-general in Liberia, under whose flag vast quantities of opium and narcotics are shipped. He was a high-ranking member of the Most Venerable Order of St. John of Jerusalem and ran its subsidiary Canadian Red Cross Ambulance Corporation.

Major Bloomfield also ran Britain's International Assassination Bureau, an entity we will soon examine in detail.

Are They Really Clean?

The answer, of course, is no. Since the days they sent their chickencock across the border to their claim as the world's finest whiskey blenders, the Bronfmans' ties to North America's crime syndicate have never been broken, but merely undergone corporate reorganization. Later, we will analyze their criminal activities at length. At this point, a few examples will suffice.

Take the case of Bronfman family intimate Murray Koffler. A leader of the Jerusalem Foundation in Canada, Koffler was the subject of a major scandal in 1976 when his business associates, Starkman stores, were busted by Canadian police after their pharmacists were caught manufacturing illegal amphetamines and funneling them into the black market.[19]

Charles Bronfman's sister Phyllis Lambert was the subject of a simultaneous scandal over her involvement in Heritage Canada, a government-funded social service program that got caught conduiting drugs onto Canadian college campuses.[20]

In 1975, the Bronfmans again made the front pages when Edgar Bronfman's eldest son Samuel II was reported kidnapped. The case revealed the chief kidnapper to be Sam II's homosexual lover. When the police found them, Sam's kidnappers pleaded that the Bronfman youth had blackmailed them into the hoax as a way of extorting money from his father. The jury agreed; the two abductors were declared innocent of kidnapping, but found guilty of the lesser charge of extortion. The press also aired the kidnappers' pleas that their lives were now in danger for having sung about Sam II.

Since he took over the reins of Seagram's New York branch in the 1950s, Sam II's father, Edgar, has built the Seagram's distilleries network into a multinational global empire. The Bronfmans, for example, have entered into a most profitable business partnership with the Cuban rum Bacardi family. After Fidel Castro took over the island in 1959, the Bacardis switched their base of operations to Puerto Rico and Miami, taking along with them a small army of anti-Castro Cuban exiles. The Bacardis, headed by Manuel Cutilla Bacardi, have been pinpointed by law enforcement agencies as the funders and political controllers of entire networks of Cuban exiles, including terrorist networks. Drug runners in the Bacardi-Cuban exile networks, José Medardo Alvero-Cruz and Antonio Cruz Vásquez, were arrested in 1978 for drug-trafficking in the Caribbean and Mexico.[21]

Seagram's has also staked a conglomerate empire in Mexico. Bronfman's contact is former Mexican President Miguel Alemán, who demanded the revival of casino gambling in Mexico, and who owned and operated Acapulco, until his death in the mid-1980s. In the 1930s, nationalist President Lázaro Cárdenas threw the casinos, and with them Meyer Lansky, out of the country.

In short, wherever Seagram's branches appear on the map, they are thoroughly intermeshed with narcotics runners, gambling, and crime.

The Bronfmans' gutter connections are most visible in the case of Mitchell Bronfman. The son of Knight of Justice Allan Bronfman, Mitchell is reportedly never without his automatic strapped to his shoulder and his stiletto strapped to his left calf. He is on record with the Montreal Police, the Quebec Provincial Justice Ministry, and the Royal Canadian Mounted Police as a kingpin of organized crime in Montreal.[22]

A 1972 report by the Montreal Crime Commission names one Willie Obront as the head of the syndicate in the area and describes the relationship between Obront and Mitchell Bronfman as "almost a brotherly relationship."[23]

This relationship extends into illegal activities in which they have mutually or jointly indulged ... the special kinds of favors they did for each other and the resulting advantages of each in the fields of loan-sharking, gambling, illegal betting, securities, tax evasion and corruption.[24]

"Everything was on a strictly friendly basis," says Mitchell.

Obront first came to the attention of the authorities after two of his Quebec nightclubs used as hangouts for Montreal's underworld were raided. It was revealed that Mitchell's friend was one of Montreal's top movers of dirty money from narcotics, prostitution, and loan-sharking.

Together with Obront, Mitchell Bronfman is a minority partner in the Pagoda North, a Miami restaurant that has been identified by U.S. and Canadian law enforcement agencies as the headquarters for a continent-wide illegal bookmaking syndicate run by Vito Genovese.

Willie Obront was convicted in 1976 of tax evasion and put behind bars. Mitchell Bronfman narrowly averted the same fate.

Another one of Mitchell Bronfman's business partners is Sidney Rosen, who was also arrested and convicted in 1975 for looting thirty-five Canadian and American companies of $7 million through an asset-stripping clearinghouse called Value Trend Holding Company. Value Trend in turn laundered these stolen assets, along with other dirty revenues from illegal gambling, extortion, and narcotics, through Corporate Bank and Trust Company of Freeport, Grand Bahamas and Flendon Ltd., of the same address. Both companies are jointly owned by Rosen and Mitchell Bronfman through another holding company called the Milton Group. When Rosen went off to jail (again leaving Mitchell Bronfman scot free), the $7 million passed unscathed into offshore accounts in Barclays Bank in Freeport.[25]

But the two major corporations out of which Mitchell has operated are the mysterious Securex and Execaire Aviation. Securex was disbanded in 1977 by Quebec Provincial Justice Minister Bedard. Although the Official Secrets Act has kept the reasons behind this hidden, it can be stated with reasonable certainty that Mitchell Bronfman and the company were discovered to be up to their necks in the wave of FLQ (Front pour la Libération du Québec) terrorism that had plagued the province since 1970—not to mention the narcotics trade.

The two directors of Securex at the time of its banning were Donald McCleary and Gilles Brunet, formerly sergeants in the Royal Canadian Mounted Police in charge of the G–4 (Secret Service Division) of the Mounties. Both were fired from the Service in 1972 when it was discovered that they were close associates of Mitchell Bronfman.[26] McCleary and Brunet were in charge of counterterror efforts in 1970 when the FLQ kidnapped a provincial official and a British government officer, an affair that led to the declaration of a state of emergency. The emergency period was used as a pretext to go after the French

Canadian networks that had been built up by Charles de Gaulle
in conjunction with the Vatican to liberate Quebec from British
colonial status.

In point of fact, the FLQ was itself funded by Bronfman family
networks as an extension of earlier efforts to assassinate French
President de Gaulle. The Bronfmans' FLQ option was the North
American version of the British Special Air Service's control
over both the Provisional Wing of the Irish Republican Army
and the British Army's counterterror efforts.

Securex advertises itself as a consulting firm specializing in
"anti-terrorism, anti-kidnapping, and guerrilla warfare training."[27] All things considered, it would have to be regarded as
both a semi-official covert branch of British intelligence in Canada and as a bridge to the criminal underworld.

Its affiliated Execaire Aviation emerges as yet another
scarcely concealed front for crime. Execaire is the largest private charter airline service in Canada, specializing in jet service
for business executives . . . and narcotics.

Is Mitchell Bronfman just the black sheep in the Bronfman
family? It is unlikely. Cemp, the Bronfman family trust, signed
a guarantee for part of Execaire's line of credit at the Bank of
Montreal.

Nevertheless, the publicity the Bronfmans have received over
the years for such exploits as Mitchell's have prevented the
family from receiving that degree of respectability they have
always coveted. In the 1950s, Mr. Sam looked across the fence
at the status of his friend then U.S.-Senator Jacob Javits and
decided that he would buy the ultimate title to confer respectability to his name: He sought to become a senator of the Canadian Parliament. All told, he spent $1.2 million in bribes. The
Liberals took his money but wouldn't give him a seat. The
Bronfman name was still too dirty to be permitted in the ranks
of Canadian politics.

In this regard, the Kennedy family fared much better.

2

The Kennedys: Organized Crime in the Government

There are some facts before the American public that hint at the reality behind the "Kennedy look": Ted's Chappaquiddick disaster, Judith Campbell Exner's revelation that Chicago mobster Sam Giancana had given her to Jack, and the stories of Papa Joe's bootlegging days. The suspicions are there but Americans aren't really sure what the Kennedys are; after all, if they're so dirty, how do they stay so clean?

Dope, Inc. supplies the answer. The Kennedys are clean because, beginning with Papa Joe, they were flea-dipped, scrubbed, and polished by the British to be the respectable front for organized crime. Whether or not a Kennedy crosses the British Crown in terms of policy—as Jack Kennedy did in 1963—does not alter the fundamental content of the political machine that gives the Kennedy dynasty its power. The Kennedy machine is organized crime in government.

Had Ted Kennedy become President in 1980 or 1984, to whom would he have owed debts? The same people who footed the bill. At the top of the list of contributors to Ted Kennedy's 1976 senatorial campaign released by the Federal Election Commission is one Joseph Linsey.[1] A Massachusetts bootlegger who maintained connections to Meyer Lansky from the 1930s, Linsey sits on the board of International Airport Hotel Systems, Inc., a Miami-based company whose board also included Lansky. Hotel Systems is also connected to Resorts International, a firm we will soon hear more of.[2]

Among the business enterprises of Kennedy financier Joseph Linsey are two liquor distributing firms, Crown and Whitehall, and a dog-racing track in Taunton, Massachusetts. Whitehall's chief "salesman" Mike Rocco was described by the McClellan Committee hearings on organized crime, in which both John and Robert Kennedy participated, as a "collection man for the mob."[3] Linsey's chief political lobbyist, Hirsch Freed, is a senior partner in the law firm of Brown, Rudnick, Freed, Gesmar. Freed and all of his law partners are generous donors to the Kennedy campaign fund.[4]

It is the character of Kennedy's friends rather than his own low personal standard of morality that explains why as a leader and former chairman of the powerful Senate Judiciary Committee he came forward as the leading sponsor of federal legalization of marijuana and why he has given his approval to decriminalization of heroin "for experimental purposes." The job of the Kennedy dynasty is to usher in British dope and the criminals who distribute it—through the front door.

The Rise to Power

Papa Joe Kennedy did not have to struggle like the Bronfmans to make a name and money in the world of crime—he was born into it. Joe's father P.J. Kennedy was one of the shanty-town mobsters of late-nineteenth-century Boston.

P.J. began his rise to fortune as a tavern keeper who bought his way into the corrupt Democratic Party machine (a machine that, like the Jacob Astor-Aaron Burr power system in New York, had its roots in opium-trafficking). Once he had obtained a seat on the ward's Democratic Committee at the age of twenty-six, P.J. gave up his tavern and went into the more lucrative wholesale liquor business. Two years later in 1886 he began the first of five consecutive terms in the Massachusetts State Legislature. By 1896, he was part of the triumvirate of Kennedy-Donovan-Corbett, known as the Board of Strategy, which controlled the Democratic organization in Boston. But it was common knowledge that the secret to P.J. Kennedy's political success was his control of the local crime ring, the "McGuire Gang."[5]

Joe Kennedy's mother sadly recognized that, given her husband's notoriety, her social pretensions could never be realized. Kennedy's public image was so filthy that he could not even qualify for entry into the "High Irish" social circles of Boston, let alone the Brahmin "elite" centered around the smuggling Perkins family. She set her hopes on her children. It was Joe Kennedy's marriage into the Fitzgerald family (over the vehement protests of his father-in-law, Boston's High Irish Mayor "Honey Fitz" Fitzgerald) that launched the Kennedy family into high society.

Nevertheless, when Joe Kennedy went to Harvard he was snubbed and ridiculed by his Brahmin classmates, who never missed a chance to remind him of his family's seedy history. Joseph bitterly referred time and again to his rejection by the exclusive "final clubs," Harvard's most desired status symbol.[6]

After World War I, Kennedy was employed by Galen Stone, a partner in the prestigious Hayden, Stone and Co., a Boston Hat Street investment house with ties to the Rothschilds. While there, he made his first contacts with the British aristocracy. Kennedy got wind that one of Hayden, Stone's clients, the British company of Robertson-Cole Pictures, was in the throes of a credit squeeze. The ambitious Irishman went to London to seek the purchase of the company's U.S. distribution affiliate, the Film Booking Company. He was turned down flat. Within a month, however, Lord Inverforth arrived in Boston to take

Kennedy up on the offer. Through a subsequent merger with Ideal Films Ltd., Kennedy founded what was described at the time as the "first genuinely reciprocal exchange of production and distribution facilities between British and American companies."[7] Kennedy's joint ventures with the British soon produced RKO studios.

Lord Inverforth later shows up during World War II working closely with British Secret Intelligence Services chief William Stephenson ("Intrepid").[8] The Robertson Cole deal was Kennedy's first contact with Britain's aristocratic high command.

In 1929, Kennedy joined with Blair and Co., a firm operated by Elisha Walker, later of Kuhn, Loeb, and Jean Monnet, to bid for control of A.P. Giannini's Transamerican Co., the controlling company for the Bank of America. The attempt failed, but Kennedy gained another invaluable contact. Jean Monnet had come to North America to represent his family's liquor business, Monnet et Cie., in dealings with the Hudson's Bay Company. In the period that Kennedy was working with Blair and Co., Monnet was traveling to Shanghai on a financial mission for the League of Nations. Given Monnet's associations with Hudson's Bay, it is likely that more was on the agenda than the financing of Chinese railroads.

Papa Joe also had business liaisons with the seamier side of the illegal distribution market. During his own bootlegging days in Prohibition, Kennedy entered into a coalition with Newark's Reinfeld Syndicate, 50% owned by the Bronfman gang. Joe retained his business dealings with the syndicate thugs until 1946. At that time, in preparation for the launching of his sons' political careers, Joe sold his liquor company, Somerset Importers Ltd., for $8 million to "Renfield Importers"—a revised version of the Reinfeld Syndicate.[9]

As the end of Prohibition approached, Kennedy again turned to London, where Winston Churchill personally approved the grant given to him for the British distillers' franchise for the American market. Through Kennedy's Somerset Importers, Ltd. and Renfield Importers, Kennedy marketed Dewar's scotch, Gordon's gin, Ron Rico rum, and Haig and Haig.[10]

But as Papa Joe made clear early in the game, he was not in

it for the money. His goal was to build a political dynasty, and his wife produced nine children in succession to guarantee it. Churchill's nod of approval and the cash flow accompanying it signaled that the British were ready to take advantage of Joe Kennedy's political ambitions.

Kennedy acknowledged the deal by placing his accumulated fortune in the hands of one of the inner circle of London finance: Lazard Brothers, Ltd. André Meyer, head of the New York branch of that house, became the manager of the Kennedy Estates. Lazard Brothers, Ltd. is owned by Viscount Cowdray (Weetman John Churchill Pearson), who is the cousin of Winston Churchill.

In 1933, Kennedy was appointed by President Franklin Roosevelt to head the new Securities and Exchange Commission. Kennedy's earlier association with the London banking circles had put him on the inside track to conduct a flurry of stock speculation on the eve of the 1929 stock market crash and walk away from it all with a pocket full of cash. When the SEC was created to regulate the market, Roosevelt returned Kennedy's favor of swinging the Boston Democratic machine behind the FDR candidacy at the 1932 nominating convention.

In 1936, FDR appointed Kennedy U.S. ambassador to Great Britain, a post Kennedy wanted more than life itself. As Joe's official biographer explained, "The old American aristocracy, with its Anglophilic leanings—the aristocrats that had rejected Kennedy at Harvard—regarded the post as the nation's highest social office.[11] Kennedy had at last succeeded in giving the Boston Brahmins a kick in the teeth. Once in London, the Royal Family further obliged the funny Irishman by posing with his family in full regalia for the newspapers.

Kennedy quickly attached himself to the most pro-Nazi British aristocrats centered around Lady Astor's Cliveden Set where Roundtable figures such as Lazard Brothers' Lord Robert Brand, the Marquess of Lothian, Fabian George Bernard Shaw, and the opium-trading Sassoon family congregated to dictate Britain's appeasement policy for the British Foreign Office.

Kennedy's antics in Britain soon got back to President Roosevelt. Kennedy's notoriety as a Nazi appeaser—like his father's earlier underworld career—could not be covered over by even the most sympathetic biographer. David E. Koskoff in his commissioned biography of Joe Kennedy reported:

> Kennedy had become intensely anglophilic: "Indeed there are unfortunate signs that Kennedy is going by way of Page." They reported that he was one of the prime exhibits of Cliveden . . . that he was a partisan of England and should be watched carefully. . . .
>
> From the beginning of the Ambassador's career to the end, the spectre of Walter Hines Page haunted Joseph Kennedy. From his position as ambassador to England, anglophile Page had conspired with the British to bring America into World War I. . . . Kennedy resented the fact that his name was always linked with Page. . . . Even Roosevelt said before the outbreak of war, "He's more British than Walter Hines Page."[12]

Kennedy's unswerving loyalty to the British monarchy was rewarded; his daughter, Kathleen Kennedy, the sister of John, Robert, and Edward, married William Cavendish, the Marquess of Hartington. Hartington was the son and heir to the tenth Duke of Devonshire and his wife, Lady Mary Alice Cecil (daughter of the fourth Marquess of Salisbury), the Duchess of Devonshire.

In the hierarchy of the British nobility, the dukes are the highest rank of royalty, taking second place only to the monarchy itself. The Duke of Devonshire is at the center of the interlocking families of the Cecils, Salisburys, and Macmillans who have run British politics since the days of Elizabeth I.

Joseph Kennedy repeated the theme many times: "If Kathleen and her husband were living, I'd be the father of the Duchess of Devonshire (first Lady-in-Waiting to the Queen) and the father-in-law of the head of all the Masons in the world."[13] Later, his son John would marry Jacqueline Bouvier, whose sister Lee married Prince Stanislaus Radziwill, a member of the Polish nobility who traces his titles back over 500 years.

The Radziwill family, which resides in England, established the Order of St. John of Jerusalem in Poland in 1610 and was instrumental in transplanting the order into the United States in the early twentieth century. While serving as ambassador in Britain, Joseph Kennedy was made an initiate in His Majesty's Most Venerable Order of St. John of Jerusalem.

Despite Joseph Kennedy's eventual unceremonious recall from the Court of St. James at the beginning of World War II, the elder Kennedy had succeeded brilliantly in restoring his tarnished reputation. During his sojourn in Britain, he turned over his sons to the British Roundtable for a "proper" education. Joseph Kennedy, Jr. and John F. Kennedy were trained at the London School of Economics, an institution founded by the Fabian Society dedicated to training and recruiting foreign cadre as future British agents within government, business, media, and educational posts in their own countries. The Kennedy brothers were trained by Fabian Society Executive member Harold Laski.

At Harvard, on the Kennedys' return to the United States, further tutoring for son John was secured from Sir John Wheeler-Bennett, the founder and head of the research division of the Royal Institute of International Affairs. Wheeler-Bennett denies that he was the writer of Kennedy's Harvard master's thesis, later published in book form as *Why England Slept*.[14]

There is little doubt that Wheeler-Bennett was aware that he had been entrusted with the training of Britain's future political kingpins in the United States. As he recalls:

I was invited one evening to dine informally at the American embassy. We were a small party, not more than ten, as I recall, and the three eldest Kennedy sons sat in a row on the far side of the table to myself. . . . "I'll tell you about these boys," said the Ambassador to me in his rasping nasal voice, as if they weren't there at all. "There's young Joe, he's going to be President of the United States. And there's Jack, he going to be a university president; and there's Bobby (tapping his nose in a cunning manner), he's the lawyer."[15]

Why the British Killed Kennedy

When John F. Kennedy became President of the United States in 1960, it is reported that André Meyer of Lazard Brothers, Ltd. went around Europe introducing himself as "the real President." Whether the story is true or not, it is the case that the Court of St. James had at least temporarily seized control of the Oval Office.

So had organized crime. The Kennedy machine moved into the Justice Department, specifically Robert Kennedy's Organized Crime Strike Force. The Organized Crime Drive, as it was called, was a highly irregular unit, even according to its nominal chief, Ed Silberling. The section was in fact run by non-lawyer Walter Sheridan, a former FBI man who had worked as chief of the Counterintelligence Section, Special Operations Division, Office of Security, and the National Security Agency. It was Sheridan who had the ear of Robert Kennedy, often as much as three times a day.[16]

According to Victor Navasky's *Kennedy Justice,* the Sheridan crew "had free access to the files of the McClellan Committee. It was in touch with grand juries through the country. It had an undercover air of mystery about it. Its modus operandi was cloak and dagger. . . . Its relations with the FBI were highly irregular in that it received little or no cooperation from the top, yet Sheridan, an ex-FBI man, had a degree of line cooperation in the field that was, in some respects, unparalleled. He actually coordinated FBI agents with his own men—told them where to go when," and, "unlike every other unit of the Justice Department, which is organized around subject areas of responsibility," reports Navasky, "the Sheridan unit's raison d'etre seemed to be not a subject area but a target: Jimmy Hoffa."[17]

If Kennedy himself was obsessed with getting Hoffa, the machine behind him found the campaign a convenient ruse for three reasons. First, it badly damaged the Teamsters, the biggest and strongest trade union in the country, which had consistently used its power to press for industrial growth. Second, the publicity it engendered was a good diversion. And third, it was a good cover for going after local mafiosi who might object to a tightened drug syndicate and the rise of the new black mafia to service the cities. The fanfare around the Valachi revelations served the same purpose.

A look at the ensuing careers of the Kennedy crimefighters underlines the point.

■ Henry Peterson of the Organized Crime and Racketeering Division joined Max Jacobs's Emprise Corporation, a money-laundering outfit.

■ His boss William Hundley and Robert Peloquin of the Criminal Division left Justice, formed their own law firm, and now sit on the board of International Intelligence (Intertel), Meyer Lansky's crime clearinghouse.

■ Stanley Mills, head of the Kennedy Antitrust Division, became general counsel for Max Jacobs's Sportsystems.

■ William O. Bittman, prosecutor for the Justice Department against Hoffa, jointed the board of Sportsystems.

■ David Holloman and Thomas Kennedy of the Organized Crime Division joined the same board.

■ Horace Webb of the department's Public Informational Services Division is the public relations man for Sportsystems.

■ Thomas J. McKeon, member of the Organized Crime Strike Force in Detroit, is assistant general counsel and vice-president of Intertel.

While Sheridan's "Terrible Twenty" burned the small fry, Meyer Lansky and Max Jacobs went untouched. Lansky's biographer, Hank Messick, could even report that "Lansky could deplore the loss of Newport and Hot Springs, but the attack on La Cosa Nostra caused him no loss of sleep. Instead, from 1960 to 1965, he succeeded in keeping his name completely out of the newspapers. That five-year period was for Lansky one of the most active, and profitable, eras he had known."[18]

Double-Cross

Meanwhile, in the White House John Kennedy was being advised by the higher echelons of the same network that had invaded the Justice Department. Almost simultaneously with Kennedy's inauguration, Harold Macmillan moved into 10 Downing Street. Macmillan was himself part of the extended Devonshire family into which Kennedy's sister Kathleen had married. His Canada-based pulp and paper company, Macmillan Bloedel, as noted, was a component of the British Columbia drug-smuggling apparat.[19]

Macmillan's newly appointed ambassador to the United States, David Ormsby-Gore (later Lord Harlech), was also a distant in-law of the President through the Cecil family. Ormsby-Gore had been a close friend of JFK since their days together at the London School of Economics. The British ambassador had daily access to the President. He was the fourth member of Kennedy's inner policy-making core, "ExComm," along with Robert Kennedy and the anglophile National Security Adviser McGeorge Bundy (also a Harvard protégé of the Roundtable's William Yandell Elliott). During the Cuban Missile Crisis, documents show that Ormsby-Gore and Macmillan made most of the minute-to-minute decisions at the point that the United States was on the brink of nuclear war.

Best estimates have it that up through the winter of 1962–1963, British directives to the White House, transmitted through Ormsby-Gore, were carried out with only minor points of difference. That special relationship began to show signs of deterioration during early 1963. Policy differences between the Kennedy and the Macmillan governments began to surface, as the U.S. President took a series of initiatives to launch the National Aeronautics and Space Administration and to buck the Bertrand Russell-McGeorge Bundy military policy of Mutual and Assured Destruction.[20]

The diaries of Macmillan testify that Kennedy had to be intensely armtwisted at the famous Nassau summit in spring 1963 before he would agree to turn over the Polaris missile program to the British.[21] That move precipitated French President Charles de Gaulle's vehement denunciation of the Anglo-American violation of the Atlantic Charter, followed by France's withdrawal from the NATO military command.

During the spring and summer months of 1963, JFK began reversing previous policies. Plans were being prepared to devolve U.S. presence in Southeast Asia. Detente discussions were opened up with the Soviet Union; in the weeks prior to his assassination, Kennedy even sent a secret emissary to Havana to open up talks with Fidel Castro. The Kennedys were showing signs of bucking the machine that had put them in power. The British had him killed. To use the language of a grade-B movie, "Kennedy tried to double-cross the syndicate and he got iced."

It is reported by Kennedy biographer Koskoff that upon JFK's death, Lord Beaverbrook (whom we shall encounter in regard to the International Assassination Bureau) sent a scarcely veiled warning to Joe Kennedy:

> Perhaps he [Joe Kennedy] was a little comforted by the kind note that his dear friend Lord Beaverbrook sent to Rose: "May Joe find solace . . . in the assurance that Bobby will repeat Jack's career."[22]

When Robert Kennedy refused to back off from the track of his brother's assassins and began to prepare his own campaign for the presidency, he too was murdered on British orders.

Playing by the rules of the game is Ted Kennedy's insurance policy. That's what makes him the foremost proponent of dope decriminalization; that's what makes him today's frontrunner for organized crime; that's what makes him the collaborator of the assassins of his brothers.

3

Britain's International Assassination Bureau: Permindex

According to an unpublished manuscript on the assassination of John F. Kennedy authored by "William Torbitt" (an apparent pseudonym), during the spring, summer, and autumn months of 1963, a series of top-secret conspiratorial meetings took place behind well-guarded closed doors at an exclusive resort spot at Montego Bay on the Caribbean island of Jamaica. The location for those meetings was the Tryall Compound, built at the close of World War II by Britain's highest-ranking secret espionage agent, Sir William Stephenson. Reportedly present at various times for the planning sessions were: Major Louis Mortimer Bloomfield, in 1963 still a top officer in Sir William Stephenson's British Special Operations Executive (SOE); Ferenc Nagy, a wartime cabinet minister in the pro-Hitler Horthy government of Hungary and later its Prime Minister; Georgio Mantello, a Rumanian-born Jew who had served as a trade minister under Mussolini; Colonel Clay Shaw, a former officer in the U.S. Office of Strategic Services (OSS) who in 1963 was the director of the New Orleans International Trade Mart; Jean de Menil, a White Russian emigré who at that moment was the president of the Houston-based Schlumberger Company, a heavy equipment manufacturer frequently used as a covert conduit for weapons; Paul Raigorodsky, another White Russian active in the right-wing Solidarist movement. The purpose of the meetings, the manuscript alleged, was to plot the assassination of President John F. Kennedy.

Whether or not the meetings took place as described in the manuscript, the authors of Dope, Inc. have been unable to confirm. But through interviews in the United States and Western Europe and through reviews of the evidence presented before the Warren Commission and before the grand jury proceedings and trial of Clay Shaw in New Orleans, the authors have established links between the named individuals and the Permindex trading company at the center of the Kennedy assassination plot.

Permindex was an obscure international trading exposition company, incorporated in Switzerland and housed in Montreal; Permindex is a contraction of "Permanent Industrial Expositions." Its president and chairman of the board from its inception in 1958 was Major Louis Mortimer Bloomfield. The individuals named as plotting at the Tryall Compound were, at the time, board members, officers, and investors in Permindex.

Each of these individuals was also a longstanding trusted asset of the British SOE. Unlike any other trade expositions company in the world, the employees and investors in Permindex had all been selected for specific operational capabilities that they represented; capabilities that would be indispensable to the conducting of high-level political assassinations.

As we delve into the Permindex international assassination bureau and discover the suppressed facts behind the assassination of President John F. Kennedy, we shall encounter three capabilities in particular already familiar to us as Dope, Inc.

First we shall encounter an international web of dirty money outfits, responsible for channeling millions of dollars in black market revenues into the hands of the professional killers deployed on behalf of Permindex and its SOE control. Not surprisingly, we shall discover that these dirty money channels are hard-wired into the Hongkong and Shanghai Bank-centered apparatus that launders the $400 billion in annual revenues from illegal drug sales.

Second, we shall discover an international band of protected killers, drawn from the ranks of the Nazi and Fascist gestapos of World War II—many now in the employ of the Soviet KGB—from the street-level crime syndicate responsible for the retail distribution of narcotics; and from a secret capability established by the Stephenson organization at the outset of World War II, operating under the cover of missionary activity in Latin America and the East bloc. Their missions? Political assassinations employing high-powered rifles at a distance of 1,000 yards.

Third, we shall encounter a British SOE fifth column embedded deeply into the American official intelligence community. This fifth column, linked directly to Permindex and its chairman Major Bloomfield, represents perhaps the single most crucial component of the international assassination bureau: its cover-up capability. Seventeen years after the assassination of John F. Kennedy, Permindex remains one of the best kept secrets in the world—despite the fact that it has been exposed on more than one occasion as the agency behind high-level political exterminations touching on top political officials of no fewer than three sovereign nations.

Louis Mortimer Bloomfield

At the time of the Kennedy assassination, Major Louis Mortimer Bloomfield was acting on behalf of his superiors in the British Special Operations Executive, including "retired" chief Sir William Stephenson, at that time a permanent resident of the Tryall Compound on Montego Bay, Jamaica.

As president and chairman of the board of Permindex, Bloomfield was the designated chief operations officer for the Kennedy hit.

Who is Louis Mortimer Bloomfield and what had brought him to the point of becoming, by 1963, the unofficial successor to Stephenson as Her Majesty's top secret agent in North America; the man entrusted to carry out the execution of John F. Kennedy, an American President who dared to violate the "special relationship" with the British Crown?

Louis Mortimer Bloomfield was recruited into the SOE in 1938,[1] the year that Stephenson, acting as personal emissary of Winston Churchill, negotiated an agreement with U.S. President Franklin Delano Roosevelt allowing British intelligence to set up shop in the United States and to effectively merge its operations with those of the FBI and military intelligence.[2] Under SOE commission, Bloomfield was given an officer's rank in the U.S. Army and assigned to the newly created Office of Strategic Services (OSS), the wartime predecessor to the Central Intelligence Agency.

As a major in the OSS, Bloomfield was detailed into the Federal Bureau of Investigation as the contracting (recruitment) agent for its counterespionage Division Five.[3] Bloomfield, described by numerous authors and associates as a practicing homosexual, developed a deeply personal friendship with FBI Director J. Edgar Hoover. Through that relationship, Bloomfield was able to retain his powerful position in Division Five long after the end of the war. As late as 1963, when Bloomfield was case officering the assassination plot against John F. Kennedy, he was still a top official in Division Five.

When the SOE "formally" dissolved its U.S. operations at the close of World War II, Bloomfield returned to Montreal, Canada to resume his career as a prominent attorney. He had been a founding partner in the prestigious law firm of Phillips, Vineberg, Bloomfield and Goodman, the firm that represents and controls the Bronfman family's holdings. Bloomfield's name was only removed from the firm's letterhead in 1968, after French President Charles de Gaulle publicly exposed the role of Bloomfield's Permindex company in acting as a conduit for funds into the Secret Army Organization (OAS) to finance the 1962 assassination attempt against him.[4]

From the outset, the British SOE had made a point of operating though commercial fronts. For example, Stephenson set up the SOE command center in the United States in the Radio Corporation of America building in New York City's Rockefeller Center under the sign of an import-export firm.[5]

Montreal attorney and SOE operative Bloomfield created a nest of corporate entities following his return to Canada, all of which served as vehicles for ongoing SOE activity. Among Bloomfield's corporate holdings were the Israeli Continental Corporation; the Canadian subsidiary of the Heineken Breweries of Holland; and Crédit Suisse of Canada, a correspondent bank to the Crédit Suisse of Geneva that was among the holding companies exposed by President de Gaulle's intelligence bureau SDECE as a laundering point for hit money into the OAS.[6] As the Bank of Boston case covered up by U.S. Attorney William Weld demonstrates, today Crédit Suisse is at the center of drug-money laundering.

All of these companies would later be documented as investors in Permindex.

Like his law partner Lazarus Phillips and his former "clients" the Bronfmans, Bloomfield also established himself at the top of the Zionist movement in Canada. Among his numerous honorary positions, Bloomfield is the annual chairman of the Histadrut campaign of Canada. No ordinary charity, the Histadrut owns over one-third of the gross national product of Israel; controls the second-largest bank in Israel, the Bank Hapoalim; and has been caught on more than one occasion laundering money into overseas operations of the Israeli secret service, the Mossad. Some of those funds, passed directly back into Major Bloomfield's Permindex, were also used to bankroll unsuccessful hit attempts against de Gaulle.

Among Bloomfield's other "charitable" activities was his chairmanship of the Canadian Red Cross Ambulance Service, a position traditionally held by a top-ranking knight in the Queen's official chivalric order, the Most Venerable Military and Hospitaller Order of St. John of Jerusalem. As an operating arm of the Sovereign Order, the Red Cross Ambulance Service is an official intelligence arm of the British Monarchy, frequently called upon to carry out espionage and terrorist activities.[7]

In addition to his corporate and "charitable" activities in his native Canada and his continuing post in Hoover's FBI Division Five, Major Bloomfield was given special responsibility following the war to develop the international network of clandestine shipping routes that would be essential to the planned skyrocketing of narcotics traffic, dirty money, and related black-marketeering.

First, Bloomfield assumed the directorship of the Israeli-Canadian Maritime League, a trade association whose significance will become clear shortly. Simultaneously, he became the consul-general in charge of the Western Hemisphere of the African state of Liberia. Liberia was a notorious tax shelter and smugglers' port of call. With no shipping regulations, Liberia—under Bloomfield's consularship—became the flag of convenience under which a sizeable portion of the ships bearing bulk cargos of Far East narcotics are registered. Liberia is also one of the secondary offshore banking centers employed by the directorate of Dope, Inc. The unregulated "banks" of Liberia account for $7 billion in average daily transfers—the vast majority of which are related to black market transfers.

The only other foreign-stationed consul-general for Liberia, as of 1978, was Bloomfield-Permindex associate and former Israeli Mossad official Dr. Tibor Rosenbaum.

One final deployment in the immediate postwar period by the SOE's Major Bloomfield would set the stage for the future emergence of the assassination bureau, Permindex. In 1952, Bloomfield became a ranking official of the United Nations Organization, one of its leading advisers on international law. Bloomfield accomplished this by assuming a position as overseas representative of the International Executive Board of the International Law Association. Established in 1873, the International Law Association was from the beginning an arm of Lord Milner's Roundtable group responsible for developing a code of law compatible with the "one world" designs of Britain's leading oligarchical families. After World War II, the ILA became an officially recognized Non-Governmental Organization of the UNO and its principal advisory body on all matters of international law.

Major Bloomfield's particular area of "expertise" on behalf of the UNO: international terrorism, piracy, and civil aviation. To this day, the United Nations' International Civil Aviation Commission is housed in Montreal, under one of Major Bloomfield's closest collaborators, Gerald Fitzgerald. Fitzgerald, on advisement from Bloomfield, has drafted every United Nations convention on hijacking, piracy, and terrorism. In 1962, the year before the Kennedy assassination, Fitzgerald and Major Bloomfield coauthored a history of political assassinations in the twentieth century, focusing particularly on the activities of the Zionist clandestine army, the Irgun, and its 1940s murder plots against Sweden's Count Bernadotte and Britain's Lord Moyne.[8]

1958: Better than ten years have passed since Major Bloomfield's "official" retirement from the SOE-OSS and his return to his native Canada. Sufficient distance has been created from his past activities as a master spy within Her Majesty's most secret spy army to warrant Major Bloomfield a place on the list of "citizens above suspicion." And so, in 1958, on orders from his superiors at Montego Bay, Bloomfield created Permindex and its international subsidiaries Centro Mondiale and the Italo-American Hotel Corporation to house an international assassination bureau.

The Permindex Board of Directors

At the outset of this chapter on Dope, Inc's international assassination bureau, we looked in on the behind-closed-doors sessions at Tryall in which the Kennedy assassination was planned out. At that time, we were introduced to several members of the board of Permindex. It is worth briefly returning to that board of directors roster to get a closer glimpse of the sorts of individuals recruited by chief of operations Major Bloomfield to carry out the most hideous crimes of the century.

According to corporate records on file in Berne, Switzerland, the following individuals were officially listed as officers and board members of Permindex at the time of its incorporation by Major Bloomfield.

- Louis Mortimer Bloomfield, president and chairman of the board of Permindex;
- Ferenc Nagy;
- Georgio Mantello;
- Roy Marcus Cohn, attorney, New York City, former general counsel to Senator Joseph McCarthy, chairman, American Jewish League Against Communism, president, Lionel Corporation;
- Joseph Bonanno, syndicate boss of Montreal and Phoenix; chairman of the board, Lionel Corporation;
- Jean de Menil, millionaire owner of the Schlumberger company of Houston; married into one of the oldest European banking families deployed to reverse the American Revolution;
- Paul Raigorodsky;
- Count Guitierez di Spadafora, former undersecretary of agriculture to Mussolini; sponsor of the Sicilian Separatist Movement;
- Hans Seligman, banker, Basel, Switzerland;
- Carlo d'Amelio, attorney, Rome, representing the financial holdings of the House of Savoy and the House of Pallavicini; attorney for "circolo Rex"; general counsel Centro Mondiale Commerciale;
- Max Hageman, editor, Munich *National Zeitung;*
- Munir Chourbagi, uncle of King Farouk of Egypt;
- Giuseppe Zigiotti, head of the Italian political party Fascist National Association for Militia Arms;
- Ferenc H. Simonfay, former Nazi collaborator in Hungary; leader of the Solidarist movement;
- Colonel Clay Shaw.

Several of these individuals represented a decade-long asset of the British SOE, called into active service for a very specific role in a very specific series of operations.

Bankrolling an Assassination

In 1967, the French Intelligence Bureau SDECE released the results of a five-year investigation into the 1962 aborted assassination attempt against General de Gaulle, carried out by the rabidly right-wing Secret Army Organization (OAS). While the SDECE report traced the origins of the assassination plot to the Brussels headquarters of NATO and to a specific group of disgruntled French and British generals, as well as the remnant of the old Nazi intelligence apparatus, it also singled out Major Bloomfield's Permindex trading company as the agency responsible for conduiting $200,000 into the OAS to bankroll the attempt. The source of the funds was FBI Division Five, the secret counterespionage branch of Hoover's agency that was run out of the Montreal law offices of Major Bloomfield.

As the result of the de Gaulle exposé of Permindex's role in the OAS hit squads, Permindex was forced to shut down its public operations in Western Europe and relocate its headquarters to Johannesburg, South Africa.

As a related feature of the de Gaulle crackdown, Israel's overseas intelligence branch, the Mossad, was temporarily kicked out of France. We have already noted that Permindex's Major Bloomfield established himself as one of the leading Zionists in Canada and had extended that "charitable" activity to a prosperous business relationship extending into international shipping and banking. We shall now see that Bloomfield's efforts "on behalf of Israel" represented an extension of British SOE penetration and control over sections of the important capabilities that were consolidated with the 1958 creation of Permindex. In the course of unraveling this piece of the Permindex web, we shall encounter those operatives within the international assassination bureau designated with the responsibility of providing the laundered millions of dollars for the financing of political violence.

We begin with Basel banker Hans Seligman. According to a suppressed manuscript on the Permindex assassination cabal, the Seligman Bank of Basel, Switzerland was a subsidiary of Permindex responsible for laundering funds into Major Bloomfield's various operations, one of a dozen such subsidiaries of the Montreal trade expositions company.

Hans Seligman is the last remaining European-based member of the Seligman family that made its vast fortune in the United States during the nineteenth century, first in dry goods and later in banking. The Seligman family of New York was one of the "Our Crowd" group that turned its experience in retailing dry goods into a lucrative black market in booze following the passage of the Eighteenth Amendment.

Like the De Hirsh family, the Seligmans originated in Bavaria as part of the entourage built up around the Wittelsbach and Hapsburg courts. It was the joint efforts of the de Hirsch and Seligman families that led to the founding of the de Hirsh Foundation and the Jewish Colonization Association, the agencies responsible for transplanting the likes of Yechiel Bronfman to Canada as an indentured servant. At the time of the Bronfman migration, the de Hirsch Foundation was being run out of New York City by Jesse Seligman.

By the 1890s, the Seligman, de Hirsh and Gunzberg interests merged with the Louis-Dreyfus family interests. Today all four families share control over the Banque Louis-Dreyfus. As we have seen in earlier chapters, Banque Louis-Dreyfus maintains financial control over the Bronfman family holdings, one of the important fronts for the channeling of the revenues of Dope, Inc. Hans Seligman's placement on the board of Permindex, headed by "former" Bronfman family attorney and financial adviser Bloomfield, constitutes one closed circle through which drug revenues can be passed to finance the activities of Permindex.

In addition to the Seligman Bank of Basel, the unpublished Permindex manuscript lists a number of additional banking entities wholly owned by Permindex. These include: Astaldo

Vaduz of Miami, De Famaco Vaduz of Liechtenstein, and De Famaco Astaldo Vaduz of Geneva.

These entities appear to have amounted to little more than post office boxes serving as money drops in locations where virtually nonexistent banking laws facilitated such blind passes.

Bloomfield ran the Canadian subsidiary of Crédit Suisse, a far more formidable banking institution with deep ties into the financial circuitry behind Dope, Inc.[9]

But the most formidable banking entity in the Permindex family was the Banque du Crédit Internationale (BCI) of Basel, Switzerland, which remained in business until 1974.

Dr. Tibor Rosenbaum, BCI, and Permindex

BCI was the creation of Dr. Tibor Rosenbaum, a Hungarian-born Jew who migrated to Palestine under the sponsorship of the Jewish Agency. Back in Hungary, Rosenbaum had been associated with Dr. Rudolph Kastner, whose activities as a personal collaborator of Adolf Eichmann in sending an estimated 800,000 Jews of Eastern Europe to the gas chambers at Auschwitz created a major scandal in Israel in the early 1950s, and served as the basis for Ben Hecht's famous suppressed book *Perfidy*.

Following Israel's statehood, Tibor Rosenbaum was appointed the first minister of supply and finance for the foreign intelligence branch, the Mossad. In 1951, Rosenbaum was deployed to Geneva, ostensibly as the director of Israeli migration, holding full diplomatic papers. As there was no migration from Switzerland to Israel during this period, speculation that Rosenbaum was already involved in setting up funds-laundering operations on behalf of the Mossad is well-founded. According to a recently published book-length exposé of the Israeli mafia, by *L'Express* journalist Jacques Derogy,[10] Rosenbaum traded his Israeli diplomatic papers for Liberian documents in the mid-1950s on the eve of his launching the Banque du Crédit

Internationale. Rosenbaum incorporated the BCI in 1958, the same year that his fellow "Liberian diplomat" Major Louis Mortimer Bloomfield established Permindex.

According to Derogy, Dr. Rosenbaum was designated as the "Swiss connection" in an international money-laundering apparatus created to facilitate the diamonds-for-dope trade that was to make up an increasingly large share of the foreign trade of Israel. Despite the cosmetic cover provided to Rosenbaum's operations by his Liberian papers, his Banque du Crédit Internationale was so deeply meshed with Israeli high finance and big time politics that when the scandal of Rosenbaum's dirty-money operations broke in Israel in the early 1970s, Israeli Finance Minister Pinchas Sapir immediately resigned, creating a government crisis.

What can be said about Rosenbaum's Swiss laundering operations and how did his BCI intersect the operations of Major Bloomfield's Permindex?

According to a 1967 *Life* magazine exposé, Rosenbaum's Banque du Crédit International was on the receiving end of $10 million in illegal funds, laundered through the World Commerce Bank of Nassau, Grand Bahamas. The Nassau bank was a joint venture of North American syndicate kingpin Meyer Lansky and several of his closest associates in the gambling, smuggling, extortion and dirty money rackets. The World Commerce Bank was managed by Lansky accountant Alvin Malnick. Another official of the Nassau laundering-hole was a Swiss national and well-known Lansky bagman, Sylvain Ferdmann. According to the *Life* magazine investigators, Ferdmann was simultaneously listed as the chief operations officer of Rosenbaum's BCI.[11]

The picture of BCI, however, remains incomplete without the inclusion of yet another board member of Dr. Rosenbaum's Swiss establishment: Ernst Israel Japhet.

Japhet's presence on the board of directors of the Banque du Crédit International brings us full circle back to the London boardrooms of the Big Five commercial banks that command the international narcotics cartel top down.

Who is Ernest Israel Japhet, in addition to being a board

member of the BCI, an entity servicing the black-market money
needs of the Mossad, the Israeli mafia and the "wizard" of North
American syndicate financing, Meyer Lansky? Japhet was, at
the time, the chairman and president of the Bank Leumi, the
largest bank in Israel—a bank that we have already identified
as a critical component of the diamonds-for-dope traffic into
Hong Kong. The current heir of a German banking family that
traces its roots back centuries, Japhet sold the family's trading
company to the Quaker Barclays Bank of London, which in
turn placed him on the board of directors of its thus-created
subsidiary Charterhouse-Japhet. Charterhouse-Japhet, like
the Japhet Company before it, deals exclusively in the diamond
trade between Israel and Hong Kong—trading those precious
stones for the same Golden Triangle opium that launched the
Japhet family's career in international finance 150 years ago.

Joining Japhet as a trustee of Bank Leumi is Baron Stormont
Bancroft, a member of the Samuel family, a former lord-in-
waiting to the Queen of England and the deputy chairman
of Cunard Lines, a shipping company strongly suspected of
shipping large volumes of Far East heroin over its Asian and
Mediterranean routes.[12]

Bank Leumi keeps its hands in the drug trade through its 100
percent-owned subsidiary Union Bank. Ernest Israel Japhet is
the chairman of Union Bank, which handles over one-third of
the world's financing in diamonds.

Bank Leumi was not the only Israeli bank to interface its
operations with the Geneva laundering-hole of Dr. Rosenbaum.
Even more heavily involved in the BCI is the Bank Hapoalim.[13]
The second largest bank in Israel, Bank Hapoalim was founded
as an offshoot of the Jewish Agency. Its founder and present
board director, British High Commissioner Viscount Erwin
Herbert Samuel, belongs to the same Samuel family behind
Bank Leumi and the Cunard Lines. Viscount Samuel presides
as head of the Israel Red Cross, an official branch of the Most
Venerable Military and Hospitaller Order of St. John of Jerusalem—the same order held by Major Louis Mortimer Bloomfield
of Permindex.[14]

According to the already cited Derogy exposé of the Israeli

mafia, Bank Hapoalim figured prominently in the same dia-monds-for-dope apparatus. Illegal revenues from the diamonds-for-dope exchange run between Israel and the Golden Triangle banks of Thailand, would be initially deposited in an escrow account in London, for transfer to protected accounts in Johan-nesburg, South Africa. From South Africa, the same funds would be laundered through the Bank Hapoalim into Dr. Rosen-baum's BCI.

The "South African connection" for this diamonds-for-dope operation, according to author Derogy, was Zwy Peer, the Is-raeli director of the Investors Overseas Service (IOS).

IOS, until its demise in 1975, was indistinguishable from the Banque du Crédit Internationale. Nominally an international mutual fund founded by Bernie Cornfeld, and eventually taken over by Robert Vesco, IOS in reality was a laundering service deploying an army of "salesmen" in every corner of the globe, often carrying phenomenal volumes of cash which the IOS di-rectors claimed were the investment deposits of thousands of small investors. These investors for the most part remained anonymous. According to author Hank Messick, a significant number of the so-called small investors were local operatives of the Meyer Lansky-Israeli mafia apparatus.[15]

The convergence of the drug syndicate and the intelligence services of Great Britain and Israel in the person of Dr. Tibor Rosenbaum is further amplified by a brief look at the Swiss-based banker's other major financial holding, the Swiss-Israel Trade Bank of Geneva.

Among its principal holdings, the Swiss-Israel Trade Bank owns one-third interest in the Paz conglomerate. Owned until the early 1950s by the Rothschild family, the Paz group of corporations maintains a virtual monopoly over the Israeli oil and petrochemical industry, including the vital shipping lines transporting oil and petrochemicals in and out of the Middle East. In 1978, police authorities in New York City seized a Paz ship as it attempted entry into New York Harbor. Police found its hold loaded with liquid hashish.

Sharing the Paz ownership with Dr. Rosenbaum's Swiss-Is-rael entity are Max Fisher, a Detroit, Michigan-based "busi-

nessman-philanthropist" about whom we shall learn a great
deal more in a later chapter; and Sir Isaac Wolfson, a London
department store magnate whose family traces its lineage back
to the thirteenth century. It was Wolfson whose family mantle
provided prestige for the Paz group following its sale by the
Rothschild interests. Sir Isaac was the chairman of the British
Board of Jewish Deputies, the most prestigious and powerful
Zionist organization in the British Empire. More recently, his
son has been a principal policy adviser to British Prime Minister Margaret Thatcher.

The Swiss-Israel Trade Bank, the third owner of Paz, is a
who's who of the combined British-Israeli Mossad apparatus,
beginning with Dr. Tibor Rosenbaum. The manager of the
Swiss-Israel Trade Bank until his recent semi-retirement was
General Julius Klein. We shall encounter General Klein on
several occasions as we unravel the complex web of front companies, offshore banks, and official government services that together comprised the Permindex international assassination
bureau.

As early as 1922, following his service as a U.S. Army counterintelligence officer during World War I, Klein was picked up
by Sir William Wiseman, then head of all British intelligence
operations in the United States and later a neighbor of Sir
William Stephenson at the Tryall Compound on Montego Bay,
Jamaica. Under Wiseman's instructions, Klein was brought
onto the staff of Colonel House, the special adviser to President
Woodrow Wilson who led the U.S. negotiating team at the
Versailles Treaty negotiations. The presidential adviser was a
neighbor of the British spook, and House rarely made a serious
political decision without first consulting Wiseman.

By 1932, the young Klein was on the inside track of the
Anglo-American intelligence establishment. In that year, he
was appointed director of the first anti-subversive section established in the U.S. Department of Justice. This appointment
brought Klein into close working relationship with FBI Director J. Edgar Hoover, and particularly with the FBI's Division
Five. In 1938, Klein's operations, for all intents and purposes,
became a subordinate feature of the British Special Operations

Executive. In addition to his Justice Department anti-subversive role, Klein that year founded a dirty tricks unit of the Jewish War Veterans, the first of several private organizations that he would create as recruiting grounds and intelligence fronts for Stephenson's SOE.

Sir William Stephenson's access to the intelligence facilities of the Zionist movement in the United States and Canada was greatly facilitated by the fact that from 1922, he had employed Chaim Weizmann as his principal adviser on scientific and technical espionage activities. The fact that Stephenson's own mentor, Sir William Wiseman, was a leading figure in the Anglo-Zionist movement also provided the future SOE head with an inside track to the resources and talents of the Zionist networks. According to Richard Deacon, a semi-official historian of British and Israeli intelligence, Stephenson was the single most important figure in establishing the Israeli intelligence services following independence.[16] As we have already seen in the case of Permindex chief Major Louis Mortimer Bloomfield, many of the postwar commercial fronts through which the SOE operated were joint ventures with the Mossad.

In the effort to create an Israeli intelligence apparatus married to the British SOE, Julius Klein would play a major role on behalf of Sir William Stephenson. From his position at the close of World War II as head of the U.S. Army Counterintelligence Corps responsible for Western Europe, Klein—by his own admission—illegally rerouted whole shiploads of medical supplies, trucks, construction equipment, etc. from earmarked destinations in Germany and Austria to the Haganah in Palestine. Throughout the early 1950s, Klein made frequent trips to Israel to aid in the training and structuring of the Mossad. We shall turn our attention once again to General Klein at a later point in our inquiry when he emerges as a principal, background figure in recruiting of the board of directors for Permindex.

Another Rosenbaum associate in the Swiss-Israel operation was Shaul Eisenberg, the top weapons procurer and scientific spy for Israeli intelligence during the 1950s and 1960s. According to the *Washington Post,* Eisenberg was officially the

Mossad station chief in Vienna during much of this period. Born in Shanghai, Eisenberg was the unoffical trade representative for the Israelis in the Far East. Official statistics show that 90 percent of the Israeli business in that region involved sales of diamonds.

Shaul Eisenberg also ran a string of scientific consulting firms in New York City that maintained contracts with the major Canadian firms engaged in the exporting of nuclear technology. These companies have been publicly identified as part of the nest of high technology firms created by the Stephenson SOE following the war.

Completing the board of directors of Dr. Tibor Rosenbaum's Swiss-Israel Trade Bank were:

■ Abe Feinberg, the head of the Americans for Haganah, a thinly veiled front for SOE-Zionist espionage and laundering operations during the pre-independence period;

■ Phillip Klutznick, self-described protégé of Julius Klein and secretary of commerce in the Carter administration;

■ David Graiver, the enigmatic Argentinian banker who was indicted in the early 1970s in New York on charges of bribery and extortion and subsequently disappeared in a mysterious plane crash over Mexico that had federal court officials and investigators debating for years whether or not he was still alive.[17] Indictments were handed down against Graiver after considerable evidence surfaced that he was serving as a "financial consultant" to a number of Latin American terrorist organizations kidnapping American executives and government officials for fantastic ransoms.

How did this enormous international network of black market banking ventures service the operations of Major Bloomfield's "trading company"?

According to the findings of the SDECE, $200,000 in black market revenues were channeled into the Banque du Crédit Internationale accounts maintained by Permindex. Among the sources of those funds was the Bank Hapoalim, the Israeli banking institution owned by the Histadrut, for which Major Bloomfield was the chief Canadian fundraiser.

Those funds were passed onto the New Orleans station chief of the FBI's Division Five, Guy Bannister. From New Orleans, Bannister deployed one of his agents, Jerry Brooks Gatlin, directly to Paris with a suitcase full of cash for hand delivery to the OAS generals.[18] In 1966, at the very outset of the Garrison investigation into the assassination of President Kennedy, Gatlin—who operated a Permindex-Division Five front called the Anti-Communist League of the Caribbean—died when he was thrown out of a sixth-floor window in a San Juan, Puerto Rico hotel. By this time, FBI Division Five spook Bannister had already died under equally mysterious circumstances.[19] Sources in New Orleans reported at the time of Bannister's death that within hours of his demise, agents of Division Five had invaded his office and his home and carted off all of his files. Those documents never materialized again.

Colonel Clay Shaw

There was no coincidence to the fact that the Permindex funds for the 1962 aborted assassination attempt against Charles de Gaulle were laundered through a New Orleans-stationed agent of Division Five. By 1962, New Orleans had already assumed the role of field operations center for the assassination cabal headquartered offshore on the island retreat at Tryall.

The reason that New Orleans assumed a special role in the cabal is that it headquartered the major U.S. subsidiary of Permindex, the International Trade Mart, directed by Colonel Clay Shaw.

Within the overall organizational chart of Permindex, Colonel Shaw maintained two principal roles. Through his International Trade Mart, Shaw retained a secondary capability for washing large volumes of money on an international scale. But first and foremost, Shaw was responsible for "handling" the nest of agents deployed through Permindex's various fronts to carry out the assassination of John F. Kennedy.

By the time that the Kennedy conspiracy was placed on a fully operational footing in the spring of 1963, Colonel Clay Shaw had already put in over twenty years of duty under the direction of Stephenson's SOE.

In order to situate the special role of the New Orleans colonel and the International Trade Mart that he presided over in the Permindex assassination cabal, it is first necessary to return briefly to the Montego Bay outpost of SOE chief Sir William Stephenson and to retrace the process through which the Special Operations Executive turned its wartime capabilities into a postwar fifth column devoted to destroying and capturing the American republic.

As we have already noted, both during and after World War II, it was the modus operandi of the SOE to operate principally through commercial fronts. In 1945, immediately following the "official" curtailment of SOE operations within the territorial United States, Sir William Stephenson founded the Newfoundland Development Corporation in partnership with Newfoundland's top colonial official Jerry Smallwood. (It was not until 1948 that Newfoundland was admitted as a province to Canada). The following year, Stephenson set up BRINCO, an energy exploration company also located on Newfoundland, with financing from Rio Tinto Zinc, an already familiar component of Britain's Dope, Inc. apparatus, and staffing by leading figures from wartime British intelligence. These Newfoundland ventures were the prototypes for the vast string of "offshore" ventures that the Stephenson apparatus would create over the next decades.

In 1949, the same year that BRINCO was launched, Stephenson relocated to Jamaica, where he founded the "retirement colony" at Montego Bay. At the same time, the Stephenson-centered group created the British-American-Canadian Corporation. According to David Ogilvy, another SOE executive who drafted the corporate prospectus, BAC was to be "a profitable company of merchant adventurers." Ogilvy himself became the vice president of the company, with John Pepper, the chief of Stephenson's wartime Washington, D.C. bureau becoming president. Ogilvy subsequently founded the New York City blue ribbon advertising agency Ogilvy & Mather, drawing upon his wartime black propaganda experience as well as his pre-war stint with the Gallup Polls organization.

BAC was financed through the Hambro's financial group in London.

British-American-Canadian Corporation was soon renamed the World Commerce Corporation. By the late 1940s, WCC was doing such a large share of the U.S. and British trade activity into Latin America that one contemporary source commented that if there were "several World Commerce Corporations, there would be no need for the Marshall Plan." Stephenson and company were quietly and systematically building up the infrastructure of trading companies, banks, and shipping lines, etc. through which to conduct their multi-billion dollar opium war against the United States.

By 1946, Colonel Clay Shaw was already a part of that covert command structure. Shaw's association with the Stephenson circle dates back to at least the outset of World War II. At that time, Shaw served as an OSS officer stationed in London. According to Shaw's own testimony, published in *The Kennedy Conspiracy* by New Orleans District Attorney Garrison's investigator Paris Flammonde, he served as an OSS liaison officer to the headquarters of British Prime Minister Winston Churchill. Through that experience, Shaw developed such a feeling of attachment to the British Empire that he seriously considered emigrating to England at the close of the war. It is not difficult to imagine the raving anglophile Shaw (another practicing homosexual in the mold of his Permindex superior Major Bloomfield) choosing instead to assume the role of agent of Her Majesty's government "behind enemy lines" in the United States.

Shaw did return to the United States, to his birthplace New Orleans to assume the directorship in 1945 of the International House/World Trade Center, a "nonprofit association fostering the development of international trade, tourism, and cultural exchange."

Almost immediately, Shaw left the World Trade Center to

found the International Trade Mart, also in New Orleans. Very much a profit-making venture, the International Trade Mart sponsored permanent industrial expositions, focused particularly on the Caribbean region then being "colonized" by the Stephenson World Commerce Corporation.

Was Shaw's New Orleans International Trade Mart a front for SOE activities from the beginning in 1946? It is a fact that in 1958, as soon as Major Bloomfield established his own "permanent industrial expositions" firm, Clay Shaw became a board member and with that, his New Orleans Mart became a subsidiary of Permindex's international arm, Centro Mondiale Commerciale.

What sort of evil design did Shaw and Stephenson share back in 1946 when they launched their International Commerce ventures?

Today, there are over fifty "world trade marts" located in thirty countries around the world. Each of these world trade marts is made up of over 1,000 corporate subscribers.

Since 1968, all of the world trade marts have been hooked together through a massive computerized data bank. That data bank now functions through an intelligence-transmitting satellite system, one of the largest privately owned satellite systems in existence. The satellite-computer control point is maintained by the World Trade Center Association—the offspring of the very New Orleans World Trade Center that Clay Shaw assumed the directorship of at the close of World War II on behalf of the Stephenson SOE apparatus.

The computer-satellite system maintains a tracking of all international trade routes, carriers and rate scales; a virtual inventory and tracking map of every air-land-sea shipping medium and bulk cargo in the world.

Among the fifty-plus world trade marts hooked into the WTCA satellite-computer complex is the Hong Kong World Trade Center—a joint venture of the Hongkong and Shanghai Bank and Jardine Matheson. HKWTC is the single largest and highest-priced chunk of real estate in Hong Kong. Dope, Inc., through this Hong Kong center, thus maintains a transnational tracking system that is more sophisticated and technologically advanced than the capabilities at the disposal of any government attempting to combat its deadly traffic.

History of an Assassination

In 1958, however, Permindex had not yet emerged as an international octopus of trading fronts hooked up through satellite-based computers, possessing the resources for global money-laundering at the push of a button on a computer console. Yet, as court records in New Orleans, Montreal, and Paris document, millions of dollars in "hit money" passed through the Permindex organization to bankroll the most deadly assassination plots of the century.

We have already met the black market bankers, many of them linked to the financial, political, and intelligence establishment of the state of Israel, whose special role in the Permindex cabal involved the laundering of the "hit money" into the hands of FBI Division Five couriers for delivery to the designated assassin teams.

We shall now investigate the second major component of the Permindex assassination bureau, the network of protected killers whose actions have irreversibly shaped the course of history for the last two decades.

Garrison Hands Down an Indictment

In February of 1969 proceedings began in the New Orleans Parish Court in the case of *The State of Louisiana v. Clay M. Shaw*. New Orleans District Attorney Jim Garrison, flouting the findings of the Warren Commission, had gone before a grand jury and successfully petitioned for a murder conspiracy indictment against Permindex board member Clay Shaw.

It would take the mysterious deaths of seventeen key prosecution witnesses and the launching of a nationwide media witchhunt against the New Orleans DA to defeat Garrison's effort to get to the bottom of the assassination of President John F. Kennedy in Dallas on November 22, 1963.

What evidence had Garrison compiled against the New Orleans colonel and his co-conspirators on the board of directors of Permindex?

At minimum, Garrison had "cracked" the Kennedy assassination plot at the operational level; at the level directed by New Orleans case officer Shaw. On March 14, 1967, Garrison brought Perry Raymond Russo, an insurance salesman from Baton Rouge, Louisiana, before a three-judge criminal district court panel. Russo testified that during the middle of September 1963, he had been witness to a conversation between Clay Shaw, David Ferrie and an individual he identified as "Leon Oswald." The topic of the conversation was the assassination of President John Kennedy. In that conversation, Ferrie, an agent of Division Five about whom we shall learn more later, emphasized the importance of using at least three marksmen in order to create a "triangulation of fire." He added, according to witness Russo, that a scapegoat would be required to secure the escape of the actual assassins.

According to the Garrison investigation, the individual introduced to Russo as "Leon Oswald" at the September 1963 meeting, was in all likelihood not the Lee Harvey Oswald charged by the Warren Commission with having conducted the "lone assassination" of President Kennedy. According to the unpublished manuscript by "William Torbitt," the individual (bearing a striking resemblance to the actual Lee Harvey Oswald) was William Seymour, an agent for a Miami-based private detective agency called Double-Chek. Double-Chek, according to "Torbitt," was a U.S. subsidiary of the Rome Centro Mondiale Commerciale, and functioned as a frequently used front for Division Five and CIA activities. Double-Chek was reported to be the CIA channel for weapons into the Bay of Pigs invasion force. Those weapons were provided through the Schlumberger Company of Houston, Texas; the Schlumberger Company whose president Jean de Menil was reported by "Torbitt" to have been present at the Tryall Compound on Montego Bay for the meetings at which the Kennedy "hit" was planned.

Seymour, according to the "Torbitt" manuscript, was one of several individuals responsible for impersonating Lee Harvey Oswald in the several months leading up to November 22, 1963. Seymour traveled throughout Texas, into Mexico under the name "Lee Oswald." He left a trail of witnesses who would testify that they had spoken with "Oswald," that "Oswald" was an avowed Cuban Communist sympathizer, and that "Oswald" had made statements that in retrospect pointed strongly toward his intention to kill the President of the United States.

Seymour and the other "Lee Oswalds" were deployed under the direction of FBI Division Five southern chief Guy Bannister, the same Bannister who oversaw the laundering of $200,000 in Permindex money into the hands of the OAS generals in France.

According to evidence presented in the course of the Garrison inquiry into the Kennedy assassination, Clay Shaw, Georgio Mantello, and Ferenc Nagy, all of the board of directors of Permindex and its subsidiary Centro Mondiale Commerciale, were in place in New Orleans, Dallas, and Los Angeles on November 22, 1963, handling aspects of the assassination and coverup. That deployment had been set by Major Bloomfield several months earlier. Evidence gathered during the Garrison grand jury and published by Garrison investigator Paris Flammonde, established that several members of the Permindex cabal were present at the airport restaurant in Winnipeg weeks before the assassination in Dallas to review the final details of the plan. Witnesses identified one of the individuals at the Winnipeg airport as Major Louis M. Bloomfield.

Who were the assassins deployed to carry out the "triangulated firing" on President Kennedy in Dallas on November 22? According to the "Torbitt" papers, the assassins—seven expert riflemen in all—were part of a special team of the most expert killers in the world that had been put together in 1943 at the combined initiative of FBI Director J. Edgar Hoover and SOE Commander Sir William Stephenson. Members of that team

would be implicated in the assassinations of Reverend Martin
Luther King, Jr. and Senator Robert F. Kennedy.

We have identified a number of the specific individuals implicated in the actual execution of John Kennedy. We have traced
their personal chain of command into the FBI's Division Five
and into the board of directors of Permindex. To fill out the
picture, however, it is now necessary to delve further into what
particular operational capabilities these individuals represented. As we probe these protected assassins, we shall return
over and over again to the unavoidable fact that Dope, Inc.
killed Kennedy.

The Solidarists

Three of the principals in the Permindex assassination of
John F.Kennedy were Eastern European and White Russian
emigrés. Each of these individuals, Jean DeMenil, Ferenc
Nagy, and Paul Raigorodsky, was a leading figure in the Solidarist movement of fascists.

As we have already noted, Ferenc Nagy was a minister in
the wartime Horthy government that ruled Hungary on behalf
of Adolf Hitler. After the war, Nagy was himself briefly installed as prime minister during 1946–47. Nagy resigned from
that post with a telephone call placed from the lobby of a Swiss
bank where he had just opened up a sealed account with the
government funds he had looted on his way out of Hungary.

On his departure from Hungary, Nagy immediately became
involved in the Solidarist movement.

What are the Solidarists?

The Solidarists were Eastern European and White Russian
feudalists and fascists, predominantly former officials of the
wartime "Quisling" governments of Eastern Europe and veterans of the Nazi eastern front intelligence apparatus.

By no later than 1943, as a part of the Yalta process accepted
by FDR, both the Soviet and Anglo-American intelligence services had begun recruiting from the ranks of the most rabid

Nazis for postwar intelligence work. (Anglo-Soviet cooperation in such projects actually reflected a longstanding deal struck between Churchill and members of the Soviet Cheka of Felix Dzherzhinsky during Lenin's lifetime.) Among those recruited were the Eastern European Solidarists who became an all-purpose asset of combined British and Soviet networks in the postwar period. Among the services rendered by these Eastern Nazis was the penetration of right-wing circles in the West.

This infiltration based on the early Bolshevik Trust operation, was facilitated by the severe shortcoming of U.S. intelligence agencies in particular, in understanding the Russian Orthodox Church. The ROC is an integral part of the Soviet state apparat, integrated into the overseas operation of the KGB. Many Russian and Eastern European exiles picked up by British Intelligence "on loan," function as shared assets of Moscow and London. It would be through this channel that Moscow, too, would add its endorsement to the plot to kill JFK. Agencies such as Permindex function as derivative agencies integrating shared objectives of multiple states—with one state, in this case Britain, directing the on the ground operation and the cover-up. Were such an operation as the JFK hit to be carried out in Eastern Europe or the Soviet Union, it would be the KGB rather than the SOE directing the derivative agency.

Among the leading components of the Solidarist movement was a highly professional espionage, sabotage and assassination network called Narodnyi Trudovoy Soyuz ("National Alliance of Solidarists"). Founded in the late 1920s out of the old Menshevik circles in Russia, NTS functioned as one of British secret intelligence's premier spy rings inside the Soviet Union. NTS was bankrolled by Royal Dutch Shell chairman Sir Henry Deterding and by Vickers Arms president Sir Basil Zaharoff.

At the close of World War II, NTS established offices in Munich and New York City. From 1939, the principal Western financial backing to the NTS and all of the other "Solidarist" groupings was provided through the Tolstoy Foundation, a self-described refugee relief and cultural fund. The current office of the Tolstoy Foundation in New York City is located in a West 57th Street building that has been the property of the British

SOE since the middle of World War II, when it housed the offices of a dozen front companies all involved in smuggling arms and other military equipment to the Haganah in Palestine. In 1978, one of the Tolstoy Foundation's neighbors in the West 57th Street office building was Julius Klein Associates, the public relations company owned by the same General Julius Klein we have already encountered in our investigation into the dirty-money branch of the Permindex organization.

Among the officially listed board members of the Tolstoy Foundation since the early 1960s height of Permindex activity were Paul Raigorodsky and Jean DeMenil.

Raigorodsky was the owner of Claiborne Oil Company of Baton Rouge, Louisiana. He later became an official United States government liaison officer to NATO.

Jean DeMenil, the millionaire owner of the Schlumberger Company of Houston, was one of the principal financial "angels" behind the cultural activities of the Tolstoy Foundation and its allied Solidarist movement. Following the Russian Revolution, DeMenil's family fled their native country, winding up in France. There, Jean DeMenil married into the powerful Schlumberger family of the de Neuflize, Schlumberger, Mallet banking empire.

As Anton Chaitkin has documented in *Treason in America,* the Mallet-de Neuflize Swiss financial networks have been at the center of evil operations against the republican institutions of the United States since the time of the French Revolution. In November 1981, Mme. Dominique Schlumberger, the wife of Jean DeMenil, hosted a gathering of the fanatical Muslim Brotherhood in Houston, Texas—to celebrate the Brotherhood's assassination of Egyptian President Anwar Sadat. It is no exaggeration to say that the Schlumbergers have been involved in every derivative assassination of political significance for the past 200 years.

In the 1950s, Schlumberger diversified into the oil diagnostic equipment industry. The company created for that purpose is now the largest company in the field worldwide, accounting for the production and sale of 50% of all of the equipment in existence. In 1958, son-in-law Jean DeMenil became president of the company, headquartered in Houston. That company, as we noted earlier, served as a weapons conduit for the CIA and FBI Division Five. Those smuggling operations were conducted in conjunction with the Double-Chek Company of Miami, Florida.[20]

During the mid-1960s, de Gaulle's intelligence services established that the de Neuflize, Schlumberger, Mallet Bank was channeling funds to Jacques Soustelle to bankroll OAS terrorist activities.

The American Council of Christian Churches

One of the principal agencies through which the Solidarist movement maintained contact with its operatives worldwide was the Old Orthodox Catholic Church of North America and its affiliated Synod of Bishops of the Russian Orthodox Church Outside Russia. This splinter church out of the Russian Orthodox Church had been established originally as a front for British intelligence espionage activities inside Russia following the Bolshevik Revolution and retained that function in North America after many of its operatives had relocated to the West following World War II. Throughout this period a section of Soviet intelligence maintained equal control over the network. This Anglo-Soviet deal came to be known as the Trust.

The Old Orthodox Catholic Church of North America was an affiliated Church of the American Council of Christian Churches (ACCC), an umbrella organization nominally representing those traditionalist churches of all denominations that opposed the ultra-liberal outlook of the World Council of Churches and its U.S. subsidiary National Council of Churches.

Many "conservative" churches are to this day affiliated with the ACCC for precisely this reason stated above. However, there is another side to the ACCC that prompted District Attorney James Garrison to identify it as one of the agencies deeply involved in the Kennedy assassination conspiracy; and to issue an indictment against the ACCC's West Coast Director E.E.

Bradley, on charges that he aided Colonel Clay Shaw in assassinating the President.

In 1941, J. Edgar Hoover, in consultation with British SOE head Sir William Stephenson and Division Five recruiter Louis M. Bloomfield, arranged for his close friend Reverend Carl McIntyre to found the American Council of Christian Churches. McIntyre was already a contract agent of Hoover's FBI Division Five. The ACCC was to conceal an extensive espionage and intelligence unit to be deployed thoughout the United States, Canada, Mexico and Latin America. The spies and saboteurs were to operate under the cover of Christian missionaries.

As part of the ACCC espionage net, Hoover, Stephenson, and Bloomfield created a secret assassination unit in 1943 under the direction of ACCC Minister Albert Osborne. It is not clear that McIntyre was ever let in on this sinister aspect of the ACCC by his "friend" Hoover. The unit consisted of twenty-five to thirty of the world's most skilled riflemen. It was housed in a missionary school for orphans in Puebla, Mexico. Up through at least 1969, the special "kill unit" remained intact under the personal supervision of J. Edgar Hoover, operating through his trusted agent of thirty years, Albert Osborne.

According to author "Torbitt," it was Osborne and a team of seven expert riflemen from the Puebla "kill unit" who carried out the assassination of John F. Kennedy in Dallas on November 22, 1963.

The records of the Warren Commission establish that Albert Osborne had been a charter member of the ACCC. In 1942, while working for the Hoover-Bloomfield Division Five, Osborne had directed a Nazi blackshirt group called the Campfire Council in the rural area around Knoxville, Tennessee. At that time he had nearly been arrested following an incident in which he burned an American flag in protest against the U.S. entry into the war against Nazi Germany. He shortly thereafter left Tennessee to relocate to Puebla, Mexico.

Garrison documented that on October 10, 1963, Osborne had visited New Orleans, making three stops in town. First he visited the offices of Clay Shaw at the International Trade Mart building. Later the same day he visited the offices of FBI

Division Five courier Jerry Brooks Gatlin, whom we encountered earlier in probing the 1962 assassination attempt against French President Charles de Gaulle. Osborne's final stop in New Orleans was at the office of FBI Division Five southern chief Guy Bannister, at 544 Camp Street.

From New Orleans, Osborne traveled directly to Mexico City where, according to the records of both the Garrison investigation and the Warren Commission, he was seen repeatedly in the company of the "Leon Oswald" whom we met earlier in New Orleans with Clay Shaw and David Ferrie.

This circle of assassins closes a bit further as we return to the case of yet another Division Five operative who maintained a cover as a priest in the employ of the American Council of Christian Churches: David Ferrie.

In 1946, Ferrie dropped out of a Roman Catholic seminary in Ohio and joined the Byelorussian Liberation Front, simultaneously being ordained as a priest in the Old Orthodox Catholic Church of North America, an agency we have already identified as a front for the Solidarist movement, the KGB, and FBI Division Five. Ferrie was subsequently redeployed to the southern region of the FBI, where he operated as a Division Five recruitment officer (placing him under the direct jurisdiction of Major Bloomfield).

According to testimony before both the Warren Commission and the Garrison grand jury, given by FBI operative Jack Martin, Lee Harvey Oswald was recruited into the FBI Division Five in 1956 by none other than David Ferrie. While nominally in the Marine Corps, Oswald received special training in covert espionage activities at the Naval Intelligence School on the Memphis Naval Base. One aspect of this training included special instruction in the Russian language, provided by an agent of the Solidarist movement operating in San Francisco under the cover of the Federation of Russian Charitable Organizations, a West Coast branch of the Tolstoy Foundation.

From 1956 until his untimely death in the basement of the Dallas Police headquarters in November 1963, Lee Harvey Oswald had been on a secret Division Five payroll, maintained through a secret account concealed in the budget of the Immigration and Naturalization Service, a unit within the Department of Justice.

During the six-month period leading up to his murder in Dallas, the real Lee Harvey Oswald had been operating out of New Orleans and Dallas under the immediate supervision of Division Five regional director Guy Bannister. In fact, the New Orleans headquarters of the pro-Castro Fair Play for Cuba Committee, a group that Oswald actively participated in during 1963, was located in the same Camp Street office building that housed Bannister. Unknown to Oswald, his "infiltration" into the pro-Castro grouping on behalf of Division Five had a far different purpose than he imagined; a purpose that would become clear only after he assumed the role of the "patsy" that David Ferrie had discussed with Clay Shaw and William Seymour.[21]

The Lionel Corporation Connection

We have now seen two components of the network of protected killers who carried out the assassination of John Kennedy on behalf of Permindex. In the case of both the Solidarists and the American Council of Christian Churches, we have seen the fruit of Sir William Stephenson's wartime penetration of the national security apparatus of the United States.

One further note must be made here concerning Stephenson's wartime activities as they would later surface in the Permindex assassination plot against Kennedy. Stephenson oversaw the recruitment of U.S. organized crime figures into the SOE-OSS during World War II. The best-known case in point was the "rehabilitation" of convicted drug runner, pimp and suspected murderer Charles "Lucky" Luciano. Luciano was dispatched to Sicily under joint SOE-OSS direction to reconstitute old networks that had been dispersed or expatriated during the Mussolini period.[22] In this effort, Luciano would actively collaborate with Count Guitierez di Spadafora, a board member of Permindex.

Luciano has been widely identified as the case officer on the scene in Sicily for the 1962 assassination of Italian oil minister and close de Gaulle collaborator Enrico Mattei.[23]

Mattei died when his plane went down over the Mediterranean after having been tampered with during a brief, unscheduled stopover at an obscure airport in Sicily.[24] According to sources, the decision to go with the plane sabotage was made by Luciano only after the options of hiring an OAS hit team or an American "leftist" controlled by a Texas oil company had been rejected as too politically explosive. The Texas oil company in question was an investor in Major Bloomfield's international trade expositions firm.

Luciano was by no means the only syndicate figure coopted into the employ of Permindex.

According to official incorporation papers on file in New York City and Berne, Switzerland, mob attorney Roy Marcus Cohn and Montreal crime boss Joseph Bonanno were both personal stockholders in Permindex through their ownership of the Lionel Corporation of Hillside, New Jersey.

At the time of Permindex's initial incorporation, 50% of the corporate stock was purchased by Major Bloomfield. A significant minority position was purchased by Lionel Corporation. Several years before the Permindex investment, Lionel had been bought up by Cohn and Bonanno. Sources indicate that the Lionel buy into Permindex was financed through a $600,000 "loan" that Cohn arranged through contacts in Hong Kong. New York City corporate records show that as of 1958, Joseph Bonanno was the chairman of the board of Lionel and attorney Roy Cohn was the president.

Lionel was principally involved in defense contract work. At the same time the nest of corporate fronts was used to carry out other "business" on behalf of Major Bloomfield's trade expositions company in which, as we noted, Lionel had been an enthusiastic investor.

At the end of 1963, Cohn, et al. sold off Lionel and all of its subsidiaries. One of the most lucrative pieces of the Lionel "empire," the Intercontinental Corporation of Garland, Texas, was sold to Robert Vesco. It became one of Vesco's earliest financial scores.

It was the same Intercontinental Corporation that author "Torbitt" identified as the front through which a group of Cuban exiles, all veterans of the Caribbean gambling and narcotics syndicate and the Bay of Pigs paramilitary operation, were assigned to Permindex board member Ferenc Nagy to play supporting roles in the assassination of John Kennedy.

We have already seen how Sir William Stephenson and a coterie of SOE spooks moved in on Montego Bay at the very close of World War II and built that spot up into a cross between paradise and Fort Knox. In the case of Acapulco, the guiding figure behind its postwar emergence as a watering hole for the super-rich and the super-secretive was former Mexican President Miguel Alemán, himself a central figure in the international narcotics and assassination cartel.

It was during Alemán's tenure as interior minister (1940–46) and President of Mexico (1946–52) that J. Edgar Hoover's Division Five was given carte blanche to set up shop in that country. Combined SOE-Division Five operations were set up all over Mexico and very few were shut down at the end of the war. Reverend Osborne's Christian boys school has already been identified as one such case in which a "hundred-year lease" was signed between Alemán and SOE-Division Five.

When President Alemán formally retired from politics in the 1950s, he built up a vast real estate empire in Mexico that today includes a string of resort hotels, among them one of the largest resort spots in Acapulco.

Not coincidentally, all of Alemán's hotel acquisitions are managed by the Canadian Pacific Corporation—the biggest covert importer of Golden Triangle narcotics into North America and a heavy investor in the Caribbean islands that house some of the most important black market money houses in the Dope, Inc. international portfolio.

Among Alemán's other major holdings is a lion's share of the stock in the fifth largest company in Mexico, Tavos de Acero de México (TAMSA). The director of TAMSA, Bruno Pagliai, is the cousin of Princess Beatrice of Savoy, herself a resident of Mexico and a frequent guest at Alemán's own Acapulco jet set parties.

It is through two Alemán confidants that the Mexican end of Dope, Inc. begins to emerge more clearly. Alemán's personal banker and one of his most intimate friends is Max Schein, president of the Banco Mercantil de México. Schein's bank is the correspondent bank to Bank Leumi, the Israeli banking giant that we have already encountered as a major laundering vehicle for the revenues of international dope traffic. Schein is the chairman of the Sociedad Technión de México, the local branch of the Israel Technion Society—the Mossad's overseas scientific espionage front. Among the board members of the Technion International is Major Louis Mortimer Bloomfield of Permindex.

Alemán's other, far more exposed flank into Dope, Inc., is Gonzalo N. Santos, a former aide and well-publicized personal friend of the ex-President. Santos was a business partner of a Guadalajara-based Cuban exile named Alberto Sicilia Falcón. Falcón, once an asset of the Division Five apparatus in Miami and later Mexico City (and also widely believed to be on the payroll of Cuban intelligence, DGI), was arrested in 1975 as the head of a major heroin-importing ring that stretched from Thailand to Turkey to Marseilles. The Falcón ring had an entire fleet of private planes that ran drug pickup and dropoff routes throughout Latin America into the United States. That ring also ran a string of heroin laboratories.

While Falcón's associate and Alemán staff officer Santos survived the 1975 bust unscathed, he was the subject of a 1977 Mexican Senate inquiry into the guns-for-dope traffic across the United States-Mexican border. Santos was labeled as the major conduit of illegal weapons acquired in the United States and smuggled into the hands of some of the leading oligarchical families in Mexico. Many of these weapons were believed to have been subsequently passed into the hands of the Liga 23 de Septiembre, Mexico's equivalent to the terrorist Italian Red Brigades.

The Coverup

As we unravel the web of government agencies, media channels, and private spook armies that were set loose both immediately after the Kennedy assassination, and once again when New Orleans DA Garrison launched his own independent probe into the Clay Shaw cabal, we shall discover that the cover-up of the Kennedy plot is perhaps the single most damning piece of evidence pointing to a high-level conspiracy behind the death of the President. Once again, we shall discover the guiding hand behind the operation to be that of Dope, Inc.

Immediately after the assassination, there were more than six months' active disruption efforts against the investigation on the part of a very special secret agent of the national security establishment. The agent was Walter Sheridan, the man that Attorney General Robert F. Kennedy had earlier entrusted to head up the highly irregular "Get Hoffa" unit of the Department of Justice. Despite such appearances of closeness to the Kennedy family machine, strong evidence suggests that Walter Sheridan had already been a longtime asset of the British SOE circuitry inside the U.S. intelligence establishment at the time of his "recruitment" into the Kennedy camp in the late 1950s.

Walter Sheridan, after graduating from the Jesuit-run Fordham University and briefly attending Albany Law School, was recruited into the Federal Bureau of Investigation, where he worked for four years. From the FBI, Sheridan moved over to the newly established National Security Agency. The NSA was established in the early 1950s as the most secretive, high technology-oriented snooping agency in the U.S. government. To this day, for example, the NSA is the one intelligence service that operates under a total Official Secrets Act screen. Neither the Congress nor any other federal agency has oversight or even access to information concerning the NSA.

Walter Sheridan evidently already had heavy backing. He was appointed chief of the Counterintelligence Section, Special Operations Division, Office of Security of the NSA. He was subsequently appointed assistant chief of the NSA Clearance Division.

The NSA had been an outgrowth of the sophisticated telecommunications and coding operations developed by the Allies during World War II. In this effort the United States had been thoroughly trained by the British Special Operations Executive. Early in the war, Sir William Stephenson had established a special "code breaking" unit at Blechley Park, England, which served as a training center as well as an encoding unit employing a select group of Americans and Englishmen. Among the Americans trained at the Blechley Park center were Robert Sarnoff and William Bundy. Sarnoff was the son of General David Sarnoff, the founder and president of the Radio Corporation of America (Robert Sarnoff would replace his father as president on the latter's retirement during the early 1950s) and a wartime member of the SOE elite in the United States. Bundy would later become the editor of the Council on Foreign Relations' quarterly journal *Foreign Affairs* while his brother assumed the National Security directorship under John F. Kennedy.

After the War, Sarnoff's RCA became the technological core of the capability that later was brought under top secret government control as the NSA. In that sense, the NSA is perhaps the branch of the U.S. intelligence establishment most directly run by the Stephenson SOE apparatus.

Sheridan's high-level placement in the NSA Counterintelligence Division—the unit most closely interfaced with the FBI Division Five—belies the popular idea that Sheridan was first and foremost a Kennedy family loyalist.

In 1958, a "church friend" introduced Sheridan to Robert Kennedy, who immediately hired the NSA veteran as the special investigator for the Senate Rackets Committee, the "McClellan committee" that RFK was then serving as general counsel. When John Kennedy was elected President, Sheridan was appointed "confidential assistant" to Attorney General Robert Kennedy—a position that placed him in the inner circle of both the Justice Department and the White House (where he maintained a secret office adjacent to the Oval Office).

As "confidential assistant" to RFK, Sheridan created the "Get Hoffa" unit of the Justice Department. According to sources who served close to Robert Kennedy at that time, the "Get Hoffa" unit rapidly became a private fiefdom of Sheridan that even the Attorney General could not penetrate.

Kennedy Justice Department historian Victor Navasky described the Sheridan unit in the following way: "Its modus operandi was pure cloak and dagger. . . . Sheridan's relations with the FBI were highly irregular, in that it received little or no cooperation from the top, yet Sheridan, an ex-FBI man, had a degree of line cooperation in the field that was, in some respects, unparalleled. He actually coordinated FBI agents with his own men—told them where to go and when, and they went."[25] Sheridan had similar access to the resources of the Internal Revenue Service, the Secret Service, the U.S. Marshals, and the Alcohol, Tobacco and Firearms Division of Treasury. In effect, Sheridan replicated the operational capabilities and the targeting methods of the wartime SOE. Sheridan's private army replicated the methods of the SOE in another significant area. In addition to the "official" channels that Sheridan was able to navigate through every federal agency even remotely involved in intelligence and enforcement, he apparently created a nest of clandestine agencies—under corporate cover—that were deployed to carry out those special operations that were so flagrantly illegal that they could not even be remotely associated with the government.

According to author Jim Hougan, Sheridan created a private investigative agency known as "Five Eyes": International Investigators Incorporated of Indianapolis, Indiana. Although the firm was officially incorporated on October 3, 1966 (two years after Sheridan left the Justice Department), Five Eyes maintained offices in Indianapolis, Chicago, Detroit, Louisville, Nashville, Memphis, and Minneapolis by no later than fall 1961. For its first five years of existence, no corporate records existed anywhere in the United States even suggesting its existence.[26]

Sheridan's Five Eyes (also frequently referred to as Three Eyes, for International Investigators, Inc.) went out of business in the late 1960s at the same time that another Three Eyes was being founded by some of Sheridan's top operatives in the "Get

Hoffa" unit. This Three Eyes, International Intelligence, Incorporated, is more commonly known as Intertel, the private security arm of the Caribbean gambling and dope center known as Resorts International. We shall return to this offshore paradise in our next chapter.

In February 1967, Walter Sheridan was hired by the National Broadcasting Company (NBC) as an "investigative journalist" attached to the NBC White Paper television documentary series. Sheridan's assignment for NBC? To do a special television report on the investigation into the assassination of President John F. Kennedy that had just been launched by New Orleans District Attorney Jim Garrison. By July of that year, Sheridan would be indicted by Garrison on four separate charges of public bribery—all revolving around Sheridan's efforts to wreck the Garrison probe.

According to evidence submitted by Garrison, Sheridan had engaged in flagrant witness-tampering aimed at both publicly discrediting the Garrison probe and preventing key witnesses from appearing before the New Orleans grand jury.

One of the witnesses targeted by Sheridan was the Baton Rouge insurance salesman Perry Raymond Russo, whom we met earlier as the "fourth man" in the assassination planning session convened by Clay Shaw.

On June 19, 1967, Assistant New Orleans District Attorney Andrew J. Sciambra delivered a memo to Garrison proving that Sheridan had used his NBC team to harass Russo on a round-the-clock basis, had gotten to Russo's employers at Equitable Life Insurance to pressure them to relocate Russo outside of the Louisiana jurisdiction of Garrison, and had succeeded in smuggling Russo out of the state for a "vacation" in California. Once out of Garrison's hands, Russo was to be put on nationwide television to denounce Garrison for having "doctored" his testimony to create a phony conspiracy case against Clay Shaw.

The Sciambra memo further reported that the NBC White Paper crew was working closely with a research team from the *Saturday Evening Post* on the "Get Garrison" operation. The *Saturday Evening Post* had just been purchased by Bert SerVaas of Indianapolis. SerVaas's name appeared in October 1966 on the incorporation papers of International Investigators, Incorporated as its president.

A second bombshell exploded in the face of the Sheridan operation on August 19, 1967 in a Chicago courtroom. There, an official of the International Brotherhood of Teamsters, Zachary Strate, testified that he had been offered a deal by Sheridan. In return for his joining Sheridan in the propaganda blitz against Garrison, Strate would be provided with classified government documents proving that his conviction on extortion in a case involving Teamster president and Sheridan target Jimmy Hoffa, had been obtained through the use of illegal wiretaps.

Extortion, blackmail, kidnapping, bribery; these were not the only weapons unleashed in the war against Garrison. By the time of the 1967 Garrison probe, over a dozen key witnesses had died under mysterious circumstances. Guy Bannister, the FBI Division Five chief in New Orleans, was dead. Lee Harvey Oswald was dead, shot at point-blank range before a nationwide television audience in the basement of the Dallas Police headquarters. His assassin, Jack Ruby, far from being the "distraught good samaritan," had been a business partner of Guy Bannister and David Ferrie in a series of Cuban casino ventures before the fall of Batista; and had been involved in the Schlumberger-Double-Chek gun-running adventures, first into Fidel Castro's forces and later into the anti-Castro army put together by the CIA after the Cuban President's turn to the Soviet Union.

David Ferrie was also dead, the victim of a "suicide" overdose of narcotics on the very eve of his appearance before District Attorney Garrison's probe. According to Jules Rocco Kimble, a witness before the Garrison probe, he and Jack Helms had entered the Ferrie apartment just hours after the former Division Five contract employee had died and removed a file cabinet full of documents. Kimble and Helms, both admitted members of the Ku Klux Klan, then fled to Canada. Their flight, and their future lodgings and safety, had been guaranteed by Walter Sheridan of NBC. Kimble "coincidentally" showed up in the files of the House Select Committee on Assassinations as a neighbor of James Earl Ray, when the assassin of Martin Luther King fled New Orleans for Montreal after his jailbreak.

Sheridan's blast at Garrison did eventually air on NBC national television and did serve as the trigger mechanism for a barrage of attacks on the New Orleans DA from the national media.

NBC was from its founding a wholly owned subsidiary of the Radio Corporation of America. At the time of the airing of the NBC White Paper on Garrison, the president of NBC was Robert Sarnoff, the wartime veteran of Sir William Stephenson's SOE retreat at Blechley Park, England. In retrospect, President Dwight Eisenhower's efforts to break up the RCA monopoly were among the clearest, most important—and unheeded— legacies of his presidency.

What apparatus within the government stood behind Walter Sheridan and his "Get Garrison" apparatus? We have already identified the NSA and FBI Division Five pedigree of this Jesuit-trained spook. Evidence further exists that another secret police agency—one that we have already encountered in our probe of Permindex—was instrumental in the effort to cover up the cabal behind the Kennedy assassination.

According to author "Torbitt," a New Orleans employee of the Double-Chek agency named Gordon Novel had infiltrated the Garrison investigation staff in spring 1967, and determined that Double-Chek and the FBI's Division Five were being actively investigated for their parts in the Kennedy assassination. Novel was put in contact with Walter Sheridan. When Garrison discovered the double-agent role being played by Novel, he subpoenaed the former "staff investigator" to appear before his grand jury probe. Novel left Louisiana under the protection of Sheridan and was delivered to a Virginia safehouse where the results of a doctored lie detector test were released to the press by Sheridan, claiming that Novel had provided conclusive proof that the Garrison probe was a pure publicity stunt with no substantive evidence.

More than two decades have passed since the assassination of John Kennedy in Dallas; and at this very moment, Permindex and the British command that ordered the cold coup by assassination remains one of the best-kept secrets in the world.

4

Permindex Unveiled: Resorts International-Intertel

In September 1974, less than four weeks after President Richard Nixon was driven out of office, Evelyn de Rothschild, Walter Hesselbach, and a handful of others conspired to bring down the Banque du Crédit Internationale.[1] The collapse caused a momentary panic on the international financial markets and more long-term financial problems for such people as Nixon and Michele Sindona, the Italian banker, whose poor judgment led them to place their money in the hands of IOS. Did this financial catastrophe spell the end of Permindex? After all, BCI had been one of the centerpieces of the dirty money side of Major Bloomfield's assassination bureau.

Not only did the International Assassination Bureau survive the September 1974 events, and the earlier shunting of Permindex to South Africa, pulling the plug on the BCI appears to have been a loud diversionary manuever to obscure the fact that quietly, systematically, over a period of years, the Permindex *capability* was upgraded, expanded, and relocated to a spot only miles off the coast of the United States: Paradise Island in the Grand Bahamas. Here stands the corporate headquarters of Resorts International and its wholly owned subsidiary security division, International Intelligence ("Intertel").

Forget about the pictures of Resorts International in glossy travel brochures or the advertisements in the Travel Section of the Sunday *New York Times*. Scarcely concealed among the palm trees, the swimming pools, and the all-night casinos and nightclubs is Major Bloomfield's Royal Commission of High Executioners—and billions of dollars in dope. Barely hidden behind the Resorts International letterhead is the *éminence grise* of organized crime, Meyer Lansky.

Beginning no later than 1960, Lansky hatched a grand scheme to create a "Hong Kong West"[2] in the Caribbean: an offshore center that would bring together gambling, narcotics, dirty money, and Murder Inc. under one unregulated and highly respectable roof.

First, Lansky picked the Grand Bahamas Island as the site for a plush casino-resort. Operating through a Canadian "cut-out," longtime business associate Louis Chesler, Lansky negotiated a purchase of a large tract of land on the island and oversaw the construction of a grand hotel, the Lucayan Beach Hotel, which was completed and opened for business before the end of 1963.[3] At the time the venture began, casino gambling was illegal in the Grand Bahamas—except for those hotels that received a Certificate of Exemption from the Bahamian government. The most powerful political figure on the island, chief of the so-called "Bay Street Boys," was Sir Stafford Sands. Several meetings between Sands and Chesler and $1,800,000 in bribery later, Lansky received his Certificate of Exemption on March 27, 1963. On January 22, 1964, the casino at Lucayan Beach was opened under festive circumstances that Hank Messick described as follows:

The international jet set was on hand to give the event some class, but Meyer Lansky's veterans were in complete control.

Red Ritter was general manager; Max Courtney was credit manager; Charley Brudner was his assistant; Dino Cellini was supervisor, and so on. As a matter of fact, Dino had operated a school in London to train the dealers and stick men who came originally from Sicily by way of the syndicate casino on the Isle of Man in the Irish Sea.[4]

Phase One of Lansky's "Operation Respectable" completed, the old wizard proceeded wth the next steps. First, he cleared the way for a consortium of "legitimate" investors headed by the Miami-based Mary Carter Paint Company to buy into Hog Island (renamed Paradise Island by its owner Huntington Hartford, the multimillionaire magnate of the Great Atlantic and Pacific Tea Company) and to receive a Certificate of Exemption for the construction of a hotel-gambling casino. Sir Stafford Sands, now in Lansky's hip pocket, saw these measures through and simultaneously announced that the Bahamian government was undertaking the construction of a bridge connecting Grand Bahamas to Hog Island, to be completed by December 31, 1967.[5]

What sort of weird entity was Mary Carter Paint and why had Meyer Lansky gone out of his way to open all the doors on Bay Sreet to it?

To begin with the obvious, Mary Carter Paint Company was involved in more than wall coverings. In 1958, it was effectively taken over by merger with the Crosby-Miller Co.—a Florida company about which little is known except that former New York Governor and two-time Republican presidential candidate Thomas Dewey was one of its biggest investors.[6] Dewey's "Mr. Clean" crimebuster reputation, dating back to his days as New York prosecutor during the 1930s, was a perfect cover for Lansky's move to Paradise Island.

Via the 1958 merger, the president of Mary Carter Paint Company was James M. Crosby. Crosby's brother, Peter Crosby, was a convicted stock swindler and close business associate of Dino Cellini. Cellini was the first lieutenant to Meyer Lansky and was known as Florida's "connection" to Canadian heroin trafficker Giuseppi Cotroni. So even with Governor Thomas

Dewey's anglophile profile on the label of every can of Mary Carter Paint, the product was severely tarnished by big-time crime.

Fidel Castro's takeover of Cuba in 1959 had been a bitter pill for the Lansky syndicate to swallow; however, it taught the old wizard a valuable lesson: Don't take politics for granted. Before he socked tens of millions of dollars into his Grand Bahamas dreamland, Lansky would make absolutely certain that he was treading on solid political ground.

So, in 1964, Lansky arranged a small scandal centered around the sudden "revelation" that Lucayan Beach promoter Lou Chesler had connections to organized crime boss Meyer Lansky! Chesler left the island no doubt laughing all the way to the bank, and Lansky became invisible.

Next, Lansky moved to overthrow the deeply entrenched and corrupted Bay Street Boys (the "Batistas of the Bahamas") and impose a new government committed to the public welfare of the Bahamian population—as long as the welfare was provided by revenues from lucrative gambling takes. Covertly, Lansky political operatives—often men like "Big Mike" McLaney, who had been Lansky's bagman for payoffs to Cuban dictator Batista—began to heavily bankroll the Progessive Liberal Party representing the island's black majority.[7]

At the same time, Lansky began releasing blackmail dossiers on the Bay Street Boys. First, James Crosby went to the Justice Department to meet with Robert Peloquin of the Organized Crime Strike Force. Crosby clinched a deal with Peloquin (representing Robert Kennedy's "secret team"). Shortly thereafter Peloquin launched a full-scale investigation into "corruption in the Grand Bahamas"—using the evidence provided through Lansky. Another Lansky frontman, Tex McCrary, began leaking material to the press. McCrary's leaks enabled the *Wall Street Journal* to win the 1966 Pulitzer prize for a lengthy series of articles exposing the connections between organized crime and the ruling political elite of the island—the Bay Streeters.[8]

Following the Crosby-Peloquin meeting, in 1965 the Internal Revenue Service—in connection with the Organized Crime sec-

tion of the Justice Department—embarked on "Operation
Tradewinds," ostensibly an investigation into "hot money" operations in the Bahamas. Heading the IRS side of the investigation was William Koler. Running the effort from the Justice
Department was Robert Peloquin, working in close contact with
Organized Crime and Racketeering section head Henry Peterson and Criminal Division head William Hundley.

By Christmas 1966, growing scandals had presented the Bay
Street Boys with a fait accompli. They called for elections and,
on January 10, 1967, were driven out of office by the Progressive
Liberal Party. Progressive Chairman Lynden O. Pindling became Premier, and he petitioned for the convening of a Royal
Commission of Inquiry to handle the organized crime penetration and control over Bay Street. The commission was convened
in February 1967 under the chairmanship of Sir Ranulph
Bacon, former head of Scotland Yard. Its investigation was
based almost exclusively on the Lansky dossiers, which were
passed on to Sir Ranulph by the Operation Tradewinds crew.[9]

By March 1967 all competitors with Mary Carter Paint Company had withdrawn their bids on the Hog Island land in fear
that they would be exposed for their corrupt ties to Bay Street.
Before the end of the month, Sir Stafford Sands packed his bags
and retired to a castle in Spain.

Lansky, as the business agent for Dope, Inc., had completed
a most silent coup d'état. In rapid succession, all the rats surfaced to claim their just rewards.

Peloquin and Hundley "retired" from the Justice Department, opened up a law firm, and within a month were retained
to manage the legal affairs of "Resorts International"—the new
name adopted by Mary Carter Paint in 1966 when it made the
bid for Hog Island. Both men became vice presidents of Paradise
Enterprise, Inc., the Resorts International subsidiary that owns
the island. By 1970, Resorts had created a wholly owned subsidiary private security army, Intertel. Its cofounders (who started
off with a $2,000,000 commission from Resorts) were Peloquin,
who became president, and Hundley who became the secretary
and the general counsel. Their initial recruits were drawn prin-

cipally from the Operation Tradewinds taskforce, beginning with former IRS Intelligence Division head Koler. What Permindex had previously done under a shroud of secrecy and multiple layers of cover, Intertel was set up to do on a grand scale—before the public eye under the cover of crime control!

Before we look at Intertel and its personnel more closely, it is important to set a few things straight about the investment capital that went into the construction of Resorts International.

Resorts International was financed largely with a transfer of funds from the Banque de Crédit Internationale of Tibor Rosenbaum and Major Louis Mortimer Bloomfield, and the Investors Overseas Service of Bernie Cornfeld and the Rothschild family. An estimated $14 million in transferred monies traveling through Meyer Lansky's World Trade Bank and the Fiduciary Trust Company of Nassau, a wholly owned subsidiary of IOS, found their way into Resorts during its half-dozen formative years.[10]

Furthermore, by the agreement that first cleared the way for the granting of the property title, the construction rights, and the vital Certificate of Exemption, 44 cents on every dollar of profit taken in at the Paradise Island casino goes to the Lucayan Beach Hotel and Casino Corporation—still largely owned by Meyer Lansky and the inheritors of Lansky's crime empire, through his Canadian business partner Lou Chesler.

From its investors' side then, Resorts International is indistinguishable from the previously Geneva and Basel-headquartered Permindex-BCI-IOS—a nexus that we have shown to be founded on the revenues of Dope, Inc. Resorts International equals big-time drug-trafficking: cocaine and marijuana from the Caribbean and South America, LSD and hashish produced in factories in the Bahamas, Costa Rica, etc., with venture capital provided through IOS. Resorts International's stationing on Paradise Island created the "Silver Triangle"—a dope route up through the Caribbean that the U.S. Drug Enforcement Administration estimates to be the source of over $7 billion a year alone in narcotics passed through the southernmost tip of Florida.

Permindex Moves to Bay Street

As the guts of BCI moved to Paradise Island, so the Permindex ring moved to Intertel. No longer was the Special Operations Executive to house its secret assassination teams in trading companies, Christian missionary schools, and commercial executive airline services. Murder, Inc. was to become part of the respectable, Kennedy "liberal establishment," flaunting itself as a private intelligence army for hire.

Of course, occasionally old methods of cover were demanded when inquiring reporters, grand juries, or congressional committees threatened to come a bit too close to the truth. Thus, when Intertel was brought before the Senate Watergate Committee for possible investigation, it was officially described as a "commercial firm that specialized in the identification of typewriters."[11]

What is International Intelligence? A *Who's Who* listing of its board and senior staff reads like a printout of British intelligence, the Mafia and Mossad.

Intertel President Robert Peloquin was a troubleshooter for the Kennedy Justice Department "secret team" under Walter Sheridan. A World War II naval intelligence officer assigned to the Office of Naval Intelligence, Peloquin was transferred to the National Security Agency where he remained until moving to the ciminal division of the Justice Department. In 1966, Peloquin was sent to Buffalo to head up the first official Organized Crime Strike Force in the country. Peloquin's "no crime here" cover-up of the Jacobs family syndicate was so well received that his boss, Henry Peterson, was gratefully hired as general counsel for the Jacobs' Sportsystems Corporation and let loose with a $1 million annual budget. Hundley and Peloquin run Intertel; Peterson runs Sportsystems; all three have been partners in the same law firm since 1976.

Hundley, the secretary and general counsel for Intertel, spent the 1951–57 years in the Internal Security section of the Justice Department. In that capacity, Hundley would have been in liaison with Division Five of the FBI headed by Permindex's Major Louis Mortimer Bloomfield. From Internal Security,

Hundley moved onto the Kennedy Justice "secret team" and participated in the prosecution of Teamster President James Hoffa.

Sir Ranulph Bacon, the former head of Scotland Yard who conducted the Royal Commission inquiry that cleaned out the Bay Street Boys for Lansky, cashed in his chips by moving on to the Intertel Board.

John D. O'Connell is the executive vice president of Intertel in charge of its New York City operations. A 24-year veteran of the FBI, O'Connell was the supervisor of all FBI intelligence activities related to organized crime.

Thomas J. McKeon, vice president and assistant general counsel, was a supervisor with Major Bloomfield's FBI Division Five before he went to Detroit to head up the Organized Crime Strike Force.

David Belisle, a member of the board, was the Deputy Director for Security at the State Department and subsequently the head of the security section of the National Security Agency at the same time Sheridan was at NSA.

Edward M. Mullin, presently Intertel's director of intelligence operations, was with Division Five of the FBI and later with the CIA as an assistant deputy director in charge of clandestine services. Mullin's private security front in Washington, D.C. was infamous as the base of operations for E. Howard Hunt during the time of the Watergate break-in. Mullin is also directly tied into the Miami Double-Chek outfit that is implicated in several Permindex-run assassinations, including the JFK killing.

Among the other board members and ranking staff of Intertel are: a retired director of the Royal Canadian Mounted Police; a president of the Bronfman family's Royal Bank of Canada Trust Company; a president of the Dreyfus corporation, an investment fund owned by the de Gunzberg family, into which the Bronfmans are intermarried.

What do we have here? First we have Resorts International, financed through the Geneva-Basel retail revenues of Dope, Inc. The manager of Paradise Island for its first half decade of operation (1968–73) was Eddie Cellini, the brother of Dino

Cellini and another well-known lieutenant of Meyer Lansky. (When Cellini's criminal record became a potential sore spot for Resorts, he was discreetly shipped off to Miami where he now handles "charter flights" between Florida and Paradise Island—flights that may shuttle more than paying customers.) In 1972, Robert Vesco came a hair's breadth away from buying majority holdings in Resorts International for $60 million—a transaction that was heartily endorsed by the "supersleuths" at Intertel.[12]

Vesco went on from IOS to become the financial kingpin of the post-1979 Latin American cocaine bonanza. It is no exaggeration to state that, on Meyer Lansky's death, Vesco emerged as the inheritor of the old wizard's Caribbean dope money empire. Vesco completed Lansky's "dream" in 1982, when, at the point that U.S. Drug Enforcement Administration began closing in on his Costa Rica safe haven, he moved to Havana as the personal guest and financial adviser of Fidel Castro, who had long since placed the resources of the DGI at the disposal of Dope, Inc.

If Resorts International is a glossy front for Meyer Lansky's retail end of the biggest business in the world, then what does that say for its wholly owned subsidiary Intertel? Is it conceivable that this collection of senior officials from the most prestigious and sophisticated intelligence services of the United States, Canada, and Britain could be oblivious to the fact that they are "riding shotgun" for one of the biggest channels of narcotics and hot money in the Western Hemisphere?

Intertel stands exposed as the successor to Major Bloomfield's Permindex, drawing on the same SOE-Division Five capabilities, the same "direct line" interface into the official intelligence branches of half the countries in the world, the same allegiance to the British oligarchy behind the $200 billion a year Dope, Inc. While the motives may vary case by case, it is sufficient to say that anyone on the inside of Intertel attempting to break from its service and spill the beans would have about the same chance for survival as a Royal Hong Kong police officer who decides to turn down his weekly bribery envelope.

With the consolidation of Resorts International, we once

again swing full circle. From a Prohibition-era jumping-off point of syndicated organized crime in the United States—fostered by the same British families that had ordered the Shanghai Massacre to safeguard the rule of Dope, Inc. in China—we now find ourselves 50 years later confronted by a criminal infrastructure lobbying for the *decriminalization of crime itself*. The Kennedy Justice Department, Scotland Yard, and RCMP boys at Intertel sell their services as "experts in cleaning out undesirable criminal elements from your corporation."[13] Through this ruse they captured the Howard Hughes fortunes and are at present taking over "security services" for all the big Las Vegas casinos.[14] They moved into New Jersey and imposed gambling, horse racing, and numbers as the three "growth industries"; they are now posing New Jersey as the model to be followed by Florida, Arizona, Rhode Island, Massachusetts, and New York.

After World War II, one of the economic warfare specialists in Sir William Stephenson's SOE, a fellow named Ian Fleming, wrote a series of coded novels describing the efforts at world conquest of a "third force"—an ultramodern international crime syndicate housed in the resort islands of the Caribbean. The weapons of "third force" conquest were drugs, political assassinations, grand-scale blackmail, and economic war against the nations of the world. With Resorts International-Intertel, Fleming's "third force"—the British oligarchy's Dope, Inc.—put itself up for trade on the stock markets of the world.

5

Max Fisher: Distributor and Retailer

"Max immediately became my protégé" said Julius Klein of Detroit's Republican Party powerbroker and philanthropist Max Fisher. "From that point on I have always kept Max well informed on all intelligence matters."

The time is 1936, the year that marks Fisher's promotion from "bagman" for Morris Dalitz's Purple Gang to the inside of Julius Klein's British intelligence section. From there, Fisher was trained for the franchise for the retail trade of Dope, Inc. Fisher's story will take us to two enterprises: The one, well-known, is United Brands, which supplies the United States with most of its bananas—and shipped an estimated 20% of its cocaine and marijuana during the 1970s, according to U.S. law enforcement sources. The other is Airborne Freight, which spirits dirty money and dope across the country.

In Detroit, the Fisher Building is owned by the Bronfman family. The connection is to be expected. What the Bronfmans are to Canada and the East Coast, Max Fisher is to the Midwest and the West Coast, and his story begins the same way.

Max Fisher was born in Pittsburgh in 1908, the son of Russian Jews who had emigrated to the United States two years earlier. In 1930, immediately upon his graduation from Ohio State University, Fisher went into the oil business. He became a young partner in the Michigan-based Aurora Oil Company, which had been founded a year earlier by a mysterious character named Henry A. Wenger. Describing himself as an "international banker," Wenger had been forced to flee to Canada during the 1920s, when indictments for stock fraud were handed down against him. By 1920—after a stop in Oklahoma—Wenger wound up in the Michigan oil-drilling business.[1]

The strange Mr. Wenger aside, the Midwest oil business was one of the first legitimate businesses to be taken over by organized crime in the reorganization handed down by Johnny Torrio in 1928. In the Midwest, this meant control by the Purple Gang, the Detroit- and Cleveland-based branch of the mob that ran all the bootlegging of whiskey during the 1920s and later narcotics.[2]

According to several sources, Max Fisher was a "runner" for the Purple Gang during the early 1930s. His job was to carry cash receipts across the Canadian border to the Bronfman gang in advance payment for the next shipment of booze and drugs for the speakeasies of Detroit, Cleveland, and Buffalo. During this period, Fisher's activities brought him into contact with the Murder, Inc. syndicate headed by Meyer Lansky.

Meanwhile, on the East Coast, Julius Klein, as an underling of William Wiseman, the official head of British intelligence in the United States, was deployed to pull together a "dirty tricks unit" that would be ready for action on behalf of British interests in the Middle East as part of the "Great Game."

Klein recruited the unit from the ranks of the Jewish War Veterans.[3]

British intelligence's Palestine operation dates officially back to the 1917 Balfour Declaration—the British oligarchy's statement of its determination to establish a "Jewish homeland" that would serve as an asset for British interests in the Middle East, especially against France. The project was run through the British Secret Intelligence Service, with the London Hofjuden families—particularly the Rothschilds—and the "Our Crowd" investment bank circles of lower Manhattan the immediate sponsors, as cutouts for the higher-ups of the British-centered black nobility we have already met.

Run out of the Manhattan offices of Kuhn, Loeb, Wiseman's "plumbers unit" continued work that had begun with Baron Edmond de Rothschild's founding of the Palestine Economics Commission in the 1920s. Under Rothschild funding, the commission established an intricate network of weapons-smuggling cells, money-laundering channels, and contraband shipping lines—utilizing criminal enterprises and respectable businesses interchangeably. Julius Klein supervised the smuggling networks stateside.[4]

In this venture he had the support of at least one agency of the U.S. government. In 1932, Klein was appointed director of the first anti-subversion section of the U.S. Justice Department. This brought Klein into close contact with J. Edgar Hoover, who himself was on intimate terms with Lansky's partner Lewis Rosenstiel of Schenley's liquor.[5]

The cover for Klein's Jewish War Veterans "plumbers' unit" was anti-Nazism. Klein's unit essentially operated as a subsidiary of William Stephenson's British Special Operations Executive, which set up shop in the United States in preparation for American entry into World War II.

When Fisher was brought to New York City in 1936, the occasion was the War Veterans' convention to call for an "Anti-Nazi Coalition." It is there that Fisher became Klein's top recruit. From that point until the mid-1940s, the shadowy strands of Fisher's life are lost, as he became submerged in the intelligence operations that Klein directed.

Sonneborn and the Syndicate

In the late 1940s and early 1950s, it is known that Klein took Fisher along on a series of missions to Israel where Klein oversaw the organization and training of the Israeli army and intelligence services. After the war, as head of the U.S. Army Counterintelligence Corps in Western Europe—the same corps that produced Henry Kissinger—Klein had illegally rerouted whole shiploads of medical supplies, trucks, construction equipment, and so forth that were earmarked for Germany and Austria into the Zionist underground terrorist organizations in Palestine.[6]

The scramble for dominance after the war had put the Palestine project on the top of the list of Britain's operational priorities. The previous allotment of funds and manpower to the project was dwarfed by the Rothschild and SOE post-1945 operations. A large part of the work was directed from the United States by the little-known organization called the Sonneborn Institute.

In 1945, Orde Wingate, the SOE officer assigned to Palestine to train an expanded Haganah, had sent future Israeli Prime Minister David Ben-Gurion to the United States to link up with Julius Klein. Klein immediately steered him to Rudolph Sonneborn, the Baltimore chemical magnate, whose wife, Dorothy Schiff, was a member of the London Warburg clan.[7]

In July 1945, Sonneborn and Henry Montor, the chairman of United Jewish Appeal, pulled together a secret meeting in New York City, that drew sixteen top Zionists in the country for a strategy session with Ben-Gurion. Out of that meeting the Sonneborn Institute was born—with the purpose of providing smuggled military equipment, trained assassins, spies and demolition experts, and military and scientific secrets to Orde Wingate's Haganah.[8]

To give an idea of the size of the project, the average annual expenditure—all in violation of U.S. law—grew from an initial figure of over $10 million into the range of $100 million by the late 1940s. By 1947, Sonneborn could report to his executive board at one of its weekly secret meetings that the initial core of sixteen in July 1945 had become a continentwide underground with an executive of seventy and over 10,000 "cadre" burrowed into every Jewish community in the United States, Canada, and Mexico; a clandestine fleet of military convoy planes; a network of schools for assassins; and one U.S. surplus aircraft carrier.[9]

Through Sonneborn, lines of daily contact were laid down between the drug syndicate, selected lawyers, bankers, businessmen, and labor leaders, seasoned Haganah operatives like Yehuda Arazi (of which more in a moment), and certain offices in the Justice Department and the FBI. At Klein's initiative, J. Edgar Hoover met with the Sonneborn executive and agreed to give it unofficial support.[10] At every level, of course, Sonneborn's net was controlled at the top by Stephenson's Special Operations Executive.

Yehuda Arazi was the ace Haganah weapons smuggler who had been sent to direct "weapons procurement" for Sonneborn. Originally trained by the British Mandatory Police in Palestine (he himself was a police commissioner), Arazi had spent the 1930s making gun deals with Nazi governments throughout Eastern Europe. In 1939 he was listed as an ambassador of the Nicaraguan government of dictator Anastasio Somoza. Responsibility: weapons procurement. Most of Arazi's "Nicaraguan" guns were bought either from Eastern Europe or Central America and found their way into the hands of the terrorist underground in Palestine.

Arazi was Sonneborn's contact man with the Lansky mob. As the official historian of the Sonneborn project, Leonard Slater, relates it:

One morning Al Robison [a New Jersey Zionist who was the number-two man in Sonneborn's group and the Institute's case carrier] arrived at Arazi's apartment to find him talking to two hard-looking individuals. "As I walked in," Robison recalls, "he said, 'I'll see you tomorrow, Al.' I realized he was having a conversation with somebody he didn't want me to meet, so I took the hint and left. The next day, he apologized. 'In my business, Al, we can't be too fussy about who we do business with. Sometimes they're not nice people. You're a nice American fellow, with good standing in your community. I don't want you to meet some of the people I have to deal with. This is an organization that comes out of Brooklyn. I think they're called Murder, Limited.' "

As Slater commented, "The British-oriented Arazi had made an understandable error in the title of Murder, Inc."[11]

Max Fisher, the protégé of Julius Klein, was Sonneborn's "glue man" for both weapons and petroleum smuggling. According to Sonneborn recruiter Sally Field of Detroit, Fisher delivered funds from Meyer Lansky into the Haganah war chest and also served as the mediator to army surplus distributors in buying up tanks, weapons systems, warplanes, and other equipment for illegal shipment to Palestine. The principal Midwest dealer in surplus at this time was the Purple Gang's Morris Dalitz.

Fisher was also important to Sonneborn as the key man in Detroit, the capital of the U.S. war production industry and a petroleum boom area. Through mob connections, Fisher's Aurora Oil Company maintained full capacity stocks of gasoline throughout the war period—despite federal rationing. Portions of the gasoline found its way onto tankers bound for Palestine.[12]

Out of the Shadows

During the early 1950s, Max Fisher was rewarded for his work with a new, "legitimate" identity. In 1952, he was named Michigan chairman of the United Jewish Appeal—the successor to the Sonneborn Institute as the largest Zionist fundraising organization. By the late 1950s, Fisher was its national director. Fisher's big break into financial prominence and respectability, however, came in 1957, at the personal initiative of Edmond de Rothschild. Max Fisher was permitted to buy one-third ownership in Paz Oil, Ltd. and Paz Chemical, Ltd., of Israel.

We have already discovered the men Fisher joined on the board of the Paz conglomerate: the leading figures in the Permindex web. But for Fisher, entry into Paz marked the beginning of his career in drug-smuggling. It is not a matter of speculation that the Paz corporations are directly involved in narcotics transport. In 1978, the *New York Times* reported a series of incidents in which tanker ships transporting Paz petroleum products on ships owned by the Israeli state sector, were caught in the New York City harbor filled not with oil, but with liquid hashish.

Fisher's part-ownership in Paz was but a stepping-stone to other advantageous corporate holdings: chairmanship of United Brands (previously United Fruit Company), chairmanship of the Fruehauf Trucking Company, and ownership of the Airborne Freight Corporation. All three companies have been implicated in dope trafficking.

Beginning in 1975, law enforcement officials in the Midwest began pointing to Fisher as a "kingpin" behind the area's dope trade, and cited his relation to Fruehauf Trucking as one component of the drug machine. Fruehauf is one of the largest distributors of tractor-trailers in the country. Certain shopping centers in the Detroit suburb of Southfield were identified as transshipment points for narcotics delivered in Fruehauf trucks. One of Max Fisher's closest associates, Charles Taubman, himself a part owner in United Brands, also conveniently owns a number of shopping centers in that city.

Airborne Freight is a joint enterprise of Max Fisher and the Jacobs brothers of Buffalo—longtime crime colleagues of Fisher's since the days of the 1920s Purple Gang. Airborne Freight shares its airlines exclusively with the Federal Reserve as the only two clients of an entity known as Midwest Airlines. The advantage of this is that the Federal Reserve contract makes Midwest Airlines' planes security-free. Airborne Freight uses the "secure" cargo planes of Midwest Airlines to make large-scale narcotics pickups and deliveries—beginning in such locations as Seattle, a 100% containerized port and a location immediately adjacent to British Columbia, the entry point of dope from Hong Kong.

It is not in the least surprising that Midwest sources also report that the pilots designated with these "most valuable" cargo deliveries are predominantly former South African mercenaries. Some are allegedly associated with Permindex directly. Reportedly, previous pilots of Midwest were forced into early retirement and paid off lucratively with shares in Resorts International.

The close proximity of Canada to Fisher's Detroit has been identified by law enforcement and intelligence agents on both sides of the border as another key component of the Fisher crime connection. Windsor, Ontario, just across the river from Detroit, is another depot stop on the Permindex underground railroad, safehousing dope traffickers and hitmen from all corners of the globe. One Windsor-based operative of the Fisher-Bronfman crowd, "Hank" Jacobsen, has recently been implicated in a Juárez City, Mexico-based cocaine and killers-for-hire apparatus that echoes the Bloomfield Permindex operation. As Bloomfield did earlier, Jacobsen enjoys the protection of high levels of the FBI and Royal Canadian Mounted Police— in large measure thanks to the good offices of Fisher and Bronfman.

United Brands: A Case History of Crime

In the spring of 1975, Max Fisher was voted in as chairman of the board of United Brands. This placed him at the helm of a corporation whose records reveal the very beginnings of organized crime in the United States.

The story begins even before the American Civil War, when New Orleans, the base of United Brands, became the receiving station for what was then known as "Mazzini's Mafia." Back in Italy, Giuseppe Mazzini, leader of the Scottish Rite in that country, commanded the "Young Italy" movement sponsored by British Prime Minister Benjamin Disraeli and funded by the Rothschilds. In New Orleans, Mazzini's protégés, Joseph Macheca and Charles Matrenga, became the "godfathers" of the city, taking the port over on behalf of the Palermo mob, which reported directly to Mazzini and thence to Disraeli. The chain of command was so well-known that the joke made the rounds that the word "mafia" was really an acronym from "Mazzini autorizza furti, incendi, e avvelenamenti"—"Mazzini authorizes theft, arson, and kidnapping."[13]

The first of the Mazzini networks drifted in before and during the Civil War. "The Mafias in New Orleans, New York, and Palermo were separate societies," wrote one leading historian of the period, "but they cooperated closely. A member who was properly sponsored could be transferred from one city to another, from one family to another."[14]

By the close of the Civil War, Disraeli's Mafia in New Orleans was in the hands of Joseph Macheca. By contemporary accounts, the activities of the Macheca gang were indistinguishable from those of the Ku Klux Klan. In 1868, Macheca organized the New Orleans side of Democratic candidate Seymour's campaign against Ulysses S. Grant. Seymour's funding and political direction came from August Belmont, the Rothschilds' official business agent in the United States. The campaign was described as follows in the *New Orleans Picayune:*

> This popular and pleasant-mannered gentleman [Macheca] organized and commanded a company of Sicilians, 150 strong, known as the Innocents. Their uniform was a white cape bearing a Maltese Cross [the insignia of the British Royal Family's Order of St. John of Jerusalem] on the left shoulder. They wore sidearms and when they marched the streets they shot at every Negro that came in sight. They left a trail of a dozen dead Negroes behind them. General James E. Steadman, managing the [Seymour] campaign, forbade them from making further parades and they were disbanded.[15]

One historian of the Mafia notes, "This matter-of-fact account is the first report of a formal Sicilian organization in New

Orleans, and it is likely that from the ranks of these armed Innocents came the nucleus of Macheca's Mafia."[16]

Belmont's presidential candidate ran on a program drafted at the Seligman and associated banking houses in New York: the repeal of Lincoln's Emancipation Proclamation. The same networks controlled General Albert Pike and his hooded goons, the Ku Klux Klan, whom Macheca's gangsters took such great pains to imitate—along with the conceit of the Maltese Cross. Pike, Macheca, and their paramilitary irregulars unleashed a wave of violence across the South that buried Lincoln's Reconstruction policy not many years after the President himself.

The historical record shows that Macheca's group in New Orleans, which started out by shooting blacks for the Copperhead banks in New York, had proved its mettle by the early 1870s. It became the jumping-off point for the organization of the mob throughout the United States. Macheca provided a base for Mazzini's syndicate organizer of the first years of the Mafia, Giuseppe Esposito. A close Mazzini associate, Esposito fled Sicily in the early 1870s, arriving in New Orleans to make contact with Macheca. Esposito traveled through the United States, pulling together Italian-speaking secret societies and establishing intercity communications where none had existed before. From Esposito's tour onward, the Sicilian-speaking secret societies became crime syndicates. Mazzini's representative on the scene had absolute authority over the local godfathers, even over the leader of the New Orleans base organization. Macheca's "Mafia leadership was eclipsed briefly," according to one historian, "from 1879 to 1881, when he temporarily deferred to Giuseppe Esposito."[17]

Macheca died at the hands of a New Orleans mob, which dragged him from a prison cell and lynched him, after he had been arrested for the murder of a policeman.[18] His old lieutenant Matrenga took over the reins. Macheca's death left a deep impression on the syndicates; possibly this is the point where the mob decided to "go legit," its strategy ever since.

The vehicle for the New Orleans mob's conversion to "legitimate business" in 1900 was an immigrant from the Romanian province of Bessarabia, whence Yechiel Bronfman had migrated to Canada some ten years earlier. The new immigrant, one Samuel Zemurray, obtained financing from a group of Boston and New York Our Crowd banks, and bought out a portion of the Macheca gang's shipping interests. A historian comments, "Joe Macheca's shipping line merged with four others to form the great United Fruit Company, which remains one of the largest of all U.S. firms."[19] United Fruit—rechartered recently as United Brands Company—traditionally brought in Our Crowd bankers for its top management. Nonetheless, the Sicilian mob was remembered with nostalgia. When Charles Matrenga died in 1943, the entire board of United Fruit turned out for the funeral.[20]

Max Fisher did not take over the helm of the huge corporation for another thirty years. Fisher's predecessor Eli Black, who had succeeded Zemurray, was killed in February of 1975 when he walked out a 44th-story window of his Pan Am Building offices in New York City. The official cause of death was suicide; however, there still exists widespread speculation that Black was shoved out of the way to make room for a more ruthless figure.[21]

Under the directorship of Max Fisher, United Brands' drug-trafficking appears to have flourished. According to 1978 estimates of the Drug Enforcement Administration, over 20% of the cocaine and marijuana smuggled into the United States enters aboard the ships and planes of United Brands.

Fisher's personal hand in this dope route (DEA official reports show that over $7 billion a year in heroin, cocaine, and marijuana is smuggled into the Florida Keys alone through this "Silver Triangle" channel) is further suggested by reports from several Midwest sources that his principal "contact man" into the Caribbean is Robert Vesco. Fisher's privately owned Marathon Oil Company, barging crude oil into the Midwest from ports of call in South America, is also suspected of joining United Brands in running the "Silver Triangle" drug traffic.

United Brands of Genocide

It is common knowledge in the United States and throughout the world that the power ruling the "banana republics" of Central America is and has been the United Fruit Company— United Brands. It is no exaggeration to say that every coup that has taken place in the region was backed by the fruit company, which ran the nations of Central America mercilessly as slave-labor plantations. In 1932, a coup in El Salvador—with United Fruit sponsorship—exterminated 300,000 peasants who had risen up in revolt against the conditions in which they were forced to live.[22] For forty years, the United Fruit Company stood behind the regime of Anastasio Somoza in Nicaragua. It is through the offices of United Fruit that Haganah gun-runner Yehuda Arazi came to be listed as an ambassador of the Nicaraguan government.

Once the state of Israel was established, the flow of weapons through Nicaragua into Palestine was reversed: A sizable part of the Israeli armaments industry (an estimated 60%) was pumped back into the Central American "banana dictatorships." Israeli weapons and military hardware sustained the Somoza regime when it came under attack and permitted Somoza to carry out his scorched earth policy against his own population.[23] When Somoza's regime finally collapsed, it was a former United Brands employee, Francisco Urcuyo, who briefly stepped into the presidency. Israeli weapons to Somoza were funneled under the cover of the Israeli Maritime Fruit Company, through the services of Max Fisher's associates, including Fisher's partner in Paz, Shaul Eisenberg. And when the United Brands mafia determined to dump the traditional dictators of the previous half-century, the same flow of Israeli and East Bloc originating arms began to flow into the Sandinistas and Moscow-backed narcoterrorist groups in Guatemala and El Salvador. All of this was simultaneous with Lansky successor Vesco's move into the Soviet-Cuban orbit.

The cocaine and marijuana consumed in the United States is the blood product of hundreds of thousands in Central America who live under the rule of United Brands. Yet today, United Brands Chairman Max Fisher is acknowledged "kingmaker" of the Michigan Republican Party, and has served as president of the United Jewish Appeal, president of the Jewish Welfare Fund, honorary chairman of the American Jewish Committee; and was until 1978 the national fundraising chairman for the Republican Party. In 1979 the *Jerusalem Post* named him "Jew of the Year."

6

The Jacobs Family's Emprise: Sports and Crime

On June 2, 1976, moments after a bomb exploded in his car and inflicted fatal injuries, dying Arizona investigative reporter Don Bolles whispered three words to the rescue team that pulled him from the wreckage: "Mafia . . . Emprise . . . Adamson."

Bolles was on the verge of completing a seven-year investigation of laundered drug-traffic money in the state of Arizona, including organized crime takeovers of dog tracks and horse racing—areas the Buffalo-based Jacobs family began moving into in 1959. A Phoenix resident, John Adamson, pleaded guilty to the murder in January 1977, naming a local real estate developer, Max Dunlop, as the man who hired him to murder Bolles. Mysteriously, no investigation ever took place of Emprise, the leading vehicle since 1916 of the Jacobs family, which had been the primary target of Bolles's investigation and the subject of his last words.

Emprise was one of the largest non-public, family-owned corporations in the world, a conglomerate with control or partial control over 450 separate companies. Its stated annual income as of the late 1970s was $350 million, from holdings in North American and British sports complexes, race tracks, and food consortia. It is probably the biggest quasi-legitimate cover for organized crime's money-laundering in the United States.

The Jacobs family's only concession to the numerous attempts by law enforcement agencies to shut them down was to change Emprise's name to Sportsystems in 1972.

The vast extent of the present Jacobs empire is approximated by Sportsystems' 1977 declared holdings. The pattern that emerges conforms to the requisites of an international laundering racket for narcotics, prostitution, and gambling receipts.

Sportsystems Corporation maintains:

■ Majority interest or significant minority interests in over twenty horse racing tracks in the United States and Canada.

■ Food concessions at over forty horse racing tracks in the United States and Canada, plus another fifteen in England. Those in Great Britain are maintained in the name of Sportsystems' wholly owned subsidiary, Letheby and Christopher, Ltd., chaired by a retired British Army colonel, Livingstone Learmouth;

■ Over ten greyhound racing tracks in the United States and Canada, including majority holdings in nearly every track in the heavily drug-trafficked state of Arizona;

■ Twenty-four concession contracts with major-league baseball teams in the United States, including Chicago's Comiskey Park and Detroit's Tiger Stadium;

■ Ownership of the Boston Garden indoor professional sports complex and the Boston Bruins professional ice hockey team;

■ Ownership of Professional Sports Publications, Inc., the largest U.S. publisher of sports events programs;

■ 161 concessions at theaters and bowling alleys in the United States;

■ Fifteen airport concessions, including in-flight and ground-level concessions at Washington, D.C. airports and Palm Springs, Florida;

■ Two jai alai stadiums (legal gambling facilities) in Florida;

■ Industrial food catering services at such locations as the Gulf of Mexico oil drilling platforms; and

■ One Alaska-to-Seattle cargo fleet comprised of six ships. This route curiously parallels the prime entry point to the United States of Chinese heroin.

Within this maze of operations, each characterized by a high volume of cash turnover, the $350 million figure is a fraud, published for tax purposes. Law enforcement sources estimate the annual flow-through of tainted cash in the range of several billions of dollars.

That is not conjecture. Emprise and its incarnation, Sportsystems, left a broad trail of investigations, indictments, and convictions, occurring mainly during the years of Nixon's War on Drugs—a trail that ended with the Bolles murder. In 1972, the family firm was convicted of conspiracy to take over a gambling casino in Las Vegas by illegal means. That incident, among other things, provoked the change of the Emprise name. Indicted along with the Jacobs brothers were some of the best-known faces in the mug files of the Justice Department's Organized Crime Strike Force. Among the co-conspirators were top racketeers, drug traffickers, and the entire leadership of the Detroit mob, including

■ Anthony Zerilli, son of Joseph Zerilli, Detroit's mob boss and an official of the Emprise subsidiary, Hazel Park Racing Association;

■ Michael B. Polizzi of Grosse Point, Michigan, an owner of the Valley Die Cast Association, identified as a Detroit mob lieutenant in police files;

■ Anthony Giordano of the "St. Louis Banana Distributing Company," the kingpin of St. Louis drug traffic;

■ Peter J. Bellanca, also a director of the Emprise-owned Hazel Park Racing Association; and Jacob Shapiro, a Detroit-

Miami mobster, with interests in Las Vegas' Silver Slipper casino.

Conviction in the same dock with known mobsters did not deter the Jacobs family. Since 1972, they have continued to act as money-movers and bagmen for a whole list of organized crime figures. Several large loans to crime syndicates are on the record, including a $2 million 1972 loan to the Montreal Expos— owned by their old sponsors and counterparts across the Canadian border, the Bronfman family of Montreal. On the list of the Jacobs' "loan" recipients are a number of associates of syndicate financier Meyer Lansky, including Morris Dalitz, according to testimony in the *Congressional Record*[1].

In 1978 a Michigan grand jury heard a case implicating the Jacobs' Sportsystems and the Jacobs brothers personally in an attempt to tamper with Michigan state criminal records involving members of the Zerilli mob and St. Louis crime figure Morris Shenker.

Despite a record of criminal activity stretching back to World War I—and never interrupted—the Jacobs family remains one of the open, "legitimate" fronts for Dope. Inc. Not only is the Jacobs family protected, but it retains a group of veterans of the Kennedy administration's Organized Crime Strike Force as its legal department.

Emprise appeared in 1916, the year that the Bronfmans and the Hudson's Bay Company began bootlegging through the "Pure Drug Distribution Company," using the three Jacobs brothers as contacts right across the border in Buffalo. The original Jacobs brothers, Louis, Marvin, and Charles, used the old smugglers' cover of "food concessions" for a chain of vaudeville theaters on the Canadian border crossing points at Buffalo and Cleveland.[2] The modus operandi is pretty much the one Mitchell Bronfman used during the early 1970s for smuggling heroin into the United States. Once established, the Jacobs machine became a leading distributor for Bronfman liquor as the United States went dry.

Functionally, Emprise represented the "throttle" through

which shipments of liquor could be turned on or off to the American mob. The Jacobs family, enduring a half-dozen criminal indictments through the 1920s, controlled the supply and financing of illegal booze for most of American organized crime. Their dependents included the Purple Gang of Detroit, the gang convicted with the Jacobs brothers in the 1972 Las Vegas incident; the Morris Dalitz Cleveland-Las Vegas crime syndicate; and the Crown-Lundheimer mob in Chicago, the controllers of the colorful "cutout," Al Capone.[3] Not only are these ties still in place; every man who tried to do something about them is either dead, like reporter Don Bolles, or broken, like former Arizona Congressman Sam Steiger.

The Steiger Investigation

Beginning in 1970, five-term Arizona conservative Congressman Sam Steiger began an investigation into Emprise's activities in his home state. Working closely with Bolles, Steiger prepared a series of reports for the House Select Committee on Crime, of which he was a member. Steiger placed two damning reports on Emprise in the *Congressional Record* in 1970 and 1972.[4] He also widely publicized the finding of an Arizona State Auditor General's report charging Emprise with falsifying figures to get a tax-break bill through the state legislature. By 1972, in conjunction with the Nixon Justice Department, he succeeded in getting grand jury charges and federal court convictions against Emprise and the six Detroit area mobsters already cited. On May 24, 1972, pressure on Emprise had reached such a public crescendo that even *Sports Illustrated* ran a lengthy exposé titled "Jacobs—Godfather of Sports"; the magazine was promptly sued for $20 million and settled out of court.

At that point, Democratic Party politicians and other prominent figures went into action in Emprise's behalf. Not coincidentally, the same forces that came forward for Emprise were also preparing the Watergate scandal to bring down President Richard Nixon.[5]

Democratic members of the House Select Panel on Crime denounced the majority report prepared by Steiger exposing Emprise's ties to organized crime. As admitted by Max and Jeremy Jacobs in congressional testimony, Emprise hired New York public relations man Hal Antin to defeat Steiger in his 1976 re-election bid. A Phoenix underworld figure, George H. Johnson, was paid to wiretap and survey Steiger and manufacture scandals against him. Arnold Weiss, a Buffalo attorney on the Emprise payroll, was sent to meet with Steiger and deliver a series of ultimatums. Weiss reportedly threatened to ruin Steiger by planting rumors that his marriage had broken up after his wife caught him in illicit relations with their three-year-old daughter. Such rumors, in fact, did appear in various Arizona media.

In 1972, Senator Robert Dole (R-Kan.), now the Senate Majority Leader, publicly protested the House Select Panel's decision to terminate the hearings on Emprise. Dole revealed that the decision had followed a private meeting between Jeremy Jacobs and Democratic National Committee Chairman Larry O'Brien. O'Brien subsequently left his Democratic Party post and assumed a lucrative job as president of the National Basketball Association—an organization with heavy representation by the Jacobs family.

As the Watergate campaign escalated, the attack against Emprise faded. By June 1976, Don Bolles was dead. On November 3, 1976, in an election heavily shaped by nationwide vote fraud, Representative Steiger lost his bid for a sixth term in Congress. By this time a broken man fearing for his life, Steiger met with Jeremy Jacobs to "apologize" for his accusations against Emprise. At this time Emprise-Sportsystems had three pending civil suits against Steiger. In a last act of humiliation, Steiger wrote to Attorney General Edward Levi *as a spokesman for Emprise* on behalf of a presidential pardon for the 1972 federal racketeering conviction. Incoming Attorney General Griffin Bell turned down the requests as "not deserving."

Jacobs and Royal Crown

The second generation of Jacobs brothers, Max, Jeremy, and Lawrence, underwent the same "washing" into respectable society as their old Prohibition business partners, the Bronfmans. Ironically, the Jacobs brothers used their longstanding association with the Bronfmans to lend them an air of respectability somewhat above that of the outright thugs with whom they still do most of their business. For example, a third-generation Jacobs, Jeremy, took his "higher education" not at a university, but at the Toronto Jockey Club, after his 1960 high school graduation. The Bronfman-run Toronto Jockey Club, like its counterpart in Hong Kong, is not only one of Canada's best protected dirty-money-gathering outfits, but a place where gangsters and "respectable people" can amiably mix in safety. Regular denizens of the Toronto Club include Viscount Hardinge and Canadian organized-crime figure Murray Koffler. Koffler's role as a retail outlet for Bronfman dope-running came into the public domain in 1976, when an associate's chain of retail drug stores was indicted for maintaining an amphetamine factory and a national army of pill-pushers. That distinction did not prevent Koffler from attending the wedding of Britain's Princess Anne, or from maintaining his close friendship with Anne's husband, Captain Mark Phillips.

The Jacobs have been awarded a respectable role in the train of the British monarchy, in a service capacity. The "crown jewel" of the Jacobs' operations is the British firm Letheby and Christopher, Ltd.—the caterers, by Her Majesty's appointment, to "all events with a royal presence." Their concessions through Letheby and Christopher include the Tate Gallery, the Ascot Races, and other gathering places of the Royal Family and the British aristocracy. L&C, as it is affectionately known in Britain, was awarded the management of Ascot through the Bank of Norfolk, whose trustees include the Marquis of Abergavemy and Lord Tyron—the Keeper of the Queen's Privy Purse, third in aristocratic rank to the Keeper of the Queen's Horse, and the Keeper of the Queen's Bedchamber.

Apart from its royal honors, the Jacobs subsidiary manages twelve other racetracks in Great Britain, including the national track at Liverpool, the site of the Grand National, and Wembley Stadium, Britain's equivalent of Madison Square Garden.

Working for the HongShang

From available evidence, the British oligarchy rates the Jacobs group's political usefulness as an intermediary for control over organized crime sufficiently important to make major efforts to rebuild the Jacobs' tarnished image. The prize that motivates Britain in this regard is the Buffalo-based Marine Midland Bank, which the Hongkong and Shanghai Bank sought to buy out.

From the American side the most important "inside agents" pushing the HongShang takeover were Leonard Rochwarger and Paul Schoelkopf, since 1973 the closest business associates of Max and Jeremy Jacobs. Rochwarger is president of Firstmark Corporation, a heavy equipment leasing company and the American leg of an international conglomerate controlled by the Rothschilds and Sebag-Montefiores.

Rochwarger was brought into the deal at a Paris meeting in 1971 with Edmond de Rothschild and Robin Sebag-Montefiore, who represented, respectively, the Isrop S.A. of Luxembourg and the Gilsyd Corporation of Liechtenstein. Under an intricate merger arrangement, Rochwarger emerged from the meeting as president of a new international subsidiary of the Rothschild and Montefiore companies, Israel-American Leasing of Tel Aviv, now the largest firm of its type in Israel.

Rochwarger is an old associate of Max Jacobs; both sit on the board of the Joint Distribution Committee, the funding center for American Zionist organizations. In addition, Rochwarger is the director of the National Jewish Centers and Youth Programs both in the United States and Canada, a regional board member of the Anti-Defamation League of B'nai B'rith, and fundraising chairman of the United Jewish Appeal.

Buffalo-based Paul Schoelkopf led the local campaign in support of HongShang's bid for Marine Midland. Schoelkopf was chairman of Buffalo's Niagara Share Corporation, an investment company that pools the resources of wealthy local investors for large investments. Among Niagara's holdings is 246,000 shares in HongShang stock. Its other holdings include investments in the Swire family's Pacific A Corporation, and 400,000 shares in two Hong Kong holding companies, Cheung Kong Holdings, Ltd., and the trading company Hutchinson Whampoa, also linked to HongShang.

Another Schoelkopf investment vehicle is the $450 million-per-year food wholesaling-retailing group, Niagara Frontier Services, whose chairman is Armand Castellani, a member of Marine Midland's board of directors. A merger was in process in 1978 between Niagara Frontier Services and Sportsystems, to double the stated "legitimate" revenue base of the Jacobs family empire.

Jacobs Joins Intertel

In the aftermath of Congressman Steiger's investigation, Sportsystems underwent a corporate personnel reorganization. The result was that Sportsystems established an interface with the center of the crime syndicates and the reincarnated Assassination Bureau—Resorts International and its subsidiary, Intertel.

The entire executive team and legal staff brought into Sportsystems in 1975 was made up exclusively of veterans of the Kennedy Justice Department—the same Kennedy Justice Department that sent the man who is now president of Intertel, Robert Peloquin, to Buffalo, to "investigate" the Emprise crime syndicate!

In early 1975, Donald Carmichael, a Kennedy Democrat who had served as a delegate both at the 1964 and 1968 Democratic conventions, as well as on the President's War on Poverty panel, became the president of Sportsystems. Carmichael ushered in a dozen Kennedy Justice Department hands over the next two years.

In 1976, Max and Jeremy Jacobs' close friend and "business associate" Max Fisher released the general counsel of his own corporation, United Brands (formerly United Fruit), so that he could accept Jacobs' offer of the post of general counsel to Sportsystems. Before his employment at United Brands, Stanley Mills had been a Justice Department aide to Attorney General Robert Kennedy.

In 1977, when the Bolles murder temporarily threatened to bring Emprise-Sportsystems under criminal investigation, Horace S. Webb joined the firm as public relations director. Webb, who assisted the Watergating of Richard Nixon on behalf of the Kennedy machine, had previously been deputy public information director for the Justice Department and later press secretary for Attorney General Elliot Richardson, a Boston Brahmin tied to the Bank of Boston.

By the time the facelift of Sportsystems was finished, four other Kennedy administration officials—each a member of Robert Kennedy's "secret team"—were brought into the firm's legal division.

Half the Kennedy "old boys" had moved into Resorts International and Intertel; the other half went over to the Jacobs group, for the same type of assignment.

Heading the "Intertel Team" at Sportsystems is Henry Peterson, the former chief of the Organized Crime and Racketeering Division of the Kennedy Justice Department. At Camelot, Peterson was the superior of Robert Peloquin, now president of Intertel.

Peterson's entire staff from the old Robert Kennedy days came with him. At Sportsystems, his chief aides were William Bittman, Daniel Hollman, and Thomas Kennedy. Kennedy worked for Peterson in the Organized Crime Division of the Department of Justice. Their big assignment in the old days came when Peterson sent them to New York State—to investigate the mob connections of Emprise!

Notes: Part VII

1: The Bronfman Gang

1. Canadian Jewish Congress Report, 1967–68, in commemoration of Samuel Bronfman.

2. Ibid.

3. Peter C. Newman, *Bronfman Dynasty, The Rothschilds of the New World* (Toronto: McClelland and Stewart Ltd., 1978), pp. 66–73.

4. Newman, *Bronfman Dynasty*, p. 64.

5. Hank Messick, *Lansky* (New York: Berkley Medallion Books, 1971), pp. 230–31.

6. James H. Gray, *Booze* (Toronto: Macmillan Co. of Canada, Alger Press, 1972).

7. Newman, *Bronfman Dynasty*, p. 127.

8. *Russell Sage Foundation, 1870–1946* (New York: Russell Sage Foundation, 1947), Volume 1. Loan-shark operation surveys were also conducted in Illinois and Kentucky.

9. Hank Messick, *Secret File* (New York: G.P. Putnam's Sons, 1969), pp. 277–78.

10. Torrio's rise to power has been chronicled in hundreds of books and press accounts dealing with the history of organized crime and with the "Capone" Chicago organization in particular. See Don Maclean, *Pictorial History of the Mafia* (New York: Pyramid Books, 1974); Ralph Salerno and John S. Tompkins, *The Crime Confederation* (New York: Doubleday & Company, Inc., 1969); Martin A. Gosch and Richard Hammer, *The Last Testament of Lucky Luciano* (New York: Dell Publishing Co., Inc., 1974). Additional insight was provided through numerous interviews with law enforcement officials at the U.S. Customs Bureau and Drug Enforcement Administration.

11. Maclean, *Pictorial History of the Mafia*, p. 150; see also Donald R. Cressey, *Theft of the Nation: The Structure and Operations of Organized Crime in America* (New York: Harper and Row, 1969), pp. 29–53.

12. Maclean, *Pictorial History of the Mafia*, p. 461. Figures vary for the death toll reached during the war period; however, on the night that New York boss Salvatore Maranzano was assassinated—Septem-

ber 11, 1931—and the immediate 48-hour period following, it is estimated that 40 gang leaders were killed in the overall purge. *See also:* Donald R. Cressey, *Theft of the Nation,* pp. 29–53, and Peter Maas, *The Valachi Papers* (New York: Bantam Books, 1968).

13. Messick, *Secret File,* pp. 96–97. Corroboration of the analysis presented here was provided through numerous and exhaustive interviews with law enforcement officials at the DEA and U.S. Customs Bureau.

14. Messick, *Lansky,* pp. 90, 97–98. Additional corroboration was provided by DEA officials in interviews in December 1977.

15. Report from Narcotics Division Agent Ralph Oyler to Narcotics Division Chief Levi Nutt, March 30, 1926 (DEA Library, Washington, D.C.).

16. Henry Aubin, *Who Owns Montreal.*

17. Ibid.

18. Newman, *Bronfman Dynasty,* pp. 55–61.

19. Starkman stores' connections to Koffler were widely publicized at the time in the Toronto *Globe and Mail.*

20. *See also* Newman, *Bronfman Dynasty,* pp. 167–169.

21. The *Washington Post,* November 6, 1978, p. 2.

22. Newman, *Bronfman Dynasty,* p. 233.

23. Ibid., p. 231.

24. Ibid., p. 225.

25. Ibid., p. 232.

26. Ibid., p. 227.

27. Ibid., p. 227.

2: The Kennedys

1. Financial Campaign Report filed by the Kennedy for Re-Election Committee, 1976, with the Clerk of the Senate.

2. *Pictorial History of Mafia;* see also Clark R. Mollenhoff, *Strike Force: Organized Crime and the Government* (Englewood Cliffs, N.J.: Prentice Hall, Inc., 1972).

3. Senate Committee Hearings on Organized Crime and Narcotics, 1963.

4. Financial Campaign Report filed by the Kennedy for Re-Election Committee, 1976.

5. David E. Koskoff, *Joseph P. Kennedy: A Life and Times* (Englewood Cliffs, N.J.: Prentice-Hall, Inc., 1974), p. 9. Additional insight and information on Kennedy was provided through interviews with law enforcement officials.

6. Koskoff, *Joseph P. Kennedy,* p. 19.

7. Ibid., pp. 28, 30.

8. Ibid., p. 28; see also *William Stephenson, A Man Called Intrepid* (New York: Ballantine Books, 1976),p. 325.

9. Interview with DEA officials, December 1977; see also Messick, *Secret File,* p. 197; and Koskoff, *Joseph P. Kennedy,* p. 53.

10. Koskoff, *Joseph P. Kennedy,* p. 53.

11. Ibid., p. 115.

12. Ibid., pp. 16, 394–95.

13. Ibid., p. 378.

14. Sir John Wheeler-Bennett, *Special Relationships: America in Peace and War* (New York: St. Martin, 1976), pp. 34–35; see also Koskoff, *Joseph P. Kennedy,* pp. 403–4.

15. Wheeler-Bennett, *Special Relationships,* pp. 34–35.

16. Victor Navasky, *Kennedy Justice* (New York: Atheneum, 1970), p. 404.

17. Ibid.

18. Messick, *Lansky,* pp. 241–42. This viewpoint was also shared by numerous law enforcement officials who were interviewed in the course of researching the history of organized crime.

19. *Who's Who in Canada.*

20. Harold Macmillan, *At the End of the Day 1961–63* (London: MacMillan London, Ltd., 1973), 6:359–60. According to Macmillan: "The President did not want to give us Polaris on political grounds, for fear of upsetting all the European nations. . . . The arrangement finally agreed was that we should be supplied with the Polaris missile. . . . Our nuclear fleet was to be 'assigned' to NATO, except in cases 'where Her Majesty's government may decide that superior national interests are at stake.' . . . Three days' hard negotiating—nearly four days in reality. The Americans pushed us very hard . . . the discussions were protracted and fiercely contested. . . ."

21. Ibid.

22. Koskoff, *Joseph P. Kennedy,* p. 439.

3: Britain's International Assassination Bureau: Permindex

1. "The Nomenclature of An Assassination Cabal," unpublished manuscript by William Torbitt, 1970, p. 21.

2. This pre-war controlling beach-head of British intelligence within the U.S. intelligence services was arranged through the services, in particular, of John J. McCloy on the American side. McCloy, then a partner of Cravath, Swaine, and Moore law firm in New York, became the post-war U.S. high commissioner for Germany. This arrangement almost immediately brought into a controlling position over U.S. wartime intelligence capabilities, the notorious British "triple agent" Kim Philby, who is now a KGB general in Moscow.

3. Torbitt, *op. cit.*, pp. 231–232.

4. A series of articles appearing in *Paese Sera* on March 4, 12, 14, 1967; see also *Les Echos* during spring 1962 for numerous news and editorial references to Permindex's role in the assassination attempts against President de Gaulle.

5. Virtually all the book-length material on Sir William Stephenson and the British Security Coordination—Special Operations Executive is "official cover story" commissioned by the SOE to provide limited exposure to aspects of its operations while withholding the most illegal and anti-American activities. Two books that fit this "official cover story" description, but which provide numerous references to Stephenson's methods of operation, including his penetration into every level of the U.S. military command with his SOE agents, are: H. Montgomery Hyde, *Room 3603* (New York: Ballantine Books, 1962); and *William Stephenson, A Man Called Intrepid,* (New York: Ballantine Books, 1976.)

6. Louis Wiznitzer, "Will Garrison's Inquiry into Kennedy Assassination Lead to Montreal?" *Le Devoir,* March 16, 1967, Montreal; also *Canadian Dimension,* Sept.–Oct., 1967 (reprint).

7. Ibid.

8. Bloomfield, Louis M. and Fitzgerald, Gerald, *Crimes Against Protected Persons: Prevention & Punishment* (New York: Praeger, 1975).

9. Canadian *Who's Who* (Toronto: TransCanada Press) Vols. 7, 8, 9, 10; and (Toronto: Who's Who Canada Publishers) Vols. 11, 12, 13.

10. Jacques Derogy, *The Israeli Connection: The Mafia in Israel* (Paris: Librarie Plon, 1980).

11. Torbitt, "Assassination Cabal," p. 105; Messick, *Lansky,* p. 248; *Life,* October 8, 1967.

12. *Who's Who in Great Britain; see also, 1977 Annual Report of the Bank Leumi.*

13. *See also New York Times* index citation on "Banque de Credit Internationale" and "Tibor Rosenbaum," particularly covering the period of exposure of Bank Hapoalim and related institutions' involvement in money-laundering; see also Katherine Burdman, "The British Crown's Secret Financial Capability: Israeli Banking," *Executive Intelligence Review* 44 (1978)

14. Col. Sir Edwin King and Sir Harry Luke, *The Knights of St. John in the British Realm—Being the Official History of the Most Venerable Order of the Hospital of St. John of Jerusalem* (London: Hills and Lacy, 1924).

15. Hank Messick, *Lansky*, p. 248.

16. Richard Deacon, *A History of the British Secret Service* (New York: Taplinger Publishing Company, 1970).

17. The U.S. government later went on record as believing that David Graiver was indeed still alive. Graiver gained notoriety when his American Bank and Trust Company in New York City went bankrupt in 1976, amid charges that Graiver had siphoned off some $50 million from the bank and then disappeared. A federal indictment was sought and those charges were dropped. In June 1978, the U.S. Attorney for the Southern District of New York petitioned for the charges to be reinstated. The petition was granted the same month. *See The New York Times* and the *Wall Street Journal* of June 3–30, 1978.

18. Torbitt, "Assassination Cabal," p. 73.

19. Ibid., p. 161.

20. Ibid., p. 213.

21. Ferrie was found murdered days after he was subpoenaed to testify before Garrison's grand jury on the Kennedy killing. See Torbitt, "Assassination Cabal," p. 164.

22. Rodney Campbell, *The Luciano Project* (New York: McGraw-Hill Book Company, 1977); see also Julian Semyonov, "Capriccio Siciliano," *Ogonyok* (Moscow), October–November, 1978.

23. Semyonov, "Capriccio Siciliano," reprinted English translation from *Ogonyok* in *Executive Intelligence Review* 43 (1978), p. 38.

24. Giuseppe Pantaleone, "An Interview," *Panorama*, April 1970.

25. Victor Navasky, *Kennedy Justice*.

26. Jim Hougan, *Spooks* (New York: Bantam Books, 1978).

4: Permindex Unveiled: Resorts International-Intertel

1. Hutchinson, *Vesco*.

2. Messick, *Lansky*, pp. 221–51. Lansky had had his eye on the Bahamas since the 1940s, but his attention was then fixed on his Cuban and Las Vegas casino empires. (Castro's refusal to play ball allegedly inspired Lansky to issue a $1 million "contract" on Castro's life.) With the 1959 fall of the Batista government, the Bahamas option became an imperative. Thus, it was no accident that the British gave the go-ahead for legalized gambling not only for their Caribbean hold-

ings, but in Britain as well. Messick reports (p. 228): "All that was needed in 1960 was to find a semirespectable front from which he [Lansky] could operate."

3. Ibid., p. 228.

4. Ibid., p. 229.

5. Ibid., pp. 230–32; see also Jim Hougan, "A Surfeit of Spies," *Harper's,* December 1974, p. 58; Frank J. Prial, "Concern Fights Crime in Business," *New York Times,* July 26, 1970, Business Section, p. 1, p. 11.

6. Messick, *Lansky,* pp. 230–231, 235.

7. Ibid., pp. 232–233.

8. Ibid., p. 232; *see also* Hougan, "Surfeit of Spies," pp. 58, 63.

9. Hougan, "Surfeit of Spies," pp. 58, 63.

10. Hutchinson, *Vesco;* see also James Hougan, *Spooks: The Haunting of America—The Private Use of Secret Agents* (New York: William Morrow and Co., 1978), pp. 390–392.

11. Hougan, "Surfeit of Spies," p. 54.

12. Ibid., pp. 66–67; see also Hutchinson, *Vesco.*

13. Hougan, "Surfeit of Spies," pp. 54, 56; *see also* Prial, "Concern Fights Crime," p. 11.

14. Hougan, "Surfeit of Spies," p. 66; Hougan's information is corroborated by the authors' interviews with law enforcement officials.

5: Max Fisher

1. Kirk Cheyfitz, "The Power Broker," *Monthly Detroit* magazine, July 1980.

2. From an interview with Mrs. Sally Fields, June 5, 1979.

3. From an interview with Julius Klein, June 4, 1979.

4. Ibid.

5. Hank Messick, *John Edgar Hoover* (New York: David McKay, Inc., 1972).

6. Interview with Klein.

7. Leonard Slater, *The Pledge* (New York: Simon and Schuster, 1970).

8. Ibid.

9. Ibid.

10. Ibid.

11. Ibid, p. 132.

12. Interview with Fields.

13. Charles William Heckethorn, *The Secret Societies of All Ages*

and Countries, Vols. I and II, 1875 (New York: University Books, Inc., 1965).

14. David Leon Chandler, *Brothers in Blood* (New York: E.P. Dutton Co., Inc., 1975).

15. Ibid.

16. Ibid.

17. Ibid.

18. Ibid.

19. Ibid.

20. Ibid.

21. This information was volunteered anonymously by persons close to the United Fruit situation in 1975.

22. Thomas McCann and Henry Scammel, *An American Company: The Tragedy of United Fruit,* (New York, Crown Publishers, 1976).

23. "Brzezinski Pushes Limited Sovereignty in Nicaraguan Crisis," *Executive Intelligence Review,* Oct. 3–9, 1978, pp. 53–56.

6: The Jacobs Family's Emprise

1. Testimony of labor racketeer James Plumeri (Jimmy Doyle) before the McClellan Subcommittee on Criminal Laws and Procedures; *see also* Congressman Sam Steiger's insertion into the *Congressional Record* of the 91st Congress, "Emprise: A Lesson in Corporate Calumny."

2. Testimony of Plumeri before the McClellan Subcommittee on Criminal Laws and Procedures.

3. From their positions in Cleveland and Buffalo, the Jacobs family was a Bronfman link into the United States in alliance with the Reinfeld Syndicate and the Big Seven Combine.

4. "Emprise: A Lesson in Corporate Calumny," 91st *Congressional Record,* p. 5888; "Emprise: A Little More of the Iceberg Exposed," 91st *Congressional Record,* p. 6830.

5. Many of the Justice Department officials who worked with Robert Kennedy in the "Get Hoffa" campaign turned up playing supporting roles in forcing Richard Nixon out of office, particularly when Nixon demonstrated a commitment to go after organized crime. This includes most especially Horace S. Webb.

PART VIII

Origins of the Counterculture

The Aquarian Conspiracy

In the spring of 1980, a book appeared called *The Aquarian Conspiracy* that put itself forward as a manifesto of the counterculture. Defining the counterculture as the conscious embracing of irrationality—from rock and drugs to biofeedback, meditation, "consciousness-raising," yoga, mountain climbing, group therapy, and psychodrama—*The Aquarian Conspiracy* declares that it is now time for the 15 million Americans involved in the counterculture to join in bringing about a "radical change in the United States."

Writes author Marilyn Ferguson: "While outlining a not-yet-titled book about the emerging social alternatives, I thought again about the peculiar form of this movement; its atypical leadership, the patient intensity of its adherents, their unlikely successes. It suddenly struck me that in their sharing of strategies, their linkage, and their recognition of each other by subtle signals, the participants were not merely cooperating with one another. They were in collusion. It—this movement—is a conspiracy!"[1]

Ferguson used a half-truth to tell a lie. The counterculture is a conspiracy—but not in the half-conscious way Ferguson claims—as she well knows. Ferguson wrote her manifesto under the direction of Willis Harman, social policy director of the Stanford Research Institute, as a popular version of a May 1974 policy study on how to transform the United States into Aldous Huxley's *Brave New World*. The counterculture is a conspiracy at the top, created as a method of social control, used to drain the United States of its commitment to scientific and technological progress.

That conspiracy goes back to the 1930s, when the British sent Aldous Huxley to the United States as the case officer for an operation to prepare the United States for the mass dissemination of drugs. We will take this conspiracy apart—step-by-step—from its small beginnings with Huxley in California to the victimization of 15 million Americans today. With *The Aquarian Conspiracy,* the British Opium War against the United States has come out into the open.

The Model

The British had a precedent for the counterculture they imposed upon the United States: the pagan cult ceremonies of the decadent Egyptian and Roman Empires. The following description of cult ceremonies dating back to the Egyptian Isis priesthood of the third millennium B.C. could just as well be a journalistic account of a "hippy be-in" circa A.D. 1969:

> The acts or gestures that accompany the incantations constitute the rite [of Isis]. In these dances, the beating of drums and the rhythm of music and repetitive movements were helped by hallucinatory substances like hashish or mescal; these were consumed as adjuvants to create the trance and

the hallucinations that were taken to be the visitation of the god. The drugs were sacred, and their knowledge was limited to the initiated. . . .

Possibly because they have the illusion of satisfied desires, and allowed the innermost feelings to escape, these rites acquired during their execution a frenzied character that is conspicuous in certain spells: "Retreat! Re is piercing thy head, slashing thy face, dividing thy head, crushing it in his hands; thy bones are shattered, thy limbs are cut to pieces!"[2]

The counterculture that was foisted on the 1960s adolescent youth of America is not merely analogous to the ancient cult of Isis. It is a literal resurrection of the cult—down to the popularization of the Isis cross as the counterculture's most frequently used symbol.

The High Priesthood

The high priest for Britain's Opium War was Aldous Huxley, the grandson of Thomas H. Huxley, a founder of the Rhodes Roundtable group and a lifelong collaborator of Arnold Toynbee. Toynbee himself sat on the RIIA council for nearly fifty years, headed the Research Division of British intelligence throughout World War II, and served as wartime briefing officer to Prime Minister Winston Churchill.

Toynbee's "theory" of history, expounded in his twenty-volume history of Western civilization, was that its determining feature has always been the rise and decline of grand imperial dynasties. At the very point that these dynasties—the "thousand year Reich" of the Egyptian pharaohs, the Roman Empire, and the British Empire—succeed in imposing their rule over the entire face of the earth, they tend to decline. Toynbee argued that this decline could be abated if the ruling oligarchy (like that of the British Roundtable) would devote itself to the recruitment and training of an ever-expanding priesthood devoted to the principles of imperial rule.[3]

Trained at Toynbee's Oxford, Aldous Huxley was one of the initiates in the "Children of the Sun," a Dionysian cult comprised of the children of Britain's Roundtable elite.[4] Among the other initiates were T.S. Eliot, W.H. Auden, Sir Oswald Mosley, and D.H. Lawrence, Huxley's homosexual lover. It was Huxley, furthermore, who would launch the legal battle in the 1950s to have Lawrence's pornographic novel *Lady Chatterley's Lover* allowed into the United States on the ground that it was a misunderstood "work of art."[5]

Aldous Huxley, along with his brother Julian, was tutored at Oxford by H.G. Wells, the head of British foreign intelligence during World War I and the spiritual grandfather of the Aquarian Conspiracy. Ferguson accurately sees the counterculture as the realization of what Wells called *The Open Conspiracy: Blue Prints for a World Revolution.*

The "Open Conspiracy," Wells wrote, "will appear first, I believe, as a conscious organization of intelligent and quite possibly in some cases, wealthy men, as a movement having distinct social and political aims, confessedly ignoring most of the existing apparatus of political control, or using it only as an incidental implement in the stages, a mere movement of a number of people in a certain direction who will presently discover with a sort of surprise the common object toward which they are all moving. . . . In all sorts of ways they will be influencing and controlling the apparatus of the ostensible government."[6]

What Ferguson left out is that Wells called his conspiracy a "one-world brain" which would function as "a police of the mind."

Such books as the *Open Conspiracy* were for the priesthood itself. But Wells's popular writings (*Time Machine, The Island of Dr. Moreau,* and so forth), and those of his protégés Aldous Huxley (*Brave New World*) and George Orwell (*1984* and *Animal Farm*), were written as "mass appeal" organizing documents on behalf of one-world order. Only in the United States are these "science fiction classics" taught in grade school as attacks against fascism.

Under Wells's tutelage, Huxley was first introduced to Aleister Crowley. Crowley was a product of the cultist circle that developed in Britain from the 1860s under the guiding influence of Edward Bulwer-Lytton—who, it will be recalled, was the colonial minister under Lord Palmerston during the Second Opium War. In 1886, Crowley, William Butler Yeats, and several other Bulwer-Lytton protégés formed the Isis-Urania Temple of Hermetic Students of the Golden Dawn. This Isis Cult was organized around the 1877 manuscript *Isis Unveiled* by Madame Helena Blavatsky, in which the Russian occultist called for the British aristocracy to organize itself into an Isis priesthood.[7]

In 1937, Huxley was sent to the United States, where he remained throughout the period of World War II. Through a Los Angeles contact, Jacob Zeitlin, Huxley and pederast Christopher Isherwood were employed as script writers for MGM, Warner Brothers, and Walt Disney Studios. Hollywood was already dominated by organized crime elements bankrolled and controlled through London. Joseph Kennedy was the front man for a British consortium that created RKO studios, and "Bugsy" Siegel, the West Coast boss of the Lansky syndicate, was heavily involved in Warner Brothers and MGM.

Huxley founded a nest of Isis cults in southern California and in San Francisco, that consisted exclusively of several hundred deranged worshippers of Isis and other cult gods. Isherwood, during the California period, translated and propagated a number of ancient Zen Buddhist documents, inspiring Zen-mystical cults along the way.[8]

In effect, Huxley and Isherwood (joined soon afterwards by Thomas Mann and his daughter Elisabeth Mann Borghese) laid the foundations during the late 1930s and the 1940s for the later LSD culture, by recruiting a core of "initiates" into the Isis cults that Huxley's mentors, Bulwer-Lytton, Blavatsky, and Crowley, had constituted while stationed in India.

LSD: 'Visitation from the Gods'

"Ironically," writes Ferguson, "the introduction of major psychedelics like LSD, in the 1960s, was largely attributable to the

Central Intelligence Agency's investigation into the substances for possible military use. Experiments on more than eighty college campuses, under various CIA code names, unintentionally popularized LSD. Thousands of graduate students served as guinea pigs. Soon they were synthesizing their own 'acid.' "[9]

The CIA operation was code named MK-Ultra, its result was not unintentional, and it began in 1952, the year Aldous Huxley returned to the United States.

Lysergic acid diethylamide, or LSD, was developed in 1943 by Albert Hoffman, a chemist at Sandoz A.B.—a Swiss pharmaceutical house owned by S.G. Warburg. While precise documentation is unavailable as to the auspices under which the LSD research was commissioned, it can be safely assumed that British intelligence and its subsidiary U.S. Office of Strategic Services were directly involved. Allen Dulles, the director of the CIA when that agency began MK-Ultra, was the OSS station chief in Berne, Switzerland throughout the early Sandoz research. One of his OSS assistants was James Warburg, of the same Warburg family, who was instrumental in the 1963 founding of the Institute for Policy Studies, and worked with both Huxley and Robert Hutchins.[10]

Aldous Huxley returned to the United States from Britain, accompanied by Dr. Humphrey Osmond, the Huxleys' private physician. Osmond had been part of a discussion group Huxley had organized at the National Hospital, Queens Square, London. Along with another seminar participant, J.R. Smythies, Osmond wrote *Schizophrenia: A New Approach,* in which he asserted that mescaline—a derivative of the mescal cactus used in ancient Egyptian and Indian pagan rites—produced a psychotic state identical in all clinical respects to schizophrenia. On this basis, Osmond and Smythies advocated experimentation with hallucinogenic drugs as a means of developing a "cure" for mental disorders.

Osmond was brought in by Allen Dulles to play a prominent role in MK-Ultra. At the same time, Osmond, Huxley, and the University of Chicago's Robert Hutchins held a series of secret planning sessions in 1952 and 1953 for a second, private LSD-mescaline project under Ford Foundation funding.[11] Hutchins, it will be recalled, was the program director of the Ford Foundation during this period. His LSD proposal incited such rage in Henry Ford II that Hutchins was fired from the foundation the following year.

It was also in 1953 that Osmond gave Huxley a supply of mescaline for his personal consumption. The next year, Huxley wrote *The Doors of Perception,* the first manifesto of the psychedelic drug cult, which claimed that hallucinogenic drugs "expand consciousness."

Although the Ford Foundation rejected the Hutchins-Huxley proposal for private foundation sponsorship of LSD, the project was not dropped. Beginning in 1962, the Rand Corporation of Santa Monica, California began a four-year experiment in LSD, peyote, and marijuana. The Rand Corporation was established simultaneously with the reorganization of the Ford Foundation during 1949. Rand was an outgrowth of the wartime Strategic Bombing Survey, a "cost analysis" study of the psychological effects of the bombings of German population centers.

According to a 1962 *Rand Abstract,* W.H. McGlothlin conducted a preparatory study on "The Long-Lasting Effects of LSD on Certain Attitudes in Normals: An Experimental Proposal." The following year, McGlothlin conducted a year-long experiment on thirty human guinea pigs, called "Short-Term Effects of LSD on Anxiety, Attitudes and Performance." The study concluded that LSD *improved* emotional attitudes and resolved anxiety problems.[12]

Huxley At Work

Huxley expanded his own LSD-mescaline project in California by recruiting several individuals who had been initially drawn into the cult circles he helped establish during his earlier stay. The two most prominent individuals were Alan Watts and the late Dr. Gregory Bateson (the former husband of Dame Margaret Mead).

Watts became a self-styled "guru" of a nationwide Zen Buddhist cult built around his well-publicized books. Bateson, an anthropologist with the OSS, became the director of a hallucinogenic drug experimental clinic at the Palo Alto Veterans Administration Hospital. Under Bateson's auspices, the initiating "cadre" of the LSD cult—the hippies—were programmed.[13]

Watts at the same time founded the Pacifica Foundation, which sponsored two radio stations—WKBW in San Francisco and WBAI-FM in New York City. The Pacifica stations were among the first to push the "Liverpool Sound"—the British-imported hard rock twanging of the Rolling Stones, the Beatles, and the Animals. They would later pioneer "acid rock" and eventually the self-avowed psychotic "punk rock."

During the fall of 1960, Huxley was appointed visiting professor at the Massachusetts Institute of Technology in Boston. Around his stay in that city, Huxley created a circle at Harvard parallel to his West Coast LSD team. The Harvard group included Huxley, Osmond, and Watts (brought in from California), Timothy Leary, and Richard Alpert.

The ostensible topic of the Harvard seminar was "Religion and its Significance in the Modern Age." The seminar was actually a planning session for the "acid rock" counterculture. Huxley established contact during this Harvard period with the president of Sandoz, which at the time was working on a CIA contract to produce large quantities of LSD and psilocybin (another synthetic hallucinogenic drug) for MK-Ultra, the CIA's official chemical warfare experiment. According to recently released CIA documents, Allen Dulles purchased over 100 million doses of LSD—almost all of which flooded the streets of the United States during the late 1960s. During the same period, Leary began privately purchasing large quantities of LSD from Sandoz as well.[14]

From the discussions of the Harvard seminar, Leary put together the book *The Psychedelic Experience*, based on the ancient cultist *Tibetan Book of the Dead*. It was this book that popularized Osmond's previously coined term, "psychedelic mind-expanding."

The Roots of the Flower People

Back in California, Gregory Bateson had maintained the Huxley operation out of the Palo Alto VA hospital. Through LSD experimentation on patients already hospitalized for psychological problems, Bateson established a core of "initiates" into the "psychedelic" Isis Cult.

Foremost among his Palo Alto recruits was Ken Kesey. In 1959, Bateson administered the first dose of LSD to Kesey. By 1962, Kesey had completed a novel, *One Flew Over the Cuckoo's Nest,* which popularized the notion that society is a prison and the only truly "free" people are the insane.[15]

Kesey subsequently organized a circle of LSD initiates called "The Merry Pranksters." They toured the country disseminating LSD (often without forewarning the receiving parties), building up local distribution connections, and establishing the pretext for a high volume of publicity on behalf of the still minuscule "counterculture."

By 1967, the Kesey cult had handed out such quantities of LSD that a sizable drug population had emerged, centered in the Haight-Ashbury district of San Francisco. Here Huxley collaborator Bateson set up a "free clinic," staffed by

- **Dr. David Smith**—later a "medical adviser" for the National Organization for the Reform of Marijuana Laws (NORML);
- **Dr. Ernest Dernberg**—an active-duty military officer, probably on assignment through MK-Ultra;
- **Roger Smith**—a street gang organizer trained by Saul Alinsky. During the Free Clinic period, Roger Smith was the parole officer of the cultist mass murderer Charles Manson;
- **Dr. Peter Bourne**—formerly President Carter's special as-

sistant on drug abuse. Bourne did his psychiatric residency at the clinic. He had previously conducted a profiling study of GI heroin addicts in Vietnam.

The Free Clinic paralleled a project at the Tavistock Institute, the psychological warfare agency for the British Secret Intelligence Service. Tavistock, founded as a clinic in London in the 1920s, had become the Psychiatric Division of the British Army during World War II under its director, Dr. John Rawlings Rees.[16]

During the 1960s, the Tavistock Clinic fostered the notion that no criteria for sanity exist and that psychedelic "mind-expanding" drugs are valuable tools of psychoanalysis. In 1967, Tavistock sponsored a Conference on the "Dialectics of Liberation," chaired by Tavistock psychoanalyst Dr. R.D. Laing, himself a popularized author and advocate of drug use. That conference drew a number of people who would soon play a prominent role in fostering terrorism; Angela Davis and Stokely Carmichael were two prominent American delegates.

Thus, by 1963, Huxley had recruited his core of "initiates." All of them—Leary, Osmond, Watts, Kesey, Alpert—became the highly publicized promoters of the early LSD counterculture. By 1967, with the cult of "Flower People" in Haight-Ashbury and the emergence of the antiwar movement, the United States was ready for the inundation of LSD, hashish, and marijuana that hit American college campuses in the late 1960s.

'The Beating of Drums . . .'

In 1963, the Beatles arrived in the United States, and with their decisive airing on the Ed Sullivan Show, the "British sound" took off in the U.S.A. For their achievement, the four rocksters were awarded the Order of the British Empire by Her Majesty the Queen. The Beatles and the Animals, Rolling Stones, and homicidal punk rock maniacs who followed were, of course, no more a spontaneous outpouring of alienated youth than was the acid culture they accompanied.

The social theory of rock was elaborated by musicologist Theodor Adorno, who came to the United States in 1939 to head the Princeton University Radio Research Project.[17] Adorno writes:

> In an imaginary but psychologically emotion-laden domain, the listener who remembers a hit song will turn into the song's ideal subject, into the person for whom the song ideally speaks. At the same time, as one of many who identify with that fictitious subject, that musical I, he will feel his isolation ease as he himself feels integrated into the community of "fans." In whistling such a song he bows to a ritual of socialization, although beyond this unarticulated subjective stirring of the moment his isolation continues unchanged. . . .
>
> The comparison with addiction is inescapable. Addicted conduct generally has a social component: it is one possible reaction to the atomization which, as sociologists have noticed, parallels the compression of the social network. Addiction to music on the part of a number of entertainment listeners would be a similar phenomenon.[18]

The hit parade is organized precisely on the same principles used by Egypt's Isis priesthood and for the same purpose: the recruitment of youth to the dionysiac counterculture.

In a report prepared for the University of Michigan's Institute for Social Research, Paul Hirsch described the product of Adorno's Radio Research Project.[19] According to Hirsch, the establishment of postwar radio's Hit Parade "transformed the mass medium into an agency of sub-cultural programming." Radio networks were converted into round-the-clock recycling machines that repeated the top forty "hits." Hirsch documents how all popular culture—movies, music, books, and fashion—is now run on the same program of preselection. Today's mass culture operates like the opium trade: The supply determines the demand.

The Vietnam War and the Anti-War Trap

But without the Vietnam War and the "anti-war" movement, the Isis cult would have been contained to a fringe phenomenon—no bigger than the beatnik cult of the 1950s that was an outgrowth of the early Huxley ventures in California. The Vietnam War created the climate of moral despair that opened America's youth to drugs.

Under Kennedy, American military involvement in Vietnam—which had been vetoed by the Eisenhower administration—was initiated on a limited scale. Under Lyndon Johnson, American military presence in Vietnam was massively escalated, at the same time that U.S. efforts were restricted to the framework of "limited war." Playing on the President's profile, the anglophile Eastern Establishment, typified by top White House national security aide McGeorge Bundy and Defense Secretary Robert McNamara, convinced President Johnson that under the nuclear "balance of terror," or the regime of Mutual and Assured Destruction, the United States could afford neither a political solution to the conflict, nor the commitment to a military victory.

The outcome of this debacle was a major strategic withdrawal from Asia by the United States, spelled out in Henry Kissinger's "Guam Doctrine," adoption of the spectacular failure known as the "China Card" strategy for containing Soviet influence, and demoralization of the American people over the war to the point that the sense of national pride and confidence in the future progress of the republic was badly damaged.

Just as Aldous Huxley began the counterculture subversion of the United States thirty years before its consequences became evident to the public, Lord Bertrand Russell began laying the foundations for the anti-war movement of the 1960s before the 1930s expired. Russell's "pacifism" was always relative—the means to his most cherished end, one-world government on the imperial model, that would curb the nation-state and its persistent tendency toward republicanism and technological progress.

Lord Russell and Aldous Huxley cofounded the Peace Pledge

Union in 1937—campaigning for peace with Hitler—just before both went to the United States for the duration of World War II.[20] During World War II, Lord Russell opposed British and American warfare against the Nazis. In 1947, when the United States was in possession of the atomic bomb and Russia was not, Russell loudly advocated that the United States order the Soviets to surrender to a one-world government that would enjoy a restrictive monopoly on nuclear weapons, under the threat of a preemptive World War III against the Soviet Union. His 1950s "Ban the Bomb" movement was directed to the same end—it functioned as an anti-technology movement against the peace-through-economic development potentials represented by President Eisenhower's "Atoms for Peace" initiative.

From the mid-1950s onward, Russell's principal assignment was to build an international anti-war and anti-American movement. Coincident with the escalation of U.S. involvement in Vietnam under British manipulation, Russell upgraded the old Peace Pledge Union (which had been used in West Germany throughout the postwar period to promote an anti-capitalist "New Left" wing of the Social Democratic Party, recruiting several future members of the Baader-Meinhof terrorist gang in the process) into the Bertrand Russell Peace Foundation.

In the United States, the New York banks provided several hundred thousand dollars to establish the Institute for Policy Studies (IPS), effectively the U.S. branch of the Russell Peace Foundation. Among the founding trustees of the IPS was James Warburg, directly representing the family's interests.

IPS drew its most active operatives from a variety of British-dominated institutions. IPS founding director Marcus Raskin was a member of the Kennedy administration's National Security Council and also a fellow of the National Training Labs, a U.S. subsidiary of the Tavistock Institute founded by Dr. Kurt Lewin.

After its creation by the League for Industrial Democracy, Students for a Democratic Society (SDS), the umbrella of the student anti-war movement, was in turn financed and run through IPS—up through and beyond its splintering into a number of terrorist and Maoist gangs in the late 1960s.[21] More broadly, the institutions and outlook of the U.S. anti-war movement were dominated by the direct political descendants of the British-dominated "socialist movement" in the U.S.A., fostered by the House of Morgan as far back as the years before World War I.

This is not to say that the majority of anti-war protesters were paid, certified British agents. On the contrary, the overwhelming majority of anti-war protesters went into SDS on the basis of outrage at the developments in Vietnam. But once caught in the environment defined by Russell and the Tavistock Institute's psychological warfare experts, and inundated with the message that hedonistic pleasure-seeking was a legitimate alternative to "immoral war," their sense of values and their creative potential went up in a cloud of hashish smoke.

'Changing Images'

Now, fifteen years later, with nearly an entire generation of American youth submerged in the drugs that flooded the nation's campuses, the Aquarian Conspiracy's Marilyn Ferguson is able to write: "There are legions of [Aquarian] conspirators. They are in corporations, universities, and hospitals, on the faculties of public schools, in factories and doctors' offices, in state and federal agencies, on city councils, and the White House staff, in state legislatures, in volunteer organizations, in virtually all arenas of policy making in the country."[22]

Like the British inundation of China with drugs in the nineteenth century, the British counterculture has succeeded in subverting the fabric of the nation, even up to the top-most levels of government.

In 1962, Huxley helped found the Esalen Institute in Big Sur, California, which became a mecca for hundreds of Americans to engage in weekends of T-Groups and Training Groups modeled on behavior group therapy, for Zen, Hindu, and Buddhist transcendental meditation, and "out of body" experiences through simulated and actual hallucinogenic drugs.[23]

As described in the Esalen Institute *Newsletter:*

> Esalen started in the fall of 1962 as a forum to bring together
> a wide variety of approaches to enhancement of the human
> potential . . . including experiential sessions involving en-
> counter groups, sensory awakening, gestalt awareness train-
> ing, related disciplines. Our latest step is to fan out into the
> community at large, running programs in cooperation with
> many different institutions, churches, schools, hospitals, and
> government.[24]

Esalen's nominal founders were two transcendental meditation
students, Michael Murphy and Richard Price, both graduates
of Stanford University. Price also participated in the experi-
ments on patients at Bateson's Palo Alto Veterans Hospital.
Today Esalen's catalogue offers: "T-Groups; Psychodrama Mar-
athon; Fight Training for Lovers and Couples; Religious Cults;
LSD Experiences and the Great Religions of the World; Are
You Sound, a weekend workshop with Alan Watts; Creating
New Forms of Worship; Hallucinogenic Psychosis; and Non-
Drug Approaches to Psychedelic Experiences."

Several tens of thousands of Americans have passed through
Esalen; millions have passed through the programs it has sired
throughout the country.

The next leap in Britain's Aquarian Conspiracy against the
United States was the May 1974 report that provided the basis
for Ferguson's work. The report is entitled "Changing Images
of Man," Contract Number URH (489)–2150, Policy Research
Report No. 4/4.74, prepared by the Stanford Research Institute
Center for the Study of Social Policy, Willis Harman, director.

The 319-page mimeographed report was prepared by a team
of fourteen researchers and supervised by a panel of twenty-
three controllers, including anthropologist Margaret Mead,
psychologist B.F. Skinner, Ervin Laszlo of the United Nations,
and Sir Geoffrey Vickers of British intelligence.

The aim of the study, the authors state, is to change the
image of mankind from that of industrial progress to one of
"spiritualism." The study asserts that in our present society,

the "image of industrial and technological man" is obsolete and must be "discarded":

> Many of our present images appear to have become dangerously obsolete, however. . . . Science, technology, and economics have made possible really significant strides toward achieving such basic human goals as physical safety and security, material comfort and better health. But many of these successes have brought with them problems of being too successful—problems that themselves seem insoluble within the set of societal value-premises that led to their emergence. . . . Our highly developed system of technology leads to higher vulnerability and breakdowns. Indeed the range and interconnected impact of societal problems that are now emerging pose a serious threat to our civilization. . . . If our projections of the future prove correct, we can expect the association problems of the trend to become more serious, more universal and to occur more rapidly.

Therefore, SRI concludes, we must change the industrial-technological image of man fast: "Analysis of the nature of contemporary societal problems leads to the conclusion that . . . the images of man that dominated the last two centuries will be inadequate for the post-industrial era."

Since the writing of the Harman report, one President of the United States, Jimmy Carter, reported sighting UFOs, his National Security Adviser Zbigniew Brzezinski made speeches proclaiming the advent of the New Age, the Joint Chiefs of Staff every morning read so-called intelligence reports on the biorhythms and horoscopes of the members of the Soviet Politburo. The House of Representatives established a new congressional committee, called the Congressional Clearinghouse on the Future, where the likes of Ferguson have come to lecture up to a hundred congressmen.[25]

What began as Britain's creation of the counterculture to open the market for its dope has come a long way.

The LSD Connection

Who provided the drugs that swamped the anti-war movement and the college campuses of the United States in the late 1960s? The organized crime infrastructure—which had set up the Peking Connection for the opium trade in 1928—provided the same services in the 1960s and 1970s it had provided during Prohibition. This was also the same network Huxley had established contact with in Hollywood during the 1930s.

The LSD connection begins with one William "Billy" Mellon Hitchcock. Hitchcock was a graduate of the University of Vienna and a scion of the millionaire Mellon banking family of Pittsburgh. (Andrew Mellon of the same family had been the U.S. treasury secretary throughout Prohibition.) In 1963, when Timothy Leary was thrown out of Harvard, Hitchcock rented a fifty-five-room mansion in Millbrook, New York, where the entire Leary-Huxley circle of initiates was housed until its later move back to California.[26]

Hitchcock was also a broker for the Lansky syndicate and for the Fiduciary Trust Co., Nassau, Grand Bahamas—a wholly owned subsidiary of Investors Overseas Services. He was formally employed by Delafield and Delafield Investments, where he worked on buying and selling vast quantities of stock in the Mary Carter Paint Co., soon to become Resorts International.

In 1967, Dr. Richard Alpert put Hitchcock in contact with Augustus Owsley Stanley III. As Owsley's agent, Hitchcock retained the law firm of Rabinowitz, Boudin and Standard[27] to conduct a feasibility study of several Caribbean countries to determine the best location for the production and distribution of LSD and hashish.

During this period, Hitchcock joined Leary and his circle in California. Leary had established an LSD cult called the Brotherhood of Eternal Love and several front companies, including Mystics Art World, Inc. of Laguna Beach, California. These California-based entities ran lucrative trafficking in Mexican marijuana and LSD brought in from Switzerland and Britain. The British connection had been established directly by Hitchcock, who contracted the Charles Bruce chemical firm to import large quantities of the chemical components of LSD. With financing from both Hitchcock and George Grant Hoag, the heir to the J.C. Penney dry goods fortune, the Brotherhood of Eternal Love set up LSD and hashish production-marketing operations in Costa Rica in 1968.[28]

Toward the end of 1968, Hitchcock expanded the LSD-hashish production operations in the Caribbean with funds provided by the Fiduciary Trust Co. (IOS). In conjunction with J. Vontobel and Co. of Zürich, Hitchcock founded a corporation called 4-Star Anstalt in Liechtenstein. This company, employing "investment funds" (that is, drug receipts) from Fiduciary Trust, bought up large tracts of land in the Grand Bahamas as well as large quantities of ergotamine tartrate, the basic chemical used in the production of LSD.[29]

Hitchcock's personal hand in the LSD connection abruptly ended several years later. Hitchcock had been working closely with Johann F. Parravacini of the Parravacini Bank Ltd. in Berne, Switzerland. From 1968, they had together funded even further expansion of the Caribbean-California LSD-hashish ventures. In the early 1970s, as the result of a Securities and Exchange Commission investigation, both Hitchcock and Parravacini were indicted and convicted of a $40 million stock fraud. Parravacini had registered a $40 million sale to Hitchcock for which Hitchcock had not put down a penny of cash or collateral. This was one of the rare instances in which federal investigators succeeded in getting inside the $200 billion drug fund as it was making its way around the "offshore" banking system.

Another channel for laundering dirty drug money—a channel yet to be compromised by federal investigative agencies—is important to note here. This is the use of tax-exempt foundations to finance terrorism and environmentalism. One immediately relevant case makes the point.

In 1957, the University of Chicago's Robert M. Hutchins established the Center for the Study of Democratic Institutions (CSDI) in Santa Barbara, California. Knight Commander Hutchins drew in Aldous Huxley, Elisabeth Mann Borghese, and some Rhodes Scholars who had originally been brought into the University of Chicago during the 1930s and 1940s.

The CSDI was originally funded 1957 to 1961 through a several-million-dollar fund that Hutchins managed to set up before his untimely departure from the Ford Foundation. From 1961 onward, the Center was principally financed by organized crime. The two funding conduits were the Fund of Funds, a tax-exempt front for Bernie Cornfeld's IOS, and the Parvin Foundation, a parallel front for Parvin-Dohrman Co. of Nevada. IOS and Parvin-Dohrman held controlling interests in the Desert Inn, the Aladdin, and the Dunes—all Las Vegas casinos associated with the Lansky syndicate. IOS, as already documented, was a conduiting vehicle for LSD, hashish, and marijuana distribution throughout the 1960s.[30] In 1967 alone, IOS channeled between $3 and $4 million to the center. Wherever there is dope, there is Dope, Inc.

Notes: Part VIII

1: Aquarian Conspiracy

1. Marilyn Ferguson, *The Aquarian Conspiracy* (Los Angeles: J.P. Tarcher, 1980), p. 19.

2. Paul Ghalioungui, *The House of Life: Magic and Medical Science in Ancient Egypt* (New York: Schram Enterprises, 1974).

3. Arnold Toynbee, *A Study of History* (New York: Oxford University Press, 1935).

4. Martin Green, *Children of the Sun: A Narrative of Decadence in England after 1918* (New York: Basic Books, 1976).

5. *See* Ronald William Clark, *The Huxleys* (New York: McGraw-Hill, 1968).

6. H.G. Wells, *Anticipations of the Reaction of Mechanical and Scientific Progress Upon Human Life and Thought* (New York: Harper and Row, 1902), p. 285.

7. Helena P. Blavatsky, *Isis Unveiled, A Master Key to the Mysteries of Ancient and Modern Science and Theology* (Los Angeles: Theosophy Co., 1931).

8. Francis King, *Sexuality, Magic and Perversion* (New York: Citadel, 1974), p. 118.

9. Ferguson, *Aquarian Conspiracy,* p. 126n.

10. Institute for Policy Studies, "The First Ten Years, 1963–1973," Washington, D.C., 1974.

11. Humphrey Osmond, *Understanding Understanding* (New York: Harper and Row, 1974).

12. Rand Corporation Catalogue of Documents.

13. Gregory Bateson, *Steps to the Ecology of the Mind* (New York: Chandler, 1972).

14. Ralph Metzner, *The Ecstatic Adventure* (New York: Macmillan, 1968).

15. *See* Clark, *The Huxleys.*

16. Michael Minnicino, "Low Intensity Operations: The Reesian Theory of War," *The Campaigner* (April 1974).

17. Theodor Adorno was a leading professor of the Frankfurt School of Social Research in Germany, founded by the British Fabian Society.

A collaborator of twelve-tone formalist and British intelligence operative Arnold Schoenberg, Adorno was brought to the United States in 1939 to head the Princeton Radio Research Project. The aim of this project, as stated in Adorno's *Introduction to the Sociology of Music,* was to program a mass "musical" culture that would steadily degrade its consumers. Punk rock is, in the most direct sense, the ultimate result of Adorno's work.

18. Theodor Adorno, *Introduction to the Sociology of Music* (New York: Seabury Press, 1976).

19. Paul Hirsch, "The Structure of the Popular Music Industry; The Filtering Process by which Records are Preselected for Public Consumption," Institute for Social Research's Survey Research Center Monograph, 1969.

20. Ronald Clark, *The Life of Bertrand Russell* (New York: Alfred A. Knopf, 1976), p. 457.

21. *Illinois Crime Commission Report,* 1969. The Institute for Policy Studies (IPS) was established in 1963 by Marcus Raskin, a former National Security Adviser under NSC Director McGeorge Bundy, and by Richard Barnet, a former State Department adviser on arms control and disarmament. Among the board of trustees of IPS were Thurmond Arnold, James Warburg, Philip Stern, and Hans Morgenthau, with seed money from the Ford Foundation (later to be headed by McGeorge Bundy). IPS has functioned as the "New Left" think tank and control center for local community control, community health centers, and direct terrorist organizations. In its report "The First Ten Years," the Institute lists among its lecturers and fellows, members of the Weathermen group, and known associates of the Japanese Red Army, the Puerto Rican terrorist Armed Forces of National Liberation (FALN), and the Black Liberation Army. See also *Carter and the Party of International Terrorism,* Special Report by the U.S. Labor Party, August 1976.

22. Ferguson, *Aquarian Conspiracy,* p. 24.

23. Criton Zoakos et al., *Stamp Out the Aquarian Conspiracy,* Citizens for LaRouche monograph, New York, 1980, pp. 60–63.

24. Ibid.

25. Ibid., pp. 10–12.

26. Mary Jo Warth, "The Story of Acid Profiteers," *Village Voice,* August 22, 1974.

27. Ibid.

28. Ibid.

29. Ibid.

30. Hutchinson, *Vesco.*

PART IX

The Dope Lobby: The Criminals Come Out Into The Open

1
Drug Pushers in Government

In California in 1978, a bill came before the state legislature that would decriminalize all drug use on the grounds that this would free law enforcement and judicial agencies to deal with "more serious crime." The sponsor of that bill was State Representative Willie Brown, a paid lobbyist for Resorts International.

That's one tip-off to the real nature of the Dope lobby. therefore, what does it say about the state of the nation that the biggest dope lobby in the United States—during the presidency of James Earl Carter—was the executive branch of the U.S. government?

As early as March 15, 1977, the *New York Times* reported the fact that the "Carter administration asked Congress today to decriminalize marijuana possession and said it was 'carefully reexamining' its position on penalties for possession of cocaine."

On August 2 of the same year, Jimmy Carter stated in his Message to Congress, "I supported a change in the laws to end federal criminal penalties for possession of up to one ounce of marijuana, leaving the states free to adopt whatever laws they wish concerning marijuana. Decriminalization is not legalization."

The Carter administration retained four members of the advisory board of the National Organization for the Reform of Marijuana Laws (NORML), the nation's official drug lobby. And Carter himself had no compunctions in taking drug money to enhance his political aspirations. His 1976 presidential campaign received $1 million in proceeds from record and ticket sales from Phil Walton, chief of Capricorn Records, a subsidiary of Warner Communications. Walton's promotional instrument was the Allman Brothers rock band, that was arrested in 1976 and convicted of cocaine-smuggling. Nevertheless, the rock band was invited to perform at Carter campaign events with the Carter family on several occasions not long after the drug conviction.[1]

The problem, however, did not end with Jimmy Carter. The dope lobby moved into the executive branch through the creation of so-called President's advisory panels on drug abuse. The first was the Drug Abuse Council, founded in 1972 by the Ford Foundation's then-director McGeorge Bundy, with an initial $1 million treasury. During the first half of the seventies, the DAC focused on promoting methadone as the primary means of dealing with heroin addiction. Once the idea of methadone had been accepted in certain circles, the DAC called for "a legal distribution system" of heroin "to compete with the illegal one." DAC was an enthusiastic supporter of marijuana "decriminalization."[2]

Following the release of its first report supporting the British system of heroin distribution, the Drug Abuse Council was granted a matching fund by the Kaiser Foundation and the Commonwealth Fund that more than doubled its annual revenues. The Commonwealth Fund is named after the British Commonwealth and is formally headed by Queen Elizabeth II of England.

DAC's final report, before it was disbanded in April 1980, caused outrage among drug enforcement officials and police departments. Titled "A Study on Drug Abuse," the report called for the legalization of marijuana and an easing of penalties for possession of cocaine, hashish, and methadone.[3]

The DAC's official founder, Dr. Andrew Weil, came to the Council from the faculty of Harvard University. He served on the advisory board of NORML, and as a contributing editor to the dope lobby's magazine, the pornographic *High Times*.

Although the DAC was disbanded, it is still correct to speak of the Council in the present tense; most of its personnel was absorbed into the Carter administration and thereafter became "respectable" publicists for the international Dope Lobby.

Dr. Norman Zinberg is one example. The co-author of the Council's "Study of Abuse," Zinberg was the chairman of the Liaison Task Panel of the President's Commission on Mental Health and adviser to the National Institute on Drug Abuse. He is also a co-founder of NORML and a current member of the organization's advisory board. A professor of psychiatry at Harvard University, Zinberg was sent by the Pentagon to Vietnam in 1971 to study the effects of heroin addiction on American soldiers. Shortly upon returning, he co-founded NORML and wrote: "Drugs should be legalized. . . . There is a lack of knowledge on how to use drugs, but if we educate the population, misuse will end. . . . After all, drugs are a part of the social setting."

The president of the Drug Abuse Council, Dr. Thomas Bryant, became the chairman of Rosalyn Carter's President's Commission on Mental Health. Bryant is also a member of the advisory board of NORML. Before the Commission was dismantled in 1978, it issued a final report, also authored by Norman Zinberg, which repeated the theme that the problem with psychoactive drugs is that Americans are not educated on the use of mind-altering drugs: hence, "misuse."

The Commission was directly connected to the National Institute of Mental Health, which was founded by Dr. Nathan Kline. An expert in Haitian voodoo, Kline recommended that voodoo be imported into the United States as a "therapeutic tool" in conjunction with drugs. In 1955, Kline testified before Congress on the need for federal funding for psychotropic drug research—funding that ultimately poured into MK-Ultra.

Kline and his colleagues are unabashed in revealing the real purpose behind the dope lobby: social control. Kline states: "Now it may well be that we could make drugs which serve some useful purpose attractive enough to become addictive. Perhaps we should build into the appropriate drugs some addicting factors so that we would be induced to use them rather than avoid them."[4]

Another of the pro-drug agencies that ringed the Carter White House was the National Institute on Drug Abuse, under the Department of Health and Human Services. Set up in the early 1970s, the Institute is a clearinghouse for funding drug treatment programs and research into the medical and social effects of drugs. It, too, recommended marijuana decriminalization.

Until 1979, the director of the Institute was Dr. Robert Du-Pont, a graduate of Emory University of Atlanta. DuPont is known for having proposed to the United Nations the international decriminalization of marijuana, adding that once this is accomplished, home cultivation should be encouraged. He was forced out of the Institute when he was charged with misuse of funds.

But the dope lobby got its real hold on the government when Jimmy Carter's personal adviser and fellow Georgian, Peter Bourne, moved into the Office of Drug Abuse Policy. Then called the Drug Policy Branch of the White House Domestic Policy Staff under Stuart Eizenstat, the Office of Drug Abuse Policy was the direct conduit into the Oval Office for every study, proposal, and scenario issued by the Drug Abuse Council, the National Institute on Drug Abuse, and NORML.

Bourne hit the front pages of the nation's press in 1979 when he was forced to resign upon discovery that he was filling out illegal prescriptions for Quaaludes for the staff members of his office. Yet Bourne remained a close confidant of Jimmy Carter. By the President's own admission, it was Bourne, who oversaw

Carter's transition to a "born again" fundamentalist. A product of Emory University, where his father directs the behavioral psychology center, Bourne did his psychiatric residency at the Haight-Ashbury Free Medical Clinic in San Francisco.

Prior to his residency with MK-Ultra in California, Bourne was a military psychiatrist in Vietnam, where he conducted "stress tests" on Green Berets and did studies on heroin-addicted soldiers. In the 1970s, Bourne returned to Georgia, where he became a special adviser on health matters and held the only license for methadone dispensing in the state under Governor Jimmy Carter.

Shortly before he came to Washington with Carter, Bourne helped found NORML. He has been a member of the lobby's advisory board ever since.

There was another NORML member within the executive branch: Mathea Falco. This member of the advisory board of NORML was the Assistant Secretary of State for Narcotics Control.

During the Carter administration, two bills were before Congress calling for the national legalization of marijuana: the Javits-Koch bill and the Senate Bill 1722 bill to revise the U.S. criminal code, sponsored by Senator Edward Kennedy.

Kennedy's Drug Death Cult

In the United States, Senator Edward Kennedy and his family's Joseph and Rose Kennedy Institute for the Study of Human Reproduction and Bioethics at Georgetown University are the spokesmen for one of the most evil operations ever run by the Most Venerable Military and Hospitaler Order of St. John of Jerusalem: the so-called hospice movement. In this country, it goes under the rubric "The Right to Die."

The Knights began their hospice movement in the eleventh century, when Knights-Hospitalers organized hospices as a "death cult" where the sick were administered hallucinogenic drugs instead of medical treatment. The hospices became known as the dissemination point for drugs and lethal poisons, often targeted at the Knights' adversaries.

In 1967, the Order of St. John resurrected its eleventh-century hospice movement at St. Christopher's Hospice in London. Here, "patients" are administered a "painkiller" called the Brompton Mixture. It consists of heroin, cocaine, alcohol, tranquilizers, and chloroform water. It is administered every three hours—until the patient dies.[5]

In 1977, the Order of St. John launched a hospice movement in the United States. It advocates the decriminalization of heroin and cocaine—on the "humanitarian" grounds that everyone has the human right to die as he or she sees fit.

To propagate the hospice movement here, the Order founded the National Committee on the Treatment of Intractable Pain (NCTIP). Its honorary chairman is Lady Mary Ward, a British specialist in the hospice movement, who founded Hospice, Inc. in Connecticut as the first operating "death clinic" in the U.S. The director of the NCTIP is another British national, Arthur Trebach. A professor at the Center for the Administration of Justice at the American University in Washington, D.C., Trebach is also the director of the Institute on Drugs, Crime and Justice in Britain. For the past five years, Trebach has sponsored hundreds of U.S. medical students, professional physicians, and others for special indoctrination sessions at the Imperial College of Science and Technology, University of London. The theme of the session is the "success" of Britain's policy of legalizing heroin in curbing the illegal drug problem.[6]

In the United States, Hospice, Inc. is financed by the Kaiser Foundation, which includes on its board Kingman Brewster, Carter's U.S. ambassador to the Court of St. James. The Kaiser Foundation's participation in Britain's Opium War dates back to at least 1958, when Dr. Timothy Leary conducted his first experiments with LSD at the Foundation's Kaiser Experimental Hospital in San Francisco.

The other institution currently involved in financing the hospice project is the Kennedy Institute for Bioethics.

In October 1978, the first annual National Hospice Organizing Meeting took place in Washington, D.C.; the two keynote speakers were Carter Secretary of Health, Education and Welfare Joseph Califano, and Senator Edward Kennedy, former chairman of the Senate Judiciary Committee and a ranking member of the Senate Public Health Committee.

How New York Became A Dope, Inc. Stronghold

Startling evidence of the relations between the late Senator Jacob Javits and the Bronfman gang surfaced in 1977 when a marijuana decriminalization bill was rammed through the New York State legislature. Subsequently a legislative investigating committee showed a 300% jump in adolescent marijuana abuse in the state following "decrim." As the sponsor since 1968 of legislation to federally decriminalize marijuana, Javits and Congressman Edward Koch, the same Ed Koch who became the Mayor of New York City, were the most outspoken organizers for the New York State marijuana legalization bill.

During the 1977 legislative session, the bill was defeated. In an unprecedented move pushed by the senior U.S. Senator, Governor Hugh Carey personally conducted a pressure campaign on behalf of a reintroduced version of the same bill, which passed by one vote in June 1977. The decisive vote was cast by a severely ill hospitalized member of the legislature who was helicoptered back and forth from his sickbed by state police on personal orders from the governor.

These extraordinary measures were perhaps clarified several weeks later when Edgar Bronfman made a personal "loan" to Carey of $350,000 to pay off the governor's outstanding 1974 campaign debts. The loan was in violation of state and federal campaign financing laws.

Kennedy's NORML

As the chairman of the Senate Judiciary Committee, Kennedy necessarily steered away from an open lobbying posture on behalf of drugs in order to maintain a modicum of credibility among the powerful law enforcement lobby. Yet the Kennedy family was directly represented on NORML's advisory board by ex-brother-in-law Peter Lawford.

Kennedy, too, is up to his neck in Lansky-Vesco offshore criminal activities. At the top of Kennedy's 1976 campaign contributors list was Joseph Linsey, a leading "philanthropist," who is also known as the kingpin of organized crime in New England. Linsey was a business partner of Meyer Lansky in the International Airport Hotel Distributing, Inc.

The Kennedy fortunes are even more directly linked to Lansky through the already documented Resorts International-Intertel interface. Nowhere is this interface more evident than in New Jersey, where a combination of Justice Department "watergating specialists" teamed with a $1 million Resorts International lobbying and payoff campaign to legalize casino gambling.

Former New Jersey Governor Brendan Byrne, who was recruited out of the Essex County prosecutor's office by the Kennedy Justice hands and installed in the Governor's mansion, was a nationally prominent spokesman for drug decriminalization. As chairman of the Law Enforcement Assistance Administration (LEAA) National Advisory Committee on Criminal Justice Standards and Goals, Byrne commissioned a series of studies supporting decriminalization of marijuana and casino gambling.

NORML, the clearinghouse organization for the various local dionysian cults and "liberal" legislators, is itself a thinly veiled cover through which the poisoning influence of organized crime is extended into the high schools and neighborhoods of the country. NORML is virtually indistinguishable from the drug cult-pornographic magazine *High Times,* which boasts a several hundred thousand circulation predominantly among high school age drug users. The magazine features dozens of pages of advertisements for drug paraphernalia, instructions on the production and use of legal and illicit drugs, and pornographic photographs and interviews with various "high priests" of the drug-rock cult. Through the revenues of *High Times,* through an average of $100,000 per year in tax-exempt grants from the Playboy Foundation, and through "frequent anonymous contributions from drug dealers," NORML is financed.

The Advisory Board of NORML has included Max Palevsky, chairman of the board of the Xerox Corporation; Hugh Hefner, owner of the Playboy Enterprises, Inc.; William F. Buckley Jr.; Burton Joseph, director of the Playboy Foundation; Canon Walter D. Dennis of the Cathedral of St. John the Divine in New York City, the "temple and headquarters" of the Order of St. John of Jerusalem in the United States; and Stewart Mott, heir to the General Motors fortune.

NORML's general counsels, Michael Kennedy and Gerald Lefcourt, also served as counsel to the terrorist Puerto Rican FALN (Armed Forces for National Liberation) and Weatherunderground leader Mark Rudd.

The Price

What has been the toll taken from our nation as Dope, Inc. extends its operations into every area of government—including the presidency?

In testimony before the Criminal Justice Subcommittee on the Senate Judiciary Committee in November 1979, Robert DuPont, then head of the National Institute on Drug Abuse, reported that the "increase in marijuana use among young people is literally off the charts in the United States. The most recent data show that one out of nine high school seniors smokes marijuana every single day of the high school year."

In November 1978 the New York State Substance Abuse Service showed that marijuana use in public schools in grades seven to twelve had increased by 300% since the decriminalization of marijuana eighteen months earlier. The report also showed a 10% experimentation rate with cocaine for the same age group.

A study by the University of Michigan released in January 1980 showed that the use of cocaine by high school seniors had soared—to 12%, double the number in 1975.

In 1978, statewide surveys in Maine and Maryland showed that one in every six high school students gets high on marijuana on a daily basis, and that a growing percentage of children under the age of twelve are smoking marijuana.

A report from the Carter administration's Department of Health and Human Services released in June 1980 reported that the proportion of persons aged eighteen to twenty-five who have used marijuana at some time in their lives jumped from 4% in 1962 to 60% in 1977 and 68% in 1979. In the young adult group surveyed, nearly half those who had used marijuana said they used it at least 100 times.

In the same age group, according to the report, 19% had tried cocaine at least once in 1977. By 1979 the figure had jumped to 28%, a nearly 50% increase.

It is estimated that each year, 500,000 to 1 million adolescents become new users of marijuana and other dangerous drugs.

Britain's Opium War against the United States is taking a generation of Americans and it will claim the nation—if it is not stopped now.

Notes: Part IX

1: Drug Pushers in Government

1. *Bust the Dope Ring in the White House,* monograph, New York: Campaigner Publications, 1977.

2. "Who's Pushing Drugs on America?" *War on Drugs* (August 1980) 1:14–27.

3. Ibid., as cited, p. 20.

4. "The Story Behind Hallucinogenic Drugs," *War on Drugs* (October 1980).

5. "The Hospice Movement—Taking the Pain Out of Genocide," *New Solidarity,* Vol. IX, No. 62, October 6, 1978. See also Sandol Stoddard, *The Hospice Movement* (Briarcliff Manor, New York: Stein and Day, 1978).

6. Seminar listings for the Fifth Institute on Drugs, Crime and Justice in Britain, held in London in July 1978. The Institute has held seven such annual conferences at the Imperial College of the University of London, bringing American university students and American public health officials to study drug abuse in Britain and the "British Model" of treatment.

APPENDICES

APPENDICES

Appendix A

A Proposed Multi-National Strategic Operation Against the Drug Traffic for the Western Hemisphere

This speech by Lyndon H. LaRouche, Jr. was read at an anti-drug conference in Mexico City, on March 9, 1985.

Distinguished members of this conference! I take this opportunity to communicate my great respect for the President of Mexico, and to acknowledge the debt we all owe to those hundreds of soldiers of the Republic who have already lost their lives fighting against the international drug traffickers.

Not long after his first inauguration in 1981, President Ronald Reagan adopted the kind of policy which my associates and I had been recommending since 1978, a War on Drugs. Since the President's second inauguration, this past January, he has escalated his commitment to fighting and winning that War against Drugs. Naturally, some influential persons and institutions inside the United States, are not in sympathy with the

President's War on Drugs; but, the President is stubbornly determined to win the War on Drugs, and there are many in our government who are in enthusiastic support of the President's policy.

It is clear to the governments fighting the international drug traffickers, that the drug traffic could never be defeated if each of our nations tried to fight this evil independently of the other nations of this Hemisphere. If the drug traffickers' laboratories are shut down in Colombia, new laboratories open up in Brazil. If the route into Florida and Georgia is attacked heavily enough, the drug traffickers reopen routes into California, through Belize and Mexico. If Mexico shuts down drug-routes through its territory, the drug traffickers will use Pacific routes into the U.S. states of Washington and Oregon, through the marijuana-traffickers of Hawaii.

The greatest political threat to democracy in Venezuela, Colombia, Peru, and other countries, is the use of the billions of revenues held by the drug traffickers to fund terrorist armies, and to bring corrupted military officers into right-wing coup-plots directed by former officials of the Nazi regime of Germany. The ability of governments to resist these bloody threats is undermined by the increase of the number of officials of governments, political parties, and private institutions, who are bribed by the drug traffickers. It is impossible to break the ominously increasing political power of the drug traffickers in Mexico, Colombia, Venezuela, and other countries, without capturing the billions of dollars of drug-revenues run through corrupt banking institutions.

Without help of closer cooperation between the United States, Mexico, Colombia, Venezuela, and other nations of this hemisphere, neither the United States nor any of the other republics could defeat the monstrously powerful complex of criminal, financial, and political forces who are behind the international drug traffic. The purpose of my remarks today, is to outline to you a proposed war-plan, for cooperative action against the international drug traffickers, by the governments of this Hemisphere committed to that action.

Before I outline that proposed war-plan itself, it is useful, and perhaps necessary, that I identify briefly my qualifications in this connection.

Since 1975, I have become an increasingly controversial public figure internationally. I became controversial, originally, because of a campaign I launched in April 1975, for reforms of the international monetary system consistent with high rates of capital-goods exports from industrialized nations essential to economic progress among the developing nations. As one of the most powerful bankers in Europe said a little over a year ago, "LaRouche's plan for monetary reform would work, but we don't like it much." Since spring 1982, I have come under increasingly violent attack by the Soviet government for my part in proposing the Strategic Defense Initiative which President Reagan announced on March 23, 1983. The most violent attacks upon me have been launched since May 1978, because of my demand that a War on Drugs be launched by all civilized nations, and because of the work of my associates in exposing the powerful financial interests of Europe, Asia, and the Americas who were collecting the major portion of the hundreds of billions of dollars gained by the international drug traffic.

My part in the War against Drugs began during the summer of 1977, as an indirect result of my being on the same Baader-Meinhof assassination-list with two West Germany figures, Juergen Ponto of the Dresdner Bank and Hans-Martin Schleyer of the Mercedes-Benz interests. To keep me alive, my associates retained the expert services of Colonel Mitchell WerBell; the specialists associated with me in our publishing activities consulted with Colonel WerBell and other specialists on the nature of the three-way connection among the drug traffic, international terrorism, and certain wicked and politically powerful financial interests. With indispensable help from law enforcement officials of many nations, my associates in 1978 produced the famous textbook on the war against drugs, *Dope, Inc.*

It was the publication of *Dope, Inc.* which caused the beginning of violent attacks upon me by the Heritage Foundation and by business associates of Robert Vesco, in May 1978. Most of the attacks upon me and my associates in the U.S., European, and Caribbean television and news-media, from 1978 to the most recent weeks, are directed by persons and agencies which are proven members or political allies of the international drug traffickers, or simply corrupt elements of political parties and governments under the control of the drug trafficking interests.

At the same time that the drug traffickers attack me and my associates so violently, the law enforcement and other agencies of governments and private institutions, have recognized that the publications with which I am associated will publish the truth about the drug problem when even most of the major news media not controlled by the drug lobby are afraid to do so. With assistance of information reported to us by law enforcement and other agencies of concerned governments in many parts of the world, the specialists associated with my publication, the *Executive Intelligence Review,* have become leading experts in the investigation of the international drug trafficking and its connections to finance and terrorism. Also, over the past seven years, experience has shown that investigation of the source of the lies published against me and my activities, in various parts of the world, is usually a part or a political ally of the drug traffic. Investigation of the sources of such attacks, has uncovered information concerning the drug traffic and international terrorism, which has proven helpful to law enforcement agencies in various governments.

Also, through my own work, and that of my collaborators, in designing a proposed strategic ballistic missile defense, my attention has been drawn to existing kinds of military capabilities which represent exactly the kinds of technology we need for detecting and destroying the production, processing and transportation of marijuana, cocaine, and opiates. The republics of the Americas possess the technology needed to locate and to confirm sites used for growing and processing these crops, to monitor routes used for transport of these drugs, and to destroy quickly and mercilessly the vulnerable major elements of these facilities and activities.

That indicates the nature of my expert qualifications in this subject. Now, I outline to you my proposed war-plan for our war against drugs.

1. What we are fighting, is not only the effects of the use of these drugs on their victims. The international drug traffic has become an evil and powerful government in its own right. It represents today a financial, political, and military power greater than that of entire nations within the Americas. It is a government which is making war against civilized nations, a government upon which we must declare war, a war which we must fight with the weapons of war, and a war which we must win in the same spirit the United States fought for the unconditional defeat of Nazism between 1941 and 1945. Law enforcement methods, by themselves, will fail; even joint law enforcement efforts by the nations bordering the Caribbean would fail. The nations of Central and South America will each and all either fall under bloody, Nazi-like dictatorships, or will be destroyed through more or less perpetual civil war, unless the international drug traffic's invasion of this hemisphere is crushed by the methods and weapons of war.

2. Law enforcement methods must support the military side of the war on drugs. The mandate given to law enforcement forces deployed in support of this war, must be the principle that collaboration with the drug traffic or with the financier or political forces of the international drug traffickers, is treason in time of war.

(a) Any person caught in trafficking of drugs, is to be classed as either a traitor in time of war, or as the foreign spy of an enemy power.

(b) Any person purchasing unlawful substances, or advocating the legalization of traffic in such substances, or advocating leniency in anti-drug military or law enforcement policy toward the production or trafficking in drugs, is guilty of the crime of giving aid and comfort to the enemy in time of war.

3. A treaty of alliance for conduct of war, should be established between the United States and the governments of Ibero-American states which join the War on Drugs alliance to which

the President of Mexico has subscribed. Other states should be
encouraged to join that military alliance.

4. Under the auspices of this treaty, provisions for actions of a
joint military command should be elaborated. These provisions
should define principles of common action, to the effect that
necessary forms of joint military and law enforcement action
do not subvert the national sovereignty of any of the allied
nations on whose territory military operations are conducted.
These provisions should include the following:

(a) The establishment of bilateral military task-forces,
pairwise, among the allied nations.

(b) The establishment of a Common Command, assigned
to provide specified classes of assistance, as such may be
requested by designated agencies of either any of the member
states, or of the bilateral command of any two states.

(c) Under the Common Command, there should be established a central anti-drug intelligence agency, operating in
the mode of the intelligence and planning function of a military general staff, and providing the functions of a combat
war-room.

(d) Rules governing the activities of foreign nationals assigned to provide technical advice and services on the sovereign territory of members of the alliance.

5. In general, insofar as each member nation has the means
to do so, military and related actions of warfare against targets
of the War on Drugs, should be conducted by assigned forces of
the nation on whose territory the action occurs. It were preferred, where practicable, to provide the member nation essential supplementary equipment and support personnel, rather
than have foreign technical-assistance personnel engaged in
combat-functions.

Insofar as possible:

(a) Combat military-type functions of foreign personnel
supplied should be restricted to operation of detection systems, and to operation of certain types of aircraft and antiair-

craft systems provided to supplement the capabilities of national forces; and

(b) Reasonable extension of intelligence, technical advice, and services supplied as allied personnel to appropriate elements of field-operations.

6. Technologies appropriate to detection and confirmation of growing, processing, and transport of drugs, including satellite-based and aircraft-based systems of detection, should be supplied with assistance of the United States. As soon as the growing of a relevant crop is confirmed for any area, military airborne assault should be deployed immediately for the destruction of that crop, and military ground-forces with close air support deployed to inspect the same area and to conduct such supplementary operations as may be required. The object is to eliminate every field of marijuana, opium, and cocaine in the Americas, excepting those fields properly licensed by governments.

7. With aid of the same technologies, processing centers must be detected and confirmed, and each destroyed promptly in the same manner as fields growing relevant crops.

8. Borders among the allied nations, and borders with other nations, must be virtually hermetically sealed against drug traffic across borders. All unlogged aircraft flying across borders or across the Caribbean waters, which fail to land according to instructions, are to be shot down by military action. A thorough search of all sea, truck, rail, and other transport, including inbound container traffic, is to be effected at all borders and other points of customs inspection. Massive concentration with aid of military forces must be made in border-crossing areas, and along relevant arteries of internal highway and waterborne transport.

9. A system of total regulation of financial institutions, to the effect of detecting deposits, outbound transfers, and inbound transfers of funds, which might be reasonably suspected of be-

ing funds secured from drug trafficking, must be established and maintained.

10. All real estate, business enterprises, financial institutions, and personal funds, shown to be employed in the growing, processing, transport, or sale of unlawful drugs, should be taken into military custody immediately, and confiscated in the manner of military actions in time of war. All business and ownership records of entities used by the drug traffickers, and all persons associated with operations and ownership of such entities, should be classed either as suspects or material witnesses.

11. The primary objective of the War on Drugs, is military in nature: to destroy the enemy quasi-state, the international drug trafficking interest, by destroying or confiscating that quasi-state's economic and financial resources, by disbanding business and political associations associated with the drug trafficking interest, by confiscating the wealth accumulated through complicity with the drug trafficker's operations, and by detaining, as "prisoners of war" or as traitors or spies, all persons aiding the drug trafficking interest.

12. Special attention should be concentrated on those banks, insurance enterprises, and other business institutions which are in fact elements of an international financial cartel coordinating the flow of hundreds of billions annually of revenues from the international drug traffic. Such entities should be classed as outlaws according to the "crimes against humanity" doctrine elaborated at the post-war Nuremberg Tribunal, and all business relations with such entities should be prohibited according to the terms of prohibition against trading with the enemy in time of war.

13. The conduct of the War on Drugs within the Americas has two general phases. The first object is to eradicate all unlicensed growing of marijuana, opium, and cocaine within the Americas, and to destroy at the same time all principal conduits within the Hemisphere for import and distribution of drugs from major

drug-producing regions of other parts of the world. These other areas are, in present order of rank:

(a) The Southeast Asia Golden Triangle, still the major and growing source of opium and its derivatives;

(b) The Golden Crescent, which is a much smaller producer than the Golden Triangle, but which has growing importance as a channel for conduiting Golden Triangle opium into the Mediterranean drug-conduits;

(c) The recently rapid revival of opium-production in southern India and Sri Lanka, a revival of the old British East India Company opium-production;

(d) The increase of production of drugs in parts of Africa. Once all significant production of drugs in the Americas is exterminated, the War on Drugs enters a second phase, in which the War concentrates on combatting the conduiting of drugs from sources outside the Hemisphere.

14. One of the worst problems we continue to face in combatting drug trafficking, especially since political developments of the 1977–1981 period, is the increasing corruption of governmental agencies and personnel, as well as influential political factions, by politically powerful financial interests associated with either the drug trafficking as such, or powerful financial and business interests associated with conduiting the revenues of the drug trafficking. For this and related reasons, ordinary law enforcement methods of combatting the drug traffic fail. In addition to corruption of governmental agencies, the drug-trafickers are protected by the growth of powerful groups which advocate either legalization of the drug traffic, or which campaign more or less efficiently to prevent effective forms of enforcement of laws against the usage and trafficking in drugs. Investigation has shown that the associations engaged in such advocacy are political arms of the financial interests associated with the conduiting of revenues from the drug traffic, and that they are therefore to be treated in the manner Nazi sympathizer operations were treated in the United States during World War II.

15. The War on Drugs should include agreed provisions for allotment of confiscated billions of dollars of assets of the drug trafficking interests to beneficial purposes of economic development, in basic economic infrastructure, agriculture, and goods-producing industry. These measures should apply the right of sovereign states to taking title of the foreign as well as domestic holdings of their nationals, respecting the lawful obligations of those nationals to the state. The fact that ill-gotten gains are transferred to accounts in foreign banks, or real estate holdings in foreign nations, does not place those holdings beyond reach of recovery by the state of that national.

On the issue of the international drug traffic, all honorable governments of Central and South America share a common purpose and avowed common interest with the government of the United States. By fighting this necessary war, as allies, we may reasonably hope to improve greatly the cooperation among the allies, in many important matters beyond the immediate issue of this war itself. Whenever allies join, as comrades-in-arms, to fight a great evil, this often proves itself the best way to promote a sense of common interest and common purpose in other matters. Many difficulties among the states of this hemisphere, which have resisted cooperative efforts at solution, should begin to become solvable, as we experience the comradeship of the War on Drugs.

Appendix B

The FBI: An American Okhrana

On February 13, 1986, Federal Bureau of Investigation Director William H. Webster, in an exclusive interview with the *Los Angeles Times,* issued a pointed denunciation of President Ronald Reagan for his January 3 press conference statement that narcoterrorism represented the "gravest threat to the security of the Western Hemisphere."

"Words like narcoterrorism," said Judge Webster, "tend to exacerbate the realities as we know them. I also do not believe that the hard evidence links the two, that we're in a situation where the terrorists have become drug dealers, or the drug dealers have become terrorists."

Explicitly defending Fidel Castro and his Havana-safehoused "drug czar" Robert Vesco, Webster continued, "I think it's a mistake to say that Cuba is in the drug-running business or that Cuba is using drugs to support terrorism."

By this point in this book, the reader is well qualified to judge the magnitude of the "big lie" spread by Judge Webster. Coming from an FBI director whose jurisdiction now includes control over the Drug Enforcement Administration (DEA), Webster's words are a stunning indictment of the FBI's lack of qualifications to run the nation's war on drugs effort.

Just months before Webster's *Los Angeles Times* interview, DEA Administrator Francis Mullen, a career FBI official who rose to the number three rank in the Bureau, resigned from government service, reportedly in the wake of expos;aaes of his past financial involvement with a New Orleans-Texas marijuana smuggling ring linked to the assassination of Texas federal judge John Wood in 1979. When the same drug mafia kidnaped and assassinated a DEA official, Enrique Camarena, in Guadalajara, Mexico in February 1985, things apparently got too complicated for DEA chief Mullen.

In fairness to Mullen, it was reported at the time of his 1985 resignation that the FBI's deputy director, Oliver "Buck" Revell, had orchestrated a "Get Mullen" campaign within the Bureau's executive offices to eliminate Mullen, his main competitor for the FBI directorship when Judge Webster's ten-year term expires in 1987.

Revell had endeared himself to Moscow in January 1986 by caustically denying reports that Libyan dictator Muammar Qaddafi had deployed assassination squads to the United States, and that there was a serious terrorist threat on United States territory.

But the tale of horrors does not stop there.

In the aftermath of the FBI's late 1970s sting operation, known as Abscam, in which a dozen ranking members of the U.S. Congress and one U.S. senator were framed up and convicted on "corruption" charges by an FBI that paid lavish fees to hardened criminals deployed to set the traps, one victim, Senator Harrison Williams, filed legal action against the Bureau on May 4, 1984. In the court papers submitted by Williams's attorneys, tape recorded evidence was submitted showing that the FBI had been running a sex-with-children blackmail ring to set up U.S. senators and other elected officials

in the "sting" operations. Among the FBI special agents cited
in the evidence was Anthony Amoroso, one of the control agents
over Abscam crook Melvin Weinberg.

The Williams court papers stated, in part:

> . . . the claim made of gross outrageous conduct has reached
> the point where the . . . FBI and Justice Department have
> become dictatorial in nature and placed themselves above
> the law. The vile, degenerate and illegal actions engaged in
> by the agents and informers . . . when coupled with all the
> other acts of outrageous conduct . . . prove . . . that the govern-
> ment has not only engaged in [such] conduct, but has been
> party to and condoned actions that are abominations and
> have violated numerous laws . . . to the point where they
> must stand accused of . . . crimes of a most degenerate nature.

Three days before the Williams court papers were filed, on
May 1, 1984, the House Judiciary Subcommittee on Civil and
Constitutional Rights released the findings of its four-year
study into FBI undercover and "sting" operations. The 100-
page report concluded that the Bureau had taken actions which
had seriously undermined the nation's "political, judicial and
financial institutions," and had "tampered with history."

In addition to the already cited creation of a child sex ring
for the exclusive purpose of blackmailing public officials listed
on the FBI's political hit list, the congressional report documented that the FBI had manufactured crimes for the purpose
of destroying the political careers of standing elected officials
and members of the judicial system; had tampered with local
elections; and had carried out witchhunts even against members of the federal prosecutorial staff of the Department of
Justice who challenged the legality of the FBI's sting programs.

To quote one example detailed in the Subcommittee's
findings:

> In Abscam . . . after prosecutors from the New Jersey United
> States Attorney's office voiced serious doubts about the super-
> vision, control, and tactics of the principal informant, Mel

Weinberg, and questioned the sufficiency of the evidence in certain aspects of the probe, instead of investigating these allegations, the Department of Justice investigated the prosecutors and, "to dissuade the courts and counsel from further inquiry," leaked an inaccurate, libelous memorandum, concerning them. Indeed, even though the assertions of these internal critics were subsequently validated, the Department has refused to release its own report exonerating them.

In yet another FBI "sting" program code-named Operation Graylord, targeted against a group of Democratic Party-linked Chicago judges and court officials, the FBI employed the services of a con man named Michael Raymond to set up the local politicos. Raymond remained a protected FBI asset, under the Federal Witness Protection Program, even after Broward County, Florida police informed the FBI that Raymond was the sole suspect in three separate murders of little old ladies in Fort Lauderdale. To this day, the FBI has refused to release Raymond to local authorities in Florida.

The FBI's marriage with leading elements of organized crime had reached such an extent by the mid-1980s, through programs such as the Federal Witness Protection Program and the hundreds of FBI "sting" operations, that today it is virtually impossible to separate out the two.

Is the FBI's entry into the world of bigtime organized crime and political corruption some recent aberration, reflecting the dying out of the old J. Edgar Hoover leadership?

Emphatically not.

As the archives of the U.S. Congress and other U.S. government agencies document, from its very inception, the FBI was an American Okhrana, a political police force at the disposal of the same Eastern Establishment families whose names are now familiar to the readers of this book as the American branch of Dope, Inc.

This is not to say that every individual FBI special agent is a witting participant in this criminality bordering on sedition. It is to say that the institution is fundamentally corrupt, and that the corruption increases exponentially as one gets closer to the executive offices at the J. Edgar Hoover Building in Washington, D.C.

A brief walk through the historical records sheds important light on the FBI. The story of Dope, Inc. would be incomplete without this documentation.

* * *

The FBI, which, until a congressional enactment of 1935, was called the Bureau of Investigation (BOI), was conceived in secrecy and in defiance of the expressed will of Congress of the United States. Congress, in fact, became the first victim of the Bureau's blackmail and of frame-up attempts, carried out at the direction of President Theodore Roosevelt and his attorney general, Charles J. Bonaparte.

Prelude to the BOI: The Lands Scandal

What were the circumstances at the turn of the century that created the congressional outrage and charges that the BOI threatened to be little more than a general "spy system" such as those used by Europe's despots?

In the post-Civil War period, a number of congressional bills were passed to promote development of our western frontiers. One such law was the Timber and Stone Act of 1878, which provided for the sale of lands generally considered unfit for cultivation although rich in valuable virgin forests. This land quickly became the target of speculators and swindlers.

Shortly after taking office, President Theodore Roosevelt was approached by Interior Secretary Ethan A. Hitchcock, who suspected that his own department may have been involved in the land fraud operations. Hitchcock conducted a preliminary investigation, and then requested that the Department of Justice pursue the matter. Attorney General Bonaparte (the grandnephew of French Emperor Napoleon I) promptly "borrowed" agents from the Treasury Department to make the inquiries.

At that time, the Department of Justice did not have its own investigatory force; thus, in 1892 it had adopted the practice of "borrowing" agents from other federal departments such as Treasury, Interior, and the Postal Service.

'Abscammed'

Bonaparte's men found that the General Lands Division of the Interior Department had indeed been involved in the land frauds. What followed were the sensational indictments and convictions of public figures including Sen. John H. Mitchell and Rep. John N. Williamson, both of Oregon; and Van Gesner, a business partner of Williamson; U.S. District Attorney John J. Hall, who was to prosecute the case but was later said to have been involved in the land swindle himself; and U.S. Commissioner Marion R. Biggs.

All were found guilty. But the actual shock came in the follow-up investigation made by the Taft administration in 1911. Taft's attorney general George W. Wickerham found that the U.S. attorney who prosecuted the Oregon case had employed a private detective to screen, threaten, and bribe jurors. Affidavits were filed stating that the detective, William J. Burns, had compelled witnesses by threats and intimidation to give perjured testimony to a grand jury.

In later years, Rep. Williamson's appeal to the Supreme Court was upheld, and the charges against him dismissed. Mitchell died before the higher courts could make a decision on his appeal.

But in 1907, the land frauds scandal was still "hot." Bonaparte went before the House Appropriations Committee and requested the creation of a permanent detective force for the Department of Justice.

The request was not well received by the congressmen. The House immediately moved to ban the existing Department of Justice practice of borrowing agents, which was accomplished

by an amendment to the Sundry Civil Appropriations Act that
passed on May 27, 1908.

Roosevelt Tries Again

Roosevelt tried to sidetrack the amendment. Writing to
House Speaker Joseph G. Cannon, he warned that "the provision about the employment of the Secret Service men will work
very great damage to the government in its endeavor to prevent
and punish crime. There is no more foolish outcry than this
against 'spies'; only criminals need fear our detectives."

The *New York Times* rallied to his side. In a typical editorial
entitled "Tools of Thieves," the *Times* stated: "It was the combination of 'land sharks,' according to the report, that persuaded
the Appropriations Committee to approve and the House to
pass the Amendment to the Sundry Civil bill. . . . The Representatives have, however, unwittingly become the tools of thieves.
The Senators are duly warned."

A typical Chicago newspaper article summarizing the opposing viewpoint during the debates was published in the Congressional Record: "There is no desire for a general detective service
or national police organization in connection with the Federal
Government. On the contrary, there is in Congress an utter
abhorrence of such a scheme. . . ."

The Backroom Birth

The Congress adjourned on June 1, 1908. On July 26, acting
at the direction of the President, Bonaparte issued the order
that gave birth to the Bureau of Investigation. Upon its return,
Congress was confronted with the Roosevelt-Bonaparte *fait accompli*.

The congressional response was both hostile and immediate.
Investigations were launched by both houses into all federal

investigative and police agencies, particularly the new force at the Justice Department. Bonaparte was forced to appear before the House and was subjected to intensive confrontation and grilling by the angered members.

At the same time, rumors and accusations were circulating that congressmen were being surveilled and their personal papers and mail were being tampered with and, in some cases, actually opened. Roosevelt publicly denied the charges. However, he admitted that "sometimes through the accidental breaking of such [a mail] package, the contents were exposed." The President then proceeded to publish the private correspondence of one of his principal foes, Sen. Benjamin R. Tillman of South Carolina. The object lesson was not lost on the opposition.

Bonaparte made one final appearance before the House Appropriations Committee in December 1908. Impatient with the persistent, however feeble, cries against the abuses by the BOI, he declared: "Anybody can shadow me as much as they please. They can watch my coming in and my going out. I do not care whether there is somebody standing at the corner and watching where I go or where I do not go."

Congressman Sherley's (Ky.) response to Bonaparte was reportedly met with a standing ovation by the House:

In my reading of history, I recall no instance where a government perished because of the absence of a secret-service force, but many there are that perished as the result of the spy system. If Anglo-Saxon civilization stands for anything, it is for a government where the humblest of citizens is safeguarded against the secret activities of the executive of the government. . . .

The Fourth Amendment declares: "The right of the people to be secure in their persons, houses, papers, and effects against unreasonable searches and seizures shall not be violated.". . .

The view of government that called it into existence is not lightly to be brushed aside.

The model for the Abscam-Brilab witchhunts of today is the FBI's first major national assignment: its investigation, toward the beginning of the century, of the "white slave trade" under the Mann Act. This first major undertaking of the FBI's predecessor organization, the Bureau of Investigation, already employed every ugly ruse in the FBI's frameups and entrapments today.

The FBI has never been a law-enforcement agency. Then, as now, the FBI's only relationship to law enforcement is as a pretext for gathering information to be used in its *jihad* against its assigned targets and its perceived foes.

In each case, the FBI has justified its gross abuses by pointing to a "menace"—a threat to citizens' safety or national security so grave as to exonerate even the FBI. "White slavery" was the FBI's first great "menace," and it was through the white slavery "investigation" that the FBI took its first steps towards obtaining the powers and prerogatives to become an American gestapo.

The First 'Menace'

In its earliest years, the FBI scrounged and strained for federal enforcement authorization. According to FBI critic Max Lowenthal, the Bureau of Investigation's first cases "were somewhat makeshift in character. . . . The Justice detectives investigated crimes committed in Indian or other government reservations . . . they prepared some District of Columbia cases involving false purchases and sales of securities; they handled a few peonage and bankruptcy fraud cases."

But under Bureau of Investigation chief Stanley W. Finch, who had been appointed by Roosevelt's attorney general and BOI co-founder Bonaparte, the Bureau seized the mandate for enforcement of the Mann Act statutes of 1910. According to author Fred J. Cook, "Finch quickly saw the Mann Act as a golden opportunity to apply to Congress for even more funds and for even more agents."

Congressional Opposition

As in the case of the founding of the BOI itself, fierce opposition from Congress greeted the new white-slave trading legislation. Congressman William C. Adamson of Georgia expressed his dislike for the "practice of piling up recitals of filth and iniquity ... and then running to Congress for more legislation. . . . States ought to take care of morals, and not overburden Congress. . . . If I understand the gentlemen . . . this is not an attempt to prevent prostitution, but to purify [interstate] commerce. . . ." And, just as congressmen who opposed the creation of the Bureau were smeared as protectors of criminals, now opponents of the Mann Act, also offering constitutional arguments based on states' rights or fear of government despotism, were maligned as promoters and proponents of vice.

'No Girl is Safe'

When the Mann Act became law, no specific guidelines for which enforcement agency would have jurisdiction were set. Finch's Bureau stepped forward to assume responsibility for the new statute.

After a few desultory months of investigations, Finch proceeded to stir up a nationwide "girl-napper" scare to pry loose from the still suspicious Congress the means to create the new national secret police.

In a tactic that has become familiar as the *modus operandi* of the FBI in dealing with Congress and other agencies, Finch painted the following chilling picture before Congress in 1911:

Unless a girl was actually confined in a room and guarded, there was no girl, regardless of her station in life, who was altogether safe. . . . There was need that every person be on his guard, because no one could tell when his daughter or his wife or his mother would be selected as a victim.

Despite the knights-to-the-rescue eloquence of Finch's warnings of danger to women everywhere, the Bureau did not use the Mann Act to break up the white-slave traffic or organized-crime prostitution. It used the Mann Act as a pretext to embark on a crusade against personal immorality—using as informants and witnesses the madames and pimps it was purportedly investigating.

As an up-and-coming assistant to Finch, J. Edgar Hoover was later to acknowledge, "The average case concerns usually one man and one woman or two men and two women"—not the gang-busting crime hunt of legend.

Finch and his detectives used their new funding and congressional mandate to travel from city to city, working with local police in mapping local houses of prostitution. When a new face appeared, especially if it were one that had crossed a state line, the agents would pounce.

In congressional testimony, Finch intimated how some of his "leads" were developed: "Some madames are very jealous of other madames . . . and they spy on other madams" for Finch's vice squad.

Finch also hired local attorneys to spy on local brothels and keep a census on patrons and prostitutes. Finch used these local relationships to place agents across the nation and turn citizens into the "eyes and ears" of the BOI.

Bureau critic Lowenthal gave some insight into how the collection of BOI informants were roped in and controlled:

Excluded in the main from direct action themselves, the agents ordered all persons enumerated in vice census to obey local laws and on occasion *threatened to furnish local police with evidence of local crime they had collected* [emphasis added].

A National Vice Squad

At most, the Bureau's Mann Act mobilization scored a few raids of houses of ill repute that had run afoul of its informant networks. More frequently, the Bureau used the Mann Act to launch inquests into the personal morality of individuals not connected to criminal activity in any way.

One victim of this aspect of Mann Act enforcement was Jack Johnson, then the world's heavyweight boxing champion. Johnson had fallen in love with a lady of ill repute, and persuaded her to leave her profession and marry him. Johnson and his fiancée were subsequently arrested by the BOI when they crossed state lines. Although there was never any question of criminal activity—Johnson intended to violate neither the law nor the woman in question—he was arrested and sentenced to prison. Johnson's real "crime" may have been the fact that he was black and his fiancee white.

In another infamous episode, BOI agents arrested the son of an aide to President Woodrow Wilson for crossing a state line in furtherance "of a private impropriety." Again, there was no suggestion that the young man's peccadillo was related to any criminal activity properly construed. Rather, as J. Edgar Hoover was to explain this and similar cases of federal indictments of private individuals, in instances of personal morality, the agency was attacking the "problem of vice in modern civilization."

It is on this model that the Abscam and Brilab cases are constructed by the FBI today—cases where weak, foolish, or even entirely innocent individuals were trapped into circumstances in which they had no intention of committing criminal actions, but were compromised nonetheless.

The result of the Mann Act period was not merely the destruction of the lives and reputations of non-criminals. Through the Mann Act period, the Bureau secured the means to become a national gestapo.

Through its informant "eyes and ears," the Bureau began to accumulate its massive bank of raw dossier material on thousands of citizens.

As Lowenthal described an aspect of this process:

> Distressed citizens from all over the country write in to give
> the detectives all kinds of information about the travels of
> strangers, acquaintances, relatives, or even themselves.
> Hundreds of thousands of such communications have found
> their way into the swelling permanent records of the Bureau,
> registering and perpetuating the names, the failings (alleged
> or real), and the private affairs of the many victims and
> victimizers.

Citizens are protected from monitoring by government until
such time as they themselves become suspects in a criminal
case or become victims or step forward as witnesses. But the
Bureau does not and has never abided by such routine law-
enforcement procedures. Instead, acting as an information-
gathering agency, not a law-enforcement agency, files are
opened on individual citizens whenever possible.

Through the Mann Act period also, the Bureau began the
practice of electronic eavesdroppoing and launched its first
"dragnet"—a mass arrest of individuals not involved in a federal crime.

In 1937, J. Edgar Hoover personally supervised a mass
roundup under the Mann Act of ten establishments in Baltimore. Of the 47 arrests made, few were found to have been
under federal jurisdiction. However, inaugurating the FBI's
now routine technique of "trial by press," the names of those
apprehended were quickly routed to the news media for public
humiliation. (To Hoover's embarrassment, however, three,
whose names were carefully concealed from the press, were
close friends of the FBI director himself!)

With prosecutions rendered impossible by lack of jurisdiction,
Hoover was pressed to explain why the Bureau had acted so
hastily. His answer was that the FBI had acted—for the first
time—on wiretap information.

In fact, the information had been gathered through a wiretap
on the phone of a Maryland legislator!

Interpreting the wiretapped conversation incorrectly, the Bureau later explained, they thought they had overheard plans to transport some of the Baltimore female offenders over state lines, but it turned out that the scheme was only entertainment for the locals.

A former FBI agent later recalled that, during the 1930s, "when we were doing investigations under the White Slave Traffic Act, there was one dependable way to find out information about call girls: by wiretapping. And we didn't hesitate a bit."

It is likely that very little of this information gathered by electronic surveillance ever found its way as evidence into a court of law. Rather, it continued to feed "raw" data dossiers that are the Bureau's famous black files.

How perceptive were those congressmen who warned the nation that the launching of the FBI would be used only "to dig up the private scandals of men."

Ultimately, the Bureau jettisoned the Mann Act rationale for its intelligence-gathering activities after a 1940s vice raid in Miami. Cries of private outrage and sober second thoughts by the Justice Department attorneys charged with prosecuting these flimsy cases led the Bureau to back off.

However, the FBI had secured its objectives. It had become an established bureaucracy with a multimillion dollar budget, and a network of offices throughout the country. More importantly, it had files, with information on thousands of Americans, information that—without being criminal material—could be used to intimidate and coerce.

The Major Leagues

Many of the abuses that were publicized under the Mann Act were swept away with a bit of political sleight-of-hand. They were blamed on the corrupt administration of William Burns, who had been appointed to head the agency under President Taft. Hoover was appointed in 1924, among public declarations and promises that he would not be politically beholden to any-

one, nor would the Bureau be used for the private peccadilloes
of the powerful in or out of office. Despite allusions to the
contrary, Hoover had crawled up the Bureau's hierarchy by
playing by the already established and very dirty rules; there
was no reason whatsoever to change anything except the public's perception. For this, Hoover created what might be considered the most prolific public relations and disinformation machine in the history of the American nation. It was from this
machine that the "G-man" mythologies were churned out for
the press, the backs of cereal boxes, the radio, and most especially the "silver screen."

Hoover's reputation within the Bureau was created prior to
and during World War I, a period in which the BOI greatly
expanded its political influence and its jurisdiction.

The American Protective League

In the years before and during World War I, British intelligence directed a concerted propaganda and dirty tricks campaign to secure U.S. entry into the war on Britain's side, using
such influence channels as Walter Lippmann's *New Republic*
magazine. Attacks were leveled against German-Americans
and German culture—including the works of such "American"
Germans as Ludwig van Beethoven and Friedrich Schiller.

One vehicle for this drive was the American Defense Society.
Formed with Teddy Roosevelt as honorary president, and his
former Attorney General Charles Bonaparte as its honorary
vice-president, the ADS opposed German business in America,
employment of Germans, and the teaching of the German language in the schools.

This line was quickly taken up by the remnants of turn-of-
the-century nativist movements, and by the time of the 1914
outbreak of hostilities, it was fueling a climate of jingoism and
xenophobia, in which self-appointed bands of vigilantes formed
throughout the nation. In March 1917, BOI chief A. Bruce
Bielaski seized upon this impulse to complement the Bureau's

network of informants with an army of thugs. Winning approval from Attorney General Thomas W. Gregory, Bielaski announced the formation of the American Protective League (APL), as a civilian adjunct of the Bureau, open to able-bodied, patriotic American men who wanted to "help their country."

Within three months, the APL grew to 100,000 members, and swelled at its height to 250,000 in chapters nationwide. For one dollar, recruits could obtain a shiny badge, describing the bearer as a member of the Secret Service Division. Later, when scandalized officials of the Treasury Department protested that the badges would invite confusion between the APL members and agents of the real Secret Service, the badges were changed to read "Auxiliary to the United States Department of Justice."

In a report to Congress dated December 4, 1917, Gregory hailed the APL as an internal security asset:

[T]he department encourages the formation of various local and volunteer citizen's committees for the purpose of being on the lookout for disloyal or enemy acvitities. . . . One of them in particular . . . the American Protective League, has proven to be invaluable, and constitutes the most important auxilliary and reserve for the Bureau of Investigations.

However, Treasury Secretary William Gibbs McAdoo sounded a warning. According to FBI critic Cook, McAdoo wrote Gregory that he was "concerned about the danger implicit in the entire movement." He recalled that a similar volunteer organization, the Sons of Liberty, had been created during the American Revolution, and that it had been responsible for abuses and injustices. McAdoo went on to say that he felt that the "Secret Service" divisions of the APL contained "the same potentialities."

However, continued Cook, the BOI "ignored McAdoo's perceptive warning about the larger issues involved and continued to bestow its prestige upon its volunteer superpatriots."

BOI and Wartime Security

During the war, the United States was woefully unprepared for the counterintelligence resource and security challenges posed by the global conflict and those in-depth capabilities of the nations involved—friends and foes alike. American intelligence capabilities barely existed within the military and civilian communities. The BOI, on the other hand, had at least 600 full-time agents at its disposal, a manpower force which had been created under the Mann Act, spread throughout the nation in regional offices in major cities. For this reason, the BOI's assistance was eagerly sought by the existing comparatively meager counterintelligence and law enforcement agencies.

However, the Bureau refused to take a back seat and place its resources at the disposal of anything outside the BOI. Instead, the Bureau concentrated its energies into two major offensives: harassing nascent labor unions and conducting mass raids against "slackers."

The APL was deployed against the labor unions, on the behalf of employers. Unions were dubbed "radical" and "anarchist" (and perhaps they were—such are the shortcomings of a republic, that protection and freedom of speech are the right of all its citizens). The point to bear in mind here, is that the vacuum created by the dissolution of the APL, would later come to be filled by organized crime. This activity, combined with Hoover's insistence on blocking any legislation that would force the Bureau into even acknowledging the existence of organized crime in the U.S. ,set the preconditions that *allowed* the mob to exert power and influence over not only labor unions, but over whole industries in this country today.

The Draft Raids

Labor was not the only target of the BOI's junior G-men. APL goons were unleashed against the entire U.S. population, through raids, with full power of arrest, against any American male hapless enough to be caught in the BOI's first great dragnet.

On August 5, 1918, Secretary of War Newton Baker wrote Attorney General Gregory claiming that the "known desertion" from the first and second draft calls totaled 308,489 persons. How this incredible figure was derived is beyond this author's realm of knowledge to explain, but it was used as the pretext for the BOI-APL draft raids. The roundups began in earnest in spring 1918. The APL did the on-the-ground dirty work, while the BOI handled the logistics of the mass roundups and arrests. According to U.S. intelligence historian William Corsan, "In return for a promise from the Justice Department that they would have sole jurisdiction over slackers, the APL members pledged to forgo" a promised $50 bounty per slacker. "On April 15, however, [Attorney General] Gregory authorized 'expense reimbursements' of up to $50 per slacker . . . in effect renewing the bounty hunter incentive."

On September 15, 1918 the first in a series of lightning raids was launched against the slackers in major cities; in New York alone, 75,000 suspected slackers were arrested and jailed, 30,000 of them on the first day. And what, you may well ask, consitituted a slacker? Any man unable to show his draft card and/or birth certificate on demand, of course! Cripples, young boys below the draft age, innumerable men legally registered and awaiting callup but caught with their pants down, so to speak, were arrested.

Basking in the publicity of the credulous press accounts and heralds for patriotic action, and amazed at their own success, the BOI proceeded to make some fairly startling declarations, e.g., that 25% to 30% of the men arrested were "willful slackers." Two days later, the BOI was forced to greatly downgrade that estimate, as thousands of men in New York City alone were released from the holding cells as tales of gross mistreatment and the horrible conditions of their imprisonment began to filter to the outside world. The BOI had to admit within 48 hours of the raids, that out of 200 persons arrested, 199 were "mistakes," and of the remaining adjudicated by the BOI as slackers, 99% turned out to be persons visiting the area from

out of town, who did not happen to be carrying the appropriate
paperwork, and could not access it until days after their arrest.

The Name of the Game Is Damage Control

In the eyes of the BOI, the only damage and fault it could
find with the draft raids, was the ensuing bad publicity and
allowing its auxiliaries—i.e. the APL—to "exceed their orders."
This has a familiar ring to it, as should the public "debate"
concerning the raids. On the one hand, the Bureau's "Nacht
und Nebel" draft raids were labeled an "outrage" and characterized as "mob rule." Public mouthpieces cultivated by the BOI
in the press and Congress came to the rescue, justifying the
BOI's actions as patriotic, arguing, for example, that the public
should willingly surrender their rights in order that justice be
done. Senator Andrieus Aristieus Jones of New Mexico stated
that "Under our system of government, it is usually the case
that some innocent people are called upon to suffer for the
crimes of others." He further argued, "Is there a Senator in this
body who would not willingly stay in jail a week, if necessary,
in order to have justice meted out to even one such criminal?"

Said William Fosgate Kirby of Arkansas, "If . . . some individuals are inconvenienced or individual rights are infringed more
or less, they must put up with that rather than that the law
shall not be enforced."

Others did not hesitate to call a spade a spade. Congressmen
called the BOI's action "terrorism." Said Congressman Joseph
Frelinghuysen of New Jersey,

I happened to be in New York on the day when the first round-
up occurred. . . . At the point of a bayonet [citizens] were put
in motor cars and driven through the streets amid the jeers
and scoffs of the crowd. . . . [The action] savors of the press
gang and not of a civil tribunal.

Congressman Charles Spaulding Thomas said, "In the west we
have another name for that sort of procedure, although we use

it against animals and not men. We call it a round-up, and even then the mavericks are cut out." The BOI held firm in its belief that the raids would be "justified if only two or three slackers had been found . . . of inestimable value even if the net had not brought in a single slacker." On pulling their operation out of Manhattan, the site of the most thoroughgoing of the sweeps, the brave crime fighters of the BOI skipped town, leaving a government clerk holding the bag, along with a stenographer, who were bombarded by frantic mothers, wives, and victims seeking information on their loved ones or issuing complaints.

Corsan reports in his book, *Armies of Ignorance,* that toward the end of the war the APL had become

> too large and had been created from too many separate opera-
> tions for anyone to control it. . . . Orders from . . . Washington
> were routinely disobeyed or ignored. For the remainder of
> the war, various segments of the APL abused their position
> through illegal wiretaps, arrests, harassments, violations of
> personal records, and general disregard of civil liberties. The
> Justice Department lacked the money and manpower to con-
> trol the APL or to do without it.

Although the APL no longer staged the slacker raids that had netted the BOI headlines (and greater appropriations), the APL continued to serve the BOI by securing information through its illegal surveillance unofficial "black bag jobs" which in turn was fed into the burgeoning "confidential files."

There is nothing in the Bureau's history to indicate that it abhorred the tactics of the draft raids. In the postwar period there were the notorious Palmer raids, carried out against the "Red Menace"; FBI files were used indiscriminately to feed the drunken exhortations of Senator Joseph McCarthy's anti-communist witchhunts.

Senator Bandagee's verdict on the BOI's tactics during World War I holds true today: "If this great government . . . is to hunt down lawbreakers, it cannot with any consistency assume to act the part of the lawbreaker itself."

Appendix C

The Anti-Defamation League: Dope, Inc.'s Public Relations Firm

1. What Is the ADL?

The Anti-Defamation League of B'nai B'rith proclaims itself to be a non-profit corporation "designed to eliminate defamation of Jews and other religious and ethnic groups; to advance proper understanding among all peoples; and to preserve and translate into greater effectiveness the principles of freedom, equality and democracy" (from the Bylaws of the ADL of B'nai B'rith, as amended by the National Commission, June 1982).

Nothing could be further from the truth.

In repeated flagrant violation of Section 501(c)3 of the Internal Revenue Service Codes, the ADL operates as a tax-exempt public interest organization, while in reality it engages in a wide range of activities that are inherently criminal in nature, including interference in the judicial and law enforcement process, support for domestic and international terrorist organizations, instigation of "hate crimes," espionage, support for suspected international narcotics traffickers, unregistered political activities, and covert activities on behalf of both hostile foreign governments and U.S. government agencies generally linked to the international social democracy. (It is a matter of historical record that before, during and immediately after World War II, the ADL functioned as a "covert action" arm of the British Special Operations Executive under its North American chief Sir William Stephenson, in close liaison with the FBI's Division Five.)

Through its 151-member National Commission and its paid staff maintaining regional offices in 31 cities in the United States and a number of locations in Europe, the Middle East, Ibero-America, and the Soviet Union (a Moscow office is in the process of being opened at the invitation of President Mikhail Gorbachov), the ADL operates as a covert strike force whose corrupting influence extends into the pores of the financial community, the legal establishment, the media, and the U.S. government at the federal, state, and local level.

Above all else, the ADL is a public-relations front for that branch of American organized crime founded by Meyer Lansky during the early decades of this century, under the patronage and sponsorship of leading Anglo-American financial interests. ADL officials, for this reason, were reportedly deeply dismayed when Lyndon LaRouche dubbed the ADL the "American Drug Lobby." More recently, the ADL has moved to deepen its ties to the Soviet foreign intelligence services operating in the West and in the newly liberated nations of Central Europe.

2. Organizational Structure and Key Personnel

The ADL, according to its bylaws, is run by a National Commission (NC), which currently consists of 151 members. It is chaired by a national chairman, currently Burton Levinson, an attorney from Beverly Hills, California. The National Commission formally meets once a year.

According to Article VII of the bylaws, in the interval between the NC annual meetings, the ADL's National Executive Committee (NEC) acts for it. The NEC is composed of a chairman (now Ronald B. Sobel, a senior rabbi at Temple Emanu-El in New York City) and vice chairman; the elected officers of the NC, the president, executive vice president, and honorary (past) presidents of B'nai B'rith, together with their counterparts from B'nai B'rith Women; the appointed chairmen of all of the ADL standing committees; and the president of the ADL Foundation, together with 15 additional members of the NC who are elected by it.

The ADL is formally affiliated with B'nai B'rith. However, this link is principally maintained through the B'nai B'rith's representation on ADL's National Commission. Unlike its parent organization, the B'nai B'rith, the ADL is not a membership organization. One cannot join the ADL; membership is by nomination or invitation only. In this sense, the ADL bears a greater likeness to the secret lodges of Freemasonry than its B'nai B'rith parent organization, which was originally conceived in the mid-19th century as a Jewish branch of British Freemasonry.

The current president of B'nai B'rith is Seymour D. Reich, a longstanding activist and officer of the ADL prior to his election to head B'nai B'rith.

Of the current 151 active National Commission members, a smaller core group directs the overall activities of the ADL's staff through participation in standing committees of the NC. The standing committees are organized in precise parallel to the ADL staff divisions and departments, thus permitting the maximum flow of marching orders and other inputs from the National Commission into the day-to-day activities of the league's paid employees. In this sense, Edgar Bronfman and other leading National Commissioners run the ADL.

Standing committee chairmen of the ADL, who, together with their committee members, are appointed by the national chairman, include: Howard P. Berkowitz, Planning; Donald R. Mintz, Civil Rights; Michael Nachman, Community Service; Sherwin Newar, Budget; Melvin I. Salberg, Communications; Michael E. Schultz, Administration; Joel Sprayregen and Lucille Kantor, International Affairs; David H. Strassler, Intergroup Relations; Robert G. Sugarman, Leadership; and, William Veprin, Development.

These committees correspond to the divisions of the ADL's full-time staff. The divisions include:

■ Administration. Concerned with the ADL's internal affairs, it is directed by Philip Shamis, who had previously been controller for the American Jewish Committee.

■ Civil Rights. This division works through departments on Fact Finding (headed by Irwin Suall), Research and Evaluation (Alan M. Schwartz), Legal Affairs (Steven M. Freeman), a Washington, D.C. office (Jess Hordes), where a Task Force on Nazi War Criminals (Elliot Welles) is based, and four regional area coordinators. Its director is Jeffrey P. Sinensky, who had previously been associate director of the division.

■ Community Service. This division directs the 31 regional offices throughout the United States, whose directors work closely with regional boards appointed by the NC. Its director is Charney V. Bromberg, who was previously the deputy director of the International Relations Department of the American Jewish Committee.

■ Communications. Handles public relations and the production of material. Until January 1990, its director was Lynne Ianniello.

■ Development. It oversees the fundraising activities of the ADL Appeal—e.g., ADL honorary vice chairman Edgar Bronfman is also head of the Greater New York Appeal.

■ Intergroup Relations. It is made up of departments on Education (Frances M. Sonnenschein); Higher Education/Campus Affairs (Jeffrey A. Ross); Interfaith Affairs (Rabbi Leon Klenicki, who is also liaison to the Vatican); Television, Radio and Film; Publications (Howard J. Langer); and an International Center for Holocaust Studies (Dennis B. Klein). Its director is

Alan Bayer, who was previously executive director of the Jewish Federation of San Antonio, Texas.

■ International Affairs. It comprises departments in the United States concerned with European, Latin American, and Middle Eastern Affairs, and is in charge of ADL's overseas operations, including the offices in Paris (Robert Goldman), Rome (Lisa Palmieri-Billig), and Jerusalem (Harry Wall). Its director is ADL National Director Abraham Foxman, who employs associate division director Kenneth Jacobson for daily operations.

■ Leadership. Recruits potential future leaders, and coordinates an ADL National Leadership Conference. Its director is Marvin S. Rappaport. The National Leadership Conference recently brought 250 ADL members from around the United States to Washington, D.C. for three days of meetings with officials of the Bush administration, the Congress, and the Israeli embassy.

The ADL has over 300 people who hold leadership or honorary leadership positions. Among this list are a number of honorary vice chairmen who are closely linked to the ADL, but who for various reasons—including government service—cannot serve as active officers. This group includes Senators Rudy Boschwitz (R-Minn.) and Howard Metzenbaum (D-Ohio), former Carter administration Secretary of Commerce Phillip Klutznick, former Reagan administration arms control negotiator Max Kampelman, and former Sen. Abraham Ribicoff (D-Conn.) and Rep. Sidney Yates (D-Ill.). World Jewish Congress president Edgar Bronfman is also an honorary vice chairman, along with two other major crime figures from the old Meyer Lansky orbit, bankers Leonard Abess and Theodore Silbert. With the exception of the members of Congress, all the above-listed honorary vice chairmen were at one time active National Commission members.

The Active Operatives
Among the active core of ADL operatives are:

■ Burton S. Levinson, ADL national chairman since 1987. His work with ADL dates back to 1950, when, as a student at Los Angeles City College, he infiltrated a group affiliated with Gerald L.K. Smith. Now he is a senior partner in the Beverly Hills-based law firm of Levinson & Lieberman.

■ Abraham H. Foxman, ADL national director since 1987. He has worked on the staff of the ADL since 1965. Born in Baronowicze, Poland in 1940, Foxman is one of the most mysterious figures in the ADL leadership. U.S. intelligence sources, and even some top-ranking ADL members, reportedly suspect Foxman may be a Soviet "illegal"—a long-term penetration agent operating without any links to the official Soviet diplomatic corps.

■ Arnold Forster was associate director of the ADL under Ben Epstein since 1946, and is now a member of the NC and ADL general counsel. He has been "Of Counsel" with the New York law firm of Shea & Gould, a firm intimately tied to the late mob lawyer Roy Cohn.

■ Kenneth J. Bialkin. This former ADL national chairman from 1982–86 is today an honorary chairman and NC member, as well as president of the ADL Foundation.

■ Theodore H. Silbert. An honorary vice chairman, he works with Edgar Bronfman in the lucrative Greater New York Appeal for the ADL. Silbert is chairman of Sterling National Bank (see below).

■ Burton M. Joseph, ADL national chairman from 1976–1978, is today an honorary chairman. His family runs the Minnesota-based agricultural products firm I.S. Joseph. After World War II, Joseph teamed up politically with liberal Democrat Hubert H. Humphrey, through whom he became friends of Max M. Kampelman (now ADL honorary vice chairman) and ADL top funder Dwayne Andreas. Together they form the "Minneapolis ADL mafia."

■ Edgar Bronfman, ADL honorary national chairman and head of its Greater New York Appeal (see below).

■ Irwin Suall. Since 1966, he has headed the Fact-Finding Department of the ADL's Civil Rights Division.

■ Meyer Eisenberg, ADL vice chairman and former head of

the National Commission's Civil Rights Committee (with over-sight over the Fact-Finding and Legal departments). He served from 1959–70 as an attorney with the U.S. Securities and Exchange Commission, attaining the position of deputy general counsel of the SEC before his retirement from government. In private law practice with a string of Washington, D.C. area firms, Eisenberg remains one of the nation's experts on securities law.

3. The ADL and Organized Crime

It was no public relations gaffe when, in 1985, the ADL gave its Torch of Liberty award to gangster Morris Dalitz, a founder of the notorious Purple Gang and longtime crime partner of the late mobster Meyer Lansky. The present leadership of the ADL is dominated by figures with longstanding ties to organized crime, particularly to the international drug money-laundering apparatus.

Foremost among these contaminated ADL officials is Kenneth Bialkin, the ex-national chairman who is still an honorary national chairman and a director of the ADL Foundation. While with the New York law firm of Willkie Farr and Gallagher throughout the 1970s, Bialkin masterminded Robert Vesco's looting of Investors Overseas Service (IOS) of more than $60 million. Vesco, the fugitive financier now living in Havana, Cuba, was an early partner of Medellín Cartel dope smuggler Carlos Lehder Rivas, helping Lehder to set up his marijuana and cocaine smuggling routes through the Bahamas. On April 17, 1989, Robert Vesco was again indicted by a federal grand jury in Jacksonville, Florida, which charged him with involvement in a Medellín Cartel cocaine-smuggling conspiracy from 1974–89.

In January 1980, a jury in the U.S. Southern District of New York ordered Willkie Farr and Gallagher to pay $35 million to victims of the IOS looting, and found that Bialkin had been instrumental in structuring the money-laundering and theft scheme at every level. Law enforcement officials believe that IOS was one of the early conduits for billions of dollars in drug profits, and was a cash repository used by Meyer Lansky.

Recently, Bialkin left Willkie Farr to join the country's largest law firm, Skadden Arps. In much the same way that Willkie Farr pioneered the elaborate offshore money-laundering schemes that today constitute the bloodstream of the international drug trade, Skadden Arps pioneered the junk bond and leveraged buyout schemes through which billions of dollars in dubious offshore money have been repatriated through hostile corporate takeovers and asset stripping of America's industrial sector. Two of Skadden Arps's most notorious clients are Drexel Burnham's Michael Milken and Ivan Boesky—both of whom, not coincidentally, have been ADL contributors.

Another ADL national chairman, Burton Joseph, played a pivotal role in the Robert Vesco takeover and looting of IOS, by putting Vesco into contact with his protégé, financier Meshulam Riklis of the Rapid American Corp. Riklis, according to court records, purchased a controlling block of IOS stock as a surrogate for Vesco. Riklis was later linked to Bialkin, Edgar Bronfman, Henry Kissinger, and other ADL figures in a real estate scandal involving the illegal purchase of large tracts in the Israeli Occupied Territories and Christian and Muslim sections of Jerusalem.

During Bialkin's tenure at Willkie Farr, the firm also handled *pro bono* legal work for the ADL, and represented major ADL donor and suspected crime figure Edmond Safra. Bialkin represented Safra in the Syrian banker's takeover of American Express, a transaction that ended years later in a fiasco, with American Express officials accusing Safra of money laundering.

On Jan. 3, 1989, officials of the U.S. Customs Service and the U.S. Drug Enforcement Administration in Berne, Switzerland identified Edmond Safra as a major figure in an international drug money-laundering scheme involving the Shakarchi Trading Co. The government reports identified Safra as a lifetime friend and business associate of Mohammed Shakarchi, and identified numbered accounts at Safra's New York City Repub-

lic National Bank as pass-through accounts for drug profits
from Syrian, Lebanese, Bulgarian, and Colombian trafficking
organizations.

According to aides to Safra, he arranged that the ADL receive
$1 million from money he won in a lawsuit in 1989.

Moneybags at Sterling National

There is one financial institution that is more closely linked
to the ADL than any other: Sterling National Bank of New
York City. On Jan. 29, 1982, Italian authorities filed civil suit
against Sterling National Bank and other U.S. financial institutions on behalf of depositors in Banca Privata Italiana, charging that $27 million had been looted. The chairman of Sterling,
both at the time of the alleged theft and today, is Theodore H.
Silbert, another honorary vice chairman of the ADL and the
former head of the ADL Appeal, its major fundraising arm.

Law enforcement sources have identified Sterling National
as a mob front since its founding in 1929 by Meyer Lansky
associate Frank Erickson. Sterling National was also implicated in a tax evasion scheme in the early 1980s through another ADL-linked bank director, Arnold Burns, a Reagan-era
U.S. deputy attorney general. Burns's law firm, Burns and
Summit, apparently set up a string of Caribbean tax shelters
which shielded millions of dollars in taxable income through
nonexistent "R&D investments" in Israel.

Former Reagan official, Ambassador to Italy Maxwell Raab,
is another longstanding Sterling National director. Raab was a
onetime business partner of Meyer Lansky in the International
Airport Hotel Corp.

Yet another mob-linked banker who sits on the ADL's National Commission and is listed in the League's most recent
"Purpose and Program" as an honorary vice chairman, is Leonard Abess of the City National Bank of Miami. In 1981, Abess
brought Colombian cartel money launderer Alberto Duque onto
the bank's board, where he remained until he was jailed on
money-laundering charges in 1986. The following year, Donald
Beasley was named City National's chairman. Beasley was the
former director of the Nugan Hand Bank, believed to have

been a major laundering conduit for Southeast Asian heroin proceeds, as well as "black" funds derived from the illicit arms trafficking of Theodore G. Shackley and other former top CIA officials later implicated in the Iran-Contra scandal.

A listing of ADL financial contributors and award recipients over the recent decades reads like a "Who's Who" of the Meyer Lansky international crime syndicate. Longtime Lansky cronies such as Victor Posner, Hollywood attorney Sidney Korshak, and Moe Dalitz all appear as ADL patrons.

The same pattern holds true at the regional levels of the ADL. For example, Phil Baskin, a Pittsburgh attorney and Democratic Party fixer known to be the chief operator of the ADL in western Pennsylvania, was forced to resign as the senior partner in his law firm after being implicated in an effort to deliver a major airport construction contract to a top figure in the New York City Gambino family, "Nicky" Sands.

Further south, Paul Lipkin, the chairman of the Virginia Regional Board of the ADL, was for decades the personal attorney for Arthur "Bootsy" Goldstein, the biggest pornography distributor in Norfolk. Goldstein was arrested 85 times and served three jail terms for crimes including selling glue to minors and peddling sex paraphernalia.

The Booze Baron

No discussion of the ADL's ties to organized crime and the drug apparatus would be complete without reference to Edgar Bronfman, ADL honorary vice chairman and chief of its New York Appeal.

Today touted as a leading international businessman, philanthropist, and the chairman of the prestigious World Jewish Congress, Bronfman has been unable to erase the taint left by the fact that his entire family fortune—Seagram's Corp., its majority share in E.I. du Pont de Nemours Co., etc.—derived from his father's Prohibition-era bootlegging activities. Known at the time as the "Bronfman Gang," the Canadian Bronfmans were the main illegal suppliers to America's crime syndicate known as "Murder, Inc." By no later than 1920, when Edgar's father Sam Bronfman and Arnold Rothstein agent Jacob Katzenberg were dispatched to Hong Kong to arrange opium supplies, the bootlegging routes were also utilized for the smuggling and retail distribution of illegal drugs.

To this day, elements of the Bronfman family remain tied to the gutter levels of organized crime, while Edgar and his brothers and cousins have managed to wrap themselves in a somewhat ragged cloak of respectability. Edgar's nephew Mitchell Bronfman was named in a 1972 Montreal Crime Commission report as an intimate of local crime boss Willy Obront: "Their relationship extends into illegal activities in which they have mutually or jointly indulged . . . the special kinds of favors they did for each other and the resulting advantages of each in the fields of loan sharking, gambling, illegal betting, securities, tax evasion and corruption" (from *The Bronfman Dynasty*, by Peter C. Newman). Obront and another Mitchell Bronfman crime partner Sidney Rosen were both jailed in the mid-1970s for drug money laundering and related crimes.

When in 1978 the links of the Bronfman family to organized crime were published in the book-length study of the international illegal drug trade, *Dope, Inc.*, commissioned by Lyndon LaRouche, Bronfman, according to Quebec police sources, ordered his attorneys to prepare a multimillion-dollar libel suit. But after careful deliberation, the attorneys strongly argued against such an action. Instead, Bronfman reportedly poured large amounts of money into the ADL. Almost immediately, the ADL began a shrill publicity and dirty-tricks campaign, slandering LaRouche as an "anti-Semite" and demanding his elimination.

4. The ADL and the Soviet Union

In its March–April 1990 edition, the West German magazine *Semit,* self-described as "the independent Jewish magazine," published a blistering exposé of ADL honorary vice chairman Edgar Bronfman's dealings with the now-toppled regime of East German communist dictator Erich Honecker. The article, by Jacob Dachauer and titled "A Whiskey for the Holocaust," documents how Bronfman used his post as president of the World Jewish Congress to make deals with the Honecker regime on behalf of his Seagram's liquor empire, and it is accompanied by a picture of Bronfman receiving the highest state medal of "People's Friendship in Gold" from Honecker in October 1988.

The essence of the *Semit* exposé is that Bronfman used his credentials as head of the once-respected World Jewish Congress to absolve the German Democratic Republic (G.D.R.) of any responsibility for the wartime Holocaust, in return for a series of lucrative concessions to market his whiskey in the German communist paradise.

As *EIR* has reported, Bronfman's courtship of the Honecker regime began in 1986, when an associate of his traveled to East Berlin to meet with Klaus Gysi, the communist regime's secretary of state for religious affairs. Klaus Gysi's son is Gregor Gysi, the "reformer" successor to Honecker as chief of the SED communist party (now called the PDS). In subsequent trips, Bronfman met with Honecker and SED Central Committee member Hermann Axen. During one visit in 1988, Bronfman pledged that he would personally arrange a state visit to Washington, D.C. by Honecker by 1990 at the latest. Subsequent events, of course, have made it impossible for him to live up to that.

Edgar's brother and business partner Charles Bronfman of Montreal became a prominent figure in Canadian-East German friendship groups, and had veto power over all G.D.R. visas issued to Canadians until the collapse of the communist regime in November 1989. These extensive G.D.R. links have led some intelligence analysts to conclude that Edgar and Charles Bronfman have especially close ties to Gen. Markus Wolf, the head of the East German Staatssicherheitsdienst (Stasi) intelligence service and a leading protégé of the late KGB and Soviet Communist Party boss Yuri Andropov.

Edgar Bronfman enjoys equally close ties to the regime in Moscow, and those links have grown even firmer since the accession to power of Mikhail Gorbachov in 1985. According to sources familiar with Bronfman's Russian links, the Canadian whiskey baron has been a longtime associate of Alexander Yakovlev, the former Soviet ambassador in Ottawa who is now one of Gorbachov's closest advisers. Yakovlev sits on both the Politburo and the newly formed Presidential Council.

In scores of speeches and commentaries written since Gorbachov's rise to power, Bronfman has called upon the United States to grant the Soviet Union Most Favored Nation status, membership in GATT, and access to the most advanced Western technologies. In a press release issued by his office on March 22, 1989, for example, Bronfman hailed Gorbachov for overturning "socialism in one country," declaring, "It is in U.S. interest to prevent even a partial reversal of perestroika."

Bronfman is a board member of the U.S.-Soviet Trade and Economic Cooperation Council (USTEC), a collection of American Fortune 500 executives and Soviet trade officials actively pushing expanded trade between the two superpowers. According to a U.S. State Department document, the Soviet delegation to USTEC is known by the CIA to be dominated by KGB and GRU (Soviet military intelligence) operatives. Up until recently, the Soviet co-chairman of the group was KGB Gen. Yevgeni Petrovich Pitrovanov, a longtime Stalin ally who survived the post-Stalin shifts and became the head of the Soviet Chamber of Commerce.

Jewish slaves for Israel

On Jan. 23, 1989, syndicated columnists Evans and Novak reported on a secret meeting at Edgar Bronfman's New York City apartment which also involved USTEC officials Dwayne Andreas and James Giffen, together with Morris Abrams and Simcha Dinitz. The group reportedly hatched plans to mobilize Zionist lobby support for the repeal of the Jackson-Vanik Amendment, in exchange for unrestricted Soviet Jewish emigration to Israel.

The genesis of that scheme dates back to January 1985, when Edgar Bronfman, at the governing board meeting of the World

Jewish Congress in Vienna, proposed that the organization oppose the Reagan administration's Strategic Defense Initiative, "on Jewish grounds." When Bronfman also announced in April of that same year that he would lead the WJC in an effort to prevent President Reagan from visiting a German cemetery at Bitburg during his state visit to the Federal Republic, Moscow reciprocated by inviting him to the Soviet Union in his official capacity as WJC chairman. The invitation, extended by Russian Federation Justice Minister Alexander Sukharev, specifically proposed to discuss Soviet Jewish emigration.

In similar gestures of support for Gorbachov, Bronfman has taken the point in forcing the resignation of the head of the West German parliament, Phillip Jenninger, for a speech delivered in November 1988 on the 50th anniversary of Nazis' "Night of the Broken Glass" anti-Jewish pogrom. In addition, at a widely publicized press conference in Budapest, Hungary on May 4, 1987, Bronfman branded Austrian President Kurt Waldheim an "essential component of the Nazi killing machine." The charges against Waldheim were based largely on Soviet-forged documents and perjured testimony, and were part of a major destabilization of Austria and the Vatican.

No wonder Bronfman became a frequent commuter between New York and Moscow.

Weeks after Bronfman's secret New York City planning session, on Feb. 11, 1989, Edgar Bronfman led the largest delegation of Jewish leaders to ever visit Moscow. On Dec. 13, 1989, Bronfman was back in Moscow again, this time heading a delegation of 100 Western Jewish leaders to attend the opening of a Jewish Cultural Center. One week later, Kenneth Jacobson, the international affairs director of the ADL, announced that an ADL delegation would also visit Moscow in early 1990 to pursue President Gorbachov's offer to open an office in the Soviet capital.

Next to Edgar Bronfman, Minneapolis grain merchant Dwayne Andreas, who participated in the Bronfman apartment meeting at which the "Jews for grain" plot was activated, is the

ADL patron most responsible for the deep ties between the League and the Gorbachov regime.

Although Andreas is not Jewish, he is one of the ADL's most generous donors. At a critical point in the late 1970s, when the ADL was financially on the skids, Andreas, at the request of ADL National Chairman Burton Joseph of the Minneapolis agricultural equipment firm I.E. Joseph, put up the seed money to establish the ADL Foundation.

Andreas's relations with the ADL date back to his early political training by ADL National Chairman Ben Epstein, a relationship that Andreas described during congressional testimony in 1987: "Mr. Ben Epstein, may he rest in peace, who was my friend for 20 years, to his everlasting credit, was my mentor and guidance on the matters of diplomatic positions. I worked with him for weeks on this problem of how to expand trade with the U.S.S.R."

The Sept. 26, 1986 *Wall Street Journal,* in a front-page piece titled "Gorbachov's Pal: Dwayne Andreas Gains a Position as the Kremlin's Apparent Favorite," identified Andreas as the successor to Occidental Petroleum's chairman Armand Hammer (now 91), as the Soviet regime's favorite "capitalist."

It was apparently Andreas, who has had more private audiences with Gorbachov than any other Westerner, who arranged the invitation for the ADL to set up shop in Moscow ostensibly in order to help combat anti-Semitism inside Russia. A former State Department intelligence officer told *EIR* that the real purpose of establishing the ADL office in Moscow was to improve ADL coordination with the KGB in running pro-Gorbachov propaganda inside the United States.

Another feature of the ADL's current "go east" push is the effort by Bronfman and others to move in on the "lucrative new markets" in the liberated nations of Central Europe—on behalf of organized crime. For instance, the Canadian real estate billionaires, the Reichmann brothers, represented by the ADL-linked law firm of Shea Gould and the ADL-linked investment house of Bear Stearns, are part of a new investment consortium seeking to establish a major financial hub in Budapest—with the blessings of both the Gorbachov regime and the U.S. State Department.

ADL Was On U.S. Watch List

ADL links to the Bolshevik regime and its intelligence services date back decades. Even during World War II, when the Soviet Union and the United States were allied against the Nazis, certain ADL officials were kept on U.S. Military Intelligence watch lists as suspected Soviet agents. According to one eyewitness account, Sanford Griffith, who headed the equivalent of the Fact-Finding Division during and immediately following World War II, was on such a list.

The April 5, 1955 issue of *Headlines And What's Behind Them* catalogues a controversial instance in which the ADL provided cover for a known Soviet intelligence asset. The Soviet agent in question, Vladimir Stepankowsky, had been deported from France and Switzerland in the mid-1930s after having been identified as the head of the Bolshevik Information Bureau, only to emigrate to the United States and immediately go to work for the ADL's Mitchell Solomon. Through Solomon's ties to U.S. Army Lt. Col. Eugene Prince, an intelligence officer in charge of immigration background checks, Stepankowsky was able to penetrate American wartime intelligence operations. In 1954, he was identified by Elizabeth Bentley as a member of a Soviet spy ring; however, he was saved from prosecution through the intervention of his ADL case officer Mitchell Solomon. By this point, the ADL had deployed the Soviet agent into the National Renaissance Party of Robert Madole, a neo-Nazi countergang that had been set up largely by ADL infiltrators in order to create the specter of a new "fascist menace" inside the United States. According to the *Headlines* account, the Madole group attracted a small core of members, principally on the basis of the ADL providing NRP founder Madole with a stable of prostitutes from the Mickey Jelke vice ring. ADL officials Ben Epstein and Arnold Forster then reportedly used Stepankowsky's information to inundate the Velde Commission (House Un-American Activities Committee) with scare stories that the NRP had swelled to 200–700 members in New York City alone.

5. The ADL and Project Democracy

ADL officials, and the ADL as an organization, are guilty of the same crimes for which Carl "Spitz" Channell and Richard Miller were indicted during the 1987 Iran-Contra probe: illegally using private, tax-exempt organizations to conduct covert operations. However, unlike Channell and Miller, who were low-level flunkies in the overall "secret parallel government" plot, the ADL was deeply involved in every facet of the Iran-Contra scandal and the Project Democracy scheme at the highest levels on both the government and private sector sides.

The ADL's central role in the official Project Democracy apparatus of the Reagan-Bush era was an outgrowth of the ADL's longstanding position as a major agency within the U.S. branch of the Socialist International, which has always been dominated by members of the old Bukharinite "Right Opposition" to Stalin. This link is typified by Fact-Finding Division head Irwin Suall, who was trained by the International Ladies Garment Workers Union of former U.S. Communist Party chairman Jay Lovestone. Suall was later schooled at the premier Fabian labor school, Ruskin College at Britain's Oxford University, and then passed through the Socialist Party and the Jewish Labor Committee before graduating to his ADL post in 1967. Today, Suall sits on the board of the League for Industrial Democracy and the Social Democrats USA.

The direct links between the ADL and the Iran-Contra fiasco run through the following key players:

■ Carl Gershman, a former paid staffer of the ADL's Fact-Finding Division, was the director of the National Endowment for Democracy (NED) throughout the Iran-Contra fiasco. From 1966–72, Gershman was employed by the Research Department of the ADL. According to Jerome Bakst, his supervisor at

DOPE, INC.

the time, Gershman used his extensive experience as a New Left activist at Yale University to provide the ADL with detailed dossiers on Students for a Democratic Society, the Black Panther Party, and the Student Non-Violent Coordinating Committee. According to documents procured under the Freedom of Information Act, as well as a recently published book-length account of the FBI's Cointelpro efforts against the black student movement in the 1960s, the ADL dossiers, apparently including Gershman's work, were regularly passed on to the FBI's Division Five.

Early this year, Gershman hired ADL Fact-Finding Division deputy director David Lowe as his executive assistant at the State Department U.S. Information Agency unit. NED was a major government funding conduit for Lt. Col. Oliver North, and for White House deputy Walter Raymond's "Public Diplomacy" project, a black propaganda and "active measures" effort launched to shape media coverage of the Sandinista regime in Nicaragua.

■ ADL Latin American Affairs director Rabbi Morton M. Rosenthal was directly financed by the NED in 1985 to conduct an electoral "fact finding" trip through Central America. Among Rosenthal's assignments for the NED was the monitoring of the presidential elections in El Salvador. On May 23, 1983, Rosenthal issued a report charging that the Sandinista regime in Nicaragua was guilty of anti-Semitism. The Rosenthal attack on the Sandinistas was part of an effort to marshal Jewish support for the Reagan administration's Contra effort. That month, Rosenthal addressed a closed-door White House meeting sponsored by Faith Whittelsey at which aspects of the covert Contra support program were apparently discussed.

In a memorandum to the Latin American Affairs Committee of the ADL dated June 9, 1983, Rosenthal described the ADL's direct role in the anti-Sandinista propaganda offensive:

The ADL's Sandinista anti-Semitism "story's unusually wide international and domestic coverage, by both print and electronic media, stimulated a flood of calls and mail to Nicaragua's Embassy and Consulates and also elicited strong comments from members of Congress. A few days after the story broke, the Nicaraguan Embassy contacted us through intermediaries and inquired if we were willing to meet and discuss the issues. The Embassy then called officially to invite ADL representatives to meet the Nicaraguan Ambassador, Antonio Jarquin. The meeting was held at the Nicaraguan Embassy in Washington on Monday, June 6."

■ Kenneth Bialkin, then the national chairman of the ADL, was the attorney for Saudi billionaire Adnan Khashoggi during 1984–85 when Khashoggi provided the initial funds through which the Iranian government purchased arms from the North-Secord-Hakim "Enterprise." At the time of these transactions, Bialkin was also a member of an administrative commission revamping U.S. federal codes. Another member of the commission was C. Boyden Gray, the general counsel to Vice President George Bush, who formally ran the administration's Special Situation Group/Crisis Pre-Planning Group, the White House interagency units set up under National Security Decision Directive 3 to oversee the Reagan-Bush government's Central America policy.

■ The Lake Resources front company in Geneva, Switzerland, through which Gen. Richard Secord and Albert Hakim laundered the Iranian profits to the Contras, was controlled from the outset by attorney Willard Zucker. A former partner of Bialkin's at Willkie Farr, Zucker had been installed by the ADL national chairman in 1972 as the chief of the IOS legal department, making him a key inside player in the Vesco looting of the fund.

■ Edmond Safra, one of the ADL's major financial "angels," was the co-owner, with Willard Zucker, of the fleet of corporate jets which were used to shuttle then-National Security Adviser Robert McFarlane and Lt. Col. Oliver North to secret meetings in Teheran.

The ADL itself was directly involved in the "active measures" department of The Enterprise, through its sponsorship of a series of propaganda broadsides attacking as "anti-Semites" leftist groups which opposed the administration's Central America policy. One such study commissioned by the ADL in 1983 resulted in a book-length attack by writer Harvey Klehr

on the group called Clergy and Laity Concerned. Another study,
by longtime ADL stringer Rael Jean Isaac, made similar attacks against the Institute for Policy Studies. In 1984, ADL
chapters around the country hosted a speaking tour by Isaac.
Both Klehr and Isaac were funded during the same period by
the Smith Richardson Foundation, a North Carolina-based tax-
exempt foundation with very strong ties to the social democratic
wing of the U.S. intelligence community. Reagan-era National
Security Adviser Richard Allen and U.N. Ambassador Jeane
Kirkpatrick both currently sit on the board of Smith Richardson.

6. The ADL and Domestic Terrorism

Today more than ever, the ADL as an organization represents
a major agent-provocateur factor within the United States, fo-
menting racial and ethnic tensions, all the while claiming to
be great defenders of civil rights.

Freedom of Information Act records show that the ADL
played a major role in the FBI's Cointelpro "Racial Matters"
and "White Hate Groups" operations, targeting the civil rights
movement as well as its opponents. Among the paid informants
used by the ADL during the civil rights struggles of the 1960s
were Ku Klux Klan members implicated in the murders of
three civil rights workers in Mississippi.

A Feb. 13, 1970 article in the *Los Angeles Times* by investigative reporter Jack Nelson first revealed FBI and ADL joint
patronage of the Roberts brothers in the June 30, 1968 murder
of a Klanswoman named Cathy Ainsworth. At the time of the
shootout in front of the Meridian, Mississippi home of ADL
official Meyer Davidson, which resulted in the death of Ainsworth and the near death of her associate Thomas A. Tarrants
III (who survived over 70 shotgun, rifle, and pistol wounds),
Alton Wayne Roberts and six other Klansmen had already been
convicted for federal civil rights violations in connection with

their infamous murder of civil rights workers Chaney, Goodman, and Schwerner in Philadelphia, Mississippi in 1964.

Roberts's case was under appeal when, according to various
newspaper accounts and local police reports, the brothers were
approached by Adolph "Sam" Botnick, who is still the ADL's
regional director in New Orleans, with the proposition that
they would be paid $69,000 to act as agents provocateurs in
setting up a Klan bombing of ADL official Meyer Davidson's
home. Botnick had been a close associate of the FBI Division
Five (counterintelligence) chief in New Orleans, the late Guy
Bannister, who had established the left-wing Fair Play for Cuba
group that was part of the milieu of President John F. Kennedy's purported assassin Lee Harvey Oswald. Bannister had
also been a controller of an agent provocateur network in the
Minutemen which, according to one well-informed U.S. intelligence source, helped break James Earl Ray out of prison, so
that he could be used as a similar patsy in the April 4, 1968
murder of Dr. Martin Luther King in Memphis, Tennessee, just
a few weeks prior to the Meridian, Mississippi shootout staged
by the Roberts brothers at the behest of the ADL and FBI.

A police file report dated June 10, 1968 by Detective Luke
Scarborough, confirms the *Los Angeles Times* report of the Ainsworth setup, namely that there was a three-way deal between
the ADL, FBI, and local police in the matter, for which the ADL
had provided the money. As the apparent result of such ADL-
FBI cooperation, the federal government "trod lightly" in pun-
ishing Alton Wayne Roberts for his part in the murder of
Schwerner, Goodman, and Chaney when, on March 17, 1970,
he was sentenced to only 10 years, and was paroled in three.
The Roberts brothers were reportedly later given the status of
"Federally Protected Witnesses," and remain on the FBI and
ADL's informant roster to this day.

As for the ADL officials, Sam Botnick still runs the ADL's
New Orleans regional office, and his then-assistant Richard
Lobenthal took over ADL operations in Detroit. Lobenthal was
later caught funding local members of the Communist Labor
Party, a violent Maoist group infiltrated into local auto plants.
Justin J. Finger, who ran the ADL's Atlanta-based Southern

legal department during the heyday of civil rights activities
and Klan murders, is now associate national director of the
ADL.

Baiting the Black Panthers

ADL dirty tricks in collusion with the FBI were later run
against segments of the anti-war movement during the late
1960s and early 1970s.

FOIA documents released by the FBI (cf. 100–530-X from the
Special Agent in Charge Los Angeles to FBI Director Hoover
on the subject "Black Panther Party"/"Racial Matter") point to
ADL-FBI collusion against the Black Panther Party as well.
The document in question is an Oct. 22, 1968 ADL report on
the Black Panther Party by Carl Gershman and Jerome Bakst,
which concludes: "For the present at least, increasingly frequent and increasingly violent encounters can be expected between the Panthers and the police." The discovery of this in-
flammatory report in FBI files corroborates a passage in the
recent book *Racial Matters* by Kenneth O'Reilly in a chapter
titled, "The Only Good Panther," which says:

"Division Five tried to disrupt the Panthers by manipulating
Rabbi Meir Kahane and the 'vigilante-type' Jewish Defense
League (JDL), leaking information to college administrators
and sources in the Anti-Defamation League, and working with
newspaper columnists. The FBI compared Panther ideology
with 'the traditional anti-Semitism of organizations like the
American Nazi Party' and the even more traditional anti-Semitism of the late Adolf Hitler. In the case of the JDL, the FBI
did not limit itself to 'the furnishing of factual information'
because Kahane's group could not 'be motivated to act' unless
'the information . . . concerning anti-Semitism and other matters were furnished . . . [with] some embellishment.' "

Doing the FBI's Dirty Work

The ADL has continued its involvement in such Cointelpro-
type operations to this day. In fact, well-informed U.S. intelligence sources charge that after the scope of the FBI's criminality in Cointelpro had been exposed and condemned by the U.S.

Congress, the FBI temporarily "shopped out" all such Cointel-pro operations to the ADL. Two illustrative cases:

■ James R. Rosenberg (a.k.a. Jimmy Mitchell, Jimmy Anderson) is a full-time paid agent of ADL Fact-Finding Division. Police reports corroborate statements to *EIR* that Rosenberg was the ADL's infiltrator into the Ku Klux Klan chapter in Trenton, New Jersey, who sought to provoke the group into bombing Trenton's chapter of the National Association for the Advancement of Colored People (NAACP). Pay stubs from the ADL to Rosenberg at this time have been recovered.

Like many provocateurs employed by both the ADL and the more overtly violent Jewish Defense League, Rosenberg was given military training in Israel as an Israeli Defense Forces soldier "on loan" from the U.S. National Guard.

In 1981, a female JDL member, using the code-name "Ricky," told *EIR:* "I met Jimmy in Israel around 1978 when I was at the Kfar Saba Kibbutz near the West Bank. . . . He was always bragging about how he worked for the Anti-Defamation League to infiltrate the Ku Klux Klan. . . . Jimmy got all messed up on Valium. He even had to go for drug treatment, and that upset him because he got impotent for about six months. . . . Jimmy really wanted to be in the Israeli military, and he made it—he sent me a picture. . . . But he's a 'jobnik,' a paper pusher; they wouldn't trust him in combat."

Rosenberg returned from Israel in 1979 to continue his work for Irwin Suall, who apparently used Jimmy's new military training to have him infiltrate the paramilitary Right, which had become a major target of the ADL. On Dec. 7, 1981, Rosenberg appeared in his undercover capacity on a WCCO Television documentary in Minneapolis, titled "Armies of the Right," where he made the most violent and anti-Semitic statements of any of the members of the Christian Patriots Defense League on the show. Either by oversight or intent, the producers never identified Rosenberg as an ADL provocateur. They simply identified him as "Jimmy Anderson," an official of the Queens, New York chapter of the Christian Defense League. Rosenberg and another ADL infiltrator/provocateur in the group were later arrested on the roof of a Manhattan brownstone brandishing automatic weapons.

■ Mordechai Levy (a.k.a. James Gutman, James Frank, Mark Levine, Mark Levy, Morty, etc.). On Aug. 10, 1989, Mordechai Levy was apprehended by the New York Police Department after he mounted the roof of his 6 Bleecker Street apartment building in Greenwich Village and wounded an innocent passerby in wild sniper fire. The shooting occurred after Jewish Defense League (JDL) leader Irv Rubin tried to deliver a subpoena to Levy, who now heads the rival Jewish Defense Organization, for a civil libel case.

The arrest of the 30-year-old terrorist on charges of attempted murder, first-degree assault, and reckless endangerment brought to light a new chapter in the pattern of FBI and ADL collusion in domestic terrorism, reminiscent of Cointelpro. In a July 18, 1984 court deposition, the ADL's Irwin Suall admitted that he has met and has had telephone conversations with Levy "from time to time for quite a long time." Suall's admissions drastically underplayed Levy's longstanding role as one of the ADL's agents provocateurs. But in an interview with *Village Voice* reporter Robert Friedman, another ADL Fact-Finding Division official, Gail Gans, confirmed Levy's status as an ADL operator. Levy was in fact a shared asset of the ADL, the FBI, and other police agencies. Two of Levy's FBI controllers are known to be FBI Special Agents Joseph Valiquette and Paul Locke, both of the New York Field Office. Freedom of Information Act documents show that the New York Field office had an official liaison with the ADL's national headquarters since at least the 1960s.

In February 1979, Levy was caught attempting to provoke a major riot in Philadelphia. Using the pseudonym James Gutman, Levy obtained a rally permit for a neo-Nazi rally at which he planned to display banners reading: "Hitler Was Right— Gas The Commie Jews." Working out of the Philadelphia offices of the JDL, Levy, under his phony "neo-Nazi" cover, was in the process of contacting all of the local KKK and Nazi groups to draw them into the event. Simultaneously, he was working with local left-wing and Jewish groups and black churches to

organize a counter-demonstration. When some local reporters
learned of Levy's scheme and informed the National Park Service, the rally permit was canceled. Local press headlines exposed the plot with headlines such as in the *Journal,* "Jew
Applied for the Permit for Nazi Rally," and the *Philadelphia
Bulletin,* "Nazi Rally-Rouser Really Jewish?"

At the same time, the ADL ordered Levy to conduct a harassment campaign against associates of Lyndon LaRouche, which
involved scores of death threats phoned into the offices of Campaigner Publications in New York City. By Levy's own admission, that effort culminated in an attempted JDL armed assault
against Lyndon LaRouche's Riverdale, New York apartment
and a menacing demonstration of JDLers and Yippies (Youth
International Party) in front of the Campaigner offices.

Jury Tampering

The ADL's direct use of Levy in criminal activities came to
light in an affidavit submitted in October 1984, during
LaRouche's civil libel suit against the National Broadcasting
Corp. and the Anti-Defamation League of B'nai B'rith in U.S.
District Court in Alexandria, Virginia. Levy admitted to a Cali-
fornia LaRouche associate that he had been ordered by the
ADL to launch a telephone harassment campaign against the
Alexandria jurors, which would be blamed on followers of
LaRouche. The ADL, according to the affidavit, provided Levy
with the names and addresses of the jurors. FBI Special Agent
Richard Wade of the Alexandria Field Office was ordered by
federal Judge James Cacheris to investigate the Levy jury-
tampering evidence, but the investigation was quashed. On
Nov. 20, 1984, Levy fired a .45 caliber slug into the Los Angeles
house of a LaRouche associate who was investigating this jury-
tampering incident.

In 1985, Levy also emerged as a suspected accomplice in
several of the most significant domestic terrorist acts in years:

■ On Aug. 15, 1985, Tscherim Soobzokov, a leader of the
Circassian Muslim community in Paterson, New Jersey, was
the target of a bombing of his home, which caused his death on

Sept. 7. Just days before the explosion, Mordechai Levy had been in Paterson, publicly attacking Soobzokov in a local synagogue with the same charges by which the U.S. Justice Department's Office of Special Investigations had unsuccessfully tried to prove Soobzokov was a "Nazi war criminal." A few days after the bombing, Levy held a press conference in Paterson applauding the attack, but denying responsibility. One week prior to the bombing, Levy had phoned a death threat to Soobzokov's attorney in the OSI case, Michael Dennis, Esq., during which Levy also vowed to kill Soobzokov.

On Oct. 11, 1985, Alex Odeh, the Santa Ana, California head of the Arab-American Anti-Discrimination Committee, died at 11:21 a.m. after a bomb rigged to the door of his office exploded as Odeh was reporting for work. The night before he was assassinated, Odeh had been interviewed on two national television shows, on the hijacking of the *Achille Lauro* cruise ship which Odeh said had been the work of an anti-Arafat terrorist splinter group from the Palestine Liberation Organization. Highly reliable sources report that Odeh had been the recipient of multiple threats from Mordechai Levy, the JDL, and the JDO.

Although FBI Director William Webster, a longtime "friend" of the ADL, was obliged to publicly identify the "Jewish underground" as the most active terrorist organization in the United States during 1985, no arrests were ever made in either the Soobzokov or Odeh cases. Sources close to the late Alex Odeh were candidly told by the FBI that there would be no arrests, because of the killers' links to Israeli intelligence. The sources were also told that Levy would not be prosecuted despite evidence of his complicity before the fact—because he was to be used by the government as a witness in upcoming federal trials of Lyndon LaRouche.

7. The ADL and International Terrorism

Top officials of the ADL are suspected accessories in a number of major international political assassinations, including the

murders of Swedish Prime Minister Olof Palme and Indian
Prime Minister Indira Gandhi. While no evidence is known to
exist linking the ADL to the actual executions, very strong
evidence does exist in all three cases implicating top ADL officials in the preparation or the coverup of those crimes.

In the case of the assassination of Indira Gandhi on Oct. 31,
1984, eyewitness accounts of a courtroom encounter with ADL
officials Irwin Suall and Barbara Wall just hours after Mrs.
Gandhi was murdered by a Sikh fanatic who was a member of
her own security detail, report that the two were visibly elated
over her assassination.

The key link between the ADL and the Sikh extremists who
murdered Prime Minister Gandhi runs through Rabbi Rosenthal, a senior ADL employee and head of the league's Latin
American Affairs Division, who is directly linked to the man
who ordered the assassination, Dr. Jagjit Singh Chauhan. It
also runs through Rosenthal's longtime intimate political collaborator and sometimes business partner Jon Speller. Speller
is widely believed to be a high-level intelligence agent for British intelligence and Scottish Rite Freemasonic networks associated with Lord Nicholas Bethel and Julian Amery, although
he also had documented links to Israeli, Soviet, and American
intelligence services.

One year before Mrs. Gandhi's assassination, Speller sponsored a U.S. visit by Jagjit Singh Chauhan, which included
meetings with conservative members of the U.S. Senate. It was
partly on the basis of that American tour that Soviet news
agencies blamed the Reagan administration for the Gandhi
assassination—even though then-Defense Secretary Caspar
Weinberger was in the process of deepening U.S.-Indian military cooperation, which was threatening Soviet influence in the
subcontinent.

After Mrs. Gandhi's death, Rabbi Rosenthal and Speller, operating through a front company they had jointly established
called Transglobal Resources, arranged a series of secret meetings in Washington, London, and Quito, Ecuador, which resulted in the Ecuadoran government offering Chauhan a large
tract of land on which to establish a Khalistani homeland. As

the ADL's full-time director of Latin American affairs, Rosen-thal had utilized the agency's channels inside the Ecuador to help establish a safe haven for Sikh extremists, some of whom had recently blown up an Air Canada flight and had plotted the assassination of Mrs. Gandhi's son and successor Rajiv Gandhi during a state visit to Washington in December 1984.

The Sikh extremists have never tried to hide their intention of eliminating Mrs. Gandhi. Jagjit Singh Chauhan, the "president-in-exile" of the nonexistent separatist state of Khalistan, issued his widely publicized call for Mrs. Gandhi's assassination on June 9, 1984—three days after Indian Army troops had stormed the Golden Temple in Amritsar and liberated it from the hands of armed Sikh radicals linked to Chauhan. Less than one week before Mrs. Gandhi's murder, Chauhan had told a caller into his Reading, England headquarters, "Some man will come forward and take off the head of Mrs. Gandhi."

Chauhan's call led immediately to the formation of the terrorist World Sikh Organization. Representatives of the WSO were soon meeting with officials of the ADL's Interfaith Affairs Department, according to Rabbi Leon Klenicki, the department's director. The meeting had been set up at the request of Landrum Bolling, the chairman of the Eli Lilly Endowment, which heavily funds the League's interfaith unit.

Surjit Singh, a top official of the WSO who has been intimately linked to Chauhan since 1947, is also a close personal friend of ADL Honorary National Chairman Kenneth Bialkin.

The Palme Assassination Coverup

If the assassination of Indira Gandhi was intended as a blow to improving U.S.-Indian relations to the benefit of the ADL's London sponsors and Soviet and Israeli friends, the assassination on Feb. 28, 1986 of Swedish Prime Minister Olof Palme appears to have been similarly motivated by a common objective of certain circles in Moscow, London, and Washington: to cover up the biggest international weapons and drug trafficking scandal in history—a scandal that only began to surface with the Iran-Contra revelations in the United States and Western Europe and the more recent "Stasi-gate" in East Germany.

When Prime Minister Olof Palme ordered Swedish police to raid the offices of Karl Erik Schmits, a prominent international arms dealer, just months before his assassination, significant evidence began to turn up concerning American, British, Israeli, as well as Soviet bloc arms trafficking to Iran, Iraq, and the Nicaraguan Contras all in apparent collusion. Palme reportedly became deeply concerned when the full extent of Swedish socialist democratic involvement in the arms trafficking and profiteering was documented in records seized in the Schmits raids, and began to crack down on the flow of arms from Sweden to the Persian Gulf. At that point, the prime minister became an expendable adversary of the very intelligence services for whom he had worked throughout his political career.

While the identity of the assassin team may never be known, a profile of the responsible agencies emerges from the massive coverup which began within hours of the Palme murder, with the first news leak that the European Labor Party (ELP), which is associated with the ideas and policies of Lyndon LaRouche, was under police investigation. The false trail of accusations linking LaRouche to the Palme murder diverted investigators from pursuing legitimate leads for the first two months of the probe, thereby wrecking any prospects of solving the crime. It was the ADL, along with KGB, which played the pivotal role in that critical coverup phase.

Since 1982, the ADL had been involved with some of the most notorious KGB agents of influence in Sweden in slandering the ELP. ADL official Irwin Suall, an active member of the Socialist International, is an intimate of Swedish Social Democrat Pierre Schori and West German Social Democrat Klauss-Henning Rosen, the chief aide to former Chancellor Willy Brandt. Schori was named by confessed Norwegian KGB spy Arne Treholt as a leading KGB "agent of influence" in Scandinavian social democratic circles.

In 1982, Suall aided Swedish television producer Goran Rosenberg in preparing a series of slanders labeling the ELP as "neo-Nazi." Two years later, the daily *Svenska Dagbladet* published a similar slander by Willy Silberman, based on "research" by journalist Hans Lindquist, a protégé of Joachim Israel. Investigations at the time revealed that Lindquist had been directed in his efforts by the ADL's European director in Paris, Shimon Stanley Samuels. Samuels, in turn, had coordinated the anti-LaRouche campaign with Gerry Gable, the London-based editor of *Searchlight* magazine and a member of the Communist Party of Great Britain. *Searchlight* is believed to be one of the KGB's major front-publications in Western Europe. Thus, at least two years before the Palme assassination and coverup, the ADL was already involved with Soviet intelligence networks in slandering LaRouche in Europe.

Within 72 hours of Palme's murder, Danish, West German, and Soviet news outlets were naming the ELP as prime suspects of the Swedish police. This set the stage for the detention nine days later of Victor Gunnarsson, a local Stockholm weirdo who had once signed a petition endorsing the ELP's party status, possibly on behalf of socialist party-run police networks who had used him for years as an informant on groups opposed to the Palme's Socialist Labor Party (SAP).

Unconfirmed reports suggest that the ADL deployed a team of operatives to Stockholm in early March 1986 to fuel the accusations against the LaRouche associates, but that the team was summoned back to the United States when two LaRouche associates won the Illinois Democratic primary elections for lieutenant governor and secretary of state on March 18, 1986.

What is confirmed is that Jonas Hafstrom, the first secretary of the Swedish embassy in Washington, was put in contact with the ADL's International Affairs Director Abe Foxman by Israeli embassy deputy chief of mission Elyahim Rubenstein-Migdal. Foxman funneled ADL "files" on LaRouche into the hands of Stockholm Police Chief Hans Holmér, the chief investigator of the Palme murder, through a Swedish Foreign Ministry official named Nils Rosenberg. Those files became an integral part of the Palme task force's coverup. At the same time, U.S. State Department Swedish desk officer Richard Christensen steered American reporters to ADL stringer Goran Rosenberg, the producer of the 1982 television slander, who was by then based in Washington, D.C.

On March 18, 1986—the same day as the Illinois primaries—
Irwin Suall appeared on NBC Nightly News in an interview
with Brian Ross, in which he said that LaRouche associates
were capable of assassinating Palme. On March 19, Swedish
police released Gunnarsson for lack of evidence, although the
"Gunnarsson-ELP" track of the investigation was pursued for
many months.

The Suall-ADL propaganda offensive intersected an identical
campaign by top Soviet officials to blame the Palme murder on
LaRouche and the ELP. The Soviet disinformation effort was
steered by Sergei Losev, the director general of the official
Soviet news agency TASS, and was coordinated in Stockholm
by Soviet ambassador Boris Pankin. Pankin, a former director
general of VAAP, the Soviet copyright office, has been identified
as a lieutenant general in the KGB and a former director of
KGB Service A, the disinformation unit, before he became ambassador in Stockholm in 1982.

On Aug. 24, 1989, the Swedish daily newspaper *Expressen*
revealed that officials of the Swedish national police (SÄPO)
counterespionage unit had bugged the home of a Soviet embassy
official and suspected KGB man and had obtained taped evidence that the Kremlin knew in advance of the Palme assassination. Thus, the ADL was not only complicit in a major international assassination coverup scheme; the scheme at least in
part concealed Soviet complicity before the fact in the assassination of a Western head of state.

8. The ADL Subverts Justice: the OSI

One of the most significant focal points of Soviet and Israeli
intelligence penetration of the U.S. government is through the
Justice Department's Office of Special Investigations (OSI), a
unit created by congressional action in 1978 to ostensibly hunt
down Nazi criminals and deport them from the United States
to stand trial for their crimes back home.

In fact, the OSI has always functioned as a pipeline for Soviet-forged evidence and other contamination of the American judicial system, and for Soviet and Israeli propaganda directed against Eastern European emigré circles within the United States. The ADL maintains a full-time liaison officer to OSI posted in Washington, and another full-time ADL official works with Israeli authorities in Tel Aviv.

Where forged documents have not been sufficient to complete the railroading of the OSI's targets, more violent means have been frequently used. The already cited case of Tscherim Soobzokov is one such example. The more recent events in Israel involving John Demjanjuk, a retired Cleveland autoworker falsely accused of being Treblinka concentration guard "Ivan the Terrible," are an even more telling case of ADL-KGB collusion.

On Nov. 29, 1988, Dov Eytan, a respected attorney and member of the Israeli establishment, plunged to his death out of the 15th floor of his office building in Tel Aviv. At the time of his death, Eytan, a former judge, was preparing Demjanjuk's appeal before the Israeli bar which would expose the Soviet KGB's hand in forged documents, witness coercion, and the suppression of exculpatory evidence by the U.S. Department of Justice's Office of Special Investigation, all of which had led an Israeli court to sentence Demjanjuk to death as "Ivan the Terrible." On Dec. 1, at Dov Eytan's funeral, after a quick ruling by the Israeli government that he had committed suicide, acid was thrown in the face of Yoram Sheftel, John Demjanjuk's other lawyer, who had argued forcefully that Demjanjuk was the victim of mistaken identity perpetrated by the OSI and Soviet KGB.

In fact, virtually all of the witnesses against Demjanjuk had either earlier given contradictory testimony, or had been proven to be liars during the course of the trial. The key piece of "evidence" against Demjanjuk, a concentration camp ID card, had been flown to Israel from Moscow by Soviet agent Armand Hammer aboard his Occidental Petroleum private jet. Demjanjuk's attorneys presented conclusive evidence that the ID card was a KGB forgery.

More recently, in the United States, the ADL launched an

attack against Rep. James Traficant (D-Ohio), because he charged on Aug. 2, 1989 that the OSI may have deliberately withheld information showing that a key witness against Demjanjuk, Otto Horn, perjured himself when he identified Demjanjuk as "Ivan" during 1981 denaturalization proceedings. The proof of the perjury was discovered in two internal OSI reports found in a trash can outside their office, which were then given to Demjanjuk's son-in-law. Traficant, who has asked Attorney General Richard Thornburgh to authorize an "objective review" of OSI work on the Demjanjuk case, said that no one "really knows" if Demjanjuk is Ivan. "We endanger the rights of all Americans by allowing John Demjanjuk to be hung out to dry under such unusual circumstances," Traficant added.

Not only had the OSI suppressed evidence of Otto Horn's perjury, but there is reason to believe that the entire case had been fabricated by the OSI. ADL honorary vice chairman Edgar Bronfman has also mobilized the World Jewish Congress, of which he is president and chief contributor, in tandem with the OSI on numerous other cases. The original list of 200 suspected Nazi war criminals living in the United States, which constituted the bulk of cases since probed by the OSI, was prepared by Charles Allen, a one time researcher for the WJC who headed up an American-East German friendship group known to be a front group for the Communist Party USA.

Two years after the OSI's founding, OSI officials Allan Ryan and Neal Sher, armed with the Charles Allen "list," traveled to Moscow, where they met with General Rudenko, a Soviet military official, to review Russian files on the accused wartime Nazis. Gen. Roman Rudenko was well-known for his handling of Moscow's genocide policy toward Ukrainians in the 1930s, when 8–10 million Ukrainians died of starvation—a performance that had earned him a promotion to be one of Josef Stalin's favorite prosecutors during the purge trials. When the OSI's Sher and Ryan met with him in 1981, they arranged to introduce the sort of KGB-manufactured evidence for which the OSI would become notorious.

As the ADL's Teitel writes: "The United States-Israel cooperation in this [Demjanjuk] case was only the tip of the iceberg.

Without similar cooperation between the U.S. and the Soviet
Union, John Demjanjuk might never have been found." And
the September 1984 edition of the *ADL Bulletin* carried a two-
page article by Neal Sher, who had succeeded Ryan as OSI
director, defending the OSI against charges from Eastern Euro-
peans that this agreement with the Soviets had introduced
KGB "forged documents" and "intimidated witness" testimony
to U.S. courts.

The Arthur Rudolph and Kurt Waldheim Capers

Edgar Bronfman was a willing accomplice in the OSI's
frameup of the rocket scientist Dr. Arthur Rudolph, who was
illegally forced into exile from the United States in the spring
of 1984 after he had been targeted as a "Nazi war criminal"
in Soviet publications. The real reason why the Soviets and
Bronfman targeted the celebrated designer of the Pershing I
and Saturn rockets, was because he was part of the Strategic
Defense Initiative project, which was then Soviet intelligence's
number-one priority to disable. Kept by lack of funds and advanced age from waging a full defense against the groundless
charges, and fearful that his wife and children would be driven
into poverty were his U.S. government pension revoked, Rudolph reached an agreement with the OSI that he would volun-
tarily return to his native Germany. A subsequent investigation by West German courts found him guiltless of any
involvement in the crimes the OSI accused him of.

Bronfman's next case of collaboration with the OSI was his
campaign against former United Nations general secretary and
current Austrian President Kurt Waldheim, whose biggest
crime appears to have been that, in agreement with the Hel-
sinki Accords, he has given Soviet Jews passing through Austria the right to settle wherever they choose—not just in Israel,
as implicitly demanded by Bronfman and the ADL. Waldheim's
defenders charge that Bronfman's WJC distorted the facts and
even solicited perjured testimony against the Austrian leader.
Noted war crimes investigator Simon Wiesenthal has been a
harsh critic of the WJC, and has defended Waldheim. Nevertheless, Bronfman's evidence led the OSI's Neal Sher to place

Waldheim on a watch list of those prohibited from entering the United States.

9. ADL Penetration of Law Enforcement

Despite the fact that the ADL has been repeatedly linked to organized crime, foreign espionage agencies, and domestic and international terrorist groups, the League has managed to conduct a highly successful campaign to insinuate itself into the day-to-day workings of virtually every major police department and sheriff's department in the United States. In doing so, it has drawn heavily upon its longstanding "special relationship" with the FBI—which has blossomed under recent directors William Webster and William Sessions—and upon its deep involvement with the Justice Department's Office of Special Investigations.

In the spring of 1989, Justin Finger, the ADL's associate national director, led a delegation of American law enforcement officials to Israel on an all-expenses-paid tour that included meetings with the Israeli National Police, the Shin Beth, the Mossad, and special anti-terrorist units. Among the police executives along on the trip were: Charles Barry, the Massachusetts Secretary of Public Safety; Cornelius Behan, the police chief of Baltimore; Lester Forst, the Connecticut Commissioner of Public Safety; Michael Hennessey, Sheriff of San Francisco County; Robert Hightower, Police Chief of Cobb County, Georgia; Leroy Martin, Superintendent of the Chicago Police Department; Charles Plummer, Sheriff of Alameda County, California; Peter Ronstadt, Police Chief of Tucson, Arizona; Jerry Williams, Police Chief of Aurora, Colorado; and Aristides Zavaras, Police Chief of Denver, Colorado.

The trip was the third in a series of ADL-sponsored visits to Israel by major urban police since 1987, and is part of the League's escalated penetration of the American law enforcement and judicial community. Since 1988, the ADL has been publishing a *Law Enforcement Bulletin,* which is distributed free of charge to police departments, private security firms, and federal government agencies.

The *Bulletin* provides a crazy quilt of accurate and severely distorted information, principally targeted at the Palestinian movement, pro-Palestinian elements within the left, all varieties of right-wing groups, and Lyndon LaRouche.

In 1986, *EIR* learned from police officials in Atlanta, Georgia that Charles Wittenstein, the regional director of the ADL, had approached police officials there with an offer to finance and manage their entire informant program. Similar approaches apparently have been made elsewhere around the country.

A review of the past decade's issues of the ADL's monthly newsletter reveals that in the 31 regional offices in the United States, staff directors devote the majority of their time to liaison with police and prosecutors, often providing information generated from the ADL's own agents provocateurs inside the radical left and right. For example:

■ In February 1984, Stan Anderman, ADL regional director in St. Louis, and Michael Lieberman, ADL Midwest regional director, addressed a Missouri Law Enforcement conference at Ozark Lake. Other speakers included Jim Winter, the director of the FBI's Counter-Terror Program; Jim Elder, head of the St. Louis office of the Bureau of Alcohol, Tobacco and Firearms (BATF); Tom Kelly, head of the Kansas Bureau of Investigations; Howard Hoffman, head of the Missouri Highway Patrol; and Mark Middleman, a former Missouri assistant attorney general who was hired as a staff consultant to the ADL.

■ On Feb. 13, 1986, two ADL officials, Michael Kozin and Midwest regional director Michael Lieberman, addressed a Chicago conference on Law Enforcement's Response to Extremism in the farmbelt. Among the other participants in the conference were Illinois U.S. Commission on Civil Rights director Rhona Stewart; Chicago FBI office chief Joseph Lewis; Chicago BATF office chief James Seaves; Illinois State Police Director James Zagel; and Chicago U.S. Attorney James Reidy.

■ In February 1987, the ADL sponsored an all-day conference on terrorism at the FBI headquarters in Indianapolis, attended by 140 police officials. The conference was ostensibly in preparation for the Pan-American Games, and the keynote speaker was Robert Kupperman of the Center for Strategic and International Studies at Georgetown University in Washington, who is a frequent participant in ADL sponsored terrorism events.

■ In other, similar conferences with local police, the ADL has inserted "experts" with longstanding known ties to the Mossad. Among them: Prof. Uri Ra'anan, the recruiter of convicted spy Jonathan Pollard, and Prof. Yonah Alexander.

10. The ADL, Israel, and the Temple Mount Plot

Since the founding of the state of Israel, the ADL has kept its own "special relationship" with the Israeli Mossad intelligence service, especially with corrupt intelligence circles linked to what author Jacques Derogy dubbed "the Israeli Mafia."

Meshulam Riklis, the protégé of ADL National Chairman Burton Joseph who was implicated in the Bialkin-Vesco looting of IOS, has been the financial "angel" of Israel's former Defense Minister Ariel Sharon for years. Riklis purchased a large ranch in the Negev Desert and gave it to Sharon, the leader of Likud's extreme militant wing, as a gift. It was at that ranch, that a series of secret meetings took place in May and November 1982 to plot out an ambitious real estate scam, aimed at consolidating permanent Israeli control over the Occupied Territories of the West Bank, the Gaza Strip, and East Jerusalem, and laying the basis for the recent years' flood of Russian Jewish immigrants.

According to eyewitness accounts, the Sharon ranch meetings brought together representatives of the Bronfmans, Britain's Lord Harlech and Lord Carrington, Henry A. Kissinger, and the ADL's Kenneth Bialkin.

Operating through an extensive network of American-based Christian fundamentalist groups, the ADL-Sharon group arranged for the illegal purchase of dozens of buildings and tracts

of land in the contested territories, and planned for their ulti-
mate settlement by militant Jewish activists. A network of
fanatical Jewish fundamentalists based in a series of yeshivas
(Jewish parochial schools) inside Jerusalem, including Ateret
Cohanim, began illegal excavations on Islamic holy sites in the
Old City, proclaiming that they would rebuild the Third Temple
on its original site—even if it meant blowing up the Dome of
the Rock on the Temple Mount, the second-most holy place of
Islam. These Jewish fanatics, many of them linked to the Meir
Kahane Jewish Defense League and Kach Movement and heavily funded by JDL and ADL financial backers in the United
States, have carried out machine-gun and hand-grenade attacks on the Dome of the Rock on dozens of occasions in recent
years. In almost every instance, Ariel Sharon defended the
actions, and even led protest rallies when Israeli police removed
militants by force.

The most dramatic confrontation occurred during the Easter
celebrations this year, when a group of 150 Ateret Cohanim
fanatics illegally obtained a sub-lease on the St. John's Hospice
in the Christian Quarter of Old Jerusalem and attempted to
occupy the building. When the Greek Orthodox Patriarch of
Jerusalem led a peaceful protest against the action, Israeli
police gassed him and other demonstrators.

On April 17, the caretaker Likud government of Yitzhak
Shamir issued a statement admitting that the Housing Ministry, headed by Morton Rosenthal and Jon Speller collaborator
David Levi, had secretly funded the Ateret Cohanim takeover
of the hospice. These incidents caused Pope John Paul II to tell
Easter pilgrims in Rome that the "grave incidents" in Jerusalem "are a cause also for me of suffering and profound concern."

Spying for Foreign Intelligence Services

The ADL's involvement in the dirty underbelly of Israeli
politics did not begin with the Sharon plot. According to court
records and other sources, the ADL has been used for decades
as a cover of convenience for Israeli Mossad operations inside
the United States. More often than not, those operations were
in direct conflict with U.S. national security interests.

In 1967, former B'nai B'rith official Saul I. Joftas filed a slander suit charging that he had been fired for his refusal to cooperate with secret Israeli intelligence spy operations being run through the B'nai B'rith and the ADL. Depositions taken in this suit show that in 1960, ADL honorary vice chairman Phillip Klutznick, then president of B'nai B'rith, established a B'nai B'rith cover for an Israeli intelligence operation in New York, that sought to penetrate U.S. intelligence by dangling bits of information about the U.S.S.R. The Mossad case officer for this operation was Uri Ra'anan, then the director of the Israeli consulate's information department in New York, who later helped recruit Israeli "false flag" agent Jonathan Pollard. Another member of this cell was ADL general counsel Arnold Forster, who was then the ADL's associate national director.

Another operation run by this group was uncovered during the court proceedings in a letter to Joftas dated July 7, 1961 by then-ADL national director Benjamin Epstein. The letter read in part: "As you know, the Anti-Defamation League for many years has maintained a very important, confidential investigative coverage of Arab activities and propaganda. . . . We have maintained an information-gathering operation since 1948 relating to activities from the Arab Consular Offices, Arab United Nations Delegations, Arab Information Center, Arab Refugee Office, and the Organization of Arab Students." The rest of the letter elaborated upon this espionage activity, then requested additional funds for it.

Behind the Pollard Spy Case

This 1960s collusion between ADL and the Mossad in running spy operations inside the U.S. apparently continued unabated until the November 1985 arrest of Jonathan J. Pollard. A Naval Investigative Service (NIS) counterterrorism analyst, Pollard was part of a spy network set up by "Dirty Rafi" Eytan, a Mossad official and intimate of Ariel Sharon who at one time headed an elite killer squad out of the prime minister's office.

Pollard was initially profiled for Mossad recruitment by Dr. Uri Ra'anan, the former Israeli Consulate official and longtime ADL collaborator who had taken up a special teaching post at

the Center for International Security Studies at the Fletcher
School of Diplomacy at Tufts University in Boston. Once recruited, Pollard was "handled" by Col. Aviem Sella, an Israeli
Air Force officer operating under the cover of attending graduate school at New York University. Sella's wife Ruth was employed during the entire time of the Pollard-Sella operation in
the Legal Department of the ADL headquarters in New York.
In protest over the sentencing of Pollard to life in prison for his
espionage activities, the Israeli government promoted Sella to
the rank of general. In response, an ADL delegation rushed
off to Israel to prevent a full diplomatic rift that might have
prompted a deeper investigation into the Pollard network leading ultimately to the ADL headquarters.

Secretary of Defense Caspar Weinberger had asked the court
to impose the maximum sentence on Pollard once U.S. intelligence "damage assessments" had revealed that much of the top-
secret information stolen by Pollard had found its way into the
hands of the KGB and GRU. Weinberger reportedly concluded
that the entire Eytan network had been working both for the
Mossad and for the Russians. Weinberger ordered a more extensive probe to determine the identity of an "X Committee" believed to have been working with Pollard. Some U.S. intelligence specialists believe that a full probe of the "X Committee"
would reveal a significant interface with the National Commission of the ADL.

While Weinberger was pressing the Pollard affair, a separate
scandal began to emerge involving another top ADL associate,
Deputy Attorney General Arnold Burns, a director of the ADL's
Sterling National Bank. His law firm Burns and Summit was
caught running a string of phony offshore tax shelters that
claimed big tax write-offs for nonexistent investments in Israeli
research and development firms. One of the attorneys linked to
the scam was Howard Katz, the paymaster for the Pollard spy
ring.

Yet another still active ADL link to the Pollard spy ring
centers around Mira Lansky Boland, the head of the ADL Fact-
Finding Division office in Washington. Lansky Boland had been
a classmate of Jonathan Pollard at the Fletcher School, and was

part of the same tightly knit group of students under Professor Ra'anan. At approximately the same time when Ra'anan was helping to place Pollard in the sensitive position with NIS, he apparently also helped to secure Lansky her job with the ADL. Lansky Boland has played a pivotal role in the federal-state "Get LaRouche" task force, serving as a principal conduit of information between different state and federal agencies, soliciting press slanders, and even producing "witnesses" for the government's cases.

11. The ADL Subverts the Farm Movement

With the heavy infusion of cash into the ADL from Minneapolis grain merchant Dwayne Andreas, the president of Archer Daniels Midland, Inc., beginning in 1978, the ADL's offices in Minneapolis, Chicago, St. Louis, Atlanta, and Omaha began to function as adjuncts to the major Midwest grain cartels, which were at that time expanding their intelligence-gathering and dirty-tricks capabilities against the mounting threat of farmer protests against foreclosures and impossible operating costs.

ADL links to the grain merchants had blossomed earlier, particularly under the chairmanship of Burton Joseph between 1976–78. Joseph was himself in the agricultural products business, running a Minneapolis firm called I.S. Joseph. Joseph and one of his ADL Vice chairmen, Max Kampelman, were known as the "Minneapolis Mafia" within ADL inner circles because of their close links to the Minnesota Farm Labor Party and the Hubert Humphrey-Walter Mondale political machine.

ADL had also benefited for years from the financial largess of the Moore family of the Nabisco Corp.—another giant in the grain industry.

Rather than using physical force to disrupt the emerging farmer populist movement, the ADL resorted to its usual bag of tricks: proclaiming the farm protest movement a hotbed of anti-Semitism and right-wing militance, the ADL churned out propaganda, spread wildly distorted "intelligence" to federal, state, and local police agencies, and worked with a network of left-wing radicals to set up farm protest "countergangs" to steer the ferment into populist and impotent directions.

On Jan. 10, 1986, the ADL's Minneapolis regional director Morton Wrywick was a keynote speaker at the founding conference of the Family Farm Resource Organizing Committee (FFROC), a coalition of left-wing farmbelt groups including the Socialist Workers Party, Groundswell, Prairie Fire, the Center for Rural Affairs, Catholic Rural Life, and the Center for Democratic Renewal. Joe Krastil was the nominal head of the group, which disseminated a just-released ADL report titled "The Farmer and The Extremist" as part of its "counseling service" to recently bankrupted farmers. According to interviews given at the time, Krastil had been trained by Ken Lawrence, a Mississippi-based left-wing activist tied to the London *Searchlight* group, a known KGB front organization. Lawrence is also a regular writer for the CIA defector Philip Agee's journal *Covert Action Information Bulletin* and the National Lawyers Guild's *The Public Eye,* which is edited by John Foster "Chip" Berlet, one of the most prominent slanderers of Lyndon LaRouche.

Another founder of the FFROC front, Lenny Zeskind, runs the Center for Democratic Renewal, formerly the Anti-Klan Committee, with Lynn Wells, a former Communist Party youth leader who later helped found the Maoist October League. Dan Levitas, a founder of Prairie Fire, another farmbelt leftist insurgency group sponsored by the ADL, recently moved to Atlanta to join Zeskind and Wells at the CDR.

Through ADL officials Morton Wrywick (Minneapolis), Michael Lieberman (Chicago), Stan Anderman (St. Louis), Justin Finger and Yitzak Santus (Omaha), Marvin Stern (Seattle), Sol Rosenthal (Denver), Mark Briskman (Dallas) and Charles Wittenstein (Atlanta), the collection of left-wing farm radicals were presented as legitimate "informants" to regional law enforcement task forces, set up at ADL urging, to deal with the threat of "extremism" in the Midwest.

In interviews conducted in early 1986, Donald Burger, the head of the U.S. Justice Department's Community Relations

Service regional office in Kansas City, Missouri, and David Tell, head of the Program and Policy Division of the U.S. Commission on Civil Rights in Washington, D.C., both confirmed that the federal government's efforts in the farmbelt were fully integrated with the ADL and ADL-linked operatives like Levitas and Zeskind. Similarly, Mark Tirchie in the office of Minnesota Gov. Rudy Perpich, and Ann Kesten in the office of Minnesota Attorney General "Skip" Humphrey, confirmed their dependence on the ADL to provide information and direction to their efforts to "combat extremism" in the farm community.

12. ADL Targets Pro-life Movement and the Vatican

In recent years, the ADL has played a major behind-the-scenes role in opposing the pro-life movement, both through the filing of a series of *amicus curiae* briefs in all the major abortion cases now up before the U.S. Supreme Court, and through the deployment of its spy and agent provocateur networks to vilify the Right to Life movement as a haven for neo-Nazis, anti-Semites and right-wing terrorists.

On May 1, 1991, members of the Civil Rights Division of the ADL confirmed in interviews with *EIR* that the ADL had intensified its campaign to destroy the pro-life movement. An ADL team of lawyers and analysts are reviewing videos and news coverage of the huge pro-life march held in Washington, D.C. on April 31, in order to identify "extremists" and "anti-Semites" who participated. Another ADL source revealed that the ADL has compiled dossiers on anti-abortion activists, with particular attention to monitoring members of Operation Rescue. The dossiers reportedly are being made available to law enforcement authorities who are trying to fraudulently apply the so-called RICO, anti-racketeering statutes to the prosecution of Operation Rescue.

The ADL has filed a series of *amicus curiae* briefs taking a radical pro-abortion stand. Honorary ADL chairman Kenneth

Bialkin filed the brief with the U.S. Supreme Court in the cases No. 88–790, No. 88–805, and Nos. 88–1125 and 88–1309. Bialkin filed his brief as the Counsel of Record for the Anti-Defamation League of B'nai B'rith, B'nai B'rith Women, Catholics for a Free Choice, and Women's American ORT. Listed as "Of Counsel" were such ADL bigwigs as Honorary Vice Chairman Meyer Eisenberg, ADL Associate National Director Justin J. Finger, and Civil Rights Division director Jeffrey P. Sinensky.

The ADL *amicus* brief argues that the anti-abortion statutes of "Illinois, Minnesota, and Ohio . . . violate the establishment clause by endorsing one religious theory of when life begins" and that they impose "an impermissible burden on a woman's free exercise of religion by restricting her fundamental religious interest in deciding whether to continue a pregnancy." The argumentation is in keeping with their dozens of *amicus curiae* briefs to remove prayer from school, in that it advocates a "value-free" school and society in which scientifically grounded moral principles have no force.

Still more to the point, Laura Kam-Issacharoff, a member of the ADL's Israel office, wrote an article for the March 6, 1990 *Jerusalem Post* entitled "Anti-Semitism in the Anti-Abortion Movement." Its opening paragraph reads: "Increasing anti-Semitic manifestations in the volatile debate on abortions are worrying Jewish leaders in the U.S. In several states, the FBI has begun probing the burgeoning hate mail that has been directed at 'pro-choice' Jewish political leaders and doctors." The remainder of the piece contains one exaggerated claim after another that somehow pro-life activists believe Jewish doctors are killing Christian babies out of revenge for the Holocaust.

Going After the Pope

One day after Pope John Paul II expressed "concern" about incidents at St. John's Hospice in Jerusalem (see above), ADL national director Abraham Foxman made the following statement, as reported in the May 3 *Washington Jewish Week:* "I am concerned and disturbed at the way the Christian community has responded by escalating this into an international religious confrontation. . . . To hear this orgy of criticism [i.e., from the Pope] has sinister undertones. It may even border on elements of Crusadism."

Foxman's remarks are only the latest of a series of dramatic confrontations between the ADL and the Vatican. The last confrontation in the fall of 1989 followed a provocation by friends of ADL-controlled terrorist Mordechai Levy in the Coalition of Concern, who attempted to shut down a Carmelite convent located just outside the grounds of the former Auschwitz concentration camp in Poland.

Glenn Richter, a friend of Levy, issued a press release after he had accompanied Rabbi Avraham Weiss, also a friend of Levy, in what became a confrontation with workmen at the convent, describing how his group had surrounded it, demanding that it be removed, and complaining "that the 24-foot cross desecrated the memory of the Jewish martyrs of Auschwitz." Rabbi Avraham Weiss issued a press statement saying that Cardinal Franciszek Macharski of Krakow, Poland was "repugnant" for blaming the Coalition of Concern for "lack of respect for the nuns and for their human and Christian dignity" and for failure to respect "the symbols of faith and piety" through "attempts at taking [the convent] over." Rabbi Weiss called "upon Jewish leaders to freeze dialogue with the Vatican" until it removed the convent. In an article in the *New York Post* he claimed that Pope John Paul II and the Vatican had done nothing to protect Jews from the Nazis.

On Aug. 15, 1989, Elan Steinberg, an aide to Edgar Bronfman, denounced the Pope for anti-Semitism arising out of the Pope's attempts to "de-Judaize the Holocaust." Steinberg said that it was "obscene" that the Pope had met with Austrian President Kurt Waldheim. Steinberg told a journalist that the chief theological problem was the Pope's "triumphalist vision," which he said was a step back from the "progressivism of Vatican II." The Pope, Steinberg warned, is mounting a "conservative international" which is regressive on issues ranging from abortion, to sexuality, to the interreligious dialogue between Catholics and Jews, to failure to support Liberation Theology in Central America, to pushing Solidarnosc in Poland on a dangerous course that might undermine Edgar Bronfman's friend, Soviet President Mikhail Gorbachov.

13. The ADL Defends Satan

Last year, when a group of Texas state legislators introduced a bill criminalizing certain Satanic ritualistic practices, the Dallas office of the ADL cried "anti-Semitism!" and attempted to mobilize the Jewish community to block its passage. The ADL effort fell on deaf ears, since most rabbis and other Jewish community leaders had been duly horrified by the recent discovery in Matamoros, Mexico of a ritualistic mass burial site on a ranch used by a notorious drug-smuggling ring. Texas Gov. William Clements summoned both houses of the state legislature into special session to unanimously pass the bill, the first of several such anti-Satanism bills to become state law around the country.

The ADL's "religious freedom" antics in Texas reflected longstanding ADL complicity in the spread of Satanism and the drug-rock-sex counterculture. The first documented instance of ADL involvement dates back to the early 1960s, when Rabbi Maurice Davis, later of Westchester County, New York, participated in Project MK-Ultra, the CIA's foray into the use of LSD–25 and other psychedelic drugs in mind control and mass social manipulation. Davis was the chaplain at the Lexington, Kentucky Addiction Research Center, a hotbed of the CIA's secret LSD testing. According to Davis's co-workers at the time, the rabbi helped track some of the LSD human guinea pigs when they were released to outpatient treatment. The full extent of Davis's involvement in the CIA project may never be known, because the CIA's chief chemist, Dr. Sidney Gottlieb, shredded millions of pages of MK-Ultra records in 1972 at the behest of outgoing CIA director Richard Helms.

It can be assumed, however, that Davis's services were appreciated, because following his transfer to Indianapolis in the mid-1960s, he became one of the first patrons of the Rev. Jim Jones and his People's Temple—what several authors have described as another Anglo-American Occult Bureau "project." Davis was joined in that effort by Episcopal priest and later Bishop Paul Moore, offspring of the same patrician Moore family that has heavily funded the ADL over the past several decades. Moore later moved to New York City where he has presided over the Cathedral of St. John the Divine, a notorious center of New Age and outright Satanic cultism, as well as terrorism. (For years the New York City Police Department's Arson and Explosives Unit identified the cathedral as a safehouse for the FALN, a Puerto Rican terrorist group that carried out dozens of bomb attacks in the Metropolitan area during the 1970s.)

(In 1978, as the ADL launched its Big Lie campaign branding Lyndon LaRouche as an "anti-Semite," Canon West, a top aide to Bishop Moore at the Episcopal Archdiocese, confided to a visitor that they had "gotten the Jews" to take care of LaRouche, an indication that the relationship between the ADL and the blueblood WASP establishment ran much deeper than the Moore-Davis tie.)

In Indianapolis, Davis and Moore sponsored Jim Jones onto a number of community boards. Davis personally arranged the sale of his own synagogue to Jones and arranged the mortgage for what would be the first People's Temple.

When Davis moved to the New York area shortly after Jones relocated his followers to San Francisco, the rabbi, by now an active figure in ADL circles, became one of the first religious figures to warn about the dangerous proliferation of coercive cults. But far from being a Damascus Road conversion, Davis's new profile as an anti-cult crusader merely represented a continuation of his involvement in the Occult Bureau efforts. Along with other MK-Ultra veterans such as Dr. Louis Jolyon West and Robert J. Lifton, Davis launched the "deprogramming" movement in the early 1970s as the "solution" to the mushrooming problem of coercive cults which Davis himself had helped to foster. Over the next decade, hundreds of members of pseudo-religion and therapy cults like the Unification Church, the Church of Scientology, The Way International, EST, and the Hare Krishnas were kidnaped and subjected to grueling round-the-clock ego stripping, physical abuse, and other forms of behavior modification—often no different than the treatment they received when they were inside the cults. In nearly every instance, the parents of the cult members paid through the teeth for the kidnaping services provided by Davis and his collaborators.

In 1974, Davis founded Citizens Engaged in Reuniting Families (CERF), a deprogrammers' front which later merged into the two major anti-cult agencies, the American Family Foundation and the Cult Awareness Network. Capitalizing on the post-Jonestown reaction, the ADL established a full-time anti-cult center, housed at the Washington, D.C. headquarters of the B'nai B'rith and run by Esther Dietz and Asya Komm. The Cult Center of B'nai B'rith maintained joint offices with the Cult Awareness Network. In this way, the ADL established formal, ongoing links to the AFF/CAN, which continue through to the present.

The 'Son of Sam,' and Dennis King

Among Davis' employees in CERF were Dennis King and Kalev Pehme, both of whom later played prominent roles in the post-1978 "Get LaRouche" drive, and worked for a mob-run weekly on the East Side of Manhattan, *Our Town*. In 1978, Pehme wrote for *Our Town* a glowing piece on the Foundation Faith of the Millennium, formerly the Process Church of the Final Judgment. This outright Satanic outfit had been so closely linked to the Manson Family murders on the West Coast in 1969 that they were forced to relocate their operations back East and change their name. According to *The Ultimate Evil* by Maury Terry, which is an account of the 1976–77 "Son of Sam" murders in New York, the Process Church, now based out of Westchester County, was suspected of links to those ritualistic killings as well.

Another person who turned up with the *Our Town* rag controlled by mobster Ed Kayatt, was Dennis King, a protégé of Maurice Davis and author of hate literature against Lyndon

LaRouche. King published one of his nastiest slanders against LaRouche in the pages of *High Times* magazine, the voice of the dope legalization lobby and drug paraphernalia industry. King's most intimate collaborator in the LaRouche-bashing effort, which mushroomed into a full-scale government frameup strike force, was John Foster "Chip" Berlet, for years the Washington, D.C. bureau chief of *High Times* and an activist in NORML, the official dope legalization lobby.

By 1979, King was a full-time asset of the ADL's Fact-Finding Division and an anti-LaRouche informant to a variety of federal and state agencies and prosecutors. Throughout that period, King was a member of the Humanist Society of New York, a secular humanist club linked to the Society for Psychical Research, SIECUS (the radical sex education movement), and other New Age kook outfits.

The ADL links to explicitly pro-Satanist circles was no low-level effort. ADL mogul Edgar Bronfman has been associated with this project since no later than April 17, 1989, when he and Britain's Prince Philip launched the Sacred Literature Trust, an effort aimed at publicizing the religious foundations of ecology and environmentalism—i.e., the revival of Mother Earth and other forms of paganism. At a United Nations press conference in New York City on that date, Bronfman aide Rabbi Arthur Hertzberg and Prince Philip's spokesman Martin Palmer announced the project. Palmer's numerous writings on various aspects of pagan and gnostic theology are published by the Lucis Trust—formerly the Lucifer Trust—an elite group which grew out of the 19th-century Theosophy movement. As for Rabbi Hertzberg, he first gained attention at a conference in Assisi, Italy in 1986, where he advocated the revival of the gnostic Jewish Cabala. The proposal for the Sacred Literary Trust was first floated at that Assisi conference.

Appendix D

The Drug-Runners in Beijing

The cover-up of the role of the People's Republic of China in producing and trafficking drugs to the West is one of the biggest lies perpetrated by a U.S. government, in this case by successive American presidential administrations, over the last two decades. The success of this coverup far exceeds even that of the Warren Commission report on the assassination of John Kennedy. Whereas over 80% of the American population believes the Warren report is a fabrication, the issue of the P.R.C.'s poisoning of American veins and minds with drugs appears to have been buried forever. As of the early 1980s, the Drug Enforcement Administration had no files on the P.R.C. at all!

Not only did the P.R.C. never stop growing and trafficking in opium—and there is no evidence to suggest that Beijing did stop—but in the 1980s, the resurgence of the Golden Triangle drug flow to the West, surpassing the heyday of the Vietnam War, shows that Beijing is on a new drug offensive.

Corroborated reports indicate that today the P.R.C. is the world's largest opium producer. According to Hong Kong reports, the P.R.C. is producing 800 metric tons of opium per year. This is the same as the record-high 800 tons produced annually *in the entire region* during the height of the Vietnam War, when Chinese drug-trafficking was an open matter of Chinese war strategy. Before 1972, it was well known that the P.R.C. produced 65% of the world's opium. The Hong Kong-based *Liberation Monthly* reported in December 1989 that the P.R.C. provides 80% of the high-quality heroin selling on the international market.

The censorship on Chinese drug-trafficking, however, is so complete that details of the P.R.C. dope trade rarely see the light of day. A *San Jose Mercury* article, published May 16, 1975, explained why: "A secret federal report, the *Mercury* has learned, pinpoints the People's Republic of China as the producer of quantities of heroin that have been detected in the Bay area. The report, completed six months ago, supposedly is being kept under wraps by the federal government for fear its release could affect detente between the U.S. and China."

Contrary to the P.R.C.'s own propaganda, drug-trafficking is not the business of independent criminals, but a prime earner of foreign exchange and directed by a state monopoly controlled by some of the top dogs of the communist hierarchy. P.R.C. leaders' occasional reports that the mainland is becoming a "transhipment point" for Golden Triangle drugs are to be laughed at as crude coverup attempts. For example, in October 1989, Liu Wen, director of criminal investigations in the Ministry of Public Security, acknowledged to an Interpol conference that farmers "have been found" growing opium poppies in the southeast border areas. Lui blamed an increasing mainland addiction problem on the P.R.C.'s increasing contact with foreigners. In July 1988, the *Beijing Review* reported that "A few people in the southwest border areas (Golden Triangle country) have adopted the habit of smoking opium." All 43 traffickers arrested in the P.R.C. since 1986, the *Review* claimed, were of foreign nationality.

How Beijing's Dope Trade Works

The China dope is smuggled out into the world labeled either as "Burmese," "Pakistani," or "Afghan." As the Dec. 19, 1985, French journal *Vendredi, Samedi, Dimanche* noted in an article, the P.R.C. drug trade "does not work in a clandestine way. One of the centers of this Chinese connection is the extreme-western part of China near Pakistan, Afghanistan, and the Soviet Union. The reporter arrived in a city called Kashi where the ethnic minority called the Uygurs are controlling the drug traffic toward Pakistan." The city is reportedly filled with Pakistanis.

It is on the public record, but certainly not in the public conscience, that the P.R.C. is the world's major supplier of the illegal drug Quaalude. This came to light in a June 30, 1982 article in the *Washington Post,* which reported that China legally exports the drug to brokers in West Germany. Ten percent of that shipped is used for legitimate medicinal purposes. The remainder—that is, the bulk the P.R.C. produces—is dispatched through West Germany to drug-trafficking networks in Mexico, Colombia, and Canada, for re-shipment to the United States. The *Post* article quotes Senator Paula Hawkins as saying that the P.R.C. "now produces about 100% of the metaqualone (generic name for Quaalude) illegally used in the U.S." That trade is estimated to reap $2 billion annually.

Other sources of illegal Quaalude—West Germany, Austria, and Hungary—cut down their Quaalude trade, since the supply many times exceeded the medicinal demand. The P.R.C. regime, however, has refused to cooperate with efforts to dry up the supply. In an admission of Beijing's determination to use any means to acquire foreign exchange while subverting the West, a Chinese foreign ministry spokesman told reporters in

June 1982 when the scandal briefly flared that: "China's sale of a certain amount of methaqualone as medicine through normal trade channels fully conforms to internatoinal practice." In 1982, Quaalude was listed by U.S. drug officials as the major cause of deaths, injuries, and mental trauma in 13 major U.S. cities, especially among teenagers. In 1984, P.R.C. Quaalude production again came to light with the report of the U.S. House Select Committee on Narcotics Abuse and Control, which stated: "Methaqualone . . . has mostly been smuggled from Colombia, where it is formulated into tablets from methaqualone powder originating in the People's Republic of China and Hungary and surreptitiously shipped to Colombia from the Free Port of Hamburg."

The Quaalude case conclusively proves that P.R.C. interest in drug-trafficking did not end with the end of the Vietnam War, the end of the Cultural Revolution, or the death of madman Mao Zedong, but continues to be the policy of China's "reformist" leadership under Kissinger crony Deng Xiaoping.

The Kissinger Coverup

The lid was clamped down on the Chinese communists' role in global drug-trafficking by Henry Kissinger. Although it was widely known and of course admitted by Beijing's leaders that the P.R.C. had produced and trafficked dope to American G.I.s in Vietnam, by the end of the Nixon administration, Kissinger had squelched all mention of the P.R.C. as a drug source, in the interests of his new "China card" policy for a Washington-Beijing rapprochement. Kissinger's effort involved not only protection of the P.R.C. but the subversion of Nixon's entire 1971 War on Drugs.

Nixon's war effort had been skewed from the very beginning. Despite massive evidence that the major source of heroin flowing into the United States came from the Golden Triangle comprised by northern Burma, Thailand, Laos, and the Yunnan Province of the P.R.C., Nixon's major political focus was the termination of poppy cultivation in Turkey. Soon agreement had been reached with Turkey for crop substitution and other measures to eradicate the poppy crop. The next step was to prepare a "world poppy map" of total opium production. This intelligence was compiled by the Nixon-created Cabinet Comitee for International Narcotics Control (CCINC), under the direction of Nelson Gross and Egil Krogh. Gross, with special cooperation from Defense Secretary Melvin Laird, began flying F–4 and SR–71 reconnaissance missions over the Golden Triangle, including sections of the P.R.C. Learning of these operations, Henry Kissinger, from his position as national security advisor, sent out orders to end the reconnaissance flights, on the grounds that they threatened the U.S.-P.R.C. "detente" Kissinger was trying to effect.

Kissinger stepped in again when Gross ordered U.S. ambassadors in opium-producing countries to draw up an action program against the drug. Gross also proposed that the United States threaten use of its veto and cutoff power in the International Monetary Fund and World Bank, to threaten loan freezes against any country refusing to cooperate.

Kissinger answered these recommendations in a policy paper countering Gross point by point. In defense of Dope, Inc., Kissinger argued that Gross's policy would 1) exasperate relations between the U.S.A. and other countries; 2) create internal repercussions for allied governments; 3) be counterproductive to other U.S. security and foreign-policy interests; 4) could not be applied to all nations; could not be applied easily by financial institutions; and set up situations in which targeted countries could easily call Washington's bluff.

At several points, Kissinger specifically intervened to protect the P.R.C. against charges that the Communists were the major source of heroin flooding U.S. installations in Vietnam, and U.S. cities. In February 1972, to "dispel" widely circulated rumors of P.R.C. drug-trafficking, the "White House" (that is, Kissinger) sent a memo on plain white stationary to select Republican members of the House of Representatives asserting that "the Government of the People's Republic of China had for years officially forbidden the private production, consumption, and distribution of opium and its derivatives. There is no reliable evidence that the P.R.C. has either engaged in or sanctioned the illicit export of opium or its derivatives to the free world nor are there any indications of P.R.C. control over the opium trade of Southest Asia and adjacent markets"—notwithstanding Zhou Enlai's confessions!

Since, of course, the P.R.C.'s opium production is under state monopoly, the carefully selected phrases "private production" and "illicit export" tended to arouse more suspicion than they disspelled.

Several months later, Kissinger took further measures with a "White House" memo ostensibly released from Drug Information Director Richard Harkness, and sent to the State, Treasury, and Defense Departments. The memo urged cabinet agencies to combat claims that the P.R.C. trafficked drugs. The memo was leaked to Jack Anderson, who wrote a May 26, 1972 column, bluntly titled, "Protecting Beijing." "A White House memo," Anderson said, "contains evidence that Richard Nixon, once the implacable foe of communist China, is now defending China" against charges that it is involved in drug-running.

Later, Rep. John Ashbrook revealed that Nixon was prepared to raise the question of Beijing's drug-trafficking when he visited Beijing, but this was vetoed by Kissinger because "it would have been too expensive in the initial meetings."

In short, the United States entered into its geopolitical alliance with the P.R.C. with the full knowledge that Beijing-produced and -trafficked drugs were being funneled into the veins of American youth, with the profits going to Beijing. (The possibilities of the profits reaped by Kissinger and his associates from the P.R.C. drug spigot will be seen below.) But, just as with the Bush administration's diplomatic embrace of the butchers of Tiananmen Square, the geopolitical relationship with Beijing was considered far more important.

The Hoax of the Golden Triangle

As Drug Enforcement Administration sources indicated, the chief Big Lie Kissinger executed on behalf of Beijing's drug lords was to order the DEA to redraw the map of the Golden

Triangle. Whereas the original map contained the P.R.C.'s Yu-
annan province—in fact the southwest section of the province
comprised the largest component of the Triangle—Kissinger
ordered that the Triangle be inverted so that the apex reached
only as far as the Yuannan-Burma border and the bottom of
the Triangle cut a far wider swath across Burma, Thailand,
and Laos. Although the original mapping of the Triangle had
been based on detailed intelligence reports, at least through the
early 1960s by Henry J. Anslinger, head of the U.S. Narcotics
Control Board, the Chinese role was quashed completely, without a shred of evidence to indicate any decrease in P.R.C. drug-
related activity.

After the end of the Vietnam War, and even more so with the
1979 Soviet invasion of Afghanistan and the overthrow of the
Shah of Iran, the Golden Triangle as a whole largely slipped
from the U.S. drug radar.

On Feb. 12, 1988, however, the DEA was forced to re-evalu-
ate, when Thai law enforcement authorities seized 1,280 kilograms of heroin in a ship in the port of Bangkok, in one of the
biggest drug busts in history. The heroin seized had a street
value of $2.1 billion. All of it was bound for New York City. The
amount seized—1.4 tons—also exceeded the DEA's estimate of
only 1.2 tons of heroin coming into the United States from the
Golden Triangle in a single year! Given that any amounts
seized represent only a small fraction of the actual flow, the
DEA estimate of the Golden Triangle flow into the United
States was off by anywhere from 50 to 90%.

The bulk of the heroin distributed in the United States is
derived from opium produced in the P.R.C., and much of that
in Yunnan province. The opium is dubbed "Burmese" because
it is brought to the outside world through Burma, thanks to the
services of the Chinese-backed Burmese Communist Party, the
Chinese-backed Kachin Independence Army and the Shan
United Army (SUA), led by the notorious drug lord Khun Sa, a
"Shah" of Yunnan-province descent who, it is believed, controls
80% of the Golden Triangle drug flow, and who directs opium
refineries scattered throughout northern Burma, Thailand, and
the Soviet client state Laos. Khun Sa's ties to Yunnan are

close. In October 1989, his top aide, Sakchai Suwannapong, also known as Ma Kuang-ting, was arrested in Hong Kong. A warrant for his arrest was issued Sept. 20, 1989, by the U.S. District Court of New York. Sakchai had been charged by Khun Sa with moving large amounts of opium and heroin through Thailand, allegedly because of his high-level Thai contacts. But Sakchai also has official ties to the P.R.C.; he is the president of the Chinese Yunnanese Association in Thailand.

Since the early 1980s successful crackdown by the Thailand government against opium growing, Thailand has become primarily a transshipment point for "Burmese" drugs. Khun Sa claims that the opium is grown in scattered one-hectare plots in Burma along the Yunnan border by hills tribesmen. However, the bulk of opium now moving out of the Triangle would be difficult to produce in Burma alone under such conditions. According to John McBeth of the *Far Eastern Economic Review*, in 1979 the normal Burma crop yield was 400–500 tons, producing 40–50 tons of heroin. But in 1979, the crop went down to 200 tons, with half of that, McBeth reported, staying in Burma. This low yield was the result of "tougher enforcement measures, both in northern Thailand and along the Burmese side of the border, [which] have combined . . . to put the squeeze on traffickers and addicts alike."

Since then, however, despite continued pressure in Burma, the "Burmese" yield has steadily risen. In 1981, the crop was 600 tons. In 1986, it is estimated 700–1,100 tons were produced; in 1988, the crop was estimated to have climbed to 1,400 tons. In June 1989, Thai Police Major General Chavalit Yodmanee predicted that Burma's 1989 harvest would increase to 2,000 tons.

The yield is more than double that of the Vietnam War high of 800 tons. The difference is a vast increase in the Asian drug market itself, with severe heroin addiction problems emerging in Malaysia, Thailand, India, and Pakistan; and a surge in the Western market, as the Bangkok seizure of 1.4 tons of heroin bound for New York attests.

No matter how much of the "Burma" crop is grown along the northern or southern side of the Burma-P.R.C. border, there is no doubt that the P.R.C. is actively involved in the trade: The connection goes back to 1954–56, when 700,000 Chinese moved into Burma from Yunnan. At the same time, the Maoist regime began cultivating the ethnic groupings of northern Burma, including the Kachins and Shans. In addition, the Chinese controlled the Burmese Communist Party. (Even in 1988, the *London Daily Telegraph* reported [April 4] that the BCP is controlling large chunks of the opium trade in Burma and that the communists have "some sort of sanctuary in China which provides them an edge.) In 1967, when the Burmese government of Ne Win attempted to challenge the P.R.C. hold on northern Burma by cracking down on the Maoist Red Guard operating in Burma, Beijing lambasted Ne Win as a "fascist dictator," a "puppet of U.S. imperialism," and broke diplomatic relations. Ne Win was forced to back down, acknowledging P.R.C. dominion over northern Burma—and the opium flow.

That opium flow—out of Yunnan into and out of Burma— was documented in detail by U.S. Commissioner Harry Anslinger. In 1953, Anslinger told the Eighth Session of the United nations Commission on Narcotic Drugs that "Despite the efforts of the Burmese government to control the illicit traffic in narcotics, hundreds of tons of cleaned and packaged opium in one-kilogram units are brought into Burma each year from Yunnan province. Routes for the smuggling are through Myitkyina in the Kachin State and through Lashio on the old Burma Road in Northern Shan States. The hub of the traffic on the Yunnan side of the border is Tangyueh. Along the border are found trucks, military vehicles, carts, mules and pack trains used for transporting the opium. About 43 tons of opium are consumed annually in one small area along the Yunnan border, but the amount of opium in the traffic through Burma far surpasses the amount consumed within the country.

"During the year 1953, opium from Yunnan province accounted for almost 100% of the opium seized at some transhipment points," Anslinger told the commission.

Anslinger reported that the big marketplace for the dope was Chiengrai in northern Thailand. "From there the opium reaches Bangkok by boat, truck, rail and plane, and three to four tons can be delivered at any time to a point outside the border at Bangkok in the open sea"—a smuggling practice that continues to this day.

In 1955, Anslinger estimated that the P.R.C. was producing over 1,200 tons, with Yunnan producing 500 tons and another 500 tons leaving the P.R.C. via Canton, adjacent to Hong Kong.

In January 1959, a major drug ring was busted in San Francisco, whose operation indicated the extensive P.R.C. use of overseas Chinese to market the mainland's heroin. A total of 21 Chinese conspirators were found to be in the ring, with 12 of them residing in Hong Kong, Macao, and Shanghai, and the rest operating in the U.S.A. in secret criminal organizations called the Tongs. Documents seized showed that the heroin originated in Deng Xiaoping's Szechuan province, and was smuggled into the United States via Hong Kong. Except for the source tag on the heroin, nothing has changed in the criminal transfer system since.

Eyewitnesses have come forward in recent years to confirm the Yunnan connection. In June 1984, writes Maj. Gen. (Ret.) Chu Sing-yu of the Society for Strategic Studies of the Republic of China, an individual by the name of Chang Yu-mu left Yunnan for Taiwan and reported that the local Yunnan authorities had assigned 36 People's Communes of Haimung Haien to grow opium. In 1982, she said, communist cadres were sent into the zone controlled by the Burmese Communist Party to buy opium and better seeds. The BCP is a satrap of the mainland party, a relationship so close that in 1973 the BCP formed with Beijing the "Chinese-Burmese Communist Composite Force" joining the BCP's Northeast Military District and the Kunming Military District. The expansion of opium production and profit-splitting from it became an integral part of the relationship in 1976, according to Wang Kang, a Chinese communist who was sent into the BCP zones as a "special product transportation officer" in the 1980s and then escaped into Thailand in 1984. Reports that Beijing has decreased its official financial support for the BCP signify only that the gross profits from expanded opium trade in the 1980s have rendered such official support unnecessary.

The opium produced under the aegis of the BCP is then brokered to Khun Sa, who oversees its refining into heroin and negotiates the deals for its transshipment through organized crime gangs. As the *Bangkok Post* reported in February 1988, Khun Sa's "Shen state is not a major producer of opium but buys the raw material from others in [the] Golden Triangle to process into heroin. According to field sources, his supply comes mainly from Burmese Communists with poppy fields east of the Salween River close to the southern Chinese province of Yunnan."

Once transported by Khun Sa into Thailand, the heroin is taxed by Yunnanese-origin Chinese based in Chiang Mai, who also provide security. Then, at least up to 1979, the Chao Chou Chinese buy and export it. However, in the late 1980s, with the expansion of the Golden Triangle heroin trade, there is evidence that suggests Beijing is moving to take over this latter leg of the heroin trade route in its own right. In 1984, gang warfare broke out in Amsterdam, the hub for the distribution of Golden Triangle dope for Western Europe. Amsterdam's flow has been controlled by various Chinese ethnic groups led by the Hong Kong-based 24,000-member 14K. In 1984, dead bodies started appearing when the "Big Circle" gang began challenging the 14K. The Big Circle is comprised of recent immigrants from the mainland—whose direct ties to Beijing are undoubtedly clear.

In addition, the *Far Eastern Economic Review* reported at the same time that the "Narcotics agencies say that there is evidence that some of these Yunnanese middlemen are now seeking to strengthen their international connections with the aim the Ch'ao Chou syndicates."

This is further corroborated by source reports that since 1985, a major reorganization of Chinese organized crime networks was carried out in New York City. In part, such a reorganization was preparation for the leap in Golden Triangle drug flow to the U.S.A. and the expanding role of ethnic-Chinese crime networks in the U.S. drug market. Beijing's aim is to push out the old Chao Chou management of the drug trade. Over the course of the decade, the P.R.C. lost its trust in the Chao Chou, since the overseas Chinese tended increasingly to reinvesting their drug funds in legitimate ventures in their resident countries, instead of sending it all back to Beijing. Control of the Beijing drug flow has been shifted, say these sources, to networks based in the port of Foochow, in Fukien province, nearly midway on the coast between Canton and Shanghai. The Foochow smuggling networks have close ties to the Fukien branch of the Ministry of Public Security. Foochow smugglers make their way illegally into the United States through Canada and Mexico. These "immigrants" leave from Canton in groups of 20 to 30, going from there to Hong Kong or Macào. Many go to Nepal, where Beijing has relaunched construction of a cross-Nepal highway linked to Tibet as part of its plan to build a new "Silk Road" stretching from China across Nepal and central Asia into the Middle East. In Nepal, the Foochow are outfitted with new identities as citizens of Singapore, Indonesia, Thailand, or Malaysia. From there, they go to their "adopted" country, and thence to the United States.

It is estimated that ethnic-Chinese gangs account for 40% of the heroin sold in the United States.

Beijing's Monopoly Control

In 1981, reports began to surface that the P.R.C. had become a transshipment point for drugs. The *Ming Pao* daily of Hong Kong reported Sept. 1 that a Guangzhou (Canton) city security agency had destroyed a network that had brought 16.95 kilos of opium from the Yunnan border with plans to pass it on to Hong Kong and from there to the rest of the world.

The report, of course, exposes a deliberate route established by the P.R.C. for marketing its Yunnan-produced opium. "Transshipment" has been actively abetted by the P.R.C. government. In 1981, the same year the new route was discovered, P.R.C. authorities moved their checkpoints back from the Hong Kong border. The new checkpoints separated the Shenzhen Special Economic Zone from the rest of Guangdong province, "to ease entry into the zone from Hong Kong."

"Border control is not handy for business," the *Review* quoted a Shenzhen official as saying. "When the new economic border is in place to the north, with Hong Kong's own checkpoints to guard against arms and narcotics smuggling, foreign businessmen and goods should be able to flow through with ease."

The same policy has been applied to all the other Special Economic Zones (SEZs) along the Chinese coast. These "free ports," a la the days of the *taipans,* are the loci for funds and goods flowing back to the P.R.C. and for smuggled goods—opium and heroin—going out.

The policy is the Opium War in reverse. The history of the Chinese Communist Party is laced with opium. As early as the 1920s, communist leaders Mao Zedong and Zhou Enlai had praised opium as a crucial demoralizing instrument in waging "people's war" against the Chinese nationalist followers of Chiang Kai-shek. The Maoists regularly used the sale of opium to fund their operations and even established a "Regulation of Harvesting and Selling of Opium" in the regions they controlled as early as 1928. Important figures such as Chu Teh and General Ho Long, who had directed huge opium-smuggling networks prior to becoming Maoists, were followed by their loyal bands of followers into the communist armies. Opium smuggling was a common occupation of many of the criminal organizations recruited into what became the People's Liberation Army.

After 1949, the communists outlawed all drug consumption, a policy which, like all others, was ruthlessly enforced. Simultaneously, Beijing expanded opium production nationally and brought it under strict state monopoly control.

As Joseph Douglass reports in his book *Red Cocaine,* "Their targets were Japan, the United States military forces in the Far East, neighboring countries throughout the Far East, and the U.S. mainland. The primary organizations involved in the early 1950s were the Chinese Foreign Ministry, the Trade Ministry, the Intelligence Service. North Korea was also producing and trafficking narcotics in cooperation with China at this time and was directly connected with the flow of drugs into Japan and into the U.S. military bases in the Far East. . . .

"China's narcotics operations . . . have been described by several Chinese officials who later left China and were granted political asylum in other countries. One such official who left in the late 1950s described a secret meeting of state officials in 1952 when the Chinese operation was reorganized and a 20-year plan adopted. At this meeting, decisions were made to standardize grades of narcotics, establish promotion regulations, set pricing schedules that would encourage aggressive marketing, dispatch sales representatives, expand research and production, and reorganize management responsibility."

As Douglass reports, "In 1957, at the third meeting of the Central Committee of the Chinese Communist Party, attention was focused on the economy. The decision was taken at that meeting to expand drug production as one solution for their economic problems. The collective farms were to be expanded by 100 percent, and similarly, research and production laboratories were to be expanded. To further ease the problems, instructions were sent out to have emigrants invest in business in China and support China's policy and interests, including the marketing of drugs and narcotics. Primary targets were Mexico, the United States and Canada."

"The organization behind the Chinese narcotics operations was extensive and involved many ministries and agencies from the national down to the local levels. These organizations oversaw the reclamation of lands for production (Ministry of Forestry and Reclamation), the cultivation and research to produce better varieties of poppies (Ministry of Agriculture), development of opiates (Committee for the Review of Austerity), management of storage and preparation for export (Ministry of Commerce), management of external trade organizations (Ministry of Foreign Trade), statistical control and programming (Central Government Production Board), finance (Ministry of Finance), marketing through special representatives and political intrigue (Ministry of Foreign Affairs), and security and covert operations (Ministry of Public Security).

"Another important overseer of opium production has been the Tobacco Monopoly Bureau of the State Council. Prior to World War I, much of Chinese opium was produced under the

direction of British tobacco interests, of which British American
Tobacco was the most important. This is the apparent basis
for the later role of the P.R.C. Tobacco Bureau in the trade.
Interestingly, George Bush's White House counsel C. Boyden
Gray, is the heir to the R.J. Reynolds tobacco fortune, which is
based on that firm's partnership with British American Tobacco
in that same period.

"The trafficking tradecraft," Douglass relates, "included classical smuggling, transport by shipping companies (both knowingly and unknowingly), use of communists and ethnic Chinese
abroad, collaboration with international organized-crime syndicates, use of foreign posts of mainland parent organizations,
abuse of diplomatic privilege, use of normal branded merchan-
dise as a cover, transport by mail, and forgery, or packaging
with misleading trademarks. . . .

"Throughout the 1950s and 1960s, probably the most important official who exercised day-to-day control over China's narcotics operations was Chou En-lai"—Kissinger's grand partner
in forging the China card policy. During a meeting in Wuhan
in 1958 convened to discuss the expansion of opium production,
Chou En-lai is quoted by Taiwan specialists as saying:

"The Center has decided to promote poppy cultivation on a
large scale. . . . Everyone of you must awake to the fact that the
war in Vietnam is likely to escalate and U.S. imperialism has
determined to fight against our revolutionary camp by increasing its military force in Vietnam. . . . From the revolutionary
point of view, the poppy is great force to assist the course of our
revolution and should be used; from the class point of view, the
poppy can also become a powerful weapon to win the proletarian
revolution. . . By exporting large quantities of morphine and
heroin, we are able to weaken the U.S. combat force and to
defeat it without even fighting at all."

Another top figure overseeing the drug industry was Bo Yibo,
formerly chief of the finance division of the "Opium Prohibition
Bureau." In the 1950s, he became finance minister and chairman of the powerful State Planning Commission. In 1973, he
led the first P.R.C. commercial delegation to the United States
after Nixon had ended the 23-year trade embargo against the

mainland. Today, Bo Yibo, who was a leading crusader of the "Anti-Spiritual Pollution" campaign of the early 1980s, is a staunch factional ally of the hardline, octogenarian butchers who put down the China democracy movement of 1989.

Another key figure in the postwar expansion of opium production is Yao Yilin, today the vice premier of the P.R.C. and who gained notoriety during the aftermath of the Tiananmen Square massacre of 1989 with his attacks on the West and threats that the P.R.C. would again ally with its communist neighbor, the Soviet Union. Former P.R.C. President Li Xiannian also sat on the P.R.C. narcotics board of directors. Li was named the "money god" for his miraculous payment of the P.R.C.'s war debt, during his tenure as finance minister from 1957 to 1975.

Index

Abbell, Michael 42
Abello, Alberto 328
Abergavemy, Marquis of 521
Abess, Leonard 607, 611
Ablon, Carl S. 174
Abrams, Elliott 22, 24, 25
Abrams, Morris 615
Abreu Burelli, Judge Alirio 357-58
Abscam 584-85, 588, 591, 594
Abshire, David 10
Abu Nidal 17
Abwehr 372
Acevedo, Sen. Valmore 328
Achille Lauro 17
Action Directe 375-76
Adamson, John 515
Adamson, William C. 592
Addams, Jane 136
Adorno, Theodor 545
A.G. Becker 100
Agca, Mehmet Ali 19, 371, 384, 386, 389
Agee, Philip 644
Ainsworth, Cathy 622
Airborne Freight 171-76, 502, 508
Air Force Military Airlift Command 174
Earl of Airlie 274
Al Fatah 375
Alberti, Gerlando 383, 386
Alemán, Miguel 438, 484-85
Alexander, Yonah 639
Alinsky, Saul 137
Aliyev, Geidar Ali-Reza Ogly 63, 294, 298-99
Al-Jabal, Shaykh xi
Al-Kassar, Mansur 17
Allen and Co. 171, 174

Allen, Charles 173, 176, 635
Allen, Richard 622
Allianz Versicherung 94
Allman Brothers 560
Alpert, Richard (a.k.a. Baba Ram Dass) 200, 542, 544, 551
Alpina Lodge 388
Amadruz, Gaston Guy 375
American Bank & Trust 20, 107
American Banker 88
American Civil Liberties Union (ACLU) 422
American Council of Christian Churches (ACCC) 479-82
American Defense Society (ADS) 597
American Express Co. 92, 95, 106-07, 234, 354, 610
American Family Foundation 650
American Financial Corp. 85
American Jewish Committee 514, 606
American Jewish League Against Communism 459
American Protective League 598-601
American Revolution 188, 264, 271, 459, 598
American Telephone & Telegraph (AT&T) 177
Amery, Julian 629
Amnesty International 23
Amoroso, Anthony 585
Andean Pact 68
Anderman, Stan 638, 644
Anderson, Jack 18
Anderson, Robert O. 320
Andreas, Dwayne 57, 608, 615-17, 643
Andreyev, M.A. 197
Andropov, Yuri xi, 71, 90, 140, 299, 614

Angiulo family 77
Anglo-American Mining 94, 101, 198, 200-201, 238, 272, 362
Anglo-American Occult Bureau 649
Animals, The 542, 544
Anne, Princess 521
Anslinger, Henry J. 225, 228, 658, 660-61
Anti-Communist League of the Caribbean 469
Anti-Defamation League of B'nai B'rith (ADL) xiii, 6-7, 10-13, 20, 27, 71-73, 106, 422, 522, 603-13, 616-24, 626-49, 651; (see also B'nai B'rith)
Anti-Nazi Coalition 504
Anti-Saloon League 135-36
Antonov, Serge Ivanov 379, 386
Antwerp Diamond Bourse 202
Anzalone, Thomas 78
Appleton family 127
Arab-American Anti-Discrimination Committee 628
Arab Bureau 368
Araven Finance Ltd. 354
Arazi, Yehuda 506-07, 513
Arbuckle, William 432
Arce Gómez 297
Archer Daniels Midland, Inc. (ADM) 643; ADM/Töpfer 57
Argomaniz, Alberto 353; Argomaniz, Enrique "Kaki" 353
Aristotelian Society 270
Arky, Steven 82-83, 85
Arnold, Benedict 416
Arrupe, Father Pedro 342
Arsan, Henri 381-83, 387
Ashbrook, Rep. John 657
Ashburton, Lord 127
Asian Research Institute 241
Aspen Institute 196
Assad, Hafez al- 6, 17; Assad, Rifaat al- 17
Assassins (Hashishins) xi
Assicurazioni Generali di Venezia e Trieste 98-99, 107-08, 314, 341-42, 355
Astaldo Vaduz (Miami) 461-62
Astor, John Jacob 125-26, 128, 249, 443; Astor family 135; Astor, Lady 445; Astor, Waldorf 128, 249
Atlantic Charter 243
Atlas Shipping Company 426
Atoms for Peace 248, 547

Auckland, Lord 122
Auden, Wystan Hugh 538
Aurora Oil Co. 503, 507
Axen, Hermann 614

Baader-Meinhof Gang 547, 575
Bacardi, Manuel Cutilla 437
Bacon, Sir Ranulph 496, 499; Bacon family 127
Bahro, Rudolf 395
Baker, Newton 600
Bakst, Jerome 619, 624
Baldwin, Stanley 270
Balfour, Arthur 264, 270
Balfour Declaration (1914) 504
Balkan Tours/Airlines 379, 386
Ball, Edward 350
Ball, George 99, 106, 341
Ban Cal Tri-State 93
Banca Commerciale d'Italia 96, 99, 104, 341-43
Banca d'America e d'Italia 105
Banca della Svizzera Italiana 99, 104, 341, 354
Banca Nazionale della Agricoltura 105
Banca Privata 72, 98, 106, 108, 611
Banco Ambrosiano 66-67, 92, 96, 98, 104-05, 109, 297, 312, 322, 341-42, 362, 381-82, 387-88
Banco Andino 341
Banco Caribe 381
Banco Consolidado 354
Banco de Colombia 326
Banco de Iberoamérica (Panama) 84
Banco de la Nación (Peru) 322
Banco del Crédito (Peru) 84
Banco del Estado 352
Banco Internacional (Peru) 84
Banco Interoceánico 25
Banco Latino (Venezuela) 354
Banco Mercantil de México 485
Banco Nacional de Cuba 351
Banco Nacional de Panamá 76, 332
Bancroft, Baron Stormont 464
Bandagee, Senator 602
Bangkok Bank 187-89
Bangkok Metropolitan Bank 187-88
Bankers Trust 79
Bank for International Settlements (BIS) 99, 159, 314
Bank Hapoalim 24-25, 180, 456, 464-65, 468
Bank Leu of Zurich 75
Bank Leumi 180, 201-02, 273, 464, 485

Bank of America 103-05, 312, 343, 444
Bank of Basel 461
Bank of Boston Corp. 50, 73, 77-78, 80, 456, 524; Bank of Boston SA of Luxembourg 75
Bank of China 218-19, 221, 239, 246-47
Bank of East Asia 108, 349
Bank of England 161
Bank of Ireland 76
Bank of Montreal 92, 256, 432, 440
Bank of Norfolk (Great Britain) 521
Bank of Nova Scotia 66, 92, 202-03, 236, 252-53, 256-58, 260, 320
Bank of the Middle East 135, 248
Bank of Tokyo 84
Bank Secrecy Act of 1980 204
Bannister, Guy 469, 475, 481-82, 490, 623
Banque Bruxelles-Lambert 98, 201
Banque Commerciale Arabe 374, 376
Banque de Paris et des Pays Bas (Paribas) 98, 100, 108
Banque du Crédit International (BCI) 168, 342-43, 462-65, 468, 492, 497-98
Banque Française et Italienne pour l'Amérique du Sud 341
Banque Louis-Dreyfus Holding Co. 107-08, 342, 434; Banque Louis-Dreyfus of Paris 461
Banque Privée (Geneva) 461
Banque Sudameris 341, 343, 354
Barbie, Klaus 297, 373, 376, 388, 401
Barclays Bank International of New York 75, 92, 102, 108, 202-03, 252, 256, 264, 273, 439, 464
Baring Brothers Bank 126-27
Baring family 114, 125-26; Baring, Francis 118
Barnabo, Count 179
Barnes, Earl 81
Barnett, A. Doak 231
Barnett Banks (Florida) 84
Barr, Henry 29
Barry, Charles 637
Barth, Dr. Karl 372
Baseler Handelsbank 161
Baskin, Phil 612
Bateman, Jaime 405-06; *Listen Brother* 406
Bateson, Dr. Gregory 542-43, 549
Batista, Fulgencio 495
Bayer, Alan 607
Bear Stearns 617

Beasley, Donald 611
Beatles, The 542, 544
Beatrice Foods 349
Beaverbrook, Lord 135, 269, 451
Beethoven, Ludwig van 597
Behan, Cornelius 637
Belisle, David 499
Belmont, August 510-11
Bell, Griffin 520
Bellanca, Peter J. 517
Ben Barka, Mehdi 382
Ben Bella, Ahmed 376
Ben-Gurion, David 505
Benoist-Mechin 373
Ben-Or, Pesach 25-26
Bensinger, Peter 293
Bentham, Jeremy 126
Bentley, Elizabeth 618
Berkowitz, Howard P. 606
Berlet, John Foster ("Chip") 7, 644, 651
Bernadotte, Count 458
Bernasconi, Paolo 40
Besser, Albert 73
Betancur, Belisario 62, 310-11, 324-26, 329
Bethel, Lord Nicholas 629
Bevill, Bresler and Schulman 86
Bialkin, Kenneth J. 7, 71, 73, 106, 608-10, 621, 630, 639, 645-46
Bielaski, Bruce 597-98
Biggs, Marion R. 588
Bingham, William 126
Binny, J.A.F. 162, 256
Bittman, William O. 524
Black, Eli 339, 512
Black Panther Party 620, 624
Black September 17, 376
Blair and Co. 444
Blair, Claude Maclary 174
Blake, George 375
Blavatsky, Helena 268-69, 380, 539
Blom-Cooper, Louis 23
Bloomfield, Louis Mortimer 342, 418-19, 436, 452-64, 467-69, 471-72, 475, 480-81, 483, 485, 492, 497-500, 509
Bludhorn, Charles 339
Blue Ribbon Commission on Central American Policy 11
B'nai B'rith 422, 605, 641; B'nai B'rith Women 646; (see also Anti-Defamation League)
Boesky, Ivan 610

Bohemian Grove xii, 10
Boland, Mira Lansky 642-43
Bolívar, Simón 394
Bolles, Don 515, 517, 519, 524
Bolling, Landrum 630
Bolshevik Information Bureau 618
Bonacossi, Franco Orsini 98
Bonanno, Joseph 459, 483
Bonaparte, Charles J. 587-91, 597
Bond, Richard 22
Boren, Sen. David 12
Borghese, Elisabeth Mann 539, 552
Bormann, Martin 373
Bosch, Orlando 353
Boschwitz, Sen. Rudy 607
Bostetter, Judge Martin V.B. 14
Boston Globe 77
Boston Herald 13
Botco, Ltd. 296
Botero Montoya, Rodrigo 325
Botnick, Adolph "Sam" 623
Bo Yibo 666-67
Bourne, Geoffrey 360; Bourne, Dr. Peter 313, 317, 360-61, 543-44, 562-63
Bouvier, Jacqueline 446; Bouvier, Lee 446
Boylston family 127
Bradley, E.E. 479-80
Braganza family 95, 378, 389
Brand, Lord Robert 445
Brandt, Willy 631
Breguet, Bruno 376
Bretton Woods System 316
Brewster, Kingman 564
Briceno, Leovigildo (a.k.a. Comisario Amilcar) 356-58
Briskman, Mark 644
British-American-Canadian Corp. 470-71
British American Tobacco 666
British Bank of the Middle East 432
British Board of Jewish Deputies 466
British Chamber of Jewish Deputies 115
British East India Co. xi, 8, 71, 93, 116, 118-20, 125-26, 186, 214, 249, 306-07, 338, 369, 372, 387, 581 (see also Dutch East India Company)
British Foreign Office 8, 239, 248, 445
British Ministry of Economic Warfare 199, 236, 270
British Newfoundland Development Corp. (BRINCO) 470

British Petroleum 237, 248, 254, 297, 387-88
British Roundtable 133, 238, 445, 447, 450, 457, 538,
British Secret Intelligence Service 135, 224, 368, 385, 444, 477, 504, 544; Special Air Service 440, 23
Broderick, Percival 319
Bromberg, Charney V. 606
Bronfman, Abe 425, 431, 434; Bronfman, Allan 434, 438; Bronfman, Charles 260, 432, 434, 437, 614; Bronfman, Edgar 6-7, 71, 78, 434, 436-37, 565, 605-08, 610, 612-16, 635-36, 647-48, 651; Bronfman family 94, 115, 136, 139, 150, 237, 252-53, 256, 260-61, 273, 347, 370, 416, 418-19, 423, 426-31, 433-38, 440, 442, 444, 456, 461, 499, 503, 509, 518, 521, 612-13, 639; Cemp (Bronfman family trust) 440; Bronfman, Harry 426; Bronfman, Minda 434; Bronfman, Mitchell 438, 440, 518, 613; Bronfman, Peter 436; Bronfman, Phyllis 434; Bronfman, Sam 180, 424-26, 431, 433-36, 440, 612; Bronfman, Samuel II 437; Bronfman, Yechiel (Ekiel) 423, 425, 433, 461, 512
Brotherhood of Eternal Love 351, 551-52
Brown, Rudnick, Freed, Gesmar 442
Brown University 175
Brown, William (Willie) 75, 559
Bruce, Charles 551
Bruce, Edward 267; Bruce family 272; Bruce, Frederick 266; Bruce, James, Earl of Elgin 265, 270; Bruce, King Robert of Scotland 265
Brudner, Charley 494
Brunet, Gilles 439
Bryan, Judge Albert Vickers, Jr. 13
Bryant, Dr. Thomas 561
Brzezinski, Zbigniew 26, 291, 421, 550
Buckley, James 421; Buckley William F., Jr. 421, 567
Bulgarian Airlines 379, 384
Bulgarian Orthodox Church 386
Bulgarian State Security (KDS) 378-80, 383
Bulwer-Lytton, Edward 263-64, 267-71, 539
Bundy, McGeorge xii, 450, 546, 560; Bundy, William 487

Bunge 57, 92
Burbridge, F.S. 432
Bureau of Investigation (BOI) 587, 589-602
Burger, Donald 644
Burns and Summit 611, 642
Burns, Arnold 12, 611, 642
Burns, William J. 588, 596
Burr, Aaron 126, 416, 443
Bush, George 4-5, 13-15, 18-19, 25, 28-31, 42, 49, 51, 621, 666; Bush administration 657
Butcher, Willard C. 175
Byelorussian Liberation Front 481

Cabinet Committee for International Narcotics Control (CCINC) 656
Cabot family 127
Cacheris, Judge James 627
Cada Supermarkets 348, 354
Cali Cartel 41-42
Califano, Joseph 565
Calvi, Roberto 66-67, 69, 92, 96, 104-05, 297, 341, 382, 387-88
Calypso Travel Agency 336
Camarena, Enrique 15-16, 584
Camorra 391
Campaigner Publications, Inc. 627
Campfire Council 480
Canadian Corporate Management Corp. 258
Canadian Council of Christians and Jews 436
Canadian Imperial Bank of Commerce 75, 252, 256, 260
Canadian Institute of International Affairs (CIIA) 236, 242, 251-53, 258, 260-61
Canadian Israeli Bond Drives 436
Canadian Jewish Committee 433
Canadian Jewish Congress 434
Canadian Pacific, Ltd. 255, 258-60, 264, 349, 390, 432-33, 484; Canadian Pacific Railroad, 425; Canadian Pacific Transport 172
Canadian Red Cross Ambulance Corp. 436, 456-57
Canadian Roundtable 135
Canning, Lord 266
Cannon, Joseph G. 589
Capo d'Istria, Count Giovanni 314
Capone, Al 137, 429, 519
Capricorn Records 560
Cárdenas, Lázaro 438

Caretas 406
Carey, Gov. Hugh 565
Carey, James H. 175-76
Cargill 57, 92
Caribbean Basin Initiative 318
Caribbean/Central American Action Group 318
Carli, Guido 343
"Carlos" 375-76
Carmichael, Donald 523
Carmichael, Stokely 544
Carnegie Foundation 241
Caro Quintero, Rafael 15-16
Carrington, Peter Lord 8, 108, 234, 314-15, 639
Carter, Edward 242
Carter, James Earl (Jimmy) 4, 6, 25, 62, 80, 82-83, 163, 291, 293, 306, 312-13, 317, 340, 346, 349-50, 360, 408, 468, 543, 550, 559-64, 568, 607; Carter, Billy 313, 350; Carter, Rosalyn 561
Casey, William 18, 24
Casino de Liban 374
Cassa San Giorgio 314
Castellammarese gang 429
Castellani, Armand 523
Castro Cervantes, Fernando 341
Castro, Fidel 71-72, 96, 313, 318-19, 325, 341, 345, 350-51, 353, 357, 360, 362, 407, 437, 451, 482, 490, 495, 500, 583
Castro, Frank 16
Cater, Jack 210
Cathedral of St. John the Divine 567, 649
Catholic Church 389; Catholic Rural Life 644; Catholics for a Free Choice 646
Cator, W.J. 189
Catto, Lord of Cairncatto 128
Cavendish, William, Marquess of Hartington 446; Cavendish, Victor C.W., Duke of Devonshire 137, 255, 446
Ceauşescu, Nicolae 26
Cecil, Mary Alice, Duchess of Devonshire 446
Cecil, Lord Robert 238-39, 267, 446, 450
Celenk, Bekir 386
Celeste, Gov. Richard 81
Celik, Oral 384, 386
Cellini, Dino 494, 499; Cellini, Eddie 499

Center for Democratic Renewal 644
Center for Rural Affairs 644
Center for the Administration of Justice at the American University 564
Center for the Study of Democratic Institutions (CSDI) 138, 552-53
Centrade Group 20-21
Central Intelligence Agency (CIA) xii, 5, 13, 15-18, 21-22, 24, 46, 193, 246, 418, 455, 474, 479, 490, 499, 540, 542, 612, 615, 644, 648
Central Narcotics Board 132
Central Selling Organization 201-02
Centro Mondiale Commerciale (CMC) 458-59, 472, 474-75
Chaitkin, Anton 478; *Treason in America* 478
Chamberlain, Houston Stewart 268
Chamoun, Camille 380-81
Chanes, Francisco 16
Chang Yu-mu 661
Channell, Carl "Spitz" 619
Chao Chou Chinese 187-88, 201-02, 229-30, 232, 662
Charris, Fausto 403
Charter Consolidated 108
Charter Oil Co. 313, 350
Chartered Bank 114, 238
Charterhouse Japhet 182, 202, 237, 273, 464
Chase Manhattan Bank 67, 92, 103-05, 107, 172, 175-77, 215, 217, 234, 312, 336, 349, 354
Chatham House (see Royal Institute of International Affairs)
Chauhan, Jagjit Singh 385, 629-30
Chavalit Yodmanee 659
Cheka 477
Chemical Bank 166, 169
Chen, K.P. 239, 246-47
Chen Pi Chen (a.k.a. Chin Sophonpanich) 187-88
Chen Yi 244
Cherne, Leo 10
Chesler, Louis 493, 495, 497
Cheung Kong Holdings, Ltd. 523
Chiang Kai-shek 245, 664
Chicago Tribune 55
Chi Ch'ao-ting 239, 246-47
Children of the Sun 538
China Association 241
China Everbright Holdings, Ltd. 233-34

Chinese Arts and Crafts (Hong Kong) 21
Chinese Central External Liaison Dept. 222
Chinese Commercial Corp. 259
Chinese Communist Intelligence Service (CCIS) 218, 223-24, 230, 232, 664
Chinese Cultural Center 259
Chinese General Chamber of Commerce 220-21
Chinese Manufacturers Assn. 211
Chinese Ministry of Investigation 222
Chinese People's Institute of Foreign Affairs 242
Chinese Yunnanese Assoc. 659
Chou En-lai (see Zhou Enlai)
Chourbagi, Munir 459
Christian Patriots Defense League 625
Chu Sing-yu, Maj. Gen. (ret.) 661
Chu Teh 240, 664
Chung, Louis 88
Church of Scientology 650
Churchill, Winston 243-44, 274, 444-45, 455, 471, 477, 537
Circle of Initiates 264
Cisneros, Antonio 348; Cisneros Fajardo, Oswaldo 345, 348, 350-51, 353, 355, 357; Cisneros family 338, 357; Cisneros Group 72; Cisneros, Gustavo 26-27, 75, 85, 318, 346-50, 354-55, 357; Cisneros Rendiles, Ricardo 348, 354
Cissell, James 82
Citibank 92, 100-103, 159, 312, 343, 348, 355
Citizens Engaged in Reuniting Families (CERF) 650
Citizens and Southern Bank (Georgia) 351-52
City National Bank of Miami 611, 337
Civil War (U.S.) 114, 129, 510
Claiborne Oil Co. 478
Clare, Robert 101
Clariden Bank 75
Clarkson and Gordon 252, 259
Clarkson, Steven 252
Clement V, Pope 265
Clements, William 648
Clergy and Laity Concerned 622
Cleveland, Harlan 196
Cleveland National City Bank 173-76
Cliveden Set 445-46
Clough, Susan 83

Club of Rome 104, 388
Codman family 127
Cohen, Lazarus 433
Cohen, Lyon 433
Cohn, Roy Marcus 459, 483, 608
Cointelpro 624-26
Colombian Coffee 337
Colombian Justice Ministry 68, 329-30
Colombian National Anti-Drug Coalition 403
Colombian Supreme Court 329
Colosimo, "Big Jim" 428
Columbia Broadcasting System (CBS) 86, 381
Combank 83-85
Commonwealth Fund 560
Communist International (Comintern) 369, 374-75; Communist Party of Azerbaijan 298; Communist Party of Bulgaria 380; Communist Party of Burma (White Flag) 227, 658, 660-62; Communist Party of China (CCP) 222, 230, 240-41, 243-45, 664-65; Communist Party of Great Britain 632; Communist Party of Indonesia (PKI) 230; Communist Party of Peru 396; Communist Party, U.S.A. 619, 635, 644; Communist Party of the Soviet Union 375
Communist Labor Party 623
Communist Workers Party 422
Consolidated Gold Fields 94, 101, 194, 196, 198, 200, 225
Continental Grain 57
Continental Illinois Bank 76
Contras 11-12, 14-16, 18, 23, 25
Cook, Fred J. 591
Coolidge family 127
Copei Party (Venezuela) 328
Cork, E. Kendall 203
Cornfeld, Bernie 96, 138, 168, 417, 465, 497, 553
Corporate Bank and Trust Co. 439
Corporate Jets 337
Corsan, William 600; *Armies of Ignorance* 602
Cortés Cadena, Arturo 405
Cotroni, Giuseppe 494
Coudert Brothers 163
Council of Christian Churches 421
Courtney, Max 494
Cowdray, Viscount (Weetman John Churchill Pearson) 445

Crédit Suisse xii, 75-76, 79-80, 213; Crédit Suisse-First Boston 74, 213, 336, 456, 462 (see also First Boston Corp.)
Credival 345-46
Crocker National Bank (Calif.) 93, 204-06, 212, 214
Cromos 405
Crosby, James M. 494-95
Crosby, Peter 494
Crosby-Miller Co. 494
Crowley, Aleister 268, 538-39
Crown Distributing Co. 442
Crown-Lundheimer mob 519
Cruz Vásquez, Antonio 437
Cuban Missile Crisis 450
Cult Awareness Network 650
Cultural Revolution 220, 396
Culverhouse, Hugh, Sr. 83, 85; Culverhouse, Hugh, Jr. 83-84
Cummings, Sam 13
Cunard Lines 464
Cunningham family 127
Curiel, Henri 375-76; Solidarity Group 375
Curtis, Lionel 238-39

D-16 (British Foreign Intelligence) 223-24
Dachauer, Jacob 614
Dalitz, Morris 502, 507, 518-19, 609, 612
D'Amato, Sen. Alfonse 22
DAP-EK 379
Davidson, Meyer 622-23
David-Weill family 98-99
Davis, Angela 544
Davis, Rabbi Maurice 648-650
DEA (See U.S. Drug Enforcement Administration)
Deacon, Richard 221-22, 224, 467; *The Chinese Secret Service* 221
Deak-Perrera 336
DeBartolo, Edward J. 85
De Beers Corp. 94, 151, 155, 198, 200-02, 238, 272 (see also Central Selling Organization)
de Comondo family 341
De Famaco Astaldo Vaduz (Geneva) 462; De Famaco Vaduz 461 (Liechtenstein)
de Gaulle, Gen. Charles 368, 440, 451, 455-56, 460 469, 479, 481, 483; Free French 374

de Gunzburg, Baron Alain 434; de Gunzburg family 461, 499
de Hirsch, Baron Maurice 424, 433; de Hirsch family 420, 433, 461; de Hirsch Foundation 424, 436
Delafield and Delafield Investments 551
Della Chiaie, Stefano 297, 388-89, 400-401
Della Torre, Franco 79
Delvalle, Eric 22
de Menil family 421; de Menil, Dominique Schlumberger 478; de Menil, Jean 374, 453, 459, 474, 476, 478
Demjanjuk, John 634-36
Democratic Party (U.S.) 5, 12, 74, 78, 81-82, 86, 136, 443, 519-20, 586, 612
de Molay, Jacques 265
de Neuflize, Schlumberger, Mallet Bank 478-79
Deng Xiaoping 216-17, 655, 661
Dennis, Canon Walter D. 567
Dennis, Michael 628
Dent family, 114, 127, 162; Dent, Lancelot 256; Dent, R.J. 256
Dernberg, Dr. Ernest 543
Dérogy, Jacques 462-65, 639
DeRusha, Floyd, 49-50
Der Weg 373
Deterding, Sir Henry 477
de Tilly, Count 126
Dewar, Lord 426
Dewey, Thomas 425, 494-95
deZulueta, Sir Philip 200, 253
DGI (Cuban Intelligence) 360, 362, 485, 500
Diamond, Legs 425, 428-29
Diario de Caracas 345, 350, 357
DiCarlo, Dominick 205
Diethelm Brothers Import-Export 373
Dietz, Esther 650
Dillon, C. Douglas 159
Dinef 381
Dinitz, Simcha 615
DISIP (Venezuelan political police) 72, 356-57
Disraeli, Benjamin 509-10
Distillery Company of London (DCL) 426
Dogoloff, Lee 360
Dome of the Rock 640
Dominion Mortgage Corp. 353

Domino Investments 337
Donahue, Phil 212
Donatelli, Richard 22
Donnell, James C. II 174
Dope, Inc. xii, 5-6, 9, 27, 41, 61-65, 71-72, 371, 390, 575, 613
Doria family 99, 314
Double-Chek Co. 474, 479, 490-91, 499
Douglass, Joseph 664-66; Red Cocaine 664
Dozier, Gen. James 391
Drake, Sir Eric 254, 273, 431-32
Draycott Trading and Finance, Ltd. 297
Dreikot Driving and Financial Co. 388
Dresdner Bank 575
Drexel Burham Lambert 98, 100, 257, 610
Dreyfus, Louis 57, 92, 499
Drug Abuse Council 560-62
Drug Abuse Warning Network (DAWN) 29, 38
Duke of Alba 99
Duke of Gloucester 261
Duke of Wellington 267
Dulles, Allen 368, 370, 372-73, 540, 542
Dunlop, Max 515
E.I. du Pont de Nemours Co. 612
DuPont, Dr. Robert 562, 567
Duque, Alberto 336-37, 363, 611
D'Urso, Mario 107
Düsseldorf Global Bank 296
Dutch East India Company 93 (see also British East India Company)
Dzherzhinsky, Felix 477

Eagleburger, Lawrence, 108, 318
Eagle Star Insurance, 92, 94, 252-53, 435
East German Army (NVA) 374
East India Company (see British East India Company)
Edper Co. 436
E.F. Hutton 68
Egan, Richard 86
Eichmann, Adolf 462
Eisenberg, Meyer 608-09, 646
Eisenberg, Shaul, 467-68, 513
Eisenhower, Gen. Dwight David 248, 491, 547
Eizenstat, Stuart 562
El Al Airline 375-76
Elder, Jim 638

El Espacio 394
Elgin, Lord 124, 266-67
Eli Lilly Endowment 630
Eliot, Charles 120-21
Eliot, Thomas Stearns 538
Elizabeth I, Queen of England 446
Elizabeth II, Queen of England, 175, 215, 250, 255, 261, 456, 544, 560
Elliott, William Yandell 450
El Mundo (Venezuela) 76, 356
ELN (National Liberation Army—Colombia) 394
Else TH 24
El Tiempo 326-27, 407
Emerald Triangle 53-54
Emory University 563
Emprise 175, 449, 515-24
Endara, Guillermo 25
Endicott, James 242, 258-59
Engelhard Minerals 101
English Property Corp., Ltd. 252, 435
Enterprise, The 17
Epstein, Benjamin 608, 617-18, 641
Equitable Life Insurance 489
Erben, Dr. Herman 369-71
Erickson, Frank 611
Esalen Institute 548-49
Escobar Gaviria, Pablo 17, 41, 326, 357, 393
ESM Government Securities 81, 83, 86
Esposito, Giuseppe 511
European Labor Party (EAP) 631-33
Ewton, Ronnie R. 82-83, 86
Execairc Aviation 439-40
Executive Intelligence Review (EIR) 7, 26, 29-30, 38, 44, 47, 93, 100, 202-03, 340, 342, 356-57, 397, 401, 404, 576, 645
Executive Order 12333, 10; Executive Order 12435, 67
Exner, Judith Campbell 441
Extraditables, the 42
Eytan, Dov 634
Eytan, Rafael ("Dirty Rafi") 641-42

Fabian Society 136, 447
Fadlallah, Sheikh 300
Fairbanks, J.K. 239
Fair Play for Cuba Committee 482, 623
Falange Party (Lebanon) 380
Falco, Mathea 563
FALN (Armed Forces for National Liberation) 567, 649

Family Farm Resource Organizing Committee (FFROC) 644
Family Weekly 360
Farmer, Victor 241, 243-44
Farmers Home Administration (FmHA) 56-57
Farouk, King of Egypt 459
Fascist National Association for Militia Arms (Italy) 459
Federal Bureau of Investigation (FBI) 4, 9-10, 12, 16, 46, 62, 71, 78, 81, 86, 88, 178, 418-19, 422, 448, 455, 457, 460, 466, 469, 473, 475-76, 479-81, 486-88, 491, 499, 506, 509, 583-87, 591-92, 594-96, 598, 602, 604, 619, 623-25, 628, 637-38, 646
Federal Bureau of Narcotics xxi, 225, 228, 369
Federal Election Commission (FEC) 442
Federal Reserve Board 56, 65, 76, 85, 172-74, 213, 306, 312-13, 332-34, 508
Federal Security Directorate 16
Federal Witness Protection Program (FWPP) 586
Federation of Jewish Philanthropists 434
Federation of Russian Charitable Organizations 481
Feinberg, Abe 468
Fequiz, Pierpaolo Luzzatto 98
Ferdmann, Sylvain 463
Ferguson, Marilyn, 535-36, 538-39, 548, 550; *The Aquarian Conspiracy* 535-36, 548
Ferguson, Robert 73, 86-87, 89
Ferrie, David 481-82, 490
Ferris, Paul 196; *The City* 196
Fiat 104
Fidelity Guards (South Africa) 225
Fiduciary Trust Co. 497, 551-52
Field, Sally 507
Figueres, José 341, 361
Film Booking Co. 443
Financial Times 186, 211, 274
Finch, Stanley W. 591, 593
Finger, Justin J. 623, 637, 644, 646
First Boston Corp. 74, 213 (see also Crédit Suisse-First Boston)
First Empire Bank 175
First Fidelity Bank of New Jersey 73, 86-89
First Interamericas Bank 41

Firstmark Corp. 522
First National Bank of Boston 75, 128
Fisher, Max 7, 71, 95, 170-71, 173-74, 176, 339-40, 418, 465, 502-14, 524
Fitzgerald, Gerald 458
Fitzgerald, "Honey Fitz" 443
Flammonde, Paris 471, 475; *The Kennedy Conspiracy* 471
Flegenheimer, Arthur (see Schultz, Dutch)
Fleming, Ian 501
Flendon, Ltd. 439
FLN (National Liberation Front—Algeria) 374
Flores, José Cupertino 76
Florida National Bank of Jacksonville 349-50
Florida State Banking Commission 180
FLQ (Front for the Liberation of Quebec) 439-40
Flynn, Errol 369
Fok, Henry 220
Fontanals de Cisneros, Ella 351; Fontanals Pérez, José 351
Forbes, John Murray 127; Forbes family 127
Forbes 361
Ford Foundation 541, 553, 560
Ford, Gerald 8
Ford, Henry II 540
Forst, Lester 637
Forster, Arnold 608, 618, 641
Foundation Faith of the Millennium 650
Four-Star Anstalt (Liechtenstein) 552
Foxman, Abraham H. 607-08, 632, 646-47
Franco, Gen. Francisco 272
Fraser family 271, 274
Freed, Hirsch 442
Free Democratic Party (Germany) 295
Freedom Savings and Loan Assn. (Florida) 85
Freeman, Steven M. 606
Freie Osterreichische, Die (bank) 75
Frelinghuysen, Joseph 601
French Revolution 478
Fribourg family 92
Friedman, Milton 211, 213; *Free to Choose* 211-12, 214, 307, 408
Friedman, Robert 626
Fruehauf Trucking Co. 508
Fund of Funds 553
Fusion 14

Gable, Gerry 632
Galán, Luis Carlos x, 21-23
Gambino family 87, 612
Gandhi, Indira 368, 384, 629-30; Gandhi, Rajiv 630
Gandhi, Mohandas K. (Mahatma) 131
Gandica, Judge Ana Luisa 356; Gandica, Luis Gregorio 358
Gang of Four 240, 396
Gans, Gail 626
Gant, Donald R. 340
García, Alan 62, 68, 72, 309-11
García Bustillos, Gonzalo 328
García Márquez, Gabriel 407
Gardner, Richard 104-05
Garrigy, Joseph 173-74
Garrison, James 418-19, 469, 471, 473-75, 479, 481, 486, 489-91
Gatlin, Jerry Brooks 469, 481
Geddes, Sir Auckland 272; Geddes, Ford Irvine 272
Gelli, Licio 96, 297, 341, 382, 387-88
General Agreement on Tariffs and Trade (GATT) 56, 615
General Coffee 337
General Motors Corp. 567
Genillard, Robert 75
Genoud, François 368, 371-76, 382, 385, 390
Genovese, Vito 439
Genscher, Hans-Dietrich 295
George, Lloyd 238
George III, King of England 264, 271
Gershman, Carl 11, 619-20, 624
Gesner, Van 588
Gestapo 369, 373, 382, 401
Giancana, Sam 441
Giannini, A.P. 444
Giffen, James 615
Gilmer, John C. 258-60
Gilsyd Corp. of Liechtenstein 522
Gimbel family 431
Giordano, Anthony 517
Girard Bank and Trust 127
Girard, Stephen 127
Giustiniani family 99, 314
Globus (see Kintex)
Glorious Revolution of 1688, 420
Gnoedinger, Walter 296
Gnostics 404, 407-08
Goebbels, Joseph 6, 368, 374
Golden Crescent 63, 292-93, 298-301, 308, 368, 377, 385, 390, 581
Golden Loop 196

Golden Temple of Amritsar 384
Golden Triangle 9, 29, 36-37, 63, 68,
    88-89, 147-48, 151, 153-54, 160,
    182, 184, 187-88, 192-93, 195, 205,
    208, 227, 229, 232, 235-36, 300,
    368, 382, 290, 464-65, 484, 581,
    653, 655-58, 662
Goldman, Robert 607
Goldman Sachs 100, 107, 340
Goldstein, Arthur "Bootsy" 612
Gorbachov, Mikhail 604, 615-18, 648
Gordon, Walter Lockhart, 242, 251-52,
    258-59
Gottlieb, Dr. Sidney 648
Govern, Robert 84-85
Graham, Robert 349
Graiver, David 20, 107, 468
Grancolombiano Group 314, 325, 359,
    407
Grand Mufti of Jerusalem 372
Grant, Gen. Ulysses S. 510
Gray, C. Boyden 621, 666
Great American Bank 82-85
Great Atlantic and Pacific Tea Co. 494
Great Britain China Committee 241
Green, Charles Fiddian 224-25
Green Gangs 239, 416
Green Party (Germany) 394-95, 408
Green, Timothy 194
Greenbaum, Greenbaum, Rowe and
    Smith 88
Gregory, Thomas W. 598, 600
Grey, Albert 264, 268
Grey Wolves 384, 386
Griffith, Sanford 618
Gross, Nelson 656
Groundswell 644
GRU (Soviet military intelligence)
    615, 642
Grupo Latino 355
Gulf and Western 339, 347, 349
Guida, Richard 29
Gunnarsson, Victor 632-33
Guzmán, Abimael 394, 402
Gyllenhammer, Per 349
Gysi, Gregor 614; Gysi, Klaus 614

Hafstrom, Jonas 632
Haganah, 434, 467, 478, 505-07, 513;
    Americans for Haganah 468
Hageman, Max 459
Hagen, Norman 172-74
Haig, Field Marshal Douglas 426
Hakim, Albert 621

Hall, John J. 588
Hambro, Sir Charles 175, 269; Hambro,
    Jocelyn 98; Hambro, Richard 175;
    Hambro's Bank 98, 108, 175-76
Hamilton, Alexander 126
Hammer, Armand 313, 617, 634
Hammerman, Stephen 74
Hans brothers 388
Hapsburg family 99, 461
Harder, F. William 171, 174
Hardinge, Viscount 521
Hare Krishna 650
Harkness, Richard 657
Harlech, Lord (David Ormsby-Gore)
    450, 639
Harmon, Willis 536, 549-50
Harrison, Laurence Victor 16
Hart, Sir Robert 128
Hartford Convention 74
Hartford, Huntington 494
Harvard University 128, 200, 445, 447,
    542, 561
Hasan, Hehir 383
Hasenfus, Eugene 14
Hashishins (see Assassins)
Haushofer, Karl 268-69
Hawkins, Sen. Paula 654
Hayden, Stone and Co. 443
Hazel Park Racing Assn. 517
Hearst, Patty 403
Hecht, Ben 462; Perfidy 462
Hefner, Hugh 567
Heikal, Mohammed 226
Helms, Jack 490
Helms, Richard 648
Hennessey, Michael 637
Heritage Canada 437
Heritage Foundation 71, 575
Hernández Cartaya, Guillermo 345-47,
    351-53, 363
Herrera, Col. Eduardo 23
Hertzberg, Rabbi Arthur 651
Hesburgh, Fr. Theodore 349
Hess, Rudolf 268
Hesselbach, Walter 492
Hezbollah (Party of God) 300
High Times 7, 313, 320, 359-60, 422,
    561, 567
Hightower, Robert 637
Hill Samuel 252-53
Hirsch, Louis 434
Hirsch, Paul 545
Histadrut Campaign of Canada 436,
    456, 469

Hitchcock, Ethan A. 587
Hitchcock, William ("Billy") Mellon 551-52
Hitler, Adolf 6, 268, 270-71, 367-69, 372-73, 389, 394-96, 404, 406, 408, 421, 452, 476, 547, 624; *Mein Kampf* 268
Hitler-Stalin Pact 369-70, 373, 395
Ho, Stanley 191, 220-221, 247
Hoag, George Grant 552
Hod Hahanit (Spearhead, Ltd.) 23-25
Hoffa, Jimmy 448-49, 486-91, 499
Hoffman, Albert 540
Hoffman, Howard 638
Hogan, Robert 24
Hogg, Fred 173-74
Holland, William 242, 246-47, 249
Hollman, Daniel 524
Holloman, David 449
Holmér, Hans 632
Ho Long, Gen. 240, 664
Home State Savings Bank 81-82, 86
Honecker, Erich 26, 613-14
Hongkong and Shanghai Banking Corp. (HongShang) xii, 64-65, 92-94, 103-04, 114, 123, 127, 131-32, 147-49, 158, 162-63, 172, 182-83, 185, 188-89, 191-99, 205-07, 209, 215, 217, 231, 234, 237, 241, 247-48, 253-54, 256, 260, 262, 264, 271-72, 274, 313, 318, 333, 336, 339-40, 432, 454, 472, 522-23
Hong Kong Jockey Club 220-21
Hong Kong Land Co., Ltd. 219
Hong Kong Seamen's Union 183, 222
Hong Kong Stock Exchange 209
Hoover, J. Edgar 418-19, 455, 457, 460, 466, 475, 480, 484, 504, 506, 586-87, 593-95, 597, 599, 624
Hordes, Jess 606
Horn, Otto 635
Horton, Buster 13
Hospice, Inc. 564
Hougan, Jim 488
House Appropriations Committee 590; House Banking Committee 173; House Foreign Affairs Committee 132; House Judiciary Committee on Civil and Constitutional Rights 585; House Select Committee on Assassinations 490; House Select Committee on Crime 519-20; House Select Committee on Narcotics Abuse and Control 47, 156, 205, 228, 655; House Un-American Activities Committee (Velde Commission) 618
House, Colonel 466
Ho Yin 221
Hoyos, Carlos Mauro x
Hua Guofeng 233
Huber, Roland 296
Hudson's Bay Company 253-54, 256, 258, 273, 525, 431-32, 444, 518
Hughes, Howard 501
Humanist Society 651
Humphrey, Hubert H. 608, 643; Humphrey, Hubert "Skip" 645; Hubert Humphrey Institute 196
Hundley, William 449, 496, 498-99
Hunt, E. Howard 499
Hunter Savings Assn. 85-86
Huseyn, Cil 383
Hustler 422
Hutchins, Robert M. 137-38, 417, 540-41, 552-53
Hutchinson Whampoa Trading Co. 523
Hutien-Fa 188; Hutien-Hsiang 188
Huxley, Aldous 536-44, 546, 548, 551-52; *Brave New World* 536, 538; *The Doors of Perception* 541; Huxley, Julian 538; Huxley, Thomas H. 270, 537

Ianniello, Lynne 606
Ideal Films, Ltd. 444
Idema 352
IFA, Inc. 88
IG Farben 373
Illinois Marijuana Initiative 55
Immobiliare Roma 342
Imperial Chemical Industries 241
Imperial Chinese Customs Service 128
Inchcape and Co. 199, 273; Inchcape family 254, 270, 272-73, 431; Inchcape, Lord 131-32, 199, 273, 432
Independent Commission Against Corruption (Hong Kong) (ICAC) 210, 221
Indian Council of South America (CISA) 399
Institute for Pacific Relations 128, 239-44, 246-47, 251-52, 258-59
Institute for Policy Studies (IPS) 422, 540, 547, 622
Institute for Social Research of the University of Michigan 545

Institute on Drugs, Crime and Justice (Great Britain) 564
Istituto per le Opere Religiose 342
Inter-Alpha 104-05
Inter-American Center of the Institute for Human Relations 340
Interbanca Spa 105
Intercontinental Corporation 484
Interkommers 379
International Affairs 243
International Airport Hotel Distributing, Inc. 442, 566, 611
International Association of the Friends of the Arab World 373
International Brotherhood of Teamsters (IBT) 448, 490
International Center for Holocaust Studies 606
International Commerce 472
International House/World Trade Center 471
International Ladies Garment Workers Union (ILGWU) 619
International Law Association (ILA) 457-58
International Monetary Fund (IMF) 6, 9, 38, 49, 69-70, 90, 92, 97, 109, 162, 213, 244, 257, 306-08, 313-17, 319-22, 398, 408, 656; *World Economic Outlook* 69
International Shipping and Investment Co. 233
International Settlements of Shanghai 431
International Student Union 375
International Trade Mart 453, 469-71, 480
International Trust Corp. (Itco) 120
International United Front (Hong Kong) 222
Interpol 653
Intertel (International Intelligence, Inc.) xii, 176, 449, 489, 493, 496-501, 523-24, 566; International Investigators, Inc. of Indianapolis, Indiana 488, 490
Intrabank 360, 362, 374-75
Inverforth, Lord 443-44
Inversiones Fénix 346, 353
Investors Overseas Service (IOS) 71, 96, 109, 138, 168, 341, 417, 465, 492, 497, 500, 551-53, 609-10, 621, 639
Ipekci, Abdi 384

Iran-Contra 11-12, 14, 18, 22, 24, 612, 619, 630
Irgun 458
Irish Republican Army 76, 440
Irving Trust 336
Isaac, Rael Jean 622
Isherwood, Christopher 539
Isis (also Isis Cult, Isis-Urania Temple of Hermetic Students of the Golden Dawn) 263-64, 268, 380, 536-37, 539, 543, 545-46
Israel-American Leasing of Tel Aviv 522
Israel Discount Bank 107, 273
Israel, Joachim 632
Israel Technion Society 485; Sociedad Techníon de México 485
Israeli Continental Co. 436, 456
Israeli Maritime League 436, 457
Israeli Military Industry 25
Isrop SA of Luxembourg 522
Italo-American Hotel Corp. 458

Jackman, Henry R. 261
Jacobs, Jeremy 520-22, 524
Jacobs, Max 164, 170, 175, 449, 498, 508, 516, 518-19, 521-24
Jacobsen, "Hank" 509
Jacobson, Kenneth 607, 616
James I, King of Scotland 267
Janer, Father, S.J. 340
Japhet Co. 464; Japhet, Ernst Israel 202, 273, 463-64; Japhet family 127, 273;
Jardine family 127; Jardine Matheson 114, 119-21, 125, 128, 182, 199, 218-19, 223, 225, 236-37, 240, 243, 254, 256, 271, 273, 390, 425, 431, 472
Jarecki, Dr. Henry 199-200, 258
Jarquin, Antonio 621
Javits, Jacob 440, 565
Jay, K.C. 221
Jefferson Insurance Co. 107-108
Jelke, Mickey 618
Jenninger, Philipp 616
Jerusalem Foundation 114, 424, 437
Jerusalem Post 514
Jewish Agency 462, 464
Jewish Colonization Assn. 424, 433, 461
Jewish Defense League (JDL) 624-28, 640

Jewish Defense Organization (JDO)
626, 628
Jewish Federation 607
Jewish Labor Committee 619
Jewish War Veterans 467, 504
Jewish Welfare Fund 514
Jibril, Ahmed 17
Jiménez, Gaspar 353
Jiménez Gómez, Carlos 326
Jiménez Nevia, Danilo 341
Joftas, Saul I. 641
John Paul II, Pope 19, 63, 95-96, 368,
378, 389, 640, 646-47
Johnson, Jack 594
Johnson, Lyndon Baines 546
Johnson Matthey 200
Joint Distribution Committee 434, 522
Jones, Andrieus Aristieus 601
Jones, Rev. Jim 408, 649
Joseph, Burton M. 567, 608, 610, 617,
639, 643
J. Vontobel and Co. 552

Kach Party 640
Kachin Independence Army 658
Kahane, Rabbi Meir 624, 640
Kahn, Otto 274
Kaiser Foundation 560, 564
Kam-Issacharoff, Laura 646
Kampelman, Max 607-08, 643
Kan Kuam Tsing Co. 197
Kan, Y.K. 108
Kantor, Lucille 606
Kao, C.H. 221
Kastner, Dr. Rudolph 462
Kattan Kasin, Isaac 84
Katz, Howard 642
Katzenberg, Jacob 272, 430-31, 612-13
Kayatt, Ed 650
Keeny, John 82
Keith, Sir Kenneth 253, 435
Kelly, Tom 638
Kemp, Elaine 84
Keng Biao 222
Kennedy, Sen. Edward 140, 441-42,
446, 450, 563, 565-66; Kennedy
family 115, 139, 440; Kennedy In-
stitute for the Study of Human
Reproduction and Bioethics,
Georgetown University 563, 565;
Kennedy, John Fitzgerald 159,
255, 368, 418, 441-42, 446-48, 450-
55, 458, 469-70, 474-77, 480, 482,
484, 486-87, 489-91, 546-47, 623,

652 Why England Slept 447; Kennedy, Joseph, Jr. 447; Kennedy,
Joseph, Sr. 134, 137, 255, 441-42,
444-47, 450, 539; Kennedy, Kathleen 446, 450; Kennedy, P.J. 442-
43; Kennedy, Robert F. 442, 446-
48, 450-51, 476, 486-88, 495, 498-
99, 501, 523-24; Kennedy, Rose
451
Kennedy, Michael 567
Kennedy, Thomas 524
Kenning, George 24
Kent, Duke of 378, 382
Kesey, Ken 543-44; One Flew Over the
Cuckoo's Nest 543
Kesten, Ann 645
Keswick, David 271; Keswick family
114-15, 199, 254, 270, 274, 425,
431; Keswick, Henry Neville Lindley 219, 254, 271-72; Keswick, J.J.
271; Keswick, Sir John Henry 199,
236-37, 239-40, 243-46, 248-
49, 270-71; Keswick, William J.
David 271; Keswick, Sir William
Johnston 243-44, 248, 254-55, 272-
73, 431-32; Keswick, William P.
271
Keynes, John Maynard 98, 244, 314
KGB xi-xiii, 17, 63, 71, 140, 221, 291,
297-300, 346, 360, 375, 385, 418,
454, 477, 481, 615-16, 631-34, 636,
642, 644; Islamic Division 368
Khashoggi, Adnan 621
Kheel, Theodore 107
Khomeini, Ayatollah Ruhollah 291-93,
295-96, 300-301, 387-88, 390
Khieu Samphon 397
Khun Sa (a.k.a. Chiang Chi Fu) 227,
658-59, 662
Kimble, Jules Rocco 490
King, Dennis 650-51
King, MacKenzie 135
King, Martin Luther, Jr. 476, 490, 623
Kintex (Globus) 19, 379-83, 385-86
Kipling, Rudyard 133, 269-70
Kirby, William Fosgate 601
Kirkpatrick, Jeane 622
Kissinger Associates 8-9, 92, 107-109,
234, 318-19; Kissinger, Henry A.
xii, 3-4, 7-12, 37, 42, 92, 100, 105-
07, 140, 216, 228, 234, 308, 313,
315, 318-21, 340, 349, 388, 505,
546, 610, 639, 655-57, 666
Kiszynski, George 16

Kiwanis Club 231
Klehr, Harvey 621
Klein, Dennis B. 606
Julius Klein Associates 478; Klein,
    Gen. Julius 418, 466-68, 502-05,
    507.
Klein, Dr. Nathan 561-62
Klein, Col. Yair 23-26
Kleinwort Benson 198-99, 254
Klenicki, Rabbi Leon 606, 630
Klinghoffer, Leon 17
Klutznick, Phillip 468, 607, 641
Knights of Malta 260, 264, 348-49
Knights Templar 265
Koch, Edward I. 565
Koffler, Murray 437, 521
Ko Lao Hui, ("Elder Brothers Society")
    240
Koler, William 496
Komm, Asya 650
Koor Co. 296
Korean War 191, 220-21, 247
Korshak, Sidney 612
Koskoff, David E. 446, 451
Kowloon Chamber of Commerce 211
Kozin, Michael 638
Krastil, Joe 644
Krogh, Egil 656
Krohn, Juan Fernandez 389-90
Kuhn family 424
Kuhn, Loeb 106-07, 135, 274, 444, 504
Kui Kwing Company 219
Ku Klux Klan 422, 490, 510-11, 622-
    26
Kuntsler, William 422
Kunz, Hans Albert 297, 388
Kuomintang 245
Kupperman, Robert 639
Kurth, Dick 45, 49-50; Kurth, Judith
    45, 49-50
Kuwait International Investment Co.
    354
Kwitny, Jonathan 87-89

La Cosa Nostra 449
Laing, Dr. R.D. 544
Laird, Melvin 656
Lake Resources 18, 621
Lambert family 100; Lambert, Jean
    434; Lambert, Phyllis 437; Lam-
    bert, Pierre 98
Langer, Howard J. 606
Langhans, Rainer 395
Lansky, Meyer xii, 5-7, 12, 21, 71, 73,

85-87, 107, 115, 134, 139, 168,
    176, 180, 339, 416-18, 429-31, 438,
    442, 449, 463-65, 493-95, 497, 499-
    500, 503-04, 506-07, 513, 518, 551,
    553, 566, 604, 607, 609-12
Lara Bonilla, Rodrigo ix, 325-27, 358,
    393
LaRouche, Lyndon H., Jr. 3-10, 12-14,
    16, 26, 41, 61-62, 73-74, 78, 80-81,
    86-87, 356-57, 397-98, 573, 575,
    604, 613, 627, 631-33, 638, 643-44,
    649-51; "The Influence of Gnostic,
    Sufi and 'Nativist' Cults in Recruit-
    ing and Controlling Terrorist and
    Separatist Insurgencies" 397-98
Laski, Harold 447
Laszlo, Ervin 549
Latourette, Dr. Kenneth 125-26
Law Enforcement Assistance Adminis-
    tration (LEAA) 89, 566
Lawford, Peter 566
Lawrence, David Herbert (D.H.) 538;
    Lady Chatterley's Lover 538
Lawrence, Ken 644
Lazard Frères 98-99, 108, 274, 445-46,
    448
League for Industrial Democracy 422,
    547
League of Armed Neutrality 118
League of Nations 131, 134, 199, 273,
    444; Opium Committee 130, 132
Learmouth, Livingstone 516
Leary, Timothy 200, 542, 544, 551,
    564; The Psychedelic Experience
    542
Ledbetter, Andrew 86
Lefcourt, Gerald 567
Lefèbvre, Archbishop Marcel 389
Legión Cubana 16
Lehder Rivas, Carlos 63, 325, 328, 351,
    359-61, 363, 393, 406-08, 609
Lehman Brothers 99, 106, 125
Lenin, Vladimir 477
Lernoux, Penny 345-46, 353; In Banks
    We Trust 345
Letheby and Christopher, Ltd. 516-21
Levant Company xi
Levi, Edward 520
Levinson, Burton S. 605, 608
Levitas, Dan 644-45
Levy, David 640
Levy, Mordechai 626-28, 647
Lewin, Dr. Kurt 547
Lewis, Gerald E. 83, 85

Lewis, Joseph 638
Liberal Party (Canada) 258, 435, 440;
    Liberal Party (Colombia) 327
Lieberman, Michael 638, 644
Life 243, 463
Lifton, Robert J. 649
Liga 23 de Septiembre 485
Likud Party 639-40
Lin, Dr. Paul 242, 258
Lincoln, Abraham 129, 511
Lindley, Frederick 272
Lindner, Carl 85, 95, 106, 339
Lindquist, Hans 632
Linowitz, Sol 163, 317-19, 340, 349
Linsey, Joseph 442, 566
Lin Tse-hsu 120-22
Lionel Corp. 459, 482-84
Lipkin, Paul 612
Lippmann, Walter 597
Litex Bank 380-81
Liu Shaoqi 234
Liu Wen 653
Li Xiannian 667
Lloyd, A.D.F. 274
Lloyds of London 252, 256, 435
Lobenthal, Richard 623
Loche, Paul 626
Lodge family 127
Loeb, Ann 434
Loeb, Rhoades 106, 420, 424
Lombard Odier Bank of Geneva 161,
    372
Londoño, Maximiliano 403; Londoño,
    Patricia Paredes de 403-05
London School of Economics 447, 450
López Michelsen, Alfonso 68, 325-27,
    337, 352, 359, 380, 404, 407
López Portillo, José 573, 478
Loser, Sergei 633
Lovestone, Jay 619
Lowe, David 620
Lowenthal, Max 591, 593, 595
Loyola University of New Orleans
    340
Lucas, Paul 166, 169
Lucayan Beach Hotel and Casino
    Corp. 497
Luce, Henry 243
Luciano, Charles "Lucky" 418, 429,
    431, 482-83
Lucis Trust (formerly Lucifer Trust)
    651
Ludlum, Robert 342; *The Matarese
    Circle* 342

Lusinchi, Jaime 309, 345, 357
Luzzatto, Bruno 105; Luzzatto, Daniele
    105; Luzzatto family 98
Lytton, Edward 269

MI-6 253
M-19 (April 19th Movment) 63, 68,
    329, 361, 392, 405-407
MacAleese, Peter 23
Macao Chamber of Commerce 221
MacDonald, Lovatt 297
Macharski, Cardinal Franciszek 647
Macheca, Joseph 509-12
Mackay, J.W. 273-74
Mackay, Katherine 273
Mackay-Tallack, Sir Hugh 273, 274
Macmillan Bloedel 255, 450
Macmillan family 446
Macmillan, Harold 255, 450
Madole, Robert 618
Mafia (see also La Cosa Nostra) 114,
    335, 428, 429, 498, 509-11, 515
Magna Development Co. 221
Malnick, Alvin 463
Malthus, Thomas 114, 307
Malvinas War 314
Mamarella, Richard 87-89
Manley, Michael 318, 320
Mann Act 591-96, 599
Mann, Thomas 539
Manson, Charles 650
Mantello, Georgio 452, 459, 475
Mao Zedong 149, 239-41, 259, 389,
    396, 655, 664
Marathon Oil Company 512
March, Juan 342
Marcinkus, Bishop Paul C. 342
Marden, John 209
Mariátegui, José Carlos 396
Marine Midland Bank 64-65, 163, 333,
    336, 340, 522-23
Marino Ospina, Iván 407
Maritime Fruit Co. 513
Márquez, José Vicente 405
Marsh, Laurie 435
Marshall Plan 105, 471
Martella, Ilario 379, 386
Martin, Jack 481
Martin, Leroy 637
Martínez de Hoz, José 349
Martinez, Robert 28-29
Mary Carter Paint Co. xii, 425, 494-
    96, 551
MAS (Death to Kidnapers) 394

Mason, Raymond 350
Massachusetts Institute of Technology
    (MIT) 542
Matheson, Donald 273; Matheson fam-
    ily 114, 125, 127, 199, 271, 273;
    Matheson, Hugh 271; Matheson,
    James Sutherland 271, 273
Matoff, Paul 426
Matrenga, Charles 509, 511-12
Matta Ballesteros, Juan Ramón 15-16
Mattei, Enrico 483
Mazzini, Giuseppe 114, 136, 382, 509-
    11
Mazzone, Judge A. David 78
McAdoo, William Gibbs 598
McBeth, John 659
McCarran Committee 242, 246
McCarthy, Sen. Joseph 459, 602
McCleary, Donald 439
McClellan Committee 442, 448, 487
McCrary, Tex 495
McFadyean, Sir Andrew 242, 244
McFarlane, Robert 17, 621
McGlothlin, W.H. 541
McIntyre, Rev. Carl 480
McKeon, Thomas J. 449, 499
McLaney, "Big Mike" 495
McLaughlin, W.E. 260
McNamara, Robert Strange 546
Mead, George 82, 86
Mead, Margaret 542, 549
Medellín Cartel 7, 17, 20-21, 23, 25,
    41-42, 609
Medina Vizcaíno, Julio 405
Meese, Edwin 62, 78, 80
Mellon, Andrew 551
Méndez, Carlos 356; Méndez, Lucía
    356
Meneses, Alvaro 322, 341
Menini, Luigi 342
Mercedes-Benz 575
Mercer, William C. 78
Merck und Finck 98
Mercury Securities 108
Merrill Lynch xii, 41, 74, 79, 82, 100
Merry Pranksters 543
Messick, Hank 449, 465, 493
Metaphysical Society 270
Metropolitan Bank (Florida) 85
Metzenbaum, Howard 607
Meyer, André 100, 108, 420, 445, 447
Meyjes, Robert Christopher Portomas
    102-103
Metro Goldwyn Mayer (MGM) 539

Michelsen Uribe, Jaime 325, 359, 363,
    407
Michener, Roland 262
Middle East 388
Middleman, Mark 638
Midland Bank 93, 200, 205, 234, 256
Midwest Air Charter, Inc. 171-74, 508-
    09
Milken, Michael 610
Mill, James 114; Mill, John Stuart 114
Miller, Clifford G. 174
Miller, G. William 313
Miller, Richard 619
Milliyet 384
Mills, Stanley 449, 524
Milner, Alfred Lord 133, 236, 238, 264,
    267, 272, 457
Milton Group 439
Minnesota Farmer Labor Party 643
Minorco 101
Mintz, Donald R. 606
Minutemen 623
Mitchell, Sen. John H. 588
Mivtza B.M. 296
MK-Ultra xii, 540, 542, 562-63, 648
Mocatta and Goldsmid 199-200, 420
Mocatta Metals 199, 258, 320
Mocca Coffee 179-80
Mohler, Armin 372; The Conservative
    Revolution in Germany (1918-
    1933) 372
Mondale, Walter 5, 643
Monnet et Cie. 444; Monnet, Jean 444
Monroe Doctrine 321
Montagu, Samuel 200, 271
Montefiore Club 436; Montefiore fam-
    ily 200, 420, 428, 433, 522; Mon-
    tefiore, Lord Harold Sebag 424;
    Montefiore, William Sebag 424;
    Moses Montefiore Jewish Coloniza-
    tion Committee 424
Montoneros 95, 107
Montor, Henry 505
Mont Pelerin Society 322, 346, 348,
    355
Moon, Rev. Sun Myung 408
Moore, George S. 75, 348
Moore, Bishop Paul 649
Morales Bermúdez, Gen. Francisco
    320-21
Morgan Bank 128, 272
Morgan Grenfell 354
Morgan Guaranty Trust 128
Morgan, House of 127

Morgan, J. Bartlett 432
Morgenthau, Robert 292
Moro, Aldo 161
Morris, Robert 177
Mosley, Sir Oswald 538
Mosquera, Christian 352; Mosquera, Jaime 352
Mossad 12, 20-21, 24, 96, 200, 456-57, 460, 462, 464, 466-68, 485, 498
Mott, Stewart 567
Moulin, Jean 376
Moyne, Lord 458
Mulack, Peter 381
Mullen, Francis 584
Mullin, Edward M. 499
Murphy, Michael 549
Muslim Brotherhood 373, 478
Mussolini, Benito 421, 428, 453, 459, 482
Mustafa, Kisakis 383
Mystics Art World, Inc. 551

Nabisco Corp. 643
Nachman, Michael 606
Nagy, Ferenc 421, 452, 459, 475-76, 484
Napoleon I 587
Narcotráfico, SA 4, 72-73, 355-56, 358, 362
Narodny Bank 346, 352, 362
Narodnyi Trodovoy Soyuz (National Alliance of Solidarists) 477
Narong Kittikachorn 188
Nassel de Lehder, Jemel 351
Nasser, Jamel Abdul 215, 226-27
National Aeronautics and Space Administration (NASA) 450
National Anti-Drug Coalition (NADC) 5, 7, 73, 404
National Association for the Advancement of Colored People (NAACP) 625
National Association of Financial Institutions 359
National Bank of South Florida 352
National Basketball Assn. 520
National Bipartisan Commission on Central America 318, 321
National Broadcasting Corp. (NBC) 86, 489, 491, 627, 633
National Cash Register 348
National Coffee Growers Federation 324

National Committee on the Treatment of Intractable Pain (NCTIP) 564
National Conference of Israeli and Jewish Rehabilitation 434
National Council of Churches 479
National Drug Control Strategy 28-29
National Endowment for Democracy 11-12, 619-20
National Guard 82
National Institute on Drug Abuse 561-62, 567
National Jewish Centers and Youth Programs 522
National Jewish People's Relief Committee 433
National Latin Civic Movement 393-94, 408
National Law Journal 78
National Lawyers Guild 644
National Narcotics Intelligence Consumers Committee (NNICC) 46-47, 334; Narcotics Intelligence Estimate 299, 301
National Organization for the Reform of Marijuana Laws (NORML) 46-48, 50, 317, 319, 360, 560-63, 566-67, 651
National Renaissance Party (NRP) 618-19
National Security Agency (NSA) 418-19
National Security Council 5, 12, 15, 18
National Security Decision Directive 3 15, 621
National Training Labs 547
National Westminister Bank 162, 256, 260
Nationalist Bank of China 246
NATO (North Atlantic Treaty Organization) 108, 390-91, 451, 460, 478
Navasky, Victor 448; Kennedy Justice 448
Nazi Party (Nazis) 367-69, 372, 382, 384-85, 388, 398, 400-401, 454, 480, 506, 577, 581, 616, 618, 624, 626, 633, 635-36, 647;
Nelson, Jack 622
Neue Zürcher Zeitung 196, 324
Newar, Sherwin 606
Newbigging, David 128
New European Order 375
Ne Win 660
Newman, Peter C. 436, 613; The Bronfman Dynasty 436, 613

New Solidarity 14
Newsweek 345
New York Council on Foreign Relations xi, 308, 487; *1980s Project* 308; *Foreign Affairs* 487
New York Diamond Dealers Club 201-02
New York State Substance Abuse Service 568
New York Times 108, 293, 329-30, 361, 508
Niagara Frontier Services 523
Niagara Share Corp. 523
Nicholson, John Robertson 259
Nietzsche, Friedrich 396
Nitti, Frank 137
Nixon, Richard M. 8, 95, 108, 140, 155, 228, 492, 514, 519-20, 524, 655-57, 666
Noranda Mines 202-03, 258
Noriega, Gen. Manuel Antonio 22-23, 25, 41
Norman Bethune Institute 243, 259
North, Lt. Col. Oliver 5, 12-18, 22, 620-21
Norwest Bank 45, 49-50
Norwick, Allen 81-82, 86
Notre Dame University 349
Novel, Gordon 491
Nugan Hand Bank 611
Núñez, Carlos 84
Nuremberg Tribunal 580
Nutt, Levi 431

OAS (see Secret Army Organization)
Oasis 372
Obront, Willy 438-39, 613
Occidental Petroleum 617, 634
Ochoa, Jorge 326, 393
O'Connell, John 499
October League 644
Odeh, Alex 628
ODESSA 372
Official Secrets Act 251
Office of Drug Abuse Policy 562
Office of Naval Intelligence 370, 374, 481
Office of Strategic Services (OSS) 246, 351, 373, 418, 453, 455, 458, 471, 482, 540, 542
Office of War Information 246
Ogden Corp. 174
Ogilvy and Mather 471
Ogilvy, David 470-71

Old Orthodox Catholic Church of North America 479, 481
Old Tie Veterans Association 240
Oltro family 372
Operación Cerberus 292, 390
Operation Condor 308
Operation Graylord 586
Operation Greenback 83-84
Operation Groper 84
Operation Polar Cap 20
Operation Rescue 645
Operation Tradewinds 496-97
Operation Wipeout 54
Opium Wars 8, 114, 116, 118, 122-23, 140, 244, 263, 266-67, 270-71, 306, 368, 378, 382, 539
Oppenheimer, Sir Ernest 201; Oppenheimer family 92, 94, 97, 100-102, 108, 322, 362, 420; Oppenheimer, Sir Harry 101, 200, 202
Order of St. John of Jerusalem (Most Venerable Military and Hospitaller) 114, 116, 137, 175-76, 250, 258-61, 264-65, 272, 424, 434, 436, 447, 457, 464, 510, 563-64, 567
Order of St. Lazarus 261
Ordine Nero 388
Ordine Nuovo 391
O'Reilly, Kenneth 624; *Racial Matters* 624
Organización Diego Cisneros (ODC) 345, 347-48, 355
Organization of American States (OAS) Special Task Force on Narcotics 309
Organization of Armed Struggle (Carlos network) 375
Organized Crime Strike Force 495, 498-99
Ormsby-Gore, David (see Harlech, Lord)
Orozco, Eduardo 335-37, 363
Orsini family 98
Ortolani, Umberto 96, 341
Orwell, George 538; *1984* 538; *Animal Farm* 538
Osborne, Albert 480, 484
Osiris 263
Osmond, Dr. Humphrey 540-44 *Schizophrenia: A New Approach* 540
Ostiguy, J.P.W. 260
Oswald, Lee Harvey 474-75, 481-82, 490, 623; Oswald, "Leon" 474, 481
Our Town 650

Overseas Chinese Industrial Construction Co. 233
Overseas Chinese Investment Corp. (OCIC) 233
Oxford University 133, 238, 268, 538, 619
Oyler, Ralph 431

Pacific A Corp. 523
Pacifica Foundation 542
Page, Walter Hines 446
Pagliai, Bruno 485
Pagliai, Pier Luigi 388
Paine, Thomas 264
Palermo, Judge Carlo 296-97, 377, 383-84
Palestine Liberation Front 17
Palestine Liberation Organization (PLO) 296, 628
Palevsky, Max 567
Pallavicini family 459
Palme, Olof 629-33
Palmer, Martin 651
Palmerston, Lord 120, 122-24, 263, 267, 269, 539
Palmieri-Billig, Lisa 607
Pan American World Airways 22, 349; Pan Am Flight 103 18-19
Pang Hock-lim 231
Pankin, Boris 633
Panorama 400
Pao San and Co. 198
Pao, Sir Y.K. 103, 215-17, 233, 313, 349
Paradise Enterprise, Inc. 496
Paramount Pictures 347
Parejo González, Enrique 329-30
Parkman family 127
Parodi, Senator 402
Parravicini Bank, Ltd. 552; Parravicini, Johann F. 552
Parry, Laurence 224-25
Parvin Foundation 138, 553
Paterno, Joseph 89
Patiwana, Rajan 294
Paytuvi, Lionel 84
Paz Oil Co. 465, 507-08, 513
Peace Pledge Union 546-47
Pease, Aline 273; Pease family 274; Pease, Richard T. 273
Peccei, Aurelio 104, 388
Peer, Zwy 465
Pehme, Kalev 650

Peloquin, Robert 449, 495-96, 498, 523-24
Peninsular and Orient Steam Navigation Co. (P&O) 114, 125, 131-32, 182, 199, 237, 254, 272-73, 431
Penn Central Railroad 85
People's Temple 408
Pepper, John 470
Pepsi-Cola 348, 350, 356-58
Perceval, Spencer 271
Percóvich, Luis 401
Pérez Alamo, Duney 353
Pérez, Carlos Andrés 27
Peñez Sandoval, Vincente 85
Perkins family xi, 127, 443; Perkins, Thomas Nelson 127-28
Permindex (Permanent Industrial Expositions) 342, 419, 421, 453-60, 463, 466, 468-71, 473-78, 482-85, 492-93, 497-500, 508-09
Perpich, Gov. Rudy 645
Peruvian Anti-Drug Coalition 72
Peterson, Henry 449, 496, 498, 524
Peterson, Rudolph 103, 105
Petrycki, John 87
Phelps family 346; Phelps, Patricia 348
Phibro 94, 100-102, 341
Philby, Harold "Kim" 370, 373, 375, 418; Philby, St. John 373
Philip, Prince of England 651
Philip the Fair 265
Phillips and Vineberg (Phillips, Vineberg, Bloomfield and Goodman) 435-36, 455
Phillips, Lazarus 256, 435-36, 456
Phillips, Capt. Mark 521
Phillips, Neil 256
Pick, Felice 343; Pick, Dr. Franz 342-43 Pick's Currency Yearbook 342
Pike, Albert 511
Pindling, Lynden O. 496
Pinochet, Gen. Augusto 380-81
Pinto, Augusto Matheus, Esq. 357
Pitrovanov, Gen. Yevgeni Petrovich 615
Pitt, William (the Younger) 117
Playboy Foundation (Playboy Enterprises, Inc.) 567; Playboy 347, 422
Plummer, Charles 637
Poe, Edgar Allan 152
Polisario (National Union of Popular Forces of Morocco) 373
Polizzi, Michael B. 517

Pollard, Jonathan Jay 12, 639, 641-43
Pol Pot 376, 397
Ponto, Jürgen 575
Paul VI, Pope 307; *Populorum Pro-*
    gressio 307
Popper, Sir Karl 270
Popular Front for the Liberation of
    Palestine—General Command 17,
    375-76
Porter, Rep. Stephen 132
Posner, Victor 339, 612
Potter, Robert 167
Prairie Fire 644
President's Commission on Mental
    Health 561
President's Commission on Organized
    Crime "The Cash Connection: Or-
    ganized Crime, Financial Institu-
    tions, and Money Laundering" 64,
    67, 77, 79, 206, 320, 331-32, 334-
    35
President's Foreign Intelligence Advi-
    sory Board (PFIAB) 10
Price, Richard 549
Prince, Lt. Col. Eugene 618
Princeton University Radio Research
    Project 545
Privy Council 250, 252, 261, 424
Process Church of the Final Judgment
    650
Production Credit Assn. (PCA) 57
Professional Sports Publications, Inc.
    516
Progressive Liberal Party (Cuba) 495-
    96
Prohibition (Volstead Act) 94, 115,
    134, 135-39, 180, 236, 250, 253,
    255-56, 273, 424, 427-28, 430, 432-
    33, 444, 501, 521, 551, 612; Eigh-
    teenth Amendment 136, 461
Project Democracy 21, 619
Propaganda-2 99, 104, 297, 382, 385,
    387-88
Prudential Life Insurance 176
Pugwash Conferences 90
Purcell, Victor 189; *The Chinese in
    Malaya* 189
Pure Drug Co. 258, 425, 431, 518
Purple Gang 502-03, 507-08, 519, 609

Qaddafi, Muammar 381, 584
Quindío Libre 394
Quintero, Rafael (see Caro Quintero,
    Rafael)

Raab, Maxwell 611
Ra'anan, Uri 639, 641, 643
Rabinowitz, Boudin and Standard 551
Radziwill family 421, 447; Radziwill,
    Prince Stanislaus 446
Raigorodsky, Paul 453, 459, 476-78
Ramat Gan 202
Ramírez Ocampo, Augusto 309
RAND Corp. 541
Rapid American Corp. 96, 339, 610
Rappaport, Bruce 24
Rappaport, Marvin S. 607
Raskin, Marcus 547
Rastafarians 320
Ray, James Earl 490, 623
Raymond, Michael 586
Raymond, Walter 620
Radio Corporation of America (RCA)
    418-19, 456, 487, 491
Reagan, Ronald xii, xiii, 5, 9-10, 62,
    67, 83, 368, 573, 575, 583, 611,
    622; Reagan administration 11,
    15, 21, 23, 26, 55-57, 62, 318, 616,
    619-21, 629
Recanati family 106
Red Brigades 351, 387, 390-91, 485
Red Cross 272
Red Guard 660
Red Orchestra 374
Rees, Dr. John Rawlings 544
Regan, Donald T. xiii, 41, 79, 214
Reich, Seymour D. 605
Reichenberg, Hans 373
Reichmann brothers 617
Reichwald, Harold P. 204
Reidy, James 638
Reinfeld Importers 444; Reinfeld, Jo-
    seph 428; Reinfeld Syndicate 428,
    444
Reinhard, H.R. 196-98
Reliance Corp. 339
Remer, Lt. Gen. Otto-Ernst 375
Rennie, Charles Tatham Ogilvy 223;
    Rennie family 223; Rennie, Gor-
    don 224; Rennie, Sir John 223-24;
    Rennies Consolidated Holdings,
    Ltd. 223-24
Republic National Bank 19, 107, 610-
    11
Republican Party 22, 81, 502, 514
Resorts International xii, 73, 170, 176,
    362, 418, 442, 489, 493, 496-97,
    499-501, 509, 523-24, 551, 559,
    566

Resumen (Venezuela) 345, 350-51, 353
Revenga, José Rafael 348, 357
Revell, Oliver "Buck" 10, 16, 584
R.J. Reynolds Tobacco Co. 666
R.H. Macy's 175-76
Rhodes, Cecil 94, 101, 133, 199, 201, 238, 263-64, 267-69, 272; Rhodes Trust 238, 270, 272
Ribicoff, Sen. Abraham 607
Ricardo, David 114
Richardson, Elliot 524
Richter, Glenn 647
Riis, Jacob 385
Riklis, Meshulam 7, 96, 339, 610, 639
Rio Tinto Zinc 198-99, 236, 254, 270-73, 470
Ritter, Red 494
Riunione Adriatica di Sicurtà 99, 107, 314
Rivet, Paul 374
RKO Studios 444, 539
Roberts, Alton Wayne 622-23
Robertson-Cole Pictures 443
Robertson, Geoffrey 23
Robison, Al 506
Rocco, Mike 442
Rochdale College 259
Rochwarger, Leonard 522
Rockefeller, David xii, 103, 105, 107, 175, 306, 312-13, 318-19, 322, 345, 348-49, 357; Rockefeller family 4, 72, 135, 346, 348; Rockefeller Foundation 135, 241; Rockefeller, John D. I 135; Rockefeller, Nelson 348
Rodríguez Gacha, José Gonzalo 21-25, 41, 393
Rogers, William 9
Roll, Eric Lord of Ipsden 108
Rolling Stones 542, 544
Ronning, Chester 242, 247-49, 258-59
Ronstadt, Peter 637
Roosa, Robert V. 159
Roosevelt, Franklin Delano 98-99, 244, 314, 445-46, 455, 476; Roosevelt, Theodore 321, 587, 589-91, 597
Ropex 20
"Rosa Dei Vente" 387
Rosen, Klauss-Henning 631
Rosen, Sidney 439, 613
Rosenbaum, Dr. Tibor 21, 96, 107, 168, 457, 462-68, 497
Rosenberg, Goran 631-32
Rosenberg, James R. 625

Rosenberg, Nils 632
Rosenstiel, Lewis 504
Rosenthal, Rabbi Morton M. 620, 629-30, 640
Rosenthal, Sol 644
Rosicrucianism 263, 267
Rosing, Michael 55
Rosone, Roberto 381
Ross, Arthur 108
Ross, Brian 633
Ross, Jeffrey A. 606
Ross, William 426
Rothschild, Baron Edmond de 96, 161, 264, 424, 504, 507, 522; Rothschild, Elie de 98; Rothschild, Evelyn de 435, 492; Rothschild family 93, 100, 114, 125, 200-201, 354, 420, 424, 431, 433-34, 443, 465-66, 497, 504-05, 509-10, 522; N.M. Rothschild and Sons 102, 135, 198, 200, 252
Rothstein, Arnold 7, 134, 255, 427-31, 612
Royal Bank of Canada 102, 256-57, 260, 346-47, 408, 435, 499
Royal Bank of Scotland 104
Royal Canadian Mounted Police (RCMP) 438-39, 499, 501, 509
Royal Dutch Shell 237, 297, 349, 387-88, 477
Royal Institute of International Affairs (RIIA) 89, 102, 128, 133, 149, 236-41, 243, 246-49, 251, 254, 259, 263, 268, 272, 447, 537
Royal Liquor Commission (London) 136
Royal Police of Hong Kong 207, 210-11
Rubenstein-Migdal, Elyahim 632
Rubin, Irv 626
Ruby, Jack 490
Rudd, Mark 567
Rudenko, Roman 635
Rudolph, Arthur 636
Runnewell family 127
Ruskin, John 264, 268, 270
Russell and Co. 127-28
Russell, Lord Arthur 240; Russell, Bertrand 90, 123, 267, 270, 450, 546-48; Bertrand Russell Peace Foundation 547; Russell family 272; Russell, Lord John 123, 267, 270;
Russell Sage Foundation 135-36, 428
Russian Orthodox Church 385, 477, 479
Russian Revolution 478

Russo, Perry Raymond 474, 489
Ryan, Allan 635-36

Sachar, Pinchas 25-26
Sacred Literature Trust 651
Sadat, Anwar 368, 478
Safra, Edmund 7, 20, 82; 95, 106, 362, 610-11, 621
Saint Augustine 404
Sakchai Suwannapong (a.k.a. Ma Kuang-ting) 659
Salberg, Melvin I. 606
Salcedo, Félix 327-28
Salerno, Ralph 138; *The Crime Confederation* 138
Salisbury family 446
Salomon Brothers 100-102
Samael Aun Weor (a.k.a. Victor Manuel Gómez) 404-05; *Keys to Mental Dynamics* 404-05
Samper Pizano, Ernesto 313, 359-60, 407
Samuel, Viscount Erwin Herbert 464
Samuels family 200, 464
Samuels, John 107
Samuels, Nathaniel 107
Samuels, Shimon Stanley 632
Sandberg, M.G. 260
Sandinistas 11, 17, 353, 380, 513
Sandoz AG 540, 542
Sands, "Nicky" 612
Sands, Sir Stafford 493-94, 496
Santos, Gonzalo N. 485
Santus, Yitzak 644
Sapir, Pinhas 96, 463
Sarfati, Maurice 21, 24-25
Sarnoff, David 418, 487; Sarnoff, Robert 487, 491
Sassoon family 127, 420-21, 431, 445; (E.D. Sassoon, Ltd.) 162
Sati 296
Savoy family 342, 421, 459; Savoy, Princess Beatrice 485
Scarborough, Luke 623
Schacht, Hjalmar 370, 373
Schein, Max 485
Schenley's Liquor 504
Schiebel, David J. 86
Schiff family 420, 505
Schiller, Friedrich 597
Schleyer, Hanns-Martin 575
Schlumberger Co. 453, 459, 474, 478, 490
Schmits, Karl Erik 631

Schoelkopf, Paul 522-23
Schori, Pierre 631
Schroeder Bank 274, 373
Schroeder family 271, 420
Schuller, Johann N. 375
Schultz, Dutch 425, 428
Schultz, Michael E. 606
Schultz, Harry 174
Schwartz, Alan M. 606
Sciambra, Andrew J. 489
Scotland Yard 226, 496, 499, 501
Scottish Rite of Freemasonry 123, 263, 265, 267-68, 382, 509
Scott, Walter 264
SDECE (French Intelligence Bureau) 456, 460, 468
Sea First 50
Seagram's Corp. 253, 256-57, 259-60, 423, 425-26, 432, 434-38, 612, 614
Sea Point 24-25
Seaga, Edward 108, 317-20
Searchlight 632, 644
Sears Roebuck 348
Seaves, James 638
Sebag family 522; Sebag-Montefiore, Robin 522;
Secord, Gen. Richard 12, 15, 621
Secret Army Organization (OAS) 374, 376, 382 456, 460, 469, 475, 479, 483
Securex 439-40
Securities and Exchange Commission (SEC) 82, 86, 209, 445, 552
Securities Industry Assn. (SIA) 100
Security Pacific Bank 178
SED (Socialist Unity Party—East Germany) 614
Sella, Aviem 642; Sella, Ruth 642
Seligman family 431, 434, 461, 511; Seligman, Hans 459, 461; Seligman, Jesse 461
Semit 614
Senate 66-67, 246; Senate Banking Committee 167, 179; Senate Church Committee 95; Senate Judiciary Committee 442, 567; Senate Permanent Investigations Subcommittee (SPIS) 64-66, 76, 167; Senate Watergate Committee 498
Sendero Luminoso 68, 305, 388-89, 392, 394, 396-402, 406
Seneca, Robert 82
Ser Vaas, Bert 489
Service, John S. 241, 243

Sessions, William 637
SETCO Air 15
Seymour, William 474-75, 482, 510
Shackley, Theodore G. 612
Shah Reza Pahlavi of Iran 291, 658
Shakarchi, Mohammed 19, 610; Sha-
    karchi Trading Co. 19, 610
Shamir, Yitzhak 640
Shamis, Philip 606
Shanghai Commercial Bank 239, 249
Shanghai International Settlements
    243-44
Shanghai Municipal Settlements 254,
    272
Shan States United Army (SUA) 227,
    658
Sharon, Ariel 96, 639-41
Sharps Pixley Ward 193, 196, 198, 254
Shaw, Col. Clay 418, 453, 459, 469-75,
    480-82, 486, 489
Shaw family 127, 220
Shaw, Frank 50
Shaw, George Bernard 445
Shapiro, Jacob 517
Shea and Gould 608, 617
Shearman and Sterling 101
Shearson Lehman American Express
    106
Sheftel, Yoram 634
Shelburne, Lord 116-18
Shelepin, Alexander 375
Shenker, Morris 518
She Pa Lang (a.k.a. Sao Fa Lan; a.k.a.
    Chang Chu-Chun) 228
Sher, Neal 635-36
Sheridan, Walter 418, 448, 486-91,
    498-99
Shin Beth 637
Shopov, Col. Gen. Grigor 379
Shulgovskii, Anatolii 400
Sicilia Falcón, Alberto 485
Siddon, Art 205
Siebert, Muriel 64
SIECUS 651
Siegel, Benjamin "Bugsy" 429, 539
Siete Días 296
Silberling, Ed 448
Silberman, Willy 631
Silbert, Theodore 72, 106, 607-08, 611
Siles Zuazo, Hernán 400
Silver Slipper Casino 518
Silver Triangle 236, 252, 497, 512
Simonfay, Ferenc H. 459
Sinclair, Ian D. 349

Sindona, Michele 72, 96, 98, 106, 108,
    339, 342, 492
Sinensky, Jeffrey P. 606, 646
Singh, Branjandan 293
Singh, Mehta Gulati 294
Singh, Surjit 630
Singh, Yoginder 384
Sinnett, A.P. 269; The Pioneer 269
Sino-British Trade Council 240
Skadden Arps 610
Skinner, B.F. 549
Skinner, William 190; Chinese Society
    in Thailand, An Analytical His-
    tory 190
Skorzeny, Otto 373-74
Slavkov, Ivan 380-81
Slater, Leonard 506-507
Slebi, Jairo 327
Smalley, Ian 296
Smallwood, Jerry 470
Smith, Adam xi, 71, 114, 118-19, 149,
    214; The Wealth of Nations 118-19
Smith, Dr. David 543
Smith, Gerald L.K. 608
Smith, Lewis du Pont 7-8
Smith, Roger 543
Smith-Richardson Foundation 622
Snow, Edgar 239
Sobel, Ronald B. 605
Socialist International 340-41, 421-22,
    619, 631; Social Democratic Party
    (Germany) 547, 421-22; Socialist
    Labor Party (SAP—Sweden) 632;
    Socialist Party (Italy) 104; Social-
    ist Party U.S.A. (Social Democrats
    U.S.A.) 421, 619
Socialist Workers Party 644
Société des Americanistes 398
Société Interlogin, SA 373
Society for Endangered Peoples 368,
    385, 390
Society for Psychical Research 651
Society of Jesus 116-17, 120, 314, 340
Solidarnosc 648
Solomon, Mitchell 618
Soltam B.M. 296
Somerset Importers, Ltd. 444
Somoza, Anastasio 353, 506, 513
Sonneborn Institute 505, 507
Sonneborn, Rudolph 505-507
Sonnenschein, Frances M. 606
Son of Sam 650
Sonoroven 347
Sons of Liberty 598

Soobzokov, Tscherim 627-28, 634
Sorg, Richard 370
Soto Pacheco, Gabriel Enrique 357-58
Soustelle, Jacques 374
South China Enterprise Co. 233
Space Research Corp. 370
Spadafora, Count Guitierez di 459,
    483; Spadafora family 421
Spanish Civil War 369
Special Operations Executive (SOE)
    175, 269-70, 368, 385, 417-18, 452-
    558, 460, 466-68, 470-71, 475, 477-
    78, 480, 482, 484, 486-87, 491,
    498, 500-501, 504-06, 604
Special Situation Group/Crisis Pre-
    Planning Group 15, 621
Speller, Jon 385, 629, 640
Sports Illustrated 519
Sportsystems Corp. 449, 498, 516-18,
    520, 523-24
Sprayregen, Joel 606
Stacchini, Mario 89
Stalin, Josef 615, 619, 635
Standard and Chartered Bank, Ltd.
    75, 177, 180, 199, 217-19, 247, 274
Standard Bank 199, 238
Stanford Research Institute 536, 549-
    50; Changing Images of Man 549
Stanford University 549
Stanley, Augustus Owsley III 551
Stark, Ronald 351
Stasi (East German secret police) 614
Steadman, James E. 510
Steiger, Sam 519-20, 523
Steinberg, Elan 647
Stepankowsky, Vladimir 618
Stephenson, Sir William ("Intrepid")
    176, 368, 418, 422, 444, 452, 454-
    56, 466-67, 470-72, 475, 480-81,
    484, 487, 491, 501, 504, 506, 604
Sterling National Bank 72, 106, 608,
    611, 642
Stern, Marvin 644
Stevenson, Robert Louis 264-65
Stewart, Rhona 638
Stipam International Transport 297,
    377-78, 381-83, 386-87
St. Louis Banana Distributing Co. 517
Stone, Galen 443
Straight, Willard 128
Strassler, David H. 606
Strategic Bombing Survey 541
Strategic Defense Initiative 11, 575,
    616, 636

Strong, Anna Louise 239-40
Strong, Sir Kenneth 253, 435
Stroup, Keith 319
Student Non-Violent Coordinating
    Committee (SNCC) 620
Students for a Democratic Society
    (SDS) 547-48, 620
Suall, Irwin 606, 608, 619, 625-26,
    629, 631, 633
Suez Crisis 248
Sugarman, Robert G. 606
Sukharev, Alexander 616
Sullivan, Ed 544
Sullivan, Laurence 118
Sun Company 219
Sun Yat-sen 245
Surrey, Walter Sterling 351
Sutherland family 125, 271
Swire family 114, 182, 523; John
    Swire and Sons 237; Swire, John
    Kidston 199, 236, 241, 271
Swiss Bank Corp. 75, 84
Swiss-Israel Trade Bank 465-66, 468
Synarchist International 369, 393

Tabatabai, Sadegh 296-98
Tablante, Carlos 357-58
Taft, William Howard 588, 596
Tajapaibul, Udhane 187-88
TAMSA (Tavos de Acero de México)
    485
Tarrants, Thomas A. III 622
Tashkent Institute 368
Taubman, Charles 508
Tavistock Institute 544, 547-48
Tell, David 644-45
Temperance Movement 136
Tennyson, Alfred Lord 270; The Lotus
    Eaters 270
Terry, Maury 650; The Ultimate Evil
    650
Thatcher, Margaret 18-19, 216, 233,
    466
Theosophy Movement 263, 268-69, 651
The Economist 40-41, 224, 274
Theology of Liberation 314, 340
The Reporter 196
The Times 124
The Trust 477, 479
Thomas, Charles Spaulding 601
Thompson, William Boyce 272
Thornburgh, Richard 28-29, 635
Thurn und Taxis family 94; Thurn und
    Taxis, Johannes von 98

Tillman, Benjamin R. 590
Tinoco, Jr., Pedro 349, 354-55
Tirchie, Mark 645
Tolstoy Foundation 477-78, 481
Tomkins, David 23
Torbitt, William 474-75, 480
Toronto Dominion Bank 252, 256
Toronto Jockey Club 521
Torres, Camilo 394
Torrio, John 428-30, 503
Townshend, Lady Caroline 434
Toynbee, Arnold 268, 537
Toynbee Hall 136
Trade Development Bank of Geneva
    106
Tradition, Family and Property 95,
    389-90
Traex 79
Trafficante, Santos 353
Traficant, Rep. James 18, 635
Transamerican Co. 444
Transcanada Transport Co. 425
Transglobal Resources 629
Treaty of Chuenpi (1841) 121
Treaty of Nanking (1842) 122-23
Treaty of Tientsin (Oct. 25, 1860) 124
Trebach, Arthur 564
Treholt, Arne 631
Trevelyan, Lord Humphrey 237, 248-
    49, 254, 432
Triad Society (Society of Heaven and
    Earth) 114, 120, 129, 188
Trilateral Commission xii, 104-05, 306,
    313, 317, 320
Trizec Corp. 252-53, 434-35
Trotsky, Leon 374
Tufts University Fletcher School of Di-
    plomacy 642
Turano, Anthony 89
Turkes, Col. al-Par Slan 384
Turner, Sir Mark 198-200, 236, 254,
    270
Turner, Sir Michael 260
Tyron, Lord 521

Ugurlu, Abuzer 386
Ulloa, Manuel 72-73, 314, 322
Ultrafin 104-05
Unibank 352-53
Unification Church 408, 649
Union Bank of Israel 202, 464
Union Bank of Switzerland 75
Union Corse 382
United Brands (UB) 85, 95, 321, 339-

    40, 418, 502, 508, 512-14, 524;
    United Fruit Co. 95, 106, 318,
    339-41, 361, 508, 512-13, 524
United Jewish Appeal 505, 507, 514,
    522
United Nations Organization (U.N.)
    309-10, 457-58; United Nations
    Confederation on Trade and De-
    velopment (UNCTAD) 156
Universal Christian Gnostic Church of
    Colombia 404-05
University of Chicago 137, 417, 540,
    552-53; Center for the Study of
    Democratic Institutions 417
University of Huamanga 402
University of Michigan 568
University of Rome 401
University of Vienna 551
University of Vladivostok 222
Urcuyo, Francisco 513
U.S. Army Counterintelligence 370,
    467, 505; U.S. Army G-2 369, 374
U.S. Congress 346 (see also individual
    House and Senate committees);
    Congressional Clearinghouse on
    the Future 550
U.S. Customs Service 19-20, 83, 96,
    172, 293, 339, 346, 357, 610
U.S. Department of Agriculture
    (USDA) 13, 49, 56-57; Economic
    Research Service 46
U.S. Department of Commerce 213
U.S. Department of Defense (Penta-
    gon) 561, 657
U.S. Department of Health and Hu-
    man Services 562, 568
U.S. Department of Interior 588
U.S. Department of Justice 4, 12-13,
    42, 49-50, 62, 71, 81-82, 84, 418,
    448, 450, 466-67, 482, 486-88, 495-
    96, 498, 501, 504, 506, 517, 519,
    523-24, 566, 585-88, 590, 596, 598,
    602, 628, 644; Criminal Division
    79; Office of Special Investigations
    (OSI) 628, 633-37; Organized
    Crime Strike Force 448,495, 498-
    99, 517-18; (see also Federal Bu-
    reau of Investigation and Law En-
    forcement Assistance Adminis-
    tration)
U.S. Department of State 15, 22, 29,
    46, 107, 239-41, 244-46, 313, 318-
    20, 499, 615, 618, 620, 657;
    Agency for International Develop-

ment (AID) 401; U.S. Information Agency (USIA) 16, 620
U.S. Department of Treasury 77, 82-83, 100, 167-68, 177-80, 204-05, 244, 313, 332-33, 336, 425, 488, 495-97, 587-88, 598, 657; Secret Service 488, 589
U.S. Drug Enforcement Admininistration (DEA) 15-16, 19-20, 29-30, 35-36, 38, 46, 48, 54, 83-84, 89, 134, 140, 151, 154, 164, 166, 169, 183, 229, 231, 292-94, 298, 300, 346, 351, 353, 378-80, 382-84, 386, 390, 497, 500, 512, 584, 610, 652, 654, 658; "The Involvement of the People's Republic of Bulgaria in International Narcotics Trafficking" 378
U.S. Immigration and Naturalization Service 481-82
U.S.-Jamaican Businessmen's Assn. 348
U.S. Labor Party 4-5, 10
U.S. Marines 321, 481
U.S. Narcotics Control Board 431, 658
U.S. National Security Agency (NSA) 486-87, 491, 498-99
U.S. Postal Service 588
U.S.-Soviet Trade and Economic Cooperation Council (USTEC) 615
U.S.S.R. Academy of Sciences 400

Valcárcel, Luis E. 397; *Peru, Paradise for the Anthropologist* 397
Valiquette, Joseph 626
Vallejo Arabeláez, Joaquín 42
Valley Die Cast Assn. 517
Valve Trend Holding Co. 439
Vance, Cyrus 313, 349
Van de Put, Karl 375
Vanderbilt family 135
Vanying Bank 219
Vásquez Medina, Luis 72-73
Vastenavondt, Ludovicus 294
Vatican 340, 440, 606, 616, 645, 647
Velasco, Gen. Juan 322
Venevisión 347-48, 356-57
Venezuelan/Jamaican Businessmen's Committee 318, 348
Veprin, William 606
Vergès, Jacques (a.k.a. Jacques Mansur) 375-76
Versailles Treaty 130, 466
Vesco, Robert 7, 63, 71, 73, 83-85, 87,

96, 168, 325, 341, 360-63, 393, 417, 465, 484, 500, 512-13, 566, 575, 583, 609-10, 621, 639
Vickers Arms 477
Vickers, Geoffrey 549
Victoria, Queen of England 122, 264
Vietnam War 9, 63, 188, 193, 229, 546, 653, 655, 658-59
Village Voice 407
Villiers, Edith 267; Villiers family 272; Villiers, George 267; Villiers, Gerald Hyde 270-71
Vineberg, Abraham Moses 436; Vineberg, Phillip F. 436
Vincent, John Carter 241
Vladimirov, Peter 241; *Vladimirov Diaries* 241
Vojta, George 101
Volcker, Paul Adolph 56, 65, 97, 306, 308, 313
Volkman, Ernest 360-61
Volstead Act (see Prohibition)
Volvo 349
von Finck, Baron August 98
von Hayek, Friedrich 307, 346
Vril Society 268

Wade, Richard 627
Wagner, Richard 268
Wakkas, Sallah Aldin 382-83
Waldheim, Kurt 616, 636-37, 647
Walker, Col. Clyde 24
Walker, Elisha 444
Walker, John M., Jr. 77, 205
Wall, Barbara 629
Wall, Harry 607
Wall Street Journal 20, 41, 87-88, 495
Walt Disney Studios 539
Walton, Phil 560
Wang Daohan 216
Wang Guangying 234
Wang Kang 661
Wang Kwan-cheng, Dr. 221
Wang Ping-nan 247-48
Warburg-Becker-Paribas 100
Warburg family 135, 420, 424, 505; Warburg, James 540, 544; S.G. Warburg 100, 108, 540
Ward, Mary Lady 564
Warner Brothers 539; Warner Communications 560
Warner, Marvin 80-83, 85
War on Drugs xiii, 31, 49

Warren Commission 453, 473-74, 480-
    81, 652
Warsaw Pact 299, 378
Washington Post 16, 42, 329, 467
Watts, Alan 541-42, 544, 549
Way International 650
Weather Underground 567
Webb, Horace S. 449, 524
Webster, William 9-10, 583-84, 628, 637
Weil, Dr. Andrew 561
Weinberg, Melvin 585-86
Weinberger, Caspar 629, 642
Weiss, Rabbi Avraham 647
Weizmann, Chaim 467
Weld, David 74-75; Weld, William xii,
    12, 73-74, 76-78, 86, 456; White
    Weld xii, 74-75, 81-82, 86
Welles, Elliot 606
Wells, Herbert George 538; *The Island
    of Dr. Moreau* 538; *The Open Con-
    spiracy: Blue Prints for a World
    Revolution* 538; *Time Machine* 538
Wells, Lynn 644
Wenger, Henry A. 503
WerBell, Col. Mitchell 575
West, Canon Edward 649
West, Dr. Louis Jolyon 649
Wheeler-Bennett, Sir John 447
Wheelock Marden 209
Whitehall Distributing Co. 442
White, Harry Dexter 244
White House Office of Drug Abuse Pol-
    icy 313
White, Kevin 78
Whitman, Peter M. 77
Whittelsey, Faith 620
Wickerham, George W. 588
Wiesenthal, Simon 636
Williams and Glyns 104
Williams, Edward Bennett 10, 82
Williams, Sen. Harrison 584-85
Williams, Jerry 637
Williamson, Rep. John N. 588
Willkie, Farr & Gallagher 71, 609-10,
    621
Wills, Frederick 315-16
Wilson, Woodrow 466, 594
Wingate, Orde 505
Winter, Jim 638
Wiseman, Sir William 135, 466-67,
    503-04
Wittelsbach family 94, 98, 461
Wittenstein, Charles 638, 644
Wolf, Gen. Markus 614

Wolfe, R.D. 257
Wolfe, Rep. Lester 228
Wolff, SS Gen. Karl 373
Wolfson, Sir Isaac 466
Wolmarano, Fred G. 225
Women's American ORT 646
Women's Christian Temperance Union
    (WCTU) 135-36
Wong Hong Hon Co. 195
Wood, Judge John 584
World Bank 6, 333, 656
World Commerce Bank 463
World Commerce Corp. 471-72
World Council of Churches 479
World Finance Corp. (WFC) 85, 345-
    46, 351-53, 355
World Jewish Congress 607, 612, 614-
    16, 635-36
World Sikh Organization 630
World Trade Bank 497
World Trade Center Assn. (WTCA)
    472; World Trade Center, Hong
    Kong 472
World War I 135, 272, 446, 466, 518,
    597, 602
World War II 62, 90, 128, 199, 220,
    236, 240, 242, 249, 253, 258, 269-
    71, 368, 385, 401, 417-18, 421,
    447, 454, 467, 470-72, 477-79, 482,
    487, 504, 547, 581, 604, 608, 618
Worldwide Shipping Corp. 215-16, 349
W.R. Grace 348
Wriston, Walter 101-02, 159
Wrywick, Morton 644

Xerox Corp. 567

Yakovlev, Alexander 615
Yale University 620
Yao Yilin 667
Yates, Sidney 607
Yeats, William Butler 539
Yet-Keung Kan 349
Ying, Tsu-li 188
Yippies (Youth International Party)
    422, 627
Yohakem, Nathaniel 88
York University 243, 259
Young, George 199
Young Men's Christian Assn. (YMCA)
    242

Zagame, John 22
Zagel, James 638

Zaharoff, Sir Basil 477
Zavaras, Aristides 637
Zeitlin, Jacob 539
Zemurray, Samuel 512
Zerilli, Anthony 517; Zerilli, Joseph
    517-18
Zeskind, Lenny 644-45
Zhivkov, Todor 378, 380; Zhivkova,
    Lyudmila 386

Zhou Enlai (Chou En-lai) 215-16, 226-
    27, 239-40, 242, 247-48, 258-59,
    267, 657, 664, 666
Zia ul-Haq, Gen. Mohammad 294
Zigiotti, Giuseppe 459
Zinberg, Dr. Norman 561
Zionist Organization of Canada 434
Zucker, Willard 621
Zwillman, Abner "Longie" 428, 430